The History of Freedom and Other Essays

John E.E. Dalberg Acton

Cosimo Classics
New York

The History of Freedom and Other Essays

For information, address:

Cosimo
P.O. Box 416
Old Chelsea Station
New York, NY 10113-0416

or visit our website at:
www.cosimobooks.com

The History of Freedom and Other Essays originally published by Macmillan and Co. in 1922.

Library of Congress Cataloging-in-Publication Data
A catalog record for this book is available from the Library of Congress

Cover design by www.wiselephant.com

ISBN: 1-59605-224-4

Acton

PREFATORY NOTE

THE Editors desire to thank the members of the Acton family for their help and advice during the preparation of this volume and of the volume of *Historical Essays and Studies*. They have had the advantage of access to many of Acton's letters, especially those to Döllinger and Lady Blennerhasset. They have thus been provided with valuable material for the Introduction. At the same time they wish to take the entire responsibility for the opinions expressed therein. They are again indebted to Professor Henry Jackson for valuable suggestions.

This volume consists of articles reprinted from the following journals: *The Quarterly Review, The English Historical Review, The Nineteenth Century, The Rambler, The Home and Foreign Review, The North British Review, The Bridgnorth Journal.* The Editors have to thank Mr. John Murray, Messrs. Longmans, Kegan Paul, Williams and Norgate, and the proprietors of *The Bridgnorth Journal* for their kind permission to republish these articles, and also the Delegacy of the Clarendon Press for allowing the reprint of the Introduction to Mr. Burd's edition of *Il Principe*. They desire to point out that in *Lord Acton and his Circle* the article on "The Protestant Theory of Persecution" is attributed to Simpson: this is an error.

J. N. F.
R. V. L.

August 24, 1907.

CONTENTS

CHRONICLE

JOHN EMERICH EDWARD DALBERG-ACTON, born at Naples, 10th January 1834, son of Sir Ferdinand Richard Edward Dalberg-Acton and Marie de Dalberg, afterwards Countess Granville.

	French school near Paris.
1843–1848.	Student at Oscott.
	,, ,, Edinburgh.
1848–1854.	,, ,, Munich University, living with Döllinger.
1855.	Visits America in company with Lord Ellesmere.
1858–1862.	Becomes editor of *The Rambler*.
1859–1865.	M.P. for Carlow.
1862–1864.	Founds, edits, and concludes *The Home and Foreign Review*.
1864.	Pius IX. issued *Quanta Cura*, with appended *Syllabus Errorum*.
1865–1866.	M.P. for Bridgnorth
1865.	Marries Countess Marie Arco-Valley.
1867–1868.	Writes for *The Chronicle*.
1869.	Created Baron Acton.
1869–1871.	Writes for *North British Review*.
1869–1870.	Vatican Council. Acton at Rome. Writes "Letters of Quirinus" in *Allgemeine Zeitung*.
1872.	Honorary degree at Munich.
1874.	Letters to *The Times* on "The Vatican Decrees."
1888.	Honorary degree at Cambridge.
1889.	,, ,, Oxford.
1890.	Honorary Fellow of All Souls'.
1892–1895.	Lord-in-Waiting.
1895–1902.	Regius Professor of Modern History at Cambridge Honorary Fellow of Trinity College.
19th June 1902.	Died at Tegernsee.

INTRODUCTION

THE two volumes here published contain but a small selection from the numerous writings of Acton on a variety of topics, which are to be found scattered through many periodicals of the last half-century. The result here displayed is therefore not complete. A further selection of nearly equal quantity might be made, and still much that is valuable in Acton's work would remain buried. Here, for instance, we have extracted nothing from the *Chronicle* ; and Acton's gifts as a leader-writer remain without illustration. Yet they were remarkable. Rarely did he show to better advantage than in the articles and reviews he wrote in that short-lived rival of the *Saturday Review.* From the two bound volumes of that single weekly, there might be made a selection which would be of high interest to all who cared to learn what was passing in the minds of the most acute and enlightened members of the Roman Communion at one of the most critical epochs in the history of the papacy. But what could never be reproduced is the general impression of Acton's many contributions to the *Rambler*, the *Home and Foreign*, and the *North British Review.* Perhaps none of his longer and more ceremonious writings can give to the reader so vivid a sense at once of the range of Acton's erudition and the strength of his critical faculty as does the perusal of these short notices. Any one who wished to understand the personality of Acton could not do better than take the published Bibliography and read a few of the articles on "contemporary literature" furnished by him to the three Reviews. In no other way could the reader so clearly realise the complexity of his mind or the vast number of subjects which he could touch with the hand of a master. In a single number there are twenty-eight such notices. His writing before he was thirty years of age shows an intimate and detailed knowledge of documents and authorities which with most students is the "hard won and hardly won" achievement of a lifetime of labour. He always writes as the student, never as the *littérateur*. Even the memorable phrases which give point to his briefest articles are judicial, not journalistic. Yet he treats of matters which range from the dawn of history through the ancient empires down to subjects so essentially modern as the vast literature of revolutionary France or the leaders of the romantic movement which replaced it. In all these writings of Acton those qualities manifest themselves, which only grew stronger with time, and gave him a distinct and unique place among his contemporaries. Here is the same austere love of truth, the same resolve to dig to the bed-rock of fact, and to exhaust all sources of possible illumination, the same breadth of view and intensity of inquiring ardour, which stimulated his studies and limited his productive power. Above all, there is the same unwavering faith in principles, as affording the only criterion of judgment amid the ever-fluctuating welter of human passions, political manœuvring, and ecclesiastical intrigue. But this is not all. We note the same value for great books as the source of wisdom, combined with the same enthusiasm for immediate justice which made Acton the despair of the mere academic student, an enigma among men of the world, and a stumbling-block to the politician of the clubs

Beyond this, we find that certainty and decision of judgment, that crisp concentration of phrase, that grave and deliberate irony and that mastery of subtlety, allusion, and wit, which make his interpretation an adventure and his judgment a sword.

A few instances may be given. In criticising a professor of history famous in every way rather than as a student, Acton says, "his Lectures are indeed not entirely unhistorical, for he has borrowed quite discriminatingly from Tocqueville." Of another writer he says that "ideas, if they occur to him, he rejects like temptations to sin." Of Ranke, thinking perhaps also of himself, he declares that "his intimate knowledge of all the contemporary history of Europe is a merit not suited to his insular readers." Of a partisan French writer under Louis Napoleon he says that "he will have a fair grievance if he fails to obtain from a discriminating government some acknowledgment of the services which mere historical science will find it hard to appreciate.' Of Laurent he says, that "sometimes it even happens that his information is not second-hand, and there are some original authorities with which he is evidently familiar. The ardour of his opinions, so different from those which have usually distorted history, gives an interest even to his grossest errors. Mr. Buckle, if he had been able to distinguish a good book from a bad one, would have been a tolerable imitation of M. Laurent." Perhaps, however, the most characteristic of these forgotten judgments is the description of Lord Liverpool and the class which supported him. Not even Disraeli painting the leader of that party which he was destined so strangely to "educate" could equal the austere and accurate irony with which Acton, writing as a student, not as a novelist, sums up the characteristics of the class of his birth.

Lord Liverpool governed England in the greatest crisis of the war, and for twelve troubled years of peace, chosen not by the nation, but by the owners of the land. The English gentry were well content with an order of things by which for a century and a quarter they had enjoyed so much prosperity and power. Desiring no change they wished for no ideas. They sympathised with the complacent respectability of Lord Liverpool's character, and knew how to value the safe sterility of his mind. He distanced statesmen like Grenville, Wellesley, and Canning, not in spite of his inferiority, but by reason of it. His mediocrity was his merit. The secret of his policy was that he had none. For six years his administration outdid the Holy Alliance. For five years it led the liberal movement throughout the world. The Prime Minister hardly knew the difference. He it was who forced Canning on the King. In the same spirit he wished his government to include men who were in favour of the Catholic claims and men who were opposed to them. His career exemplifies, not the accidental combination but the natural affinity, between the love of conservatism and the fear of ideas.

The longer essays republished in these volumes exhibit in most of its characteristics a personality which even those who disagreed with his views must allow to have been one of the most remarkable products of European culture in the nineteenth century. They will show in some degree how Acton's mind developed in the three chief periods of his activity, something of the influences which moulded it, a great deal of its preferences and its antipathies, and nearly all its directing ideals. During the first period—roughly to be dated from 1855 to 1863—he was hopefully striving, under the influence of Döllinger (his teacher from the age of seventeen), to educate his co-religionists in breadth and sympathy, and to place before his countrymen ideals of right in politics, which were to him bound up with the Catholic faith. The combination of scientific inquiry with true rules of political justice he claimed, in a letter to Döllinger, as the aim of the *Home and Foreign Review*. The result is to be seen in a quarterly, forgotten, like all such quarterlies to-day, but far surpassing, alike in knowledge, range, and certainty, any of the other quarterlies, political, or ecclesiastical, or specialist, which the nineteenth century produced. There is indeed no general periodical which comes near to it for thoroughness of erudition and strength of thought, if not for brilliance and ease; while it touches on topics contemporary and political in a way impossible to any specialist journal. A comparison with the *British Critic* in the religious sphere, with the *Edinburgh* in the political, will show how in all the weightier matters of learning and thought, the *Home and Foreign* (indeed the *Rambler*) was their superior, while it displayed a cosmopolitan interest foreign to most English journals.

We need not recapitulate the story so admirably told already by Doctor Gasquet of the beginning and end of the various journalistic enterprises with which Acton was connected. So far as he was concerned, however, the time may be regarded as that of youth and hope.

Next came what must be termed the "fighting period," when he stood forth as the leader among laymen of the party opposed to that "insolent and aggressive faction" which achieved its imagined triumph at the Vatican Council. This period, which may perhaps be dated from the issue of the Syllabus by Pius IX. in 1864, may be considered to close with the reply to Mr. Gladstone's pamphlet on "The Vatican Decrees," and with the attempt of the famous Cardinal, in whose mind history was identified with heresy, to drive from the Roman communion its most illustrious English layman. Part of this story tells itself in the letters published by the Abbot Gasquet; and more will be known when those to Döllinger are given to the world.

We may date the third period of Acton's life from the failure of Manning's attempt, or indeed a little earlier.

He had now given up all attempt to contend against the dominant influence of the Court of Rome, though feeling that loyalty to the Church of his Baptism, as a living body, was independent of the disastrous policy of its hierarchy. During this time he was occupied with the great unrealised project of the history of liberty or in movements of English politics and in the usual avocations of a student. In the earlier part of this period are to be placed some of the best things that Acton ever wrote, such as the lectures on Liberty, here republished. It is characterised by his discovery in the "eighties" that Döllinger and he were divided on the question of the severity of condemnation to be passed on persecutors and their approvers. Acton found to his dismay that Döllinger (like Creighton) was willing to accept pleas in arrest of judgment or at least mitigation of sentence, which the layman's sterner code repudiated. Finding that he had misunderstood his master, Acton was for a time profoundly discouraged, declared himself isolated, and surrendered the outlook of literary work as vain. He found, in fact, that in ecclesiastical as in general politics he was alone, however much he might sympathise with others up to a certain point. On the other hand, these years witnessed a gradual mellowing of his judgment in regard to the prospects of the Church, and its capacity to absorb and interpret in a harmless sense the dogma against whose promulgation he had fought so eagerly. It might also be correct to say that the English element in Acton came out most strongly in this period, closing as it did with the Cambridge Professorship, and including the development of the friendship between himself and Mr. Gladstone.

We have spoken both of the English element in Acton and of his European importance. This is the only way in which it is possible to present or understand him. There were in him strains of many races. On his father's side he was an English country squire, but foreign residence and the Neapolitan Court had largely affected the family, in addition to that flavour of cosmopolitan culture which belongs to the more highly placed Englishmen of the Roman Communion. On his mother's side he was a member of one of the oldest and greatest families in Germany, which was only not princely. The Dalbergs, moreover, had intermarried with an Italian family, the Brignoli. Trained first at Oscott under Wiseman, and afterwards at Munich under Döllinger, in whose house he lived, Acton by education as well as birth was a cosmopolitan, while his marriage with the family of Arco-Valley introduced a further strain of Bavarian influence into his life. His mother's second marriage with Lord Granville brought him into connection with the dominant influences of the great Whig Houses. For a brief period, like many another county magnate, he was a member of the House of Commons, but he never became accustomed to its atmosphere. For a longer time he lived at his house in Shropshire, and was a stately and sympathetic host, though without much taste for the avocations of country life. His English birth and Whig surroundings were largely responsible for that intense constitutionalism, which was to him a religion, and in regard both to ecclesiastical and civil politics formed his guiding criterion. This explains his detestation of all forms of absolutism on the one hand, and what he always called "the revolution" on the other.

It was not, however, the English strain that was most obvious in Acton, but the German. It was natural that he should become fired under Döllinger's influence with the ideals of continental scholarship and exact and minute investigation. He had a good deal of the massive solidity of the German intellect. He liked, as in the "Letter to a

German Bishop," to make his judgment appear as the culmination of so much weighty evidence, that it seemed to speak for itself. He had, too, a little of the German habit of breaking a butterfly upon a wheel, and at times he makes reading difficult by a more than Teutonic allusiveness. It was not easy for Acton to bear in mind that the public is often ignorant of even the names of distinguished scholars, and that "a European reputation" is sometimes confined to the readers of specialist publications.

The Italian strain in Acton is apparent in another quality, which is perhaps his one point of kinship with Machiavelli, the absence of hesitation from his thought, and of mystery from his writing. Subtle and ironic as his style is, charged with allusion and weighted with passion, it is yet entirely devoid both of German sentiment and English vagueness. There was no haze in his mind. He judges, but does not paint pictures. It may have been this absence of half-tones in his vein of thought, and of *chiaroscuro* in his imagination that made Manning, an intelligent however hostile critic, speak of "the ruthless talk of undergraduates."

But however much or little be allowed to the diverse strains of hereditary influence or outward circumstances, the interest of Acton to the student lies in his intense individuality. That austerity of moral judgment, that sense of the greatness of human affairs, and of the vast issues that lie in action and in thought, was no product of outside influences, and went beyond what he had learnt from his master Döllinger. To treat politics as a game, to play with truth or make it subservient to any cause other than itself, to take trivial views, was to Acton as deep a crime as to waste in pleasure or futility the hours so brief given for salvation of the soul would have seemed to Baxter or Bunyan ; indeed, there was an element of Puritan severity in his attitude towards statesmen both ecclesiastical and civil. He was no "light half-believer of a casual creed," but had a sense of reality more like Dante than many moderns.

This, perhaps, it was that drew him ever closer to Mr. Gladstone, while it made the House of Commons and the daily doings of politicians uncongenial. There is no doubt that he had learned too well "the secret of intellectual detachment." Early in his life his shrewd and kindly stepfather had pointed out to him the danger of losing influence by a too unrestrained desire to escape worshipping the idols of the market-place. There are, it is true, not wanting signs that his view of the true relations of States and Churches may become one day more dominant, for it appears as though once more the earlier Middle Ages will be justified, and religious bodies become the guardians of freedom, even in the political sphere. Still, a successful career in public life could hardly be predicted for one who felt at the beginning that "I agree with nobody, and nobody agrees with me," and towards the close admitted that he "never had any contemporaries." On the other hand, it may be questioned whether, in the chief of his self-imposed tasks, he failed so greatly as at first appeared. If he did not prevent "infallibility" being decreed, the action of the party of Strossmayer and Hefele assuredly prevented the form of the decree being so dangerous as they at first feared. We can only hazard a guess that the mild and minimising terms of the dogma, especially as they have since been interpreted, were in reality no triumph to Veuillot and the Jesuits. In later life Acton seems to have felt that they need not have the dangerous consequences, both in regard to historical judgments or political principles, which he had feared from the registered victory of ultramontane reaction. However this may be, Acton's whole career is evidence of his detachment of mind, and entire independence even of his closest associates. It was a matter to him not of taste but of principle. What mainly marked him out among men was the intense reality of his faith. This gave to all his studies their practical tone. He had none of the pedant's contempt for ordinary life, none of the æsthete's contempt for action as a "little vulgar," and no desire to make of intellectual pursuits an end in themselves. His scholarship was to him as practical as his politics, and his politics as ethical as his faith. Thus his whole life was a unity. All his various interests were inspired by one unconquered resolve, the aim of securing universally, alike in Church and in State, the recognition of the paramountcy of principles over interests, of liberty over tyranny, of truth over all forms of evasion or equivocation. His ideal in the political world was, as he said, that of securing *suum cuique* to every individual or association of human life, and to prevent any institution, however holy its aims, acquiring more.

To understand the ardour of his efforts it is necessary to bear in mind the world into which he was born, and the crises intellectual, religious, and political which he lived to witness and sometimes to influence. Born in the early days of the July monarchy, when reform in England was a novelty, and Catholic freedom a late-won boon, Acton as he grew to manhood in Munich and in England had presented to his regard a series of scenes well calculated to arouse a thoughtful mind to consideration of the deepest problems, both of politics and religion. What must have been the "long, long thoughts" of a youth, naturally reflective and acutely observant, as he witnessed the break-up of the old order in '48 and the years that followed. In the most impressionable age of life he was driven to contemplate a Europe in solution; the crash of the kingdoms; the Pope a Liberal, an exile, and a reactionary; the principle of nationality claiming to supersede all vested rights, and to absorb and complete the work of '89; even socialism for once striving to reduce theory to practice, till there came the "saviour of society" with the *coup d'état* and a new era of authority and despotism. This was the outward aspect. In the world of thought he looked upon a period of moral and intellectual anarchy. Philosopher had succeeded philosopher, critic had followed critic, Strauss and Baur were names to conjure with, and Hegel was still unforgotten in the land of his birth. Materialistic science was in the very heyday of its parvenu and tawdry intolerance, and historical knowledge in the splendid dawn of that new world of knowledge, of which Ranke was the Columbus. Everywhere faith was shaken, and except for a few resolute and unconquered spirits, it seemed as though its defence were left to a class of men who thought the only refuge of religion was in obscurity, the sole bulwark of order was tyranny, and the one support of eternal truth plausible and convenient fiction. What wonder then that the pupil of Döllinger should exhaust the intellectual and moral energies of a lifetime, in preaching to those who direct the affairs of men the paramount supremacy of principle. The course of the plebiscitary Empire, and that gradual campaign in the United States by which the will of the majority became identified with that necessity which knows no law, contributed further to educate his sense of right in politics, and to augment the distrust of power natural to a pupil of the great Whigs, of Burke, of Montesquieu, of Madame de Staël. On the other hand, as a pupil of Döllinger, his religious faith was deeper than could be touched by the recognition of facts, of which too many were notorious to make it even good policy to deny the rest; and he demanded with passion that history should set the follies and the crimes of ecclesiastical authority in no better light than those of civil.

We cannot understand Acton aright, if we do not remember that he was an English Roman Catholic, to whom the penal laws and the exploitation of Ireland were a burning injustice. They were in his view as foul a blot on the Protestant establishment and the Whig aristocracy as was the St. Bartholomew's medal on the memory of Gregory XIII., or the murder of the duc d'Enghien on the genius of Napoleon, or the burning of Servetus on the sanctity of Calvin, or the permission of bigamy on the character of Luther, or the September Massacres on Danton.

Two other tendencies dominant in Germany—tendencies which had and have a great power in the minds of scholars, yet to Acton, both as a Christian and a man, seemed corrupting—compelled him to a search for principles which might deliver him from slavery alike to traditions and to fashion, from the historian's vice of condoning whatever has got itself allowed to exist, and from the politician's habit of mere opportunist acquiescence in popular standards.

First of these is the famous maxim of Schiller, *Die Welt-Geschichte ist das Welt-Gericht*, which, as commonly interpreted, definitely identifies success with right, and is based, consciously or unconsciously, on a pantheistic philosophy. This tendency, especially when envisaged by an age passing through revolutionary nationalism back to Machiavelli's ideals and *Realpolitik*, is clearly subversive of any system of public law or morality, and indeed is generally recognised as such nowadays even by its adherents.

The second tendency against which Acton's moral sense revolted, had arisen out of the laudable determination of historians to be sympathetic towards men of distant ages and of alien modes of thought. With the romantic movement the early nineteenth century placed a check upon the habit of despising mediæval ideals, which had been increasing from the days of the Renaissance and had culminated in Voltaire. Instead of this, there arose a sentiment of admiration for the past, while the general growth of historical methods of thinking supplied a sense of the relativity of moral principles, and led to a desire to condone if not to commend the crimes of other ages. It became almost a trick of style to talk of judging men by the standard of their day and to allege the spirit of the age in excuse for the Albigensian Crusade or the burning of Hus. Acton felt that this was to destroy the very bases of moral judgment and to open the way to a boundless scepticism. Anxious as he was to uphold the doctrine of growth in theology, he allowed nothing for it in the realm of morals, at any rate in the Christian era, since the thirteenth century. He demanded a code of moral judgment independent of place and time, and not merely relative to a particular civilisation. He also demanded that it should be independent of religion. His reverence for scholars knew no limits of creed or church, and he desired some body of rules which all might recognise, independently of such historical phenomena as religious institutions. At a time when such varied and contradictory opinions, both within and without the limits of Christian belief, were supported by some of the most powerful minds and distinguished investigators, it seemed idle to look for any basis of agreement beyond some simple moral principles. But he thought that all men might agree in admitting the sanctity of human life and judging accordingly every man or system which needlessly sacrificed it. It is this preaching in season and out of season against the reality of wickedness, and against every interference with the conscience, that is the real inspiration both of Acton's life and of his writings.

It is related of Frederick Robertson of Brighton, that

during one of his periods of intellectual perplexity he found that the only rope to hold fast by was the conviction, "it must be right to do right." The whole of Lord Acton's career might be summed up in a counterphrase, "it must be wrong to do wrong." It was this conviction, universally and unwaveringly applied, and combined with an unalterable faith in Christ, which gave unity to all his efforts, sustained him in his struggle with ecclesiastical authority, accounted for all his sympathies, and accentuated his antipathies, while it at once expanded and limited his interests. It is this that made his personality so much greater a gift to the world than any book which he might have written—had he cared less for the end and more for the process of historical knowledge.

He was interested in knowledge — that it might diminish prejudice and break down barriers. To a world in which the very bases of civilisation seemed to be dissolving he preached the need of directing ideals.

Artistic interests were not strong in him, and the decadent pursuit of culture as a mere luxury had no stronger enemy. Intellectual activity, apart from moral purpose, was anathema to Acton. He has been censured for bidding the student of his hundred best books to steel his mind against the charm of literary beauty and style. Yet he was right. His list of books was expressly framed to be a guide, not a pleasure; it was intended to supply the place of University direction to those who could not afford a college life, and it throws light upon the various strands that mingled in Acton and the historical, scientific, and political influences which formed his mind. He felt the danger that lurks in the charm of literary beauty and style, for he had both as a writer and a reader a strong taste for rhetoric, and he knew how young minds are apt to be enchained rather by the persuasive spell of the manner than the living thought beneath it. Above all, he detested the modern journalistic craze for novelty, and despised the shallowness which rates cleverness above wisdom.

In the same way his eulogy of George Eliot has been censured far more than it has been understood. It was not as an artist superior to all others that he praised the author of *Daniel Deronda* and the translator of Strauss. It was because she supplied in her own person the solution of the problem nearest to his heart, and redeemed (so far as teaching went) infidelity in religion from immorality in ethics. It was, above all, as a constructive teacher of morals that he admired George Eliot, who might, in his view, save a daily increasing scepticism from its worst dangers, and preserve morals which a future age of faith might once more inspire with religious ideals. Here was a writer at the summit of modern culture, saturated with materialistic science, a convinced and unchanging atheist, who, in spite of this, proclaimed in all her work that moral law is binding, and upheld a code of ethics, Christian in content, though not in foundation.

In the same way his admiration for Mr. Gladstone is to be explained. It was not his successes so much as his failures that attracted Acton, and above all, his refusal to admit that nations, in their dealings with one another, are subject to no law but that of greed. Doubtless one who gave himself no credit for practical aptitude in public affairs, admired a man who had gifts that were not his own. But what Acton most admired was what many condemned. It was because he was not like Lord Palmerston, because Bismarck disliked him, because he gave back the Transvaal to the Boers, and tried to restore Ireland to its people, because his love of liberty never weaned him from loyalty to the Crown, and his politics were part of his religion, that Acton used of Gladstone language rarely used, and still more rarely applicable, to any statesman. For this very reason—his belief that political differences do, while religious differences do not, imply a different morality—he censured so severely the generous eulogy of Disraeli, just as in Döllinger's case he blamed the praise of Dupanloup. For Acton was intolerant of all leniency towards methods and individuals whom he thought immoral. He could give quarter to the infidel more easily than to the Jesuit.

We may, of course, deny that Acton was right. But few intelligent observers can dispute the accuracy of his diagnosis, or deny that more than anything else the disease of Western civilisation is a general lack of directing ideals other than those which are included in the gospel of commercialism. It may surely be further admitted that even intellectual activity has too much of triviality about it to-day; that if people despise the schoolmen, it is rather owing to their virtues than their defects, because impressionism has taken the place of thought, and brilliancy that of labour. On the other hand, Acton's dream of ethical agreement, apart from religion, seems further off from realisation than ever.

Acton, however, wrote for a world which breathed in the atmosphere created by Kant. His position was something as follows: After the discovery of facts, a matter of honesty and industry independent of any opinions, history needs a criterion of judgment by which it may appraise men's actions. This criterion cannot be afforded by religion, for religion is one part of the historic process of which we are tracing the flow. The principles on which all can combine are the inviolable sanctity of human life, and the unalterable principle of even justice and toleration. Wherever these are violated our course is clear. Neither custom nor convenience, neither distance of time nor difference of culture may excuse or even limit our condemnation. Murder is always murder, whether it be committed by populace or patricians, by councils or kings or popes. Had they had their dues, Paolo Sarpi would have been in Newgate and George I. would have died at Tyburn.

The unbending severity of his judgment, which is sometimes carried to an excess almost ludicrous, is further explained by another element in his experience. In his letters to Döllinger and others he more than once relates how in early life he had sought guidance in the difficult historical and ethical questions which beset the history of the papacy from many of the most eminent ultramontanes. Later on he was able to test their answers in the light of his constant study of original authorities and his careful investigation of archives. He found that the answers given him had been at the best but plausible evasions. The letters make it clear that the harshness with which Acton always regarded ultramontanes was due to that bitter feeling which arises in any reflecting mind on the discovery that it has been put off with explanations that did not explain, or left in ignorance of material facts.

Liberalism, we must remember, was a religion to Acton—*i.e.* liberalism as he understood it, by no means always what goes by the name. His conviction that ultramontane theories lead to immoral politics prompted his ecclesiastical antipathies. His anger was aroused, not by any feeling that Papal infallibility was a theological error, but by the belief that it enshrined in the Church monarchical autocracy, which could never maintain itself apart from crime committed or condoned. It was not intellectual error but moral obliquity that was to him here, as everywhere, the enemy. He could tolerate unbelief, he could not tolerate sin. Machiavelli represented to him the worst of political principles, because in the name of the public weal he destroyed the individual's conscience. Yet he left a loophole in private life for religion, and a sinning statesman might one day become converted. But when the same principles are applied, as they have been applied by the Jesuit organisers of ultramontane reaction (also on occasion by Protestants), *ad majorem dei gloriam*, it is clear that the soul is corrupted at its highest point, and the very means of serving God are made the occasion of denying him. Because for Acton there was no comparison between goodness and knowledge, and because life was to him more than thought, because the passion of his life was to secure for all souls the freedom to live as God would have them live, he hated in the Church the politics of ultramontanism, and in the State the principles of Machiavelli. In the same way he denied the legitimacy of every form of government, every economic wrong, every party creed, which sacrificed to the pleasures or the safety of the few the righteousness and salvation of the many. His one belief was the right of every man not to have, but to be, his best.

This fact gives the key to what seems to many an unsolved contradiction, that the man who said what he did say and fought as he had fought should yet declare in private that it had never occurred to him to doubt any single dogma of his Church, and assert in public that communion with it was "dearer than life itself." Yet all the evidence both of his writings and his most intimate associates confirms this view. His opposition to the doctrine of infallibility was ethical and political rather than theological. As he wrote to Döllinger, the evil lay deeper, and Vaticanism was but the last triumph of a policy that was centuries old. Unless he were turned out of her he would see no more reason to leave the Church of his baptism on account of the Vatican Decrees than on account of those of the Lateran Council. To the dogma of the Immaculate Conception he had no hostility, and could not understand Döllinger's condemnation of it, or reconcile it with his previous utterances. He had great sympathy with the position of Liberal High Anglicans; but there is not the slightest reason to suppose that he ever desired to join the English Church. Even with the old Catholic movement he had no sympathy, and dissuaded his friends from joining it.[1] All forms of Gallicanism were distasteful to Acton, and he looked to the future for the victory of his ideas. His position in the Roman Church symbolises in an acute form what may be called the soul's tragedy of the whole nineteenth century, but Acton had not the smallest inclination to follow either Gavazzi or Lamennais. It was, in truth, the unwavering loyalty of his churchmanship and his far-reaching historical sense that enabled him to attack with such vehemence evils which he believed to be accidental and temporary, even though they might have endured for a millennium. Long searching of the vista of history preserved Acton from the common danger of confusing the eternal with what is merely lengthy. To such a mind as his, it no more occurred to leave the Church because he disapproved some of its official procedure, than it would to an Englishman to surrender his nationality when his political opponents came into office. He distinguished, as he said Froschammer ought to have done, between the authorities and the authority of the Church. He had a strong belief in the doctrine of development, and felt that it would prove impossible in the long run to bind the Christian community to any explanation of the faith which should have a non-Christian or immoral tendency. He left it to time and the common

[1] There is no foundation for the statement of Canon Meyrick in his *Reminiscences*, that Acton, had he lived on the Continent, would have undoubtedly become an Old Catholic. He did very largely live on the Continent. Nor did even Döllinger, of whom Dr. Meyrick also asserts it, ever become an adherent of that movement.

conscience to clear the dogma from association with dangerous political tendencies, for his loyalty to the institution was too deep to be affected by his dislike of the *Camarilla* in power. He not only did not desire to leave the Church, but took pains to make his confession and receive absolution immediately after his letters appeared in the *Times*. It must also be stated that so far from approving Mr. Gladstone's attack on Vaticanism, he did his utmost to prevent its publication, which he regarded as neither fair nor wise.

It is true that Acton's whole tendency was individualistic, and his inner respect for mere authority apart from knowledge and judgment was doubtless small. But here we must remember what he said once of the political sphere—that neither liberty nor authority is conceivable except in an ordered society, and that they are both relative to conditions remote alike from anarchy and tyranny. Doubtless he leaned away from those in power, and probably felt of Manning as strongly as the latter wrote of him. Yet his individualism was always active within the religious society, and never contemplated itself as outside. He showed no sympathy for any form of Protestantism, except the purely political side of the Independents and other sects which have promoted liberty of conscience.

Acton's position as a churchman is made clearer by a view of his politics. At once an admirer and an adviser of Mr. Gladstone, he probably helped more than any other single friend to make his leader a Home Ruler. Yet he was anything but a modern Radical: for liberty was his goddess, not equality, and he dreaded any single power in a State, whether it was the King, or Parliament, or People. Neither popes nor princes, not even Protestant persecutors, did Acton condemn more deeply than the crimes of majorities and the fury of uncontrolled democracy. It was not the rule of one or many that was his ideal, but a balance of powers that might preserve freedom and keep every kind of authority subject to law. For, as he said, "liberty is not a means to a higher end, it is itself the highest political end." His preference was, therefore, not for any sovereign one or number, such as formed the ideal of Rousseau or the absolutists; but for a monarchy of the English type, with due representation to the aristocratic and propertied classes, as well as adequate power to the people. He did not believe in the doctrine of numbers, and had no sympathy with the cry *Vox populi Vox Dei*; on the other hand, he felt strongly that the stake in the country argument really applied with fullest force to the poor, for while political error means mere discomfort to the rich, it means to the poor the loss of all that makes life noble and even of life itself. As he said in one of his already published letters:—

> The men who pay wages ought not to be the political masters of those who earn them, for laws should be adapted to those who have the heaviest stake in the country, for whom misgovernment means not mortified pride or stinted luxury, but want and pain and degradation, and risk to their own lives and to their children's souls.

While he felt the dangers of Rousseau's doctrine of equality, declaring that in the end it would be destructive alike of liberty and religion, he was yet strongly imbued with the need of reconciling some of the socialists' ideals with the regard due to the principles which he respected. He was anxious to promote the study of Roscher and the historical economists, and he seems to have thought that by their means some solution of the great economic evils of the modern world might be found, which should avoid injustice either to the capitalist or the wage-earner. He had a burning hatred of injustice and tyranny, which made him anxious to see the horrors of the modern proletariat system mitigated and destroyed: but combined with this there was a very deep sense of the need of acting on principles universally valid, and a distrust of any merely emotional enthusiasm which might, in the future, create more evils than it cured. Acton was, in truth, the incarnation of the "spirit of Whiggism," although in a very different sense of the phrase from that in which it became the target for the arrows of Disraeli's scorn and his mockery of the Venetian constitution. He was not the Conservative Whig of the "glorious revolution," for to him the memory of William of Orange might be immortal but was certainly not pious: yet it was "revolution principles" of which he said that they were the great gift of England to the world. By this he meant the real principles by which the events of 1688 could be philosophically justified, when purged of all their vulgar and interested associations, raised above their connection with a territorial oligarchy, and based on reasoned and universal ideals. Acton's liberalism was above all things historical, and rested on a consciousness of the past. He knew very well that the roots of modern constitutionalism were mediæval, and declared that it was the stolid conservatism of the English character, which had alone enabled it to preserve what other nations had lost in the passion for autocracy that characterised the men of the Renaissance and the Reformation. Constitutional government was for him the sole eternal truth in politics, the rare but the only guardian of freedom. He loved to trace the growth of the principle of power limiting itself and law triumphant alike over king, aristocracies, and majorities; and to show how it arose out of the cruel conflicts of the religious wars and rested upon the achievements of Constance and the efforts of Basle, and how it was influenced in expression by the thinkers of the ancient world and the theologians of the modern, by the politics of Aristotle, by the maxims of Ulpian and of Gaius, by the theology of St. Thomas and Ockham, and even by Suarez and Molina.

What Acton feared and hated was the claim of absolutism to crush the individuality and destroy the conscience of men. It was indifferent to him whether this claim was exercised by Church or State, by Pope or Council, or King or Parliament. He felt, however, that it was more dangerous because more absorbing when exercised in religious matters, and thus condemned the Protestant theory more deeply than the Catholic permission of persecution. He also felt that monarchy was more easily checked than pure democracy, and that the risk of tyranny was greater in the latter.

Provided that freedom was left to men to do their duty, Acton was not greatly careful of mere rights. He had no belief in the natural equality of men, and no dislike of the subordination of classes on the score of birth. His ideal of freedom as of the Church was in some respects that of the earlier Middle Ages. He did not object to serfdom, provided that it safeguarded the elementary rights of the serf to serve God as well as man. In the great struggle in America, he had no sympathy with the North, which seemed to him to make majority rule the only measure of right: and he wrote, if not in favour, at least in palliation, of slavery. It may be doubted how far he would have used the same language in later life, but his reasons were in accord with all his general views. Slavery might be rendered harmless by the State, and some form of compulsion might be the only way of dealing with child-races, indeed, it might be merely a form of education no more morally blameworthy than the legal disabilities of minors. But the absolute state recognising no limits but its own will, and bound by no rule either of human or Divine law, appeared to him definitely immoral.

Acton's political conscience was also very broad on the side technically called moral. No one had higher ideals of purity. Yet he had little desire to pry into the private morality of kings or politicians. It was by the presence or absence of *political* principles that he judged them. He would have condemned Pope Paul the Fourth more than Rodrigo Borgia, and the inventor of the "dragonnades" more than his great-grandson. He did not view personal morality as relevant to political judgment.

In this, if in nothing else, he agreed with Creighton. His correspondence with the latter throws his principles into the strongest light, and forms the best material for a judgment. For it must, we think, be admitted that he applied these doctrines with a rigidity which human affairs will not admit, and assumed a knowledge beyond our capacity. To declare that no one could be in a state of grace who praised S. Carlo Borromeo, because the latter followed the evil principle of his day in the matter of persecution, is not merely to make the historian a hanging judge, but to ignore the great truth that if crime is always crime, degrees of temptation are widely variable. The fact is, Acton's desire to maintain the view that "morality is not ambulatory," led him at times to ignore the complementary doctrine that it certainly develops, and that the difficulties of statesmen or ecclesiastics, if they do not excuse, at least at times explain their less admirable courses. At the very close of his life Acton came to this view himself. In a pathetic conversation with his son, he lamented the harshness of some of his judgments, and hoped the example would not be followed.

Still, Acton, if he erred here, erred on the nobler side. The doctrine of moral relativity had been overdone by historians, and the principles of Machiavelli had become so common a cry of politicians, that severe protest was necessary. The ethics of Nietzsche are the logical expansion of Machiavelli, and his influence is proof that, in the long-run, men cannot separate their international code from their private one. We must remember that Acton lived in a time when, as he said, the course of history had been "twenty-five times diverted by actual or attempted crime," and when the old ideals of liberty seemed swallowed up by the pursuit of gain. To all those who reflect on history or politics, it was a gain of the highest order that at the very summit of historical scholarship and profound political knowledge there should be placed a leader who erred on the unfashionable side, who denied the statesmen's claim to subject justice to expediency, and opposed the partisan's attempt to palter with facts in the interest of his creed.

It is these principles which both explain Acton's work as a student, and make it so difficult to understand. He believed, that as an investigator of facts the historian must know no passion, save that of a desire to sift evidence; and his notion of this sifting was of the remorseless scientific school of Germany, which sometimes, perhaps, expects more in the way of testimony than human life affords. At any rate, Acton demanded that the historian must never misconceive the case of the adversaries of his views, or leave in shade the faults of his own side. But on the other hand, when he comes to interpret facts or to trace their relation, his views and even his temperament will affect the result. It is only the barest outline that can be quite objective. In Acton's view the historian as investigator is one thing, the historian as judge another. In an early essay on Döllinger he makes a distinction of this kind. The reader must bear it in mind in considering Acton's own writing. Some of the essays here printed, and still more the lectures, are anything but colourless; they show very distinctly the predilections of the writer, and it is hardly conceivable that they should have been written by a defender of absolutism, or even by an old-fashioned Tory. What Acton really demanded was not the academic aloofness of the pedant who stands apart from the strife of principles, but the honesty of purpose which "throws itself into the mind of one's opponents, and accounts for their mistakes," giving their case the best possible colouring. For, to be sure of one's ground, one must meet one's adversaries' strongest arguments, and not be content with merely picking holes in his armour. Otherwise one's own belief may be at the mercy of the next clever opponent. The reader may doubt how far Acton succeeded in his own aim, for there was a touch of intolerance in his hatred of absolutism, and he believed himself to be divided from his ecclesiastical and political foes by no mere intellectual difference but by a moral cleavage. Further, his writing is never half-hearted. His convictions were certitudes based on continual reading and reflection, and admitting in his mind of no qualification. He was eminently a Victorian in his confidence that he was right. He had none of the invertebrate tendency of mind which thinks it is impartial, merely because it is undecided, and regards the judicial attitude as that which refrains from judging. Acton's was not a doubting mind. If he now and then suspended his judgment, it was as an act of deliberate choice, because he had made up his mind that the matter could not be decided, not because he could not decide to make up his mind. Whether he was right or wrong, he always knew what he thought, and his language was as exact an expression of his meaning as he could make it. It was true that his subtle and far-sighted intelligence makes his style now and then like a boomerang, as when he says of Ranke's method "it is a discipline we shall all do well to adopt, and also do well to relinquish." Indeed, it is hardly possible to read a single essay without observing this marked characteristic. He has been called a "Meredith turned historian," and that there is truth in this judgment, any one who sees at once the difficulty and the suggestiveness of his reviews can bear witness. He could hardly write the briefest note without stamping his personality upon it and exhibiting the marks of a very complex culture. But the main characteristic of his style is that it represents the ideals of a man to whom every word was sacred. Its analogies are rather in sculpture than painting. Each paragraph, almost every sentence is a perfectly chiselled whole, impressive by no brilliance or outside polish, so much as by the inward intensity of which it is the symbol. Thus his writing is never fluent or easy, but it has a moral dignity rare and unfashionable.

Acton, indeed, was by no means without a gift of rhetoric, and in the "Lecture on Mexico," here republished, there is ample evidence of a power of handling words which should impress a popular audience. It is in gravity of judgment and in the light he can draw from small details that his power is most plainly shown. On the other hand, he had a little of the scholar's love of clinging to the bank, and, as the notes to his "Inaugural" show, he seems at times too much disposed to use the crutches of quotation to prop up positions which need no such support. It was of course the same habit—the desire not to speak before he had read everything that was relevant, whether in print or manuscript—that hindered so severely his output. His projected *History of Liberty* was, from the first, impossible of achievement. It would have required the intellects of Napoleon and Julius Cæsar combined, and the lifetime of the patriarchs, to have executed that project as Acton appears to have planned it. A *History of Liberty*, beginning with the ancient world and carried down to our own day, to be based entirely upon original sources, treating both of the institutions which secured it, the persons who fought for it, and the ideas which expressed it, and taking note of all that scholars had written about every several portion of the subject, was and is beyond the reach of a single man. Probably towards the close of his life Acton had felt this. The *Cambridge Modern History*, which required the co-operation of so many specialists, was to him really but a fragment of this great project.

Two other causes limited Acton's output. Towards the close of the seventies he began to suspect, and eventually discovered, that he and Döllinger were not so close together as he had believed. That is to say, he found that in regard to the crimes of the past, Döllinger's position was more like that of Creighton than his own—that, while he was willing to say persecution was always wrong, he was not willing to go so far as Acton in rejecting every kind of mitigating plea and with mediæval certainty consigning the persecutors to perdition. Acton, who had, as he thought, learnt all this from Döllinger, was distressed at what seemed to him the weakness and the sacerdotal prejudice of his master, felt that he was now indeed alone, and for the time surrendered, as he said, all views of literary work. This was the time when he had been gathering materials for a *History of the Council of Trent.* That this cleavage, coming when it did, had a paralysing effect on Acton's productive energy is most probable, for it made him feel that he was no longer one of a school, and was without sympathy and support in the things that lay nearest his heart.

Another cause retarded production—his determination to know all about the work of others. Acton desired to be in touch with university life all over Europe, to be aware, if possible through personal knowledge, of the trend of investigation and thought of scholars working in all the cognate branches of his subject. To keep up thoroughly with other people's work, and do much original writing of one's own, is rarely possible. At any rate we may say that the same man could not have produced the essay on German schools of history, and written a *magnum opus* of his own.

His life marks what, in an age of minute specialism, must always be at once the crown and the catastrophe of those who take all knowledge for their province. His achievement is something different from any book. Acton's life-work was, in fact, himself. Those who lament what he might have written as a historian would do well to reflect on the unique position which he held in the world of letters, and to ask themselves how far he could have wielded the influence that was his, or held the standard so high, had his own achievement been greater. Men such as Acton and Hort give to the world, by their example and disposition, more than any written volume could convey. In both cases a great part of their published writings has had, at least in book form, to be posthumous. But their influence on other workers is incalculable, and has not yet determined.

To an age doubting on all things, and with the moral basis of its action largely undermined, Acton gave the spectacle of a career which was as moving as it was rare. He stood for a spirit of unwavering and even childlike faith united to a passion for scientific inquiry, and a scorn of consequences, which at times made him almost an iconoclast. His whole life was dedicated to one high end, the aim of preaching the need of principles based on the widest induction and the most penetrating thought, as the only refuge amid the storm and welter of sophistical philosophies and ecclesiastical intrigues. The union of faith with knowledge, and the eternal supremacy of righteousness, this was the message of Acton to mankind.

It may be thought that he sometimes exaggerated his thesis, that he preached it out of season, that he laid himself open to the charge of being doctrinaire, and that in fighting for it he failed to utter the resources of his vast learning. Enough, however, is left to enable the world to judge what he was. No books ever do more than that for any man. Those who are nice in comparisons may weigh against the book lost the man gained. Those who loved him will know no doubt.

The following document was found among Lord Acton's Papers. It records in an imaginative form the ideals which he set before him. Perhaps it forms the most fitting conclusion to this Introduction.

This day's post informed me of the death of Adrian, who was the best of all men I have known. He loved retirement, and avoided company, but you might sometimes meet him coming from scenes of sorrow, silent and appalled, as if he had seen a ghost, or in the darkest corner of churches, his dim eyes radiant with light from another world. In youth he had gone through much anxiety and contention; but he lived to be trusted and honoured. At last he dropped out of notice and the memory of men, and that part of his life was the happiest.

Years ago, when I saw much of him, most people had not found him out. There was something in his best qualities themselves that baffled observation, and fell short of decided excellence. He looked absent and preoccupied, as if thinking of things he cared not to speak of, and seemed but little interested in the cares and events of the day. Often it was hard to decide whether he had an opinion, and when he showed it, he would defend it with more eagerness and obstinacy than we liked. He did not mingle readily with others or co-operate in any common undertaking, so that one could not rely on him socially, or for practical objects. As he never spoke harshly of persons, so he seldom praised them warmly, and there was some apparent indifference and want of feeling. Ill success did not depress, but happy prospects did not elate him, and though never impatient, he was not actively hopeful. Facetious friends called him the weather-cock, or Mr. Facingbothways, because there was no heartiness in his judgments, and he satisfied nobody, and said things that were at first sight grossly inconsistent, without attempting to reconcile them. He was reserved about himself, and gave no explanations, so that he was constantly misunderstood, and there was a sense of failure, of disappointment, of perplexity about him.

These things struck me, as well as others, and at first repelled me. I could see indeed, at the same time, that his conduct was remarkably methodical, and was guided at every step by an inexhaustible provision of maxims. He had meditated on every contingency in life, and was prepared with rules and precepts, which he never disobeyed. But I doubted whether all this was not artificial,—a contrivance to satisfy the pride of intellect and establish a cold superiority. In time I discovered that it was the perfection of a developed character. He had disciplined his soul with such wisdom and energy as to make it the obedient and spontaneous instrument of God's will, and he moved in an orbit of thoughts beyond our reach.

It was part of his religion to live much in the past, to realise every phase of thought, every crisis of controversy, every stage of progress the Church has gone through. So that the events and ideas of his own day lost much of their importance in comparison, were old friends with new faces, and impressed him less than the multitude of those that went before. This caused him to seem absent and indifferent, rarely given to admire, or to expect. He respected other men's opinions, fearing to give pain, or to tempt with anger by contradiction, and when forced to defend his own he felt bound to assume that every one would look sincerely for the truth, and would gladly recognise it. But he could not easily enter into their motives when they were mixed, and finding them generally mixed, he avoided contention by holding much aloof. Being quite sincere, he was quite impartial, and pleaded with equal zeal for what seemed true, whether it was on one side or on the other. He would have felt dishonest if he had unduly favoured people of his own country, his own religion, or his own party, or if he had entertained the shadow of a prejudice against those who were against them, and when he was asked why he did not try to clear himself from misrepresentation, he said that he was silent both from humility and pride.

At last I understood that what we had disliked in him was his virtue itself.

J. N. F.
R. V. L.

I

THE HISTORY OF FREEDOM IN ANTIQUITY[1]

LIBERTY, next to religion, has been the motive of good deeds and the common pretext of crime, from the sowing of the seed at Athens, two thousand four hundred and sixty years ago, until the ripened harvest was gathered by men of our race. It is the delicate fruit of a mature civilisation; and scarcely a century has passed since nations, that knew the meaning of the term, resolved to be free. In every age its progress has been beset by its natural enemies, by ignorance and superstitution, by lust of conquest and by love of ease, by the strong man's craving for power, and the poor man's craving for food. During long intervals it has been utterly arrested, when nations were being rescued from barbarism and from the grasp of strangers, and when the perpetual struggle for existence, depriving men of all interest and understanding in politics, has made them eager to sell their birthright for a mess of pottage, and ignorant of the treasure they resigned. At all times sincere friends of freedom have been rare, and its triumphs have been due to minorities, that have prevailed by associating themselves with auxiliaries whose objects often differed from their own; and this association, which is always dangerous, has been sometimes disastrous, by giving to opponents just grounds of opposition, and by kindling dispute over the spoils in the hour of success.

[1] An address delivered to the members of the Bridgnorth Institution at the Agricultural Hall, 26th February 1877.

No obstacle has been so constant, or so difficult to overcome, as uncertainty and confusion touching the nature of true liberty. If hostile interests have wrought much injury, false ideas have wrought still more; and its advance is recorded in the increase of knowledge, as much as in the improvement of laws. The history of institutions is often a history of deception and illusions; for their virtue depends on the ideas that produce and on the spirit that preserves them, and the form may remain unaltered when the substance has passed away.

A few familiar examples from modern politics will explain why it is that the burden of my argument will lie outside the domain of legislation. It is often said that our Constitution attained its formal perfection in 1679, when the Habeas Corpus Act was passed. Yet Charles II. succeeded, only two years later, in making himself independent of Parliament. In 1789, while the States-General assembled at Versailles, the Spanish Cortes, older than Magna Charta and more venerable than our House of Commons, were summoned after an interval of generations, but they immediately prayed the King to abstain from consulting them, and to make his reforms of his own wisdom and authority. According to the common opinion, indirect elections are a safeguard of conservatism. But all the Assemblies of the French Revolution issued from indirect elections. A restricted suffrage is another reputed security for monarchy. But the Parliament of Charles X., which was returned by 90,000 electors, resisted and overthrew the throne; while the Parliament of Louis Philippe, chosen by a Constitution of 250,000, obsequiously promoted the reactionary policy of his Ministers, and in the fatal division which, by rejecting reform, laid the monarchy in the dust, Guizot's majority was obtained by the votes of 129 public functionaries. An unpaid legislature is, for obvious reasons, more independent than most of the Continental legislatures which receive pay. But it would be unreasonable in America to send a member as far as from here to Constantinople to live for twelve months at his own expense in the dearest of capital cities. Legally and to outward seeming the American President is the successor of Washington, and still enjoys powers devised and limited by the Convention of Philadelphia. In reality the new President differs from the Magistrate imagined by the Fathers of the Republic as widely as Monarchy from Democracy, for he is expected to make 70,000 changes in the public service; fifty years ago John Quincy Adams dismissed only two men. The purchase of judicial appointments is manifestly indefensible; yet in the old French monarchy that monstrous practice created the only corporation able to resist the king. Official corruption, which would ruin a commonwealth, serves in Russia as a salutary relief from the pressure of absolutism. There are conditions in which it is scarcely a hyperbole to say that slavery itself is a stage on the road to freedom. Therefore we are not so much concerned this evening with the dead letter of edicts and of statutes as with the living thoughts of men. A century ago it was perfectly well known that whoever had one audience of a Master in Chancery was made to pay for three, but no man heeded the enormity until it suggested to a young lawyer that it might be well to question and examine with rigorous suspicion every part of a system in which such things were done. The day on which that gleam lighted up the clear hard mind of Jeremy Bentham is memorable in the political calendar beyond the entire administration of many statesmen. It would be easy to point out a paragraph in St. Augustine, or a sentence of Grotius that outweighs in influence the Acts of fifty Parliaments, and our cause owes more to Cicero and Seneca, to Vinet and Tocqueville, than to the laws of Lycurgus or the Five Codes of France.

By liberty I mean the assurance that every man shall be protected in doing what he believes his duty against the influence of authority and majorities, custom and opinion. The State is competent to assign duties and draw the line between good and evil only in its immediate sphere. Beyond the limits of things necessary for its well-being, it can only give indirect help to fight the battle of life by promoting the influences which prevail against temptation,—religion, education, and the distribution of wealth. In ancient times the State absorbed authorities not its own, and intruded on the domain of personal freedom. In the Middle Ages it possessed too little authority, and suffered others to intrude. Modern States fall habitually into both excesses. The most certain test by which we judge whether a country is really free is the amount of security enjoyed by minorities. Liberty, by this definition, is the essential condition and guardian of religion; and it is in the history of the Chosen People, accordingly, that the first illustrations of my subject are obtained. The government of the Israelites was a Federation, held together by no political authority, but by the unity of race and faith, and founded, not on physical force, but on a voluntary covenant. The principle of self-government was carried out not only in each tribe, but in every group of at least 120 families; and there was neither privilege of rank nor inequality before the law. Monarchy was so alien to the primitive spirit of the community that it was resisted by Samuel in that momentous protestation and warning which all the kingdoms of Asia and many of the kingdoms of Europe have unceasingly confirmed. The throne was erected on a compact; and the king was deprived of the right of legislation among a people that recognised no lawgiver but God, whose highest aim in politics was to restore the original purity of the constitution, and to make its government conform to the ideal type that was hallowed by the sanctions of heaven. The inspired men who rose in unfailing succession to prophesy against the usurper and the tyrant, constantly proclaimed that the laws, which were divine, were paramount over sinful rulers, and appealed from the established authorities, from the king, the priests, and the princes of the people, to the healing forces that slept in the uncorrupted consciences of the masses. Thus the example of the Hebrew nation laid down the parallel lines on which all freedom has been won—the doctrine of national tradition and the doctrine of the higher law; the principle that a constitution grows from a root, by process of development, and not of essential change; and the principle that all political authorities must be tested and reformed according to a code which was not made by man. The operation of these principles, in unison, or in antagonism, occupies the whole of the space we are going over together.

The conflict between liberty under divine authority and the absolutism of human authorities ended disastrously. In the year 622 a supreme effort was made at Jerusalem to reform and preserve the State. The High Priest produced from the temple of Jehovah the book of the deserted and forgotten Law, and both king and people bound themselves by solemn oaths to observe it. But that early example of limited monarchy and of the supremacy of law neither lasted nor spread; and the forces by which freedom has conquered must be sought elsewhere. In the very year 586, in which the flood of Asiatic despotism closed over the city which had been, and was destined again to be, the sanctuary of freedom in the East, a new home was prepared for it in the West, where, guarded by the sea and the mountains, and by valiant hearts, that stately plant was reared under whose shade we dwell, and which is extending its invincible arms so slowly and yet so surely over the civilised world.

According to a famous saying of the most famous authoress of the Continent, liberty is ancient, and it is despotism that is new. It has been the pride of recent historians to vindicate the truth of that maxim. The heroic age of Greece confirms it, and it is still more conspicuously true of Teutonic Europe. Wherever we can trace the earlier life of the Aryan nations we discover germs which favouring circumstances and assiduous culture might have developed into free societies. They exhibit some sense of common interest in common concerns, little reverence for external authority, and an imperfect sense of the function and supremacy of the State. Where the division of property and labour is incomplete there is little division of classes and of power. Until societies are tried by the complex problems of civilisation they may escape despotism, as societies that are undisturbed by religious diversity avoid persecution. In general, the forms of the patriarchal age failed to resist the growth of absolute States when the difficulties and temptations of advancing life began to tell; and with one sovereign exception, which is not within my scope to-day, it is scarcely possible to trace their survival in the institutions of later times. Six hundred years before the birth of Christ absolutism held unbounded sway. Throughout the East it was propped by the unchanging influence of priests and armies. In the West, where there were no sacred books requiring trained interpreters, the priesthood acquired no preponderance, and when the kings were overthrown their powers passed to aristocracies of birth. What followed, during many generations, was the cruel domination of class over class, the oppression of the poor by the rich, and of the ignorant by the wise. The spirit of that domination found passionate utterance in the verses of the aristocratic poet Theognis, a man of genius and refinement, who avows that he longed to drink the blood of his political adversaries. From these oppressors the people of many cities sought deliverance in the less intolerable tyranny of revolutionary usurpers. The remedy gave new shape and energy to the evil. The tyrants were often men of surprising capacity and merit, like some of those who, in the fourteenth century, made themselves lords of Italian cities; but rights secured by equal laws and by sharing power existed nowhere.

From this universal degradation the world was rescued by the most gifted of the nations. Athens, which like other cities was distracted and oppressed by a privileged class, avoided violence and appointed Solon to revise its laws. It was the happiest choice that history records. Solon was not only the wisest man to be found in Athens, but the most profound political genius of antiquity; and the easy, bloodless, and pacific revolution by which he accomplished the deliverance of his country was the first step in a career which our age glories in pursuing, and instituted a power which has done more than anything, except revealed religion, for the regeneration of society. The upper class had possessed the right of making and administering the laws, and he left them in possession, only transferring to wealth what had been the privilege of birth. To the rich, who alone had the means of sustaining the burden of public service in taxation and war, Solon gave a share of power proportioned to the demands made on their resources. The poorest classes were exempt from direct taxes, but were excluded from office. Solon gave them a voice in electing magistrates from the classes above them, and the right of calling them to account. This concession, apparently so slender, was the beginning of a mighty change. It introduced the idea that a man ought to have a voice in selecting those to whose rectitude and wisdom he is compelled to trust his fortune, his family, and his life. And this idea completely inverted the notion of human authority, for it inaugurated the reign of moral influence where all political power had depended on moral force. Government by consent superseded government by compulsion, and the pyramid which had stood on a point was made to stand upon its base. By making every citizen the guardian of his own interest Solon admitted the element of Democracy into the State. The greatest glory of a ruler, he said, is to create a popular government. Believing that no man can be entirely trusted, he subjected all who exercised power to the vigilant control of those for whom they acted.

The only resource against political disorders that had been known till then was the concentration of power. Solon undertook to effect the same object by the distribution of power. He gave to the common people as much influence as he thought them able to employ, that the State might be exempt from arbitrary government. It is the essence of Democracy, he said, to obey no master but the law. Solon recognised the principle that political forms are not final or inviolable, and must adapt themselves to facts; and he provided so well for the revision of his constitution, without breach of continuity or loss of stability, that for centuries after his death the Attic orators attributed to him, and quoted by his name, the whole structure of Athenian law. The direction of its growth was determined by the fundamental doctrine of Solon, that political power ought to be commensurate with public service. In the Persian war the services of the Democracy eclipsed those of the Patrician orders, for the fleet that swept the Asiatics from the Egean Sea was manned by the poorer Athenians. That class, whose valour had saved the State and had preserved European civilisation, had gained a title to increase of influence and privilege. The offices of State, which had been a monopoly of the rich, were thrown open to the poor, and in order to make sure that they should obtain their share, all but the highest commands were distributed by lot.

Whilst the ancient authorities were decaying, there was no accepted standard of moral and political right to make the framework of society fast in the midst of change. The instability that had seized on the forms threatened the very principles of government. The national beliefs were yielding to doubt, and doubt was not yet making way for knowledge. There had been a time when the obligations of public as well as private life were identified with the will of the gods. But that time had passed. Pallas, the ethereal goddess of the Athenians, and the Sun god whose oracles, delivered from the temple between the twin summits of Parnassus, did so much for the Greek nationality, aided in keeping up a lofty ideal of religion; but when the enlightened men of Greece learnt to apply their keen faculty of reasoning to the system of their inherited belief, they became quickly conscious that the conceptions of the gods corrupted the life and degraded the minds of the public. Popular morality could not be sustained by the popular religion. The moral instruction which was no longer supplied by the gods could not yet be found in books. There was no venerable code expounded by experts, no doctrine proclaimed by men of reputed sanctity like those teachers of the far East whose words still rule the fate of nearly half mankind. The effort to account for things by close observation and exact reasoning began by destroying. There came a time when the philosophers of the Porch and the Academy wrought the dictates of wisdom and virtue into a system so consistent and profound that it has vastly shortened the task of the Christian divines. But that time had not yet come.

The epoch of doubt and transition during which the Greeks passed from the dim fancies of mythology to the fierce light of science was the age of Pericles, and the endeavour to substitute certain truth for the prescriptions of impaired authorities, which was then beginning to absorb the energies of the Greek intellect, is the grandest movement in the profane annals of mankind, for to it we owe, even after the immeasurable progress accomplished by Christianity, much of our philosophy and far the better part of the political knowledge we possess. Pericles, who was at the head of the Athenian Government, was the first statesman who encountered the problem which the rapid weakening of traditions forced on the political world. No authority in morals or in politics remained unshaken by the motion that was in the air. No guide could be confidently trusted; there was no available criterion to appeal to, for the means of controlling or denying convictions that prevailed among the people. The popular sentiment as to what was right might be mistaken, but it was subject to no test. The people were, for practical purposes, the seat of the knowledge of good and evil. The people, therefore, were the seat of power.

The political philosophy of Pericles consisted of this conclusion. He resolutely struck away all the props that still sustained the artificial preponderance of wealth. For the ancient doctrine that power goes with land, he introduced the idea that power ought to be so equitably diffused as to afford equal security to all. That one part of the community should govern the whole, or that one class should make laws for another, he declared to be tyrannical. The abolition of privilege would have served only to transfer the supremacy from the rich to the poor, if Pericles had not redressed the balance by restricting the right of citizenship to Athenians of pure descent. By this measure the class which formed what we should call the third estate was brought down to 14,000 citizens, and became about equal in numbers with the higher ranks. Pericles held that every Athenian who neglected to take his part in the public business inflicted an injury on the commonwealth. That none might be excluded by poverty, he caused the poor to be paid for their attendance out of the funds of the State; for his administration of the federal tribute had brought together a treasure of more than two million sterling. The instrument of his sway was the art of speaking. He governed by persuasion. Everything was decided by argument in open deliberation, and every influence bowed before the ascendency of mind. The idea that the object of constitutions is not to confirm the predominance of any interest, but to prevent it; to preserve with equal care the independence of labour and the security of property; to make the rich safe against envy, and the poor against oppression, marks the highest level attained by the statesmanship of Greece. It hardly survived the great patriot who conceived it; and all history has been occupied with the endeavour to upset the balance of power by giving the advantage to money, land, or numbers. A generation followed that has never been equalled in talent—a generation of men whose works, in poetry and eloquence, are still the envy of the world, and in history, philosophy, and politics remain unsurpassed. But it produced no successor to Pericles, and no man was able to wield the sceptre that fell from his hand.

It was a momentous step in the progress of nations when the principle that every interest should have the right and the means of asserting itself was adopted by the Athenian Constitution. But for those who were beaten in the vote there was no redress. The law did not check the triumph of majorities or rescue the minority from the dire penalty of having been outnumbered. When the overwhelming influence of Pericles was removed, the conflict between classes raged without restraint, and the slaughter that befell the higher ranks in the Peloponnesian war gave an irresistible preponderance to the lower. The restless and inquiring spirit of the Athenians was prompt to unfold the reason of every institution and the consequences of every principle, and their Constitution ran its course from infancy to decrepitude with unexampled speed.

Two men's lives span the interval from the first admission of popular influence, under Solon, to the downfall of the State. Their history furnishes the classic example of the peril of Democracy under conditions singularly favourable. For the Athenians were not only brave and patriotic and capable of generous sacrifice, but they were the most religious of the Greeks. They venerated the Constitution which had given them prosperity, and equality, and freedom, and never questioned the fundamental laws which regulated the enormous power of the Assembly. They tolerated considerable variety of opinion and great licence of speech; and their humanity towards their slaves roused the indignation even of the most intelligent partisan of aristocracy. Thus they became the only people of antiquity that grew great by democratic institutions. But the possession of unlimited power, which corrodes the conscience, hardens the heart, and confounds the understanding of monarchs, exercised its demoralising influence on the illustrious democracy of Athens. It is bad to be oppressed by a minority, but it is worse to be oppressed by a majority. For there is a reserve of latent power in the masses which, if it is called into play, the minority can seldom resist. But from the absolute will of an entire people there is no appeal, no redemption, no refuge but treason. The humblest and most numerous class of the Athenians united the legislative, the judicial, and, in part, the executive power. The philosophy that was then in the ascendant taught them that there is no law superior to that of the State—the lawgiver is above the law.

It followed that the sovereign people had a right to do whatever was within its power, and was bound by no rule of right or wrong but its own judgment of expediency. On a memorable occasion the assembled Athenians declared it monstrous that they should be prevented from doing whatever they chose. No force that existed could restrain them; and they resolved that no duty should restrain them, and that they would be bound by no laws that were not of their own making. In this way the emancipated people of Athens became a tyrant; and their Government, the pioneer of European freedom, stands condemned with a terrible unanimity by all the wisest of the ancients. They ruined their city by attempting to conduct war by debate in the market-place. Like the French Republic, they put their unsuccessful commanders to death. They treated their dependencies with such injustice that they lost their maritime Empire. They plundered the rich until the rich conspired with the public enemy, and they crowned their guilt by the martyrdom of Socrates.

When the absolute sway of numbers had endured for near a quarter of a century, nothing but bare existence was left for the State to lose; and the Athenians, wearied and despondent, confessed the true cause of their ruin. They understood that for liberty, justice, and equal laws, it is as necessary that Democracy should restrain itself as it had been that it should restrain the Oligarchy. They resolved to take their stand once more upon the ancient ways, and to restore the order of things which had subsisted when the monopoly of power had been taken from the rich and had not been acquired by the poor. After a first restoration had failed, which is only memorable because Thucydides, whose judgment in politics is never at fault, pronounced it the best Government Athens had enjoyed, the attempt was renewed with more experience and greater singleness of purpose. The hostile parties were reconciled, and proclaimed an amnesty, the first in history. They resolved to govern by concurrence. The laws, which had the sanction of tradition, were reduced to a code; and no act of the sovereign assembly was valid with which they might be found to disagree. Between the sacred lines of the Constitution which were to remain inviolate, and the decrees which met from time to time the needs and notions of the day, a broad distinction was drawn; and the fabric of a law which had been the work of generations was made independent of momentary variations in the popular will. The repentance of the Athenians came too late to save the Republic. But the lesson of their experience endures for all times, for it teaches that government by the whole people, being the government of the most numerous and most powerful class, is an evil of the same nature as unmixed monarchy, and requires, for nearly the same reasons, institutions that shall protect it against itself, and shall uphold the permanent reign of law against arbitrary revolutions of opinion.

Parallel with the rise and fall of Athenian freedom, Rome was employed in working out the same problems, with greater constructive sense, and greater temporary success, but ending at last in a far more terrible catastrophe. That which among the ingenious Athenians had been a development carried forward by the spell of plausible argument, was in Rome a conflict between rival forces. Speculative politics had no attraction for the grim and practical genius of the Romans. They did not consider what would be the cleverest way of getting over a difficulty, but what way was indicated by analogous cases; and they assigned less influence to the impulse and spirit of the moment, than to precedent and example. Their peculiar character prompted them to ascribe the origin of their laws to early times, and in their desire to justify the continuity of their institutions, and to get rid of the reproach of innovation, they imagined the legendary history of the kings of Rome. The energy of their adherence to traditions made their progress slow, they advanced only under compulsion of almost unavoidable necessity, and the same questions recurred often, before they were settled. The constitutional history of the Republic turns on the endeavours of the aristocracy, who claimed to be the only true Romans, to retain in their hands the power they had wrested from the kings, and of the plebeians to get an equal share in it. And this controversy, which the eager and restless Athenians went through in one generation, lasted for more than two centuries, from a time when the *plebs* were excluded from the government of the city, and were taxed, and made to serve without pay, until, in the year 286, they were admitted to political equality. Then followed one hundred and fifty years of unexampled prosperity and glory; and then, out of the original conflict which had been compromised, if not theoretically settled, a new struggle arose which was without an issue.

The mass of poorer families, impoverished by incessant service in war, were reduced to dependence on an aristocracy of about two thousand wealthy men, who divided among themselves the immense domain of the State. When the need became intense the Gracchi tried to relieve it by inducing the richer classes to allot some share in the public lands to the common people. The old and famous aristocracy of birth and rank had made a stubborn resistance, but it knew the art of yielding. The later and more selfish aristocracy was unable to learn it. The character of the people was changed by the sterner motives of dispute. The fight for political power had been carried on with the moderation which is so honourable a quality of party contests in England. But the struggle for the objects of material existence grew to be as ferocious as civil controversies in France. Repulsed by the rich, after a struggle of twenty-two years, the people, three hundred and twenty thousand of whom depended on public rations for food, were ready to follow any man who promised to obtain for them by revolution what they could not obtain by law.

For a time the Senate, representing the ancient and

threatened order of things, was strong enough to overcome every popular leader that arose, until Julius Cæsar, supported by an army which he had led in an unparalleled career of conquest, and by the famished masses which he won by his lavish liberality, and skilled beyond all other men in the art of governing, converted the Republic into a Monarchy by a series of measures that were neither violent nor injurious.

The Empire preserved the Republican forms until the reign of Diocletian; but the will of the Emperors was as uncontrolled as that of the people had been after the victory of the Tribunes. Their power was arbitrary even when it was most wisely employed, and yet the Roman Empire rendered greater services to the cause of liberty than the Roman Republic. I do not mean by reason of the temporary accident that there were emperors who made good use of their immense opportunities, such as Nerva, of whom Tacitus says that he combined monarchy and liberty, things otherwise incompatible; or that the Empire was what its panegyrists declared it, the perfection of Democracy. In truth it was at best an ill-disguised and odious despotism. But Frederic the Great was a despot; yet he was a friend to toleration and free discussion. The Bonapartes were despotic; yet no liberal ruler was ever more acceptable to the masses of the people than the First Napoleon, after he had destroyed the Republic, in 1805, and the Third Napoleon at the height of his power in 1859. In the same way, the Roman Empire possessed merits which, at a distance, and especially at a great distance of time, concern men more deeply than the tragic tyranny which was felt in the neighbourhood of the Palace. The poor had what they had demanded in vain of the Republic. The rich fared better than during the Triumvirate. The rights of Roman citizens were extended to the people of the provinces. To the imperial epoch belong the better part of Roman literature and nearly the entire Civil Law; and it was the Empire that mitigated slavery, instituted religious toleration, made a beginning of the law of nations, and created a perfect system of the law of property. The Republic which Cæsar overthrew had been anything but a free State. It provided admirable securities for the rights of citizens; it treated with savage disregard the rights of men; and allowed the free Roman to inflict atrocious wrongs on his children, on debtors and dependants, on prisoners and slaves. Those deeper ideas of right and duty, which are not found on the tables of municipal law, but with which the generous minds of Greece were conversant, were held of little account, and the philosophy which dealt with such speculations was repeatedly proscribed, as a teacher of sedition and impiety.

At length, in the year 155, the Athenian philosopher Carneades appeared at Rome, on a political mission. During an interval of official business he delivered two public orations, to give the unlettered conquerors of his country a taste of the disputations that flourished in the Attic schools. On the first day he discoursed of natural justice. On the next he denied its existence, arguing that all our notions of good and evil are derived from positive enactment. From the time of that memorable display, the genius of the vanquished held its conquerors in thrall. The most eminent of the public men of Rome, such as Scipio and Cicero, formed their minds on Grecian models, and her jurists underwent the rigorous discipline of Zeno and Chrysippus.

If, drawing the limit in the second century, when the influence of Christianity becomes perceptible, we should form our judgment of the politics of antiquity by its actual legislation, our estimate would be low. The prevailing notions of freedom were imperfect, and the endeavours to realise them were wide of the mark. The ancients understood the regulation of power better than the regulation of liberty. They concentrated so many prerogatives in the State as to leave no footing from which a man could deny its jurisdiction or assign bounds to its activity. If I may employ an expressive anachronism, the vice of the classic State was that it was both Church and State in one. Morality was undistinguished from religion and politics from morals; and in religion, morality, and politics there was only one legislator and one authority. The State, while it did deplorably little for education, for practical science, for the indigent and helpless, or for the spiritual needs of man, nevertheless claimed the use of all his faculties and the determination of all his duties. Individuals and families, associations and dependencies were so much material that the sovereign power consumed for its own purposes. What the slave was in the hands of his master, the citizen was in the hands of the community. The most sacred obligations vanished before the public advantage. The passengers existed for the sake of the ship. By their disregard for private interests, and for the moral welfare and improvement of the people, both Greece and Rome destroyed the vital elements on which the prosperity of nations rests, and perished by the decay of families and the depopulation of the country. They survive not in their institutions, but in their ideas, and by their ideas, especially on the art of government, they are—

> The dead, but sceptred sovereigns who still rule
> Our spirits from their urns.

To them, indeed, may be tracked nearly all the errors that are undermining political society—Communism, Utilitarianism, the confusion between tyranny and authority, and between lawlessness and freedom.

The notion that men lived originally in a state of nature, by violence and without laws, is due to Critias. Communism in its grossest form was recommended by Diogenes of Sinope. According to the Sophists, there is no duty above expediency and no virtue apart from pleasure. Laws are an invention of weak men to rob their betters of the reasonable enjoyment of their superiority. It is better to inflict than to suffer wrong; and as there is no greater good than to do evil without fear of retribution, so there is no worse evil than to suffer without the consolation of revenge. Justice is the mask of a craven spirit; injustice is worldly wisdom; and duty, obedience, self-denial are the impostures of hypocrisy.

Government is absolute, and may ordain what it pleases, and no subject can complain that it does him wrong, but as long as he can escape compulsion and punishment, he is always free to disobey. Happiness consists in obtaining power and in eluding the necessity of obedience; and he that gains a throne by perfidy and murder, deserves to be truly envied.

Epicurus differed but little from the propounders of the code of revolutionary despotism. All societies, he said, are founded on contract for mutual protection. Good and evil are conventional terms, for the thunderbolts of heaven fall alike on the just and the unjust. The objection to wrongdoing is not the act, but in its consequences to the wrongdoer. Wise men contrive laws, not to bind, but to protect themselves; and when they prove to be unprofitable they cease to be valid. The illiberal sentiments of even the most illustrious metaphysicians are disclosed in the saying of Aristotle, that the mark of the worst governments is that they leave men free to live as they please.

If you will bear in mind that Socrates, the best of the pagans, knew of no higher criterion for men, of no better guide of conduct, than the laws of each country; that Plato, whose sublime doctrine was so near an anticipation of Christianity that celebrated theologians wished his works to be forbidden, lest men should he content with them, and indifferent to any higher dogma—to whom was granted that prophetic vision of the Just Man, accused, condemned and scourged, and dying on a Cross—nevertheless employed the most splendid intellect ever bestowed on man to advocate the abolition of the family and the exposure of infants; that Aristotle, the ablest moralist of antiquity, saw no harm in making raids upon a neighbouring people, for the sake of reducing them to slavery—still more, if you will consider that, among the moderns, men of genius equal to these have held political doctrines not less criminal or absurd—it will be apparent to you how stubborn a phalanx of error blocks the paths of truth; that pure reason is as powerless as custom to solve the problem of free government; that it can only be the fruit of long, manifold, and painful experience; and that the tracing of the methods by which divine wisdom has educated the nations to appreciate and to assume the duties of freedom, is not the least part of that true philosophy that studies to

> Assert eternal Providence,
> And justify the ways of God to men.

But, having sounded the depth of their errors, I should give you a very inadequate idea of the wisdom of the ancients if I allowed it to appear that their precepts were no better than their practice. While statesmen and senates and popular assemblies supplied examples of every description of blunder, a noble literature arose, in which a priceless treasure of political knowledge was stored, and in which the defects of the existing institutions were exposed with unsparing sagacity. The point on which the ancients were most nearly unanimous is the right of the people to govern, and their inability to govern alone. To meet this difficulty, to give to the popular element a full share without a monopoly of power, they adopted very generally the theory of a mixed Constitution. They differed from our notion of the same thing, because modern Constitutions have been a device for limiting monarchy; with them they were invented to curb democracy. The idea arose in the time of Plato—though he repelled it—when the early monarchies and oligarchies had vanished, and it continued to be cherished long after all democracies had been absorbed in the Roman Empire. But whereas a sovereign prince who surrenders part of his authority yields to the argument of superior force, a sovereign people relinquishing its own prerogative succumbs to the influence of reason. And it has in all times proved more easy to create limitations by the use of force than by persuasion.

The ancient writers saw very clearly that each principle of government standing alone is carried to excess and provokes a reaction. Monarchy hardens into despotism. Aristocracy contracts into oligarchy. Democracy expands into the supremacy of numbers. They therefore imagined that to restrain each element by combining it with the others would avert the natural process of self-destruction, and endow the State with perpetual youth. But this harmony of monarchy, aristocracy, and democracy blended together, which was the ideal of many writers, and which they supposed to be exhibited by Sparta, by Carthage, and by Rome, was a chimera of philosophers never realised by antiquity. At last Tacitus, wiser than the rest, confessed that the mixed Constitution, however admirable in theory, was difficult to establish and impossible to maintain. His disheartening avowal is not disowned by later experience.

The experiment has been tried more often than I can tell, with a combination of resources that were unknown to the ancients—with Christianity, parliamentary government, and a free press. Yet there is no example of such a balanced Constitution having lasted a century. If it has succeeded anywhere it has been in our favoured country and in our time; and we know not yet how long the wisdom of the nation will preserve the equipoise. The Federal check was as familiar to the ancients as the Constitutional. For the type of all their Republics was the government of a city by its own inhabitants meeting in the public place. An administration embracing many cities was known to them only in the form of the oppression which Sparta exercised over the Messenians, Athens over her Confederates, and Rome over Italy. The resources which, in modern times, enabled a great people to govern itself through a single centre did not exist. Equality could be preserved only by Federalism; and it occurs more often amongst them than in the modern world. If the distribution of power among the several parts of the State is the most efficient restraint on monarchy, the distribution of power among several States is the best check on democracy. By multiplying centres of government and discussion it promotes the diffusion of political knowledge and the maintenance of healthy and independent opinion. It is the protectorate of minorities, and the consecration of self-government. But although it must be enumerated among the better achievements of practical genius in antiquity, it arose from necessity, and its properties were imperfectly investigated in theory.

When the Greeks began to reflect on the problems of society, they first of all accepted things as they were, and did their best to explain and defend them. Inquiry, which with us is stimulated by doubt, began with them in wonder. The most illustrious of the early philosophers, Pythagoras, promulgated a theory for the preservation of political power in the educated class, and ennobled a form of government which was generally founded on popular ignorance and on strong class interests. He preached authority and subordination, and dwelt more on duties than on rights, on religion than on policy; and his system perished in the revolution by which oligarchies were swept away. The revolution afterwards developed its own philosophy, whose excesses I have described.

But between the two eras, between the rigid didactics of the early Pythagoreans and the dissolving theories of Protagoras, a philosopher arose who stood aloof from both extremes, and whose difficult sayings were never really understood or valued until our time. Heraclitus, of Ephesus, deposited his book in the temple of Diana. The book has perished, like the temple and the worship, but its fragments have been collected and interpreted with incredible ardour, by the scholars, the divines, the philosophers, and politicians who have been engaged the most intensely in the toil and stress of this century. The most renowned logician of the last century adopted every one of his propositions; and the most brilliant agitator among Continental Socialists composed a work of eight hundred and forty pages to celebrate his memory.

Heraclitus complained that the masses were deaf to truth, and knew not that one good man counts for more than thousands; but he held the existing order in no superstitious reverence. Strife, he says, is the source and the master of all things. Life is perpetual motion, and repose is death. No man can plunge twice into the same current, for it is always flowing and passing, and is never the same. The only thing fixed and certain in the midst of change is the universal and sovereign reason, which all men may not perceive, but which is common to all. Laws are sustained by no human authority, but by virtue of their derivation from the one law that is divine. These sayings, which recall the grand outlines of political truth which we have found in the Sacred Books, and carry us forward to the latest teaching of our most enlightened contemporaries, would bear a good deal of elucidation and comment. Heraclitus is, unfortunately, so obscure that Socrates could not understand him, and I won't pretend to have succeeded better.

If the topic of my address was the history of political science, the highest and the largest place would belong to Plato and Aristotle. The *Laws* of the one, the *Politics* of the other, are, if I may trust my own experience, the books from which we may learn the most about the principles of politics. The penetration with which those great masters of thought analysed the institutions of Greece, and exposed their vices, is not surpassed by anything in later literature; by Burke or Hamilton, the best political writers of the last century; by Tocqueville or Roscher, the most eminent of our own. But Plato and Aristotle were philosophers, studious not of unguided freedom, but of intelligent government. They saw the disastrous effects of ill-directed striving for liberty; and they resolved that it was better not to strive for it, but to be content with a strong administration, prudently adapted to make men prosperous and happy.

Now liberty and good government do not exclude each other; and there are excellent reasons why they should go together. Liberty is not a means to a higher political end. It is itself the highest political end. It is not for the sake of a good public administration that it is required, but for security in the pursuit of the highest objects of civil society, and of private life.

Increase of freedom in the State may sometimes promote mediocrity, and give vitality to prejudice ; it may even retard useful legislation, diminish the capacity for war, and restrict the boundaries of Empire. It might be plausibly argued that, if many things would be worse in England or Ireland under an intelligent despotism, some things would be managed better ; that the Roman Government was more enlightened under Augustus and Antoninus than under the Senate, in the days of Marius or of Pompey. A generous spirit prefers that his country should be poor, and weak, and of no account, but free, rather than powerful, prosperous, and enslaved. It is better to be the citizen of a humble commonwealth in the Alps, without a prospect of influence beyond the narrow frontier, than a subject of the superb autocracy that overshadows half of Asia and of Europe. But it may be urged, on the other side, that liberty is not the sum or the substitute of all the things men ought to live for ; that to be real it must be circumscribed, and that the limits of circumscription vary ; that advancing civilisation invests the State with increased rights and duties, and imposes increased burdens and constraint on the subject ; that a highly instructed and intelligent community may perceive the benefit of compulsory obligations which, at a lower stage, would be thought unbearable ; that liberal progress is not vague or indefinite, but aims at a point where the public is subject to no restrictions but those of which it feels the advantage; that a free country may be less capable of doing much for the advancement of religion, the prevention of vice, or the relief of suffering, than one that does not shrink from confronting great emergencies by some sacrifice of individual rights, and some concentration of power ; and that the supreme political object ought to be sometimes postponed to still higher moral objects. My argument involves no collision with these qualifying reflections. We are dealing, not with the effects of freedom, but with its causes. We are seeking out the influences which brought arbitrary government under control, either by the diffusion of power, or by the appeal to an authority which transcends all government, and among those influences the greatest philosophers of Greece have no claim to be reckoned.

It is the Stoics who emancipated mankind from its subjugation to despotic rule, and whose enlightened and elevated views of life bridged the chasm that separates the ancient from the Christian state, and led the way to freedom. Seeing how little security there is that the laws of any land shall be wise or just, and that the unanimous will of a people and the assent of nations are liable to err, the Stoics looked beyond those narrow barriers, and above those inferior sanctions, for the principles that ought to regulate the lives of men and the existence of society. They made it known that there is a will superior to the collective will of man, and a law that overrules those of Solon and Lycurgus. Their test of good government is its conformity to principles that can be traced to a higher legislator. That which we must obey, that to which we are bound to reduce all civil authorities, and to sacrifice every earthly interest, is that immutable law which is perfect and eternal as God Himself, which proceeds from His nature, and reigns over heaven and earth and over all the nations.

The great question is to discover, not what governments prescribe, but what they ought to prescribe; for no prescription is valid against the conscience of mankind. Before God, there is neither Greek nor barbarian, neither rich nor poor, and the slave is as good as his master, for by birth all men are free; they are citizens of that universal commonwealth which embraces all the world, brethren of one family, and children of God. The true guide of our conduct is no outward authority, but the voice of God, who comes down to dwell in our souls, who knows all our thoughts, to whom are owing all the truth we know, and all the good we do; for vice is voluntary, and virtue comes from the grace of the heavenly spirit within.

What the teaching of that divine voice is, the philosophers who had imbibed the sublime ethics of the Porch went on to expound: It is not enough to act up to the written law, or to give all men their due; we ought to give them more than their due, to be generous and beneficent, to devote ourselves for the good of others, seeking our reward in self-denial and sacrifice, acting from the motive of sympathy and not of personal advantage. Therefore we must treat others as we wish to be treated by them, and must persist until death in doing good to our enemies, regardless of unworthiness and ingratitude. For we must be at war with evil, but at peace with men, and it is better to suffer than to commit injustice. True freedom, says the most eloquent of the Stoics, consists in obeying God. A State governed by such principles as these would have been free far beyond the measure of Greek or Roman freedom; for they open a door to religious toleration, and close it against slavery. Neither conquest nor purchase, said Zeno, can make one man the property of another.

These doctrines were adopted and applied by the great jurists of the Empire. The law of nature, they said, is superior to the written law, and slavery contradicts the law of nature. Men have no right to do what they please with their own, or to make profit out of another's loss. Such is the political wisdom of the ancients, touching the foundations of liberty, as we find it in its highest development, in Cicero, and Seneca, and Philo, a Jew of Alexandria. Their writings impress upon us the greatness of the work of preparation for the Gospel which had been accomplished among men on the eve of the mission of the Apostles. St. Augustine, after quoting Seneca, exclaims: "What more could a Christian say than this Pagan has said?" The enlightened pagans had reached nearly the last point attainable without a new dispensation, when the fulness of time was come. We have seen the breadth and the splendour of the domain of Hellenic thought, and it has brought us to the threshold of a greater kingdom. The best of the later classics speak almost the language of Christianity, and they border on its spirit.

But in all that I have been able to cite from classical literature, three things are wanting, — representative government, the emancipation of the slaves, and liberty of conscience. There were, it is true, deliberative assemblies, chosen by the people ; and confederate cities, of which, both in Asia and Africa, there were so many leagues, sent their delegates to sit in Federal Councils. But government by an elected Parliament was even in theory a thing unknown. It is congruous with the nature of Polytheism to admit some measure of toleration. And Socrates, when he avowed that he must obey God rather than the Athenians, and the Stoics, when they set the wise man above the law, were very near giving utterance to the principle. But it was first proclaimed and established by enactment, not in polytheistic and philosophical Greece, but in India, by Asoka, the earliest of the Buddhist kings, two hundred and fifty years before the birth of Christ.

Slavery has been, far more than intolerance, the perpetual curse and reproach of ancient civilisation, and although its rightfulness was disputed as early as the days of Aristotle, and was implicitly, if not definitely, denied by several Stoics, the moral philosophy of the Greeks and Romans, as well as their practice, pronounced decidedly in its favour. But there was one extraordinary people who, in this as in other things, anticipated the purer precept that was to come. Philo of Alexandria is one of the writers whose views on society were most advanced. He applauds not only liberty but equality in the enjoyment of wealth. He believes that a limited democracy, purged of its grosser elements, is the most perfect government, and will extend itself gradually over all the world. By freedom he understood the following of God. Philo, though he required that the condition of the slave should be made compatible with the wants and claims of his higher nature, did not absolutely condemn slavery. But he has put on record the customs of the Essenes of Palestine, a people who, uniting the wisdom of the Gentiles with the faith of the Jews, led lives which were uncontaminated by the surrounding civilisation, and were the first to reject slavery both in principle and practice. They formed a religious community rather than a State, and their numbers did not exceed 4000. But their example testifies to how great a height religious men were able to raise their conception of society even without the succour of the New Testament, and affords the strongest condemnation of their contemporaries.

This, then, is the conclusion to which our survey brings us: There is hardly a truth in politics or in the system of the rights of man that was not grasped by the wisest of the Gentiles and the Jews, or that they did not declare with a refinement of thought and a nobleness of expression that later writers could never surpass. I might go on for hours, reciting to you passages on the law of nature and the duties of man, so solemn and religious that though they come from the profane theatre on the Acropolis, and from the Roman Forum, you would deem that you were listening to the hymns of Christian Churches and the discourse of ordained divines. But although the maxims of the great classic teachers, of Sophocles, and Plato, and Seneca, and the glorious examples of public virtue were in the mouths of all men, there was no power in them to avert the doom of that civilisation for which the blood of so many patriots and the genius of such incomparable writers had been wasted in vain. The liberties of the ancient nations were crushed beneath a hopeless and inevitable despotism, and their vitality was spent, when the new power came forth from Galilee, giving what was wanting to the efficacy of human knowledge to redeem societies as well as men.

It would be presumptuous if I attempted to indicate the numberless channels by which Christian influence gradually penetrated the State. The first striking phenomenon is the slowness with which an action destined to be so prodigious became manifest. Going forth to all nations, in many stages of civilisation and under almost every form of government, Christianity had none of the character of a political apostolate, and in its absorbing mission to individuals did not challenge public authority. The early Christians avoided contact with the State, abstained from the responsibilities of office, and were even reluctant to serve in the army. Cherishing their citizenship of a kingdom not of this world, they despaired of an empire which seemed too powerful to be resisted and too corrupt to be converted, whose institutions, the work and the pride of untold centuries of paganism, drew their sanctions from the gods whom the Christians accounted devils, which plunged its hands from age to age in the blood of martyrs, and was beyond the hope of regeneration and foredoomed to perish. They were so much overawed as to imagine that the fall of the State would be the end of the Church and of the world, and no man dreamed of the boundless future of spiritual and social influence that awaited their religion among the race of destroyers that were bringing the empire of Augustus and of Constantine to humiliation and ruin. The duties of government were less in their thoughts than the private virtues and duties of subjects; and it was long before they became aware of the burden of power in their faith. Down almost to the time of Chrysostom, they shrank from contemplating the obligation to emancipate the slaves.

Although the doctrine of self-reliance and self-denial, which is the foundation of political economy, was written as legibly in the New Testament as in the *Wealth of Nations*, it was not recognised until our age. Tertullian boasts of the passive obedience of the Christians. Melito writes to a pagan Emperor as if he were incapable of giving an unjust command; and in Christian times Optatus thought that whoever presumed to find fault with his sovereign exalted himself almost to the level of a god. But this political quietism was not universal. Origen, the ablest writer of early times, spoke with approval of conspiring for the destruction of tyranny.

After the fourth century the declarations against slavery are earnest and continual. And in a theological but yet pregnant sense, divines of the second century insist on liberty, and divines of the fourth century on equality. There was one essential and inevitable transformation in politics. Popular governments had existed, and also mixed and federal governments, but there had been no limited government, no State the circumference of whose authority had been defined by a force external to its own. That was the great problem which philosophy had raised, and which no statesmanship had been able to solve. Those who proclaimed the assistance of a higher authority had indeed drawn a metaphysical barrier before the governments, but they had not known how to make it real. All that Socrates could effect by way of protest against the tyranny of the reformed democracy was to die for his convictions. The Stoics could only advise the wise man to hold aloof from politics, keeping the unwritten law in his heart. But when Christ said: "Render unto Cæsar the things that are Cæsar's, and unto God the things that are God's," those words, spoken on His last visit to the Temple, three days before His death, gave to the civil power, under the protection of conscience, a sacredness it had never enjoyed, and bounds it had never acknowledged; and they were the repudiation of absolutism and the inauguration of freedom. For our Lord not only delivered the precept, but created the force to execute it. To maintain the necessary immunity in one supreme sphere, to reduce all political authority within defined limits, ceased to be an aspiration of patient reasoners, and was made the perpetual charge and care of the most energetic institution and the most universal association in the world. The new law, the new spirit, the new authority, gave to liberty a meaning and a value it had not possessed in the philosophy or in the constitution of Greece or Rome before the knowledge of the truth that makes us free.

II

THE HISTORY OF FREEDOM IN CHRISTIANITY[1]

WHEN Constantine the Great carried the seat of empire from Rome to Constantinople he set up in the market-place of the new capital a porphyry pillar which had come from Egypt, and of which a strange tale is told. In a vault beneath he secretly buried the seven sacred emblems of the Roman State, which were guarded by the virgins in the temple of Vesta, with the fire that might never be quenched. On the summit he raised a statue of Apollo, representing himself, and enclosing a fragment of the Cross; and he crowned it with a diadem of rays consisting of the nails employed at the Crucifixion, which his mother was believed to have found at Jerusalem.

The pillar still stands, the most significant monument that exists of the converted empire; for the notion that the nails which had pierced the body of Christ became a fit ornament for a heathen idol as soon as it was called by the name of a living emperor indicates the position designed for Christianity in the imperial structure of Constantine. Diocletian's attempt to transform the Roman Government into a despotism of the Eastern type had brought on the last and most serious persecution of the Christians; and Constantine, in adopting their faith, intended neither to abandon his predecessor's scheme of

[1] An address delivered to the members of the Bridgnorth Institution at the Agricultural Hall, 28th May 1877.

policy nor to renounce the fascinations of arbitrary authority, but to strengthen his throne with the support of a religion which had astonished the world by its power of resistance, and to obtain that support absolutely and without a drawback he fixed the seat of his government in the East, with a patriarch of his own creation.

Nobody warned him that by promoting the Christian religion he was tying one of his hands, and surrendering the prerogative of the Cæsars. As the acknowledged author of the liberty and superiority of the Church, he was appealed to as the guardian of her unity. He admitted the obligation; he accepted the trust; and the divisions that prevailed among the Christians supplied his successors with many opportunities of extending that protectorate, and preventing any reduction of the claims or of the resources of imperialism.

Constantine declared his own will equivalent to a canon of the Church. According to Justinian, the Roman people had formally transferred to the emperors the entire plenitude of its authority, and, therefore, the Emperor's pleasure, expressed by edict or by letter, had force of law. Even in the fervent age of its conversion the Empire employed its refined civilisation, the accumulated wisdom of ancient sages, the reasonableness and sublety of Roman law, and the entire inheritance of the Jewish, the Pagan, and the Christian world, to make the Church serve as a gilded crutch of absolutism. Neither an enlightened philosophy, nor all the political wisdom of Rome, nor even the faith and virtue of the Christians availed against the incorrigible tradition of antiquity. Something was wanted beyond all the gifts of reflection and experience—a faculty of self-government and self-control, developed like its language in the fibre of a nation, and growing with its growth. This vital element, which many centures of warfare, of anarchy, of oppression had extinguished in the countries that were still draped in the pomp of ancient civilisation, was deposited on the soil of Christendom by the fertilising stream of migration that overthrew the empire of the West.

In the height of their power the Romans became aware of a race of men that had not abdicated freedom in the hands of a monarch; and the ablest writer of the empire pointed to them with a vague and bitter feeling that, to the institutions of these barbarians, not yet crushed by despotism, the future of the world belonged. Their kings, when they had kings, did not preside at their councils; they were sometimes elective; they were sometimes deposed; and they were bound by oath to act in obedience with the general wish. They enjoyed real authority only in war. This primitive Republicanism, which admits monarchy as an occasional incident, but holds fast to the collective supremacy of all free men, of the constituent authority over all constituted authorities, is the remote germ of Parliamentary government. The action of the State was confined to narrow limits; but, besides his position as head of the State, the king was surrounded by a body of followers attached to him by personal or political ties. In these, his immediate dependants, disobedience or resistance to orders was no more tolerated than in a wife, a child, or a soldier; and a man was expected to murder his own father if his chieftain required it. Thus these Teutonic communities admitted an independence of government that threatened to dissolve society; and a dependence on persons that was dangerous to freedom. It was a system very favourable to corporations, but offering no security to individuals. The State was not likely to oppress its subjects; and was not able to protect them.

The first effect of the great Teutonic migration into the regions civilised by Rome was to throw back Europe many centuries to a condition scarcely more advanced than that from which the institutions of Solon had rescued Athens. Whilst the Greeks preserved the literature, the arts, and the science of antiquity and all the sacred monuments of early Christianity with a completeness of which the rended fragments that have come down to us give no commensurate idea, and even the peasants of Bulgaria knew the New Testament by heart, Western

Europe lay under the grasp of masters the ablest of whom could not write their names. The faculty of exact reasoning, of accurate observation, became extinct for five hundred years, and even the sciences most needful to society, medicine and geometry, fell into decay, until the teachers of the West went to school at the feet of Arabian masters. To bring order out of chaotic ruin, to rear a new civilisation and blend hostile and unequal races into a nation, the thing wanted was not liberty but force. And for centuries all progress is attached to the action of men like Clovis, Charlemagne, and William the Norman, who were resolute and peremptory, and prompt to be obeyed.

The spirit of immemorial paganism which had saturated ancient society could not be exorcised except by the combined influence of Church and State; and the universal sense that their union was necessary created the Byzantine despotism. The divines of the Empire who could not fancy Christianity flourishing beyond its borders, insisted that the State is not in the Church, but the Church in the State. This doctrine had scarcely been uttered when the rapid collapse of the Western Empire opened a wider horizon; and Salvianus, a priest at Marseilles, proclaimed that the social virtues, which were decaying amid the civilised Romans, existed in greater purity and promise among the Pagan invaders. They were converted with ease and rapidity; and their conversion was generally brought about by their kings.

Christianity, which in earlier times had addressed itself to the masses, and relied on the principle of liberty, now made its appeal to the rulers, and threw its mighty influence into the scale of authority. The barbarians, who possessed no books, no secular knowledge, no education, except in the schools of the clergy, and who had scarcely acquired the rudiments of religious instruction, turned with childlike attachment to men whose minds were stored with the knowledge of Scripture, of Cicero, of St. Augustine; and in the scanty world of their ideas, the Church was felt to be something infinitely vaster, stronger, holier than their newly founded States. The clergy supplied the means of conducting the new governments, and were made exempt from taxation, from the jurisdiction of the civil magistrate, and of the political administrator. They taught that power ought to be conferred by election; and the Councils of Toledo furnished the framework of the Parliamentary system of Spain, which is, by a long interval, the oldest in the world. But the monarchy of the Goths in Spain, as well as that of the Saxons in England, in both of which the nobles and the prelates surrounded the throne with the semblance of free institutions, passed away; and the people that prospered and overshadowed the rest were the Franks, who had no native nobility, whose law of succession to the Crown became for one thousand years the fixed object of an unchanging superstition, and under whom the feudal system was developed to excess.

Feudalism made land the measure and the master of all things. Having no other source of wealth than the produce of the soil, men depended on the landlord for the means of escaping starvation; and thus his power became paramount over the liberty of the subject and the authority of the State. Every baron, said the French maxim, is sovereign in his own domain. The nations of the West lay between the competing tyrannies of local magnates and of absolute monarchs, when a force was brought upon the scene which proved for a time superior alike to the vassal and his lord.

In the days of the Conquest, when the Normans destroyed the liberties of England, the rude institutions which had come with the Saxons, the Goths, and the Franks from the forests of Germany were suffering decay, and the new element of popular government afterwards supplied by the rise of towns and the formation of a middle class was not yet active. The only influence capable of resisting the feudal hierarchy was the ecclesiastical hierarchy; and they came into collision, when the process of feudalism threatened the independence of the Church by subjecting the prelates severally to that form of personal dependence on the kings which was peculiar to the Teutonic state.

To that conflict of four hundred years we owe the rise of civil liberty. If the Church had continued to buttress the thrones of the kings whom it anointed, or if the struggle had terminated speedily in an undivided victory, all Europe would have sunk down under a Byzantine or Muscovite despotism. For the aim of both contending parties was absolute authority. But although liberty was not the end for which they strove, it was the means by which the temporal and the spiritual power called the nations to their aid. The towns of Italy and Germany won their franchises, France got her States-General, and England her Parliament out of the alternate phases of the contest; and as long as it lasted it prevented the rise of divine right. A disposition existed to regard the crown as an estate descending under the law of real property in the family that possessed it. But the authority of religion, and especially of the papacy, was thrown on the side that denied the indefeasible title of kings. In France what was afterwards called the Gallican theory maintained that the reigning house was above the law, and that the sceptre was not to pass away from it as long as there should be princes of the royal blood of St. Louis. But in other countries the oath of fidelity itself attested that it was conditional, and should be kept only during good behaviour; and it was in conformity with the public law to which all monarchs were held subject, that King John was declared a rebel against the barons, and that the men who raised Edward III. to the throne from which they had deposed his father invoked the maxim *Vox populi Vox Dei.*

And this doctrine of the divine right of the people to raise up and pull down princes, after obtaining the sanctions of religion, was made to stand on broader grounds, and was strong enough to resist both Church and king. In the struggle between the House of Bruce and the House of Plantagenet for the possession of Scotland and Ireland, the English claim was backed by the censures of Rome. But the Irish and the Scots refused it, and the address in which the Scottish Parliament informed the Pope of their resolution shows how firmly the popular doctrine had taken root. Speaking of Robert Bruce, they say: "Divine Providence, the laws and customs of the country, which we will defend till death, and the choice of the people, have made him our king. If he should ever betray his principles, and consent that we should be subjects of the English king, then we shall treat him as an enemy, as the subverter of our rights and his own, and shall elect another in his place. We care not for glory or for wealth, but for that liberty which no true man will give up but with his life." This estimate of royalty was natural among men accustomed to see those whom they most respected in constant strife with their rulers. Gregory VII. had begun the disparagement of civil authorities by saying that they are the work of the devil; and already in his time both parties were driven to acknowledge the sovereignty of the people, and appealed to it as the immediate source of power.

Two centuries later this political theory had gained both in definiteness and in force among the Guelphs, who were the Church party, and among the Ghibellines, or Imperialists. Here are the sentiments of the most celebrated of all the Guelphic writers: "A king who is unfaithful to his duty forfeits his claim to obedience. It is not rebellion to depose him, for he is himself a rebel whom the nation has a right to put down. But it is better to abridge his power, that he may be unable to abuse it. For this purpose, the whole nation ought to have a share in governing itself; the Constitution ought to combine a limited and elective monarchy, with an aristocracy of merit, and such an admixture of democracy as shall admit all classes to office, by popular election. No government has a right to levy taxes beyond the limit determined by the people. All political authority is derived from popular suffrage, and all laws must be made by the people or their representatives. There is no security for us as long as we depend on the will of another man." This language, which contains the earliest exposition of the Whig theory of the revolution, is taken from the works of St. Thomas Aquinas, of whom Lord Bacon says that he had the largest heart of the school divines. And it is worth while to observe that he wrote at the very moment when Simon de Montfort summoned the Commons; and that the politics of the Neapolitan friar are centuries in advance of the English statesman's.

The ablest writer of the Ghibelline party was Marsilius of Padua. "Laws," he said, "derive their authority from the nation, and are invalid without its assent. As the whole is greater than any part, it is wrong that any part should legislate for the whole; and as men are equal, it is wrong that one should be bound by laws made by another. But in obeying laws to which all men have agreed, all men, in reality, govern themselves. The monarch, who is instituted by the legislature to execute its will, ought to be armed with a force sufficient to coerce individuals, but not sufficient to control the majority of the people. He is responsible to the nation, and subject to the law; and the nation that appoints him, and assigns him his duties, has to see that he obeys the Constitution, and has to dismiss him if he breaks it. The rights of citizens are independent of the faith they profess; and no man may be punished for his religion." This writer, who saw in some respects farther than Locke or Montesquieu, who, in regard to the sovereignty of the nation, representative government, the superiority of the legislature over the executive, and the liberty of conscience, had so firm a grasp of the principles that were to sway the modern world, lived in the reign of Edward II., five hundred and fifty years ago.

It is significant that these two writers should agree on so many of the fundamental points which have been, ever since, the topic of controversy; for they belonged to hostile schools, and one of them would have thought the other worthy of death. St. Thomas would have made the papacy control all Christian governments. Marsilius would have had the clergy submit to the law of the land;

and would have put them under restrictions both as to property and numbers. As the great debate went on, many things gradually made themselves clear, and grew into settled convictions. For these were not only the thoughts of prophetic minds that surpassed the level of contemporaries ; there was some prospect that they would master the practical world. The ancient reign of the barons was seriously threatened. The opening of the East by the Crusades had imparted a great stimulus to industry. A stream set in from the country to the towns, and there was no room for the government of towns in the feudal machinery. When men found a way of earning a livelihood without depending for it on the good will of the class that owned the land, the landowner lost much of his importance, and it began to pass to the possessors of moveable wealth. The townspeople not only made themselves free from the control of prelates and barons, but endeavoured to obtain for their own class and interest the command of the State.

The fourteenth century was filled with the tumult of this struggle between democracy and chivalry. The Italian towns, foremost in intelligence and civilisation, led the way with democratic constitutions of an ideal and generally an impracticable type. The Swiss cast off the yoke of Austria. Two long chains of free cities arose, along the valley of the Rhine, and across the heart of Germany. The citizens of Paris got possession of the king, reformed the State, and began their tremendous career of experiments to govern France. But the most healthy and vigorous growth of municipal liberties was in Belgium, of all countries on the Continent, that which has been from immemorial ages the most stubborn in its fidelity to the principle of self-government. So vast were the resources concentrated in the Flemish towns, so widespread was the movement of democracy, that it was long doubtful whether the new interest would not prevail, and whether the ascendency of the military aristocracy would not pass over to the wealth and intelligence of the men that lived by trade. But Rienzi, Marcel, Artevelde, and the other champions of the unripe democracy of those days, lived and died in vain. The upheaval of the middle class had disclosed the need, the passions, the aspirations of the suffering poor below; ferocious insurrections in France and England caused a reaction that retarded for centuries the readjustment of power, and the red spectre of social revolution arose in the track of democracy. The armed citizens of Ghent were crushed by the French chivalry; and monarchy alone reaped the fruit of the change that was going on in the position of classes, and stirred the minds of men.

Looking back over the space of a thousand years, which we call the Middle Ages, to get an estimate of the work they had done, if not towards perfection in their institutions, at least towards attaining the knowledge of political truth, this is what we find: Representative government, which was unknown to the ancients, was almost universal. The methods of election were crude; but the principle that no tax was lawful that was not granted by the class that paid it—that is, that taxation was inseparable from representation—was recognised, not as the privilege of certain countries, but as the right of all. Not a prince in the world, said Philip de Commines, can levy a penny without the consent of the people. Slavery was almost everywhere extinct; and absolute power was deemed more intolerable and more criminal than slavery. The right of insurrection was not only admitted but defined, as a duty sanctioned by religion. Even the principles of the Habeas Corpus Act, and the method of the Income Tax, were already known. The issue of ancient politics was an absolute state planted on slavery. The political produce of the Middle Ages was a system of states in which authority was restricted by the representation of powerful classes, by privileged associations, and by the acknowledgment of duties superior to those which are imposed by man.

As regards the realisation in practice of what was seen to be good, there was almost everything to do. But the great problems of principle had been solved, and we come to the question, How did the sixteenth century husband the treasure which the Middle Ages had stored up? The most visible sign of the times was the decline of the religious influence that had reigned so long. Sixty years passed after the invention of printing, and thirty thousand books had issued from European presses, before anybody undertook to print the Greek Testament. In the days when every State made the unity of faith its first care, it came to be thought that the rights of men, and the duties of neighbours and of rulers towards them, varied according to their religion; and society did not acknowledge the same obligations to a Turk or a Jew, a pagan or a heretic, or a devil worshipper, as to an orthodox Christian. As the ascendency of religion grew weaker, this privilege of treating its enemies on exceptional principles was claimed by the State for its own benefit; and the idea that the ends of government justify the means employed was worked into system by Machiavelli. He was an acute politican, sincerely anxious that the obstacles to the intelligent government of Italy should be swept away. It appeared to him that the most vexatious obstacle to intellect is conscience, and that the vigorous use of statecraft necessary for the success of difficult schemes would never be made if governments allowed themselves to be hampered by the precepts of the copy-book.

His audacious doctrine was avowed in the succeeding age by men whose personal character stood high. They saw that in critical times good men have seldom strength for their goodness, and yield to those who have grasped the meaning of the maxim that you cannot make an omelette if you are afraid to break the eggs. They saw that public morality differs from private, because no Government can turn the other cheek, or can admit that mercy is better than justice. And they could not define the difference or draw the limits of exception; or tell what other standard for a nation's acts there is than the judgment which Heaven pronounces in this world by success.

Machiavelli's teaching would hardly have stood the test of Parliamentary government, for public discussion demands at least the profession of good faith. But it gave an immense impulse to absolutism by silencing the consciences of very religious kings, and made the good and the bad very much alike. Charles V. offered 5000 crowns for the murder of an enemy. Ferdinand I. and Ferdinand II., Henry III. and Louis XIII., each caused his most powerful subject to be treacherously despatched. Elizabeth and Mary Stuart tried to do the same to each other. The way was paved for absolute monarchy to triumph over the spirit and institutions of a better age, not by isolated acts of wickedness, but by a studied philosophy of crime and so thorough a perversion of the moral sense that the like of it had not been since the Stoics reformed the morality of paganism.

The clergy, who had in so many ways served the cause of freedom during the prolonged strife against feudalism and slavery, were associated now with the interest of royalty. Attempts had been made to reform the Church on the Constitutional model; they had failed, but they had united the hierarchy and the crown against the system of divided power as against a common enemy. Strong kings were able to bring the spirituality under subjection in France and Spain, in Sicily and in England. The absolute monarchy of France was built up in the two following centuries by twelve political cardinals. The kings of Spain obtained the same effect almost at a single stroke by reviving and appropriating to their own use the tribunal of the Inquisition, which had been growing obsolete, but now served to arm them with terrors which effectually made them despotic. One generation beheld the change all over Europe, from the anarchy of the days of the Roses to the passionate submission, the gratified acquiescence in tyranny that marks the reign of Henry VIII. and the kings of his time.

The tide was running fast when the Reformation began at Wittenberg, and it was to be expected that Luther's influence would stem the flood of absolutism. For he was confronted everywhere by the compact alliance of the Church with the State; and great part of his country was governed by hostile potentates who were prelates of the Court of Rome. He had, indeed, more to fear from temporal than from spiritual foes. The leading German bishops wished that the Protestant demands should be conceded; and the Pope himself vainly urged on the Emperor a conciliatory policy. But Charles V. had outlawed Luther, and attempted to waylay him; and the Dukes of Bavaria were active in beheading and burning his disciples, whilst the democracy of the towns generally took his side. But the dread of revolution was the deepest of his political sentiments; and the gloss by which the Guelphic divines had got over the passive obedience of the apostolic age was characteristic of that mediæval method of interpretation which he rejected. He swerved for a moment in his later years; but the substance of his political teaching was eminently conservative, the Lutheran States became the stronghold of rigid immobility, and Lutheran writers constantly condemned the democratic literature that arose in the second age of the Reformation. For the Swiss reformers were bolder than the Germans in mixing up their cause with politics. Zürich and Geneva were Republics, and the spirit of their governments influenced both Zwingli and Calvin.

Zwingli indeed did not shrink from the mediæval doctrine that evil magistrates must be cashiered; but he was killed too early to act either deeply or permanently on the political character of Protestantism. Calvin, although a Republican, judged that the people are unfit to govern themselves, and declared the popular assembly an abuse that ought to be abolished. He desired an aristocracy of the elect, armed with the means of punishing not only crime but vice and error. For he thought that the severity of the mediæval laws was insufficient for the need of the times; and he favoured the most irresistible weapon which the inquisitorial procedure put into the hand of the Government, the right of subjecting prisoners to intolerable torture, not because they were guilty, but because their guilt could not be proved. His teaching, though not calculated to promote popular institutions, was so adverse to the authority of the surrounding monarchs, that he softened down the expression of his political views in the French edition of his *Institutes.*

The direct political influence of the Reformation effected less than has been supposed. Most States were strong enough to control it. Some, by intense exertion, shut out the pouring flood. Others, with consummate skill, diverted it to their own uses. The Polish Government alone at that time left it to its course. Scotland was the only kingdom in which the Reformation triumphed over the resistance of the State; and Ireland was the only instance where it failed, in spite of Government support. But in almost every other case, both the princes that spread their canvas to the gale and those that faced it, employed the zeal, the alarm, the passions it aroused as instruments for the increase of power. Nations eagerly invested their rulers with every prerogative needed to preserve their faith, and all the care to keep Church and State asunder, and to prevent the confusion of their powers, which had been the work of ages, was renounced in the intensity of the crisis. Atrocious deeds were done, in which religious passion was often the instrument, but policy was the motive.

Fanaticism displays itself in the masses, but the masses were rarely fanaticised, and the crimes ascribed to it were commonly due to the calculations of dispassionate politicians. When the King of France undertook to kill all the Protestants, he was obliged to do it by his own agents. It was nowhere the spontaneous act of the population, and in many towns and in entire provinces the magistrates refused to obey. The motive of the Court was so far from mere fanaticism that the Queen immediately challenged Elizabeth to do the like to the English Catholics. Francis I. and Henry II. sent nearly a hundred Huguenots to the stake, but they were cordial and assiduous promoters of the Protestant religion in

Germany. Sir Nicholas Bacon was one of the ministers who suppressed the mass in England. Yet when the Huguenot refugees came over he liked them so little that he reminded Parliament of the summary way in which Henry V. at Agincourt dealt with the Frenchmen who fell into his hands. John Knox thought that every Catholic in Scotland ought to be put to death, and no man ever had disciples of a sterner or more relentless temper. But his counsel was not followed.

All through the religious conflict policy kept the upper hand. When the last of the Reformers died, religion, instead of emancipating the nations, had become an excuse for the criminal art of despots. Calvin preached and Bellarmine lectured, but Machiavelli reigned. Before the close of the century three events occurred which mark the beginning of a momentous change. The massacre of St. Bartholomew convinced the bulk of Calvinists of the lawfulness of rebellion against tyrants, and they became advocates of that doctrine in which the Bishop of Winchester had led the way,[1] and which Knox and Buchanan had received, through their master at Paris, straight from the mediæval schools. Adopted out of aversion to the King of France, it was soon put in practice against the King of Spain. The revolted Netherlands, by a solemn Act, deposed Philip II., and made themselves independent under the Prince of Orange, who had been, and continued to be, styled his Lieutenant. Their example was important, not only because subjects of one religion deposed a monarch of another, for that had been seen in Scotland, but because, moreover, it put a republic in the place of a monarchy, and forced the public law of Europe to recognise the accomplished revolution. At the same time, the French Catholics, rising against Henry III., who was the most contemptible of tyrants, and against his heir, Henry of Navarre, who, as a Protestant, repelled the majority of the nation, fought for the same principles with sword and pen.

[1] [Poynet, in his *Treatise on Political Power.*]

Many shelves might be filled with the books which came out in their defence during half a century, and they include the most comprehensive treatises on laws ever written. Nearly all are vitiated by the defect which disfigured political literature in the Middle Ages. That literature, as I have tried to show, is extremely remarkable, and its services in aiding human progress are very great. But from the death of St. Bernard until the appearance of Sir Thomas More's *Utopia*, there was hardly a writer who did not make his politics subservient to the interest of either Pope or King. And those who came after the Reformation were always thinking of laws as they might affect Catholics or Protestants. Knox thundered against what he called *the Monstrous Regiment of Women*, because the Queen went to mass, and Mariana praised the assassin of Henry III. because the King was in league with Huguenots. For the belief that it is right to murder tyrants, first taught among Christians, I believe, by John of Salisbury, the most distinguished English writer of the twelfth century, and confirmed by Roger Bacon, the most celebrated Englishman of the thirteenth, had acquired about this time a fatal significance. Nobody sincerely thought of politics as a law for the just and the unjust, or tried to find out a set of principles that should hold good alike under all changes of religion. Hooker's *Ecclesiastical Polity* stands almost alone among the works I am speaking of, and is still read with admiration by every thoughtful man as the earliest and one of the finest prose classics in our language. But though few of the others have survived, they contributed to hand down masculine notions of limited authority and conditional obedience from the epoch of theory to generations of free men. Even the coarse violence of Buchanan and Boucher was a link in the chain of tradition that connects the Hildebrandine controversy with the Long Parliament, and St. Thomas with Edmund Burke.

That men should understand that governments do not exist by divine right, and that arbitrary government is the violation of divine right, was no doubt the medicine suited to the malady under which Europe languished. But although the knowledge of this truth might become an element of salutary destruction, it could give little aid to progress and reform. Resistance to tyranny implied no faculty of constructing a legal government in its place. Tyburn tree may be a useful thing, but it is better still that the offender should live for repentance and reformation. The principles which discriminate in politics between good and evil, and make States worthy to last, were not yet found.

The French philosopher Charron was one of the men least demoralised by party spirit, and least blinded by zeal for a cause. In a passage almost literally taken from St. Thomas, he describes our subordination under a law of nature, to which all legislation must conform ; and he ascertains it not by the light of revealed religion, but by the voice of universal reason, through which God enlightens the consciences of men. Upon this foundation Grotius drew the lines of real political science. In gathering the materials of international law, he had to go beyond national treaties and denominational interests for a principle embracing all mankind. The principles of law must stand, he said, even if we suppose that there is no God. By these inaccurate terms he meant that they must be found independently of revelation. From that time it became possible to make politics a matter of principle and of conscience, so that men and nations differing in all other things could live in peace together, under the sanctions of a common law. Grotius himself used his discovery to little purpose, as he deprived it of immediate effect by admitting that the right to reign may be enjoyed as a freehold, subject to no conditions.

When Cumberland and Pufendorf unfolded the true significance of his doctrine, every settled authority, every triumphant interest recoiled aghast. None were willing to surrender advantages won by force or skill, because they might be in contradiction, not with the Ten

Commandments, but with an unknown code, which Grotius himself had not attempted to draw up, and touching which no two philosophers agreed. It was manifest that all persons who had learned that political science is an affair of conscience rather than of might or expediency, must regard their adversaries as men without principle, that the controversy between them would perpetually involve morality, and could not be governed by the plea of good intentions, which softens down the asperities of religious strife. Nearly all the greatest men of the seventeenth century repudiated the innovation. In the eighteenth, the two ideas of Grotius, that there are certain political truths by which every State and every interest must stand or fall, and that society is knit together by a series of real and hypothetical contracts, became, in other hands, the lever that displaced the world. When, by what seemed the operation of an irresistible and constant law, royalty had prevailed over all enemies and all competitors, it became a religion. Its ancient rivals, the baron and the prelate, figured as supporters by its side. Year after year, the assemblies that represented the self-government of provinces and of privileged classes, all over the Continent, met for the last time and passed away, to the satisfaction of the people, who had learned to venerate the throne as the constructor of their unity, the promoter of prosperity and power, the defender of orthodoxy, and the employer of talent.

The Bourbons, who had snatched the crown from a rebellious democracy, the Stuarts, who had come in as usurpers, set up the doctrine that States are formed by the valour, the policy, and the appropriate marriages of the royal family; that the king is consequently anterior to the people, that he is its maker rather than its handiwork, and reigns independently of consent. Theology followed up divine right with passive obedience. In the golden age of religious science, Archbishop Ussher, the most learned of Anglican prelates, and Bossuet, the ablest of the French, declared that resistance to kings is a crime, and that they may lawfully employ compulsion against the faith of their subjects. The philosophers heartily supported the divines. Bacon fixed his hope of all human progress on the strong hand of kings. Descartes advised them to crush all those who might be able to resist their power. Hobbes taught that authority is always in the right. Pascal considered it absurd to reform laws, or to set up an ideal justice against actual force. Even Spinoza, who was a Republican and a Jew, assigned to the State the absolute control of religion.

Monarchy exerted a charm over the imagination, so unlike the unceremonious spirit of the Middle Ages, that, on learning the execution of Charles I., men died of the shock; and the same thing occurred at the death of Louis XVI. and of the Duke of Enghien. The classic land of absolute monarchy was France. Richelieu held that it would be impossible to keep the people down if they were suffered to be well off. The Chancellor affirmed that France could not be governed without the right of arbitrary arrest and exile; and that in case of danger to the State it may be well that a hundred innocent men should perish. The Minister of Finance called it sedition to demand that the Crown should keep faith. One who lived on intimate terms with Louis XIV. says that even the slightest disobedience to the royal will is a crime to be punished with death. Louis employed these precepts to their fullest extent. He candidly avows that kings are no more bound by the terms of a treaty than by the words of a compliment; and that there is nothing in the possession of their subjects which they may not lawfully take from them. In obedience to this principle, when Marshal Vauban, appalled by the misery of the people, proposed that all existing imposts should be repealed for a single tax that would be less onerous, the King took his advice, but retained all the old taxes whilst he imposed the new. With half the present population, he maintained an army of 450,000 men; nearly twice as large as that which the late Emperor Napoleon assembled to attack Germany. Meanwhile the people starved on grass.

France, said Fénelon, is one enormous hospital. French historians believe that in a single generation six millions of people died of want. It would be easy to find tyrants more violent, more malignant, more odious than Louis XIV., but there was not one who ever used his power to inflict greater suffering or greater wrong; and the admiration with which he inspired the most illustrious men of his time denotes the lowest depth to which the turpitude of absolutism has ever degraded the conscience of Europe.

The Republics of that day were, for the most part, so governed as to reconcile men with the less opprobrious vices of monarchy. Poland was a State made up of centrifugal forces. What the nobles called liberty was the right of each of them to veto the acts of the Diet, and to persecute the peasants on his estates—rights which they refused to surrender up to the time of the partition, and thus verified the warning of a preacher spoken long ago: "You will perish, not by invasion or war, but by your infernal liberties." Venice suffered from the opposite evil of excessive concentration. It was the most sagacious of Governments, and would rarely have made mistakes if it had not imputed to others motives as wise as its own, and had taken account of passions and follies of which it had little cognisance. But the supreme power of the nobility had passed to a committee, from the committee to a Council of Ten, from the Ten to three Inquisitors of State; and in this intensely centralised form it became, about the year 1600, a frightful despotism. I have shown you how Machiavelli supplied the immoral theory needful for the consummation of royal absolutism; the absolute oligarchy of Venice required the same assurance against the revolt of conscience. It was provided by a writer as able as Machiavelli, who analysed the wants and resources of aristocracy, and made known that its best security is poison. As late as a century ago, Venetian senators of honourable and even religious lives employed assassins for the public good with no more compunction than Philip II. or Charles IX.

The Swiss Cantons, especially Geneva, profoundly

influenced opinion in the days preceding the French Revolution, but they had had no part in the earlier movement to inaugurate the reign of law. That honour belongs to the Netherlands alone among the Commonwealths. They earned it, not by their form of government, which was defective and precarious, for the Orange party perpetually plotted against it, and slew the two most eminent of the Republican statesmen, and William III. himself intrigued for English aid to set the crown upon his head ; but by the freedom of the press, which made Holland the vantage-ground from which, in the darkest hour of oppression, the victims of the oppressors obtained the ear of Europe.

The ordinance of Louis XIV., that every French Protestant should immediately renounce his religion, went out in the year in which James II. became king. The Protestant refugees did what their ancestors had done a century before. They asserted the deposing power of subjects over rulers who had broken the original contract between them, and all the Powers, excepting France, countenanced their argument, and sent forth William of Orange on that expedition which was the faint dawn of a brighter day.

It is to this unexampled combination of things on the Continent, more than to her own energy, that England owes her deliverance. The efforts made by the Scots, by the Irish, and at last by the Long Parliament to get rid of the misrule of the Stuarts had been foiled, not by the resistance of Monarchy, but by the helplessness of the Republic. State and Church were swept away ; new institutions were raised up under the ablest ruler that had ever sprung from a revolution ; and England, seething with the toil of political thought, had produced at least two writers who in many directions saw as far and as clearly as we do now. But Cromwell's Constitution was rolled up like a scroll ; Harrington and Lilburne were laughed at for a time and forgotten, the country confessed the failure of its striving, disavowed its aims, and flung itself with enthusiasm, and without any effective stipulations, at the feet of a worthless king.

If the people of England had accomplished no more than this to relieve mankind from the pervading pressure of unlimited monarchy, they would have done more harm than good. By the fanatical treachery with which, violating the Parliament and the law, they contrived the death of King Charles, by the ribaldry of the Latin pamphlet with which Milton justified the act before the world, by persuading the world that the Republicans were hostile alike to liberty and to authority, and did not believe in themselves, they gave strength and reason to the current of Royalism, which, at the Restoration, overwhelmed their work. If there had been nothing to make up for this defect of certainty and of constancy in politics England would have gone the way of other nations.

At that time there was some truth in the old joke which describes the English dislike of speculation by saying that all our philosophy consists of a short catechism in two questions: "What is mind? No matter. What is matter? Never mind." The only accepted appeal was to tradition. Patriots were in the habit of saying that they took their stand upon the ancient ways, and would not have the laws of England changed. To enforce their argument they invented a story that the constitution had come from Troy, and that the Romans had allowed it to subsist untouched. Such fables did not avail against Strafford; and the oracle of precedent sometimes gave responses adverse to the popular cause. In the sovereign question of religion, this was decisive, for the practice of the sixteenth century, as well as of the fifteenth, testified in favour of intolerance. By royal command, the nation had passed four times in one generation from one faith to another, with a facility that made a fatal impression on Laud. In a country that had proscribed every religion in turn, and had submitted to such a variety of penal measures against Lollard and Arian, against Augsburg and Rome, it seemed there could be no danger in cropping the ears of a Puritan.

But an age of stronger conviction had arrived; and

men resolved to abandon the ancient ways that led to the scaffold and the rack, and to make the wisdom of their ancestors and the statutes of the land bow before an unwritten law. Religious liberty had been the dream of great Christian writers in the age of Constantine and Valentinian, a dream never wholly realised in the Empire, and rudely dispelled when the barbarians found that it exceeded the resources of their art to govern civilised populations of another religion, and unity of worship was imposed by laws of blood and by theories more cruel than the laws. But from St. Athanasius and St. Ambrose down to Erasmus and More, each age heard the protest of earnest men in behalf of the liberty of conscience, and the peaceful days before the Reformation were full of promise that it would prevail.

In the commotion that followed, men were glad to get tolerated themselves by way of privilege and compromise, and willingly renounced the wider application of the principle. Socinus was the first who, on the ground that Church and State ought to be separated, required universal toleration. But Socinus disarmed his own theory, for he was a strict advocate of passive obedience.

The idea that religious liberty is the generating principle of civil, and that civil liberty is the necessary condition of religious, was a discovery reserved for the seventeenth century. Many years before the names of Milton and Taylor, of Baxter and Locke were made illustrious by their partial condemnation of intolerance, there were men among the Independent congregations who grasped with vigour and sincerity the principle that it is only by abridging the authority of States that the liberty of Churches can be assured. That great political idea, sanctifying freedom and consecrating it to God, teaching men to treasure the liberties of others as their own, and to defend them for the love of justice and charity more than as a claim of right, has been the soul of what is great and good in the progress of the last two hundred years. The cause of religion, even under the unregenerate influence of worldly passion, had as much to do as any clear notions of policy in making this country the foremost of the free. It had been the deepest current in the movement of 1641, and it remained the strongest motive that survived the reaction of 1660.

The greatest writers of the Whig party, Burke and Macaulay, constantly represented the statesmen of the Revolution as the legitimate ancestors of modern liberty. It is humiliating to trace a political lineage to Algernon Sidney, who was the paid agent of the French king; to Lord Russell, who opposed religious toleration at least as much as absolute monarchy; to Shaftesbury, who dipped his hands in the innocent blood shed by the perjury of Titus Oates; to Halifax, who insisted that the plot must be supported even if untrue; to Marlborough, who sent his comrades to perish on an expedition which he had betrayed to the French; to Locke, whose notion of liberty involves nothing more spiritual than the security of property, and is consistent with slavery and persecution; or even to Addison, who conceived that the right of voting taxes belonged to no country but his own. Defoe affirms that from the time of Charles II. to that of George I. he never knew a politician who truly held the faith of either party; and the perversity of the statesmen who led the assault against the later Stuarts threw back the cause of progress for a century.

When the purport of the secret treaty became suspected by which Louis XIV. pledged himself to support Charles II. with an army for the destruction of Parliament, if Charles would overthrow the Anglican Church, it was found necessary to make concession to the popular alarm. It was proposed that whenever James should succeed, great part of the royal prerogative and patronage should be transferred to Parliament. At the same time, the disabilities of Nonconformists and Catholics would have been removed. If the Limitation Bill, which Halifax supported with signal ability, had passed, the monarchical constitution would have advanced, in the seventeenth century, farther than it was destined to do until the second quarter of the nineteenth. But the enemies of James, guided by the Prince of Orange, preferred a Protestant king who should be nearly absolute, to a constitutional king who should be a Catholic. The scheme failed. James succeeded to a power which, in more cautious hands, would have been practically uncontrolled, and the storm that cast him down gathered beyond the sea.

By arresting the preponderance of France, the Revolution of 1688 struck the first real blow at Continental despotism. At home it relieved Dissent, purified justice, developed the national energies and resources, and ultimately, by the Act of Settlement, placed the crown in the gift of the people. But it neither introduced nor determined any important principle, and, that both parties might be able to work together, it left untouched the fundamental question between Whig and Tory. For the divine right of kings it established, in the words of Defoe, the divine right of freeholders; and their domination extended for seventy years, under the authority of John Locke, the philosopher of government by the gentry. Even Hume did not enlarge the bounds of his ideas; and his narrow materialistic belief in the connection between liberty and property captivated even the bolder mind of Fox.

By his idea that the powers of government ought to be divided according to their nature, and not according to the division of classes, which Montesquieu took up and developed with consummate talent, Locke is the originator of the long reign of English institutions in foreign lands. And his doctrine of resistance, or, as he finally termed it, the appeal to Heaven, ruled the judgment of Chatham at a moment of solemn transition in the history of the world. Our Parliamentary system, managed by the great revolution families, was a contrivance by which electors were compelled, and legislators were induced to vote against their convictions; and the intimidation of the constituencies was rewarded by the corruption of their representatives. About the year 1770 things had been brought back, by indirect ways, nearly to the condition which the Revolution had been designed to remedy for ever. Europe seemed incapable of becoming the home of free States. It was from America that the plain ideas that men ought to mind their own business, and that the nation is responsible to Heaven for the acts of the State,—ideas long locked in the breast of solitary thinkers, and hidden among Latin folios,—burst forth like a conqueror upon the world they were destined to transform, under the title of the Rights of Man. Whether the British legislature had a constitutional right to tax a subject colony was hard to say, by the letter of the law. The general presumption was immense on the side of authority; and the world believed that the will of the constituted ruler ought to be supreme, and not the will of the subject people. Very few bold writers went so far as to say that lawful power may be resisted in cases of extreme necessity. But the colonisers of America, who had gone forth not in search of gain, but to escape from laws under which other Englishmen were content to live, were so sensitive even to appearances that the Blue Laws of Connecticut forbade men to walk to church within ten feet of their wives. And the proposed tax, of only £12,000 a year, might have been easily borne. But the reasons why Edward I. and his Council were not allowed to tax England were reasons why George III. and his Parliament should not tax America. The dispute involved a principle, namely, the right of controlling government. Furthermore, it involved the conclusion that the Parliament brought together by a derisive election had no just right over the unrepresented nation, and it called on the people of England to take back its power. Our best statesmen saw that whatever might be the law, the rights of the nation were at stake. Chatham, in speeches better remembered than any that have been delivered in Parliament, exhorted America to be firm. Lord Camden, the late Chancellor, said: "Taxation and representation are inseparably united. God hath joined them. No British Parliament can separate them."

From the elements of that crisis Burke built up the noblest political philosophy in the world. "I do not know the method," said he, "of drawing up an indictment against a whole people. The natural rights of mankind are indeed sacred things, and if any public measure is proved mischievously to affect them, the objection ought to be fatal to that measure, even if no charter at all could be set up against it. Only a sovereign reason, paramount to all forms of legislation and administration, should dictate." In this way, just a hundred years ago, the opportune reticence, the politic hesitancy of European statesmanship, was at last broken down; and the principle gained ground, that a nation can never abandon its fate to an authority it cannot control. The Americans placed it at the foundation of their new government. They did more; for having subjected all civil authorities to the popular will, they surrounded the popular will with restrictions that the British legislature would not endure.

During the revolution in France the example of England, which had been held up so long, could not for a moment compete with the influence of a country whose institutions were so wisely framed to protect freedom even against the perils of democracy. When Louis Philippe became king, he assured the old Republican, Lafayette, that what he had seen in the United States had convinced him that no government can be so good as a Republic. There was a time in the Presidency of Monroe, about fifty-five years ago, which men still speak of as "the era of good feeling," when most of the incongruities that had come down from the Stuarts had been reformed, and the motives of later divisions were yet inactive. The causes of old-world trouble,—popular ignorance, pauperism, the glaring contrast between rich and poor, religious strife, public debts, standing armies and war,—were almost unknown. No other age or country had solved so successfully the problems that attend the growth of free societies, and time was to bring no further progress.

But I have reached the end of my time, and have

hardly come to the beginning of my task. In the ages of which I have spoken, the history of freedom was the history of the thing that was not. But since the Declaration of Independence, or, to speak more justly, since the Spaniards, deprived of their king, made a new government for themselves, the only known forms of liberty, Republics and Constitutional Monarchy, have made their way over the world. It would have been interesting to trace the reaction of America on the Monarchies that achieved its independence; to see how the sudden rise of political economy suggested the idea of applying the methods of science to the art of government; how Louis XVI., after confessing that despotism was useless, even to make men happy by compulsion, appealed to the nation to do what was beyond his skill, and thereby resigned his sceptre to the middle class, and the intelligent men of France, shuddering at the awful recollections of their own experience, struggled to shut out the past, that they might deliver their children from the prince of the world and rescue the living from the clutch of the dead, until the finest opportunity ever given to the world was thrown away, because the passion for equality made vain the hope of freedom.

And I should have wished to show you that the same deliberate rejection of the moral code which smoothed the paths of absolute monarchy and of oligarchy, signalised the advent of the democratic claim to unlimited power,—that one of its leading champions avowed the design of corrupting the moral sense of men, in order to destroy the influence of religion, and a famous apostle of enlightenment and toleration wished that the last king might be strangled with the entrails of the last priest. I would have tried to explain the connection between the doctrine of Adam Smith, that labour is the original source of all wealth, and the conclusion that the producers of wealth virtually compose the nation, by which Sieyès subverted historic France; and to show that Rousseau's definition of the social compact as a voluntary association of equal partners conducted Marat, by short and unavoidable stages, to declare that the poorer classes were absolved, by the law of self-preservation, from the conditions of a contract which awarded to them misery and death ; that they were at war with society, and had a right to all they could get by exterminating the rich, and that their inflexible theory of equality, the chief legacy of the Revolution, together with the avowed inadequacy of economic science to grapple with problems of the poor, revived the idea of renovating society on the principle of self-sacrifice, which had been the generous aspiration of the Essenes and the early Christians, of Fathers and Canonists and Friars, of Erasmus, the most celebrated precursor of the Reformation, of Sir Thomas More, its most illustrious victim, and of Fénelon, the most popular of bishops, but which, during the forty years of its revival, has been associated with envy and hatred and bloodshed, and is now the most dangerous enemy lurking in our path.

Last, and most of all, having told so much of the unwisdom of our ancestors, having exposed the sterility of the convulsion that burned what they adored, and made the sins of the Republic mount up as high as those of the monarchy, having shown that Legitimacy, which repudiated the Revolution, and Imperialism, which crowned it, were but disguises of the same element of violence and wrong, I should have wished, in order that my address might not break off without a meaning or a moral, to relate by whom, and in what connection, the true law of the formation of free States was recognised, and how that discovery, closely akin to those which, under the names of development, evolution, and continuïty, have given a new and deeper method to other sciences, solved the ancient problem between stability and change, and determined the authority of tradition on the progress of thought ; how that theory, which Sir James Mackintosh expressed by saying that Constitutions are not made, but grow ; the theory that custom and the national qualities of the governed, and not the will of the government, are the makers of the law ; and therefore that the nation, which is the source of its own organic institutions, should be charged with the perpetual custody of their integrity, and with the duty of bringing the form into harmony with the spirit, was made, by the singular co-operation of the purest Conservative intellect with red-handed revolution, of Niebuhr with Mazzini, to yield the idea of nationality, which, far more than the idea of liberty, has governed the movement of the present age.

I do not like to conclude without inviting attention to the impressive fact that so much of the hard fighting, the thinking, the enduring that has contributed to the deliverance of man from the power of man, has been the work of our countrymen, and of their descendants in other lands. We have had to contend, as much as any people, against monarchs of strong will and of resources secured by their foreign possession, against men of rare capacity, against whole dynasties of born tyrants. And yet that proud prerogative stands out on the background of our history. Within a generation of the Conquest, the Normans were compelled to recognise, in some grudging measure, the claims of the English people. When the struggle between Church and State extended to England, our Churchmen learned to associate themselves with the popular cause; and, with few exceptions, neither the hierarchical spirit of the foreign divines, nor the monarchical bias peculiar to the French, characterised the writers of the English school. The Civil Law, transmitted from the degenerate Empire to be the common prop of absolute power, was excluded from England. The Canon Law was restrained, and this country never admitted the Inquisition, nor fully accepted the use of torture which invested Continental royalty with so many terrors. At the end of the Middle Ages foreign writers acknowledged our superiority, and pointed to these causes. After that, our gentry maintained the means of local self-government such as no other country possessed. Divisions in religion forced toleration. The confusion of the common law taught the people that their best safeguard was the independence and the integrity of the judges.

All these explanations lie on the surface, and are as visible as the protecting ocean; but they can only be successive effects of a constant cause which must lie in the same native qualities of perseverance, moderation, individuality, and the manly sense of duty, which give to the English race its supremacy in the stern art of labour, which has enabled it to thrive as no other can on inhospitable shores, and which (although no great people has less of the bloodthirsty craving for glory and an army of 50,000 English soldiers has never been seen in battle) caused Napoleon to exclaim, as he rode away from Waterloo, "It has always been the same since Crecy."

Therefore, if there is reason for pride in the past, there is more for hope in the time to come. Our advantages increase, while other nations fear their neighbours or covet their neighbours' goods. Anomalies and defects there are, fewer and less intolerable, if not less flagrant than of old.

But I have fixed my eyes on the spaces that Heaven's light illuminates, that I may not lay too heavy a strain on the indulgence with which you have accompanied me over the dreary and heart-breaking course by which men have passed to freedom; and because the light that has guided us is still unquenched, and the causes that have carried us so far in the van of free nations have not spent their power; because the story of the future is written in the past, and that which hath been is the same thing that shall be.

III

SIR ERSKINE MAY'S DEMOCRACY IN EUROPE[1]

SCARCELY thirty years separate the Europe of Guizot and Metternich from these days of universal suffrage both in France and in United Germany; when a condemned insurgent of 1848 is the constitutional Minister of Austria; when Italy, from the Alps to the Adriatic, is governed by friends of Mazzini; and statesmen who recoiled from the temerities of Peel have doubled the electoral constituency of England. If the philosopher who proclaimed the law that democratic progress is constant and irrepressible had lived to see old age, he would have been startled by the fulfilment of his prophecy. Throughout these years of revolutionary change Sir Thomas Erskine May has been more closely and constantly connected with the centre of public affairs than any other Englishman, and his place, during most of the time, has been at the table of the House of Commons, where he has sat, like Canute, and watched the rising tide. Few could be better prepared to be the historian of European Democracy than one who, having so long studied the mechanism of popular government in the most illustrious of assemblies at the height of its power, has written its history, and taught its methods to the world.

It is not strange that so delicate and laborious a task should have remained unattempted. Democracy is a gigantic current that has been fed by many springs.

[1] *The Quarterly Review*, January 1878.

Physical and spiritual causes have contributed to swell it. Much has been done by economic theories, and more by economic laws. The propelling force lay sometimes in doctrine and sometimes in fact, and error has been as powerful as truth. Popular progress has been determined at one time by legislation, at others by a book, an invention, or a crime; and we may trace it to the influence of Greek metaphysicians and Roman jurists, of barbarian custom and ecclesiastical law, of the reformers who discarded the canonists, the sectaries who discarded the reformers, and the philosophers who discarded the sects. The scene has changed, as nation succeeded nation, and during the most stagnant epoch of European life the new world stored up the forces that have transformed the old.

A history that should pursue all the subtle threads from end to end might be eminently valuable, but not as a tribute to peace and conciliation. Few discoveries are more irritating than those which expose the pedigree of ideas. Sharp definitions and unsparing analysis would displace the veil beneath which society dissembles its divisions, would make political disputes too violent for compromise and political alliances too precarious for use, and would embitter politics with all the passion of social and religious strife. Sir Erskine May writes for all who take their stand within the broad lines of our constitution. His judgment is averse from extremes. He turns from the discussion of theories, and examines his subject by the daylight of institutions, believing that laws depend much on the condition of society, and little on notions and disputations unsupported by reality. He avows his disbelief even in the influence of Locke, and cares little to inquire how much self-government owes to Independency, or equality to the Quakers; and how democracy was affected by the doctrine that society is founded on contract, that happiness is the end of all government, or labour the only source of wealth; and for this reason, because he always touches ground, and brings to bear, on a vast array of sifted fact, the light of sound sense and tried experience rather than dogmatic precept, all men will read his book with profit, and almost all without offence.

Although he does not insist on inculcating a moral, he has stated in his introductory pages the ideas that guide him; and, indeed, the reader who fails to recognise the lesson of the book in every chapter will read in vain. Sir Erskine May is persuaded that it is the tendency of modern progress to elevate the masses of the people, to increase their part in the work and the fruit of civilisation, in comfort and education, in self-respect and independence, in political knowledge and power. Taken for a universal law of history, this would be as visionary as certain generalisations of Montesquieu and Tocqueville; but with the necessary restrictions of time and place, it cannot fairly be disputed. Another conclusion, supported by a far wider induction, is that democracy, like monarchy, is salutary within limits and fatal in excess; that it is the truest friend of freedom or its most unrelenting foe, according as it is mixed or pure; and this ancient and elementary truth of constitutional government is enforced with every variety of impressive and suggestive illustration from the time of the Patriarchs down to the revolution which, in 1874, converted federal Switzerland into an unqualified democracy governed by the direct voice of the entire people.

The effective distinction between liberty and democracy, which has occupied much of the author's thoughts, cannot be too strongly drawn. Slavery has been so often associated with democracy, that a very able writer pronounced it long ago essential to a democratic state; and the philosophers of the Southern Confederation have urged the theory with extreme fervour. For slavery operates like a restricted franchise, attaches power to property, and hinders Socialism, the infirmity that attends mature democracies. The most intelligent of Greek tyrants, Periander, discouraged the employment of slaves; and Pericles designates the freedom from manual labour as the distinguishing prerogative of Athens. At Rome a tax on manumissions immediately followed the establishment of political equality by Licinius. An impeachment of England for having imposed slavery on America was carefully expunged from the Declaration of Independence; and the French Assembly, having proclaimed the Rights of Man, declared that they did not extend to the colonies. The abolition controversy has made everybody familiar with Burke's saying, that men learn the price of freedom by being masters of slaves.

From the best days of Athens, the days of Anaxagoras, Protagoras, and Socrates, a strange affinity has subsisted between democracy and religious persecution. The bloodiest deed committed between the wars of religion and the revolution was due to the fanaticism of men living under the primitive republic in the Rhætian Alps; and of six democratic cantons only one tolerated Protestants, and that after a struggle which lasted the better part of two centuries. In 1578 the fifteen Catholic provinces would have joined the revolted Netherlands but for the furious bigotry of Ghent; and the democracy of Friesland was the most intolerant of the States. The aristocratic colonies in America defended toleration against their democratic neighbours, and its triumph in Rhode Island and Pennsylvania was the work not of policy but of religion. The French Republic came to ruin because it found the lesson of religious liberty too hard to learn. Down to the eighteenth century, indeed, it was understood in monarchies more often than in free commonwealths. Richelieu acknowledged the principle whilst he was constructing the despotism of the Bourbons; so did the electors of Brandenburg, at the time when they made themselves absolute; and after the fall of Clarendon, the notion of Indulgence was inseparable from the design of Charles II. to subvert the constitution.

A government strong enough to act in defiance of public feeling may disregard the plausible heresy that prevention is better than punishment, for it is able to punish. But a government entirely dependent on opinion looks for some security what that opinion shall be, strives for the control of the forces that shape it, and is fearful of suffering the people to be educated in sentiments hostile to its institutions. When General Grant attempted to grapple with polygamy in Utah, it was found necessary to pack the juries with Gentiles; and the Supreme Court decided that the proceedings were illegal, and that the prisoners must be set free. Even the murderer Lee was absolved, in 1875, by a jury of Mormons.

Modern democracy presents many problems too various and obscure to be solved without a larger range of materials than Tocqueville obtained from his American authorities or his own observation. To understand why the hopes and the fears that it excites have been always inseparable, to determine under what conditions it advances or retards the progress of the people and the welfare of free states, there is no better course than to follow Sir Erskine May upon the road which he has been the first to open.

In the midst of an invincible despotism, among paternal, military, and sacerdotal monarchies, the dawn rises with the deliverance of Israel out of bondage, and with the covenant which began their political life. The tribes broke up into smaller communities, administering their own affairs under the law they had sworn to observe, but which there was no civil power to enforce. They governed themselves without a central authority, a legislature, or a dominant priesthood; and this polity, which, under the forms of primitive society, realised some aspirations of developed democracy, resisted for above three hundred years the constant peril of anarchy and subjugation. The monarchy itself was limited by the same absence of a legislative power, by the submission of the king to the law that bound his subjects, by the perpetual appeal of prophets to the conscience of the people as its appointed guardian, and by the ready resource of deposition. Later still, in the decay of the religious and national constitution, the same ideas appeared with intense energy, in an extraordinary association of men who lived in austerity and self-denial, rejected slavery, maintained equality, and held their property in common, and who constituted in miniature an almost perfect Republic. But the Essenes perished with the city and the Temple, and for many ages the example of the Hebrews was more serviceable to authority than to freedom. After the Reformation, the sects that broke resolutely with the traditions of Church and State as they came down from Catholic times, and sought for their new institutions a higher authority than custom, reverted to the memory of a commonwealth founded on a voluntary contract, on self-government, federalism, equality, in which election was preferred to inheritance, and monarchy was an emblem of the heathen; and they conceived that there was no better model for themselves than a nation constituted by religion, owning no lawgiver but Moses, and obeying no king but God. Political thought had until then been guided by pagan experience.

Among the Greeks, Athens, the boldest pioneer of republican discovery, was the only democracy that prospered. It underwent the changes that were the common lot of Greek society, but it met them in a way that displayed a singular genius for politics. The struggle of competing classes for supremacy, almost everywhere a cause of oppression and bloodshed, became with them a genuine struggle for freedom; and the Athenian constitution grew, with little pressure from below, under the intelligent action of statesmen who were swayed by political reasoning more than by public opinion. They avoided violent and convulsive change, because the rate of their reforms kept ahead of the popular demand. Solon, whose laws began the reign of mind over force, instituted democracy by making the people, not indeed the administrators, but the source of power. He committed the Government not to rank or birth, but to land; and he regulated the political influence of the landowners by their share in the burdens of the public service. To the lower class, who neither bore arms nor paid taxes, and were excluded from the Government, he granted the privilege of choosing and of calling to account the men by whom they were governed, of confirming or rejecting the acts of the legislature and the judgments of the courts. Although he charged the Areopagus with the preservation of his laws, he provided that they might be revised according to need; and the ideal before his mind was government by all free citizens. His concessions to the popular element were narrow, and were carefully guarded. He yielded no more than was necessary to guarantee the attachment of the whole people to the State. But he admitted principles that went further than the claims which he conceded. He took only one step towards democracy, but it was the first of a series.

When the Persian wars, which converted aristocratic Athens into a maritime state, had developed new sources of wealth and a new description of interests, the class which had supplied many of the ships and most of the men that had saved the national independence and founded an empire, could not be excluded from power. Solon's principle, that political influence should be commensurate with political service, broke through the forms in which he had confined it, and the spirit of his constitution was too strong for the letter. The fourth estate was admitted to office, and in order that its candidates might obtain their share, and no more than their share, and that neither interest nor numbers might prevail, many public functionaries were appointed by lot. The Athenian idea of a Republic was to substitute the impersonal supremacy of law for the government of men. Mediocrity was a safeguard against the pretensions of superior capacity, for the established order was in danger, not from the average citizens, but from men, like Miltiades, of exceptional renown. The people of Athens venerated their constitution as a gift of the gods, the source and title of their power, a thing too sacred for wanton change. They had demanded a code, that the unwritten law might no longer be intrepreted at will by Archons and Areopagites; and a well-defined and authoritative legislation was a triumph of the democracy.

So well was this conservative spirit understood, that

the revolution which abolished the privileges of the aristocracy was promoted by Aristides and completed by Pericles, men free from the reproach of flattering the multitude. They associated all the free Athenians with the interest of the State, and called them, without distinction of class, to administer the powers that belonged to them. Solon had threatened with the loss of citizenship all who showed themselves indifferent in party conflicts, and Pericles declared that every man who neglected his share of public duty was a useless member of the community. That wealth might confer no unfair advantage, that the poor might not take bribes from the rich, he took them into the pay of the State during their attendance as jurors. That their numbers might give them no unjust superiority, he restricted the right of citizenship to those who came from Athenian parents on both sides; and thus he expelled more than 4000 men of mixed descent from the Assembly. This bold measure, which was made acceptable by a distribution of grain from Egypt among those who proved their full Athenian parentage, reduced the fourth class to an equality with the owners of real property. For Pericles, or Ephialtes—for it would appear that all their reforms had been carried in the year 460, when Ephialtes died—is the first democratic statesman who grasped the notion of political equality. The measures which made all citizens equal might have created a new inequality between classes, and the artificial privilege of land might have been succeeded by the more crushing preponderance of numbers. But Pericles held it to be intolerable that one portion of the people should be required to obey laws which others have the exclusive right of making; and he was able, during thirty years, to preserve the equipoise, governing by the general consent of the community, formed by free debate. He made the undivided people sovereign; but he subjected the popular initiative to a court of revision, and assigned a penalty to the proposer of any measure which should be found to be unconstitutional. Athens, under Pericles, was the most successful

Republic that existed before the system of representation; but its splendour ended with his life.

The danger to liberty from the predominance either of privilege or majorities was so manifest, that an idea arose that equality of fortune would be the only way to prevent the conflict of class interests. The philosophers, Phaleas, Plato, Aristotle, suggested various expedients to level the difference between rich and poor. Solon had endeavoured to check the increase of estates; and Pericles had not only strengthened the public resources by bringing the rich under the control of an assembly in which they were not supreme, but he had employed those resources in improving the condition and the capacity of the masses. The grievance of those who were taxed for the benefit of others was easily borne so long as the tribute of the confederates filled the treasury. But the Peloponnesian war increased the strain on the revenue and deprived Athens of its dependencies. The balance was upset; and the policy of making one class give, that another might receive, was recommended not only by the interest of the poor, but by a growing theory, that wealth and poverty make bad citizens, that the middle class is the one most easily led by reason, and that the way to make it predominate is to depress whatever rises above the common level, and to raise whatever falls below it. This theory, which became inseparable from democracy, and contained a force which alone seems able to destroy it, was fatal to Athens, for it drove the minority to treason. The glory of the Athenian democrats is, not that they escaped the worst consequences of their principle, but that, having twice cast out the usurping oligarchy, they set bounds to their own power. They forgave their vanquished enemies; they abolished pay for attendance in the assembly; they established the supremacy of law by making the code superior to the people; they distinguished things that were constitutional from things that were legal, and resolved that no legislative act should pass until it had been pronounced consistent with the constitution.

The causes which ruined the Republic of Athens illustrate the connection of ethics with politics rather than the vices inherent to democracy. A State which has only 30,000 full citizens in a population of 500,000, and is governed, practically, by about 3000 people at a public meeting, is scarcely democratic. The short triumph of Athenian liberty, and its quick decline, belong to an age which possessed no fixed standard of right and wrong. An unparalleled activity of intellect was shaking the credit of the gods, and the gods were the givers of the law. It was a very short step from the suspicion of Protagoras, that there were no gods, to the assertion of Critias that there is no sanction for laws. If nothing was certain in theology, there was no certainty in ethics and no moral obligation. The will of man, not the will of God, was the rule of life, and every man and body of men had the right to do what they had the means of doing. Tyranny was no wrong, and it was hypocrisy to deny oneself the enjoyment it affords. The doctrine of the Sophists gave no limits to power and no security to freedom; it inspired that cry of the Athenians, that they must not be hindered from doing what they pleased, and the speeches of men like Athenagoras and Euphemus, that the democracy may punish men who have done no wrong, and that nothing that is profitable is amiss. And Socrates perished by the reaction which they provoked.

The disciples of Socrates obtained the ear of posterity. Their testimony against the government that put the best of citizens to death is enshrined in writings that compete with Christianity itself for influence on the opinions of men. Greece has governed the world by her philosophy, and the loudest note in Greek philosophy is the protest against Athenian democracy. But although Socrates derided the practice of leaving the choice of magistrates to chance, and Plato admired the bloodstained tyrant Critias, and Aristotle deemed Theramenes a greater statesman than Pericles, yet these are the men who laid the first stones of a purer system, and became the lawgivers of future commonwealths.

The main point in the method of Socrates was essentially democratic. He urged men to bring all things to the test of incessant inquiry, and not to content themselves with the verdict of authorities, majorities, or custom; to judge of right and wrong, not by the will or sentiment of others, but by the light which God has set in each man's reason and conscience. He proclaimed that authority is often wrong, and has no warrant to silence or to impose conviction. But he gave no warrant to resistance. He emancipated men for thought, but not for action. The sublime history of his death shows that the superstition of the State was undisturbed by his contempt for its rulers.

Plato had not his master's patriotism, nor his reverence for the civil power. He believed that no State can command obedience if it does not deserve respect; and he encouraged citizens to despise their government if they were not governed by wise men. To the aristocracy of philosophers he assigned a boundless prerogative; but as no government satisfied that test, his plea for despotism was hypothetical. When the lapse of years roused him from the fantastic dream of his Republic, his belief in divine government moderated his intolerance of human freedom. Plato would not suffer a democratic polity; but he challenged all existing authorities to justify themselves before a superior tribunal; he desired that all constitutions should be thoroughly remodelled, and he supplied the greatest need of Greek democracy, the conviction that the will of the people is subject to the will of God, and that all civil authority, except that of an imaginary state, is limited and conditional. The prodigious vitality of his writings has kept the glaring perils of popular government constantly before mankind; but it has also preserved the belief in ideal politics and the notion of judging the powers of this world by a standard from heaven. There has been no fiercer enemy of democracy; but there has been no stronger advocate of revolution.

In the *Ethics* Aristotle condemns democracy, even with a property qualification, as the worst of governments.

But near the end of his life, when he composed his *Politics*, he was brought, grudgingly, to make a memorable concession. To preserve the sovereignty of law, which is the reason and the custom of generations, and to restrict the realm of choice and change, he conceived it best that no class of society should preponderate, that one man should not be subject to another, that all should command and all obey. He advised that power should be distributed to high and low; to the first according to their property, to the others according to numbers; and that it should centre in the middle class. If aristocracy and democracy were fairly combined and balanced against each other, he thought that none would be interested to disturb the serene majesty of impersonal government. To reconcile the two principles, he would admit even the poorer citizens to office and pay them for the discharge of public duties; but he would compel the rich to take their share, and would appoint magistrates by election and not by lot. In his indignation at the extravagance of Plato, and his sense of the significance of facts, he became, against his will, the prophetic exponent of a limited and regenerated democracy. But the *Politics*, which, to the world of living men, is the most valuable of his works, acquired no influence on antiquity, and is never quoted before the time of Cicero. Again it disappeared for many centuries; it was unknown to the Arabian commentators, and in Western Europe it was first brought to light by St. Thomas Aquinas, at the very time when an infusion of popular elements was modifying feudalism, and it helped to emancipate political philosophy from despotic theories and to confirm it in the ways of freedom.

The three generations of the Socratic school did more for the future reign of the people than all the institutions of the States of Greece. They vindicated conscience against authority, and subjected both to a higher law; and they proclaimed that doctrine of a mixed constitution, which has prevailed at last over absolute monarchy, and still has to contend against extreme Republicans and Socialists, and against the masters of a hundred legions. But their views of liberty were based on expediency, not on justice. They legislated for the favoured citizens of Greece, and were conscious of no principle that extended the same rights to the stranger and the slave. That discovery, without which all political science was merely conventional, belongs to the followers of Zeno.

The dimness and poverty of their theological speculation caused the Stoics to attribute the government of the universe less to the uncertain design of gods than to a definite law of nature. By that law, which is superior to religious traditions and national authorities, and which every man can learn from a guardian angel who neither sleeps nor errs, all are governed alike, all are equal, all are bound in charity to each other, as members of one community and children of the same God. The unity of mankind implied the existence of rights and duties common to all men, which legislation neither gives nor takes away. The Stoics held in no esteem the institutions that vary with time and place, and their ideal society resembled a universal Church more than an actual State. In every collision between authority and conscience they preferred the inner to the outer guide; and, in the words of Epictetus, regarded the laws of the gods, not the wretched laws of the dead. Their doctrine of equality, of fraternity, of humanity; their defence of individualism against public authority; their repudiation of slavery, redeemed democracy from the narrowness, the want of principle and of sympathy, which are its reproach among the Greeks. In practical life they preferred a mixed constitution to a purely popular government. Chrysippus thought it impossible to please both gods and men; and Seneca declared that the people is corrupt and incapable, and that nothing was wanting, under Nero, to the fulness of liberty, except the possibility of destroying it. But their lofty conception of freedom, as no exceptional privilege but the birthright of mankind, survived in the law of nations and purified the equity of Rome.

Whilst Dorian oligarchs and Macedonian kings crushed

the liberties of Greece, the Roman Republic was ruined, not by its enemies, for there was no enemy it did not conquer, but by its own vices. It was free from many causes of instability and dissolution that were active in Greece—the eager quickness, the philosophic thought, the independent belief, the pursuit of unsubstantial grace and beauty. It was protected by many subtle contrivances against the sovereignty of numbers and against legislation by surprise. Constitutional battles had to be fought over and over again; and progress was so slow, that reforms were often voted many years before they could be carried into effect. The authority allowed to fathers, to masters, to creditors, was as incompatible with the spirit of freedom as the practice of the servile East. The Roman citizen revelled in the luxury of power; and his jealous dread of every change that might impair its enjoyment portended a gloomy oligarchy. The cause which transformed the domination of rigid and exclusive patricians into the model Republic, and which out of the decomposed Republic built up the archetype of all despotism, was the fact that the Roman Commonwealth consisted of two States in one. The constitution was made up of compromises between independent bodies, and the obligation of observing contracts was the standing security for freedom. The plebs obtained self-government and an equal sovereignty, by the aid of the tribunes of the people, the peculiar, salient, and decisive invention of Roman statecraft. The powers conferred on the tribunes, that they might be the guardians of the weak, were ill defined, but practically were irresistible. They could not govern, but they could arrest all government. The first and the last step of plebeian progress was gained neither by violence nor persuasion, but by seceding; and, in like manner, the tribunes overcame all the authorities of the State by the weapon of obstruction. It was by stopping public business for five years that Licinius established democratic equality. The safeguard against abuse was the right of each tribune to veto the acts of his colleagues. As they were independent of their electors, and as there could hardly fail to be one wise and honest man among the ten, this was the most effective instrument for the defence of minorities ever devised by man. After the Hortensian law, which in the year 286 gave to the plebeian assembly co-ordinate legislative authority, the tribunes ceased to represent the cause of a minority, and their work was done.

A scheme less plausible or less hopeful than one which created two sovereign legislatures side by side in the same community would be hard to find. Yet it effectually closed the conflict of centuries, and gave to Rome an epoch of constant prosperity and greatness. No real division subsisted in the people, corresponding to the artificial division in the State. Fifty years passed away before the popular assembly made use of its prerogative, and passed a law in opposition to the senate. Polybius could not detect a flaw in the structure as it stood. The harmony seemed to be complete, and he judged that a more perfect example of composite government could not exist. But during those happy years the cause which wrought the ruin of Roman freedom was in full activity; for it was the condition of perpetual war that brought about the three great changes which were the beginning of the end—the reforms of the Gracchi, the arming of the paupers, and the gift of the Roman suffrage to the people of Italy.

Before the Romans began their career of foreign conquest they possessed an army of 770,000 men; and from that time the consumption of citizens in war was incessant. Regions once crowded with the small freeholds of four or five acres, which were the ideal unit of Roman society and the sinew of the army and the State, were covered with herds of cattle and herds of slaves, and the substance of the governing democracy was drained. The policy of the agrarian reform was to reconstitute this peasant class out of the public domains, that is, out of lands which the ruling families had possessed for generations, which they had bought and sold, inherited, divided, cultivated, and improved. The conflict of interests that had so long slumbered revived with a fury unknown in the controversy between the patricians and the plebs. For it was now a question not of equal rights but of subjugation. The social restoration of democratic elements could not be accomplished without demolishing the senate; and this crisis at last exposed the defect of the machinery and the peril of divided powers that were not to be controlled or reconciled. The popular assembly, led by Gracchus, had the power of making laws; and the only constitutional check was, that one of the tribunes should be induced to bar the proceedings. Accordingly, the tribune Octavius interposed his veto. The tribunician power, the most sacred of powers, which could not be questioned because it was founded on a covenant between the two parts of the community and formed the keystone of their union, was employed, in opposition to the will of the people, to prevent a reform on which the preservation of the democracy depended. Gracchus caused Octavius to be deposed. Though not illegal, this was a thing unheard of, and it seemed to the Romans a sacrilegious act that shook the pillars of the State, for it was the first significant revelation of democratic sovereignty. A tribune might burn the arsenal and betray the city, yet he could not be called to account until his year of office had expired. But when he employed against the people the authority with which they had invested him, the spell was dissolved. The tribunes had been instituted as the champions of the oppressed, when the plebs feared oppression. It was resolved that they should not interfere on the weaker side when the democracy were the strongest. They were chosen by the people as their defence against the aristocracy. It was not to be borne that they should become the agents of the aristocracy to make them once more supreme. Against a popular tribune, whom no colleague was suffered to oppose, the wealthy classes were defenceless. It is true that he held office, and was inviolable, only for a year. But the younger Gracchus was re-elected. The nobles accused him of aiming at the crown. A tribune who should be practically irremovable, as well as legally irresistible, was little less than an emperor. The senate carried on the conflict as men do who fight, not for public interests but for their own existence. They rescinded the agrarian laws. They murdered the popular leaders. They abandoned the constitution to save themselves, and invested Sylla with a power beyond all monarchs, to exterminate their foes. The ghastly conception of a magistrate legally proclaimed superior to all the laws was familiar to the stern spirit of the Romans. The decemvirs had enjoyed that arbitrary authority; but practically they were restrained by the two provisions which alone were deemed efficacious in Rome, the short duration of office, and its distribution among several colleagues. But the appointment of Sylla was neither limited nor divided. It was to last as long as he chose. Whatever he might do was right; and he was empowered to put whomsoever he pleased to death, without trial or accusation. All the victims who were butchered by his satellites suffered with the full sanction of the law.

When at last the democracy conquered, the Augustan monarchy, by which they perpetuated their triumph, was moderate in comparison with the licensed tyranny of the aristocratic chief. The Emperor was the constitutional head of the Republic, armed with all the powers requisite to master the senate. The instrument which had served to cast down the patricians was efficient against the new aristocracy of wealth and office. The tribunician power, conferred in perpetuity, made it unnecessary to create a king or a dictator. Thrice the senate proposed to Augustus the supreme power of making laws. He declared that the power of the tribunes already supplied him with all that he required. It enabled him to preserve the forms of a simulated republic. The most popular of all the magistracies of Rome furnished the marrow of Imperialism. For the Empire was created, not by usurpation, but by the legal act of a jubilant people, eager to close the era of bloodshed and to secure the largess of grain and coin, which amounted, at last, to 900,000 pounds a year. The people transferred to the Emperor the plenitude of their own sovereignty. To limit his delegated power was to challenge their omnipotence, to renew the issue between the many and the few which had been decided at Pharsalus and Philippi. The Romans upheld the absolutism of the Empire because it was their own. The elementary antagonism between liberty and democracy, between the welfare of minorities and the supremacy of masses, became manifest. The friend of the one was a traitor to the other. The dogma, that absolute power may, by the hypothesis of a popular origin, be as legitimate as constitutional freedom, began, by the combined support of the people and the throne, to darken the air.

Legitimate, in the technical sense of modern politics, the Empire was not meant to be. It had no right or claim to subsist apart from the will of the people. To limit the Emperor's authority was to renounce their own; but to take it away was to assert their own. They gave the Empire as they chose. They took it away as they chose. The Revolution was as lawful and as irresponsible as the Empire. Democratic institutions continued to develop. The provinces were no longer subject to an assembly meeting in a distant capital. They obtained the privileges of Roman citizens. Long after Tiberius had stripped the inhabitants of Rome of their electoral function, the provincials continued in undisturbed enjoyment of the right of choosing their own magistrates. They governed themselves like a vast confederation of municipal republics; and, even after Diocletian had brought in the forms as well as the reality of despotism, provincial assemblies, the obscure germ of representative institutions, exercised some control over the Imperial officers.

But the Empire owed the intensity of its force to the popular fiction. The principle, that the Emperor is not subject to laws from which he can dispense others, *princeps legibus solutus*, was interpreted to imply that he was above all legal restraint. There was no appeal from his sentence. He was the living law. The Roman jurists, whilst they adorned their writings with the exalted philosophy of the Stoics, consecrated every excess of Imperial prerogative with those famous maxims which have been balm to so many consciences and have sanctioned so much wrong; and the code of Justinian became the greatest obstacle, next to feudalism, with which liberty had to contend.

Ancient democracy, as it was in Athens in the best days of Pericles, or in Rome when Polybius described it, or even as it is idealised by Aristotle in the Sixth Book of his *Politics*, and by Cicero in the beginning of the Republic, was never more than a partial and insincere solution of the problem of popular government. The ancient politicians aimed no higher than to diffuse power among a numerous class. Their liberty was bound up with slavery. They never attempted to found a free State on the thrift and energy of free labour. They never divined the harder but more grateful task that constitutes the political life of Christian nations.

By humbling the supremacy of rank and wealth; by forbidding the State to encroach on the domain which belongs to God; by teaching man to love his neighbour as himself; by promoting the sense of equality; by condemning the pride of race, which was a stimulus of conquest, and the doctrine of separate descent, which formed the philosopher's defence of slavery; and by addressing not the rulers but the masses of mankind, and making opinion superior to authority, the Church that preached the Gospel to the poor had visible points of contact with democracy. And yet Christianity did not directly influence political progress. The ancient watchword of the Republic was translated by Papinian into the language of the Church: "Summa est ratio quæ pro religione fiat:" and for eleven hundred years, from the first to the last of the Constantines, the Christian Empire was as despotic as the pagan.

Meanwhile Western Europe was overrun by men who in their early home had been Republicans. The primitive constitution of the German communities was based on association rather than on subordination. They were accustomed to govern their affairs by common deliberation, and to obey authorities that were temporary and defined. It is one of the desperate enterprises of historical science to trace the free institutions of Europe and America, and Australia, to the life that was led in the forests of Germany. But the new States were founded on conquest, and in war the Germans were commanded by kings. The doctrine of self-government, applied to Gaul and Spain, would have made Frank and Goth disappear in the mass of the conquered people. It needed all the resources of a vigorous monarchy, of a military aristocracy, and of a territorial clergy, to construct States that were able to last. The result was the feudal system, the most absolute contradiction of democracy that has coexisted with civilisation.

The revival of democracy was due neither to the Christian Church nor to the Teutonic State, but to the quarrel between them. The effect followed the cause instantaneously. As soon as Gregory VII. made the Papacy independent of the Empire, the great conflict began ; and the same pontificate gave birth to the theory of the sovereignty of the people. The Gregorian party argued that the Emperor derived his crown from the nation, and that the nation could take away what it had bestowed. The Imperialists replied that nobody could take away what the nation had given. It is idle to look for the spark either in flint or steel. The object of both parties was unqualified supremacy. Fitznigel has no more idea of ecclesiastical liberty than John of Salisbury of political. Innocent IV. is as perfect an absolutist as Peter de Vineis. But each party encouraged democracy in turn, by seeking the aid of the towns ; each party in turn appealed to the people, and gave strength to the constitutional theory. In the fourteenth century English Parliaments judged and deposed their kings, as a matter of right ; the Estates governed France without king or noble ; and the wealth and liberties of the towns, which had worked out their independence from the centre of Italy to the North Sea, promised for a moment to transform European society. Even in the capitals of great princes, in Rome, in Paris, and, for two terrible days, in London, the commons obtained sway. But the curse of instability was on the municipal republics. Strasburg, according to Erasmus and Bodin, the best governed of all, suffered from perpetual commotions. An ingenious historian has reckoned seven thousand revolutions in the Italian cities. The democracies succeeded no better than feudalism in regulating the balance between rich and poor. The atrocities of the Jacquerie, and of Wat Tyler's rebellion, hardened the hearts of men against the common people. Church and State combined to put them down. And the last memorable struggles of mediæval liberty—the insurrection of the Comuneros in Castile, the Peasants' War in Germany, the Republic of Florence, and the Revolt of Ghent—were suppressed by Charles V. in the early years of the Reformation.

The middle ages had forged a complete arsenal of constitutional maxims: trial by jury, taxation by representation, local self-government, ecclesiastical independence, responsible authority. But they were not secured by institutions, and the Reformation began by making the dry bones more dry. Luther claimed to be the first divine who did justice to the civil power. He made the Lutheran Church the bulwark of political stability, and bequeathed to his disciples the doctrine of divine right and passive obedience. Zwingli, who was a staunch republican, desired that all magistrates should be elected, and should be liable to be dismissed by their electors; but he died too soon for his influence, and the permanent action of the Reformation on democracy was exercised through the Presbyterian constitution of Calvin.

It was long before the democratic element in Presbyterianism began to tell. The Netherlands resisted Philip II. for fifteen years before they took courage to depose him, and the scheme of the ultra-Calvinist Deventer, to subvert the ascendency of the leading States by the sovereign action of the whole people, was foiled by Leicester's incapacity, and by the consummate policy of Barnevelt. The Huguenots, having lost their leaders in 1572, reconstituted themselves on a democratic footing, and learned to think that a king who murders his subjects forfeits his divine right to be obeyed. But Junius Brutus and Buchanan damaged their credit by advocating regicide; and Hotoman, whose *Franco-Gallia* is the most serious work of the group, deserted his liberal opinions when the chief of his own party became king. The most violent explosion of democracy in that age proceeded from the opposite quarter. When Henry of Navarre became the next heir to the throne of France, the theory of the deposing power, which had proved ineffectual for more than a century, awoke with a new and more vigorous life. One-half of the nation accepted the view, that they were not bound to submit to a king they would not have chosen. A Committee of Sixteen made itself master of Paris, and, with the aid of Spain, succeeded for years in excluding Henry from his capital. The impulse thus given endured in literature for a whole generation, and produced a library of treatises on the right of Catholics to choose, to control, and to cashier their magistrates. They were on the losing side. Most of them were bloodthirsty, and were soon forgotten. But the greater part of the political ideas of Milton, Locke, and Rousseau, may be found in the ponderous Latin of Jesuits who were subjects of the Spanish Crown, of Lessius, Molina, Mariana, and Suarez.

The ideas were there, and were taken up when it suited them by extreme adherents of Rome and of Geneva; but they produced no lasting fruit until, a century after the Reformation, they became incorporated in new religious systems. Five years of civil war could not exhaust the royalism of the Presbyterians, and it required the expulsion of the majority to make the Long Parliament abandon monarchy. It had defended the constitution against the crown with legal arts, defending precedent against innovation, and setting up an ideal in the past which, with all the learning of Selden and of Prynne, was less certain than the Puritan statesmen supposed. The Independents brought in a new principle. Tradition had no authority for them, and the past no virtue. Liberty of conscience, a thing not to be found in the constitution, was more prized by many of them than all the statutes of the Plantagenets. Their idea that each congregation should govern itself abolished the force which is needed to preserve unity, and deprived monarchy of the weapon which made it injurious to freedom. An immense revolutionary energy resided in their doctrine, and it took root in America, and deeply coloured political thought in later times. But in England the sectarian democracy was strong only to destroy. Cromwell refused to be bound by it; and John Lilburne, the boldest thinker among English democrats, declared that it would be better for liberty to bring back Charles Stuart than to live under the sword of the Protector.

Lilburne was among the first to understand the real conditions of democracy, and the obstacle to its success in England. Equality of power could not be preserved, except by violence, together with an extreme inequality of possessions. There would always be danger, if power was not made to wait on property, that property would go to those who had the power. This idea of the necessary balance of property, developed by Harrington, and adopted by Milton in his later pamphlets, appeared to Toland, and even to John Adams, as important as the invention of printing, or the discovery of the circulation of the blood. At least it indicates the true explanation of the strange completeness with which the Republican party had vanished, a dozen years after the solemn trial and execution of the King. No extremity of misgovernment was able to revive it. When the treason of Charles II. against the constitution was divulged, and the Whigs plotted to expel the incorrigible dynasty, their aspirations went no farther than a Venetian oligarchy, with Monmouth for Doge. The Revolution of 1688 confined power to the aristocracy of freeholders. The conservatism of the age was unconquerable. Republicanism was distorted even in Switzerland, and became in the eighteenth century as oppressive and as intolerant as its neighbours.

In 1769, when Paoli fled from Corsica, it seemed that, in Europe at least, democracy was dead. It had, indeed, lately been defended in books by a man of bad reputation, whom the leaders of public opinion treated with contumely, and whose declamations excited so little alarm that George III. offered him a pension. What gave to Rousseau a power far exceeding that which any political writer had ever attained was the progress of events in America. The Stuarts had been willing that the colonies should serve as a refuge from their system of Church and State, and of all their colonies the one most favoured was the territory granted to William Penn. By the principles of the Society to which he belonged, it was necessary that the new State should be founded on liberty and equality. But Penn was further noted among Quakers as a follower of the new doctrine of Toleration. Thus it came to pass that Pennsylvania enjoyed the most democratic constitution in the world, and held up to the admiration of the eighteenth century an almost solitary example of freedom. It was principally through Franklin and the Quaker State that America influenced political opinion in Europe, and that the fanaticism of one revolutionary epoch was converted into the rationalism of another. American independence was the beginning of a new era, not merely as a revival of Revolution, but because no other Revolution ever proceeded from so slight a cause, or was ever conducted with so much moderation. The European monarchies supported it. The greatest statesmen in England averred that it was just. It established a pure democracy; but it was democracy in its highest perfection, armed and vigilant, less against aristocracy and monarchy than against its own weakness and excess. Whilst England was admired for the safeguards with which, in the course of many centuries, it had fortified liberty against the power of the crown, America appeared still more worthy of admiration for the safeguards which, in the deliberations of a single memorable year, it had set up against the power of its own sovereign people. It resembled no other known democracy, for it respected freedom, authority, and law. It resembled no other constitution, for it was contained in half a dozen intelligible articles. Ancient Europe opened its mind to two new ideas—that Revolution with very little provocation may be just; and that democracy in very large dimensions may be safe.

Whilst America was making itself independent, the spirit of reform had been abroad in Europe. Intelligent ministers, like Campomanes and Struensee, and well-meaning monarchs, of whom the most liberal was Leopold of Tuscany, were trying what could be done to make men happy by command. Centuries of absolute and intolerant rule had bequeathed abuses which nothing but the most vigorous use of power could remove. The age preferred the reign of intellect to the reign of liberty. Turgot, the ablest and most far-seeing reformer then living, attempted to do for France what less gifted men were doing with success in Lombardy, and Tuscany, and Parma. He attempted to employ the royal power for the good of the people, at the expense of the higher classes. The higher classes proved too strong for the crown alone; and Louis XVI. abandoned internal reforms in despair, and turned for compensation to a war with England for the deliverance of her American Colonies. When the increasing debt obliged him to seek heroic remedies, and he was again repulsed by the privileged orders, he appealed at last to the nation. When the States-General met, the power had already passed to the middle class, for it was by them alone that the country could be saved. They were strong enough to triumph by waiting. Neither the Court, nor the nobles, nor the army, could do anything against them. During the six months from January 1789 to the fall of the Bastille in July, France travelled as far as England in the six hundred years between the Earl of Leicester and Lord Beaconsfield. Ten years after the American alliance, the Rights of Man, which had been proclaimed at Philadelphia, were repeated at Versailles. The alliance had borne fruit on both sides of the Atlantic, and for France, the fruit was the triumph of American ideas over English. They were more popular, more simple, more effective against privilege, and, strange to say, more acceptable to the King. The new French constitution allowed no privileged orders, no parliamentary ministry, no power of dissolution, and only a suspensive veto. But the characteristic safeguards of the American Government were rejected: Federalism, separation of Church and State, the Second Chamber, the political arbitration of the supreme judicial body. That which weakened the Executive was taken: that which restrained the Legislature was left. Checks on the crown abounded; but should the crown be vacant, the powers that remained would be without a check. The precautions were all in one direction. Nobody would contemplate the contingency that there might be no king. The constitution was inspired by a profound disbelief in Louis XVI. and a pertinacious belief in monarchy. The assembly voted without debate, by acclamation, a Civil List three times as large as that of Queen Victoria. When Louis fled, and the throne was actually vacant, they brought him back to it, preferring the phantom of a king who was a prisoner to the reality of no king at all.

Next to this misapplication of American examples, which was the fault of nearly all the leading statesmen, excepting Mounier, Mirabeau, and Sieyès, the cause of the Revolution was injured by its religious policy. The most novel and impressive lesson taught by the fathers of the American Republic was that the people, and not the administration, should govern. Men in office were salaried agents, by whom the nation wrought its will. Authority submitted to public opinion, and left to it not only the control, but the initiative of government. Patience in waiting for a wind, alacrity in catching it, the dread of exerting unnecessary influence, characterise the early presidents. Some of the French politicians shared this view, though with less exaggeration than

Washington. They wished to decentralise the government, and to obtain, for good or evil, the genuine expression of popular sentiment. Necker himself, and Buzot, the most thoughtful of the Girondins, dreamed of federalising France. In the United States there was no current of opinion, and no combination of forces, to be seriously feared. The government needed no security against being propelled in a wrong direction. But the French Revolution was accomplished at the expense of powerful classes. Besides the nobles, the Assembly, which had been made supreme by the accession of the clergy, and had been led at first by popular ecclesiastics, by Sieyès, Talleyrand, Cicé, La Luzerne, made an enemy of the clergy. The prerogative could not be destroyed without touching the Church. Ecclesiastical patronage had helped to make the crown absolute. To leave it in the hands of Louis and his ministers was to renounce the entire policy of the constitution. To disestablish, was to make it over to the Pope. It was consistent with the democratic principle to introduce election into the Church. It involved a breach with Rome; but so, indeed, did the laws of Joseph II., Charles III., and Leopold. The Pope was not likely to cast away the friendship of France, if he could help it; and the French clergy were not likely to give trouble by their attachment to Rome. Therefore, amid the indifference of many, and against the urgent, and probably sincere, remonstrances of Robespierre and Marat, the Jansenists, who had a century of persecution to avenge, carried the Civil Constitution. The coercive measures which enforced it led to the breach with the King, and the fall of the monarchy; to the revolt of the provinces, and the fall of liberty. The Jacobins determined that public opinion should not reign, that the State should not remain at the mercy of powerful combinations. They held the representatives of the people under control, by the people itself. They attributed higher authority to the direct than to the indirect voice of the democratic oracle. They armed themselves with power to crush every adverse, every independent force, and especially to put down the Church, in whose cause the provinces had risen against the capital. They met the centrifugal federalism of the friends of the Gironde by the most resolute centralisation. France was governed by Paris; and Paris by its municipality and its mob. Obeying Rousseau's maxim, that the people cannot delegate its power, they raised the elementary constituency above its representatives. As the greatest constituent body, the most numerous accumulation of primary electors, the largest portion of sovereignty, was in the people of Paris, they designed that the people of Paris should rule over France, as the people of Rome, the mob as well as the senate, had ruled, not ingloriously, over Italy, and over half the nations that surround the Mediterranean. Although the Jacobins were scarcely more irreligious than the Abbé Sieyès or Madame Roland, although Robespierre wanted to force men to believe in God, although Danton went to confession and Barère was a professing Christian, they imparted to modern democracy that implacable hatred of religion which contrasts so strangely with the example of its Puritan prototype.

The deepest cause which made the French Revolution so disastrous to liberty was its theory of equality. Liberty was the watchword of the middle class, equality of the lower. It was the lower class that won the battles of the third estate; that took the Bastille, and made France a constitutional monarchy; that took the Tuileries, and made France a Republic. They claimed their reward. The middle class, having cast down the upper orders with the aid of the lower, instituted a new inequality and a privilege for itself. By means of a taxpaying qualification it deprived its confederates of their vote. To those, therefore, who had accomplished the Revolution, its promise was not fulfilled. Equality did nothing for them. The opinion, at that time, was almost universal, that society is founded on an agreement which is voluntary and conditional, and that the links which bind men to it are terminable, for sufficient reason, like those which subject them to authority. From these popular premises the logic of Marat drew his sanguinary conclusions. He told the famished people that the conditions on which they had consented to bear their evil lot, and had refrained from violence, had not been kept to them. It was suicide, it was murder, to submit to starve and to see one's children starving, by the fault of the rich. The bonds of society were dissolved by the wrong it inflicted. The state of nature had come back, in which every man had a right to what he could take. The time had come for the rich to make way for the poor. With this theory of equality, liberty was quenched in blood, and Frenchmen became ready to sacrifice all other things to save life and fortune.

Twenty years after the splendid opportunity that opened in 1789, the reaction had triumphed everywhere in Europe; ancient constitutions had perished as well as new; and even England afforded them neither protection nor sympathy. The liberal, at least the democratic revival, came from Spain. The Spaniards fought against the French for a king, who was a prisoner in France. They gave themselves a constitution, and placed his name at the head of it. They had a monarchy, without a king. It required to be so contrived that it would work in the absence, possibly the permanent absence, of the monarch. It became, therefore, a monarchy only in name, composed, in fact, of democratic forces. The constitution of 1812 was the attempt of inexperienced men to accomplish the most difficult task in politics. It was smitten with sterility. For many years it was the standard of abortive revolutions among the so-called Latin nations. It promulgated the notion of a king who should flourish only in name, and should not even discharge the humble function which Hegel assigns to royalty, of dotting i's for the people.

The overthrow of the Cadiz constitution, in 1823, was the supreme triumph of the restored monarchy of France. Five years later, under a wise and liberal minister, the Restoration was advancing fairly on the constitutional paths, when the incurable distrust of the Liberal party defeated Martignac, and brought in the ministry of extreme royalists that ruined the monarchy. In labouring to transfer power from the class which the Revolution had enfranchised to those which it had overthrown, Polignac and La Bourdonnaie would gladly have made terms with the working men. To break the influence of intellect and capital by means of universal suffrage, was an idea long and zealously advocated by some of their supporters. They had not foresight or ability to divide their adversaries, and they were vanquished in 1830 by the united democracy.

The promise of the Revolution of July was to reconcile royalists and democrats. The King assured Lafayette that he was a republican at heart; and Lafayette assured France that Louis Philippe was the best of republics. The shock of the great event was felt in Poland, and Belgium, and even in England. It gave a direct impulse to democratic movements in Switzerland.

Swiss democracy had been in abeyance since 1815. The national will had no organ. The cantons were supreme; and governed as inefficiently as other governments under the protecting shade of the Holy Alliance. There was no dispute that Switzerland called for extensive reforms, and no doubt of the direction they would take. The number of the cantons was the great obstacle to all improvement. It was useless to have twenty-five governments in a country equal to one American State, and inferior in population to one great city. It was impossible that they should be good governments. A central power was the manifest need of the country. In the absence of an efficient federal power, seven cantons formed a separate league for the protection of their own interests. Whilst democratic ideas were making way in Switzerland, the Papacy was travelling in the opposite direction, and showing an inflexible hostility for ideas which are the breath of democratic life. The growing democracy and the growing Ultramontanism came into collision. The Sonderbund could aver with truth that there was no safety for its rights under the Federal Constitution. The others could reply, with equal truth, that there was no safety for the constitution with the Sonderbund. In 1847, it came to a war between national sovereignty and cantonal sovereignty. The Sonderbund was dissolved, and a new Federal Constitution was adopted, avowedly and ostensibly charged with the duty of carrying out democracy, and repressing the adverse influence of Rome. It was a delusive imitation of the American system. The President was powerless. The Senate was powerless. The Supreme Court was powerless. The sovereignty of the cantons was undermined, and their power centred in the House of Representatives. The Constitution of 1848 was a first step towards the destruction of Federalism. Another and almost a final step in the direction of centralisation was taken in 1874. The railways, and the vast interests they created, made the position of the cantonal governments untenable. The conflict with the Ultramontanes increased the demand for vigorous action; and the destruction of State Rights in the American war strengthened the hands of the Centralists. The Constitution of 1874 is one of the most significant works of modern democracy. It is the triumph of democratic force over democratic freedom. It overrules not only the Federal principle, but the representative principle. It carries important measures away from the Federal Legislature to submit them to the votes of the entire people, separating decision from deliberation. The operation is so cumbrous as to be generally ineffective. But it constitutes a power such as exists, we believe, under the laws of no other country. A Swiss jurist has frankly expressed the spirit of the reigning system by saying, that the State is the appointed conscience of the nation.

The moving force in Switzerland has been democracy relieved of all constraint, the principle of putting in action the greatest force of the greatest number. The prosperity of the country has prevented complications such as arose in France. The ministers of Louis Philippe, able and enlightened men, believed that they would make the people prosper if they could have their own way, and could shut out public opinion. They acted as if the intelligent middle class was destined by heaven to govern. The upper class had proved its unfitness before 1789; the lower class, since 1789. Government by professional men, by manufacturers and scholars, was sure to be safe, and almost sure to be reasonable and practical. Money became the object of a political superstition, such as had formerly attached to land, and afterwards attached to labour. The masses of the people, who had fought against Marmont, became aware that they had not fought for their own benefit. They were still governed by their employers.

When the King parted with Lafayette, and it was found that he would not only reign but govern, the indignation of the republicans found a vent in street fighting. In 1836, when the horrors of the infernal machine had armed the crown with ampler powers, and had silenced the republican party, the term Socialism made its appearance in literature. Tocqueville, who was writing the philosophic chapters that conclude his work, failed to discover the power which the new system was destined to exercise on democracy. Until then, democrats and communists had stood apart. Although the socialist doctrines were defended by the best intellects of France, by Thierry, Comte, Chevalier, and Georges Sand, they excited more attention as a literary curiosity than as the cause of future revolutions. Towards 1840, in the recesses of secret societies, republicans and socialists coalesced. Whilst the Liberal leaders, Lamartine and Barrot, discoursed on the surface concerning reform, Ledru Rollin and Louis Blanc were quietly digging a grave for the monarchy, the Liberal party, and the reign of wealth. They worked so well, and the vanquished republicans recovered so thoroughly, by this coalition, the influence they had lost by a long series of crimes and follies, that, in 1848, they were able to conquer without fighting. The fruit of their victory was universal suffrage.

From that time the promises of socialism have supplied the best energy of democracy. Their coalition has been the ruling fact in French politics. It created the "saviour of society," and the Commune; and it still entangles the footsteps of the Republic. It is the only shape in which democracy has found an entrance into Germany. Liberty has lost its spell; and democracy maintains itself by the promise of substantial gifts to the masses of the people.

Since the Revolution of July and the Presidency of Jackson gave the impulse which has made democracy preponderate, the ablest political writers, Tocqueville, Calhoun, Mill, and Laboulaye, have drawn, in the name of freedom, a formidable indictment against it. They have shown democracy without respect for the past or care for the future, regardless of public faith and of national honour, extravagant and inconstant, jealous of talent and of knowledge, indifferent to justice but servile towards opinion, incapable of organisation, impatient of authority, averse from obedience, hostile to religion and to established law. Evidence indeed abounds, even if the true cause be not proved. But it is not to these symptoms that we must impute the permanent danger and the irrepressible conflict. As much might be made good against monarchy, and an unsympathising reasoner might in the same way argue that religion is intolerant, that conscience makes cowards, that piety rejoices in fraud. Recent experience has added little to the observations of those who witnessed the decline after Pericles, of Thucydides, Aristophanes, Plato, and of the writer whose brilliant tract against the Athenian Republic is printed among the works of Xenophon. The manifest, the avowed difficulty is that democracy, no less than monarchy or aristocracy, sacrifices everything to maintain itself, and strives, with an energy and a plausibility that kings and nobles cannot attain, to override representation, to annul all the forces of resistance and deviation, and to secure, by Plébiscite, Referendum, or Caucus, free play for the will of the majority. The true democratic principle, that none shall have power over the people, is taken to mean that none shall be able to restrain or to elude its power. The true democratic principle, that the people shall not be made to do what it does not like, is taken to mean that it shall never be required to tolerate what it does not like. The true democratic principle, that every man's free will shall be as unfettered as possible, is taken to mean that the free will of the collective people shall be fettered in nothing. Religious toleration, judicial independence, dread of centralisation, jealousy of State interference, become obstacles to freedom instead of safeguards, when the centralised force of the State is wielded by the hands of the people. Democracy claims to be not only supreme, without authority above, but absolute, without independence below; to be its own master, not a trustee. The old sovereigns of the world are exchanged for a new one, who may be flattered and deceived, but whom it is impossible to corrupt or to resist, and to whom must be rendered the things that are Cæsar's and also the things that are God's. The enemy to be overcome is no longer the absolutism of the State, but the liberty of the subject. Nothing is more significant than the relish with which Ferrari, the most powerful democratic writer since Rousseau, enumerates the merits of tyrants, and prefers devils to saints in the interest of the community.

For the old notions of civil liberty and of social order did not benefit the masses of the people. Wealth increased, without relieving their wants. The progress of knowledge left them in abject ignorance. Religion flourished, but failed to reach them. Society, whose laws were made by the upper class alone, announced that the best thing for the poor is not to be born, and the next best, to die in childhood, and suffered them to live in misery and crime and pain. As surely as the long reign of the rich has been employed in promoting the accumulation of wealth, the advent of the poor to power will be followed by schemes for diffusing it. Seeing how little was done by the wisdom of former times for education and public health, for insurance, association, and savings, for the protection of labour against the law of self-interest, and how much has been accomplished in this generation, there is reason in the fixed belief that a great change was needed, and that democracy has not striven in vain. Liberty, for the mass, is not happiness; and institutions are not an end but a means. The thing they seek is a force sufficient to sweep away scruples and the obstacle of rival interests, and, in some degree, to better their condition. They mean that the strong hand that heretofore has formed great States, protected religions, and defended the independence of nations, shall help them by preserving life, and endowing it for them with some, at least, of the things men live for. That is the notorious danger of modern democracy. That is also its purpose and its strength. And against this threatening power the weapons that struck down other despots do not avail. The greatest happiness principle positively confirms it. The principle of equality, besides being as easily applied to property as to power, opposes the existence of persons or groups of persons exempt from the common law, and independent of the common will; and the principle, that authority is a matter of contract, may hold good against kings, but not against the sovereign people, because a contract implies two parties.

If we have not done more than the ancients to develop and to examine the disease, we have far surpassed them in studying the remedy. Besides the French Constitution of the year III., and that of the American Confederates,—the most remarkable attempts that have been made since the archonship of Euclides to meet democratic evils with the antidotes which democracy itself supplies,—our age has been prolific in this branch of experimental politics.

Many expedients have been tried, that have been evaded or defeated. A divided executive, which was an important phase in the transformation of ancient monarchies into republics, and which, through the advocacy of Condorcet, took root in France, has proved to be weakness itself.

The constitution of 1795, the work of a learned priest, confined the franchise to those who should know how to read and write; and in 1849 this provision was rejected by men who intended that the ignorant voter should help them to overturn the Republic. In our time no democracy could long subsist without educating the masses; and the scheme of Daunou is simply an indirect encouragement to elementary instruction.

In 1799 Sieyès suggested to Bonaparte the idea of a great Council, whose function it should be to keep the acts of the Legislature in harmony with the constitution—a function which the *Nomophylakes* discharged at Athens, and the Supreme Court in the United States, and which produced the Sénat Conservateur, one of the favourite implements of Imperialism. Sieyès meant that his Council should also serve the purpose of a gilded ostracism, having power to absorb any obnoxious politician, and to silence him with a thousand a year.

Napoleon the Third's plan of depriving unmarried men of their votes would have disfranchised the two greatest Conservative classes in France, the priest and the soldier.

In the American constitution it was intended that the chief of the executive should be chosen by a body of carefully selected electors. But since, in 1825, the popular candidate succumbed to one who had only a minority of votes, it has become the practice to elect the President by the pledged delegates of universal suffrage.

The exclusion of ministers from Congress has been one of the severest strains on the American system; and the law which required a majority of three to one enabled Louis Napoleon to make himself Emperor. Large constituencies make independent deputies; but experience proves that small assemblies, the consequence of large constituencies, can be managed by Government.

The composite vote and the cumulative vote have been almost universally rejected as schemes for baffling the majority. But the principle of dividing the representatives equally between population and property has never had fair play. It was introduced by Thouret into the constitution of 1791. The Revolution made it inoperative; and it was so manipulated from 1817 to

1848 by the fatal dexterity of Guizot as to make opinion ripe for universal suffrage.

Constitutions which forbid the payment of deputies and the system of imperative instructions, which deny the power of dissolution, and make the Legislature last for a fixed term, or renew it by partial re-elections, and which require an interval between the several debates on the same measure, evidently strengthen the independence of the representative assembly. The Swiss veto has the same effect, as it suspends legislation only when opposed by a majority of the whole electoral body, not by a majority of those who actually vote upon it.

Indirect elections are scarcely anywhere in use out of Germany, but they have been a favourite corrective of democracy with many thoughtful politicians. Where the extent of the electoral district obliges constituents to vote for candidates who are unknown to them, the election is not free. It is managed by wire-pullers, and by party machinery, beyond the control of the electors. Indirect election puts the choice of the managers into their hands. The objection is that the intermediate electors are generally too few to span the interval between voters and candidates, and that they choose representatives not of better quality, but of different politics. If the intermediate body consisted of one in ten of the whole constituency, the contact would be preserved, the people would be really represented, and the ticket system would be broken down.

The one pervading evil of democracy is the tyranny of the majority, or rather of that party, not always the majority, that succeeds, by force or fraud, in carrying elections. To break off that point is to avert the danger. The common system of representation perpetuates the danger. Unequal electorates afford no security to majorities. Equal electorates give none to minorities. Thirty-five years ago it was pointed out that the remedy is proportional representation. It is profoundly democratic, for it increases the influence of thousands who would otherwise have no voice in the government; and it brings men more near an equality by so contriving that no vote shall be wasted, and that every voter shall contribute to bring into Parliament a member of his own opinions. The origin of the idea is variously claimed for Lord Grey and for Considérant. The successful example of Denmark and the earnest advocacy of Mill gave it prominence in the world of politics. It has gained popularity with the growth of democracy, and we are informed by M. Naville that in Switzerland Conservatives and Radicals combined to promote it.

Of all checks on democracy, federalism has been the most efficacious and the most congenial; but, becoming associated with the Red Republic, with feudalism, with the Jesuits, and with slavery, it has fallen into disrepute, and is giving way to centralism. The federal system limits and restrains the sovereign power by dividing it, and by assigning to Government only certain defined rights. It is the only method of curbing not only the majority but the power of the whole people, and it affords the strongest basis for a second chamber, which has been found the essential security for freedom in every genuine democracy.

The fall of Guizot discredited the famous maxim of the Doctrinaires, that Reason is sovereign, and not king or people; and it was further exposed to the scoffer by the promise of Comte that Positivist philosophers shall manufacture political ideas, which no man shall be permitted to dispute. But putting aside international and criminal law, in which there is some approach to uniformity, the domain of political economy seems destined to admit the rigorous certainty of science. Whenever that shall be attained, when the battle between Economists and Socialists is ended, the evil force which Socialism imparts to democracy will be spent. The battle is raging more violently than ever, but it has entered into a new phase, by the rise of a middle party. Whether that remarkable movement, which is promoted by some of the first economists in Europe, is destined to shake the authority of their science, or to conquer socialism, by robbing it of that which is the secret of its strength, it must be recorded here as the latest and the most serious effort that has been made to disprove the weighty sentence of Rousseau, that democracy is a government for gods, but unfit for man.

We have been able to touch on only a few of the topics that crowd Sir Erskine May's volumes. Although he has perceived more clearly than Tocqueville the contact of democracy with socialism, his judgment is untinged with Tocqueville's despondency, and he contemplates the direction of progress with a confidence that approaches optimism. The notion of an inflexible logic in history does not depress him, for he concerns himself with facts and with men more than with doctrines, and his book is a history of several democracies, not of democracy. There are links in the argument, there are phases of development which he leaves unnoticed, because his object has not been to trace out the properties and the connection of ideas, but to explain the results of experience. We should consult his pages, probably, without effect, if we wished to follow the origin and sequence of the democratic dogmas, that all men are equal; that speech and thought are free; that each generation is a law to itself only; that there shall be no endowments, no entails, no primogeniture; that the people are sovereign; that the people can do no wrong. The great mass of those who, of necessity, are interested in practical politics have no such antiquarian curiosity. They want to know what can be learned from the countries where the democratic experiments have been tried; but they do not care to be told how M. Waddington has emended the *Monumentum Ancyranum*, what connection there was between Mariana and Milton, or between Penn and Rousseau, or who invented the proverb *Vox Populi Vox Dei*. Sir Erskine May's reluctance to deal with matters speculative and doctrinal, and to devote his space to the mere literary history of politics, has made his touch somewhat uncertain in treating of the political action of Christianity, perhaps the most complex and comprehensive question that can embarrass a historian. He disparages the influence of the mediæval Church on nations just emerging from a barbarous paganism, and he exalts it when it had become associated with despotism and persecution. He insists on the liberating action of the Reformation in the sixteenth century, when it gave a stimulus to absolutism; and he is slow to recognise, in the enthusiasm and violence of the sects in the seventeenth, the most potent agency ever brought to bear on democratic history. The omission of America creates a void between 1660 and 1789, and leaves much unexplained in the revolutionary movement of the last hundred years, which is the central problem of the book. But if some things are missed from the design, if the execution is not equal in every part, the praise remains to Sir Erskine May, that he is the only writer who has ever brought together the materials for a comparative study of democracy, that he has avoided the temper of party, that he has shown a hearty sympathy for the progress and improvement of mankind, and a steadfast faith in the wisdom and the power that guide it.

IV

THE MASSACRE OF ST. BARTHOLOMEW[1]

THE way in which Coligny and his adherents met their death has been handed down by a crowd of trustworthy witnesses, and few things in history are known in more exact detail. But the origin and motives of the tragedy, and the manner of its reception by the opinion of Christian Europe, are still subject to controversy. Some of the evidence has been difficult of access, part is lost, and much has been deliberately destroyed. No letters written from Paris at the time have been found in the Austrian archives. In the correspondence of thirteen agents of the House of Este at the Court of Rome, every paper relating to the event has disappeared. All the documents of 1572, both from Rome and Paris, are wanting in the archives of Venice. In the Registers of many French towns the leaves which contained the records of August and September in that year have been torn out. The first reports sent to England by Walsingham and by the French Government have not been recovered. Three accounts printed at Rome, when the facts were new, speedily became so rare that they have been forgotten. The Bull of Gregory XIII. was not admitted into the official collections; and the reply to Muretus has escaped notice until now. The letters of Charles IX. to Rome, with the important exception of that which he wrote on the 24th of August, have been dispersed and lost. The letters of Gregory XIII. to France have never been seen by persons willing to make

[1] *North British Review*, Oct. 1869.

them public. In the absence of these documents the most authentic information is that which is supplied by the French Ambassador and by the Nuncio. The despatches of Ferralz, describing the attitude of the Roman court, are extant, but have not been used. Those of Salviati have long been known. Chateaubriand took a copy when the papal archives were at Paris, and projected a work on the events with which they are concerned. Some extracts were published, with his consent, by the continuator of Mackintosh; and a larger selection, from the originals in the Vatican, appeared in Theiner's *Annals of Gregory XIII.* The letters written under Pius V. are beyond the limits of that work; and Theiner, moreover, has omitted whatever seemed irrelevant to his purpose. The criterion of relevancy is uncertain; and we shall avail ourselves largely of the unpublished portions of Salviati's correspondence, which were transcribed by Chateaubriand. These manuscripts, with others of equal importance not previously consulted, determine several doubtful questions of policy and design.

The Protestants never occupied a more triumphant position, and their prospects were never brighter, than in the summer of 1572. For many years the progress of their religion had been incessant. The most valuable of the conquests it has retained were already made; and the period of its reverses had not begun. The great division which aided Catholicism afterwards to recover so much lost ground was not openly confessed; and the effectual unity of the Reformed Churches was not yet dissolved. In controversial theology the defence was weaker than the attack. The works to which the Reformation owed its popularity and system were in the hands of thousands, while the best authors of the Catholic restoration had not begun to write. The press continued to serve the new opinions better than the old; and in literature Protestantism was supreme. Persecuted in the South, and established by violence in the North, it had overcome the resistance of princes in Central Europe, and had won toleration without ceasing to be intolerant. In

France and Poland, in the dominions of the Emperor and under the German prelates, the attempt to arrest its advance by physical force had been abandoned. In Germany it covered twice the area that remained to it in the next generation, and, except in Bavaria, Catholicism was fast dying out. The Polish Government had not strength to persecute, and Poland became the refuge of the sects. When the bishops found that they could not prevent toleration, they resolved that they would not restrict it. Trusting to the maxim, "Bellum Haereticorum pax est Ecclesiae," they insisted that liberty should extend to those whom the Reformers would have exterminated.[1] The Polish Protestants, in spite of their dissensions, formed themselves into one great party. When the death of the last of the Jagellons, on the 7th of July 1572, made the monarchy elective, they were strong enough to enforce their conditions on the candidates; and it was thought that they would be able to decide the election, and obtain a king of their own choosing. Alva's reign of Terror had failed to pacify the Low Countries, and he was about to resign the hopeless task to an incapable successor. The taking of the Brill in April was the first of those maritime victories which led to the independence of the Dutch. Mons fell in May; and in July the important province of Holland declared for the Prince of Orange. The Catholics believed that all was lost if Alva remained in command.[2]

The decisive struggle was in France. During the minority of Charles IX. persecution had given way to civil war, and the Regent, his mother, had vainly striven, by submitting to neither party, to uphold the authority of the Crown. She checked the victorious Catholics, by granting to the Huguenots terms which constituted them, in spite of continual disaster in the field, a vast and organised power in the State. To escape their influence

[1] Satius fore ducebam, si minus profligari possent omnes, ut ferrentur omnes, quo mordentes et comedentes invicem, consumerentur ab invicem (Hosius to Karnkowsky, Feb. 26, 1568).

[2] The Secretary of Medina Celi to Çayas, June 24, 1572 (*Correspondance de Philippe II.*, ii. 264).

it would have been necessary to invoke the help of Philip II., and to accept protection which would have made France subordinate to Spain. Philip laboured to establish such an alliance; and it was to promote this scheme that he sent his queen, Elizabeth of Valois, to meet her mother at Bayonne. In 1568 Elizabeth died; and a rumour came to Catherine touching the manner of her death which made it hard to listen to friendly overtures from her husband. Antonio Perez, at that time an unscrupulous instrument of his master's will, afterwards accused him of having poisoned his wife. "On parle fort sinistrement de sa mort, pour avoir été advancée," says Brantôme. After the massacre of the Protestants, the ambassador at Venice, a man distinguished as a jurist and a statesman, reproached Catherine with having thrown France into the hands of him in whom the world recognised her daughter's murderer. Catherine did not deny the truth of the report. She replied that she was "bound to think of her sons in preference to her daughters, that the foul-play was not fully proved, and that if it were it could not be avenged so long as France was weakened by religious discord."[1] She wrote as she could not have written if she had been convinced that the suspicion was unjust.

When Charles IX. began to be his own master he seemed resolved to follow his father and grandfather in their hostility to the Spanish Power. He wrote to a trusted servant that all his thoughts were bent on thwarting Philip.[2] While the Christian navies were fighting at Lepanto, the King of France was treating with the Turks. His menacing attitude in the following year kept Don

[1] Quant à ce qui me touche à moy en particulier, encores que j'ayme unicquement tous mes enffans, je veulx préférer, comme il est bien raysonnable, les filz aux filles; et pour le regard de ce que me mandez de celluy qui a faict mourir ma fille, c'est chose que l'on ne tient point pour certaine, et où elle le seroit, le roy monsieur mondit filz n'en pouvoit faire la vengence en l'estat que son royaulme estoit lors; mais à présent qu'il est tout uni, il aura assez de moien et de forces pour sen ressentir quant l'occasion s'en présentera (Catherine to Du Ferrier, Oct. 1, 1572; Bib. Imp. F. Fr. 15,555). The despatches of Fourquevaulx from Madrid, published by the Marquis Du Prat in the *Histoire d'Elisabeth de Valois*, do not confirm the rumour.

[2] Toutes mes fantaisies sont bandées pour m'opposer à la grandeur des Espagnols, et délibère m'y conduire le plus dextrement qu'il me sera possible (Charles IX. to Noailles, May 2, 1572; Noailles, *Henri de Valois*, i. 8).

Juan in Sicilian waters, and made his victory barren for Christendom. Encouraged by French protection, Venice withdrew from the League. Even in Corsica there was a movement which men interpreted as a prelude to the storm that France was raising against the empire of Spain. Rome trembled in expectation of a Huguenot invasion of Italy; for Charles was active in conciliating the Protestants both abroad and at home. He married a daughter of the tolerant Emperor Maximilian II.; and he carried on negotiations for the marriage of his brother with Queen Elizabeth, not with any hope of success, but in order to impress public opinion.[1] He made treaties of alliance, in quick succession, with England, with the German Protestants, and with the Prince of Orange. He determined that his brother Anjou, the champion of the Catholics, of whom it was said that he had vowed to root out the Protestants to a man,[2] should be banished to the throne of Poland. Disregarding the threats and entreaties of the Pope, he gave his sister in marriage to Navarre. By the peace of St. Germains the Huguenots had secured, within certain limits, freedom from persecution and the liberty of persecuting; so that Pius V. declared that France had been made the slave of heretics. Coligny was now the most powerful man in the kingdom. His scheme for closing the civil wars by an expedition for the conquest of the Netherlands began to be put in motion. French auxiliaries followed Lewis of Nassau into Mons; an army of Huguenots had already gone to his assistance; another was being collected near the frontier, and Coligny was preparing to take the command in a war which might become a Protestant crusade, and which left the Catholics no hope of victory. Meanwhile many hundreds of his officers followed him to Paris, to attend the wedding which was to reconcile the factions, and cement the peace of religion.

[1] Il fault, et je vous prie ne faillir, quand bien il seroit du tout rompu, et que verriés qu'il n'y auroit nulle espérance, de trouver moyen d'en entrettenir toujours doucement le propos, d'ici à quelque temps; car cella ne peut que bien servir à establir mes affaires et aussy pour ma réputation (Charles IX. to La Mothe, Aug. 9, 1572; *Corr. de La Mothe*, vii. 311).

[2] This is stated both by his mother and by the Cardinal of Lorraine (Michelet, *La Ligue*, p. 26).

In the midst of those lofty designs and hopes, Coligny was struck down. On the morning of the 22nd of August he was shot at and badly wounded. Two days later he was killed; and a general attack was made on the Huguenots of Paris. It lasted some weeks, and was imitated in about twenty places. The chief provincial towns of France were among them.

Judged by its immediate result, the massacre of St. Bartholomew was a measure weakly planned and irresolutely executed, which deprived Protestantism of its political leaders, and left it for a time to the control of zealots. There is no evidence to make it probable that more than seven thousand victims perished. Judged by later events, it was the beginning of a vast change in the conflict of the churches. At first it was believed that a hundred thousand Huguenots had fallen. It was said that the survivors were abjuring by thousands,[1] that the children of the slain were made Catholics, that those whom the priest had admitted to absolution and communion were nevertheless put to death.[2] Men who were far beyond the reach of the French Government lost their faith in a religion which Providence had visited with so tremendous a judgment;[3] and foreign princes took heart to employ severities which could excite no horror after the scenes in France.

Contemporaries were persuaded that the Huguenots had been flattered and their policy adopted only for their destruction, and that the murder of Coligny and his followers was a long premeditated crime. Catholics and Protestants vied with each other in detecting proofs of that which they variously esteemed a sign of supernatural inspiration or of diabolical depravity. In the last forty years a different opinion has prevailed. It has been

[1] In reliqua Gallia fuit et est incredibilis defectio, quae tamen usque adeo non pacavit immanes illas feras, ut etiam eos qui defecerunt (qui pene sunt innumerabiles) semel ad internecionem una cum integris familiis trucidare prorsus decreverint (Beza, Dec. 3, 1572; *Ill. vir. Epp. Sel.*, p. 621, 1617).

[2] Languet to the Duke of Saxony, Nov. 30, 1572 (*Arcana*, sec. xvi. 183).

[3] Vidi et cum dolore intellexi lanienam illam Gallicam perfidissimam et atrocissimam plurimos per Germaniam ita offendisse, ut jam etiam de veritate nostrae Religionis et doctrinae dubitare incoeperint (Bullinger to Wittgenstein. Feb. 23, 1573; Friedländer, *Beiträge zur rel. Gesch.*, p. 254).

deemed more probable, more consistent with testimony and with the position of affairs at the time, that Coligny succeeded in acquiring extraordinary influence over the mind of Charles, that his advice really predominated, and that the sanguinary resolution was suddenly embraced by his adversaries as the last means of regaining power. This opinion is made plausible by many facts. It is supported by several writers who were then living, and by the document known as the Confession of Anjou. The best authorities of the present day are nearly unanimous in rejecting premeditation.

The evidence on the opposite side is stronger than they suppose. The doom which awaited the Huguenots had been long expected and often foretold. People at a distance, Monluc in Languedoc, and the Protestant Mylius in Italy, drew the same inference from the news that came from the court. Strangers meeting on the road discussed the infatuation of the Admiral.[1] Letters brought from Rome to the Emperor the significant intimation that the birds were all caged, and now was the time to lay hands on them.[2] Duplessis-Mornay, the future chief of the Huguenots, was so much oppressed with a sense of coming evil, that he hardly ventured into the streets on the wedding-day. He warned the Admiral of the general belief among their friends that the marriage concealed a plot for their ruin, and that the festivities would end in some horrible surprise.[3] Coligny was proof against suspicion. Several of his followers left Paris, but he remained unmoved. At one moment the excessive readiness to grant all his requests shook the confidence of his son-in-law Téligny; but the doubt vanished so completely that Téligny himself prevented the flight of his partisans after the attempt on the Admiral's life. On the morning of the fatal day, Montgomery sent word to Walsingham that Coligny was safe under protection of

[1] De Thou, *Mémoires*, p. 9.

[2] Il me dist qu'on luy avoist escript de Rome, n'avoit que trois semaines ou environ, sur le propos des noces du roy de Navarre en ces propres termes ; Que à ceste heure que tous les oiseaux estoient en cage, on les pouvoit prendre tous ensemble (Vulcob to Charles IX., Sept. 26, 1572 ; Noailles, iii. 214).

[3] *Mémoires de Duplessis-Mornay*, i. 38 ; Ambert, *Duplessis-Mornay*, p. 38.

the King's Guards, and that no further stir was to be apprehended.[1]

For many years foreign advisers had urged Catherine to make away with these men. At first it was computed that half a dozen victims would be enough.[2] That was the original estimate of Alva, at Bayonne.[3] When the Duke of Ferrara was in France, in 1564, he proposed a larger measure, and he repeated this advice by the mouth of every agent whom he sent to France.[4] After the event, both Alva and Alfonso reminded Catherine that she had done no more than follow their advice.[5] Alva's letter explicitly confirms the popular notion which connects the massacre with the conference of Bayonne; and it can no longer now be doubted that La Roche-sur-Yon, on his death-bed, informed Coligny that murderous resolutions had been taken on that occasion.[6] But the Nuncio, Santa Croce, who was present, wrote to Cardinal Borromeo that the Queen had indeed promised to punish the infraction of the Edict of Pacification, but that this was a very different thing from undertaking to extirpate heresy. Catherine affirmed that in this way the law could reach all the Huguenot ministers; and Alva professed to believe her.[7] Whatever studied ambiguity

[1] Digges, *Compleat Ambassador*, pp. 276, 255.

[2] Correr, *Relazione;* Tommaseo, ii. 116.

[3] He said to Catherine: Que quando quisiesen usar de otro y averlo, con no mas personas que con cinc o seys que son el cabo de todo esto, los tomasen a su mano y les cortasen las cabeças (Alva to Philip II., June 21, 1565; *Papiers de Granvelle*, ix. 298)..

[4] Ci rallegriamo con la maestà sua con tutto l' affetto dell' animo, ch' ella habbia presa quella risolutione così opportunamente sopra la quale noi stesso l' ultima volta che fummo in Francia parlammo con la Regina Madre. . . . Dipoi per diversi gentilhuomini che in varie occorrenze habbiamo mandato in corte siamo instati nel suddetto ricordo (Alfonso II. to Fogliani, Sept. 13, 1572; Modena Archives).

[5] Muchas vezes me ha accordado de aver dicho a Su Mag. esto mismo en Bayona, y de lo que mi offrecio, y veo que ha muy bien desempeñado su palabra (Alva to Zuñiga, Sept. 9, 1572; Coquerel, *La St. Barthélemy*, p. 12).

[6] Kluckhohn, *Zur Geschichte des angeblichen Bündnisses von Bayonne*, p. 36, 1868.

[7] Il signor duca di Alva . . . mi disse, che come in questo abboccamento negotio alcuno non havevano trattato, ne volevano trattare, altro che della religione, cosi la lor differenza era nata per questo, perchè non vedeva che la regina ci pigliasse risolutione a modo suo ne de altro, che di buone parole ben generali. . . . È stato risoluto che alla tornata in Parigi si farà una ricerca di quelli che hanno contravenuto all' editto, e si castigaranno; nel che dice S. M. che gli Ugonotti ci sono talmente compresi, che spera con questo mezzo solo cacciare i

of language she may have used, the action of 1572 was uninfluenced by deliberations which were seven years old.

During the spring and summer the Tuscan agents diligently prepared their master for what was to come. Petrucci wrote on the 19th of March that, for a reason which he could not trust to paper, the marriage would certainly take place, though not until the Huguenots had delivered up their strongholds. Four weeks later Alamanni announced that the Queen's pious design for restoring unity of faith would, by the grace of God, be speedily accomplished. On the 9th of August Petrucci was able to report that the plan arranged at Bayonne was near execution.[1] Yet he was not fully initiated. The Queen afterwards assured him that she had confided the secret to no foreign resident except the Nuncio,[2] and Petrucci resentfully complains that she had also consulted the Ambassador of Savoy. Venice, like Florence and Savoy, was not taken by surprise. In February the ambassador Contarini explained to the Senate the specious tranquillity in France, by saying that the Government reckoned on the death of the Admiral or the Queen of Navarre to work a momentous change.[3] Cavalli, his successor, judged that a business so grossly mismanaged showed no signs of deliberation.[4] There was another Venetian at Paris who was better informed. The Republic was seeking to withdraw from the league against the Turks; and her most illustrious statesman, Giovanni Michiel, was sent to solicit the help of France in negotiating peace.[5] The account which he gave of his mission has been pronounced by a consummate judge

Ministri di Francia. . . . Il Signor Duca di Alva si satisfa piu di questa deliberatione di me, perchè io non trovo che serva all' estirpation dell' heresia il castigar quelli che hanno contravenuto all' editto (Santa Croce to Borromeo, Bayonne, July 1, 1565, MS.).

[1] Desjardins, *Négociations avec la Toscane*, iii. 756, 765, 802.

[2] Io non ho fatto intendere cosa alcuna a nessuno principe; ho ben parlato al nunzio solo (Desp. Aug. 31; Desjardins, iii. 828).

[3] Alberi, *Relazioni Venete*, xii. 250.

[4] Alberi, xii. 328.

[5] Son principal but et dessein estoit de sentir quelle espérance ilz pourroient avoir de parvenir à la paix avec le G. S. dont il s'est ouvert et a demandé ce qu'il en pouvoit espérer et attendre (Charles IX. to Du Ferrier, Sept. 28, 1572; Charrière, *Négociations dans le Levant*, iii. 310).

of Venetian State-Papers the most valuable report of the sixteenth century.[1] He was admitted almost daily to secret conference with Anjou, Nevers, and the group of Italians on whom the chief odium rests; and there was no counsellor to whom Catherine more willingly gave ear.[2] Michiel affirms that the intention had been long entertained, and that the Nuncio had been directed to reveal it privately to Pius V.[3]

Salviati was related to Catherine, and had gained her good opinion as Nuncio in the year 1570. The Pope had sent him back because nobody seemed more capable of diverting her and her son from the policy which caused so much uneasiness at Rome.[4] He died many years later, with the reputation of having been one of the most eminent Cardinals at a time when the Sacred College was unusually rich in talent. Personally, he had always favoured stern measures of repression. When the Countess of Entremont was married to Coligny, Salviati declared that she had made herself liable to severe penalties by entertaining proposals of marriage with so notorious a heretic, and demanded that the Duke of Savoy should, by all the means in his power, cause that wicked bride to be put out of the way.[5] When the peace of St. Germains was concluded, he assured Charles and Catherine that their lives were in danger, as the Huguenots were seeking to pull down the throne as well as the altar. He believed that all intercourse with them was sinful, and that the sole remedy was utter extermination by the sword. "I am convinced," he wrote, "that it will come to this." "If they do the tenth part of what I have advised, it will be well for them."[6] After an audience of two hours, at which he had presented a letter from Pius V., prophesying the wrath of Heaven, Salviati perceived that his exhortations made some impression.

[1] Ranke, *Französische Geschichte*, v. 76.

[2] Digges, p. 258; Cosmi, *Memorie di Morosini*, p. 26.

[3] Alberi, xii. 294.

[4] Mittit eo Antonium Mariam Salviatum, reginae affinem eique pergratum, qui eam in officio contineat (Cardinal of Vercelli, *Comment. de Rebus Gregorii* XIII.; Ranke, *Päpste*, App. 85).

[5] Desp. Aug. 30, 1570.

[6] Oct. 14, 1570.

The King and Queen whispered to him that they hoped to make the peace yield such fruit that the end would more than countervail the badness of the beginning; and the King added, in strict confidence, that his plan was one which, once told, could never be executed.[1] This might have been said to delude the Nuncio; but he was inclined on the whole to believe that it was sincerely meant. The impression was confirmed by the Archbishop of Sens, Cardinal Pellevé, who informed him that the Huguenot leaders were caressed at Court in order to detach them from their party, and that after the loss of their leaders it would not take more than three days to deal with the rest.[2] Salviati on his return to France was made aware that his long-deferred hopes were about to be fulfilled. He shadowed it forth obscurely in his despatches. He reported that the Queen allowed the Huguenots to pass into Flanders, believing that the admiral would become more and more presumptuous until he gave her an opportunity of retribution; for she excelled in that kind of intrigue. Some days later he knew more, and wrote that he hoped soon to have good news for his Holiness.[3] At the last moment his heart misgave him. On the morning of the 21st of August the Duke of Montpensier and the Cardinal of Bourbon spoke with so much unconcern, in his presence, of what was then so near, that he thought it hardly possible the secret could be kept.[4]

The foremost of the French prelates was the Cardinal of Lorraine. He had held a prominent position at the council of Trent; and for many years he had wielded the

[1] Sept. 24, 1570. [2] Nov. 28, 1570.

[3] Quando scrissi ai giorni passati alla S. V. Illma in cifra, che l' ammiraglio s' avanzava troppo et che gli darebbero su l' unge, gia mi ero accorto, che non lo volevano più tollerare, et molto più mi confermai nell' opinione, quando con caratteri ordinarii glie scrivevo che speravo di dover haver occasione di dar qualche buona nova a Sua Beatitudine, benchè mai havrei creduto la x. parte di quello, che al presente veggo con gli occhi (Desp. Aug. 24; Theiner, *Annales*, i. 329).

[4] Che molti siano stati consapevoli del fatto è necessario, potendogli dizer che a 21 la mattina, essendo col Cardinal di Borbone et M. de Montpensier, viddi che ragionavano si domesticamente di quello che doveva seguire, che in me medesimo restando confuso, conobbi che la prattica andava gagliarda, e piutosto disperai di buon fine che altrimente (same Desp.; Mackintosh, *History of England*, ii. 355).

influence of the House of Guise over the Catholics of France. In May 1572 he went to Rome; and he was still there when the news came from Paris in September. He at once made it known that the resolution had been taken before he left France, and that it was due to himself and his nephew, the Duke of Guise.[1] As the spokesman of the Gallican Church in the following year he delivered a harangue to Charles IX., in which he declared that Charles had eclipsed the glory of preceding kings by slaying the false prophets, and especially by the holy deceit and pious dissimulation with which he had laid his plans.[2]

There was one man who did not get his knowledge from rumour, and who could not be deceived by lies. The King's confessor, Sorbin, afterwards Bishop of Nevers, published in 1574 a narrative of the life and death of Charles IX. He bears unequivocal testimony that that clement and magnanimous act, for so he terms it, was resolved upon beforehand, and he praises the secrecy as well as the justice of his hero.[3]

Early in the year a mission of extraordinary solemnity had appeared in France. Pius V., who was seriously alarmed at the conduct of Charles, had sent the Cardinal of Alessandria as Legate to the Kings of Spain and Portugal, and directed him, in returning, to visit the Court at Blois. The Legate was nephew to the Pope, and the man whom he most entirely trusted.[4] His character stood so high that the reproach of nepotism was never raised by his promotion. Several prelates destined to future eminence attended him. His chief adviser

[1] Attribuisce a se, et al nipote, et a casa sua, la morte del' ammiraglio, gloriandosene assai (Desp. Oct. 1; Theiner, p. 331). The Emperor told the French ambassador "que, depuis les choses avenues, on lui avoit mandé de Rome que Mr. le Cardinal de Lorraine avoit dit que tout le fait avoit esté délibéré avant qu'il partist de France" (Vulcob to Charles IX., Nov. 8; Groen van Prinsterer, *Archives de Nassau*, iv. App. 22).

[2] Marlot, *Histoire de Reims*, iv. 426. This language excited the surprise of Dale, Walsingham's successor (Mackintosh, iii. 226).

[3] *Archives Curieuses*, viii. 305.

[4] Egli solo tra tutti gli altri è solito particolarmente di sostenere le nostre fatiche. . . . Essendo partecipe di tutti i nostri consigli, et consapevole de segreti dell' intimo animo nostro (Pius V. to Philip II., June 20, 1571; Zucchi, *Idea del Segretario*, i. 544).

was Hippolyto Aldobrandini, who, twenty years later, ascended the papal chair as Clement VIII. The companion whose presence conferred the greatest lustre on the mission was the general of the Jesuits, Francis Borgia, the holiest of the successors of Ignatius, and the most venerated of men then living. Austerities had brought him to the last stage of weakness; and he was sinking under the malady of which he was soon to die. But it was believed that the words of such a man, pleading for the Church, would sway the mind of the King. The ostensible purpose of the Legate's journey was to break off the match with Navarre, and to bring France into the Holy League. He gained neither object. When he was summoned back to Rome it was understood in France that he had reaped nothing but refusals, and that he went away disappointed.[1] The jeers of the Protestants pursued him.[2] But it was sufficiently certain beforehand that France could not plunge into a Turkish war.[3] The real business of the Legate, besides proposing a Catholic husband for the Princess, was to ascertain the object of the expedition which was fitting out in the Western ports. On both points he had something favourable to report. In his last despatch, dated Lyons, the 6th of March, he wrote that he had failed to prevent the engagement with Navarre, but that he had something for the Pope's private ear, which made his journey not altogether unprofitable.[4] The secret was soon divulged in Italy. The King had met the earnest remonstrances of the Legate by assuring him that the marriage afforded the only prospect of wreaking vengeance on the Huguenots: the event would show; he could say no more, but desired his promise to

[1] Serranus, *Commentarii*, iv. 14; Davila, ii. 104.

[2] Digges, p. 193.

[3] Finis hujus legationis erat non tam suadere Regi ut foedus cum aliis Christianis principibus iniret (id nempe notum erat impossibile illi regno esse); sed ut rex ille praetermissus non videretur, et revera ut sciretur quo tenderent Gallorum cogitationes. Non longe nempe a Rocella naves quasdam praegrandes instruere et armare coeperat Philippus Strozza praetexens velle ad Indias a Gallis inventas navigare (*Relatio gestorum in Legatione Card. Alexandrini MS.*).

[4] Con alcuni particulari che io porto, de' quali ragguaglierò N. Signore a bocca, posso dire di non partirmi affatto mal espedito (Ranke, *Zeitschrift*, iii. 598). Le temps et les effectz luy témoigneront encores d'advantage (*Mémoire baillé au légat Alexandrin*, Feb. 1572; Bib. Imp. F. Dupuy, 523).

be carried to the Pope. It was added that he had presented a ring to the Legate, as a pledge of sincerity, which the Legate refused. The first to publish this story was Capilupi, writing only seven months later. It was repeated by Folieta,[1] and is given with all details by the historians of Pius V.—Catena and Gabuzzi. Catena was secretary to the Cardinal of Alessandria as early as July 1572, and submitted his work to him before publication.[2] Gabuzzi wrote at the instance of the same Cardinal, who supplied him with materials; and his book was examined and approved by Borghese, afterwards Paul V. Both the Cardinal of Alessandria and Paul V., therefore, were instrumental in causing it to be proclaimed that the Legate was acquainted in February 1572 with the intention which the King carried out in August.

The testimony of Aldobrandini was given still more distinctly, and with greater definiteness and authority. When he was required, as Pope, to pronounce upon the dissolution of the ill-omened marriage, he related to Borghese and other Cardinals what had passed in that interview between the Legate and the King, adding that, when the report of the massacre reached Rome, the Cardinal exclaimed: "God be praised! the King of France has kept his word." Clement referred D'Ossat to a narrative of the journey which he had written himself, and in which those things would be found.[3] The clue thus given has been unaccountably neglected, although the Report was known to exist. One copy is mentioned by Giorgi; and Mazzuchelli knew of another. Neither of them had read it; for they both ascribe it to Michele Bonelli, the Cardinal of Alessandria. The first page would have satisfied them that it was not his work. Clement VIII. describes the result of the mission to Blois

[1] *De Sacro Foedere, Graevius Thesaurus*, i. 1038.

[2] Catena, *Vita di Pio V.*, p. 197; Gabutius, *Vita Pii V.*, p. 150, and the Dedication.

[3] D'Ossat to Villeroy, Sept. 22, 1599; *Lettres*, iii. 503. An account of the Legate's journey was found by Mendham among Lord Guildford's manuscripts, and is described in the Supplement to his life of Pius V., p. 13. It is written by the Master of Ceremonies, and possesses no interest. The *Relatio* already quoted, which corresponds to the description given by Clement VIII. of his own work, is among the manuscripts of the Marquis Capponi, No. 164.

in these words: "Quae rationes eo impulerunt regem ut semel apprehensa manu Cardinalis in hanc vocem proruperit: Significate Pontifici illumque certum reddite me totum hoc quod circa id matrimonium feci et facturus sum, nulla alia de causa facere, quam ulciscendi inimicos Dei et hujus regni, et puniendi tam infidos rebelles, ut eventus ipse docebit, nec aliud vobis amplius significare possum. Quo non obstante semper Cardinalis eas subtexuit difficultates quas potuit, objiciens regi possetne contrahi matrimonium a fidele cum infidele, sitve dispensatio necessaria; quod si est nunquam Pontificem inductum iri ut illam concedat. Re ipsa ita in suspenso relicta discedendum esse putavit, cum jam rescivisset qua de causa naves parabantur, qui apparatus contra Rocellam tendebant."

The opinion that the massacre of St. Bartholomew was a sudden and unpremeditated act cannot be maintained; but it does not follow that the only alternative is to believe that it was the aim of every measure of the Government for two years before. Catherine had long contemplated it as her last expedient in extremity; but she had decided that she could not resort to it while her son was virtually a minor.[1] She suggested the idea to him in 1570. In that year he gave orders that the Huguenots should be slaughtered at Bourges. The letter is preserved in which La Chastre spurned the command: "If the people of Bourges learn that your Majesty takes pleasure in such tragedies, they will repeat them often. If these men must die, let them first be tried; but do not reward my services and sully my reputation by such a stain."[2]

In the autumn of 1571 Coligny came to Blois. Walsingham suspected, and was afterwards convinced that the intention to kill him already existed. The Pope was much displeased by his presence at Court; but he

[1] Vuol andar con ogni quiete et dissimulatione, fin che il Rè suo figliolo sia in età (Santa Croce, Desp. June 27, 1563; *Lettres du Card. Santa Croce*, p. 243).

[2] La Chastre to Charles IX., Jan. 21, 1570; Raynal, *Histoire du Berry*, iv. 105; Lavallée, *Histoire des Français*, ii. 478. Both Raynal and Lavallée had access to the original.

received assurances from the ambassador which satisfied him. It was said at the time that he at first believed that Coligny was to be murdered, but that he soon found that there was no such praiseworthy design.[1]

In December the King knew that, when the moment came, the burghers of Paris would not fail him. Marcel, the Prévôt des Marchands, told him that the wealth was driven out of the country by the Huguenots: "The Catholics will bear it no longer. . . . Let your Majesty look to it. Your crown is at stake, Paris alone can save it."[2] By the month of February 1572 the plan had assumed a practical shape. The political idea before the mind of Charles was the same by which Richelieu afterwards made France the first Power in the world; to repress the Protestants at home, and to encourage them abroad. No means of effectual repression was left but murder. But the idea of raising up enemies to Spain by means of Protestantism was thoroughly understood. The Huguenots were allowed to make an expedition to aid William of Orange. Had they gained some substantial success, the Government would have followed it up, and the scheme of Coligny would have become for the moment the policy of France. But the Huguenot commander Genlis was defeated and taken. Coligny had had his chance. He had played and lost. It was useless now to propose his great venture against the King of Spain.[3]

Philip II. perfectly understood that this event was decisive. When the news came from Hainaut, he sent to

[1] Il Papa credeva che la pace fatta, e l'aver consentito il Rè che l'Ammiraglio venisse in corte, fusse con disegno di ammazzarlo; ma accortosi come passa il fatto, non ha creduto che nel Rè Nostro sia quella brava resoluzione (Letter of Nov. 28, 1571; Desjardins, iii. 732). Pour le regard de M. l'Admiral, je n'ay failly de luy faire entendre ce que je devois, suyvant ce qu'il a pleu à V. M. me commander, dont il est demeuré fort satisfaict (Ferralz to Charles IX., Dec. 25, 1571; Bib. Imp. F. Fr. 16,039: Walsingham to Herbert, Oct. 10, 1571; to Smith, Nov. 26, 1572; Digges, p. 290).

[2] Marcel to Charles IX., December 20, 1571; *Cabinet Historique*, ii. 253.

[3] Le Roy estoit d'intelligence, ayant permis à ceux de la Religion de l'assister, et, cas advenant que leurs entreprises succédassent, qu'il les favoriserait ouvertement . . . Genlis, menant un secours dans Mons, fut défait par le duc d'Alve, qui avoit comme investi la ville. La journée de Saint-Barthélemi se résolut (Bouillon, *Mémoires*, p. 9).

the Nuncio Castagna to say that the King of France would gain more than himself by the loss of so many brave Protestants, and that the time was come for him, with the aid of the people of Paris, to get rid of Coligny and the rest of his enemies.[1] It appears from the letters of Salviati that he also regarded the resolution as having been finally taken after the defeat of Genlis.

The Court had determined to enforce unity of faith in France. An edict of toleration was issued for the purpose of lulling the Huguenots; but it was well known that it was only a pretence.[2] Strict injunctions were sent into the provinces that it should not be obeyed;[3] and Catherine said openly to the English envoy, "My son will have exercise but of one Religion in his Realm." On the 26th the King explained his plan to Mondoucet, his agent at Brussels: "Since it has pleased God to bring matters to the point they have now reached, I mean to use the opportunity to secure a perpetual repose in my kingdom, and to do something for the good of all Christendom. It is probable that the conflagration will spread to every town in France, and that they will follow the example of Paris, and lay hands on all the Protestants. . . . I have written to the governors to assemble forces in order to cut to pieces those who may resist."[4] The great object was to accomplish the extirpation of Protestantism in such a way as might leave intact the friendship with Protestant States. Every step was governed by this consideration; and the difficulty of the task caused the inconsistencies and the vacillation that ensued. By assassinating Coligny alone it was expected that such an agitation would be provoked among his

[1] Si potria distruggere il resto, maxime che l' ammiraglio si trova in Parigi, populo Catholico et devoto del suo Rè, dove potria se volesse facilmente levarselo dinnanzi per sempre (Castagna, Desp. Aug. 5, 1572; Theiner, i. 327).

[2] *Mémoires de Claude Haton*, 687.

[3] En quelque sorte que ce soit ledict Seigneur est résollu faire vivre ses subjectz en sa religion, et ne permettre jamais ny tollérer, quelque chose qui puisse advenir, qu'il n'y ait aultre forme ny exercice de religion en son royaulme que de la catholique (Instruction for the Governors of Normandy, Nov. 3, 1572; La Mothe, vii. 390).

[4] Charles IX. to Mondoucet, Aug. 26, 1572; *Compte Rendu de la Commission Royale d Histoire*, 2e Série, iv. 327.

partisans as would make it appear that they were killed by the Catholics in self-defence. Reports were circulated at once with that object. A letter written on the 23rd states that, after the Admiral was wounded on the day before, the Huguenots assembled at the gate of the Louvre, to avenge him on the Guises as they came out.[1] And the first explanation sent forth by the Government on the 24th was to the effect that the old feud between the Houses of Guise and of Châtillon had broken out with a fury which it was impossible to quell. This fable lasted only for a single day. On the 25th Charles writes that he has begun to discover traces of a Huguenot conspiracy;[2] and on the following day this was publicly substituted for the original story. Neither the vendetta of the Guises nor the conspiracy at Paris could be made to explain the massacre in the provinces. It required to be so managed that the King could disown it; Salviati describes the plan of operations. It was intended that the Huguenots should be slaughtered successively by a series of spontaneous outbreaks in different parts of the country. While Rochelle held out, it was dangerous to proceed with a more sweeping method.[3] Accordingly, no written instructions from the King are in existence; and the governors were expressly informed that they were to expect none.[4] Messengers went into the provinces with letters requiring that the verbal orders which they brought should be obeyed.[5] Many governors refused to act upon directions so vague and so hard to verify. Burgundy was preserved in this way. Two gentlemen arrived with letters of recommendation from the King, and declared his

[1] Li Ugonotti si ridussero alla porta del Louvre, per aspettare che Mons. di Guisa e Mons. d'Aumale uscissero per ammazzarli (Borso Trotti, Desp. Aug. 23; Modena Archives).

[2] L'on a commencé à descouvrir la conspiration que ceux de la religion prétendue réformée avoient faicte contre moy mesmes, ma mère et mes frères (Charles IX. to La Mothe, Aug. 25; La Mothe, vii. 325).

[3] Desp. Sept. 19, 1572.

[4] Il ne fault pas attendre d'en avoir d'autre commandement du Roy ne de Monseigneur, car ils ne vous en feront point (Puygaillard to Montsoreau, Aug. 26, 1572; Mourin, *La Réforme en Anjou*, p. 106).

[5] Vous croirez le présent porteur de ce que je luy ay donné charge de vous dire (Charles IX. to Mandelot, Aug. 24, 1572; *Corr. de Charles IX. avec Mandelot*, p. 42).

commands. They were asked to put them on paper; but they refused to give in writing what they had received by word of mouth. Mandelot, the Governor of Lyons, the most ignoble of the instruments in this foul deed, complained that the intimation of the royal wishes sent to him was obscure and insufficient.[1] He did not do his work thoroughly, and incurred the displeasure of the King. The orders were complicated as well as obscure. The public authorities were required to collect the Huguenots in some prison or other safe place, where they could be got at by hired bands of volunteer assassins. To screen the King it was desirable that his officers should not superintend the work themselves. Mandelot, having locked the gates of Lyons, and shut up the Huguenots together, took himself out of the way while they were being butchered. Carouge, at Rouen, received a commission to visit the other towns in his province. The magistrates implored him to remain, as nobody, in his absence, could restrain the people. When the King had twice repeated his commands, Carouge obeyed; and five hundred Huguenots perished.[2]

It was thought unsafe even for the King's brother to give distinct orders under his own hand. He wrote to his lieutenant in Anjou that he had commissioned Puygaillard to communicate with him on a matter which concerned the King's service and his own, and desired that his orders should be received as if they came directly from himself. They were, that every Huguenot in Angers, Saumur, and the adjoining country should be put to death without delay and without exception.[3] The Duke of Montpensier himself sent the same order to Brittany; but it was indignantly rejected by the municipality of Nantes.

When reports came in of the manner in which the

[1] Je n'en ay aucune coulpe, n'ayant sceu quelle estoit la volunté que par umbre, encores bien tard et à demy (Mandelot to Charles IX., Sept. 17, p. 73).

[2] Floquet, *Histoire du Parlement de Normandie*, iii. 121.

[3] Anjou to Montsoreau, Aug. 26; Mourin, p. 107; Falloux, *Vie de Pie V.*, i. 358; Port, *Archives de la Mairie d'Angers*, pp. 41, 42.

event had been received in foreign countries, the Government began to waver, and the sanguinary orders were recalled. Schomberg wrote from Germany that the Protestant allies were lost unless they could be satisfied that the King had not decreed the extermination of their brethren.[1] He was instructed to explain the tumult in the provinces by the animosity bequeathed by the wars of religion.[2] The Bishop of Valence was intriguing in Poland on behalf of Anjou. He wrote that his success had been made very doubtful, and that, if further cruelties were perpetrated, ten millions of gold pieces would not bribe the venal Poles. He advised that a counterfeit edict, at least, should be published.[3] Charles perceived that he would be compelled to abandon his enterprise, and set about appeasing the resentment of the Protestant Powers. He promised that an inquiry should be instituted, and the proofs of the conspiracy communicated to foreign Governments. To give a judicial aspect to the proceedings, two prominent Huguenots were ceremoniously hanged. When the new ambassador from Spain praised the long concealment of the plan, Charles became indignant.[4] It was repeated everywhere that the thing had been arranged with Rome and Spain; and he was especially studious that there should be no symptoms of a private understanding with either power.[5] He was able to flatter himself that he had at least partially succeeded. If he had not exterminated his Protestant subjects, he had preserved his Protestant allies. William the Silent continued to solicit his aid; Elizabeth consented to stand godmother to the daughter who was born to him in October; he was allowed to raise mercenaries in Switzerland; and the Polish Protestants agreed to the election of his brother. The promised evidence of the Huguenot conspiracy was forgotten; and the King suppressed the

[1] Schomberg to Brulart, Oct. 10, 1572; Capefigue, *La Réforme*, iii. 264.

[2] Instructions for Schomberg, Feb. 15, 1573; Noailles, iii. 305.

[3] Monluc to Brulart, Nov. 20, 1572; Jan. 20, 1573: to Charles IX., Jan. 22, 1573; Noailles, iii. 218, 223, 220.

[4] Charles IX. to St. Goard, Jan. 20, 1573; Groen, iv. App. 29.

[5] Letter from Paris in Strype's *Life of Parker*, iii. 110; "Tocsain contre les Massacreurs," *Archives Curieuses*, vii. 7.

materials which were to have served for an official history of the event.[1]

Zeal for religion was not the motive which inspired the chief authors of this extraordinary crime. They were trained to look on the safety of the monarchy as the sovereign law, and on the throne as an idol that justified sins committed in its worship. At all times there have been men, resolute and relentless in the pursuit of their aims, whose ardour was too strong to be restricted by moral barriers or the instinct of humanity. In the sixteenth century, beside the fanaticism of freedom, there was an abject idolatry of power; and laws both human and divine were made to yield to the intoxication of authority and the reign of will. It was laid down that kings have the right of disposing of the lives of their subjects, and may dispense with the forms of justice The Church herself, whose supreme pontiff was now an absolute monarch, was infected with this superstition. Catholic writers found an opportune argument for their religion in the assertion that it makes the prince master of the consciences as well as the bodies of the people, and enjoins submission even to the vilest tyranny.[2] Men whose lives were precious to the Catholic cause could be murdered by royal command, without protest from Rome. When the Duke of Guise, with the Cardinal his brother, was slain by Henry III., he was the most powerful and devoted upholder of Catholicism in France. Sixtus V. thundered against the sacrilegious tyrant who was stained with the blood of a prince of the Church; but he let it be known very distinctly that the death of the Duke caused him little concern.[3]

[1] Afin que ce que vous avez dressé des choses passées à la Saint-Barthélemy ne puisse être publié parmi le peuple, et mêmement entre les étrangers, comme il y en a plusieurs qui se mêlent d'écrire et qui pourraient prendre occasion d'y répondre, je vous prie qu'il n'en soit rien imprimé ni en français ni en Latin, mais si vous en avez retenu quelque chose, le garder vers vous (Charles IX. to the President de Cély, March 24, 1573; *Revue Rétrospective*, 2 Série, iii. 195).

[2] Botero, *Della Ragion di Stato*, 92. A contemporary says that the Protestants were cut to pieces out of economy, "pour afin d'éviter le coust des exécutions qu'il eust convenu payer pour les faire pendre"; and that this was done "par permission divine" (*Relation des troubles de Rouen par un témoin oculaire*, ed. Pottier, 36, 46).

[3] Del resto poco importerebbe a Roma (Card. Montalto to Card. Morosini; Tempesti, *Vita di Sisto V.*, ii. 116).

Catherine was the daughter of that Medici to whom Machiavelli had dedicated his *Prince*. So little did religion actuate her conduct that she challenged Elizabeth to do to the Catholics of England what she herself had done to the Protestants of France, promising that if they were destroyed there would be no loss of her good will.[1] The levity of her religious feelings appears from her reply when asked by Gomicourt what message he should take to the Duke of Alva: "I must give you the answer of Christ to the disciples of St. John, 'Ite et nuntiate quae vidistis et audivistis; caeci vident, claudi ambulant, leprosi mundantur.'" And she added, "Beatus qui non fuerit in me scandalizatus."[2]

If mere fanaticism had been their motive, the men who were most active in the massacre would not have spared so many lives. While Guise was galloping after Ferrières and Montgomery, who had taken horse betimes, and made for the coast, his house at Paris was crowded with families belonging to the proscribed faith, and strangers to him. A young girl who was amongst them has described his return, when he sent for the children, spoke to them kindly, and gave orders that they should be well treated as long as his roof sheltered them.[3] Protestants even spoke of him as a humane and chivalrous enemy.[4] Nevers was considered to have disgraced himself by the number of those whom he enabled to escape.[5] The Nuncio was shocked at their ill-timed generosity. He reported to Rome that the only one who had acted in the spirit of a Christian, and had refrained from mercy, was the King; while the other princes, who pretended to be good Catholics, and to deserve the favour of the Pope, had striven, one and all, to save as many Huguenots as they could.[6]

[1] Quand ce seroit contre touts les Catholiques, que nous ne nous en empescherions, ny altérerions aucunement l'amitié d'entre elle et nous (Catherine to La Mothe, Sept. 13, 1572; La Mothe, vii. 349).

[2] Alva's Report; *Bulletins de l'Académie de Bruxelles*, ix. 564.

[3] Jean Diodati, *door Schotel*, 88.

[4] *Œuvres de Brantôme*, ed. Lalanne, iv. 38.

[5] Otros que salvò el Duque de Nevers con harto vituperio suyo (Cabrera de Cordova, *Felipe Segundo*, p. 722).

[6] Il Rè Christianissimo in tutti questi accidenti, in luogo di giudicio e di valore

The worst criminals were not the men who did the deed. The crime of mobs and courtiers, infuriated by the lust of vengeance and of power, is not so strange a portent as the exultation of peaceful men, influenced by no present injury or momentary rage, but by the permanent and incurable perversion of moral sense wrought by a distorted piety.

Philip II., who had long suspected the court of France, was at once relieved from the dread which had oppressed him, and betrayed an excess of joy foreign to his phlegmatic nature.[1] He immediately sent six thousand crowns to the murderer of Coligny.[2] He persuaded himself that the breach between France and her allies was irreparable, that Charles would now be driven to seek his friendship, and that the Netherlands were out of danger.[3] He listened readily to the French ambassador, who assured him that his court had never swerved from the line of Catholic policy, but had intended all along to effect this great change.[4] Ayamonte carried his congratulations to Paris, and pretended that his master had been in the secret. It suited Philip that this should be believed by Protestant princes, in order to estrange them still more from France; but he wrote on the margin of Ayamonte's instructions, that it was uncertain how long previously the purpose had subsisted.[5] Juan and Diego de Zuñiga, his ambassadors at Rome and at Paris, were convinced that the long display of enmity to Spain was genuine, that the death

ha mostrato animo christiano, con tutto habbia salvato alcuno. Ma li altri principi che fanno gran professione di Cattolici et di meritar favori e gratie del papa hanno poi con estrema diligenza cercato a salvare quelli più di Ugonotti che hanno potuto, e se non gli nomino particolarmente, non si maravigli, per che indiferentemente tutti hanno fatto a un modo (Salviati, Desp. Sept. 2, 1572).

[1] Estque dictu mirum, quantopere Regem exhilaravit nova Gallica (Hopperus to Viglius, Madrid, Sept. 7, 1572; *Hopperi Epp.* 360).

[2] Ha avuto, con questa occasione, dal Rè di Spagna, sei mila scudi a conto della dote di sua moglie e a richiesta di casa di Guise (Petrucci, Desp. Sept. 16, 1572; Desjardins, iii. 838). On the 27th of December 1574, the Cardinal of Guise asks Philip for more money for the same man (Bouillé, *Histoire des Ducs de Guise*, ii. 505).

[3] Siendo cosa clara que, de hoy mas, ni los protestantes de Alemania, ni la reyna de Inglaterra se fiaran dél (Philip to Alva, Sept. 18, 1572; *Bulletins de Bruxelles*, xvi. 255).

[4] St. Goard to Charles IX., Sept. 12, 1572; Groen, iv. App. 12; Raumer, *Briefe aus Paris*, i. 191.

[5] *Archives de l'Empire*, K. 1530, B. 34, 299.

of Coligny had been decided at the last moment, and that the rest was not the effect of design.[1] This opinion found friends at first in Spain. The General of the Franciscans undertook to explode it. He assured Philip that he had seen the King and the Queen-mother two years before, and had found them already so intent on the massacre that he wondered how anybody could have the courage to detract from their merit by denying it.[2] This view generally prevailed in Spain. Mendoça knows not which to admire more, the loyal and Catholic inhabitants of Paris, or Charles, who justified his title of the most Christian King by helping with his own hands to slaughter his subjects.[3] Mariana witnessed the carnage, and imagined that it must gladden every Catholic heart. Other Spaniards were gratified to think that it had been contrived with Alva at Bayonne.

Alva himself did not judge the event by the same light as Philip. He also had distrusted the French Government; but he had not feared it during the ascendency of the Huguenots. Their fall appeared to him to strengthen France. In public he rejoiced with the rest. He complimented Charles on his valour and his religion, and claimed his own share of merit. But he warned Philip that things had not changed favourably for Spain, and that the King of France was now a formidable neighbour.[4] For himself, he said, he never would have committed so base a deed.

The seven Catholic Cantons had their own reason for congratulation. Their countrymen had been busy actors on the scene; and three soldiers of the Swiss guard of Anjou were named as the slayers of the Admiral.[5] On the 2nd of October they agreed to raise 6000 men for the King's service. At the following Diet they demanded

[1] Zuñiga to Alva, Aug. 31, 1572: No fue caso pensado sino repentino (*Archives de l'Empire*, K. 1530, B. 34, 66).

[2] St. Goard to Catherine, Jan. 6, 1573; Groen, iv. App. 28.

[3] *Comment. de B. de Mendoça*, i. 344.

[4] Alva to Philip, Oct. 13, 1572; *Corr. de Philippe II.*, ii. 287. On the 23rd of August Zuñiga wrote to Philip that he hoped that Coligny would recover from his wound, because, if he should die, Charles would be able to obtain obedience from all men (*Archives de l'Empire*, K. 1530, B. 34, 65).

[5] *Bulletins de la Société pour l'Histoire du Protestantisme Français*, viii. 292.

the expulsion of the fugitive Huguenots who had taken refuge in the Protestant parts of the Confederation. They made overtures to the Pope for a secret alliance against their Confederates.[1]

In Italy, where the life of a heretic was cheap, their wholesale destruction was confessed a highly politic and ingenious act. Even the sage Venetians were constrained to celebrate it with a procession. The Grand Duke Cosmo had pointed out two years before that an insidious peace would afford excellent opportunities of extinguishing Protestantism; and he derived inexpressible consolation from the heroic enterprise.[2] The Viceroy of Naples, Cardinal Granvelle, received the tidings coldly. He was surprised that the event had been so long postponed, and he reproved the Cardinal of Lorraine for the unstatesmanlike delay.[3] The Italians generally were excited to warmer feelings. They saw nothing to regret but the death of certain Catholics who had been sacrificed to private revenge. Profane men approved the skill with which the trap was laid; and pious men acknowledged the presence of a genuine religious spirit in the French court.[4] The nobles and the Parisian populace were admired for their valour in obeying the sanctified commands of the good King. One fervent enthusiast praises God for the heavenly news, and also St. Bartholomew for having lent his extremely penetrating knife for the salutary sacrifice.[5] A month after the event the renowned preacher Panigarola delivered from the pulpit a panegyric on the monarch who had achieved what none had ever heard or read before, by banishing heresy in a single day, and by a single word, from the Christian land of France.[6]

[1] *Eidgenössische Abschiede*, iv. 2, 501, 503, 506, 510.

[2] Cosmo to Camaiani, Oct. 6, 1570 (Cantù, *Gli Eretici d'Italia*, iii. 15); Cosmo to Charles IX., Sept. 4, 1572 (Gachard, *Rapport sur les Archives de Lille*, 199).

[3] Grappin, *Mémoire Historique sur le Card. de Granvelle*, 73.

[4] Bardi, *Età del Mondo*, 1581, iv. 2011; Campana, *Historie del Mondo*, 1599, i. 145; B. D. da Fano, *Aggiunte all' Historie di Mambrino Roseo*, 1583, v. 252; Pellini, *Storia di Perugia*, vol. iii. MS.

[5] Si è degnato di prestare alli suoi divoti il suo taglientissimo coltello in così salutifero sacrificio (Letter of Aug. 26; Alberi, *Vita di Caterina de' Medici*, 401).

[6] Labitte, *Démocratie chez les Prédicateurs de la Ligue*, 10.

The French churches had often resounded with furious declamations; and they afterwards rang with canticles of unholy joy. But the French clergy does not figure prominently in the inception or the execution of the sanguinary decree. Conti, a contemporary indeed, but too distant for accurate knowledge, relates that the parish priest went round, marking with a white cross the dwellings of the people who were doomed.[1] He is contradicted by the municipal Registers of Paris.[2] Morvilliers, Bishop of Orleans, though he had resigned the seals which he received from L'Hôpital, still occupied the first place at the royal council. He was consulted at the last moment, and it is said that he nearly fainted with horror. He recovered, and gave his opinion with the rest. He is the only French prelate, except the cardinals, whose complicity appears to be ascertained. But at Orleans, where the bloodshed was more dreadful in proportion than at Paris, the signal is said to have been given, not by the bishop, but by the King's preacher, Sorbin.

Sorbin is the only priest of the capital who is distinctly associated with the act of the Government. It was his opinion that God has ordained that no mercy shall be shown to heretics, that Charles was bound in conscience to do what he did, and that leniency would have been as censurable in his case as precipitation was in that of Theodosius. What the Calvinists called perfidy and cruelty seemed to him nothing but generosity and kindness.[3] These were the sentiments of the man from whose hands Charles IX. received the last consolations of his religion. It has been related that he was tortured in his last moments with remorse for the blood he had shed. His spiritual adviser was fitted to dispel such scruples. He tells us that he heard the last confession of the dying

[1] Natalis Comes, *Historiae sui temporis*, 512.

[2] Capefigue, iii. 150.

[3] Pourront-ils arguer de trahison le feu roy, qu'ils blasphèment luy donnant le nom de tyran, veu qu'il n'a rien entrepris et exécuté que ce qu'il pouvoit faire par l'expresse parole de Dieu . . . Dieu commande qu'on ne pardonne en façon que ce soit aux inventeurs ou sectateurs de nouvelles opinions ou hérésies. . . . Ce que vous estimez cruauté estre plutôt vraye magnanimité et doulceur (Sorbin, *Le Vray resveille-matin des Calvinistes*, 1576, pp. 72, 74, 78).

King, and that his most grievous sorrow was that he left the work unfinished.[1] In all that blood-stained history there is nothing more tragic than the scene in which the last words preparing the soul for judgment were spoken by such a confessor as Sorbin to such a penitent as Charles.

Edmond Auger, one of the most able and eloquent of the Jesuits, was at that time attracting multitudes by his sermons at Bordeaux. He denounced with so much violence the heretics and the people in authority who protected them, that the magistrates, fearing a cry for blood, proposed to silence or to moderate the preacher. Montpezat, Lieutenant of Guienne, arrived in time to prevent it. On the 30th of September he wrote to the King that he had done this, and that there were a score of the inhabitants who might be despatched with advantage. Three days later, when he was gone, more than two hundred Huguenots were murdered.[2]

Apart from these two instances it is not known that the clergy interfered in any part of France to encourage the assassins.

[1] Il commanda à chacun de se retirer au cabinet et à moy de m'asseoir au chevet de son lict, tant pour ouyr sa confession, et luy donner ministérialement absolution de ses péchez, que aussi pour le consoler durant et après la messe (Sorbin, *Vie de Charles IX.*; *Archives Curieuses*, viii. 287). Est très certain que le plus grand regret qu'il avoit à l'heure de sa mort estoit de ce qu'il voyoit l'idole Calvinesque n'estre encores du tout chassée (*Vray resveille-matin*, 88).

[2] The charge against the clergy of Bordeaux is brought by D'Aubigné (*Histoire Universelle*, ii. 27) and by De Thou. De Thou was very hostile to the Jesuits, and his language is not positive. D'Aubigné was a furious bigot. The truth of the charge would not be proved, without the letters of the President L'Agebaston and of the Lieutenant Montpezat: "Quelques prescheurs se sont par leurs sermons (ainsi que dernièrement j'ai escript plus amplement à votre majesté) estudié de tout leur pouvoir de troubler ciel et terre, et conciter le peuple à sédition, et en ce faisant à passer par le fil de l'espée tous ceulx de la prétendue religion réformée. . . . Après avoir des le premier et deuxième de ceste mois fait courrir un bruit sourd que vous, Sire, aviez envoyé nom par nom un rolle signé de votre propre main au Sieur de Montferaud, pour par voie de fait et sans aultre forme de justice, mettre à mort quarante des principaulx de cette ville . . ." (L'Agebaston to Charles IX., Oct. 7, 1572; Mackintosh, iii. 352). "J'ai trouvé que messieurs de la cour de parlement avoyent arresté que Monsieur Edmond, prescheur, seroit appellé en ladicte court pour luy faire des remonstrances sur quelque langaige qu'il tenoit en ses sermons, tendant à sédition, à ce qu'ils disoyent. Ce que j'ay bien voullu empescher, craignant que s'il y eust esté appellé cella eust animé plusieurs des habitants et estre cause de quelque émotion, ce que j'eusse voluntiers souffert quant j'eusse pansé qu'il n'y en eust qu'une vingtaine de despéchés" (Montpezat to Charles IX., Sept. 30, 1572; *Archives de la Gironde*, viii. 337).

The belief was common at the time, and is not yet extinct, that the massacre had been promoted and sanctioned by the Court of Rome. No evidence of this complicity, prior to the event, has ever been produced; but it seemed consistent with what was supposed to have occurred in the affair of the dispensation. The marriage of Margaret of Valois with the King of Navarre was invalid and illicit in the eyes of the Church; and it was known that Pius V. had sworn that he would never permit it. When it had been celebrated by a Cardinal, in the presence of a splendid court, and no more was heard of resistance on the part of Rome, the world concluded that the dispensation had been obtained. De Thou says, in a manuscript note, that it had been sent, and was afterwards suppressed by Salviati; and the French bishop, Spondanus, assigns the reasons which induced Gregory XIII. to give way.[1] Others affirmed that he had yielded when he learned that the marriage was a snare, so that the massacre was the price of the dispensation.[2] The Cardinal of Lorraine gave currency to the story. As he caused it to be understood that he had been in the secret, it seemed probable that he had told the Pope; for they had been old friends.[3] In the commemorative inscription which he put up in the Church of St. Lewis he spoke of the King's gratitude to the Holy See for its assistance and for its advice in the matter—"consiliorum ad eam rem datorum." It is probable that he inspired the narrative which has contributed most to sustain the imputation.

Among the Italians of the French faction who made it their duty to glorify the act of Charles IX., the Capilupi family was conspicuous. They came from Mantua, and appear to have been connected with the French interest through Lewis Gonzaga, who had become by marriage Duke of Nevers, and one of the foremost personages in France. Hippolyto Capilupi, Bishop of Fano, and formerly Nuncio at Venice, resided at Rome, busy with

[1] *Annal. Baronii Contin.* ii. 734; Bossuet says: "La dispense vint telle qu'on la pouvoit désirer" (*Histoire de France*, p. 820).
[2] Ormegregny, *Réflexions sur la Politique de France*, p. 121.
[3] De Thou, iv. 537.

French politics and Latin poetry. When Charles refused to join the League, the Bishop of Fano vindicated his neutrality in a letter to the Duke of Urbino.[1] When he slew the Huguenots, the Bishop addressed him in verse,—

> Fortunate puer, paret cui Gallica tellus,
> Quique vafros ludis pervigil arte viros,
> Ille tibi debet, toti qui praesidet Orbi,
> Cui nihil est cordi religione prius. . . .
>
> Qui tibi saepe dolos struxit, qui vincla paravit,
> Tu puer in laqueos induis arte senem. . . .
>
> Nunc florent, tolluntque caput tua lilia, et astris
> Clarius hostili tincta cruore micant.[2]

Camillo Capilupi, a nephew of the Mantuan bard, held office about the person of the Pope, and was employed on missions of consequence.[3] As soon as the news from Paris reached Rome he drew up the account which became so famous under the title of *Lo Stratagemma di Carlo IX*. The dedication is dated the 18th of September 1572.[4] This tract was suppressed, and was soon so rare that its existence was unknown in 1574 to the French translator of the second edition. Capilupi republished his book with alterations, and a preface dated the 22nd of October. The substance and purpose of the two editions is the same. Capilupi is not the official organ of the Roman court: he was not allowed to see the letters of the Nuncio. He wrote to proclaim the praises of the King of France and the Duke of Nevers. At that moment the French party in Rome was divided by the quarrel between the ambassador Ferralz and the Cardinal of Lorraine, who had contrived to get the management of French affairs into his own hands.[5] Capilupi was on the

[1] Charrière, iii. 154.

[2] *Carmina Ill. Poetarum Italorum*, iii. 212, 216.

[3] Tiepolo, Desp. Aug. 6, 1575; Mutinelli, *Storia Arcana*, i. 111.

[4] Parendomi, che sia cosa, la quale possa apportar piacere, e utile al mondo, si per la qualità del soggetto istesso, come anco per l' eleganza, e bello ordine con che viene cosi leggiadramente descritto questo nobile, e glorioso fatto . . . a fine che una cosi egregia attione non resti defraudata dell' honor, che merita (The editor, Gianfrancesco Ferrari, to the reader).

[5] Huc accedit, Oratorem Ser^mi^ Regis Galliae, et impulsu inimicorum saepedicti Domini Cardinalis, et quia summopere illi displicuit, quod superioribus mensibus Illma Sua Dominatio operam dedisset, hoc sibi mandari, ut omnia Regis negotia

side of the Cardinal, and received information from those who were about him. The chief anxiety of these men was that the official version which attributed the massacre to a Huguenot conspiracy should obtain no credence at Rome. If the Cardinal's enemies were overthrown without his participation, it would confirm the report that he had become a cipher in the State. He desired to vindicate for himself and his family the authorship of the catastrophe. Catherine could not tolerate their claim to a merit which she had made her own; and there was competition between them for the first and largest share in the gratitude of the Holy See. Lorraine prevailed with the Pope, who not only loaded him with honours, but rewarded him with benefices worth 4000 crowns a year for his nephew, and a gift of 20,000 crowns for his son. But he found that he had fallen into disgrace at Paris, and feared for his position at Rome.[1] In these circumstances Capilupi's book appeared, and enumerated a series of facts proving that the Cardinal was cognisant of the royal design. It adds little to the evidence of premeditation. Capilupi relates that Santa Croce, returning from France, had assured Pius V., in the name of Catherine,

secum communicaret, nullam praetermisisse occasionem ubi ei potuit adversari (Cardinal Delfino to the Emperor, Rome, Nov. 29, 1572; Vienna Archives).

[1] Fà ogni favor et gratia gli addimanda il Cardinale di Lorena, il consiglio del quale usa in tutte le più importanti negotiationi l' occorre di haver a trattar (Cusano to the Emperor, Rome, Sept. 27, 1572).—Conscia igitur Sua Dominatio Illma quorundam arcanorum Regni Galliae, creato Pontifice sibi in Concilio Tridentino cognito et amico, statuit huc se recipere, ut privatis suis rebus consuleret, et quia tunc foederati contra Thurcam, propter suspicionem Regi Catholico injectam de Orangio, et Gallis, non admodum videbantur concordes, et non multo post advenit nuncius mortis Domini de Colligni, et illius asseclarum; Pontifex justa de causa existimavit dictum Ill^mum Cardinalem favore et gratia sua merito esse complectendum. Evenit postmodum, ut ad Serenissimam Reginam Galliarum deferretur, bonum hunc Dominum jactasse se, quod particeps fuerit consiliorum contra dictum Colligni; id quod illa Serenissima Domina iniquo animo tulit, quae neminem gloriae socium vult habere; sibi enim totam vendicat, quod sola talis facinoris auctor, et Dux extiterit. Idcirco commorationem ipsius Lotharingiae in hac aula improbare, ac reprehendere aggressa est. Haec cum ille Illustrissimus Cardinalis perceperit, oblata sibi occasione utens, exoravit a Sua Sanctitate gratuitam expeditionem quatuor millia scutorum reditus pro suo Nepote, et 20 millia pro filio praeter sollicitationem, quam prae se fert, ut dictus Nepos in Cardinalium numerum cooptetur. . . . Cum itaque his de causis authoritas hujus Domini in Gallia imminuta videatur, ipseque praevideat, quanto in Gallia minoris aestimabitur, tanto minori etiam loco hic se habitum iri, statuit optimo judicio, ac pro eo quod suae existimacioni magis conducit, in Galliam reverti (Delfino, *ut supra*, both in the Vienna Archives).

that she intended one day to entrap Coligny, and to make a signal butchery of him and his adherents, and that letters in which the Queen renewed this promise to the Pope had been read by credible witnesses. Santa Croce was living, and did not contradict the statement. The *Stratagema* had originally stated that Lorraine had informed Sermoneta of the project soon after he arrived at Rome. In the reprint this passage was omitted. The book had, therefore, undergone a censorial revision, which enhances the authenticity of the final narrative.

Two other pieces are extant, which were printed at the Stamperia Camerale, and show what was believed at Rome. One is in the shape of a letter written at Lyons in the midst of scenes of death, and describing what the author had witnessed on the spot, and what he heard from Paris.[1] He reports that the King had positively commanded that not one Huguenot should escape, and was overjoyed at the accomplishment of his orders. He believes the thing to have been premeditated, and inspired by Divine justice. The other tract is remarkable because it strives to reconcile the pretended conspiracy with the hypothesis of premeditation.[2] There were two plots which went parallel for months. The King knew that Coligny was compassing his death, and deceived him by feigning to enter into his plan for the invasion of the Low Countries; and Coligny, allowing himself to be overreached, summoned his friends to Paris, for the purpose of killing Charles, on the 23rd of August. The writer expects that there will soon be no Huguenots in France. Capilupi at first borrowed several of his facts, which he afterwards corrected.

The real particulars relative to the marriage are set forth minutely in the correspondence of Ferralz; and they absolutely contradict the supposition of the complicity of Rome.[3] It was celebrated in flagrant defiance of the Pope, who persisted in refusing the dispensation, and

[1] *Intiera Relatione della Morte dell' Ammiraglio.*

[2] *Ragguaglio degli ordini et modi tenuti dalla Majesta Christianissima nella distruttione della setta degli Ugonotti Con la morte dell' Ammiraglio*, etc.

[3] Bib. Imp. F. Fr. 16,139.

therefore acted in a way which could only serve to mar the plot. The accusation has been kept alive by his conduct after the event. The Jesuit who wrote his life by desire of his son, says that Gregory thanked God in private, but that in public he gave signs of a tempered joy.[1] But the illuminations and processions, the singing of Te Deum and the firing of the castle guns, the jubilee, the medal, and the paintings whose faded colours still vividly preserve to our age the passions of that day, nearly exhaust the modes by which a Pope could manifest delight.

Charles IX. and Salviati both wrote to Rome on St. Bartholomew's Day; and the ambassador's nephew, Beauville, set off with the tidings. They were known before he arrived. On the 27th, Mandelot's secretary despatched a secret messenger from Lyons with orders to inform the Pope that the Huguenot leaders were slain, and that their adherents were to be secured all over France. The messenger reached Rome on the 2nd of September, and was immediately carried to the Pope by the Cardinal of Lorraine. Gregory rewarded him for the welcome intelligence with a present of a hundred crowns, and desired that Rome should be at once illuminated. This was prevented by Ferralz, who tried the patience of the Romans by declining their congratulations as long as he was not officially informed.[2] Beauville and the courier of the Nuncio arrived on the 5th. The King's letter, like

[1] Maffei, *Annali di Gregorio XIII.*, i. 34.

[2] La nouvelle qui arriva le deuxième jour du présent par ung courrier qui estoit depesché secrétement de Lyon par ung nommé Danes, secrétaire de M. de Mandelot . . . à ung commandeur de Sainct Anthoine, nommé Mr. de Gou, il luy manda qu'il allast advertir le Pape, pour en avoir quelque présant ou bienfaict, de la mort de tous les chefs de ceulx de la religion prétendue refformée, et de tous les Huguenotz de France, et que V. M. avoit mandé et commandé à tous les gouverneurs de se saisir de tous iceulx huguenotz en leurs gouvernemens ; ceste nouvelle, Sire, apporta si grand contentement a S. S., que sans ce que je luy remonstray lors me trouvant sur le lieu, en presence de Monseigneur le C[l] de Lorraine, qu'elle devoit attendre ce que V. M. m'en manderoit et ce que son nonce luy en escriroit, elle en vouloit incontinent faire des feux de joye. . . . Et pour ce que je ne voulois faire ledict feu de joye la première nuict que ledit courrier envoyé par ledict Danes feust arrivé, ny en recevoir les congratulations que l'on m'en envoyoit faire, que premièrement je n'eusse eu nouvelles de V. M. pour sçavoir et sa voulanté et comme je m'avoys a conduire, aucuns commençoient desjà de m'en regarder de maulvais œills (Ferralz to Charles IX., Rome,

all that he wrote on the first day, ascribed the outbreak to the old hatred between the rival Houses, and to the late attempt on the Admiral's life. He expressed a hope that the dispensation would not now be withheld, but left all particulars to Beauville, whose own eyes had beheld the scene.[1] Beauville told his story, and repeated the King's request; but Gregory, though much gratified with what he heard, remained inflexible.[2]

Salviati had written on the afternoon of the 24th. He desired to fling himself at the Pope's feet to wish him joy. His fondest hopes had been surpassed. Although he had known what was in store for Coligny, he had not expected that there would be energy and prudence to seize the occasion for the destruction of the rest. A new era had commenced; a new compass was required for French affairs. It was a fair sight to see the Catholics in the streets wearing white crosses, and cutting down heretics; and it was thought that, as fast as the news spread, the same thing would be done in all the towns of France.[3] This letter was read before the assembled Cardinals at the Venetian palace, and they thereupon attended the Pope to a Te Deum in the nearest church.[4]

Sept. 11, 1572; Bib. Imp. F. Fr. 16,040). Al corriero che porto tal nuova Nostro Signore diede 100 Scudi oltre li 200 che hebbe dall' Illustrissimo Lorena, che con grandissima allegrezza se n'ando subito a dar tal nuova per allegrarsene con Sua Santita (Letter from Rome to the Emperor, Sept. 6, 1572; Vienna Archives).

[1] Charles IX. to Ferralz, Aug. 24, 1572; Mackintosh, iii. 348.

[2] Elle fust merveilheusement ayse d'entendre le discours que mondit neueu de Beauville luy en feist. Lequel, après luy avoir conté le susdit affayre, supplia sadicte Saincteté, suyvant la charge expresse qu'il avoit de V. M. de vouloir concéder, pour le fruict de ceste allegresse, la dispense du mariage du roy et royne de Navarre, datée de quelques jours avant que les nopces en feussent faictes, ensemble l'absolution pour Messeigneurs les Cardinaux de Bourbon et de Ramboilhet, et pour tous les aultres evesques et prélatz qui y avoient assisté. . . . Il nous feit pour fin response qu'il y adviseroit (Ferralz, *ut supra*).

[3] Pensasi che per tutte le citta di Francia debba seguire il simile, subitoche arrivi la nuova dell' esecutione di Parigi. . . . A N. S. mi faccia gratia di basciar i piedi in nome mio, col quale mi rallegro con le viscere del cuore che sia piaciuto alla Dio. Mtà. d' incaminar nel principio del suo pontificato si felicemente e honoratamente le cose di questo regno, havendo talmente havuto in protettione il Rè e Regina Madre che hanno saputo e potuto sbarrare queste pestifere radici con tanta prudenza, in tempo tanto opportuno, che tutti lor ribelli erano sotto chiave in gabbia (Salviati, Desp. Aug. 24; Theiner, i. 329; Mackintosh, iii. 355).

[4] Sexta Septembris, mane, in Senatu Pontificis et Cardinalium lectae sunt literae a legato Pontificio e Gallia scriptae, admiralium et Huguenotos, destinata Regis voluntate atque consensu, trucidatos esse. Ea re in eodem Senatu decretum

The guns of St. Angelo were fired in the evening, and the city was illuminated for three nights. To disregard the Pope's will in this respect would have savoured of heresy. Gregory XIII. exclaimed that the massacre was more agreeable to him than fifty victories of Lepanto. For some weeks the news from the French provinces sustained the rapture and excitement of the Court.[1] It was hoped that other countries would follow the example of France; the Emperor was informed that something of the same kind was expected of him.[2] On the 8th of September the Pope went in procession to the French Church of St. Lewis, where three-and-thirty Cardinals attended at a mass of thanksgiving. On the 11th he proclaimed a jubilee. In the Bull he said that forasmuch as God had armed the King of France to inflict vengeance on the heretics for the injuries done to religion, and to punish the leaders of the rebellion which had devastated his

esse, ut inde recta Pontifex cum Cardinalibus in aedem D. Marci concederet, Deoque Opt. Max. pro tanto beneficio Sedi Romanae orbique Christiano collato gratias solemni more ageret (*Scriptum Roma missum* in Capilupi, 1574, p. 84). Quia Die 2ª praedicti mensis Septembris Smus D. N. certior factus fuerat Colignium Franciae Ammiralium a populo Parisien. occisum fuisse et cum eo multos ex Ducibus et primoribus Ugonotarum haereticorum eius sequacibus Rege ipso Franciae approbante, ex quo spes erat tranquillitatem in dicto Regno redituram expulsis haereticis, idcirco Stas Sua expleto concistorio descendit ad ecclesiam Sancti Marci, praecedente cruce et sequentibus Cardinalibus et genuflexus ante altare maius, ubi positum fuerat sanctissimum Sacramentum, oravit gratias Deo agens, et inchoavit cantando hymnum Te Deum (*Fr. Mucantii Diaria*, B. M. Add. MSS. 26,811).

[1] Après quelques autres discours qu'il me feist sur le contentement que luy et le collége des Cardinaux avoient receu de ladicte execution faicte et des nouvelles qui journellement arrivoient en ceste court de semblables exécutions que l'on a faicte et font encore en plusieurs villes de vostre royaume, qui, à dire la vérité, sont les nouvelles les plus agréables que je pense qu'on eust sceu apporter en ceste ville, sadicte Saincteté pour fin me commanda de vous escrire que cest évènement luy a esté cent fois plus agréable que cinquante victoires semblables à celle que ceulx de la ligue obtindrent l'année passée contre le Turcq, ne voulant oublier vous dire, Sire, les commandemens estroictz qu'il nous feist à tous, mesmement aux françois d'en faire feu de joye, et qui ne l'eust faict eust mal senty de la foy (Ferralz, *ut supra*).

[2] Tutta Roma stà in allegria di tal fatto et frà i più grandi si dice, che 'l Rè di Francia ha insegnato alli Principi christiani ch' hanno de simili vassalli nè stati loro a liberarsene, et dicono che vostra Maestà Cesara dovrebbe castigare il conte Palatino tanto nemico della Serenissima casa d' Austria, et della Religione cattolica, come l' anni passati fece contra il Duca di Sassonia tiene tuttavia prigione, che a un tempo vendicarebbe le tante ingiurie ha fatto detto Palatino alla Chiesa di Dio, et poveri Christiani, et alla Maestà Vostra et sua Casa Serenissima sprezzando li suoi editti et commandamenti, et privarlo dell' elettione dell'Imperio et darlo al Duca di Baviera (Cusano to the Emperor, Rome, Sept. 6, 1572; Vienna Archives).

kingdom, Catholics should pray that he might have grace to pursue his auspicious enterprise to the end, and so complete what he had begun so well.[1] Before a month had passed Vasari was summoned from Florence to decorate the hall of kings with paintings of the massacre.[2] The work was pronounced his masterpiece; and the shameful scene may still be traced upon the wall, where, for three centuries, it has insulted every pontiff that entered the Sixtine Chapel.

The story that the Huguenots had perished because they were detected plotting the King's death was known at Rome on the 6th of September. While the sham edict and the imaginary trial served to confirm it in the eyes of Europe, Catherine and her son took care that it should not deceive the Pope. They assured him that they meant to disregard the edict. To excuse his sister's marriage, the King pleaded that it had been concluded for no object but vengeance; and he promised that there would soon be not a heretic in the country.[3] This was corroborated by Salviati. As to the proclaimed toleration, he knew that it was a device to disarm foreign enmity, and prevent a popular commotion. He testified that the Queen spoke truly when she said that she had confided to him, long before, the real purpose of her daughter's engagement.[4]

[1] The Bull, as published in Paris, is printed by Strype (*Life of Parker*, iii. 197). La prima occasione che a ciò lo mosse fù per lo stratagemma fatto da Carlo Nono Christianissimo Rè di Francia contra Coligno Ammiraglio, capo d' Ugonotti, et suoi seguaci, tagliati a pezzi in Parigi (Ciappi, *Vita di Gregorio XIII.*, 1596, p. 63).

[2] Vasari to Borghini, Oct. 5, 1572; March 5, 1573; to Francesco Medici, Nov. 17, 1572; Gaye, *Carteggio d' Artisti*, iii. 328, 366, 341.

[3] Indubitatamente non si osservarà interamente, havendomi in questo modo, punto che torno dall' audienza promesso il Rè, imponendomi di darne conto in suo nome a Nostro Signore, di volere in breve tempo liberare il Regno dalli Ugonotti. . . . Mi ha parlato della dispensa, escusandosi non haver fatto il Parentado per ultro, che per liberarsi da suoi inimici (Salviati, Desp. Sept. 3, Sept. 2, Oct. 11, 1572).

[4] Si vede che l' editto non essendo osservato ne da popoli, ne dal principe, non è per pigliar piede (Salviati, Desp. Sept. 4). Qual Regina in progresso di tempo intende pur non solo di revocare tal editto, ma per mezzo della giustitia di restituir la fede cattolica nell' antica osservanza, parendogli che nessuno ne debba dubitare adesso, che hanno fatto morire l' ammiraglio con tanti altri huomini di valore, conforme ai raggionamenti altre volte havuti con esso meco essendo a Bles, et trattando del parentado di Navarra, et dell' altre cose che correvano in quei tempi, il che essendo vero, ne posso rendere testimonianza, e a Nostro Signore e a tutto il mondo (Aug. 27; Theiner, i. 329, 330).

He exposed the hollow pretence of the plot. He announced that its existence would be established by formalities of law, but added that it was so notoriously false that none but an idiot could believe in it.[1] Gregory gave no countenance to the official falsehood. At the reception of the French ambassador, Rambouillet, on the 23rd of December, Muretus made his famous speech. He said that there could not have been a happier beginning for a new pontificate, and alluded to the fabulous plot in the tone exacted of French officials. The Secretary, Boccapaduli, replying in behalf of the Pope, thanked the King for destroying the enemies of Christ; but strictly avoided the conventional fable.[2]

Cardinal Orsini went as Legate to France. He had been appointed in August, and he was to try to turn the King's course into that line of policy from which he had strayed under Protestant guidance. He had not left Rome when the events occurred which altered the whole situation. Orsini was now charged with felicitations, and was to urge Charles not to stop half-way.[3] An ancient and obsolete ceremonial was suddenly revived; and the Cardinals accompanied him to the Flaminian gate.[4] This journey of Orsini, and the pomp with which it was surrounded, were exceedingly unwelcome at Paris. It was likely to be taken as proof of that secret understanding with Rome which threatened to rend the delicate web in which Charles was striving to hold the confidence of

[1] Desp. Sept. 2, 1572.

[2] The reply of Boccapaduli is printed in French, with the translation of the oration of Muretus, Paris, 1573.

[3] Troverà le cose cosi ben disposte, che durarà poca fattica in ottener quel tanto si desidera per Sua Beatitudine, anzi haverà più presto da ringratiar quella Maestà Christianissima di cosi buona et sant' opera, ha fatto far, che da durare molta fatica in persuaderli l' unione con la Santa Chiesa Romana (Cusano to the Emperor, Rome, Sept. 6). Sereno (*Comment. della guerra di Cipro*, p. 329) understands the mission in the same light.

[4] Omnes mulas ascendentes cappis et galeris pontificalibus induti associarunt Rmum D. Cardinalem Ursinum Legatum usque ad portam Flaminiam et extra eam ubi factis multis reverentiis eum ibi reliquerunt, juxta ritum antiquum in ceremoniali libro descriptum qui longo tempore intermissus fuerat, ita Pontifice iubente in Concistorio hodierno (*Mucantii Diaria*). Ista associatio fuit determinata in Concistorio vocatis X. Cardinalibus et ex improviso exequuti fuimus (*C. Firmani Diaria*, B. M. Add. MSS. 8448).

the Protestant world.[1] He requested that the Legate might be recalled; and the Pope was willing that there should be some delay. While Orsini tarried on his way, Gregory's reply to the announcement of the massacre arrived at Paris. It was a great consolation to himself, he said, and an extraordinary grace vouchsafed to Christendom. But he desired, for the glory of God and the good of France, that the Huguenots should be extirpated utterly; and with that view he demanded the revocation of the edict. When Catherine knew that the Pope was not yet satisfied, and sought to direct the actions of the King, she could hardly restrain her rage. Salviati had never seen her so furious. The words had hardly passed his lips when she exclaimed that she wondered at such designs, and was resolved to tolerate no interference in the government of the kingdom. She and her son were Catholics from conviction, and not through fear or influence. Let the Pope content himself with that.[2] The Nuncio had at once foreseen that the court, after crushing the Huguenots, would not become more amenable to the counsels of Rome. He wrote, on the very day of St. Bartholomew, that the King would be very jealous of his authority, and would exact obedience from both sides alike.

At this untoward juncture Orsini appeared at Court. To Charles, who had done so much, it seemed unreasonable that he should be asked for more. He represented to Orsini that it was impossible to eradicate all the remnants of a faction which had been so strong. He had put seventy thousand Huguenots to the sword; and, if he had shown compassion to the rest, it was in order that they might become good Catholics.[3]

1 Mette in consideratione alla Santità Sua che havendo deputato un Legato apostolico sù la morte dell' ammiraglio, et altri capi Ugonotti, ha fatti ammazzare a Parigi, saria per metterla in molto sospetto et diffidenza delli Principi Protestanti, et della Regina d' Inghilterra, ch' ella fosse d' accordo con la sede Apostolica, et Principi Cattolici per farli guerra, i quali cerca d' acquettar con accertarli tutti, che non ha fatto ammazzar l' ammiraglio et suoi seguaci per conto della Religione (Cusano to the Emperor, Sept. 27).

2 Salviati, Desp. Sept. 22, 1572.

3 Charles IX. to S. Goard, Oct. 5, 1572; Charrière, iii. 330. Ne poteva esser bastante segno l' haver egli doppo la morte dell' Ammiraglio fatto un editto,

The hidden thoughts which the Court of Rome betrayed by its conduct on this memorable occasion have brought upon the Pope himself an amount of hatred greater than he deserved. Gregory XIII. appears as a pale figure between the two strongest of the modern Popes, without the intense zeal of the one and the ruthless volition of the other. He was not prone to large conceptions or violent resolutions. He had been converted late in life to the spirit of the Tridentine Reformation; and when he showed rigour it was thought to be not in his character, but in the counsels of those who influenced him.[1] He did not instigate the crime, nor the atrocious sentiments that hailed it. In the religious struggle a frenzy had been kindled which made weakness violent, and turned good men into prodigies of ferocity; and at Rome, where every loss inflicted on Catholicism and every wound was felt, the belief that, in dealing with heretics, murder is better than toleration prevailed for half a century. The predecessor of Gregory had been Inquisitor-General. In his eyes Protestants were worse than Pagans, and Lutherans more dangerous than other Protestants.[2] The Capuchin preacher, Pistoja, bore witness that men were hanged and quartered almost daily at Rome;[3] and Pius declared that he would release a culprit guilty of a hundred murders rather than one obstinate heretic.[4] He seriously contemplated razing the town of Faenza because it was infested with religious error, and he recommended a similar expedient to the King of France.[5] He adjured him to

che in tutti i luoghi del suo regno fossero posti a fil di spada quanti heretici vi si trovassero, onde in pochi giorni n' erano stati ammazzati settanta milla e d' avantaggio (Cicarelli, *Vita di Gregori XIII.*; Platina, *Vite de' Pontefici*, 1715, 592).

[1] Il tengono quasiche in filo et il necessitano a far cose contra la sua natura e la sua volontà perche S. Sta è sempre stato di natura piacevole e dolce (*Relatione di Gregorio XIII.*; Ranke, *Päpste*, App. 80). Faict Cardinal par le pape Pie IV., le 12e de Mars 1559, lequel en le créant, dit qu'il n'avoit créé un cardinal ains un pape (Ferralz to Charles IX., May 14, 1572).

[2] Smus Dominus Noster dixit nullam concordiam vel pacem debere nec posse esse inter nos et hereticos, et cum eis nullum foedus ineundum et habendum . . . verissimum est deteriores esse haereticos gentilibus, eo quod sunt adeo perversi et obstinati, ut propemodum infideles sint (*Acta Concistorialia*, June 18, 1571; Bib. Imp. F. Lat. 12,561).

[3] Ogni giorno faceva impiccare e squartare ora uno, ora un altro (Cantù, ii. 410).

[4] *Legazioni di Serristori*, 436, 443.

[5] Elle desire infiniment que vostre Majesté face quelque ressentement plus

hold no intercourse with the Huguenots, to make no terms with them, and not to observe the terms he had made. He required that they should be pursued to the death, that not one should be spared under any pretence, that all prisoners should suffer death.[1] He threatened Charles with the punishment of Saul when he forebore to exterminate the Amalekites.[2] He told him that it was his mission to avenge the injuries of the Lord, and that nothing is more cruel than mercy to the impious [3] When he sanctioned the murder of Elizabeth he proposed that it should be done in execution of his sentence against her.[4] It became usual with those who meditated assassination or regicide on the plea of religion to look upon the representatives of Rome as their natural advisers. On the 21st of January 1591, a young Capuchin came, by permission of his superiors, to Sega, Bishop of Piacenza, then Nuncio at Paris. He said that he was inflamed with the desire of a martyr's death; and having been assured by divines that it would be meritorious to kill that heretic and tyrant, Henry of Navarre, he asked to be dispensed from the rule of his Order while he prepared his measures and watched his opportunity. The Nuncio would not do this without authority from Rome; but the prudence, courage, and humility which he discerned in the friar made him believe that the design was really inspired from above. To make this certain, and to remove all scruples, he submitted the matter to the Pope, and asked his blessing upon it, promising that whatever he decided should be executed with all discretion.[5]

qu'elle n'a faict jusques à ceste heure contre ceux qui lui font la guerre, comme de raser quelques-unes de leurs principales maisons pour une perpétuelle mémoyre (Rambouillet to Charles IX., Rome, Jan. 17, 1569; Bib. Imp. F. Fr. 17,989).

[1] Pius V. to Catherine, April 13, 1569.

[2] Pius V. to Charles IX., March 28, 1569.

[3] Sa Saincteté m'a dict que j'escrive à vostre majesté que icelle se souvienne qu'elle combat pour la querelle de Dieu, et que ceste à elle de faire ses vengeances (Rambouillet to Charles IX., Rome, March 14, 1569; Bib. Imp. F. Fr. 16,039). Nihil est enim ea pietate misericordiaque crudelius, quae in impios et ultima supplicia meritos confertur (Pius V. to Charles IX., Oct. 20, 1569).

[4] *Correspondance de Philippe II.*, ii. 185.

[5] Inspirato più d' un anno fa di esporre la vita al martirio col procurare la liberatione della religione, et delle patria per mezzo della morte del tiranno, et assicurato da Theologi che il fatto saria stato meritorio, non ne haveva con tutto ciò mai potuto ottenere da superiori suoi la licenza o dispensa. . . . Io quantunque

The same ideas pervaded the Sacred College under Gregory. There are letters of profuse congratulation by the Cardinals of Lorraine, Este, and Pellevé. Bourbon was an accomplice before the fact. Granvelle condemned not the act but the delay. Delfino and Santorio approved. The Cardinal of Alessandria had refused the King's gift at Blois, and had opposed his wishes at the conclave. Circumstances were now so much altered that the ring was offered to him again, and this time it was accepted.[1] The one dissentient from the chorus of applause is said to have been Montalto. His conduct when he became Pope makes it very improbable; and there is no good authority for the story. But Leti has it, who is so far from a panegyrist that it deserves mention.

The theory which was framed to justify these practices has done more than plots and massacres to cast discredit on the Catholics. This theory was as follows: Confirmed heretics must be rigorously punished whenever it can be done without the probability of greater evil to religion. Where that is feared, the penalty may be suspended or delayed for a season, provided it be inflicted whenever the danger is past.[2] Treaties made with heretics, and promises given to them must not be kept, because sinful promises do not bind, and no agreement is lawful which may injure religion or ecclesiastical authority. No

mi sia parso di trovarlo pieno di tale humiltà, prudenza, spirito et core che arguiscono che questa sia inspiratione veramente piuttosto che temerità o legerezza, non cognoscendo tuttavia di potergliela concedere l' ho persuaso a tornarsene nel suo covento raccommandarsi a Dio et attendere all' obbedienza delli suoi superiori finchè io attendessi dallo assenso o ripulsa del Papa che haverei interpellato per la sua santa beneditione, se questo spirito sia veramente da Dio donde si potrà conjetturare che sia venendo approvato da Sua S[tà], e perciò sarà più sicuro da essere eseguito. . . . Resta hora che V. S. Illma mi favorisca di communicare a S. B. il caso, et scrivermene come la supplico quanto prima per duplicate et triplicate lettere la sua santa determinatione assicurandosi che per quanto sarà in me il negotio sarà trattato con la debita circumspetione (Sega, Desp. Paris, Jan. 23, 1591; deciphered in Rome, March 26).

[1] Ferralz to Charles IX., Nov. 18, Dec. 23, 1572.

[2] De Castro, *De Justa Haeret. Punitione*, 1547, p. 119. Iure Divino obligantur eos extirpare, si absque maiori incommodo possint (Lancelottus, *Haereticum quare per Catholicum quia*, 1615, p. 579). Ubi quid indulgendum sit, ratio semper exacta habeatur, an Religioni Ecclesiae, et Reipublicae quid vice mutua accedat quod majoris sit momenti, et plus prodesse possit (Pamelius, *De Relig. diversis non admittendis*, 1589, p. 159). Contagium istud sic grassatum est, ut corrupta massa non ferat antiquissimas leges, severitasque tantisper remittenda sit (Possevinus, *Animadv. in Thuanum*; Zachariae, *Iter Litterarium*, p. 321).

civil power may enter into engagements which impede the free scope of the Church's law.[1] It is part of the punishment of heretics that faith shall not be kept with them.[2] It is even mercy to kill them that they may sin no more.[3]

Such were the precepts and the examples by which the French Catholics learned to confound piety and ferocity, and were made ready to immolate their countrymen. During the civil war an association was formed in the South for the purpose of making war upon the Huguenots; and it was fortified by Pius V. with blessings and indulgences. "We doubt not," it proclaimed, "that we shall be victorious over these enemies of God and of all humankind; and if we fall, our blood will be as a second baptism, by which, without impediment, we shall join the other martyrs straightway in heaven."[4] Monluc, who told Alva at Bayonne that he had never spared an enemy, was shot through the face at the siege of Rabasteins. Whilst he believed that he was dying, they came to tell him that the place was taken. "Thank God!" he said, "that I have lived long enough to behold our victory; and now I care not for death. Go back, I beseech you, and give me a last proof of friendship, by seeing that not one man of the garrison escapes alive."[5] When Alva had defeated and captured Genlis, and expected to make many more Huguenot prisoners in the garrison of Mons, Charles IX. wrote to Mondoucet "that it would be for the service of God, and of the King of Spain, that they should die. If the Duke of Alva answers that this is a tacit request to have all the prisoners cut to pieces, you will tell him that that is what he must do, and that he will

[1] Principi saeculari nulla ratione permissum est, haereticis licentiam tribuere haereses suas docendi, atque adeo contractus ille iniustus. . . . Si quid Princeps saecularis attentet in praeiudicium Ecclesiasticae potestatis, aut contra eam aliquid statuat et paciscatur, pactum illud nullum futurum (R. Sweertii, *De Fide Haereticis servanda*, 1611, p. 36).

[2] Ad poenam quoque pertinet et odium haereticorum quod fides illis data servanda non sit (Simancha, *Inst. Cath.* pp. 46, 52).

[3] Si nolint converti, expedit eos citius tollere e medio, ne gravius postea damnentur, unde non militat contra mansuetudinem christianam, occidere Haereticos, quin potius est opus maximae misericordiae (Lancelottus, p. 579).

[4] De Rozoy, *Annales de Toulouse*, iii. 65.

[5] Alva to Philip, June 5, 1565; *Pap. de Granvelle*, ix. 288; *Comment. de Monluc*, iii. 425.

injure both himself and all Christendom if he fails to do it."[1] This request also reached Alva through Spain. Philip wrote on the margin of the despatch that, if he had not yet put them out of the world, he must do so immediately, as there could be no reason for delay.[2] The same thought occurred to others. On the 22nd of July Salviati writes that it would be a serious blow to the faction if Alva would kill his prisoners; and Granvelle wrote that, as they were all Huguenots, it would be well to throw them all into the river.[3]

Where these sentiments prevailed, Gregory XIII. was not alone in deploring that the work had been but half done. After the first explosion of gratified surprise men perceived that the thing was a failure, and began to call for more. The clergy of Rouen Cathedral instituted a procession of thanksgiving, and prayed that the King might continue what he had so virtuously begun, until all France should profess one faith.[4] There are signs that Charles was tempted at one moment, during the month of October, to follow up the blow.[5] But he died without pursuing the design; and the hopes were turned to his successor. When Henry III. passed through Italy on his way to assume the crown, there were some who hoped that the Pope would induce him to set resolutely about the extinction of the Huguenots. A petition was addressed to Gregory for this purpose, in which the writer says that hitherto the French court has erred on the side of mercy, but that the new king might make good the error if rejecting that pernicious maxim that noble blood spilt weakens a kingdom, he would appoint an execution which would be cruel only in appearance, but in reality glorious and holy, and destroy the heretics totally, sparing neither life nor property.[6] Similar

[1] Charles IX. to Mondoucet, Aug. 31, 1572; *Compte Rendu*, iv. 349.

[2] *Bulletins de Bruxelles*, xvi. 256.

[3] Granvelle to Morillon, Sept. 11, 1572; Michelet, p. 475.

[4] Floquet, iii. 137.

[5] Walsingham to Smith, Nov. 1, 1572; Digges, p. 279. Ita enim statutum ab illis fuit die 27 Octobris (Beza, Dec. 3, 1572; *Ill. vir. Epp. Sel.* 621). La Mothe, v. 164; Faustino Tasso, *Historie de nostri tempi*, 1583, p. 343.

[6] *Discorso di Monsignor Terracina à Gregorio XIII.*; *Thesauri Politici Contin.* 1618, pp. 73-76.

exhortations were addressed from Rome to Henry himself by Muzio, a layman who had gained repute, among other things, by controversial writings, of which Pius V. said that they had preserved the faith in whole districts, and who had been charged with the task of refuting the Centuriators. On the 17th of July 1574, Muzio wrote to the King that all Italy waited in reliance on his justice and valour, and besought him to spare neither old nor young, and to regard neither rank nor ties of blood.[1] These hopes also were doomed to disappointment; and a Frenchman, writing in the year of Henry's death, laments over the cruel clemency and inhuman mercy that reigned on St. Bartholomew's Day.[2]

This was not the general opinion of the Catholic world. In Spain and Italy, where hearts were hardened and consciences corrupted by the Inquisition; in Switzerland, where the Catholics lived in suspicion and dread of their Protestant neighbours; among ecclesiastical princes in Germany, whose authority waned as fast as their subjects abjured their faith, the massacre was welcomed as an act of Christian fortitude. But in France itself the great mass of the people was struck with consternation.[3] "Which maner of proceedings," writes Walsingham on the 13th of September, "is by the Catholiques themselves utterly condemned, who desire to depart hence out of this country, to quit themselves of this strange kind of government, for that they see here none can assure themselves of either goods or life." Even in places still steeped in mourning for the atrocities suffered at the hands of Huguenots during the civil war, at Nîmes, for instance, the King's orders produced no act of vengeance. At Carcassonne, the ancient seat of the Inquisition, the Catholics concealed the Protestants in their houses.[4] In

[1] Infin che ne viverà grande, o picciolo di loro, mai non le mancheranno insidie (*Lettere del Muzio*, 1590, p. 232).

[2] Coupez, tronquez, cisaillez, ne pardonnez à parens ny amis, princes et subiets, ny à quelque personne de quelque condition qu'ils soient (D'Orléans, *Premier advertissement des Catholiques Anglois aux François Catholiques*, 1590, p. 13). The notion that Charles had displayed an extreme benignity recurs in many books: "Nostre Prince a surpassé tout mesure de clémence" (Le Frère de Laval *Histoire des Troubles*, 1576, p. 527).

[3] Serranus, *Comment.* iv. 51.

[4] Bouges, *Histoire de Carcassonne*, p. 343.

Provence, the news from Lyons and the corpses that came down in the poisoned waters of the Rhone awakened nothing but horror and compassion.[1] Sir Thomas Smith wrote to Walsingham that in England "the minds of the most number are much alienated from that nation, even of the very Papists."[2] At Rome itself Zuñiga pronounced the treachery of which the French were boasting unjustifiable, even in the case of heretics and rebels;[3] and it was felt as an outrage to public opinion when the murderer of Coligny was presented to the Pope.[4] The Emperor was filled with grief and indignation. He said that the King and Queen-mother would live to learn that nothing could have been more iniquitously contrived or executed: his uncle Charles V., and his father Ferdinand, had made war on the Protestants, but they had never been guilty of so cruel an act.[5] At that moment Maximilian was seeking the crown of Poland for his son; and the events in France were a weapon in his hands against his rival, Anjou. Even the Czar of Muscovy, Ivan the Terrible, replying to his letters, protested that all Christian princes must lament the barbarous and needless shedding of so much innocent blood. It was not the rivalry of the moment that animated Maximilian. His whole life proves him to have been an enemy of violence and cruelty; and his celebrated letter to Schwendi, written long after, shows that his judgment remained unchanged. It was the Catholic Emperor who roused the Lutheran Elector of Saxony to something like resentment of the butchery in France.[6]

[1] *Sommaire de la Félonie commise à Lyon.* A contemporary tract reprinted by Gonon, 1848, p. 221.

[2] On this point Smith may be trusted rather than Parker (*Correspondence*, p. 399).

[3] *Bulletins de Bruxelles*, xvi. 249.

[4] Qui è venuto quello che dette l' archibusata all' ammiraglio di Francia, et è stato condotto dal Cardinal di Lorena et dall' Ambasciator di Francia, al papa. A molti non è piaciuto che costui sia venuto in Roma (Prospero Count Arco to the Emperor, Rome, Nov. 15, 1572; Vienna Archives).

[5] Zuñiga to Philip, March 4, 1573; *Arch. de l'Empire*, K. 1531, B. 35, 70. Zuñiga heard it from Lorraine.

[6] Et est toute la dispute encores sur les derniers évènemens de la France, contre lesquels l'Electeur est beaucoup plus aigre qu'il n'estoyt à mon aultre voyage, depuys qu'il a esté en l'escole à Vienne (Schomberg to Brulart, May 12, 1573; Groen, iv. App. 76).

For the Lutherans were not disposed to recognise the victims of Charles IX. as martyrs for the Protestant cause. During the wars of religion Lutheran auxiliaries were led by a Saxon prince, a margrave of Baden, and other German magnates, to aid the Catholic forces in putting down the heresy of Calvin. These feelings were so well known that the French Government demanded of the Duke of Wirtemberg the surrender of the Huguenots who had fled into his dominions.[1] Lutheran divines flattered themselves at first with the belief that it was the Calvinistic error, not the Protestant truth, that had invited and received the blow.[2] The most influential of them, Andreæ, declared that the Huguenots were not martyrs but rebels, who had died not for religion but sedition; and he bade the princes beware of the contagion of their spirit, which had deluged other lands with blood. When Elizabeth proposed a league for the defence of Protestantism, the North German divines protested against an alliance with men whose crime was not only religious error but blasphemous obstinacy, the root of many dreadful heresies. The very proposal, they said, argued a disposition to prefer human succour rather than the word of God.[3] When another invitation came from Henry of Navarre, the famous divine Chemnitz declared union with the disciples of Calvin a useless abomination.[4]

The very men whose own brethren had perished in France were not hearty or unanimous in execrating the deed.[5] There were Huguenots who thought that their party had brought ruin on itself, by provoking its enemies, and following the rash counsels of ambitious men.[6] This

[1] Sattler, *Geschichte von Würtemberg*, v. 23.

[2] Audio quosdam etiam nostralium theologorum cruentam istam nuptiarum feralium celebrationem pertinaciae Gallorum in semel recepta de sacramentalibus mysteriis sententia acceptam referre et praeter illos pati neminem somniare (Steinberger to Crato, Nov. 23, 1572; Gillet, *Crato von Crafftheim*, ii. 519).

[3] Heppe, *Geschichte des deutschen Protestantismus*, iv. 37, 47, 49.

[4] Hachfeld, *Martin Chemnitz*, p. 137.

[5] Sunt tamen qui hoc factum et excusare et defendere tentant (Bullinger to Hotoman, Oct. 11, 1572; Hotoman, *Epis.* 35).

[6] Nec dubium est melius cum ipsis actum fuisse, si quemadmodum a principio instituerant, cum disciplinam ecclesiasticam introduxere, viros modestos et piae veraeque reformationis cupidos tantum in suos coetus admisissent, reiectis

was the opinion of their chief, Theodore Beza, himself. Six weeks before, he wrote that they were gaining in numbers but losing in quality, and he feared lest, after destroying superstition, they should destroy religion: "Valde metuo ne superstitioni successerit impietas."[1] And afterwards he declared that nobody who had known the state of the French Protestants could deny that it was a most just judgment upon them.[2]

Beza held very stringent doctrines touching the duty of the civil magistrate to repress religious error. He thought that heresy is worse than murder, and that the good of society requires no crime to be more severely punished.[3] He declared toleration contrary to revealed religion and the constant tradition of the Church, and taught that lawful authority must be obeyed, even by those whom it persecutes. He expressly recognised this function in Catholic States, and urged Sigismund not to rest until he had got rid of the Socinians in Poland;[4] but he could not prevail against the vehement resistance of Cardinal Hosius. It was embarrassing to limit these principles when they were applied against his own Church. For a moment Beza doubted whether it had not received its death-blow in France. But he did not qualify the propositions which were open to be interpreted so fatally,[5] or deny that his people, by their vices, if not by their errors, had deserved what they had suffered.

The applause which greeted their fate came not from the Catholics generally, nor from the Catholics alone. While the Protestants were ready to palliate or excuse it, the majority of the Catholics who were not under the

petulantibus et fervidis ingeniis, quae eos in diros tumultus, et inextricabilia mala coniecerunt (Dinothus, *De Bello Civili*, 1582, p. 243).

[1] Beza to Tilius, July 5, 1572; *Ill. vir. Epp. Sel.* 607.

[2] Quoties autem ego haec ipse praedixi! quoties praemonui! Sed sic Deo visum est, iustissimis de causis irato, et tamen servatori (Beza to Tilius, Sept. 10, 1572, 614). Nihil istorum non iustissimo iudicio accidere necesse est fateri, qui Galliarum statum norunt (Beza to Crato, Aug. 26, 1573; Gillet, ii. 521).

[3] Ut mihi quidem magis absurde facere videantur quam si sacrilegas parricidas puniendos negarent, quum sint istis omnibus haeretici infinitis partibus deteriores. . . . In nullos unquam homines severius quam in haereticos, blasphemos et impios debet animadvertere (*De Haereticis puniendis*, Tract. Theol. i. 143, 152).

[4] *Epist. Theolog.* 1575, p. 338.

[5] Beza to Wittgenstein, Pentecost, 1583; Friedländer, 143.

direct influence of Madrid or Rome recognised the inexpiable horror of the crime. But the desire to defend what the Pope approved survived sporadically, when the old fierceness of dogmatic hatred was extinct. A generation passed without any perceptible change in the judgment of Rome. It was a common charge against De Thou that he had condemned the blameless act of Charles IX. The blasphemies of the Huguenots, said one of his critics, were more abominable than their retribution.[1] His History was put on the Index; and Cardinal Barberini let him know that he was condemned because he not only favoured Protestants to the detriment of Catholics, but had even disapproved the Massacre of St. Bartholomew.[2] Eudæmon-Johannes, the friend of Bellarmine, pronounces it a pious and charitable act, which immortalised its author.[3] Another Jesuit, Bompiani, says that it was grateful to Gregory, because it was likely to relieve the Church.[4] The well-known apology for Charles IX. by Naudé is based rather on political than religious grounds; but his contemporary Guyon, whose History of Orleans is pronounced by the censors full of sound doctrine and pious sentiment, deems it unworthy of Catholics to speak of the murder of heretics as if it were a crime, because, when done under lawful authority, it is a blessed thing.[5] When Innocent XI. refused to approve the Revocation of the Edict of Nantes, Frenchmen wondered that he should so far depart from the example which was kept before him by one of the most conspicuous ornaments

[1] Lobo de Silveis to De Thou, July 7, 1616; *Histoire*, XV. 371; J. B. Gallus, *Ibid.* p. 435.

[2] Le Cardinal Barberin, que je tiens pour Serviteur du Roy, a parlé franchement sur ceste affaire, et m'a dit qu'il croyoit presqu'impossible qu'il se trouve jamais remede, si vous ne la voulez recommencer; disant que depuis le commencement jusqu'à la fin vous vous estes monstré du tout passionné contre ce qui est de l'honneur et de la grandeur de l'Église, qu'il se trouvera dans vostre histoire que vous ne parlez jamais des Catholiques qu'avec du mépris et de la louange de ceux de la religion; que mesme vous avez blasmé ce que feu Monsieur le président de Thou vostre père avoit approuvé, qui est la S. Barthelemy (De Brèves to De Thou, Rome, Feb. 18, 1610; Bib. Imp. F. Dupuy, 812).

[3] Crudelitatisne tu esse ac non clementiae potius, pietatisque putas? (*Resp. ad Ep. Casauboni*, 1612, p. 118).

[4] Quae res uti Catholicae Religioni sublevandae opportuna, ita maxime jucunda Gregorio accidit (*Hist. Pontif. Gregori XIII.*, p. 30).

[5] *Histoire d'Orléans*, pp. 421, 424.

of his palace.[1] The old spirit was decaying fast in France, and the superb indignation of Bossuet fairly expresses the general opinion of his time. Two works were published on the medals of the Popes, by a French and an Italian writer. The Frenchman awkwardly palliates the conduct of Gregory XIII.; the Italian heartily defends it.[2] In Italy it was still dangerous ground. Muratori shrinks from pronouncing on the question,[3] while Cienfuegos, a Jesuit whom his Order esteemed one of the most distinguished Cardinals of the day, judges that Charles IX. died too soon for his fame.[4] Tempesti, who lived under the enlightened rule of Benedict XIV., accuses Catherine of having arrested the slaughter, in order that some cause should remain to create a demand for her counsels.[5] The German Jesuit Biner and the Papal historian Piatti, just a century ago, are among the last downright apologists.[6]

Then there was a change. A time came when the Catholics, having long relied on force, were compelled to appeal to opinion. That which had been defiantly acknowledged and defended required to be ingeniously explained away. The same motive which had justified the murder now prompted the lie. Men shrank from the conviction that the rulers and restorers of their Church had been murderers and abetters of murder, and that so much infamy had been coupled with so much zeal. They feared to say that the most monstrous of crimes had been solemnly approved at Rome, lest they should devote the Papacy to the execration of mankind. A swarm of facts were invented to meet the difficulty: The victims were insignificant in number; they were slain for no reason

[1] Germain to Bretagne, Rome, Dec. 24, 1685; Valery, *Corresp. de Mabillon*, i. 192.

[2] Du Molinet, *Hist. S. Pont. per Numismata*, 1679, 93; Buorranni, *Numismata Pontificum*, i. 336.

[3] *Annali d' Italia* ad ann. 1572.

[4] Si huviera respirado mas tiempo, huviera dado a entender al mundo, que avia Rey en la Francia, y Dios en Israel (*Vida de S. Francisco De Borja*, 446).

[5] *Vita di Sisto V.*, i. 119.

[6] Quo demum res evaderent, si Regibus non esset integrum, in rebelles, subditos, quietisque publicae turbatores animadvertere? (*Apparatus Eruditionis*, vii. 503; Piatti, *Storia de' Pontefici XI.*, p. 271).

connected with religion; the Pope believed in the existence of the plot; the plot was a reality; the medal is fictitious; the massacre was a feint concerted with the Protestants themselves; the Pope rejoiced only when he heard that it was over.[1] These things were repeated so often that they have been sometimes believed; and men have fallen into this way of speaking whose sincerity was unimpeachable, and who were not shaken in their religion by the errors or the vices of Popes. Möhler was pre-eminently such a man. In his lectures on the history of the Church, which were published only last year,[2] he said that the Catholics, as such, took no part in the massacre; that no cardinal, bishop, or priest shared in the councils that prepared it; that Charles informed the Pope that a conspiracy had been discovered; and that Gregory made his thanksgiving only because the King's life was saved.[3] Such things will cease to be written when men perceive that truth is the only merit that gives dignity and worth to history.

[1] Per le notizie che ricevette della cessata strage (Moroni, *Dizionario di Erudizione Ecclesiastica*, xxxii. 298).

[2] [1868.]

[3] *Kirchengeschichte*, iii. 211.

V

THE PROTESTANT THEORY OF PERSECUTION[1]

THE manner in which Religion influences State policy is more easily ascertained in the case of Protestantism than in that of the Catholic Church: for whilst the expression of Catholic doctrines is authoritative and unvarying, the great social problems did not all arise at once, and have at various times received different solutions. The reformers failed to construct a complete and harmonious code of doctrine; but they were compelled to supplement the new theology by a body of new rules for the guidance of their followers in those innumerable questions with regard to which the practice of the Church had grown out of the experience of ages. And although the dogmatic system of Protestantism was not completed in their time, yet the Protestant spirit animated them in greater purity and force than it did any later generation. Now, when a religion is applied to the social and political sphere, its general spirit must be considered, rather than its particular precepts. So that in studying the points of this application in the case of Protestantism, we may consult the writings of the reformers with greater confidence than we could do for an exposition of Protestant theology; and accept them as a greater authority, because they agree more entirely among themselves. We can be more sure that we have the true Protestant opinion in a political or social question on which all the reformers are agreed, than in a theological question on which they

[1] *The Rambler*, March 1862.

differ; for the concurrent opinion must be founded on an element common to all, and therefore essential. If it should further appear that this opinion was injurious to their actual interests, and maintained at a sacrifice to themselves, we should then have an additional security for its necessary connection with their fundamental views.

The most important example of this law is the Protestant theory of toleration. The views of the reformers on religious liberty are not fragmentary, accidental opinions, unconnected with their doctrines, or suggested by the circumstances amidst which they lived; but the product of their theological system, and of their ideas of political and ecclesiastical government. Civil and religious liberty are so commonly associated in people's mouths, and are so rare in fact, that their definition is evidently as little understood as the principle of their connection. The point at which they unite, the common root from which they derive their sustenance, is the right of self-government. The modern theory, which has swept away every authority except that of the State, and has made the sovereign power irresistible by multiplying those who share it, is the enemy of that common freedom in which religious freedom is included. It condemns, as a State within the State, every inner group and community, class or corporation, administering its own affairs; and, by proclaiming the abolition of privileges, it emancipates the subjects of every such authority in order to transfer them exclusively to its own. It recognises liberty only in the individual, because it is only in the individual that liberty can be separated from authority, and the right of conditional obedience deprived of the security of a limited command. Under its sway, therefore, every man may profess his own religion more or less freely; but his religion is not free to administer its own laws. In other words, religious profession is free, but Church government is controlled. And where ecclesiastical authority is restricted, religious liberty is virtually denied.

For religious liberty is not the negative right of being

without any particular religion, just as self-government is not anarchy. It is the right of religious communities to the practice of their own duties, the enjoyment of their own constitution, and the protection of the law, which equally secures to all the possession of their own independence. Far from implying a general toleration, it is best secured by a limited one. In an indifferent State, that is, in a State without any definite religious character (if such a thing is conceivable), no ecclesiastical authority could exist. A hierarchical organisation would not be tolerated by the sects that have none, or by the enemies of all definite religion; for it would be in contradiction to the prevailing theory of atomic freedom. Nor can a religion be free when it is alone, unless it makes the State subject to it. For governments restrict the liberty of the favoured Church, by way of remunerating themselves for their service in preserving her unity. The most violent and prolonged conflicts for religious freedom occurred in the Middle Ages between a Church which was not threatened by rivals and States which were most attentive to preserve her exclusive predominance. Frederic II., the most tyrannical oppressor of the Church among the German emperors, was the author of those sanguinary laws against heresy which prevailed so long in many parts of Europe. The Inquisition, which upheld the religious unity of the Spanish nation, imposed the severest restrictions on the Spanish Church; and in England conformity has been most rigorously exacted by those sovereigns who have most completely tyrannised over the Established Church. Religious liberty, therefore, is possible only where the co-existence of different religions is admitted, with an equal right to govern themselves according to their own several principles. Tolerance of error is requisite for freedom; but freedom will be most complete where there is no actual diversity to be resisted, and no theoretical unity to be maintained, but where unity exists as the triumph of truth, not of force, through the victory of the Church, not through the enactment of the State.

This freedom is attainable only in communities where rights are sacred, and where law is supreme. If the first duty is held to be obedience to authority and the preservation of order, as in the case of aristocracies and monarchies of the patriarchal type, there is no safety for the liberties either of individuals or of religion. Where the highest consideration is the public good and the popular will, as in democracies, and in constitutional monarchies after the French pattern, majority takes the place of authority; an irresistible power is substituted for an idolatrous principle, and all private rights are equally insecure. The true theory of freedom excludes all absolute power and arbitrary action, and requires that a tyrannical or revolutionary government shall be coerced by the people; but it teaches that insurrection is criminal, except as a corrective of revolution and tyranny. In order to understand the views of the Protestant reformers on toleration, they must be considered with reference to these points.

While the Reformation was an act of individual resistance and not a system, and when the secular Powers were engaged in supporting the authority of the Church, the authors of the movement were compelled to claim impunity for their opinions, and they held language regarding the right of governments to interfere with religious belief which resembles that of friends of toleration. Every religious party, however exclusive or servile its theory may be, if it is in contradiction with a system generally accepted and protected by law, must necessarily, at its first appearance, assume the protection of the idea that the conscience is free.[1] Before a new authority can be set up in the place of one that exists, there is an interval when the right of dissent must be proclaimed. At the beginning of Luther's contest with the Holy See

[1] "Le vrai principe de Luther est celui-ci : La volonté est esclave par nature. . . . Le libre examen a été pour Luther un moyen et non un principe. Il s'en est servi, et était contraint de s'en servir pour établir son vrai principe, qui était la toute-puissance de la foi et de la grâce. . . . C'est ainsi que le libre examen s'imposa au Protestantisme. L'accessoire devint le principal, et la forme dévora plus ou moins le fond" (Janet, *Histoire de la Philosophie Morale*, ii. 38, 39).

there was no rival authority for him to appeal to. No ecclesiastical organism existed, the civil power was not on his side, and not even a definite system had yet been evolved by controversy out of his original doctrine of justification. His first efforts were acts of hostility, his exhortations were entirely aggressive, and his appeal was to the masses. When the prohibition of his New Testament confirmed him in the belief that no favour was to be expected from the princes, he published his book on the Civil Power, which he judged superior to everything that had been written on government since the days of the Apostles, and in which he asserts that authority is given to the State only against the wicked, and that it cannot coerce the godly. "Princes," he says, "are not to be obeyed when they command submission to superstitious errors, but their aid is not to be invoked in support of the Word of God."[1] Heretics must be converted by the Scriptures, and not by fire, otherwise the hangman would be the greatest doctor.[2] At the time when this was written Luther was expecting the bull of excommunication and the ban of the empire, and for several years it appeared doubtful whether he would escape the treatment he condemned. He lived in constant fear of assassination, and his friends amused themselves with his terrors. At one time he believed that a Jew had been hired by the Polish bishops to despatch him; that an invisible physician was on his way to Wittenberg to murder him; that the pulpit from which he preached was impregnated with a subtle

[1] "If they prohibit true doctrine, and punish their subjects for receiving the entire sacrament, as Christ ordained it, compel the people to idolatrous practices, with masses for the dead, indulgences, invocation of saints, and the like, in these things they exceed their office, and seek to deprive God of the obedience due to Him. For God requires from us this above all, that we hear His Word, and follow it; but where the Government desires to prevent this, the subjects must know that they are not bound to obey it" (Luther's *Werke*, xiii. 2244). "Non est, mi Spalatine, principum et istius saeculi Pontificum tueri verbum Dei, nec ea gratia ullorum peto praesidium" (Luther's *Briefe*, ed. De Wette, i. 521, Nov. 4, 1520). "I will compel and urge by force no man; for the faith must be voluntary and not compulsory, and must be adopted without violence" ("Sermonen an Carlstadt," *Werke*, xx. 24, 1522).

[2] "Schrift an den christlichen Adel" (*Werke*, x. 574, June 1520). His proposition, *Haereticos comburi esse contra voluntatem spiritus*, was one of those condemned by Leo X. as pestilent, scandalous, and contrary to Christian charity.

poison.[1] These alarms dictated his language during those early years. It was not the true expression of his views, which he was not yet strong enough openly to put forth.[2]

The Zwinglian schism, the rise of the Anabaptists, and the Peasants' War altered the aspect of affairs. Luther recognised in them the fruits of his theory of the right of private judgment and of dissent,[3] and the moment had arrived to secure his Church against the application of the same dissolving principles which had served him to break off from his allegiance to Rome.[4] The excesses of the social war threatened to deprive the movement of the sympathy of the higher classes, especially of the governments; and with the defeat of the peasants the popular phase of the Reformation came to an end on the Continent. "The devil," Luther said, "having failed to put him down by the help of the Pope, was seeking his

[1] "Nihil non tentabunt Romanenses, nec potest satis Huttenus me monere, adeo mihi de veneno timet" (De Wette, i. 487). "Etiam inimici mei quidam miserti per amicos ex Halberstadio fecerunt moneri me: esse quemdam doctorem medicinae, qui arte magica factus pro libito invisibilis, quemdam occidit, mandatum habentem et occidendi Lutheri, venturumque ad futuram Dominicam ostensionis reliquiarum: valde hoc constanter narratur" (De Wette, i. 441). "Est hic apud nos Judaeus Polonus, missus sub pretio 2000 aureorum, ut me veneno perdat, ab amicis per literas mihi proditus. Doctor est medicinae, et nihil non audere et facere paratus incredibili astutia et agilitate" (De Wette, ii. 616). See also Jarcke, *Studien zur Geschichte der Reformation*, p. 176.

[2] "Multa ego premo et causa principis et universitatis nostrae cohibeo, quae (si alibi essem) evomerem in vastatricem Scripturae et Ecclesiae Romanae. . . . Timeo miser, ne forte non sim dignus pati et occidi pro tali causa: erit ista felicitas meliorum hominum, non tam foedi peccatoris. Dixi tibi semper me paratum esse cedere loco, si qua ego principi ill. viderer periculo hic vivere. Aliquando certe moriendum est, quanquam jam edita vernacula quadam apologia satis aduler Romanae Ecclesiae et Pontifici, si quid forte id prosit" (De Wette, i. 260, 261). "Ubi periculum est, ne iis protectoribus tutus saevius in Romanenses sim grassaturus, quam si sub principis imperio publicis militarem officiis docendi. . . . Ego vicissim, nisi ignem habere nequeam damnabo, publiceque concremabo jus pontificium totum, id est, lernam illam haeresium; et finem habebit humilitatis exhibitae hactenusque frustratae observantia qua nolo amplius inflari hostes Evangelii" (*Ibid.* pp. 465, 466, July 10, 1520).

[3] "Out of the Gospel and divine truth come devilish lies; . . . from the blood in our body comes corruption; out of Luther come Müntzer, and rebels, Anabaptists, Sacramentarians, and false brethren" (*Werke*, i. 75).

[4] "Habemus," wrote Erasmus, "fructum tui spiritus. . . . Non agnoscis hosce seditiosos, opinor, sed illi te agnoscunt . . . nec tamen efficis quominus credant homines per tuos libellos . . . pro libertate evangelica, contra tyrannidem humanam, hisce tumultibus fuisse datam occasionem." "And who will deny," adds a Protestant classic, "that the fault was partly owing to them?" (Planck, *Geschichte der protestantischen Kirche*, ii. 183).

destruction through the preachers of treason and blood."[1] He instantly turned from the people to the princes;[2] impressed on his party that character of political dependence, and that habit of passive obedience to the State, which it has ever since retained, and gave it a stability it could never otherwise have acquired. In thus taking refuge in the arms of the civil power, purchasing the safety of his doctrine by the sacrifice of its freedom, and conferring on the State, together with the right of control, the duty of imposing it at the point of the sword, Luther in reality reverted to his original teaching.[3] The notion of liberty, whether civil or religious, was hateful to his despotic nature, and contrary to his interpretation of Scripture. As early as 1519 he had said that even the Turk was to be reverenced as an authority.[4] The demoralising servitude and lawless oppression which the peasants endured, gave them, in his eyes, no right to relief; and when they rushed to arms, invoking his name as their deliverer, he exhorted the nobles to take a merciless revenge.[5] Their crime was, that they were animated by the sectarian spirit, which it was the most important interest of Luther to suppress.

[1] "Ich sehe das wohl, dass der Teufel, so er mich bisher nicht hat mögen umbringen durch den Pabst, sucht er mich durch die blutdürstigen Mordpropheten und Rottengeisten, so unter euch sind, zu vertilgen und auffressen" (*Werke*, xvi. 77).

[2] Schenkel, *Wesen des Protestantismus*, iii. 348, 351; Hagen, *Geist der Reformation*, ii. 146, 151; Menzel, *Neuere Geschichte der Deutschen*, i. 115.

[3] See the best of his biographies, Jürgens, *Luther's Leben*, iii. 601.

[4] "Quid hoc ad me? qui sciam etiam Turcam honorandum et ferendum potestatis gratia. Quia certus sum non nisi volente Deo ullam potestatem consistere" (De Wette, i. 236).

[5] "I beg first of all that you will not help to mollify Count Albert in these matters, but let him go on as he has begun. . . . Encourage him to go on briskly, to leave things in the hands of God, and obey His divine command to wield the sword as long as he can." "Do not allow yourselves to be much disturbed, for it will redound to the advantage of many souls that will be terrified by it, and preserved." "If there are innocent persons amongst them, God will surely save and preserve them, as He did with Lot and Jeremiah. If He does not, then they are certainly not innocent. . . . We must pray for them that they obey, otherwise this is no time for compassion; just let the guns deal with them." "Sentio melius esse omnes rusticos caedi quam principes et magistratus, eo quod rustici sine autoritate Dei gladium accipiunt. Quam nequitiam Satanae sequi non potest nisi mera Satanica vastitas regni Dei, et mundi principes etsi excedunt, tamen gladium autoritate Dei gerunt. Ibi utrumque regnum consistere potest, quare nulla misericordia, nulla patientia rusticis debetur, sed ira et indignatio Dei et hominum" (De Wette, ii. 653, 655, 666, 669, 671).

The Protestant authorities throughout Southern Germany were perplexed by their victory over the Anabaptists. It was not easy to show that their political tenets were revolutionary, and the only subversive portion of their doctrine was that they held, with the Catholics, that the State is not responsible for religion.[1] They were punished, therefore, because they taught that no man ought to suffer for his faith. At Nuremberg the magistrates did not know how to proceed against them. They seemed no worse than the Catholics, whom there was no question at that time of exterminating. The celebrated Osiander deemed these scruples inconsistent. The Papists, he said, ought also to be suppressed; and so long as this was not done, it was impossible to proceed to extremities against the Anabaptists, who were no worse than they. Luther also was consulted, and he decided that they ought not to be punished unless they refused to conform at the command of the Government.[2] The Margrave of Brandenburg was also advised by the divines that a heretic who could not be converted out of Scripture might be condemned; but that in his sentence nothing should be said about heresy, but only about sedition and murderous intent, though he should be guiltless of these.[3] With the aid of this artifice great numbers were put to death.

Luther's proud and ardent spirit despised such pretences. He had cast off all reserve, and spoke his mind openly on the rights and duties of the State towards the Church and the people. His first step was to proclaim

[1] "Wir lehren die christlich Obrigkeit möge nicht nur, sondern solle auch sich der Religion und Glaubenssachen mit Ernst annehmen; davon halten die Wiedertäufer steif das Widerspiel, welches sie auch zum Theil gemein haben mit den Prälaten der römischen Kirche" (Declaration of the Protestants, quoted in Jörg, *Deutschland von* 1522 *bis* 1526, p. 709).

[2] "As to your question, how they are to be punished, I do not consider them blasphemers, but regard them in the light of the Turks, or deluded Christians, whom the civil power has not to punish, at least bodily. But if they refuse to acknowledge and to obey the civil authority, then they forfeit all they have and are, for then sedition and murder are certainly in their hearts" (De Wette, ii. 622; Osiander's opinion in Jörg, p. 706).

[3] "Dass in dem Urtheil und desselben öffentlicher Verkündigung keines Irrthums oder Ketzereien . . . sondern allein der Aufruhr und fürgenommenen Morderei, die ihm doch laut seiner Urgicht nie lieb gewesen, gedacht werde' (Jörg, p. 708).

it the office of the civil power to prevent abominations.[1] He provided no security that, in discharging this duty, the sovereign should be guided by the advice of orthodox divines;[2] but he held the duty itself to be imperative. In obedience to the fundamental principle, that the Bible is the sole guide in all things, he defined the office and justified it by scriptural precedents. The Mosaic code, he argued, awarded to false prophets the punishment of death, and the majesty of God is not to be less deeply reverenced or less rigorously vindicated under the New Testament than under the Old; in a more perfect revelation the obligation is stronger. Those who will not hear the Church must be excluded from the communion; but the civil power is to intervene when the ecclesiastical excommunication has been pronounced, and men must be compelled to come in. For, according to the more accurate definition of the Church which is given in the Confession of Schmalkald, and in the Apology of the Confession of Augsburg, excommunication involves damnation. There is no salvation to be hoped for out of the Church, and the test of orthodoxy against the Pope, the devil, and all the world, is the dogma of justification by faith.[3]

The defence of religion became, on this theory, not only the duty of the civil power, but the object of its institution. Its business was solely the coercion of those who were out of the Church. The faithful could not be the objects of its action; they did of their own accord more than any laws required. "A good tree," says Luther, "brings forth good fruit by nature, without compulsion; is it not madness to prescribe laws to an apple-tree that it shall bear apples and not thorns?"[4] This view naturally proceeded from the axiom of the certainty of the salvation

[1] "Principes nostri non cogunt ad fidem et Evangelion, sed cohibent externas abominationes" (De Wette, iii. 50). "Wenn die weltliche Obrigkeit die Verbrechen wider die zweite Gesetzestafel bestrafen, und aus der menschlichen Gesellschaft tilgen solle, wie vielmehr denn die Verbrechen wider die erste?" (Luther, *apud* Bucholtz, *Geschichte Ferdinands I.*, iii. 571).

[2] Planck, iv. 61, explains why this was not thought of.

[3] Linde, *Staatskirche*, p. 23. "Der Papst sammt seinem Haufen glaubt nicht; darum bekennen wir, er werde nicht selig, das ist verdammt werden" (*Table-Talk*, ii. 350).

[4] Kaltenborn, *Vorläufer des Grotius*, 208.

of all who believe in the Confession of Augsburg.[1] It is the most important element in Luther's political system, because, while it made all Protestant governments despotic, it led to the rejection of the authority of Catholic governments. This is the point where Protestant and Catholic intolerance meet. If the State were instituted to promote the faith, no obedience could be due to a State of a different faith. Protestants could not conscientiously be faithful subjects of Catholic Powers, and they could not therefore be tolerated. Misbelievers would have no rights under an orthodox State, and a misbelieving prince would have no authority over orthodox subjects. The more, therefore, Luther expounded the guilt of resistance and the Divine sanction of authority, the more subversive his influence became in Catholic countries. His system was alike revolutionary, whether he defied the Catholic powers or promoted a Protestant tyranny. He had no notion of political right. He found no authority for such a claim in the New Testament, and he held that righteousness does not need to exhibit itself in works.

It was the same helpless dependence on the letter of Scripture which led the reformers to consequences more subversive of Christian morality than their views on questions of polity. When Carlstadt cited the Mosaic law in defence of polygamy, Luther was indignant. If the Mosaic law is to govern everything, he said, we should be compelled to adopt circumcision.[2] Nevertheless, as there is no prohibition of polygamy in the New Testament, the reformers were unable to condemn it. They did not forbid it as a matter of Divine law, and referred it entirely to the decision of the civil legislator.[3] This, accordingly

[1] Möhler, *Symbolik*, 428.

[2] "Quodsi unam legem Mosi cogimur servare, eadem ratione et circumcidemur, et totam legem servare oportebit. . . . Nunc vero non sumus amplius sub lege Mosi, sed subjecti legibus civilibus in talibus rebus" (Luther to Barnes, Sept. 5, 1531; De Wette, iv. 296).

[3] "All things that we find done by the patriarchs in the Old Testament ought to be free and not forbidden. Circumcision is abolished, but not so that it would be a sin to perform it, but optional, neither sinful nor acceptable. . . . In like manner it is not forbidden that a man should have more than one wife. Even at the present day I could not prohibit it; but I would not recommend it"

was the view which guided Luther and Melanchthon in treating the problem, the ultimate solution of which was the separation of England from the Church.[1] When the Landgrave Philip afterwards appealed to this opinion, and to the earlier commentaries of Luther, the reformers were compelled to approve his having two wives. Melanchthon was a witness at the wedding of the second, and the only reservation was a request that the matter should not be allowed to get abroad.[2] It was the same portion of Luther's theology, and the same opposition to the spirit of the Church in the treatment of Scripture, that induced him to believe in astrology and to ridicule the Copernican system.[3]

(Commentary on Genesis, 1528; see Jarcke, *Studien*, p. 108). "Ego sane fateor, me non posse prohibere, siquis plures velit uxores ducere, nec repugnat sacris literis: verum tamen apud Christianos id exempli nollem primo introduci, apud quos decet etiam ea intermittere, quae licita sunt, pro vitando scandalo, et pro honestate vitae" (De Wette, ii. 459, Jan. 13, 1524). "From these instances of bigamy (Lamech, Jacob) no rule can be drawn for our times; and such examples have no power with us Christians, for we live under our authorities, and are subject to our civil laws" (*Table-Talk*, v. 64).

[1] "Antequam tale repudium, probarem potius regi permitterem alteram reginam quoque ducere, et exemplo patrum et regum duas simul uxores seu reginas habere. . . . Si peccavit ducendo uxorem fratris mortui, peccavit in legem humanam seu civilem; si autem repudiaverit, peccabit in legem mere divinam" (De Wette, iv. 296). "Haud dubio rex Angliae uxorem fratris mortui ductam retinere potest . . . docendus quod has res politicas commiserit Deus magistratibus, neque nos alligaverit ad Moisen. . . . Si vult rex successioni prospicere, quanto satius est, id facere sine infamia prioris conjugii. Ac potest id fieri sine ullo periculo conscientiae cujuscunque aut famae per polygamiam. Etsi enim non velim concedere polygamiam vulgo, dixi enim supra, nos non ferre leges, tamen in hoc casu propter magnam utilitatem regni, fortassis etiam propter conscientiam regis, ita pronuncio: tutissimum esse regi, si ducat secundam uxorem, priore non abjecta, quia certum est polygamiam non esse prohibitam jure divino, nec res est omnino inusitata" (*Melanthonis Opera*, ed. Bretschneider, ii. 524, 526). "Nolumus esse auctores divortii, cum conjugium cum jure divino non pugnet. Hi, qui diversum pronunciant, terribiliter exaggerant et exasperant jus divinum. Nos contra exaggeramus in rebus politicis auctoritatem magistratus, quae profecto non est levis, multaque justa sunt propter magistratus auctoritatem, quae alioqui in dubium vocantur" (Melanchthon to Bucer, Bretschneider, ii. 552).

[2] "Suadere non possumus ut introducatur publice et velut lege sanciatur permissio, plures quam unam uxores ducendi. . . . Primum ante omnia cavendum, ne haec res inducatur in orbem ad modum legis, quam sequendi libera omnibus sit potestas. Deinde considerare dignetur vestra celsitudo scandalum, nimirum quod Evangelio hostes exclamaturi sint, nos similes esse Anabaptistis, qui plures simul duxerunt uxores" (De Wette, v. 236. Signed by Luther, Melanchthon, and Bucer).

[3] "He that would appear wise will not be satisfied with anything that others do; he must do something for himself, and that must be better than anything. This fool (Copernicus) wants to overturn the whole science of astronomy. But, as the holy Scriptures tell us, Joshua told the sun to stand still, and not the earth" (*Table-Talk*, iv. 575).

His view of the authority of Scripture and his theory of justification both precluded him from appreciating freedom. "Christian freedom," he said, "consists in the belief that we require no works to attain piety and salvation."[1] Thus he became the inventor of the theory of passive obedience, according to which no motives or provocation can justify a revolt; and the party against whom the revolt is directed, whatever its guilt may be, is to be preferred to the party revolting, however just its cause.[2] In 1530 he therefore declared that the German princes had no right to resist the Emperor in defence of their religion. "It was the duty of a Christian," he said, "to suffer wrong, and no breach of oath or of duty could deprive the Emperor of his right to the unconditional obedience of his subjects."[3] Even the empire seemed to him a despotism, from his scriptural belief that it was a continuation of the last of the four monarchies.[4] He preferred submission, in the hope of seeing a future Protestant Emperor, to a resistance which might have dismembered the empire if it had succeeded, and in which failure would have been fatal to the Protestants; and he was always afraid to draw the logical consequences of his theory of the duty of Protestants towards Catholic sovereigns. In consequence of this fact, Ranke affirms that the great reformer was also one of the greatest conservatives that ever lived; and his biographer, Jürgens, makes the more discriminating remark that history knows of no man who was at once so great an insurgent and so great

[1] "Das ist die christliche Freiheit, der einige Glaube, der da macht, nicht dass wir müssig gehen oder übel thun mögen, sondern dass wir keines Werks bedürfen, die Frömmigkeit und Seligkeit zu erlangen" (*Sermon von der Freiheit*). A Protestant historian, who quotes this passage, goes on to say: "On the other hand, the body must be brought under discipline by every means, in order that it may obey and not burden the inner man. Outward servitude, therefore, assists the progress towards internal freedom" (Bensen, *Geschichte des Bauernkriegs*, 269.)

[2] *Werke*, x. 413.

[3] "According to Scripture, it is by no means proper that one who would be a Christian should set himself against his superiors, whether by God's permission they act justly or unjustly. But a Christian must suffer violence and wrong, especially from his superiors. . . . As the emperor continues emperor, and princes princes, though they transgress all God's commandments, yea, even if they be heathen, so they do even when they do not observe their oath and duty. . . . Sin does not suspend authority and allegiance" (De Wette, iii. 560).

[4] Ranke, *Reformation*, iii. 183.

an upholder of order as he.[1] Neither of these writers understood that the same principle lies at the root both of revolution and of passive obedience, and that the difference is only in the temper of the person who applies it, and in the outward circumstances.

Luther's theory is apparently in opposition to Protestant interests, for it entitles Catholicism to the protection of Catholic Powers. He disguised from himself this inconsistency, and reconciled theory with expediency by the calculation that the immense advantages which his system offered to the princes would induce them all to adopt it. For, besides the consolatory doctrine of justification,—"a doctrine original, specious, persuasive, powerful against Rome, and wonderfully adapted, as if prophetically, to the genius of the times which were to follow,"[2]—he bribed the princes with the wealth of the Church, independence of ecclesiastical authority, facilities for polygamy, and absolute power. He told the peasants not to take arms against the Church unless they could persuade the Government to give the order; but thinking it probable, in 1522, that the Catholic clergy would, in spite of his advice, be exterminated by the fury of the people, he urged the Government to suppress them, because what was done by the constituted authority could not be wrong.[3] Persuaded that the sovereign power would be on his side, he allowed no limits to its extent. It is absurd, he says, to imagine that, even with the best intentions, kings can avoid committing occasional injustice; they stand, therefore, particularly in need—not of safeguards against the abuse of power, but—of the forgiveness of sins.[4] The power thus concentrated in the hands of the rulers for the guardianship of the faith, he wished to be used with the utmost severity against

[1] Ranke, iv. 7; Jürgens, iii. 601.

[2] Newman, *Lectures on Justification*, p. 386.

[3] "Was durch ordentliche Gewalt geschieht, ist nicht für Aufruhr zu halten" (Bensen, p. 269; Jarcke, *Studien*, p. 312; Janet, ii. 40).

[4] "Princes, and all rulers and governments, however pious and God-fearing they may be, cannot be without sin in their office and temporal administration. . . . They cannot always be so exactly just and successful as some wiseacres suppose; therefore they are above all in need of the forgiveness of sins" (see Kaltenborn, p. 209).

unregenerate men, in whom there was neither moral virtue nor civil rights, and from whom no good could come until they were converted. He therefore required that all crimes should be most cruelly punished and that the secular arm should be employed to convert where it did not destroy. The idea of mercy tempering justice he denounced as a Popish superstition.[1]

The chief object of the severity thus recommended was, of course, efficaciously to promote the end for which Government itself was held to be instituted. The clergy had authority over the conscience, but it was thought necessary that they should be supported by the State with the absolute penalties of outlawry, in order that error might be exterminated, although it was impossible to banish sin.[2] No Government, it was maintained, could tolerate heresy without being responsible for the souls that were seduced by it;[3] and as Ezechiel destroyed the brazen serpent to prevent idolatry, the mass must be suppressed, for the mass was the worst kind of idolatry.[4] In 1530, when it was proposed to leave the matters in dispute to the decision of the future Council, Luther declared that the mass and monastic life could not be tolerated in the meantime, because it was unlawful to connive at error.[5] "It will lie heavy on your conscience," he writes to the Duke of Saxony, "if you tolerate the Catholic worship; for no secular prince can permit his

1 "Of old, under the Papacy, princes and lords, and all judges, were very timid in shedding blood, and punishing robbers, murderers, thieves, and all manner of evil-doers; for they knew not how to distinguish a private individual who is not in office from one in office, charged with the duty of punishing. . . . The executioner had always to do penance, and to apologise beforehand to the convicted criminal for what he was going to do to him, just as if it was sinful and wrong." "Thus they were persuaded by monks to be gracious, indulgent, and peaceable. But authorities, princes and lords ought not to be merciful" (*Table-Talk*, iv. 159, 160).

2 "Den weltlichen Bann sollten Könige und Kaiser wieder aufrichten, denn wir können ihn jetzt nicht anrichten. . . . Aber so wir nicht können die Sünde des Lebens bannen und strafen, so bannen wir doch die Sünde der Lehre" (Bruns, *Luther's Predigten*, 63).

3 "Wo sie solche Rottengeister würden zulassen und leiden, so sie es doch wehren und vorkommen können, würden sie ihre Gewissen gräulich beschweren, und vielleicht nimmermehr widder stillen können, nicht allein der Seelen halben, die dadurch verführt und verdammt werden . . . sondern auch der ganzen heiligen Kirchen halben" (De Wette, iv. 355).

4 "Nu ist alle Abgötterey gegen die Messe ein geringes" (De Wette, v. 191; sec. iv. 307)

5 Bucholtz, iii. 570.

subjects to be divided by the preaching of opposite doctrines. The Catholics have no right to complain, for they do not prove the truth of their doctrine from Scripture, and therefore do not conscientiously believe it."[1] He would tolerate them only if they acknowledged themselves, like the Jews, enemies of Christ and of the Emperor, and consented to exist as outcasts of society.[2] "Heretics," he said, "are not to be disputed with, but to be condemned unheard, and whilst they perish by fire, the faithful ought to pursue the evil to its source, and bathe their hands in the blood of the Catholic bishops, and of the Pope, who is a devil in disguise."[3]

The persecuting principles which were involved in Luther's system, but which he cared neither to develop, to apply, nor to defend, were formed into a definite theory by the colder genius of Melanchthon. Destitute of Luther's confidence in his own strength, and in the infallible success of his doctrine, he clung more eagerly to the hope of achieving victory by the use of physical force. Like his master he too hesitated at first, and opposed the use of severe measures against the Zwickau prophets; but when he saw the development of that early germ of dissent, and the gradual dissolution of Lutheran unity, he repented of his ill-timed clemency.[4] He was not deterred from asserting the duty of persecution by the risk of putting arms into the hands of the enemies of the Reformation. He acknowledged the danger, but he denied the right. Catholic powers, he deemed, might justly persecute, but they could only persecute error. They must apply the same criterion which the Lutherans applied,

[1] "Sie aber verachten die Schrift muthwilliglich, darum wären sie billig aus der einigen Ursach zu stillen, oder nicht zu leiden" (De Wette, iii. 90).

[2] "Wollen sie aber wie die Juden seyn, nicht Christen heissen, noch Kaisers Glieder, sondern sich lassen Christus und Kaisers Feinde nennen, wie die Juden; wohlan, so wollen wir's auch leiden, dass sie in ihren Synagogen, wie die Juden, verschlossen lästern, so lang sie wollen" (De Wette, iv. 94).

[3] Riffel, *Kirchengeschichte*, ii. 9; *Table-Talk*, iii. 175.

[4] "Ego ab initio, cum primum caepi nosse Ciconiam et Ciconiae factionem, unde hoc totum genus Anabaptistarum exortum est, fui stulte clemens. Sentiebant enim et alii haereticos non esse ferro opprimendos. Et tunc dux Fridericus vehementer iratus erat Ciconiae: ac nisi a nobis tectus esset, fuisset de homine furioso et perdite malo sumtum supplicium. Nunc me ejus clementiae non parum poenitet. . . . Brentius nimis clemens est" (Bretschneider, ii. 17. Feb. 1530).

and then they were justified in persecuting those whom the Lutherans also proscribed. For the civil power had no right to proscribe a religion in order to save itself from the dangers of a distracted and divided population. The judge of the fact and of the danger must be, not the magistrate, but the clergy.[1] The crime lay, not in dissent, but in error. Here, therefore, Melanchthon repudiated the theory and practice of the Catholics, whose aid he invoked; for all the intolerance in the Catholic times was founded on the combination of two ideas—the criminality of apostasy, and the inability of the State to maintain its authority where the moral sense of a part of the community was in opposition to it. The reformers, therefore, approved the Catholic practice of intolerance, and even encouraged it, although their own principles of persecution were destitute not only of connection, but even of analogy, with it. By simply accepting the inheritance of the mediæval theory of the religious unity of the empire, they would have been its victims. By asserting that persecution was justifiable only against error, that is, only when purely religious, they set up a shield for themselves, and a sword against those sects for whose destruction they were more eager than the Catholics. Whether we refer the origin of Protestant intolerance to the doctrines or to the interests of the Reformation, it appears totally unconnected with the tradition of Catholic ages, or the atmosphere of Catholicism. All severities exercised by Catholics before that time had a practical motive; but Protestant persecution was based on a purely speculative foundation, and was due partly to the influence of Scripture examples, partly to the supposed interests of the Protestant party. It never admitted the exclusion of dissent to be a political right of the State, but maintained

[1] "Sed objiciunt exemplum nobis periculosum: si haec pertinent ad magistratus, quoties igitur magistratus judicabit aliquos errare, saeviet in eos. Caesar igitur debet nos opprimere, quoniam ita judicat nos errare. Respondeo: certe debet errores et prohibere et punire. . . . Non est enim solius Caesaris cognitio, sicut in urbibus haec cognitio non est tantum magistratus prophani, sed est doctorum. Viderit igitur magistratus ut recte judicet" (Bretschneider, ii. 712). "Deliberent igitur principes, non cum tyrannis, non cum pontificibus, non cum hypocritis, monachis aut aliis, sed cum ipsa Evangelii voce, cum probatis scriptoribus" (Bretschneider, iii. 254).

the suppression of error to be its political duty. To say, therefore, that the Protestants learnt persecution from the Catholics, is as false as to say that they used it by way of revenge. For they founded it on very different and contradictory grounds, and they admitted the right of the Catholics to persecute even the Protestant sects.

Melanchthon taught that the sects ought to be put down by the sword, and that any individual who started new opinions ought to be punished with death.[1] He carefully laid down that these severities were requisite, not in consideration of the danger to the State, nor of immoral teaching, nor even of such differences as would weaken the authority or arrest the action of the ecclesiastical organisation, but simply on account of a difference, however slight, in the theologumena of Protestantism.[2] Thamer, who held the possibility of salvation among the

[1] "Quare ita sentias, magistratum debere uti summa severitate in coercendis hujusmodi spiritibus. . . . Sines igitur novis exemplis timorem incuti multitudini . . . ad haec notae tibi sint causae seditionum, quas gladio prohiberi oportet. . . . Propterea sentio de his qui etiamsi non defendunt seditiosos articulos, habent manifeste blasphemos, quod interfici a magistratu debeant" (ii. 17, 18). "De Anabaptistis tulimus hic in genere sententiam: quia constat sectam diabolicam esse, non esse tolerandam: dissipari enim ecclesias per eos, cum ipsi nullam habeant certam doctrinam. . . . Ideo in capita factionum in singulis locis ultima supplicia constituenda esse judicavimus" (ii. 549). "It is clear that it is the duty of secular government to punish blasphemy, false doctrine, and heresy, on the bodies of those who are guilty of them. . . . Since it is evident that there are gross errors in the articles of the Anabaptist sect, we conclude that in this case the obstinate ought to be punished with death" (iii. 199). "Propter hanc causam Deus ordinavit politias ut Evangelium propagari possit . . . nec revocamus politiam Moysi, sed lex moralis perpetua est omnium aetatum . . . quandocumque constat doctrinam esse impiam, nihil dubium est quin sanior pars Ecclesiae debeat malos pastores removere et abolere impios cultus. Et hanc emendationem praecipue adjuvare debent magistratus, tanquam potiora membra Ecclesiae" (iii. 242, 244). "Thammerus, qui Mahometicas seu Ethnicas opiniones spargit, vagatur in dioecesi Mindensi, quem publicis suppliciis adficere debebant. . . . Evomuit blasphemias, quae refutandae sunt non tantum disputatione aut scriptis, sed etiam justo officio pii magistratus" (ix. 125, 131).

[2] "Voco autem blasphemos qui articulos habent, qui proprie non pertinent ad civilem statum, sed continent θεωρίας ut de divinitate Christi et similes. Etsi enim gradus quidam sunt, tamen huc etiam refero baptismum infantum. . . . Quia magistratui commissa est tutela totius legis, quod attinet ad externam disciplinam et externa facta. Quare delicta externa contra primam tabulam prohibere ac punire debet. . . . Quare non solum concessum est, sed etiam mandatum est magistratui, impias doctrinas abolere, et tueri pias in suis ditionibus" (ii. 711). "Ecclesiastica potestas tantum judicat et excommunicat haereticos, non occidit. Sed potestas civilis debet constituere poenas et supplicia in haereticos, sicut in blasphemos constituit supplicia. . . . Non enim plectitur fides, sed haeresis" (xii. 697).

heathen; Schwenkfeld, who taught that not the written Word, but the internal illumination of grace in the soul was the channel of God's influence on man; the Zwinglians, with their error on the Eucharist, all these met with no more favour than the fanatical Anabaptists.[1] The State was held bound to vindicate the first table of the law with the same severity as those commandments on which civil society depends for its existence. The government of the Church being administered by the civil magistrates, it was their office also to enforce the ordinances of religion; and the same power whose voice proclaimed religious orthodoxy and law held in its hand the sword by which they were enforced. No religious authority existed except through the civil power.[2] The Church was merged in the State; but the laws of the State, in return, were identified with the commandments of religion.[3]

In accordance with these principles, the condemnation of Servetus by a civil tribunal, which had no authority over him, and no jurisdiction over his crime—the most aggressive and revolutionary act, therefore, that is conceivable in the casuistry of persecution — was highly approved by Melanchthon. He declared it a most useful example for all future ages, and could not understand that there should be any who did not regard it in the same favourable light.[4] It is true that Servetus,

[1] "Notum est etiam, quosdam tetra et δύσφημα dixisse de sanguine Christi, quos puniri oportuit, et propter gloriam Christi, et exempli causa" (viii. 553). "Argumentatur ille praestigiator (Schwenkfeld), verbum externum non esse medium, quo Deus est efficax. Talis sophistica principum severitate compescenda erat" (ix. 579).

[2] "The office of preacher is distinct from that of governor, yet both have to contribute to the praise of God. Princes are not only to protect the goods and bodily life of their subjects, but the principal function is to promote the honour of God, and to prevent idolatry and blasphemy" (iii. 199). "Errant igitur magistratus, qui divellunt gubernationem a fine, et se tantum pacis ac ventris custodes esse existimant. . . . At si tantum venter curandus esset, quid differrent principes ab armentariis? Nam longe aliter sentiendum est. Politias divinitus admirabili sapientia et bonitate constitutas esse, non tantum ad quaerenda et fruenda ventris bona, sed multo magis, ut Deus in societate innotescat, ut aeterna bona quaerantur" (iii. 246).

[3] "Neque illa barbarica excusatio audienda est, leges illas pertinere ad politiam Mosaicam, non ad nostram. Ut Decalogus ipse ad omnes pertinet, ita judex ubique omnia Decalogi officia in externa disciplina tueatur" (viii. 520).

[4] "Legi scriptum tuum, in quo refutasti luculenter horrendas Serveti

by denying the divinity of Christ, was open to the charge of blasphemy in a stricter sense than that in which the reformers generally applied it. But this was not the case with the Catholics. They did not represent, like the sects, an element of dissolution in Protestantism, and the bulk of their doctrine was admitted by the reformers. They were not in revolt against existing authority; they required no special innovations for their protection; they demanded only that the change of religion should not be compulsory. Yet Melanchthon held that they too were to be proscribed, because their worship was idolatrous.[1] In doing this he adopted the principle of aggressive intolerance, which was at that time new to the Christian world; and which the Popes and Councils of the Catholic Church had condemned when the zeal of laymen had gone beyond the lawful measure. In the Middle Ages there had been persecution far more sanguinary than any that has been inflicted by Protestants. Various motives had occasioned it and various arguments had been used in its defence. But the principle on which the Protestants oppressed the Catholics was new. The Catholics had never admitted the theory of absolute toleration, as it was defined at first by Luther, and afterwards by some of the sects. In principle, their tolerance differed from that of the Protestants as widely as their intolerance. They had exterminated sects which, like the Albigenses, threatened to overturn the fabric of Christian society. They had

blasphemias, ac filio Dei gratias ago, qui fuit βραβευτὴς hujus tui agonis. Tibi quoque Ecclesia et nunc et ad posteros gratitudinem debet et debebit. Tuo judicio prorsus adsentior. Affirmo etiam, vestros magistratus juste fecisse, quod hominem blasphemum, re ordine judicata, interfecerunt" (Melanchthon to Calvin, Bretschneider, viii. 362). "Judico etiam Senatum Genevensem recte fecisse, quod hominem pertinacem et non omissurum blasphemias sustulit. Ac miratus sum, esse, qui severitatem illam improbent" (viii. 523). "Dedit vero et Genevensis reip. magistratus ante annos quatuor punitae insanabilis blasphemiae adversus filium Dei, sublato Serveto Arragone pium et memorabile ad omnem posteritatem exemplum" (ix. 133).

[1] "Abusus missae per magistratus debet tolli. Non aliter, atque sustulit aeneum serpentem Ezechias, aut excelsa demolitus est Josias" (i. 480). "Politicis magistratibus severissime mandatum est, ut suo quisque loco manibus et armis tollant statuas, ad quas fiunt hominum concursus et invocationes, et puniant suppliciis corporum insanabiles, qui idolorum cultum pertinaciter retinent, aut blasphemias serunt" (ix. 77).

proscribed different religions where the State was founded on religious unity, and where this unity formed an integral part of its laws and administration. They had gone one step further, and punished those whom the Church condemned as apostates; thereby vindicating, not, as in the first case, the moral basis of society, nor, as in the second, the religious foundation of the State, but the authority of the Church and the purity of her doctrine, on which they relied as the pillar and bulwark of the social and political order. Where a portion of the inhabitants of any country preferred a different creed Jew, Mohammedan, heathen, or schismatic, they had been generally tolerated, with enjoyment of property and personal freedom, but not with that of political power or autonomy. But political freedom had been denied them because they did not admit the common ideas of duty which were its basis. This position, however, was not tenable, and was the source of great disorders. The Protestants, in like manner, could give reasons for several kinds of persecution. They could bring the Socinians under the category of blasphemers; and blasphemy, like the ridicule of sacred things, destroys reverence and awe, and tends to the destruction of society. The Anabaptists, they might argue, were revolutionary fanatics, whose doctrines were subversive of the civil order; and the dogmatic sects threatened the ruin of ecclesiastical unity within the Protestant community itself. But by placing the necessity of intolerance on the simple ground of religious error, and in directing it against the Church which they themselves had abandoned, they introduced a purely subjective test, and a purely revolutionary system. It is on this account that the *tu quoque*, or retaliatory argument, is inadmissible between Catholics and Protestants. Catholic intolerance is handed down from an age when unity subsisted, and when its preservation, being essential for that of society, became a necessity of State as well as a result of circumstances. Protestant intolerance, on the contrary was the peculiar fruit of a dogmatic system in contradiction with the facts and principles on which the intolerance actually existing among Catholics was founded. Spanish intolerance has been infinitely more sanguinary than Swedish; but in Spain, independently of the interests of religion, there were strong political and social reasons to justify persecution without seeking any theory to prop it up; whilst in Sweden all those practical considerations have either been wanting, or have been opposed to persecution, which has consequently had no justification except the theory of the Reformation. The only instance in which the Protestant theory has been adopted by Catholics is the revocation of the Edict of Nantes.

Towards the end of his life, Melanchthon, having ceased to be a strict Lutheran, receded somewhat from his former uncompromising position, and was adverse to a strict scrutiny into minor theological differences. He drew a distinction between errors that required punishment and variations that were not of practical importance.[1] The English Calvinists who took refuge in Germany in the reign of Mary Tudor were ungraciously received by those who were stricter Lutherans than Melanchthon. He was consulted concerning the course to be adopted towards the refugees, and he recommended toleration. But both at Wesel and at Frankfort his advice was, to his great disgust, overruled.[2]

[1] "If the French and English community at Frankfort shared the errors of Servetus or Thamer, or other enemies of the Symbols, or the errors of the Anabaptists on infant baptism, against the authority of the State, etc., I should faithfully advise and strongly recommend that they should be soon driven away; for the civil power is bound to prevent and to punish proved blasphemy and sedition. But I find that this community is orthodox in the symbolical articles on the Son of God, and in other articles of the Symbol. . . . If the faith of the citizens in every town were inquired into, what trouble and confusion would not arise in many countries and towns!" (ix. 179).

[2] Schmidt, *Philipp Melanchthon*, p. 640. His exhortations to the Landgrave to put down the Zwinglians are characteristic: "The Zwinglians, without waiting for the Council, persecute the Papists and the Anabaptists; why must it be wrong for others to prohibit their indefensible doctrine independent of the Council?" Philip replied: "Forcibly, to prohibit a doctrine which neither contradicts the articles of faith nor encourages sedition, I do not think right. . . . When Luther began to write and to preach, he admonished and instructed the Government that it had no right to forbid books or to prevent preaching, and that its office did not extend so far, but that it had only to govern the body and goods. . . . I had not heard before that the Zwinglians persecute the Papists; but if they abolish

The severities of the Protestants were chiefly provoked by the Anabaptists, who denied the lawfulness of civil government, and strove to realise the kingdom of God on earth by absorbing the State in the Church.[1] None protested more loudly than they against the Lutheran intolerance, or suffered from it more severely. But while denying the spiritual authority of the State, they claimed for their religious community a still more absolute right of punishing error by death. Though they sacrificed government to religion, the effect was the same as that of absorbing the Church in the State. In 1524 Münzer published a sermon, in which he besought the Lutheran princes to extirpate Catholicism. "Have no remorse," he says; "for He to whom all power is given in heaven and on earth means to govern alone."[2] He demanded the punishment of all heretics, the destruction of all who were not of his faith, and the institution of religious unity. "Do not pretend," he says, "that the power of God will accomplish it without the use of your sword, or it will grow rusty in the scabbard. The tree that bringeth not forth good fruit must be cut down and cast into the fire." And elsewhere, "the ungodly have no right to live, except so far as the elect choose to grant it them."[3] When the Anabaptists were supreme at Münster, they exhibited the same intolerance. At seven in the morning of Friday, 27th February 1534, they ran through the streets crying, "Away with the ungodly!" Breaking into the houses of those who refused their baptism, they drove the men out of the town, and forcibly rebaptized the women who remained behind.[4] Whilst, therefore, the Anabaptists

abuses, it is not unjust, for the Papists wish to deserve heaven by their works, and so blaspheme the Son of God. That they should persecute the Anabaptists is also not wrong, for their doctrine is in part seditious." The divines answered: "If by God's grace our true and necessary doctrine is tolerated as it has hitherto been by the emperor, though reluctantly, we think that we ought not to prevent it by undertaking the defence of the Zwinglian doctrine, if that should not be tolerated. . . . As to the argument that we ought to spare the people while persecuting the leaders, our answer is, that it is not a question of persons, but only of doctrine, whether it be true or false" (Correspondence of Brenz and Melanchthon with Landgrave Philip of Hesse, Bretschneider, ii. 95, 98, 101).

[1] Hardwicke, *Reformation*, p. 274.

[2] Seidemann, *Thomas Münzer*, p. 35.

[3] Schenkel, iii. 381.

[4] Heinrich Grosbeck's *Bericht*, ed. Cornelius, 19.

were punished for questioning the authority of the Lutherans in religious matters, they practically justified their persecution by their own intolerant doctrines. In fact, they carried the Protestant principles of persecution to an extreme. For whereas the Lutherans regarded the defence of truth and punishment of error as being, in part, the object of the institution of civil government, they recognised it as an advantage by which the State was rewarded for its pains; but the Anabaptists repudiated the political element altogether, and held that error should be exterminated solely for the sake of truth, and at the expense of all existing States.

Bucer, whose position in the history of the Reformation is so peculiar, and who differed in important points from the Saxon leaders, agreed with them on the necessity of persecuting. He was so anxious for the success of Protestantism, that he was ready to sacrifice and renounce important doctrines, in order to save the appearance of unity;[1] but those opinions in which he took so little dogmatic interest, he was resolved to defend by force. He was very much dissatisfied with the reluctance of the Senate of Strasburg to adopt severe measures against the Catholics. His colleague Capito was singularly tolerant; for the feeling of the inhabitants was not decidedly in favour of the change.[2] But Bucer, his biographer tells us, was, in spite of his inclination to mediate, not friendly to this temporising system; partly because he had an organising intellect, which relied greatly on practical discipline to preserve what had been conquered, and on restriction of liberty to be the most certain security for its preservation; partly because he had a deep insight into the nature of various religious tendencies, and was justly alarmed at their consequences for Church and State.[3] This point in the character of Bucer provoked a powerful resistance to his system of ecclesiastical discipline, for it was feared that he

[1] Herzog, *Encyclopädie für protestantische Theologie*, ii. 418.
[2] Bussierre, *Establissement du Protestantisme en Alsace*, p. 429.
[3] Baum, *Capito und Butzer*, p. 489.

would give to the clergy a tyrannical power.[1] It is true that the demoralisation which ensued on the destruction of the old ecclesiastical authority rendered a strict attention on the part of the State to the affairs of religion highly necessary.[2] The private and confidential communications of the German reformers give a more hideous picture of the moral condition of the generation which followed the Reformation than they draw in their published writings of that which preceded it. It is on this account that Bucer so strongly insisted on the necessity of the interference of the civil power in support of the discipline of the Church.

The Swiss reformers, between whom and the Saxons Bucer forms a connecting link, differ from them in one respect, which greatly influenced their notions of government. Luther lived under a monarchy which was almost absolute, and in which the common people, who were of Slavonic origin, were in the position of the most abject servitude; but the divines of Zürich and Bern were republicans. They did not therefore entertain his exalted views as to the irresistible might of the State; and instead of requiring as absolute a theory of the indefectibility of the civil power as he did, they were satisfied with obtaining a preponderating influence for themselves. Where the power was in hands less favourable to their cause, they had less inducement to exaggerate its rights.

Zwingli abolishes both the distinction between Church and State and the notion of ecclesiastical authority. In his system the civil rulers possess the spiritual functions; and, as their foremost duty is the preservation and promotion of the true religion, it is their business to preach. As magistrates are too much occupied with other things, they must delegate the ministry of the word to preachers, for whose orthodoxy they have to provide. They are bound to establish uniformity of doctrine, and to defend it

[1] Baum, p. 492; Erbkam, *Protestantische Sekten*, p. 581.

[2] Ursinus writes to Bullinger: "Liberavit nos Deus ab idolatria: succedit licentia infinita et horribilis divini nominis, ecclesiae doctrinae purioris et sacramentorum prophanatio et sub pedibus porcorum et canum, conniventibus atque utinam non defendentibus iis qui prohibere suo loco debebant, conculcatio" (Sudhoff, *Olevianus und Ursinus*, p. 340).

against Papists and heretics. This is not only their right, but their duty; and not only their duty, but the condition on which they retain office.[1] Rulers who do not act in accordance with it are to be dismissed. Thus Zwingli combined persecution and revolution in the same doctrine. But he was not a fanatical persecutor, and his severity was directed less against the Catholics than against the Anabaptists,[2] whose prohibition of all civil offices was more subversive of order in a republic than in a monarchy. Even, however, in the case of the Anabaptists the special provocation was—not the peril to the State, nor the scandal of their errors, but—the schism which weakened the Church.[3] The punishment of heresy for the glory of God was almost inconsistent with the theory that there is no ecclesiastical power. It was not so much provoked in Zürich as elsewhere, because in a small republican community, where the governing body was supreme over both civil and religious affairs, religious unity was a matter of course. The practical necessity of maintaining unity put out of sight the speculative question of the guilt and penalty of error.

Soon after Zwingli's death, Leo Judæ called for severer measures against the Catholics, expressly stating, however, that they did not deserve death. "Excommunication," he said, "was too light a punishment to be inflicted by the State which wields the sword, and the faults in question were not great enough to involve the danger of death."[4] Afterwards he fell into doubts as to the propriety of severe measures against dissenters, but his friends Bullinger and Capito succeeded in removing his scruples, and in obtaining his acquiescence in that intolerance, which was, says his biographer, a question of life and death for the Protestant Church.[5] Bullinger took, like Zwingli, a

[1] "Adserere audemus, neminem magistratum recte gerere ne posse quidem, nisi Christianus sit" (Zuingli, *Opera*, iii. 296). "If they shall proceed in an unbrotherly way, and against the ordinance of Christ, then let them be deposed, in God's name" (Schenkel, iii. 362).

[2] Christoffel, *Huldreich Zwingli*, p. 251.

[3] Zwingli's advice to the Protestants of St. Gall, in Pressel, *Joachim Vadian*, p. 45.

[4] Pestalozzi, *Heinrich Bullinger*, p. 95.

[5] *Ibid.*, *Leo Judä*, p. 50.

more practical view of the question than was common in Germany. He thought it safer strictly to exclude religious differences than to put them down with fire and sword; "for in this case," he says, "the victims compare themselves to the early martyrs, and make their punishment a weapon of defence."[1] He did not, however, forbid capital punishment in cases of heresy. In the year 1535 he drew up an opinion on the treatment of religious error, which is written in a tone of great moderation. In this document he says "that all sects which introduce division into the Church must be put down, and not only such as, like the Anabaptists, threaten to subvert society, for the destruction of order and unity often begins in an apparently harmless or imperceptible way. The culprit should be examined with gentleness. If his disposition is good he will not refuse instruction; if not, still patience must be shown until there is no hope of converting him. Then he must be treated like other malefactors, and handed over to the torturer and the executioner."[2] After this time there were no executions for religion in Zürich, and the number, even in the lifetime of Zwingli, was less considerable than in many other places. But it was still understood that confirmed heretics would be put to death. In 1546, in answer to the Pope's invitation to the Council of Trent, Bullinger indignantly repudiates the insinuation that the Protestant cantons were heretical, "for, by the grace of God, we have always punished the vices of heresy and sodomy with fire, and have looked upon them, and still look upon them, with horror."[3] This accusation of heresy inflamed the zeal of the reformers against heretics, in order to prove to the Catholics that they had no sympathy with them. On these grounds Bullinger recommended the execution of Servetus. "If the high Council inflicts on him the fate due to a worthless blasphemer, all the world will see that the people of Geneva hate blasphemers, and that they punish with the sword of justice heretics who are obstinate in their heresy. . . . Strict fidelity and vigilance are needed, because our

[1] Pestalozzi, *Heinrich Bullinger*, p. 146. [2] *Ibid.* p. 149. [3] *Ibid.* p. 270.

churches are in ill repute abroad, as if we were heretics and friends of heresy. Now God's holy providence has furnished an opportunity of clearing ourselves of this evil suspicion."[1] After the event he advised Calvin to justify it, as there were some who were taken aback. "Everywhere," he says, "there are excellent men who are convinced that godless and blaspheming men ought not only to be rebuked and imprisoned, but also to be put to death. . . . How Servetus could have been spared I cannot see."[2]

The position of Œcolampadius in reference to these questions was altogether singular and exceptional. He dreaded the absorption of the ecclesiastical functions by the State, and sought to avoid it by the introduction of a council of twelve elders, partly magistrates, partly clergy, to direct ecclesiastical affairs. "Many things," he said, "are punished by the secular power less severely than the dignity of the Church demands. On the other hand, it punishes the repentant, to whom the Church shows mercy. Either it blunts the edge of its sword by not punishing the guilty, or it brings some hatred on the Gospel by severity."[3] But the people of Basel were deaf to the arguments of the reformer, and here, as elsewhere, the civil power usurped the office of the Church. In harmony with this jealousy of political interference, Œcolampadius was very merciful to the Anabaptists. "Severe penalties," he said, "were likely to aggravate the evil; forgiveness would hasten the cure."[4] A few months later, however, he regretted this leniency. "We perceive," he writes to a friend, "that we have sometimes shown too much indulgence; but this is better than to proceed tyrannically, or to surrender the keys of the Church."[5] Whilst, on the

[1] Pestalozzi, *Heinrich Bullinger*, p. 426.

[2] In the year 1555 he writes to Socinus: "I too am of opinion that heretical men must be cut off with the spiritual sword. . . . The Lutherans at first did not understand that sectaries must be restrained and punished, but after the fall of Münster, when thousands of poor misguided men, many of them orthodox, had perished, they were compelled to admit that it is wiser and better for the Government not only to restrain wrong-headed men, but also, by putting to death a few that deserve it, to protect thousands of inhabitants" (*Ibid.* p. 428).

[3] Herzog, *Leben Oekolampads*, ii. 197.

[4] *Ibid.* p. 189.

[5] *Ibid.* p. 206.

other hand, he rejoiced at the expulsion of the Catholics, he ingeniously justified the practice of the Catholic persecutors. "In the early ages of the Church, when the divinity of Christ manifested itself to the world by miracles, God incited the Apostles to treat the ungodly with severity. When the miracles ceased, and the faith was universally adopted, He gained the hearts of princes and rulers, so that they undertook to protect with the sword the gentleness and patience of the Church. They rigorously resisted, in fulfilment of the duties of their office, the contemners of the Church."[1] "The clergy," he goes on to say, "became tyrannical because they usurped to themselves a power which they ought to have shared with others; and as the people dread the return of this tyranny of ecclesiastical authority, it is wiser for the Protestant clergy to make no use of the similar power of excommunication which is intrusted to them."

Calvin, as the subject of an absolute monarch, and the ruling spirit in a republic, differed both from the German and the Swiss reformers in his idea of the State both in its object and in its duty towards the Church. An exile from his own country, he had lost the associations and habits of monarchy, and his views of discipline as well as doctrine were matured before he took up his abode in Switzerland.[2] His system was not founded on existing facts; it had no roots in history, but was purely ideal, speculative, and therefore more consistent and inflexible than any other. Luther's political ideas were bounded by the horizon of the monarchical absolutism under which he lived. Zwingli's were influenced by the democratic forms of his native country, which gave to the whole community the right of appointing the governing body. Calvin, independent of all such considerations, studied only how his doctrine could best be realised, whether through the instrumentality of existing authorities, or at their expense. In his eyes its interests were paramount,

[1] Herzog, *Leben Oekolampads*, ii. 195. Herzog finds an excuse for the harsh treatment of the Lutherans at Basel in the still greater severity of the Lutheran Churches against the followers of the Swiss reformation (*Ibid.* 213).

[2] Hundeshagen, *Conflikte des Zwinglianismus und Calvinismus*, 41.

their promotion the supreme duty, opposition to them an unpardonable crime. There was nothing in the institutions of men, no authority, no right, no liberty, that he cared to preserve, or towards which he entertained any feelings of reverence or obligation.

His theory made the support of religious truth the end and office of the State,[1] which was bound therefore to protect, and consequently to obey, the Church, and had no control over it. In religion the first and highest thing was the dogma: the preservation of morals was one important office of government; but the maintenance of the purity of doctrine was the highest. The result of this theory is the institution of a pure theocracy. If the elect were alone upon the earth, Calvin taught, there would be no need of the political order, and the Anabaptists would be right in rejecting it;[2] but the elect are in a minority; and there is the mass of reprobates who must be coerced by the sword, in order that all the world may be made subject to the truth, by the conquerors imposing their faith upon the vanquished.[3] He wished to extend religion by the sword, but to reserve death as the punishment of apostasy; and as this law would include the Catholics, who were in Calvin's eyes apostates from the truth, he narrowed it further to those who were

[1] "Huc spectat (politia) . . . ne idololatria, ne in Dei nomen sacrilegia, ne adversus ejus veritatem blasphemiae aliaeque religionis offensiones publice emergant ac in populum spargantur. . . . Politicam ordinationem probo, quae in hoc incumbit, ne vera religio, quae Dei lege continetur, palam, publicisque sacrilegiis impune violetur" (*Institutio Christianae Religionis*, ed. Tholuck, ii. 477). "Hoc ergo summopere requiritur a regibus, ut gladio quo praediti sunt utantur ad cultum Dei asserendum" (*Praelectiones in Prophetas*, *Opera*, v. 233, ed. 1667).

[2] "Huic etiam colligere promptum est, quam stulta fuerit imaginatio eorum qui volebant usum gladii tollere e mundo, Evangelii praetextu. Scimus Anabaptistas fuisse tumultuatos, quasi totus ordo politicus repugnaret Christi regno, quia regnum Christi continetur sola doctrina; deinde nulla futura sit vis. Hoc quidem verum esset, si essemus in hoc mundo angeli: sed quemadmodum jam dixi, exiguus est piorum numerus: ideo necesse est reliquam turbam cohiberi violento freno: quia permixti sunt filii Dei vel saevis belluis, vel vulpibus et fraudulentis hominibus" (*Pr. in Michaeam*, v. 310). "In quo non suam modo inscitiam, sed diabolicum fastum produnt, dum perfectionem sibi arrogant; cujus ne centesima quidem pars in illis conspicitur" (*Institutio*, ii. 478).

[3] "Tota igitur excellentia, tota dignitas, tota potentia Ecclesiae debet huc referri, ut omnia subjaceant Deo, et quicquid erit in gentibus hoc totum sit sacrum, ut scilicet cultus Dei tam apud victores quam apud victos vigeat" (*Pr. in Michaeam*, v. 317).

apostates from the community. In this way, he said, there was no pretext given to the Catholics to retaliate.[1] They, as well as the Jews and Mohammedans, must be allowed to live: death was only the penalty of Protestants who relapsed into error; but to them it applied equally whether they were converted to the Church or joined the sects and fell into unbelief. Only in cases where there was no danger of his words being used against the Protestants, and in letters not intended for publication, he required that Catholics should suffer the same penalties as those who were guilty of sedition, on the ground that the majesty of God must be as strictly avenged as the throne of the king.[2]

If the defence of the truth was the purpose for which power was intrusted to princes, it was natural that it should be also the condition on which they held it. Long before the revolution of 1688, Calvin had decided that princes who deny the true faith, "abdicate" their crowns, and are no longer to be obeyed;[3] and that no oaths are binding which are in contradiction to the interests of Protestantism.[4] He painted the princes of his age in the blackest colours,[5] and prayed to God for

[1] "Ita tollitur offensio, quae multos imperitos fallit, dum metuunt ne hoc praetextu ad saeviendum armentur Papae carnifices." Calvin was warned by experience of the imprudence of Luther's language. "In Gallis proceres in excusanda saevitia immani allegant autoritatem Lutheri" (Melanchthon, *Opera*, v. 176).

[2] "Vous avez deux espèces de mutins qui se sont eslevez entre le roy et l'estat du royaume: Les uns sont gens fantastiques, qui soubs couleur de l'évangile vouldroient mettre tout en confusion. Les aultres sont gens obstinés aux superstitions de l'Antéchrist de Rome. Tous ensemble méritent bien d'estre réprimés par le glayve qui vous est commis, veu qu'ils s'attaschent non seulement au roy, mais à Dieu qui l'a assis au siège royal" (Calvin to Somerset, Oct. 22, 1540; *Lettres de Calvin*, ed. Bonnet, i. 267. See also Henry, *Leben Calvins*, ii. Append. 30).

[3] "Abdicant enim se potestate terreni principes dum insurgunt contra Deum: imo indigni sunt qui censeantur in hominum numero. Potius ergo conspuere oportet in ipsorum capita, quam illis parere, ubi ita proterviunt ut velint etiam spoliare Deum jure suo, et quasi occupare solium ejus, acsi possent eum a coelo detrahere" (*Pr. in Danielem*, v. 91).

[4] "Quant au serment qu'on vous a contraincte de faire, comme vous avez failli et offensé Dieu en le faisant, aussi n'estes-vous tenue de le garder" (Calvin to the Duchess of Ferrara, *Bonnet*, ii. 338). She had taken an oath, at her husband's death, that she would not correspond with Calvin.

[5] "In aulis regum videmus primas teneri a bestiis. Nam hodie, ne repetamus veteres historias, ut reges fere omnes fatui sunt ac bruti, ita etiam sunt quasi equi et asini brutorum animalium. . . . Reges sunt hodie fere mancipia" (*Pr. in Danielem*, v. 82). "Videmus enim ut hodie quoque pro sua libidine com-

their destruction;[1] though at the same time he condemned all rebellion on the part of his friends, so long as there were great doubts of their success.[2] His principles, however, were often stronger than his exhortations, and he had difficulty in preventing murders and seditious movements in France.[3] When he was dead, nobody prevented them, and it became clear that his system, by subjecting the civil power to the service of religion, was more dangerous to toleration than Luther's plan of giving to the State supremacy over the Church.

Calvin was as positive as Luther in asserting the duty of obedience to rulers irrespective of their mode of government.[4] He constantly declared that tyranny was not to be resisted on political grounds; that no civil rights could outweigh the divine sanction of government; except in cases where a special office was appointed for

moveant totum orbem principes; quia produnt alii aliis innoxios populos, et exercent foedam nundinationem, dum quisque commodum suum venatur, et sine ullo pudore, tantum ut augeat suam potentiam, alios tradit in manum inimici" (*Pr. in Nahum*, v. 363). "Hodie pudet reges aliquid prae se ferre humanum, sed omnes gestus accommodant ad tyrannidem" (*Pr. in Jeremiam*, v. 257).

[1] "Sur ce que je vous avais allégué, que David nous instruict par son exemple de haïr les ennemis de Dieu, vous respondez que c'estoit pour ce temps-là duquel sous la loi de rigueur il estoit permis de haïr les ennemis. Or, madame, ceste glose seroit pour renverser toute l'Escriture, et partant il la fault fuir comme une peste mortelle. . . . Combien que j'aye tousjours prié Dieu de luy faire mercy, si est-ce que j'ay souvent désiré que Dieu mist la main sur luy (Guise) pour en deslivrer son Eglise, s'il ne le vouloit convertir" (Calvin to the Duchess of Ferrara, *Bonnet*, ii. 551). Luther was in this respect equally unscrupulous: "This year we must pray Duke Maurice to death, we must kill him with our prayers; for he will be an evil man" (MS. quoted in Döllinger, *Reformation*, iii. 266).

[2] "Quod de praepostero nostrorum fervore scribis, verissimum est, neque tamen ulla occurrit moderandi ratio, quia sanis consiliis non obtemperant. Passim denuntio, si judex essem me non minus severe in rabioso, istos impetus vindicaturum, quam rex suis edictis mandat. Pergendum nihilominus, quando nos Deus voluit stultis esse debitores" (Calvin to Beza; Henry, *Leben Calvins*, iii. Append. 164).

[3] "Il n'a tenu qu'à moi que, devant la guerre, gens de faict et d'exécution ne se soyent efforcez de l'exterminer du monde (Guise) lesquels ont esté retenus par ma seule exhortation."—*Bonnet*, ii. 553.

[4] "Hoc nobis si assidue ob animos et oculos obversetur, eodem decreto constitui etiam nequissimos reges, quo regum auctoritas statuitur; nunquam in animum nobis seditiosae illae cogitationes venient, tractandum esse pro meritis regem nec aequum esse, ut subditos ei nos praestemus, qui vicissim regem nobis se non praestet. . . . De privatis hominibus semper loquor. Nam si qui nunc sint populares magistratus ad moderandam regum libidinem constituti (quales olim erant . . . ephori . . . tribuni . . . demarchi: et qua etiam forte potestate, ut nunc res habent, funguntur in singulis regnis tres ordines, quum primarios conventus peragunt) . . . illos ferocienti regum licentiae pro officio intercedere non veto" (*Institutio*, ii. 493, 495).

the purpose. Where there was no such office—where, for instance, the estates of the realm had lost their independence—there was no protection. This is one of the most important and essential characteristics of the politics of the reformers. By making the protection of their religion the principal business of government, they put out of sight its more immediate and universal duties, and made the political objects of the State disappear behind its religious end. A government was to be judged, in their eyes, only by its fidelity to the Protestant Church. If it fulfilled those requirements, no other complaints against it could be entertained. A tyrannical prince could not be resisted if he was orthodox; a just prince could be dethroned if he failed in the more essential condition of faith. In this way Protestantism became favourable at once to despotism and to revolution, and was ever ready to sacrifice good government to its own interests. It subverted monarchies, and, at the same time, denounced those who, for political causes, sought their subversion; but though the monarchies it subverted were sometimes tyrannical, and the seditions it prevented sometimes revolutionary, the order it defended or sought to establish was never legitimate and free, for it was always invested with the function of religious proselytism,[1] and with the obligation of removing every traditional, social, or political right or power which could oppose the discharge of that essential duty.

The part Calvin had taken in the death of Servetus obliged him to develop more fully his views on the punishment of heresy. He wrote a short account of the trial,[2] and argued that governments are bound to suppress

[1] "Quum ergo ita licentiose omnia sibi permittent (Donatistae), volebant tamen impune manere sua scelera: et in primis tenebant hoc principium: non esse poenas sumendas, si quis ab aliis dissideret in religionis doctrina: quemadmodum hodie videmus quosdam de hac re nimis cupide contendere. Certum est quid cupiant. Nam si quis ipsos respiciat, sunt impii Dei contemptores: saltem vellent nihil certum esse in religione; ideo labefactare, et quantum in se est etiam convellere nituntur omnia pietatis principia. Ut ergo liceat ipsis evomere virus suum, ideo tantopere litigant pro impunitate, et negant poenas de haereticis et blasphemis sumendas esse" (*Pr. in Danielem*, v. 51).

[2] "Defensio Orthodoxae Fidei . . . ubi ostenditur Haereticos jure gladii coercendos esse," 1554.

heresy, and that those who deny the justice of the punishment, themselves deserve it.[1] The book was signed by all the clergy of Geneva, as Calvin's compurgators. It was generally considered a failure; and a refutation appeared, which was so skilful as to produce a great sensation in the Protestant world.[2] This famous tract, now of extreme rarity, did not, as has been said, "contain the pith of those arguments which have ultimately triumphed in almost every part of Europe;" nor did it preach an unconditional toleration.[3] But it struck hard at Calvin by quoting a passage from the first edition of his *Institutes*, afterwards omitted, in which he spoke for toleration. "Some of those," says the author, "whom we quote have subsequently written in a different spirit. Nevertheless, we have cited the earlier opinion as the true one, as it was expressed under the pressure of persecution."[4] The first edition, we are informed by Calvin himself, was written for the purpose of vindicating the Protestants who were put to death, and of putting a stop

[1] "Non modo liberum esse magistratibus poenas sumere de coelestis doctrinae corruptoribus, sed divinitus esse mandatum, ut pestiferis erroribus impunitatem dare nequeant, quin desciscant ab officii sui fide. . . . Nunc vero quisquis haereticis et blasphemis injuste paenam infligi contenderet, sciens et volens se obstringet blasphemiae reatu. . . . Ubi a suis fundamentis convellitur religio, detestandae in Deum blasphemiae proferuntur, impiis et pestiferis dogmatibus in exitium rapiuntur animae; denique ubi palam defectio ab unico Deo puraque doctrina tentatur, ad extremum illud remedium descendere necesse" (see Schenkel, iii. 389; Dyer, *Life of Calvin*, p. 354; Henry, iii. 234).

[2] *De Haereticis an sint persequendi*, Magdeburgi, 1554. Chataillon, to whom it is generally attributed, was not the author (see Heppe, *Theodor Beza*, p. 37).

[3] Hallam, *Literature of Europe*, ii. 81; Schlosser, *Leben des Beza*, p. 55. This is proved by the following passage from the dedication: "This I say not to favour the heretics, whom I abhor, but because there are here two dangerous rocks to be avoided. In the first place, that no man should be deemed a heretic when he is not, . . . and that the real rebel be distinguished from the Christian who, by following the teaching and example of his Master, necessarily causes separation from the wicked and unbelieving. The other danger is, lest the real heretics be not more severely punished than the discipline of the Church requires" (Baum, *Theodor Beza*, i. 215).

[4] "Multis piis hominibus in Gallia exustis grave passim apud Germanos odium ignes illi excitaverant, sparsi sunt, ejus restinguendi causa, improbi ac mendaces libelli, non alios tam crudeliter tractari, quam Anabaptistas ac turbulentos homines, qui perversis deliriis non religionem modo sed totum ordinem politicum convellerent. . . . Haec mihi edendae Institutionis causa fuit, primum ut ab iniusta contumelia vindicarem fratres meos, quorum mors pretiosa erat in conspectu Domini; deinde quum multis miseris eadem visitarent supplicia, pro illis dolor saltem aliquis et sollicitudo exteras gentes tangeret" (*Praefatio in Psalmos*. See "Historia Litteraria de Calvini Institutione," in *Scrinium Antiquarium*, ii. 452).

to the persecution. It was anonymous, and naturally dwelt on the principles of toleration.

Although this book did not denounce all intolerance, and although it was extremely moderate, Calvin and his friends were filled with horror. "What remains of Christianity," exclaimed Beza, "if we silently admit what this man has expectorated in his preface? . . . Since the beginning of Christianity no such blasphemy was ever heard."[1] Beza undertook to defend Calvin in an elaborate work,[2] in which it was easy for him to cite the authority of all the leading reformers in favour of the practice of putting heretics to death, and in which he reproduced all the arguments of those who had written on the subject before him. More systematic than Calvin, he first of all excludes those who are not Christians—the Jews, Turks, and heathen—whom his inquiry does not touch; "among Christians," he proceeds to say, "some are schismatics, who sin against the peace of the Church, or disbelievers, who reject her doctrine. Among these, some err in all simplicity; and if their error is not very grave, and if they do not seduce others, they need not be punished."[3] "But obstinate heretics are far worse than parricides, and deserve death, even if they repent."[4] "It is the duty of the State to punish them, for the whole ecclesiastical order is upheld by the political."[5] In early ages this power was

[1] Baum, i. 206. "Telles gens," says Calvin, "seroient contents qu'il n'y eust ne loy, ne bride au monde. Voilà pourquoy ils ont basti ce beau libvre *De non comburendis Haereticis*, où ils ont falsifié les noms tant des villes que des personnes, non pour aultre cause sinon pource que le dit livre est farcy de blasphèmes insupportables" (Bonnet, ii. 18).

[2] *De Haereticis a civili Magistratu puniendis*, 1554.

[3] "Absit autem a nobis, ut in eos, qui vel simplicitate peccant, sine aliorum pernicie et insigni blasphemia, vel in explicando quopiam Scripturae loco dissident a recepta opinione, magistratum armemus" (*Tractatus Theologici*, i. 95).

[4] This was sometimes the practice in Catholic countries, where heresy was equivalent to treason. Duke William of Bavaria ordered obstinate Anabaptists to be burnt; those who recanted to be beheaded. "Welcher revocir, den soll man köpfen; welcher nicht revocir, den soll man brennen" (Jörg, p. 717).

[5] "Ex quibus omnibus una conjunctio efficitur, istos quibus haeretici videntur non esse puniendi, opinionem in Ecclesiam Dei conari longe omnium pestilentissimam invehere et ex diametro repugnantem doctrinae primum a Deo Patre proditae, deinde a Christo instauratae, ab universa denique Ecclesia orthodoxa perpetuo consensu usurpatae, ut mihi quidem magis absurde facere videantur quam si sacrilegas aut parricidas puniendos negarent, quum sint istis omnibus haeretici infinitis partibus deteriores" (*Tract. Theol.* i. 143).

exercised by the temporal sovereigns; they convoked councils, punished heretics, promulgated dogmas. The Papacy afterwards arose, in evil times, and was a great calamity; but it was preferable a hundred times to the anarchy which was defended under the name of merciful toleration.

The circumstances of the condemnation of Servetus make it the most perfect and characteristic example of the abstract intolerance of the reformers. Servetus was guilty of no political crime; he was not an inhabitant of Geneva, and was on the point of leaving it, and nothing immoral could be attributed to him. He was not even an advocate of absolute toleration.[1] The occasion of his apprehension was a dispute between a Catholic and a Protestant, as to which party was most zealous in suppressing egregious errors. Calvin, who had long before declared that if Servetus came to Geneva he should never leave it alive,[2] did all he could to obtain his condemnation by the Inquisition at Vienne. At Geneva he was anxious that the sentence should be death,[3] and in this he was encouraged by the Swiss churches, but especially by

1 "Verum est quod correctione non exspectata Ananiam et Sapphiram occidit Petrus. Quia Spiritus Sanctus tunc maxime vigens, quem spreverant, docebat esse incorrigibiles, in malitia obstinatos. Hoc crimen est morte simpliciter dignum et apud Deum et apud homines. In aliis autem criminibus, ubi Spiritus Sanctus speciale quid non docet, ubi non est inveterata malitia, aut obstinatio certa non apparet aut atrocitas magna, correctionem per alias castigationes sperare potius debemus" (Servetus, *Restitutio Christianismi*, 656; Henry, iii. 235).

2 "Nam si venerit, modo valeat mea authoritas, vivum exire nunquam patiar" (Calvin to Farel, in Henry, iii. Append. 65; Audin, *Vie de Calvin*, ii. 314; Dyer, 544).

3 "Spero capitale saltem fore judicium: poenae vero atrocitatem remitti cupio" (Calvin to Farel, Henry, iii. 189). Dr. Henry makes no attempt to clear Calvin of the imputation of having caused the death of Servetus. Nevertheless he proposed, some years later, that the three-hundredth anniversary of the execution should be celebrated in the Church of Geneva by a demonstration. "It ought to declare itself in a body, in a manner worthy of our principles, admitting that in past times the authorities of Geneva were mistaken, loudly proclaiming toleration, which is truly the crown of our Church, and paying due honour to Calvin, because he had no hand in the business (parcequ'il n'a pas trempé dans cette affaire), of which he has unjustly borne the whole burden." The impudence of this declaration is surpassed by the editor of the French periodical from which we extract it. He appends to the words in our parenthesis the following note: "We underline in order to call attention to this opinion of Dr. Henry, who is so thoroughly acquainted with the whole question" (*Bulletin de la Société de l Histoire du Protestantisme Français*, ii. 114).

Beza, Farel, Bullinger, and Peter Martyr.[1] All the Protestant authorities, therefore, agreed in the justice of putting a writer to death in whose case all the secondary motives of intolerance were wanting. Servetus was not a party leader. He had no followers who threatened to upset the peace and unity of the Church. His doctrine was speculative, without power or attraction for the masses, like Lutheranism; and without consequences subversive of morality, or affecting in any direct way the existence of society, like Anabaptism.[2] He had nothing to do with Geneva, and his persecutors would have rejoiced if he had been put to death elsewhere. "Bayle," says Hallam,[3] "has an excellent remark on this controversy." Bayle's remark is as follows: "Whenever Protestants complain, they are answered by the right which Calvin and Beza recognised in magistrates; and to this day there has been nobody who has not failed pitiably against this *argumentum ad hominem*."

No question of the merits of the Reformation or of persecution is involved in an inquiry as to the source and

[1] "Qui scripserunt de non plectendis haereticis, semper mihi visi sunt non parum errare" (Farel to Blaarer, Henry, iii. 202). During the trial he wrote to Calvin: "If you desire to diminish the horrible punishment, you will act as a friend towards your most dangerous enemy. If I were to seduce anybody from the true faith, I should consider myself worthy of death; I cannot judge differently of another than of myself" (Schmidt, *Farel und Viret*, p. 33).

Before sentence was pronounced Bullinger wrote to Beza: "Quid vero amplissimus Senatus Genevensis ageret cum blasphemo illo nebulone Serveto. Si sapit et officium suum facit, caedit, ut totus orbis videat Genevam Christi gloriam cupere servatam" (Baum, i. 204). With reference to Socinus he wrote: "Sentio ego spirituali gladio abscindendos esse homines haereticos" (Henry, iii. 225).

Peter Martyr Vermili also gave in his adhesion to Calvin's policy: "De Serveto Hispano, quid aliud dicam non habeo, nisi eum fuisse genuinum Diaboli filium, cujus pestifera et detestanda doctrina undique profliganda est, neque magistratus, qui de illo supplicium extremum sumpsit, accusandus est, cum emendationis nulla indiçia in eo possent deprehendi, illiusque blasphemiae omnino intolerabiles essent" (*Loci Communes*, 1114. See Schlosser, *Leben des Beza und des Peter Martyr Vermili*, 512).

Zanchi, who at the instigation of Bullinger also published a treatise, *De Haereticis Coercendis*, says of Beza's work: "Non poterit non probari summopere piis omnibus. Satis superque respondit quidem ille novis istis academicis, ita ut supervacanea et inutilis omnino videatur mea tractatio" (Baum, i. 232).

[2] "The trial of Servetus," says a very ardent Calvinist, "is illegal only in one point—the crime, if crime there be, had not been committed at Geneva; but long before the Councils had usurped the unjust privilege of judging strangers stopping at Geneva, although the crimes they were accused of had not been committed there" (Haag, *La France Protestante*, iii. 129).

[3] *Literature of Europe*, ii. 82.

connection of the opinions on toleration held by the Protestant reformers. No man's sentiments on the rightfulness of religious persecution will be affected by the theories we have described, and they have no bearing whatever on doctrinal controversy. Those who—in agreement with the principle of the early Church, that men are free in matters of conscience — condemn all intolerance, will censure Catholics and Protestants alike. Those who pursue the same principle one step farther and practically invert it, by insisting on the right and duty not only of professing but of extending the truth, must, as it seems to us, approve the conduct both of Protestants and Catholics, unless they make the justice of the persecution depend on the truth of the doctrine defended, in which case they will divide on both sides. Such persons, again, as are more strongly impressed with the cruelty of actual executions than with the danger of false theories, may concentrate their indignation on the Catholics of Languedoc and Spain; while those who judge principles, not by the accidental details attending their practical realisation, but by the reasoning on which they are founded, will arrive at a verdict adverse to the Protestants. These comparative inquiries, however, have little serious interest. If we give our admiration to tolerance, we must remember that the Spanish Moors and the Turks in Europe have been more tolerant than the Christians; and if we admit the principle of intolerance, and judge its application by particular conditions, we are bound to acknowledge that the Romans had better reason for persecution than any modern State, since their empire was involved in the decline of the old religion, with which it was bound up, whereas no Christian polity has been subverted by the mere presence of religious dissent. The comparison is, moreover, entirely unreasonable, for there is nothing in common between Catholic and Protestant intolerance. The Church began with the principle of liberty, both as her claim and as her rule; and external circumstances forced intolerance upon her, after her spirit of unity had triumphed, in spite both of the freedom she proclaimed and of the persecutions she suffered. Protestantism set up intolerance as an imperative precept and as a part of its doctrine, and it was forced to admit toleration by the necessities of its position, after the rigorous penalties it imposed had failed to arrest the process of internal dissolution.[1]

At the time when this involuntary change occurred the sects that caused it were the bitterest enemies of the toleration they demanded. In the same age the Puritans and the Catholics sought a refuge beyond the Atlantic from the persecution which they suffered together under the Stuarts. Flying for the same reason, and from the same oppression, they were enabled respectively to carry out their own views in the colonies which they founded in Massachusetts and Maryland, and the history of those two States exhibits faithfully the contrast between the two Churches. The Catholic emigrants established, for the first time in modern history, a government in which religion was free, and with it the germ of that religious liberty which now prevails in America. The Puritans, on the other hand, revived with greater severity the penal laws of the mother country. In process of time the liberty of conscience in the Catholic colony was forcibly abolished by the neighbouring Protestants of Virginia; while on the borders of Massachusetts the new State of Rhode Island was formed by a party of fugitives from the intolerance of their fellow-colonists.

[1] This is the ground taken by two Dutch divines in answer to the consultation of John of Nassau in 1579: "Neque in imperio, neque in Galliis, neque in Belgio speranda esset unquam libertas in externo religionis exercitio nostris . . . si non diversarum religionum exercitia in una eademque provincia toleranda. . . . Sic igitur gladio adversus nos armabimus Pontificios, si hanc hypothesin tuebimur, quod exercitium religionis alteri parti nullum prorsus relinqui debeat" (*Scrinium Antiquarium*, i. 335).

VI

POLITICAL THOUGHTS ON THE CHURCH[1]

THERE is, perhaps, no stronger contrast between the revolutionary times in which we live and the Catholic ages, or even the period of the Reformation, than in this: that the influence which religious motives formerly possessed is now in a great measure exercised by political opinions. As the theory of the balance of power was adopted in Europe as a substitute for the influence of religious ideas, incorporated in the power of the Popes, so now political zeal occupies the place made vacant by the decline of religious fervour, and commands to an almost equal extent the enthusiasm of men. It has risen to power at the expense of religion, and by reason of its decline, and naturally regards the dethroned authority with the jealousy of a usurper. This revolution in the relative position of religious and political ideas was the inevitable consequence of the usurpation by the Protestant State of the functions of the Church, and of the supremacy which, in the modern system of government, it has assumed over her. It follows also that the false principles by which religious truth was assailed have been transferred to the political order, and that here, too, Catholics must be prepared to meet them; whilst the objections made to the Church on doctrinal grounds have lost much of their attractiveness and effect, the enmity she provokes on political grounds is more intense. It is the same old enemy with a new face. No reproach is more common, no argument better suited to the temper of these times,

[1] *The Rambler*, 1858.

than those which are founded on the supposed inferiority or incapacity of the Church in political matters. As her dogma, for instance, is assailed from opposite sides,—as she has had to defend the divine nature of Christ against the Ebionites, and His humanity against Docetism, and was attacked both on the plea of excessive rigorism and excessive laxity (Clement Alex., *Stromata*, iii. 5),—so in politics she is arraigned on behalf of the political system of every phase of heresy. She was accused of favouring revolutionary principles in the time of Elizabeth and James I., and of absolutist tendencies under James II. and his successors. Since Protestant England has been divided into two great political parties, each of these reproaches has found a permanent voice in one of them. Whilst Tory writers affirm that the Catholic religion is the enemy of all conservatism and stability, the Liberals consider it radically opposed to all true freedom.

"What are we to think," says the *Edinburgh Review* (vol. ciii. p. 586), "of the penetration or the sincerity of a man who professes to study and admire the liberties of England and the character of her people, but who does not see that English freedom has been nurtured from the earliest times by resistance to Papal authority, and established by the blessing of a reformed religion? That is, under Heaven, the basis of all the rights we possess; and the weight we might otherwise be disposed to concede to M. de Montalembert's opinions on England is materially lessened by the discovery that, after all, he would, if he had the power, place this free country under that spiritual bondage which broods over the empires of Austria or of Spain."

On the other hand, let us hearken to the Protestant eloquence of the *Quarterly Review* (vol. xcii. p. 41):—

Tyranny, fraud, base adulation, total insensibility, not only to the worth of human freedom, but to the majesty of law and the sacredness of public and private right; these are the malignant and deadly features which we see stamped upon the conduct of the Roman hierarchy.

Besides which, we have the valuable opinion of Lord Derby, which no Catholic, we should suppose, east of the Shannon has forgotten, that Catholicism is "religiously corrupt, and politically dangerous." Lord Macaulay tells us that it exclusively promoted the power of the Crown;

Ranke, that it favours revolution and regicide. Whilst the Belgian and Sardinian Liberals accuse the Church of being the enemy of constitutional freedom, the celebrated Protestant statesman, Stahl, taunts her with the reproach of being the sole support and pillar of the Belgian constitution. Thus every error pronounces judgment on itself when it attempts to apply its rules to the standard of truth.

Among Catholics the state of opinion on these questions, whether it be considered the result of unavoidable circumstances, or a sign of ingenious accommodation, or a thing to be deplored, affords at least a glaring refutation of the idea that we are united, for good or for evil, in one common political system. The Church is vindicated by her defenders, according to their individual inclinations, from the opposite faults imputed to her; she is lauded, according to circumstances, for the most contradictory merits, and her authority is invoked in exclusive support of very various systems. O'Connell, Count de Montalembert, Father Ventura, proclaim her liberal, constitutional, not to say democratic, character; whilst such writers as Bonald and Father Taparelli associate her with the cause of absolute government. Others there are, too, who deny that the Church has a political tendency or preference of any kind; who assert that she is altogether independent of, and indifferent to, particular political institutions, and, while insensible to their influence, seeks to exercise no sort of influence over them. Each view may be plausibly defended, and the inexhaustible arsenal of history seems to provide impartially instances in corroboration of each. The last opinion can appeal to the example of the Apostles and the early Christians, for whom, in the heathen empire, the only part was unconditional obedience. This is dwelt upon by the early apologists: "Oramus etiam pro imperatoribus, pro ministris eorum et potestatibus, pro statu saeculi, pro rerum quiete, pro mora finis."[1] It has the authority, too, of

[1] Tertullian, *Apologeticum*, 39; see also 30, 32. "We pray also for the emperors, for the ministers of their Government, for the State, for the peace of the world, for the delay of the last day."

those who thought with St. Augustine that the State had a sinful origin and character: "Primus fuit terrenae civitatis conditor fratricida."[1] The Liberals, at the same time, are strong in the authority of many scholastic writers, and of many of the older Jesuit divines, of St. Thomas and Suarez, Bellarmine, and Mariana. The absolutists, too, countenanced by Bossuet and the Gallican Church, and quoting amply from the Old Testament, can point triumphantly to the majority of Catholic countries in modern times. All these arguments are at the same time serviceable to our adversaries; and those by which one objection is answered help to fortify another.

The frequent recurrence of this sort of argument which appears to us as treacherous for defence as it is popular as a weapon of attack, shows that no very definite ideas prevail on the subject, and makes it doubtful whether history, which passes sentence on so many theories, is altogether consistent with any of these. Nevertheless it is obviously an inquiry of the greatest importance, and one on which controversy can never entirely be set at rest; for the relation of the spiritual and the secular power is, like that of speculation and revelation, of religion and nature, one of those problems which remain perpetually open, to receive light from the meditations and experience of all ages, and the complete solution of which is among the objects, and would be the end, of all history.

At a time when the whole system of ecclesiastical government was under discussion, and when the temporal power was beginning to predominate over the Church in France, the greatest theologian of the age made an attempt to apply the principles of secular polity to the Church. According to Gerson (*Opera*, ii. 254), the fundamental forms into which Aristotle divides all government recur in the ecclesiastical system. The royal power is represented in the Papacy, the aristocracy by the

[1] *De Civit. Dei*, xv. 5. "The fratricide was the first founder of the secular State."

college of cardinals, whilst the councils form an ecclesiastical democracy (*timocratia*). Analogous to this is the idea that the constitution of the Church served as the model of the Christian States, and that the notion of representation, for instance, was borrowed from it. But it is not by the analogy of her own forms that the Church has influenced those of the State; for in reality there is none subsisting between them, and Gerson's adoption of a theory of Grecian origin proves that he scarcely understood the spirit of that mediæval polity which, in his own country especially, was already in its decay. For not only is the whole system of government, whether we consider its origin, its end, or its means absolutely and essentially different, but the temporal notion of power is altogether unknown in the Church. "Ecclesia subjectos non habet ut servos, sed ut filios."[1] Our Lord Himself drew the distinction: "Reges gentium dominantur eorum; et qui potestatem habent super eos, benefici vocantur. Vos autem non sic: sed qui major est in vobis, fiat sicut minor; et qui praedecessor, sicut minor" (Luc. xxii. 25, 26). The supreme authority is not the will of the rulers, but the law of the Church, which binds those who are its administrators as strictly as those who have only to obey it. No human laws were ever devised which could so thoroughly succeed in making the arbitrary exercise of power impossible, as that prodigious system of canon law which is the ripe fruit of the experience and the inspiration of eighteen hundred years. Nothing can be more remote from the political notions of monarchy than the authority of the Pope. With even less justice can it be said that there is in the Church an element of aristocracy, the essence of which is the possession of hereditary personal privileges. An aristocracy of merit and of office cannot, in a political sense, legitimately bear the name. By baptism all men are equal before the Church. Yet least of all can anything be detected corresponding to the democratic principle, by which all authority resides in the mass

[1] "The Church reckons her subjects not as her servants but as her children."

of individuals, and which gives to each one equal rights. All authority in the Church is delegated, and recognises no such thing as natural rights.

This confusion of the ideas belonging to different orders has been productive of serious and dangerous errors. Whilst heretics have raised the episcopate to a level with the papacy, the priesthood with the episcopate, the laity with the clergy, impugning successively the primacy, the episcopal authority, and the sacramental character of orders, the application of ideas derived from politics to the system of the Church led to the exaggeration of the papal power in the period immediately preceding the Reformation, to the claim of a permanent aristocratic government by the Council of Basel, and to the democratic extravagance of the Observants in the fourteenth century.

If in the stress of conflicting opinions we seek repose and shelter in the view that the kingdom of God is not of this world; that the Church, belonging to a different order, has no interest in political forms, tolerates them all, and is dangerous to none; if we try to rescue her from the dangers of political controversy by this method of retreat and evasion, we are compelled to admit her inferiority, in point of temporal influence, to every other religious system. Every other religion impresses its image on the society that professes it, and the government always follows the changes of religion. Pantheism and Polytheism, Judaism and Islamism, Protestantism, and even the various Protestant as well as Mahometan sects, call forth corresponding social and political forms. All power is from God, and is exercised by men in His stead. As men's notions are, therefore, in respect to their position towards God, such must their notion of temporal power and obedience also be. The relation of man to man corresponds with his relations to God — most of all his relations towards the direct representative of God.

The view we are discussing is one founded on timidity and a desire of peace. But peace is not a good great enough to be purchased by such sacrifices. We must be prepared to do battle for our religious system in every other sphere as well as in that of doctrine. Theological error affects men's ideas on all other subjects, and we cannot accept in politics the consequences of a system which is hateful to us in its religious aspect. These questions cannot be decided by mere reasoning, but we may obtain some light by inquiring of the experience of history; our only sure guide is the example of the Church herself. "Insolentissima est insania, non modo disputare, contra id quod videmus universam ecclesiam credere sed etiam contra id quod videmus eam facere. Fides enim ecclesiae non modo regula est fidei nostrae, sed etiam actiones ipsius actionum nostrarum, consuetudo ipsius consuetudinis quam observare debemus."[1]

The Church which our Lord came to establish had a twofold mission to fulfil. Her system of doctrine, on the one hand, had to be defined and perpetually maintained. But it was also necessary that it should prove itself more than a mere matter of theory,—that it should pass into practice, and command the will as well as the intellect of men. It was necessary not only to restore the image of God in man, but to establish the divine order in the world. Religion had to transform the public as well as the private life of nations, to effect a system of public right corresponding with private morality and without which it is imperfect and insecure. It was to exhibit and confirm its victory and to perpetuate its influence by calling into existence, not only works of private virtue, but institutions which are the product of the whole life of nations, and bear an unceasing testimony to their religious sentiments. The world, instead of being external to the Church, was to be adopted by her and imbued with her ideas. The first, the doctrinal or intellectual part of the work, was chiefly performed in the Roman empire, in

[1] "It is the maddest insolence, not only to dispute against that which we see the universal Church believing, but also against what we see her doing. For not only is the faith of the Church the rule of our faith, but also her actions of ours, and her customs of that which we ought to observe" (Morinus, *Comment. de Discipl. in administ. Poenitentiae*, Preface).

the midst of the civilisation of antiquity and of that unparalleled intellectual excitement which followed the presence of Christ on earth. There the faith was prepared for the world whilst the world was not yet ready to receive it. The empire in which was concentrated all the learning and speculation of ancient times was by its intellectual splendour, and in spite, we might even say by reason, of its moral depravity, the fit scene of the intellectual establishment of Christianity. For its moral degradation ensured the most violent antipathy and hostility to the new faith ; while the mental cultivation of the age ensured a very thorough and ingenious opposition, and supplied those striking contrasts which were needed for the full discussion and vigorous development of the Christian system. Nowhere else, and at no other period, could such advantages have been found.

But for the other, equally essential part of her work the Church met with an insurmountable obstacle, which even the official conversion of the empire and all the efforts of the Christian emperors could not remove. This obstacle resided not so much in the resistance of paganism as a religion, as in the pagan character of the State. It was from a certain political sagacity chiefly that the Romans, who tolerated all religions,[1] consistently opposed that religion which threatened inevitably to revolutionise a state founded on a heathen basis. It appeared from the first a pernicious superstition ("exitiabilem superstitionem," Tacit. *Annal.* xv. 44), that taught its followers to be bad subjects ("exuere patriam," Tacitus, *Hist.* v. 5), and to be constantly dissatisfied ("quibus praesentia semper tempora cum enormi libertate displicent," Vopiscus, *Vit. Saturn.* 7). This hostility continued in spite of the protestations of every apologist, and of the submissiveness and sincere patriotism of the early Christians. They were so far from recognising what their enemies so vaguely felt, that the empire could not stand in the presence of the new faith, that it was the common belief amongst them, founded perhaps on the words of St. Paul,

[1] "Apud vos quodvis colere jus est Deum verum" (Tertullian, *Apolog.* xxiv.).

2 Thess. ii. 7,[1] that the Roman empire would last to the end of the world.[2]

The persecution of Julian was caused by the feeling of the danger which menaced the pagan empire from the Christian religion. His hostility was not founded on his attachment to the old religion of Rome, which he did not attempt to save. He endeavoured to replace it by a new system which was to furnish the State with new vigour to withstand the decay of the old paganism and the invasion of Christianity. He felt that the old religious ideas in which the Roman State had grown up had lost their power, and that Rome could only be saved by opposing at all hazards the new ideas. He was inspired rather with a political hatred of Christianity than with a religious love of paganism. Consequently Christianity was the only religion he could not tolerate. This was the beginning of the persecution of the Church on principles of liberalism and religious toleration, on the plea of political necessity, by men who felt that the existing forms of the State were incompatible with her progress. It is with the same feeling of patriotic aversion for the Church that Symmachus says (*Epist.* x. 61): "We demand the restoration of that religion which has so long been beneficial to the State . . . of that worship which has subdued the universe to our laws, of those sacrifices which repulsed Hannibal from our walls and the Gauls from the Capitol."

Very soon after the time of Constantine it began to appear that the outward conversion of the empire was a boon of doubtful value to religion. "Et postquam ad Christianos principes venerint, potentia quidem et divitiis major sed virtutibus minor facta est," says St. Jerome (in *Vita Malchi*). The zeal with which the emperors applied the secular arm for the promotion of Christianity was felt

[1] August. *de Civ. Dei*, xx. 19, 3.

[2] "Christianus nullius est hostis, nedum imperatoris, quem . . . necesse est ut . . . salvum velit cum toto Romano imperio quousque saeculum stabit; tamdiu enim stabit" (Tert. *ad Scapulam*, 2). "Cum caput illud orbis occiderit et ῥύμη esse coeperit, quod Sibyllae fore aiunt, quis dubitet venisse jam finem rebus humanis orbique terrarum?" (Lactantius, *Inst. Div.* vii. 25). "Non prius veniet Christus, quam regni Romani defectio fiat" (Ambrose *ad ep.* i. *ad Thess.*).

to be incompatible with its spirit and with its interest as well. "Religion," says Lactantius (*Inst. Div.* v. 19), "is to be defended by exhorting, not by slaying, not by severity, but by patience; not by crime, but by faith: . . . *nihil enim est tam voluntarium quam religio*."[1] "Deus," says St. Hilary of Poitiers ("ad Constantium," *Opp.* i. p. 1221 C), "obsequio non eget necessario, non requirit coactam confessionem."[2] St. Athanasius and St. John Chrysostom protest in like manner against the intemperate proselytism of the day.[3] For the result which followed the general adoption of Christianity threw an unfavourable light on the motives which had caused it. It became evident that the heathen world was incapable of being regenerated, that the weeds were choking the good seed. The corruption increased in the Church to such a degree that the Christians, unable to divest themselves of the Roman notion of the *orbis terrarum*, deemed the end of the world at hand. St. Augustine (*sermo* cv.) rebukes this superstitious fear: "Si non manet civitas quae nos carnaliter genuit, manet quae nos spiritualiter genuit. Numquid (Dominus) dormitando aedificium suum perdidit, aut non custodiendo hostes admisit? . . . Quid expavescis quia pereunt regna terrena? Ideo tibi coeleste promissum est, ne cum terrenis perires. . . . Transient quae fecit ipse Deus; quanto citius quod condidit Romulus. . . . Non ergo deficiamus, fratres: finis erit terrenis omnibus regnis."[4] But even some of the fathers themselves were filled with despair at the spectacle of the universal demoralisation: "Totius mundi una vox Christus est . . . Horret animus temporum nostrorum ruinas persequi. . . . Romanus orbis

[1] "There is nothing so voluntary as religion."

[2] "God does not want unwilling worship, nor does he require a forced repentance."

[3] Athanas. i. 363 B and 384 C μὴ ἀναγκάζειν ἀλλὰ πείθειν "not compulsion, but persuasion" (Chrysost. ii. 540 A and C).

[4] "If the State of which we are the secular children passes away, that of which we are spiritual children passes not. Has God gone to sleep and let the house be destroyed, or let in the enemy through want of watchfulness? Why fearest thou when earthly kingdoms fall? Heaven is promised thee, that thou mightest not fall with them. The works of God Himself shall pass: how much sooner the works of Romulus! Let us not quail, my brethren; all earthly kingdoms must come to an end."

ruit, et tamen cervix nostra erecta non flectitur. . . . Nostris peccatis barbari fortes sunt. Nostris vitiis Romanus superatur exercitus. . . . Nec amputamus causas morbi, ut morbus pariter auferatur. . . . Orbis terrarum ruit, in nobis peccata non ruunt."[1] St. Ambrose announces the end still more confidently: "Verborum coelestium nulli magis quam nos testes sumus, quos mundi finis invenit. . . . Quia in occasu saeculi sumus, praecedunt quaedam aegritudines mundi."[2] Two generations later Salvianus exclaims: "Quid est aliud paene omnis coetus Christianorum quam sentina vitiorum?"[3] And St. Leo declares, "Quod temporibus nostris auctore diabolo sic vitiata sunt omnia, ut paene nihil sit quod absque idolatria transigatur."[4]

When, early in the fifth century, the dismemberment of the Western empire commenced, it was clear that Christianity had not succeeded in reforming the society and the polity of the ancient world. It had arrested for a time the decline of the empire, but after the Arian separation it could not prevent its fall. The Catholics could not dissociate the interests of the Church and those of the Roman State, and looked with patriotic as well as religious horror at the barbarians by whom the work of destruction was done. They could not see that they had come to build up as well as to destroy, and that they supplied a field for the exercise of all that influence which had failed among the Romans. It was very late before they understood that the world had run but half its course; that a new skin had been prepared to contain the new wine; and that the barbarous tribes were to

[1] "The cry of the whole world is 'Christ.' The mind is horrified in reviewing the ruins of our age. The Roman world is falling, and yet our stiff neck is not bent. The barbarians' strength is in our sins; the defeat of the Roman armies in our vices. We will not cut off the occasions of the malady, that the malady may be healed. The world is falling, but in us there is no falling off from sin" (St. Jerome, *ep.* 35, *ad Heliodorum*; *ep.* 98, *ad Gaudentium*).

[2] "None are better witnesses of the words of heaven than we, on whom the end of the world has come. We assist at the world's setting, and diseases precede its dissolution" (*Expos. Ep. sec. Lucam*, x.).

[3] "What is well-nigh all Christendom but a sink of iniquity?" (*De Gub. Dei*, iii. 9).

[4] "In our age the devil has so defiled everything that scarcely a thing is done without idolatry."

justify their claim to the double inheritance of the faith and of the power of Rome. There were two principal things which fitted them for their vocation. The Romans had been unable to be the instruments of the social action of Christianity on account of their moral depravity. It was precisely for those virtues in which they were most deficient that their barbarous enemies were distinguished. Salvianus expresses this in the following words (*De Gubern. Dei*, vii. 6): "Miramur si terrae . . . nostrorum omnium a Deo barbaris datae sunt, cum eas quae Romani polluerant fornicatione, nunc mundent barbari castitate?"[1] Whilst thus their habits met half-way the morality of the Christian system, their mythology, which was the very crown and summit of all pagan religions, predisposed them in like manner for its adoption, by predicting its own end, and announcing the advent of a system which was to displace its gods. "It was more than a mere worldly impulse," says a famous northern divine, "that urged the northern nations to wander forth, and to seek, like birds of passage, a milder clime." We cannot, however, say more on the predisposition for Christianity of that race to whose hands its progress seems for ever committed, or on the wonderful facility with which the Teutonic invaders accepted it, whether presented to them in the form of Catholicism or of Arianism.[2] The great marvel in their history, and their chief claim to the dominion of the world, was, that they had preserved so long, in the bleak regions in which the growth of civilisation was in every way retarded, the virtues together with the ignorance of the barbarous State.

At a time when Arianism was extinct in the empire, it assumed among the Teutonic tribes the character of a national religion, and added a theological incitement to their animosity against the Romans. The Arian tribes,

[1] "Do we wonder that God has granted all our lands to the barbarians, when they now purify by their chastity the places which the Romans had polluted with their debauchery?"

[2] Pope Anastasius writes to Clovis: "Sedes Petri in tanta occasione non potest non laetari, cum plenitudinem gentium intuetur ad eam veloci gradu concurrere" (Bouquet, iv. 50).

to whom the work of destruction was committed, did it thoroughly. But they soon found that their own preservation depended on their submission to the Church. Those that persisted in their heresy were extirpated. The Lombards and Visigoths saved themselves by a tardy conversion from the fate with which they were threatened so long, as their religion estranged them from the Roman population, and cut them off from the civilisation of which the Church was already the only guardian. For centuries the pre-eminence in the West belonged to that race which alone became Catholic at once, and never swerved from its orthodoxy. It is a sense of the importance of this fidelity which dictated the well-known preamble of the Salic law: "Gens Francorum inclita, Deo auctore condita, ad Catholicam fidem conversa et immunis ab haeresi," etc.[1]

Then followed the ages which are not unjustly called the Dark Ages, in which were laid the foundations of all the happiness that has been since enjoyed, and of all the greatness that has been achieved, by men. The good seed, from which a new Christian civilisation sprang, was striking root in the ground. Catholicism appeared as the religion of masses. In those times of simple faith there was no opportunity to call forth an Augustine or an Athanasius. It was not an age of conspicuous saints, but sanctity was at no time so general. The holy men of the first centuries shine with an intense brilliancy from the midst of the surrounding corruption. Legions of saints—individually for the most part obscure, because of the atmosphere of light around them—throng the five illiterate centuries, from the close of the great dogmatic controversies to the rise of a new theology and the commencement of new contests with Hildebrand, Anselm, and Bernard. All the manifestations of the Catholic spirit in those days bear a character of vastness and popularity. A single idea—the words of one man—electrified hundreds of thousands. In such a state of the world, the Christian ideas were able to become incarnate, so to speak, in durable

[1] "The noble people of the Franks, founded by God, converted to the Catholic faith, and free from heresy."

forms, and succeeded in animating the political institutions as well as the social life of the nations.

The facility with which the Teutonic ideas of Government shaped themselves to the mould of the new religion, was the second point in which that race was so peculiarly adapted for the position it has ever since occupied towards Christianity. They ceased to be barbarians only in becoming Christians. Their political system was in its infancy, and was capable of being developed variously, according to the influences it might undergo. There was no hostile civilisation to break down, no traditions to oppose which were bound up with the recollections of the national greatness. The State is so closely linked with religion, that no nation that has changed its religion has ever survived in its old political form. In Rome it had proved to be impossible to alter the system, which for a thousand years had animated every portion of the State; it was incurably pagan. The conversion of the people and the outward alliance with the Church could not make up for this inconsistency.

But the Teutonic race received the Catholic ideas wholly and without reserve. There was no region into which they failed to penetrate. The nation was collectively Catholic, as well as individually. The union of the Church with the political system of the Germans was so complete, that when Hungary adopted the religion of Rome, it adopted at the same time, as a natural consequence, the institutions of the empire. The ideas of Government which the barbarians carried with them into every land which they conquered were always in substance the same. The *Respublica Christiana* of the Middle Ages, consisting of those States in which the Teutonic element combined with the Catholic system, was governed by nearly the same laws. The mediæval institutions had this also in common, that they grew up everywhere under the protection and guidance of the Church; and whilst they subsisted in their integrity, her influence in every nation, and that of the Pope over all the nations, attained their utmost height. In proportion as they have since degenerated or disappeared, the political influence of religion has declined. As we have seen that the Church was baffled in the full performance of her mission before Europe was flooded by the great migration, so it may be said that she has never permanently enjoyed her proper position and authority in any country where it did not penetrate. No other political system has yet been devised, which was consistent with the full development and action of Catholic principles, but that which was constructed by the northern barbarians who destroyed the Western empire.

From this it does not seem too much to conclude, that the Catholic religion tends to inspire and transform the public as well as the private life of men; that it is not really master of one without some authority over the other. Consequently, where the State is too powerful by long tradition and custom, or too far gone in corruption, to admit of the influence of religion, it can only prevail by ultimately destroying the political system. This helps us to understand the almost imperceptible progress of Christianity against Mahometanism, and the slowness of its increase in China, where its growth must eventually undermine the whole fabric of government. On the other hand, we know with what ease comparatively savage tribes—as the natives of California and Paraguay—were converted to a religion which first initiated them in civilisation and government. There are countries in which the natural conditions are yet wanting for the kingdom of grace. There is a fulness of time for every nation—a time at which it first becomes capable of receiving the faith.[1] It is not harder to believe that certain political conditions are required to make a nation fit for conversion than that a certain degree of intellectual development is indispensable; that the language, for instance, must have reached a point which that of some nations has not attained before it is capable of conveying the truths of Christianity.

We cannot, therefore, admit that political principles

[1] "Vetati sunt a Spiritu sancto loqui verbum Dei in Asia . . . Tentabant ire in Bithyniam, et non permisit eos spiritus Jesu" (*Acts* xvi. 6, 7).

are a matter of utter indifference to the Church. To what sort of principles it is that she inclines may be indicated by a single example. The Christian notion of conscience imperatively demands a corresponding measure of personal liberty. The feeling of duty and responsibility to God is the only arbiter of a Christian's actions. With this no human authority can be permitted to interfere. We are bound to extend to the utmost, and to guard from every encroachment, the sphere in which we can act in obedience to the sole voice of conscience, regardless of any other consideration. The Church cannot tolerate any species of government in which this right is not recognised. She is the irreconcilable enemy of the despotism of the State, whatever its name or its forms may be, and through whatever instruments it may be exercised. Where the State allows the largest amount of this autonomy, the subject enjoys the largest measure of freedom, and the Church the greatest legitimate influence. The republics of antiquity were as incapable as the Oriental despotisms of satisfying the Christian notion of freedom, or even of subsisting with it. The Church has succeeded in producing the kind of liberty she exacts for her children only in those States which she has herself created or transformed. Real freedom has been known in no State that did not pass through her mediæval action. The history of the Middle Ages is the history of the gradual emancipation of man from every species of servitude, in proportion as the influence of religion became more penetrating and more universal. The Church could never abandon that principle of liberty by which she conquered pagan Rome. The history of the last three centuries exhibits the gradual revival of declining slavery, which appears under new forms of oppression as the authority of religion has decreased. The efforts of deliverance have been violent and reactionary, the progress of dependence sure and inevitable. The political benefits of the mediæval system have been enjoyed by no nation which is destitute of Teutonic elements. The Slavonic races of the north-east, the Celtic tribes of the north-west, were deprived of them. In the centre of mediæval civilisation, the republic of Venice, proud of its unmixed descent from the Romans, was untouched by the new blood, and that Christian people failed to obtain a Christian government. Where the influence of the ideas which prevailed in those times has not been felt, the consequence has been the utmost development of extreme principles, such as have doomed Asia for so many ages to perpetual stagnation, and America to endless heedless change. It is a plain fact, that that kind of liberty which the Church everywhere and at all times requires has been attained hitherto only in States of Teutonic origin. We need hardly glance at the importance of this observation in considering the missionary vocation of the English race in the distant regions it has peopled and among the nations it has conquered; for, in spite of its religious apostacy, no other country has preserved so pure that idea of liberty which gave to religion of old its power in Europe, and is still the foundation of the greatness of England. Other nations that have preserved more faithfully their allegiance to the Church have more decidedly broken with those political traditions, without which the action of the Church is fettered.

It is equally clear that, in insisting upon one definite principle in all government, the Church has at no time understood that it could be obtained only by particular political forms. She attends to the substance, not to the form, in politics. At various times she has successively promoted monarchy, aristocracy, and democracy; and at various times she has been betrayed by each. The three fundamental forms of all government are founded on the nature of things. Sovereignty must reside with an individual, or with a minority, or with the majority. But there are seasons and circumstances where one or the other is impossible, where one or the other is necessary; and in a growing nation they cannot always remain in the same relative proportions. Christianity could neither produce nor abolish them. They are all compatible with liberty and religion, and are all liable to diverge into tyranny by the exclusive exaggeration of their principle. It is this exaggeration that has ever been the great danger to religion and to liberty, and the object of constant resistance, the source of constant suffering for the Church.

Christianity introduced no new forms of government, but a new spirit, which totally transformed the old ones. The difference between a Christian and a pagan monarchy, or between a Christian and a rationalist democracy, is as great, politically, as that between a monarchy and a republic. The Government of Athens more nearly resembled that of Persia than that of any Christian republic, however democratic. If political theorists had attended more to the experience of the Christian Ages, the Church and the State would have been spared many calamities. Unfortunately, it has long been the common practice to recur to the authority of the Greeks and the Jews. The example of both was equally dangerous; for in the Jewish as in the Gentile world, political and religious obligations were made to coincide; in both, therefore,—in the theocracy of the Jews as in the *πολιτέια* of the Greeks,—the State was absolute. Now it is the great object of the Church, by keeping the two spheres permanently distinct,—by rendering to Cæsar the things that are Cæsar's, and to God the things that are God's—to make all absolutism, of whatever kind, impossible.

As no form of government is in itself incompatible with tyranny, either of a person or a principle, nor necessarily inconsistent with liberty, there is no natural hostility or alliance between the Church and any one of them. The same Church which, in the confusion and tumult of the great migrations, restored authority by raising up and anointing kings, held in later times with the aristocracy of the empire, and called into existence the democracies of Italy. In the eighth century she looked to Charlemagne for the reorganisation of society; in the eleventh she relied on the people to carry out the reformation of the clergy. During the first period of the Middle Ages, when social and political order had to be reconstructed out of ruins, the Church everywhere addresses herself to the kings, and seeks to strengthen and to sanctify their power. The royal as well as the imperial dignity received from her their authority and splendour. Whatever her disputes on religious grounds with particular sovereigns, such as Lothar, she had in those ages as yet no contests with the encroachments of monarchical power. Later on in the Middle Ages, on the contrary, when the monarchy had prevailed almost everywhere, and had strengthened itself beyond the limits of feudal ideas by the help of the Roman law and of the notions of absolute power derived from the ancients, it stood in continual conflict with the Church. From the time of Gregory VII., all the most distinguished pontiffs were engaged in quarrels with the royal and imperial power, which resulted in the victory of the Church in Germany and her defeat in France. In this resistance to the exaggeration of monarchy, they naturally endeavoured to set barriers to it by promoting popular institutions, as the Italian democracies and the aristocratic republics of Switzerland, and the capitulations which in the thirteenth and fourteenth centuries were imposed on almost every prince. Times had greatly changed when a Pope declared his amazement at a nation which bore in silence the tyranny of their king.[1] In modern times the absolute monarchy in Catholic countries has been, next to the Reformation, the greatest and most formidable enemy of the Church. For here she again lost in great measure her natural influence. In France, Spain, and Germany, by Gallicanism, Josephism, and the Inquisition, she came to be reduced to a state of dependence, the more fatal and deplorable that the clergy were often instrumental in maintaining it. All these phenomena

[1] Innocent IV. wrote in 1246 to the Sicilians: "In omnem terram vestrae sonus tribulationis exivit . . . multis pro miro vehementi ducentibus, quod pressi tam dirae servitutis opprobrio, et personarum ac rerum gravati multiplici detrimento, neglexeritis habere concilium, per quod vobis, sicut gentibus caeteris, aliqua provenirent solatia libertatis . . . super hoc apud sedem apostolicam vos excusante formidine. . . . Cogitate itaque corde vigili, ut a collo vestrae servitutis catena decidat, et universitas vestra in libertatis et quietis gaudio reflorescat; sitque ubertate conspicuum, ita divina favente potentia secura sit libertate decorum" (Raynaldus, *Ann.* ad ann. 1246).

were simply an adaptation of Catholicism to a political system incompatible with it in its integrity; an artifice to accommodate the Church to the requirements of absolute government, and to furnish absolute princes with a resource which was elsewhere supplied by Protestantism. The consequence has been, that the Church is at this day more free under Protestant than under Catholic governments—in Prussia or England than in France or Piedmont, Naples or Bavaria.

As we have said that the Church commonly allied herself with the political elements which happened to be insufficiently represented, and to temper the predominant principle by encouraging the others, it might seem hardly unfair to conclude that that kind of government in which they are all supposed to be combined,—"aequatum et temperatum ex tribus optimis rerum publicarum modis" (Cicero, *Rep.* i. 45),—must be particularly suited to her. Practically—and we are not here pursuing a theory—this is a mere fallacy. If we look at Catholic countries, we find that in Spain and Piedmont the constitution has served only to pillage, oppress, and insult the Church; whilst in Austria, since the empire has been purified in the fiery ordeal of the revolution, she is free, secure, and on the highroad of self-improvement. In constitutional Bavaria she has but little protection against the Crown, or in Belgium against the mob. The royal power is against her in one place, the popular element in the other. Turning to Protestant countries, we find that in Prussia the Church is comparatively free; whilst the more popular Government of Baden has exhibited the most conspicuous instance of oppression which has occurred in our time. The popular Government of Sweden, again, has renewed the refusal of religious toleration at the very time when despotic Russia begins to make a show, at least, of conceding it. In the presence of these facts, it would surely be absurd to assume that the Church must look with favour on the feeble and transitory constitutions with which the revolution has covered half the Continent. It does not actually appear that she has derived greater benefits from them than she may be said to have done from the revolution itself, which in France, for instance in 1848, gave to the Church, at least for a season, that liberty and dignity for which she had struggled in vain during the constitutional period which had preceded.

The political character of our own country bears hardly more resemblance to the Liberal Governments of the Continent,—which have copied only what is valueless in our institutions,—than to the superstitious despotism of the East, or to the analogous tyranny which in the Far West is mocked with the name of freedom. Here, as elsewhere, the progress of the constitution, which it was the work of the Catholic Ages to build up, on the principles common to all the nations of the Teutonic stock, was interrupted by the attraction which the growth of absolutism abroad excited, and by the Reformation's transferring the ecclesiastical power to the Crown. The Stuarts justified their abuse of power by the same precepts and the same examples by which the Puritans justified their resistance to it. The liberty aimed at by the Levellers was as remote from that which the Middle Ages had handed down, as the power of the Stuarts from the mediæval monarchy. The Revolution of 1688 destroyed one without favouring the other. Unlike the rebellion against Charles I., that which overthrew his son did not fall into a contrary extreme. It was a restoration in some sort of the principles of government, which had been alternately assailed by absolute monarchy and by a fanatical democracy. But, as it was directed against the abuse of kingly and ecclesiastical authority, neither the Crown nor the established Church recovered their ancient position; and a jealousy of both has ever since subsisted. There can be no question but that the remnants of the old system of polity—the utter disappearance of which keeps the rest of Christendom in a state of continual futile revolution—exist more copiously in this country than in any other. Instead of the revolutions and the religious wars by which, in other Protestant countries,

Catholics have obtained toleration, they have obtained it in England by the force of the very principles of the constitution. "I should think myself inconsistent," says the chief expounder of our political system, "in not applying my ideas of civil liberty to religious." And speaking of the relaxation of the penal laws, he says: "To the great liberality and enlarged sentiments of those who are the furthest in the world from you in religious tenets, and the furthest from acting with the party which, it is thought, the greater part of the Roman Catholics are disposed to espouse, it is that you owe the whole, or very nearly the whole, of what has been done both here and in Ireland."[1] The danger which menaces the continuance of our constitution proceeds simply from the oblivion of those Christian ideas by which it was originally inspired. It should seem that it is the religious as well as the political duty of Catholics to endeavour to avert this peril, and to defend from the attacks of the Radicals and from the contempt of the Tories the only constitution which bears some resemblance to those of Catholic times, and the principles which are almost as completely forgotten in England as they are misunderstood abroad. If three centuries of Protestantism have not entirely obliterated the ancient features of our government, if they have not been so thoroughly barren of political improvement as some of its enemies would have us believe,—there is surely nothing to marvel at, nothing at which we may rejoice. Protestants may well have, in some respects, the same terrestrial superiority over Catholics that the Gentiles had over the people of God. As, at the fall of paganism, the treasures it had produced and accumulated during two thousand years became the spoils of the victor,—when the day of reckoning shall come for the great modern apostasy, it will surrender all that it has gathered in its diligent application to the things of this world; and those who have remained in the faith will have into the bargain those products of the Protestant civilisation on which its claims of superiority are founded.

[1] Burke's *Works*, i. 391, 404.

When, therefore, in the political shipwreck of modern Europe, it is asked which political form of party is favoured by the Church, the only answer we can give is, that she is attached to none; but that though indifferent to existing forms, she is attached to a spirit which is nearly extinct. Those who, from a fear of exposing her to political animosity, would deny this, forget that the truth is as strong against political as against religious error, and shut their eyes to the only means by which the political regeneration of the modern world is a possibility. For the Catholic religion alone will not suffice to save it, as it was insufficient to save the ancient world, unless the Catholic idea equally manifests itself in the political order. The Church alone, without influence on the State, is powerless as a security for good government. It is absurd to pretend that at the present day France, or Spain, or Naples, are better governed than England, Holland, or Prussia. A country entirely Protestant may have more Catholic elements in its government than one where the population is wholly Catholic. The State which is Catholic *par excellence* is a by-word for misgovernment, because the orthodoxy and piety of its administrators are deemed a substitute for a better system. The demand for a really Catholic system of government falls with the greatest weight of reproach on the Catholic States.

Yet it is important to remember that in the ages of faith the same unity prevailed in political ideas, and that the civil as well as the religious troubles of our time are in great measure due to the Reformation. It is common to advise Catholics to make up their minds to accept the political doctrines of the day; but it would be more to the purpose to recall the ideas of Catholic times. It is not in the results of the political development of the last three centuries that the Church can place her trust; neither in absolute monarchy, nor in the revolutionary liberalism, nor in the infallible constitutional scheme. She must create anew or revive her former creations, and instil a new life and spirit into those remains of the mediæval system which will bear the mark of the ages when heresy and unbelief, Roman law, and heathen philosophy, had not obscured the idea of the Christian State. These remains are to be found, in various stages of decay, in every State,—with the exception, perhaps, of France,—that grew out of the mediæval civilisation. Above all they will be found in the country which, in the midst of its apostasy, and in spite of so much guilt towards religion, has preserved the Catholic forms in its Church establishment more than any other Protestant nation, and the Catholic spirit in her political institutions more than any Catholic nation. To renew the memory of the times in which this spirit prevailed in Europe, and to preserve the remains of it, to promote the knowledge of what is lost, and the desire of what is most urgently needed,—is an important service and an important duty which it behoves us to perform. We are greatly mistaken if these are not reflections which force themselves on every one who carefully observes the political history of the Church in modern Europe.

VII

INTRODUCTION TO L. A. BURD'S EDITION OF IL PRINCIPE BY MACHIAVELLI

MR. BURD has undertaken to redeem our long inferiority in Machiavellian studies, and it will, I think, be found that he has given a more completely satisfactory explanation of *The Prince* than any country possessed before. His annotated edition supplies all the solvents of a famous problem in the history of Italy and the literature of politics. In truth, the ancient problem is extinct, and no reader of this volume will continue to wonder how so intelligent and reasonable a man came to propose such flagitious counsels. When Machiavelli declared that extraordinary objects cannot be accomplished under ordinary rules, he recorded the experience of his own epoch, but also foretold the secret of men since born. He illustrates not only the generation which taught him, but the generations which he taught, and has no less in common with the men who had his precepts before them than with the Viscontis, Borgias, and Baglionis who were the masters he observed. He represents more than the spirit of his country and his age. Knowledge, civilisation, and morality have increased; but three centuries have borne enduring witness to his political veracity. He has been as much the exponent of men whom posterity esteems as of him whose historian writes: "Cet homme que Dieu, après l'avoir fait si grand, avait fait bon aussi, n'avait rien de la vertu." The authentic interpreter of Machiavelli, the *Commentarius Perpetuus* of the *Discorsi* and *The Prince*, is the whole of later history

Michelet has said: "Rapportons-nous-en sur ceci à quelqu'un qui fut bien plus Machiavéliste que Machiavel, à la republique de Venise." Before his day, and long after, down almost to the time when a price was set on the heads of the Pretender and of Pontiac, Venice employed assassins. And this was not the desperate resource of politicians at bay, but the avowed practice of decorous and religious magistrates. In 1569 Soto hazards an impersonal doubt whether the morality of the thing was sound: "Non omnibus satis probatur Venetorum mos, qui cum complures a patria exules habeant condemnatos, singulis facultatem faciunt, ut qui alium eorum interfecerit, vita ac libertate donetur." But his sovereign shortly after obtained assurance that murder by royal command was unanimously approved by divines: "A los tales puede el Principe mandarlos matar, aunque esten fuera de su distrito y reinos.—Sin ser citado, secretamente se le puede quitar la vita.—Esta es doctrina comun y cierta y recevida de todos los theologos." When the King of France, by despatching the Guises, had restored his good name in Europe, a Venetian, Francesco da Molino, hoped that the example would not be thrown away on the Council of Ten: "Permeti sua divina bontà che questo esempio habbi giovato a farlo proceder come spero con meno fretta e più sodamente a cose tali e d' importanza." Sarpi, their ablest writer, their official theologian, has a string of maxims which seem to have been borrowed straight from the Florentine predecessor: "Proponendo cosa in apparenza non honesta, scusarla come necessaria, come praticata da altri, come propria al tempo, che tende a buon fine, et conforme all' opinione de' molti.—La vendetta non giova se non per fugir lo sprezzo.—Ogn' huomo ha opinione che il mendacio sia buono in ragion di medicina, et di far bene a far creder il vero et utile con premesse false." One of his countrymen, having examined his writings, reports: "I ricordi di questo grand' uomo furono più da politico che da christiano." To him was attributed the doctrine of secret punishment, and the use of poison against public enemies: "In casi d' eccessi incorrigibili si punissero secretamente, a fine che il sangue patrizio non resti profanato.—Il veleno deve esser l' unico mezzo per levarli dal mondo, quando alla giustizia non complisse farli passare sotto la manaia del carnefice." Venice, otherwise unlike the rest of Europe, was, in this particular, not an exception.

Machiavelli enjoyed a season of popularity even at Rome. The Medicean popes refused all official employment to one who had been the brain of a hostile government; but they encouraged him to write, and were not offended by the things he wrote for them. Leo's own dealings with the tyrant of Perugia were cited by jurists as a suggestive model for men who have an enemy to get rid of. Clement confessed to Contarini that honesty would be preferable, but that honest men get the worst of it: "Io cognosco certo che voi dicete il vero, et che ad farla da homo da bene, et a far il debito, seria proceder come mi aricordate; ma bisognerebbe trovar la corrispondentia. Non vedete che il mondo è ridutto a un termine che colui il qual è più astuto et cum più trame fa il fatto suo, è più laudato, et estimato più valente homo, et più celebrato, et chi fa il contrario vien detto di esso; quel tale è una bona persona, ma non val niente? Et se ne sta cum quel titulo solo di bona persona.—Chi va bonamente vien trata da bestia." Two years after this speech the astute Florentine authorised *The Prince* to be published at Rome.

It was still unprinted when Pole had it pressed on his attention by Cromwell, and Brosch consequently suspects the story. Upon the death of Clement, Pole opened the attack; but it was not pursued during the reaction against things Medicean which occupied the reign of Farnese. Machiavelli was denounced to the Inquisition on the 11th of November 1550, by Muzio, a man much employed in controversy and literary repression, who, knowing Greek, was chosen by Pius V. for the work afterwards committed to Baronius: "Senza rispetto alcuno insegna a non servar ne fede, ne charità, ne religione; et dice che di queste cosi, gli huomini se ne debbono servire per parer buoni, et per le grandezze temporali, alle quali quando non servono non se ne dee fare stima. Et non è questo peggio che heretica dottrina? Vedendosi che ciò si comporta, sono accetate come opere approvate dalla Santa Madre chiesa." Muzio, who at the same time recommended the *Decamerone*, was not acting from ethical motives. His accusation succeeded. When the Index was instituted, in 1557, Machiavelli was one of the first writers condemned, and he was more rigorously and implacably condemned than anybody else. The Trent Commissioners themselves prepared editions of certain prohibited authors, such as Clarius and Flaminius; Guicciardini was suffered to appear with retrenchments; and the famous revision of Boccaccio was carried out in 1573. This was due to the influence of Victorius, who pleaded in vain for a castigated text of Machiavelli. He continued to be specially excepted when permission was given to read forbidden books. Sometimes there were other exceptions, such as Dumoulin, Marini, or Maimbourg; but the exclusion of Machiavelli was permanent, and when Lucchesini preached against him at the Gesù, he had to apply to the Pope himself for licence to read him. Lipsius was advised by his Roman censors to mix a little Catholic salt in his Machiavellism, and to suppress a seeming protest against the universal hatred for a writer *qui misera qua non manu hodie vapulat.* One of the ablest but most contentious of the Jesuits, Raynaud, pursued his memory with a story like that with which Tronchin improved the death of Voltaire: "Exitus impiissimi nebulonis metuendus est eius aemulatoribus, nam blasphemans evomuit reprobum spiritum."

In spite of this notorious disfavour, he has been associated with the excesses of the religious wars. The daughter of the man to whom he addressed *The Prince* was Catharine of Medici, and she was reported to have taught her children "surtout des traictz de cet athée Machiavel." Boucher asserted that Henry III. carried him in his pocket: "qui perpetuus ei in sacculo atque manibus est"; and Montaigne confirms the story when he says: "Et dict on, de ce temps, que Machiavel est encores ailleurs en crédit." The pertinently appropriate quotation by which the Queen sanctified her murderous resolve was supplied, not by her father's rejected and discredited monitor, but by a bishop at the Council of Trent, whose sermons had just been published: "Bisogna esser severo et acuto, non bisogna esser clemente; è crudeltà l' esser pietoso, è pietà l' esser crudele." And the argument was afterwards embodied in the *Controversies* of Bellarmin: "Haereticis obstinatis beneficium est, quod de hac vita tollantur, nam quo diutius vivunt, eo plures errores excogitant; plures pervertunt, et majorem sibi damnationem acquirunt."

The divines who held these doctrines received them through their own channels straight from the Middle Ages. The germ theory, that the wages of heresy is death, was so expanded as to include the rebel, the usurper, the heterodox or rebellious town, and it continued to develop long after the time of Machiavelli. At first it had been doubtful whether a small number of culprits justified the demolition of a city: "Videtur quod si aliqui haeretici sunt in civitate potest exuri tota civitas." Under Gregory XIII. the right is asserted unequivocally: "Civitas ista potest igne destrui, quando in ea plures sunt haeretici." In case of sedition, fire is a less suitable agent: "Propter rebellionem civitas quandoque supponitur aratro et possunt singuli decapitari." As to heretics the view was: "Ut hostes latronesque occidi possunt etiamsi sunt clerici." A king, if he was judged a usurper, was handed over to extinction: "Licite potest a quolibet de populo occidi, pro libertate populi, quando non est recursus ad superiorem, a quo possit iustitia fieri." Or, in the words of the scrupulous Soto: "Tunc quisque ius habet ipsum extinguendi." To the end of the seventeenth century theologians taught: "Occidatur, seu occidendus proscribatur, quando non alitur potest haberi tranquillitas Reipublicae."

This was not mere theory, or the enforced logic of men in thrall to mediæval antecedents. Under the most carnal and unchristian king, the Vaudois of Provence were exterminated in the year 1545, and Paul Sadolet wrote as follows to Cardinal Farnese just before and just after the event: "Aggionta hora questa instantia del predetto paese di Provenza a quella che da Mons. Nuntio s' era fatta a Sua Maestà Christianissima a nome di Sua Beatitudine et di Vostra Reverendissima Signoria, siamo in ferma speranza, che vi si debbia pigliare qualche bono expediente et farci qualche gagliarda provisione.—È seguito, in questo paese, quel tanto desiderato et tanto necessario effetto circa le cose di Cabrieres, che da vostra Signoria Reverendissima è stato si lungamente ricordato et sollicitato et procurato." Even Melanchthon was provoked by the death of Cromwell to exclaim that there is no better deed than the slaughter of a tyrant; "Utinam Deus alicui forti viro hanc mentem inserat!" And in 1575 the Swedish bishops decided that it would be a good work to poison their king in a basin of soup—an idea particularly repugnant to the author of *De Rege et Regis Institutione.* Among Mariana's papers I have seen the letter from Paris describing the murder of Henry III., which he turned to such account in the memorable sixth chapter: "Communicò con sus superiores, si peccaria mortalmente un sacerdote que matase a un tirano. Ellos le diceron que non era pecado, mas que quedaria irregular. Y no contentandose con esto, ni con las disputas que avia de ordinario en la Sorbona sobre la materia, continuando siempre sus oraciones, lo preguntò a otros theologos, que le afirmavan lo mismo; y con esto se resolviò enteramente de executarlo. Por el successo es de collegir que tuvo el fraile alguna revelacion de Nuestro Señor en particular, y inspiracion para executar el caso." According to Maffei, the Pope's biographer, the priests were not content with saying that killing was no sin: "Cum illi posse, nec sine magno quidem merito censuissent." Regicide was so acceptable a work that it seemed fitly assigned to a divine interposition.

When, on the 21st of January 1591, a youth offered his services to make away with Henry IV., the Nuncio remitted the matter to Rome: "Quantunque mi sia parso di trovarlo pieno di tale humilità, prudenza, spirito et cose che arguiscono che questa sia inspiratione veramente piuttosto che temerità e leggerezza." In a volume which, though recent, is already rare, the Foreign Office published D'Avaux's advice to treat the Protestants of Ireland much as William treated the Catholics of Glencoe; and the argument of the Assassination Plot came originally from a Belgian seminary. There were at least three men living far into the eighteenth century who defended the massacre of St. Bartholomew in their books; and it was held as late as 1741 that culprits may be killed before they are condemned: "Etiam ante sententiam impune occidi possunt, quando de proximo erant banniendi, vel quando eorum delictum est notorium, grave, et pro quo poena capitis infligenda esset."

Whilst these principles were current in religion as well as in society, the official censures of the Church and the protests of every divine since Catharinus were ineffectual. Much of the profaner criticism uttered by such authorities as the Cardinal de Retz, Voltaire, Frederic the Great, Daunou, and Mazzini is not more convincing or more real. Linguet was not altogether wrong in suggesting that the assailants knew Machiavelli at second hand: "Chaque fois que je jette les yeux sur les ouvrages de ce grand génie, je ne saurais concevoir, je l'avoue, la cause du décri où il est tombé. Je soupçonne fortement que ses plus grands ennemis sont ceux qui ne l'ont pas lu." Retz attributed to him a proposition which is not in his writings. Frederic and Algernon Sidney had read only one of his books, and Bolingbroke, a congenial spirit, who quotes him so often, knew him very little. Hume spoils a serious remark by a glaring eighteenth-century comment: "There is scarcely any maxim in *The Prince* which subsequent experience has not entirely refuted. The errors of this politician proceeded, in a great measure, from his having lived in too early an age of the world to be a good judge of political truth." Bodin had previously written: "Il n'a jamais sondé le gué de la science politique."

Mazzini complains of his *analisi cadaverica ed ignoranza della vita*; and Barthélemy St. Hilaire, verging on paradox, says: "On dirait vraiment que l'histoire ne lui a rien appris, non plus que la conscience." That would be more scientific treatment than the common censure of moralists and the common applause of politicians. It is easier to expose errors in practical politics than to remove the ethical basis of judgments which the modern world employs in common with Machiavelli.

By plausible and dangerous paths men are drawn to the doctrine of the justice of History, of judgment by results, the nursling of the nineteenth century, from which a sharp incline leads to *The Prince*. When we say that public life is not an affair of morality, that there is no available rule of right and wrong, that men must be judged by their age, that the code shifts with the longitude, that the wisdom which governs the event is superior to our own, we carry obscurely tribute to the system which bears so odious a name. Few would scruple to maintain with Mr. Morley that the equity of history requires that we shall judge men of action by the standards of men of action; or with Retz: "Les vices d'un archevêque peuvent être, dans une infinité de rencontres, les vertus d'un chef de parti." The expounder of Adam Smith to France, J. B. Say, confirms the ambitious coadjutor: "Louis XIV. et son despotisme et ses guerres n'ont jamais fait le mal qui serait résulté des conseils de ce bon Fénelon, l'apôtre et le martyr de la vertu et du bien des hommes." Most successful public men deprecate what Sir Henry Taylor calls much weak sensibility of conscience, and approve Lord Grey's language to Princess Lieven: "I am a great lover of morality, public and private; but the intercourse of nations cannot be strictly regulated by that rule." While Burke was denouncing the Revolution, Walpole wrote: "No great country was ever saved by good men, because good men will not go the lengths that may be necessary." All which had been formerly anticipated by Pole: "Quanto quis privatam vitam agens Christi similior erit tanto minus aptus ad regendum id munus iudicio hominum existimabitur." The main principle of Machiavelli is asserted by his most eminent English disciple: "It is the solecism of power to think, to command the end, and yet not to endure the means." And Bacon leads up to the familiar Jesuit: "Cui licet finis, illi et media permissa sunt."

The austere Pascal has said: "On ne voit rien de juste ou d'injuste qui ne change de qualité en changeant de climat" (the reading *presque* rien was the precaution of an editor). The same underlying scepticism is found not only in philosophers of the Titanic sort, to whom remorse is a prejudice of education, and the moral virtues are "the political offspring which flattery begat upon pride," but among the masters of living thought. Locke, according to Mr. Bain, holds that we shall scarcely find any rule of morality, excepting such as are necessary to hold society together, and these too with great limitations, but what is somewhere or other set aside, and an opposite established by whole societies of men. Maine de Biran extracts this conclusion from the *Esprit des Lois*: "Il n'y a rien d'absolu ni dans la religion, ni dans la morale, ni, à plus forte raison, dans la politique." In the mercantile economists Turgot detects the very doctrine of Helvetius: "Il établit qu'il n'y a pas lieu à la probité entre les nations, d'où suivroit que la monde doit être éternellement un coupe-gorge. En quoi il est bien d'accord avec les panégyristes de Colbert."

These things survive, transmuted, in the edifying and popular epigram: "Die Weltgeschichte ist das Weltgericht." Lacordaire, though he spoke so well of "L'empire et les ruses de la durée," recorded his experience in these words: "J'ai toujours vu Dieu se justifier à la longue." Reuss, a teacher of opposite tendency and greater name, is equally consoling: "Les destinées de l'homme s'accomplissent ici-bas; la justice de Dieu s'exerce et se manifeste sur cette terre." In the infancy of exact observation Massillon could safely preach that wickedness ends in ignominy: "Dieu aura son tour." The indecisive Providentialism of Bossuet's countrymen is shared by English divines.

"Contemporaries," says Hare, "look at the agents, at their motives and characters; history looks rather at the acts and their consequences." Thirlwall hesitates to say that whatever is, is best; "but I have a strong faith that it is for the best, and that the general stream of tendency is toward good." And Sedgwick, combining induction with theology, writes: "If there be a superintending Providence, and if His will be manifested by general laws, operating both on the physical and moral world, then must a violation of those laws be a violation of His will, and be pregnant with inevitable misery."

Apart from the language of Religion, an optimism ranging to the bounds of fatalism is the philosophy of many, especially of historians: "Le vrai, c'est, en toutes choses, le fait." Sainte-Beuve says: "Il y a dans tout fait général et prolongé une puissance de démonstration insensible"; and Scherer describes progress as "une espèce de logique objective et impersonelle qui résout les questions sans appel." Ranke has written: "Der beste Prüfstein ist die Zeit"; and Sybel explains that this was not a short way out of confusion and incertitude, but a profound generalisation: "Ein Geschlecht, ein Volk löst das andere ab, und der Lebende hat Recht." A scholar of a different school and fibre, Stahr the Aristotelian, expresses the same idea: "Die Geschichte soll die Richtigkeit des Denkens bewähren." Richelieu's maxim: "Les grands desseins et notables entreprises ne se vérifient jamais autrement que par le succès"; and Napoleon's: "Je ne juge les hommes que par les résultats," are seriously appropriated by Fustel de Coulanges: "Ce qui caractérise le véritable homme d'état, c'est le succès, on le reconnaît surtout à ce signe, qu'il réussit." One of Machiavelli's gravest critics applied it to him: "Die ewige Aufgabe der Politik bleibt unter den gegebenen Verhältnissen und mit den vorhandenen Mitteln etwas zu erreichen. Eine Politik die das verkennt, die auf den Erfolg verzichtet, sich auf eine theoretische Propaganda, auf ideale Gesichtspunkte beschränkt, von einer verlorenen Gegenwart an eine künftige Gerechtigkeit appellirt, ist keine Politik mehr." One of the mediæval pioneers, Stenzel, delivered a formula of purest Tuscan cinquecento: "Was bei anderen Menschen gemeine Schlechtigkeit ist, erhält, bei den ungewöhnlichen Geistern, den Stempel der Grösse, der selbst dem Verbrechen sich aufdrückt. Der Maassstab ist anders; denn das Ausserordentliche lässt sich nur durch Ausserordentliches bewirken." Treitschke habitually denounces the impotent Doctrinaires who do not understand "dass der Staat Macht ist und der Welt des Willens angehört," and who know not how to rise "von der Politik des Bekenntnisses zu der Politik der That." Schäfer, though a less pronounced partisan, derides Macaulay for thinking that human happiness concerns political science: "Das Wesen des Staates ist die Macht, und die Politik die Kunst ihn zu erhalten." Rochau's *Realpolitik* was a treatise in two volumes written to prove "dass der Staat durch seine Selbsterhaltung das oberste Gebot der Sittlichkeit erfüllt." Wherefore, nobody finds fault when a State in its decline is subjugated by a robust neighbour. In one of those telling passages which moved Mr. Freeman to complain that he seems unable to understand that a small State can have any rights, or that a generous or patriotic sentiment can find a place anywhere except in the breast of a fool, Mommsen justifies the Roman conquests: "Kraft des Gesetzes dass das zum Staat entwickelte Volk die politisch unmündigen, das civilisirte die geistig unmündigen in sich auflöst." The same idea was imparted into the theory of ethics by Kirchmann, and appears, with a sobering touch, in the *Geschichte Jesu* of Hase, the most popular German divine: "Der Einzelne wird nach der Grösse seiner Ziele, nach den Wirkungen seiner Thaten für das Wohl der Völker gemessen, aber nicht nach dem Maasse der Moral und des Rechts.—Vom Leben im Geiste seiner Zeit hängt nicht der sittliche Werth eines Menschen, aber seine geschichtliche Wirksamkeit ab." Rümelin, both in politics and literature the most brilliant Suabian of his time, and a strenuous adversary of Machiavelli, wrote thus in 1874: "Für den Einzelnen im Staat gilt das Princip der Selbsthingabe, für den Staat das der Selbstbehauptung. Der Einzelne dient dem Recht; der Staat handhabt, leitet und schafft dasselbe. Der Einzelne ist nur ein flüchtiges Glied in dem sittlichen Ganzen; der Staat ist, wenn nicht dieses Ganze selbst, doch dessen reale, ordnende Macht; er ist unsterblich und sich selbst genug.—Die Erhaltung des Staats rechtfertigt jedes Opfer und steht über jedem Gebot." Nefftzer, an Alsatian borderer, says: "Le devoir suprême des individus est de se dévouer, celui des nations est de se conserver, et se confond par conséquent avec leur intérêt." Once, in a mood of pantheism, Renan wrote: "L'humanité a tout fait, et, nous voulons le croire, tout bien fait." Or, as Michelet abridges the *Scienza Nuova*: "L'humanité est son œuvre à elle-même. Dieu agit sur elle, mais par elle." Mr. Leslie Stephen thus lays down the philosophy of history according to Carlyle, "that only succeeds which is based on divine truth, and permanent success therefore proves the right, as the effect proves the cause." Darwin, having met Carlyle, notes that "in his eyes might was right," and adds that he had a narrow and unscientific mind; but Mr. Goldwin Smith discovers the same lesson: "History, of itself, if observed as science observes the facts of the physical world, can scarcely give man any principle or any object of allegiance, unless it be success." Dr. Martineau attributes this doctrine to Mill: "Do we ask what determines the moral quality of actions? We are referred, not to their spring, but to their consequences." Jeremy Bentham used to relate how he found the greatest happiness principle in 1768, and gave a shilling for it, at the corner of Queen's College. He found it in Priestley, and he might have gone on finding it in Beccaria and Hutcheson, all of whom trace their pedigree to the *Mandragola*: "Io credo che quello sia bene che facci bene a' più, e che i più se ne contentino." This is the centre of unity in all Machiavelli, and gives him touch, not with unconscious imitators only, but with the most conspicuous race of reasoners in the century.

English experience has not been familiar with a line of thought plainly involving indulgence to Machiavelli. Dugald Stewart raises him high, but raises him for a heavy fall: "No writer, certainly, either in ancient or in modern times, has ever united, in a more remarkable degree, a greater variety of the most dissimilar and seemingly the most discordant gifts and attainments.—To his maxims the royal defenders of the Catholic faith have been indebted for the spirit of that policy which they have uniformly opposed to the innovations of the reformers." Hallam indeed has said: "We continually find a more flagitious and undisguised abandonment of moral rules for the sake of some idol of a general principle than can be imputed to *The Prince* of Machiavel." But the unaccustomed hyperbole had been hazarded a century before in the obscurity of a Latin dissertation by Feuerlein: "Longe detestabiliores errores apud alios doctores politicos facile invenias, si eidem rigorosae censurae eorum scripta subiicienda essent." What has been, with us, the occasional aphorism of a masterful mind, encountered support abroad in accredited systems, and in a vast and successful political movement. The recovery of Machiavelli has been essentially the product of causes operating on the Continent.

When Hegel was dominant to the Rhine, and Cousin beyond it, the circumstances favoured his reputation. For Hegel taught: "Der Gang der Weltgeschichte steht ausserhalb der Tugend, des Lasters, und der Gerechtigkeit." And the great eclectic renewed, in explicit language, the worst maxim of the *Istorie Fiorentine*: "L'apologie d'un siècle est dans son existence, car son existence est un arrêt et un jugement de Dieu même, ou l'histoire n'est qu'une fastasmagorie insignifiante.—Le caractère propre, le signe d'un grand homme, c'est qu'il réussit.—Ou nul guerrier ne doit être appelé grand homme, ou, s'il est grand, il faut l'absoudre, et absoudre en masse tout ce qu'il a fait.—Il faut prouver que le vainqueur non seulement sert la civilisation, mais qu'il est meilleur, plus moral, et que c'est pour cela qu'il est vainqueur. Maudire la puissance (j'entends une puissance longue et durable) c'est blasphémer l'humanité."

This primitive and everlasting problem assumed a peculiar shape in theological controversy. The Catholic divines urged that prosperity is a sign by which, even in the militant period, the true Church may be known; coupling *Felicitas Temporalis illis collata qui ecclesiam defenderunt* with *Infelix exitus eorum qui ecclesiam oppugnant.* Le Blanc de Beaulieu, a name famous in the history of pacific disputation, holds the opposite opinion: "Crucem et perpessiones esse potius ecclesiae notam, nam denunciatum piis in verbo Dei fore ut in hoc mundo persecutionem patiantur, non vero ut armis sint adversariis suis superiores." Renan, outbidding all, finds that honesty is the worst policy: "En général, dans l'histoire, l'homme est puni de ce qu'il fait de bien, et récompensé de ce qu'il fait de mal.—L'histoire est tout le contraire de la vertu récompensée."

The national movement which united, first Italy and then Germany, opened a new era for Machiavelli. He had come down, laden with the distinctive reproach of abetting despotism; and the men who, in the seventeenth century, levelled the course of absolute monarchy, were commonly known as *novi politici et Machiavellistae.* In the days of Grotius they are denounced by Besold: "Novi politici, ex Italia redeuntes qui quavis fraude principibus a subditis pecuniam extorquere fas licitumque esse putant, Machiavelli plerumque praeceptis et exemplis principum, quorum rationes non capiunt, ad id abutentes." But the immediate purpose with which Italians and Germans effected the great change in the European constitution was unity, not liberty. They constructed, not securities, but forces. Machiavelli's time had come. The problems once more were his own: and in many forward and resolute minds the spirit also was his, and displayed itself in an ascending scale of praise. He was simply a faithful observer of facts, who described the fell necessity that governs narrow territories and unstable fortunes; he discovered the true line of progress and the law of future society; he was a patriot, a republican, a Liberal, but above all this, a man sagacious enough to know that politics is an inductive science. A sublime purpose justifies him, and he has been wronged by dupes and fanatics, by irresponsible dreamers and interested hypocrites.

The Italian Revolution, passing from the Liberal to the national stage, at once adopted his name and placed itself under his invocation. Count Sclopis, though he declared him *Penseur profond*, *écrivain admirable*, deplored this untimely preference: "Il m'a été pénible de voir le gouvernement provisoire de la Tuscane, en 1859, le lendemain du jour où ce pays recouvrait sa liberté, publier un décret, portant qu'une édition complète des œuvres de Machiavel serait faite aux frais de l'état." The research even of our best masters, Villari and Tommasini, is prompted by admiration. Ferrari, who comes so near him in many qualities of the intellect, proclaims him the recorder of fate: "Il décrit les rôles que la fatalité distribue aux individus et aux masses dans ces moments funestes et glorieux où ils sont appelés à changer la loi et la foi des nations." His advice, says La Farina, would have saved Italy. Canello believes that he is disliked because he is mistaken for a courtier: "L' orrore e l' antipatia che molti critici hanno provato per il Machiavelli son derivati dal pensare che tutti i suoi crudi insegnamenti fossero solo a vantaggio del Principe." One biographer, Mordenti, exalts him as the very champion of conscience: "Risuscitando la dignità del-l' umana coscienza, ne affermò l' esistenza in faccia alla ragione." He adds, more truly, "È uno dei personaggi del dramma che si va svolgendo nell' età nostra."

That is the meaning of Laurent when he says that he has imitators but no defenders: "Machiavel ne trouve plus un seul partisan au XIXe siècle.—La postérité a voué son nom à l'infamie, tout en pratiquant sa doctrine." His characteristic universality has been recognised by Baudrillart: "En exprimant ce mauvais côté, mais ce mauvais côté, hélas, éternel! Machiavel n'est plus seulement le publiciste de son pays et de son temps; il est le politique de tous les siècles.—S'il fait tout dépendre de la puissance individuelle, et de ses facultés de force, d'habileté, de ruse, c'est que, plus le théâtre se rétrécit, plus l'homme influe sur la marche des événements." Matter finds the same merits which are applauded by the Italians: "Il a plus innové pour la liberté que pour le despotisme, car autour de lui la liberté était inconnue, tandis que le despotisme lui posait partout." And his reviewer, Longpérier, pronounces the doctrine "parfaitement appropriée aux états d'Italie." Nourrisson, with Fehr, one of the few religious men who still have a good word for the Secretary, admires his sincerity: "*Le Prince* est un livre de bonne foi, où l'auteur, sans songer à mal, n'a fait que traduire en maximes les pratiques habituelles à ses contemporains." Thiers, though he surrendered *The Prince*, clung to the *Discorsi*—the *Discorsi*, with the pointed and culminating text produced by Mr. Burd. In the archives of the ministry he might have found how the idea struck his successful predecessor, Vergennes: "Il est des choses plus fortes que les hommes, et les grands intérêts des nations sont de ce genre, et doivent par conséquent l'emporter sur la façon de penser de quelques particuliers."

Loyalty to Frederic the Great has not restrained German opinion, and philosophers unite with historians in rejecting his youthful moralities. Zimmerman wonders what would have become of Prussia if the king had practised the maxims of the crown prince; and Zeller testifies that the *Anti-Machiavel* was not permitted to influence his reign: "Wird man doch weder in seiner Staatsleitung noch in seinen politischen Grundsätzen etwas von dem vermissen, worauf die Ueberlegenheit einer gesunden Realpolitik allem liberalen oder conservativen, radikalen oder legitimistischen, Doktrinarismus gegenüber beruht." Ahrens and Windelband insist on the virtue of a national government: "Der Staat ist sich selbst genug, wenn er in einer Nation wurzelt,—das ist der Grundgedanke Machiavelli's." Kirchmann celebrates the emancipation of the State from the moral yoke: "Man hat Machiavelli zwar in der Theorie bekämpft, allein die Praxis der Staaten hat seine Lehren immer eingehalten. —Wenn seine Lehre verletzt, so kommt diess nur von der Kleinheit der Staaten und Fürsten, auf die er sie verwendet.—Es spricht nur für seine tiefe Erkenntniss des Staatswesens, dass er die Staatsgewalt nicht den Regeln der Privatmoral unterwirft, sondern selbst vor groben Verletzungen dieser Moral durch den Fürsten nicht zurückschreckt, wenn das Wohl des Ganzen und die Freiheit des Vaterlandes nicht anders vorbereitet und vermittelt werden kann." In Kuno Fischer's progress through the systems of metaphysics Machiavelli appears at almost every step; his influence is manifest to Dr. Abbott throughout the whole of Bacon's political writings; Hobbes followed up his theory to the conclusions which he abstained from; Spinoza gave him the benefit of a liberal interpretation; Leibniz, the inventor of the acquiescent doctrine which Bolingbroke transmitted to the *Essay on Man*, said that he drew a good likeness of a bad prince; Herder reports him to mean that a rogue need not be a fool; Fichte frankly set himself to rehabilitate him. In the end, the great master of modern philosophy pronounces in his favour, and declares it absurd to robe a prince in the cowl of a monk: "Ein politischer Denker und Künstler dessen erfahrener und tiefer Verstand aus den geschichtlich gegebenen Verhältnissen besser, als aus den Grundsätzen der Metaphysik, die politischen Nothwendigkeiten, den Charakter, die Bildung und Aufgabe weltlicher Herrschaft zu begreifen wusste.—Da man weiss, dass politische Machtfragen nie, am Wenigsten in einem verderbten Volke, mit den Mitteln der Moral zu lösen sind, so ist es unverständig, das Buch vom Fürsten zu verschreien. Machiavelli hatte einen Herrscher zu schildern, keinen Klosterbruder."

Ranke was a grateful student of Fichte when he spoke of Machiavelli as a meritorious writer, maligned by people who could not understand him: "Einem Autor von höchstem Verdienst, und der keineswegs ein böser Mensch war.—Die falsche Auffassung des *Principe* beruht eben darauf, dass man die Lehren Machiavells als allgemeine betrachtet, während sie bloss Anweisungen für einen bestimmten Zweck sind." To Gervinus, in 1853, he is "der grosse Seher," the prophet of the modern world: "Er errieth den Geist der neuern Geschichte." Gervinus was a democratic Liberal, and, taken with Gentz from another quarter, he shows how widely the elements of the Machiavellian restoration were spread over Europe. Gentz had not forgotten his classics in the service of Austria when he wrote to a friend: "Wenn selbst das Recht je verletzt werden darf, so geschehe es, um die rechtmässige Macht zu erhalten; in allem Uebrigen herrsche es unbedingt." Twesten is as well persuaded as Machiavelli that the world cannot be governed "con Pater nostri in mano," and he deemed that patriotism atoned for his errors: "Dass der weltgeschichtliche Fortschritt nicht mit Schonung und Gelindigkeit, nicht in den Formen des Rechts vollzogen werden konnte, hat die Geschichte aller Länder bestätigt.—Auch Machiavellis Sünden mögen wir als gesühnt betrachten, durch das hochsinnige Streben für das Grosse und das Ansehen seines Volkes." One censor of Frederic, Boretius, makes him answerable for a great deal of presuming criticism: "Die Gelehrten sind bis heute in ihrem Urtheil über Machiavelli nicht einig, die öffentliche Meinung ist hierin glücklicher.—Die öffentliche Meinung kann sich für alle diese Weisheit beim alten Fritz bedanken." On the eve of the campaign in Bohemia, Herbst pointed out that Machiavelli, though previously a republican, sacrificed liberty to unity: "Der Einheit soll die innere Freiheit—Machiavelli war kurz zuvor noch begeisterter Anhänger der Republik—geopfert werden." According to Feuerlein the heart of the writer was loyal, but the conditions of the problem were inexorable; and Klein detects in *The Prince*, and even in the *Mandragola*, "die reformatorische Absicht eines Sittenspiegels." Chowanetz wrote a book to hold up Machiavelli as a teacher of all ages, but especially of our own: "Die

Absicht aber, welche Machiavel mit seinem Buche verband, ist trefflich für alle Zeiten." And Weitzel hardly knows a better writer, or one less worthy of an evil name: "Im Interesse der Menschheit und gesetzmässiger Verfassungen kann kaum ein besseres Werk geschrieben werden.—Wohl ist mancher in der Geschichte, wie in der Tradition der Völker, auf eine unschuldige Weise um seinen verdienten, oder zu einem unverdienten Rufe gekommen, aber keiner vielleicht unschuldiger als Machiavelli."

These are remote and forgotten names. Stronger men of the imperial epoch have resumed the theme with better means of judging, and yet with no harsher judgment. Hartwig sums up his penetrating and severe analysis by confessing that the world as Machiavelli saw it, without a conscience, is the real world of history as it is: "Die Thatsachen selbst scheinen uns das Geheimniss ihrer Existenz zu verrathen; wir glauben vor uns die Fäden sich verknüpfen und verschlingen zu sehen, deren Gewebe die Weltgeschichte ist." Gaspary thinks that he hated iniquity, but that he knew of no righteousness apart from the State: "Er lobte mit Wärme das Gute und tadelte mit Abscheu das Böse; aber er studirte auch dieses mit Interesse.—Er erkennt eben keine Moral, wie keine Religion, über dem Staate, sondern nur in demselben; die Menschen sind von Natur schlecht, die Gesetze machen sie gut.—Wo es kein Gericht giebt, bei dem man klagen könnte, wie in den Handlungen der Fürsten, betrachtet man immer das Ende." The common opinion is expressed by Baumgarten in his *Charles the Fifth*, that the grandeur of the purpose assures indulgence to the means proposed: "Wenn die Umstände zum Wortbruch, zur Grausamkeit, Habgier, Lüge treiben, so hat man sich nicht etwa mit Bedauern, dass die Not dazu zwinge, sondern schlechtweg, weil es eben politisch zweckmässig ist und ohne alles Bedenken so zu verhalten.—Ihre Deduktionen sind uns unerträglich, wenn wir nicht sagen können: alle diese schrecklichen Dinge empfahl Machiavelli, weil er nur durch sie die Befreiung seines Vaterlandes zu erreichen hoffte. Dieses erhabene Ziel macht uns die fürchterlichen Mittel annehmbar, welche Machiavelli seinem Fürsten empfiehlt." Hillebrand was a more international German; he had swum in many European waters, and wrote in three languages. He is scarcely less favourable in his interpretation: "Cette dictature, il ne faut jamais le perdre de vue, ne serait jamais que transitoire, et devrait faire place à un gouvernement libre dès que la grande réforme nationale et sociale serait accomplie.—Il a parfaitement conscience du mal. L'atmosphère ambiante de son siècle et de son pays n'a nullement oblitéré son sens moral.—Il a si bien conscience de l'énormité de ces crimes, qu'il la condamne hautement lorsque la dernière nécessité ne les impose pas."

Among these utterances of capable and distinguished men, it will be seen that some are partially true, and others, without a particle of truth, are at least representative and significant, and serve to bring Machiavelli within fathomable depth. He is the earliest conscious and articulate exponent of certain living forces in the present world. Religion, progressive enlightenment, the perpetual vigilance of public opinion, have not reduced his empire, or disproved the justice of his conception of mankind. He obtains a new lease of life from causes that are still prevailing, and from doctrines that are apparent in politics, philosophy, and science. Without sparing censure, or employing for comparison the grosser symptoms of the age, we find him near our common level, and perceive that he is not a vanishing type, but a constant and contemporary influence. Where it is impossible to praise, to defend, or to excuse, the burden of blame may yet be lightened by adjustment and distribution, and he is more rationally intelligible when illustrated by lights falling not only from the century he wrote in, but from our own, which has seen the course of its history twenty-five times diverted by actual or attempted crime.

VIII

MR. GOLDWIN SMITH'S IRISH HISTORY[1]

WHEN Macaulay republished his Essays from the *Edinburgh Review*, he had already commenced the great work by which his name will be remembered; and he had the prudence to exclude from the collection his early paper on the art of historical writing. In the maturity of his powers, he was rightly unwilling to bring into notice the theories of his youth. At a time when he was about to claim a place among the first historians, it would have been injudicious to remind men of the manner in which he had described the objects of his emulation or of his rivalry—how in his judgment the speeches of Thucydides violate the decencies of fiction, and give to his book something of the character of the Chinese pleasure-grounds, whilst his political observations are very superficial; how Polybius has no other merit than that of a faithful narrator of facts; and how in the nineteenth century, from the practice of distorting narrative in conformity with theory, "history proper is disappearing." But in that essay, although the judgments are puerile, the ideal at which the writer afterwards aimed is distinctly drawn, and his own character is prefigured in the description of the author of a history of England as it ought to be, who "gives to truth those attractions which have been usurped by fiction," "intersperses the details which are the charm of historical romances," and "reclaims those materials which the novelist has appropriated."

Mr. Goldwin Smith, like Macaulay, has written on

[1] *The Rambler*, March 1862.

the study of history, and he has been a keen critic of other historians before becoming one himself. It is a bold thing for a man to bring theory so near to execution, and, amidst dispute on his principles and resentment at his criticism, to give an opportunity of testing his theories by his own practice, and of applying his own canons to his performance. It reminds us of the professor of Cologne, who wrote the best Latin poem of modern times, as a model for his pupils; and of the author of an attack on Dryden's *Virgil*, who is styled by Pope the "fairest of critics," "because," says Johnson, "he exhibited his own version to be compared with that which he condemned." The work in which the professor of history and critic of historians teaches by example is not unworthy of his theory, whilst some of its defects may be explained by it.

The point which most closely connects Mr. Goldwin Smith's previous writings with his *Irish History* is his vindication of a moral code against those who identify moral with physical laws, who consider the outward regularity with which actions are done to be the inward reason why they must be done, and who conceive that all laws are opposed to freedom. In his opposition to this materialism, he goes in one respect too far, in another not far enough.

On the one hand, whilst defending liberty and morality, he has not sufficient perception of the spiritual element; and on the other, he seems to fear that it would be a concession to his antagonists to dwell on the constant laws by which nature asserts herself, and on the regularity with which like causes produce like effects. Yet it is on the observation of these laws that political, social, and economical science rests; and it is by the knowledge of them that a scientific historian is guided in grouping his matter. In this he differs from the artist, whose principle of arrangement is drawn from himself, not from external nature; and from the annalist, who has no arrangement, since he sees, not the connection, but the succession of events. Facts are intelligible and instructive,—or, in other words, history exhibits truths as well as facts,—when they are seen not merely as they follow, but as they correspond; not merely as they have happened, but as they are paralleled. The fate of Ireland is to be understood not simply from the light of English and Irish history, but by the general history of other conquests, colonies, dependencies, and establishments. In this sort of illustration by analogy and contrast Mr. Goldwin Smith is particularly infelicitous. Nor does Providence gain what science loses by his treatment of history. He rejects materialism, but he confines his view to motives and forces which are purely human.

The Catholic Church receives, therefore, very imperfect measure at his hands. Her spiritual character and purpose he cannot discern behind the temporal instruments and appendages of her existence; he confounds authority with influence, devotion with bigotry, power with force of arms, and estimates the vigour and durability of Catholicism by criterions as material as those of the philosophers he has so vehemently and so ably refuted. Most Protestant writers fail in approbation; he fails in appreciation. It is not so much a religious feeling that makes him unjust, as a way of thinking which, in great measure, ignores the supernatural, and therefore precludes a just estimate of religion in general, and of Catholicism in particular. Hence he is unjust rather to the nature than to the actions of the Church. He caricatures more than he libels her. He is much less given to misrepresentation and calumny than Macaulay, but he has a less exalted idea of the history and character of Catholicism. As he underrates what is divine, so he has no very high standard for the actions of men, and he is liberal in admitting extenuating circumstances. Though he never suspends the severity of his moral judgment in consideration of the purpose or the result, yet he is induced by a variety of arguments to mitigate its rigour. In accordance with the theory he has formerly developed, he is constantly sitting in judgment; and he discusses the morality of men and actions far oftener than history—which has very different problems to solve—either requires or tolerates. De Maistre says that in our time compassion is reserved for the guilty. Mr. Goldwin Smith is a merciful judge, whose compassion generally increases in proportion to the greatness of the culprit; and he has a sympathy for what is done in the grand style, which balances his hatred of what is wrongly done.

It would not be fair to judge of an author's notion and powers of research by a hasty and popular production. Mr. Goldwin Smith has collected quite enough information for the purpose for which he has used it, and he has not failed through want of industry. The test of solidity is not the quantity read, but the mode in which the knowledge has been collected and used. Method, not genius, or eloquence, or erudition, makes the historian. He may be discovered most easily by his use of authorities. The first question is, whether the writer understands the comparative value of sources of information, and has the habit of giving precedence to the most trustworthy informant. There are some vague indications that Mr. Goldwin Smith does not understand the importance of this fundamental rule. In his Inaugural Lecture, published two years ago, the following extravagant sentence occurs: "Before the Revolution, the fervour and the austerity of Rousseau had cast out from good society the levity and sensuality of Voltaire" (p. 15). This view—which he appears to have abandoned, for in his *Irish History* he tells us that France "has now become the eldest daughter of Voltaire"—he supports by a reference to an abridgment of French history, much and justly esteemed in French schools, but, like all abridgments, not founded on original knowledge, and disfigured by exaggeration in the colouring. Moreover, the passage he refers to has been misinterpreted. In the *Irish History* Mr. Goldwin Smith quotes, for the character of the early Celts, without any sufficient reason, another French historian, Martin, who has no great authority, and the younger Thierry, who has none at all. This is a point of very little weight by itself;

but until our author vindicates his research by other writings, it is not in his favour.

The defects of Mr. Goldwin Smith's historic art, his lax criticism, his superficial acquaintance with foreign countries, his occasional proneness to sacrifice accuracy for the sake of rhetorical effect, his aversion for spiritual things, are all covered by one transcendent merit, which, in a man of so much ability, promises great results.

Writers the most learned, the most accurate in details, and the soundest in tendency, frequently fall into a habit which can neither be cured nor pardoned,—the habit of making history into the proof of their theories. The absence of a definite didactic purpose is the only security for the good faith of a historian. This most rare virtue Mr. Goldwin Smith possesses in a high degree. He writes to tell the truths he finds, not to prove the truths which he believes. In character and design he is eminently truthful and fair, though not equally so in execution. His candour never fails him, and he is never betrayed by his temper; yet his defective knowledge of general history, and his crude notions of the Church, have made him write many things which are untrue, and some which are unjust. Prejudice is in all men of such early growth, and so difficult to eradicate, that it becomes a misfortune rather than a reproach, especially if it is due to ignorance and not to passion, and if it has not its seat in the will. In the case of Mr. Goldwin Smith it is of the curable and harmless kind. The fairness of his intention is far beyond his knowledge. When he is unjust, it is not from hatred; where he is impartial, it is not always from the copiousness of his information. His prejudices are of a nature which his ability and honesty will in time inevitably overcome.

The general result and moral of his book is excellent. He shows that the land-question has been from the beginning the great difficulty in Ireland; and he concludes with a condemnation of the Established Church, and a prophecy of its approaching fall. The weakness of

Ireland and the guilt of England are not disguised; and the author has not written to stimulate the anger of one nation or to attenuate the remorse of the other. To both he gives wise and statesman-like advice, that may soon be very opportune. The first American war was the commencement of the deliverance of Ireland, and it may be that a new American war will complete the work of regeneration which the first began. Agreeing as we do with the policy of the author, and admiring the spirit of his book, we shall not attempt either to enforce or to dispute his conclusions, and we shall confine our remarks to less essential points on which he appears to us in the wrong.

There are several instances of inaccuracy and negligence which, however trivial in themselves, tend to prove that the author is not always very scrupulous in speaking of things he has not studied. A purist so severe as to write "Kelt" for "Celt" ought not to call Mercury, originally a very different personage from Hermes, one of "the legendary authors of Greek civilisation" (p. 43); and we do not believe that anybody who had read the writings of the two primates could call Bramhall "an inferior counterpart of Laud" (p. 105). In a loftier mood, and therefore apparently with still greater license, Mr. Goldwin Smith declares that "the glorious blood of Orange could scarcely have run in a low persecutor's veins" (p. 123). The blood of Orange ran in the veins of William the Silent, the threefold hypocrite, who confessed Catholicism whilst he hoped to retain his influence at court, Lutheranism when there was a chance of obtaining assistance from the German princes, Calvinism when he was forced to resort to religion in order to excite the people against the crown, and who persecuted the Protestants in Orange and the Catholics in Holland. These, however, are matters of no consequence whatever in a political history of Ireland; but we find ourselves at issue with the author on the important question of political freedom. "Even the highly civilised Kelt of France, familiar as he is with theories of political liberty, seems almost incapable of sustaining free institutions. After a moment of constitutional government, he reverts, with a bias which the fatalist might call irresistible, to despotism in some form" (p. 18). The warning so frequently uttered by Burke in his last years, to fly from the liberty of France, is still more needful now that French liberty has exhibited itself in a far more seductive light. The danger is more subtle, when able men confound political forms with popular rights. France has never been governed by a Constitution since 1792, if by a Constitution is meant a definite rule and limitation of the governing power. It is not that the French failed to preserve the forms of parliamentary government, but that those forms no more implied freedom than the glory which the Empire has twice given in their stead. It is a serious fault in our author that he has not understood so essential a distinction. Has he not read the *Rights of Man*, by Tom Paine?—

> It is not because a part of the government is elective that makes it less a despotism, if the persons so elected possess afterwards, as a parliament, unlimited powers. Election, in this case, becomes separated from representation, and the candidates are candidates for despotism.[1]

Napoleon once consulted the cleverest among the politicians who served him, respecting the durability of some of his institutions. "Ask yourself," was the answer, "what it would cost you to destroy them. If the destruction would cost no effort, you have created nothing; for politically, as well as physically, only that which resists endures." In the year 1802 the same great writer said: "Nothing is more pernicious in a monarchy than the principles and the forms of democracy, for they allow no alternative, but despotism and revolutions." With the additional experience of half a century, a writer not inferior to the last repeats exactly the same idea:—

> Of all societies in the world, those which will always have most difficulty in permanently escaping absolute government will be pre-

[1] *Works*, ii. 47. This is one of the passages which, seventy years ago, were declared to be treasonable. We trust we run no risk in confessing that we entirely agree with it.

cisely those societies in which aristocracy is no more, and can no more be.[1]

French constitutionalism was but a form by which the absence of self-government was concealed. The State was as despotic under Villèle or Guizot as under either of the Bonapartes. The Restoration fenced itself round with artificial creations, having no root in the condition or in the sympathies of the people; these creations simply weakened it by making it unpopular. The hereditary peerage was an anomaly in a country unused to primogeniture, and so was the revival, in a nation of sceptics, of the Gallican union between Church and State. The monarchy of July, which was more suited to the nature of French society, and was thus enabled to crush a series of insurrections, was at last forced, by its position and by the necessity of self-preservation, to assume a very despotic character. After the fortifications of Paris were begun, a tendency set in which, under a younger sovereign, would have led to a system hardly distinguishable from that which now prevails; and there are princes in the House of Orleans whose government would develop the principle of democracy in a manner not very remote from the institutions of the second Empire. It is liberalism more than despotism that is opposed to liberty in France; and it is a most dangerous error to imagine that the Governments of the French Charter really resemble ours. There are States without any parliament at all, whose principles and fundamental institutions are in much closer harmony with our system of autonomy. Mr. Goldwin Smith sees half the truth, that there is something in the French nation which incapacitates it for liberty; but he does not see that what they have always sought, and sometimes enjoyed, is not freedom; that their liberty must diminish in proportion as their ideal is attained; and that they are not yet familiar with the theory of political rights. With this false notion of what constitutes liberty, it is not surprising that he should repeatedly

[1] Tocqueville, *L'Ancien Régime et la Révolution*, Préface, p. xvi.

dwell on its connection with Protestantism, and talk of "the political liberty which Protestantism brought in its train" (p. 120). Such phrases may console a Protestant reader of a book fatal to the Protestant ascendency in Ireland; but as there are no arguments in support of them, and as they are strangely contradicted by the facts in the context, Mr. Goldwin Smith resorts to the ingenious artifice of calling to mind as many ugly stories about Catholics as he can. The notion constantly recurs that, though the Protestants were very wicked in Ireland, it was against their principles and general practice, and is due to the Catholics, whose system naturally led them to be tyrannical and cruel, and thus provoked retaliation. Mr. Smith might have been reminded by Peter Plymley that when Protestantism has had its own way it has uniformly been averse to freedom: "What has Protestantism done for liberty in Denmark, in Sweden, throughout the north of Germany, and in Prussia?"—not much less than democracy has done in France. An admirer of the constitutions of 1791, 1814, or 1830 may be excused if he is not very severe on the absolutism of Protestant countries.

Mr. Goldwin Smith mistakes the character of the invasion of Ireland because he has not understood the relative position of the civilisation of the two countries at the time when it occurred. That of the Celts was in many respects more refined than that of the Normans. The Celts are not among the progressive, initiative races, but among those which supply the materials rather than the impulse of history, and are either stationary or retrogressive. The Persians, the Greeks, the Romans, and the Teutons are the only makers of history, the only authors of advancement. Other races possessing a highly developed language, a copious literature, a speculative religion, enjoying luxury and art, attain to a certain pitch of cultivation which they are unable either to communicate or to increase. They are a negative element in the world; sometimes the barrier, sometimes the instrument, sometimes the material of those races to whom it is given to originate and to advance. Their existence is either passive, or reactionary and destructive, when, after intervening like the blind forces of nature, they speedily exhibit their uncreative character, and leave others to pursue the course to which they have pointed. The Chinese are a people of this kind. They have long remained stationary, and succeeded in excluding the influences of general history. So the Hindoos; being Pantheists, they have no history of their own, but supply objects for commerce and for conquest. So the Huns, whose appearance gave a sudden impetus to a stagnant world. So the Slavonians, who tell only in the mass, and whose influence is ascertainable sometimes by adding to the momentum of active forces, sometimes by impeding through inertness the progress of mankind.

To this class of nations also belong the Celts of Gaul. The Roman and the German conquerors have not altered their character as it was drawn two thousand years ago. They have a history, but it is not theirs; their nature remains unchanged, their history is the history of the invaders. The revolution was the revival of the conquered race, and their reaction against the creations of their masters. But it has been cunning only to destroy; it has not given life to one constructive idea, or durability to one new institution; and it has exhibited to the world an unparalleled political incapacity, which was announced by Burke, and analysed by Tocqueville, in works which are the crowning pieces of two great literatures.

The Celts of these islands, in like manner, waited for a foreign influence to set in action the rich treasure which in their own hands could be of no avail. Their language was more flexible, their poetry and music more copious, than those of the Anglo-Normans. Their laws, if we may judge from those of Wales, display a society in some respects highly cultivated. But, like the rest of that group of nations to which they belong, there was not in them the incentive to action and progress which is given by the consciousness of a part in human destiny, by the inspiration of a high idea, or even by the natural development of institutions. Their life and literature were aimless and wasteful. Without combination or concentration, they had no star to guide them in an onward course; and the progress of dawn into day was no more to them than to the flocks and to the forests.

Before the Danish wars, and the decay, which is described by St. Bernard in terms which must not be taken quite literally, had led to the English invasion, there was probably as much material, certainly as much spiritual, culture in Ireland as in any country in the West; but there was not that by whose sustaining force alone these things endure, by which alone the place of nations in history is determined—there was no political civilisation. The State did not keep pace with the progress of society. This is the essential and decisive inferiority of the Celtic race, as conspicuous among the Irish in the twelfth century as among the French in our own. They gave way before the higher political aptitude of the English.

The issue of an invasion is generally decided by this political aptitude, and the consequences of conquest always depend on it. Subjection to a people of a higher capacity for government is of itself no misfortune; and it is to most countries the condition of their political advancement. The Greeks were more highly cultivated than the Romans, the Gauls than the Franks; yet in both cases the higher political intelligence prevailed. For a long time the English had, perhaps, no other superiority over the Irish; yet this alone would have made the conquest a great blessing to Ireland, but for the separation of the races. Conquering races necessarily bring with them their own system of government, and there is no other way of introducing it. A nation can obtain political education only by dependence on another. Art, literature, and science may be communicated by the conquered to the conqueror; but government can be taught only by governing, therefore only by the governors; politics can only be learnt in this school. The most uncivilised of the barbarians, whilst they slowly and imperfectly learned the arts of Rome, at once remodelled its laws. The two kinds of civilisation, social and political, are wholly unconnected with each other. Either may subsist, in high perfection, alone. Polity grows like language, and is part of a people's nature, not dependent on its will. One or the other can be developed, modified, corrected; but they cannot be subverted or changed by the people itself without an act of suicide. Organic change, if it comes at all, must come from abroad. Revolution is a malady, a frenzy, an interruption of the nation's growth, sometimes fatal to its existence, often to its independence. In this case revolution, by making the nation subject to others, may be the occasion of a new development. But it is not conceivable that a nation should arbitrarily and spontaneously cast off its history, reject its traditions, abrogate its law and government, and commence a new political existence.

Nothing in the experience of ages, or in the nature of man, allows us to believe that the attempt of France to establish a durable edifice on the ruins of 1789, without using the old materials, can ever succeed, or that she can ever emerge from the vicious circle of the last seventy years, except by returning to the principle which she then repudiated, and by admitting, that if States would live, they must preserve their organic connection with their origin and history, which are their root and their stem; that they are not voluntary creations of human wisdom; and that men labour in vain who would construct them without acknowledging God as the artificer.

Theorists who hold it to be a wrong that a nation should belong to a foreign State are therefore in contradiction with the law of civil progress. This law, or rather necessity, which is as absolute as the law that binds society together, is the force which makes us need one another, and only enables us to obtain what we need on terms, not of equality, but of dominion and subjection, in domestic, economic, or political relations. The political theory of nationality is in contradiction with the historic nation. Since a nation derives its ideas and instincts of government, as much as its temperament and its language, from God, acting through the influences of nature and of history, these ideas and instincts are originally and essentially peculiar to it, and not separable from it; they have no practical value in themselves when divided from the capacity which corresponds to them. National qualities are the incarnations of political ideas. No people can receive its government from another without receiving at the same time the ministers of government. The workman must travel with the work. Such changes can only be accomplished by submission to a foreign State, or to another race. Europe has seen two great instances of such conquests, extending over centuries,—the Roman Empire, and the settlement of the barbarians in the West. This it is which gives unity to the history of the Middle Ages. The Romans established a universal empire by subjecting all countries to the authority of a single power. The barbarians introduced into all a single system of law, and thus became the instrument of a universal Church. The same spirit of freedom, the same notions of the State, pervade all the *Leges Barbarorum*, and all the polities they founded in Europe and Asia. They differ widely in the surrounding conditions, in the state of society, in the degree of advancement, in almost all external things. The principle common to them all is to acknowledge the freedom of the Church as a corporation and a proprietor, and in virtue of the principle of self-government to allow religion to develop her influence in the State. The great migration which terminated in the Norman conquests and in the Crusades gave the dominion of the Latin world to the Teutonic chivalry, and to the Church her proper place. All other countries sank into despotism, into schism, and at last into barbarism, under the Tartars or the Turks. The union between the Teutonic races and the Holy See was founded on their political qualities more than on their religious fervour. In modern times, the most pious Catholics have often tyrannised over the Church. In the Middle Ages her liberty was often secured and respected where her spiritual injunctions were least obeyed.

The growth of the feudal system coinciding with the general decay of morals led, in the eleventh century, to new efforts of the Church to preserve her freedom. The Holy See was delivered from the Roman factions by the most illustrious of the emperors, and a series of German Popes commenced the great reform. Other princes were unwilling to submit to the authority of the imperial nominees, and the kings of France and Castile showed symptoms of resistance, in which they were supported by the heresy of Berengarius. The conduct of Henry IV. delivered the Church from the patronage of the Empire, whilst the Normans defended her against the Gallican tendencies and the feudal tyranny. In Sicily, the Normans consented to hold their power from the Pope; and in Normandy, Berengarius found a successful adversary, and the King of France a vassal who compelled him to abandon his designs. The chaplain of the Conqueror describes his government in terms which show how singularly it fulfilled the conditions which the Church requires. He tells us that William established in Normandy a truly Christian order; that every village, town, and castle enjoyed its own privileges; and that, while other princes either forbade the erection of churches or seized their endowments, he left his subjects free to make pious gifts. In his reign and by his conduct the word "bigot" ceased to be a term of reproach, and came to signify what we now should call "ultramontane." He was the foremost of those Normans who were called by the Holy See to reclaim what was degenerate, and to renovate the declining States of the North.

Where the Church addressed herself to the conversion of races of purely Teutonic origin, as in Scandinavia, her missionaries achieved the work. In other countries, as in Poland and Hungary, political dependence on the Empire was the channel and safeguard of her influence. The Norman conquest of England and of Ireland differs from all of these. In both islands the faith had been freely preached, adopted, and preserved. The rulers and the people were Catholic. The last Saxon king who died before the Conquest was a saint. The last archbishop of Dublin appointed before the invasion was a saint. Neither of the invasions can be explained simply by the demoralisation of the clergy, or by the spiritual destitution of the people.

Catholicism spreads among the nations, not only as a doctrine, but as an institution. "The Church," says Mr. Goldwin Smith, "is not a disembodied spirit, but a spirit embodied in human society." Her teaching is directed to the inner man, and is confined to the social order; but her discipline touches on the political. She cannot permanently ignore the acts and character of the State, or escape its notice. Whilst she preaches submission to authorities ordained by God, her nature, not her interest, compels her to exert an involuntary influence upon them. The jealousy so often exhibited by governments is not without reason, for the free action of the Church is the test of the free constitution of the State; and without such free constitution there must necessarily ensue either persecution or revolution. Between the settled organisation of Catholicism and every form of arbitrary power, there is an incompatibility which must terminate in conflict. In a State which possesses no security for authority or freedom, the Church must either fight or succumb. Now, as authority and freedom, the conditions of her existence, can only be obtained through the instrumentality of certain nations, she depends on the aid of these nations. Religion alone cannot civilise men, or secure its own conquest. It promotes civilisation where it has power; but it has not power where its way is not prepared. Its civilising influence is chiefly indirect, and acts by its needs and wants as much as by the fulness of its ideas. So Christianity extends itself by the aid of the secular power, relying, not on the victories of Christian arms, but on the progress of institutions and ideas that harmonise with ecclesiastical freedom. Hence, those who have most actively served the interests of the Church are not always those who have been most faithful to her doctrines. The work which the Goth and the

Frank had done on the continent of Europe the Normans came to do in England, where it had been done before but had failed, and in Ireland, where neither Roman nor German influences had entered.

Thus the theory of nationality, unknown to Catholic ages, is inconsistent both with political reason and with Christianity, which requires the dominion of race over race, and whose path was made straight by two universal empires. The missionary may outstrip, in his devoted zeal, the progress of trade or of arms; but the seed that he plants will not take root, unprotected by those ideas of right and duty which first came into the world with the tribes who destroyed the civilisation of antiquity, and whose descendants are in our day carrying those ideas to every quarter of the world. It was as impossible to realise in Ireland the mediæval notions of ecclesiastical liberty without a great political reform, as to put an end to the dissolution of society and the feuds of princes without the authority of a supreme lord.

There is one institution of those days to which Mr. Goldwin Smith has not done entire justice.

> It is needless to say that the Eric, or pecuniary composition for blood, in place of capital or other punishment, which the Brehon law sanctioned, is the reproach of all primitive codes, and of none. It is the first step from the license of savage revenge to the ordered justice of a regular law (p. 41).

Pecuniary composition for blood belongs to an advanced period of defined and regular criminal jurisprudence. In the lowest form of civil society, when the State is not yet distinct from the family, the family is compelled to defend itself; and the only protection of society is the vendetta. It is the private right of self-defence combined with the public office of punishment, and therefore not only a privilege but an obligation. The whole family is bound to avenge the injury; but the duty rests first of all with the heir. Precedency in the office of avenger is naturally connected with a first claim in inheritance; and the succession to property is determined by the law of revenge. This leads both to primogeniture, because the eldest son is most likely to be capable of punishing the culprit; and, for the same reason, to modifications of primogeniture, by the preference of the brother before the grandson, and of the male line before the female. A practice which appears barbarous is, therefore, one of the foundations of civilisation, and the origin of some of the refinements of law. In this state of society there is no distinction between civil and criminal law; an injury is looked upon as a private wrong, not, as religion considers it, a sin, or, as the State considers it, a crime.

Something very similar occurs in feudal society. Here all the barons were virtually equal to each other, and without any superior to punish their crimes or to avenge their wrongs. They were, therefore, compelled to obtain safety or reparation, like sovereigns, by force of arms. What war is among States, the feud is in feudal society, and the vengeance of blood in societies not yet matured into States—a substitute for the fixed administration of justice.

The assumption of this duty by the State begins with the recognisance of acts done against the State itself. At first, political crimes alone are visited with a public penalty; private injuries demand no public expiation, but only satisfaction of the injured party. This appears in its most rudimentary form in the *lex talionis*. Society requires that punishment should be inflicted by the State, in order to prevent continual disorders. If the injured party could be satisfied, and his duty fulfilled without inflicting on the criminal an injury corresponding to that which he had done, society was obviously the gainer. At first it was optional to accept or to refuse satisfaction; afterwards it was made obligatory.

Where property was so valuable that its loss was visited on the life or limb of the robber, and injuries against property were made a question of life and death, it soon followed that injury to life could be made a question of payment. To expiate robbery by death, and to expiate murder by the payment of a fine, are correlative ideas.

Practically this custom often told with a barbarous inequality against those who were too poor to purchase forgiveness; but it was otherwise both just and humane in principle, and it was generally encouraged by the Church. For in her eyes the criminal was guilty of an act of which it was necessary that he should repent; this made her desire, not his destruction, but his conversion. She tried, therefore, to save his life, and to put an end to revenge, mutilation, and servitude; and for all this the alternative was compensation. This purpose was served by the right of asylum. The Church surrendered the fugitive only on condition that his life and person should be spared in consideration of a lawful fine, which she often paid for him herself. "Concedatur ei vita et omnia membra. Emendat autem causam in quantum potuerit," says a law of Charlemagne, given in the year 785, when the influence of religion on legislation was most powerful in Europe.

No idea occurs more frequently in the work we are reviewing than that of the persecuting character of the Catholic Church; it is used as a perpetual apology for the penal laws in Ireland:—

"When the Catholics writhe under this wrong, let them turn their eyes to the history of Catholic countries, and remember that, while the Catholic Church was stripped of her endowments and doomed to political degradation by Protestant persecutors in Ireland, the Protestant churches were exterminated with fire and sword by Catholic persecutors in France, Austria, Flanders, Italy, and Spain" (p. 92). He speaks of Catholicism as "a religion which all Protestants believed to be idolatrous, and knew by fearful experience to be persecuting" (p. 113). "It would not be difficult to point to persecuting laws more sanguinary than these. Spain, France, and Austria will at once supply signal examples. . . . That persecution was the vice of an age and not only of a particular religion, that it disgraced Protestantism as well as Catholicism, is true. But no one who reads the religious history of Europe with an open mind can fail to perceive that the persecutions carried on by Protestants were far less bloody and less extensive than those carried on by Catholics; that they were more frequently excusable as acts of retaliation; that they arose more from political alarm, and less from the spirit of the religion; and that the temper of their authors yielded more rapidly to the advancing influence of humanity and civilisation" (pp. 127, 129).

All these arguments are fallacies; but as the statements at the same time are full of error, we believe that the author is wrong because he has not studied the question, not because he has designed to misrepresent it. The fact that he does not distinguish from each other the various kinds and occasions of persecution, proves that he is wholly ignorant of the things with which it is connected.

Persecution is the vice of particular religions, and the misfortune of particular stages of political society. It is the resource by which States that would be subverted by religious liberty escape the more dangerous alternative of imposing religious disabilities. The exclusion of a part of the community by reason of its faith from the full benefit of the law is a danger and disadvantage to every State, however highly organised its constitution may otherwise be. But the actual existence of a religious party differing in faith from the majority is dangerous only to a State very imperfectly organised. Disabilities are always a danger. Multiplicity of religions is only dangerous to States of an inferior type. By persecution they rid themselves of the peculiar danger which threatens them, without involving themselves in a system universally bad. Persecution comes naturally in a certain period of the progress of society, before a more flexible and comprehensive system has been introduced by that advance of religion and civilisation whereby Catholicism gradually penetrates into hostile countries, and Christian powers acquire dominion over infidel populations. Thus it is the token of an epoch in the political, religious, and intellectual life of mankind, and it disappears with its epoch, and with the advance of the Church militant in her Catholic vocation. Intolerance of dissent and impatience of contradiction are a characteristic of youth. Those that have no knowledge of the truth that underlies opposite opinions, and no experience of their consequent force, cannot believe that men are sincere in holding them. At a certain point of mental growth, tolerance implies indifference, and intolerance is inseparable from sincerity. Thus intolerance, in itself a defect, becomes in this case a merit. Again, although the political conditions of intolerance belong to the youth and immaturity of nations, the motives of intolerance may at any time be just and the principle high. For the theory of religious unity is founded on the most elevated and truest view of the character and function of the State, on the perception that its ultimate purpose is not distinct from that of the Church. In the pagan State they were identified; in the Christian world the end remains the same, but the means are different.

The State aims at the things of another life but indirectly. Its course runs parallel to that of the Church; they do not converge. The direct subservience of the State to religious ends would imply despotism and persecution just as much as the pagan supremacy of civil over religious authority. The similarity of the end demands harmony in the principles, and creates a decided antagonism between the State and a religious community whose character is in total contradiction with it. With such religions there is no possibility of reconciliation. A State must be at open war with any system which it sees would prevent it from fulfilling its legitimate duties. The danger, therefore, lies not in the doctrine, but in the practice. But to the pagan and to the mediæval State, the danger was in the doctrine. The Christians were the best subjects of the emperor, but Christianity was really subversive of the fundamental institutions of the Roman Empire. In the infancy of the modern States, the civil power required all the help that religion could give in order to establish itself against the lawlessness of barbarism and feudal dissolution. The existence of the State at that time depended on the power of the Church. When, in the thirteenth century, the Empire renounced this support, and made war on the Church, it fell at once into a number of small sovereignties. In those cases persecution was self-defence. It was wrongly defended as an absolute, not as a conditional principle; but such a principle was false only as the modern theory of religious liberty is false. One was a wrong generalisation from the true character of the State; the other is a true conclusion from a false notion of the State. To say that because of the union between Church and State it is right to persecute, would condemn all toleration; and to say that the objects of the State have nothing to do with religion, would condemn all persecution. But persecution and toleration are equally true in principle, considered politically; only one belongs to a more highly developed civilisation than the other. At one period toleration would destroy society; at another, persecution is fatal to liberty. The theory of intolerance is wrong only if founded absolutely upon religious motives; but even then the practice of it is not necessarily censurable. It is opposed to the Christian spirit, in the same manner as slavery is opposed to it. The Church prohibits neither intolerance nor slavery, though in proportion as her influence extends, and civilisation advances, both gradually disappear.

Unity and liberty are the only legitimate principles on which the position of a Church in a State can be regulated, but the distance between them is immeasurable, and the transition extremely difficult. To pass from religious unity to religious liberty is to effect a complete inversion in the character of the State, a change in the whole spirit of legislation, and a still greater revolution in the minds and habits of men. So great a change seldom happens all at once. The law naturally follows the condition of society, which does not suddenly change. An intervening stage from unity to liberty, a compromise between toleration and persecution, is a common but irrational, tyrannical, and impolitic arrangement. It is idle to talk of the guilt of persecution, if we do not distinguish the various principles on which religious dissent can be treated by the State. The exclusion of other religions—the system of Spain, of Sweden, of Mecklenburg, Holstein, and Tyrol—is reasonable in principle, though practically untenable in the present state of European society. The system of expulsion or compulsory conformity, adopted by Lewis XIV. and the Emperor Nicholas, is defensible neither on religious nor political grounds. But the system applied to Ireland, which uses religious disabilities for the purpose of political oppression,[1] stands alone in solitary infamy among the crimes and follies of the rulers of men.

The acquisition of real definite freedom is a very slow and tardy process. The great social independence enjoyed in the early periods of national history is not yet political freedom. The State has not yet developed its authority, or assumed the functions of government. A period follows when all the action of society is absorbed by the ruling power, when the license of early times is gone, and the liberties of a riper age are not yet acquired. These liberties are the product of a long conflict with absolutism, and of a gradual development, which, by establishing definite rights revives in positive form the negative liberty of an unformed society. The object and the result of this process is the organisation of self-government, the substitution of right for force, of authority for power, of duty for necessity, and of a moral for a physical relation between government and people. Until this point is reached, religious liberty is an anomaly. In a State which possesses all power and all authority there is no room for the autonomy of religious communities. Those States, therefore, not only refuse liberty of conscience, but deprive the favoured Church of ecclesiastical freedom. The principles of religious unity and liberty are so opposed that no modern State has at once denied toleration and allowed freedom to its established Church. Both of these are unnatural in a State which rejects self-government, the only secure basis of all freedom, whether

[1] "From what I have observed, it is pride, arrogance, and a spirit of domination, and not a bigoted spirit of religion, that has caused and kept up those oppressive statutes. I am sure I have known those who have oppressed Papists in their civil rights exceedingly indulgent to them in their religious ceremonies, and who really wished them to continue Catholics, in order to furnish pretences for oppression. These persons never saw a man (by converting) escape out of their power but with grudging and regret" (Burke, "On the Penal Laws against Irish Catholics," *Works*, iv. 505).

"I vow to God, I would sooner bring myself to put a man to immediate death for opinions I disliked, and so to get rid of the man and his opinions at once, than to fret him into a feverish being tainted with the jail-distemper of a contagious servitude, to keep him above ground, an animated mass of putrefaction, corrupted himself, and corrupting all about him" (Speech at Bristol, *ibid.* iii. 427).

religious or political. For religious freedom is based on political liberty; intolerance, therefore, is a political necessity against all religions which threaten the unity of faith in a State that is not free, and in every State against those religions which threaten its existence. Absolute intolerance belongs to the absolute State; special persecution may be justified by special causes in any State. All mediæval persecution is of the latter kind, for the sects against which it was directed were revolutionary parties. The State really defended, not its religious unity, but its political existence.

If the Catholic Church was naturally inclined to persecute, she would persecute in all cases alike, when there was no interest to serve but her own. Instead of adapting her conduct to circumstances, and accepting theories according to the character of the time, she would have developed a consistent theory out of her own system, and would have been most severe when she was most free from external influences, from political objects, or from temporary or national prejudices. She would have imposed a common rule of conduct in different countries in different ages, instead of submitting to the exigencies of each time and place. Her own rule of conduct never changed. She treats it as a crime to abandon her, not to be outside her. An apostate who returns to her has a penance for his apostasy; a heretic who is converted has no penance for his heresy. Severity against those who are outside her fold is against her principles. Persecution is contrary to the nature of a universal Church; it is peculiar to the national Churches.

While the Catholic Church by her progress in freedom naturally tends to push the development of States beyond the sphere where they are still obliged to preserve the unity of religion, and whilst she extends over States in all degrees of advancement, Protestantism, which belongs to a particular age and state of society, which makes no claim to universality, and which is dependent on political connection, regards persecution, not as an accident, but as a duty.

Wherever Protestantism prevailed, intolerance became a principle of State, and was proclaimed in theory even where the Protestants were in a minority, and where the theory supplied a weapon against themselves. The Reformation made it a general law, not only against Catholics by way of self-defence or retaliation, but against all who dissented from the reformed doctrines, whom it treated, not as enemies, but as criminals,—against the Protestant sects, against Socinians, and against atheists. It was not a right, but a duty; its object was to avenge God, not to preserve order. There is no analogy between the persecution which preserves and the persecution which attacks; or between intolerance as a religious duty, and intolerance as a necessity of State. The Reformers unanimously declared persecution to be incumbent on the civil power; and the Protestant Governments universally acted upon their injunctions, until scepticism escaped the infliction of penal laws and condemned their spirit.

Doubtless, in the interest of their religion, they acted wisely. Freedom is not more decidedly the natural condition of Catholicism than intolerance is of Protestantism; which by the help of persecution succeeded in establishing itself in countries where it had no root in the affections of the people, and in preserving itself from the internal divisions which follow free inquiry. Toleration has been at once a cause and an effect of its decline. The Catholic Church, on the other hand, supported the mediæval State by religious unity, and has saved herself in the modern State by religious freedom. No longer compelled to devise theories in justification of a system imposed on her by the exigencies of half-organised societies, she is enabled to revert to a policy more suited to her nature and to her most venerable traditions; and the principle of liberty has already restored to her much of that which the principle of unity took away. It was not, as our author imagines (p. 119), by the protection of Lewis XIV. that she was formidable; nor is it true that in consequence of the loss of temporalities, "the chill of death is gathering round the heart of the great theocracy" (p. 94); nor that "the visible decline of the papacy" is at hand because it no longer wields "the more efficacious arms of the great Catholic monarchies" (p. 190).

The same appeal to force, the same principles of intolerance which expelled Catholicism from Protestant countries, gave rise in Catholic countries to the growth of infidelity. The Revolutions of 1789 in France, and of 1859 in Italy, attest the danger of a practice which requires for its support the doctrines of another religion, or the circumstances of a different age. Not till the Church had lost those props in which Mr. Goldwin Smith sees the secret of her power, did she recover her elasticity and her expansive vigour. Catholics may have learnt this truth late, but Protestants, it appears, have yet to learn it.

In one point Mr. Goldwin Smith is not so very far from the views of the Orange party. He thinks, indeed, that the Church is no longer dangerous, and would not therefore have Catholics maltreated; but this is due, not to her merits, but to her weakness.

> Popes might now be as willing as ever, if they had the power, to step between a Protestant State and the allegiance of its subjects (p. 190).

Mr. Smith seems to think that the Popes claim the same authority over the rulers of a Protestant State that they formerly possessed over the princes of Catholic countries. Yet this political power of the Holy See was never a universal right of jurisdiction over States, but a special and positive right, which it is as absurd to censure as to fear or to regret at the present time. Directly, it extended only over territories which were held by feudal tenure of the Pope, like the Sicilian monarchy. Elsewhere the authority was indirect, not political but religious, and its political consequences were due to the laws of the land. The Catholic countries would no more submit to a king not of their communion than Protestant countries, England for instance, or

Denmark. This is as natural and inevitable in a country where the whole population is of one religion, as it is artificial and unjust in a country where no sort of religious unity prevails, and where such a law might compel the sovereign to be of the religion of the minority.

At any rate, nobody who thinks it reasonable that any prince abandoning the Established Church should forfeit the English throne, can complain of a law which compelled the sovereign to be of the religion, not of a majority, but of the whole of his subjects. The idea of the Pope stepping between a State and the allegiance of its subjects is a mere misapprehension. The instrument of his authority is the law, and the law resides in the State. The Pope could intervene, therefore, only between the State and the occupant of the throne; and his intervention suspended, not the duty of obeying, but the right of governing. The line on which his sentence ran separated, not the subjects from the State, but the sovereign from the other authorities. It was addressed to the nation politically organised against the head of the organism, not to the mass of individual subjects against the constituted authorities. That such a power was inconsistent with the modern notion of sovereignty is true; but it is also true that this notion is as much at variance with the nature of ecclesiastical authority as with civil liberty. The Roman maxim, *princeps legibus solutus*, could not be admitted by the Church; and an absolute prince could not properly be invested in her eyes with the sanctity of authority, or protected by the duty of submission. A moral, and *à fortiori* a spiritual, authority moves and lives only in an atmosphere of freedom.

There are, however, two things to be considered in explanation of the error into which our author and so many others have fallen. Law follows life, but not with an equal pace. There is a time when it ceases to correspond to the existing order of things, and meets an invincible obstacle in a new society. The exercise of the mediæval authority of the Popes was founded on the religious unity of the State, and had no basis in a divided community. It was not easy in the period of transition to tell when the change took place, and at what moment the old power lost its efficacy; no one could foresee its failure, and it still remained the legal and recognised means of preventing the change. Accordingly, it was twice tried during the wars of religion, in France with success, in England with disastrous effects. It is a universal rule that a right is not given up until the necessity of its surrender is proved. But the real difficulty arises, not from the mode in which the power was exercised, but from the way in which it was defended. The mediæval writers were accustomed to generalise; they disregarded particular circumstances, and they were generally ignorant of the habits and ideas of their age. Living in the cloister, and writing for the school, they were unacquainted with the polity and institutions around them, and sought their authorities and examples in antiquity, in the speculations of Aristotle, and the maxims of the civil law. They gave to their political doctrines as abstract a form, and attributed to them as universal an application, as the modern absolutists or the more recent liberals. So regardless were they of the difference between ancient times and their own, that the Jewish chronicles, the Grecian legislators, and the Roman code supplied them indifferently with rules and instances; they could not imagine that a new state of things would one day arise in which their theories would be completely obsolete. Their definitions of right and law are absolute in the extreme, and seem often to admit of no qualification. Hence their character is essentially revolutionary, and they contradict both the authority of law and the security of freedom. It is on this contradiction that the common notion of the danger of ecclesiastical pretensions is founded. But the men who take alarm at the tone of the mediæval claims judge them with a theory just as absolute and as excessive. No man can fairly denounce imaginary pretensions in the Church of the nineteenth century, who does not understand that rights which are now impossible may have been reasonable and legitimate in the days when they were actually exercised.

The zeal with which Mr. Goldwin Smith condemns the Irish establishment and the policy of the ascendency is all the more meritorious because he has no conception of the amount of iniquity involved in them.

> The State Church of Ireland, however anomalous and even scandalous its position may be as the Church of a dominant minority upheld by force in the midst of a hostile people, does not, in truth, rest on a principle different from that of other State Churches. To justify the existence of any State Church, it must be assumed as an axiom that the State is the judge of religious truth; and that it is bound to impose upon its subjects, or at least to require them as a community to maintain, the religion which it judges to be true (p. 91).

No such analogy in reality subsists as is here assumed. There is a great difference between the Irish and the English establishment; but even the latter has no similarity of principle with the Catholic establishments of the continent.

The fundamental distinction is, that in one case the religion of the people is adopted by the State, whilst in the other the State imposes a religion on the people. For the political justification of Catholic establishments, no more is required than the theory that it is just that the religion of a country should be represented in, and protected by, its government. This is evidently and universally true; for the moral basis which human laws require can only be derived from an influence which was originally religious as well as moral. The unity of moral consciousness must be founded on a precedent unity of spiritual belief. According to this theory, the character of the nation determines the forms of the State. Consequently it is a theory consistent with freedom. But Protestant establishments, according to our author's definition, which applies to them, and to them alone, rest on the opposite theory, that the will of the State is independent of the condition of the community; and that it may, or indeed must, impose on the nation a faith which may be that of a minority, and which in some cases has been that of the sovereign alone. According to the Catholic view, government may preserve in its laws, and by its authority, the religion of the community; according to the Protestant view it may be bound to change it. A government which has power to change the faith of its subjects must be absolute in other things; so that one theory is as favourable to tyranny as the other is opposed to it. The safeguard of the Catholic system of Church and State, as contrasted with the Protestant, was that very authority which the Holy See used to prevent the sovereign from changing the religion of the people, by deposing him if he departed from it himself. In most Catholic countries the Church preceded the State; some she assisted to form; all she contributed to sustain. Throughout Western Europe Catholicism was the religion of the inhabitants before the new monarchies were founded. The invaders, who became the dominant race and the architects of a new system of States, were sooner or later compelled, in order to preserve their dominion, to abandon their pagan or their Arian religion, and to adopt the common faith of the immense majority of the people. The connection between Church and State was therefore a natural, not an arbitrary, institution; the result of the submission of the Government to popular influence, and the means by which that influence was perpetuated. No Catholic Government ever imposed a Catholic establishment on a Protestant community, or destroyed a Protestant establishment. Even the revocation of the Edict of Nantes, the greatest wrong ever inflicted on the Protestant subjects of a Catholic State, will bear no comparison with the establishment of the religion of a minority. It is a far greater wrong than the most severe persecution, because persecution may be necessary for the preservation of an existing society, as in the case of the early Christians and of the Albigenses; but a State Church can only be justified by the acquiescence of the nation. In every other case it is a great social danger, and is inseparable from political oppression.

Mr. Goldwin Smith's vision is bounded by the Protestant horizon. The Irish establishment has one great mark in common with the other Protestant establishments, —that it is the creature of the State, and an instrument of political influence. They were all imposed on the nation by the State power, sometimes against the will of the people, sometimes against that of the Crown. By the help of military power and of penal laws, the State strove to provide that the Established Church should not be the religion of the minority. But in Ireland the establishment was introduced too late—when Protestantism had spent its expansive force, and the attraction of its doctrine no longer aided the efforts of the civil power. Its position was false from the beginning, and obliged it to resort to persecution and official proselytism in order to put an end to the anomaly. Whilst, therefore, in all cases, Protestantism became the Established Church by an exercise of authority tyrannical in itself, and possible only from the absolutism of the ruling power, in Ireland the tyranny of its institution was perpetuated in the system by which it was upheld, and in the violence with which it was introduced; and this tyranny continues through all its existence. It is the religion of the minority, the church of an alien State, the cause of suffering and of disturbance, an instrument, a creature, and a monument of conquest and of tyranny. It has nothing in common with Catholic establishments, and none of those qualities which, in the Anglican Church, redeem in part the guilt of its origin. This is not, however, the only point on which our author has mistaken the peculiar and enormous character of the evils of Ireland.

With the injustice which generally attends his historical parallels, he compares the policy of the Orange faction to that of the Jacobins in France.

The ferocity of the Jacobins was in a slight degree redeemed by their fanaticism. Their objects were not entirely selfish. They murdered aristocrats, not only because they hated and feared them, but because they wildly imagined them to stand in the way of the social and political millennium, which, according to Rousseau, awaited the acceptance of mankind (p. 175).

No comparison can be more unfair than one which places the pitiless fanaticism of an idea in the same line with the cruelty inspired by a selfish interest. The Reign of Terror is one of the most portentous events in history, because it was the consistent result of the simplest and most acceptable principle of the Revolution; it saved France from the coalition, and it was the greatest attempt ever made to mould the form of a society by force into harmony with a speculative form of Government. An explanation which treats self-interest as its primary motive, and judges other elements as merely qualifying it, is ludicrously inadequate.

The Terrorism of Robespierre was produced by the theory of equality, which was not a mere passion, but a political doctrine, and at the same time a national necessity. Political philosophers who, since the time of Hobbes, derive the State from a social compact, necessarily assume that the contracting parties were equal among themselves. By nature, therefore, all men possess equal rights, and a right to equality. The introduction of the civil power and of private property brought inequality into the world. This is opposed to the condition and to the rights of the natural state. The writers of the eighteenth century attributed to this circumstance the evils and sufferings of society. In France, the ruin of the public finances and the misery of the lower orders were both laid at the door of the classes whose property was exempt from taxation. The endeavours of successive ministers — of Turgot, Necker, and Calonne—to break down the privileges of the aristocracy and of the clergy were defeated by the resistance of the old society. The Government attempted to save itself by obtaining concessions from the Notables, but without success, and then the great reform which the State was impotent to carry into execution was effected by the people. The destruction of the aristocratic society, which the absolute monarchy had failed to reform, was the object and the triumph of the Revolution; and the Constitution of 1791 declared all men equal, and withdrew the sanction of the law from every privilege.

This system gave only an equality in civil rights, a political equality such as already subsisted in America; but it did not provide against the existence or the growth of those social inequalities by which the distribution of political power might be affected. But the theory of the natural equality of mankind understands equal rights as rights to equal things in the State, and requires not only an abstract equality of rights, but a positive equality of power. The varieties of condition caused by civilisation were so objectionable in the eyes of this school, that Rousseau wrote earnest vindications of natural society, and condemned the whole social fabric of Europe as artificial, unnatural, and monstrous. His followers laboured to destroy the work of history and the influence of the past, and to institute a natural, reasonable order of things which should dispose all men on an equal level, which no disparity of wealth or education should be permitted to disturb. There were, therefore, two opinions in the revolutionary party. Those who overthrew the monarchy, established the republic, and commenced the war, were content with having secured political and legal equality, and wished to leave the nation in the enjoyment of those advantages which fortune distributes unequally. But the consistent partisans of equality required that nothing should be allowed to raise one man above another. The Girondists wished to preserve liberty, education, and property; but the Jacobins, who held that an absolute equality should be maintained by the despotism of the government over the people, interpreted more justly the democratic principles which were common to both parties; and, fortunately for their country, they triumphed over their illogical and irresolute adversaries. "When the revolutionary movement was once established," says De Maistre, "nothing but Jacobinism could save France."

Three weeks after the fall of the Gironde, the Constitution of 1793, by which a purely ideal democracy was instituted, was presented to the French people. Its adoption exactly coincides with the supremacy of Robespierre in the Committee of Public Safety, and with the inauguration of the Reign of Terror. The danger of invasion made the new tyranny possible, but the political doctrine of the Jacobins made it necessary. Robespierre explains the system in his report on the principles of political morality, presented to the Convention at the moment of his greatest power :—

> If the principle of a popular government in time of peace is virtue, its principle during revolution is virtue and terror combined : virtue, without which terror is pernicious ; terror, without which virtue is powerless. Terror is nothing but rapid, severe, inflexible justice ; therefore a product of virtue. It is not so much a principle in itself, as a consequence of the universal principle of democracy in its application to the urgent necessities of the country.

This is perfectly true. Envy, revenge, fear, were motives by which individuals were induced or enabled to take part in the administration of such a system ; but its introduction was not the work of passion, but the inevitable result of a doctrine. The democratic Constitution required to be upheld by violence, not only against foreign arms, but against the state of society and the nature of things. The army could not be made its instrument, because the rulers were civilians, and feared, beyond all things, the influence of military officers in the State. Officers were frequently arrested and condemned as traitors, compelled to seek safety in treason, watched and controlled by members of the Convention. In the absence of a military despotism, the revolutionary tribunal was the only resource.

The same theory of an original state of nature, from which the principle of equality was deduced, also taught men where they might find the standard of equality ; as civilisation, by means of civil power, education, and wealth, was the source of corruption, the purity of virtue was to be found in the classes which had been least exposed to those disturbing causes. Those who were least tainted by the temptations of civilised society remained in the natural state. This was the definition of the new notion of the people, which became the measure of virtue and of equality. The democratic theory required that the whole nation should be reduced to the level of the lower orders in all those things in which society creates disparity, in order to be raised to the level of that republican virtue which resides among those who have retained a primitive simplicity by escaping the influence of civilisation.

The form of government and the condition of society must always correspond. Social equality is therefore a postulate of pure democracy. It was necessary that it should exist if the Constitution was to stand, and if the great ideal of popular enthusiasm was ever to be realised. The Revolution had begun by altering the social condition of the country; the correction of society by the State had already commenced. It did not, therefore, seem impossible to continue it until the nation should be completely remodelled in conformity with the new principles. The system before which the ancient monarchy had fallen, which was so fruitful of marvels, which was victorious over a more formidable coalition than that which had humbled Lewis XIV., was deemed equal to the task of completing the social changes which had been so extensively begun, and of moulding France according to the new and simple pattern. The equality which was essential to the existence of the new form of government did not in fact exist. Privilege was abolished, but influence remained. All the inequality founded on wealth, education, ability, reputation, even on the virtues of a code different from that of republican morality, presented obstacles to the establishment of the new *régime*, and those who were thus distinguished were necessarily enemies of the State. With perfect reason, all that rose above the common level, or did not conform to the universal rule, was deemed treasonable. The difference between the actual society and the ideal equality was so great that it could be removed only by violence. The great mass of those who perished were really, either by attachment or by their condition, in antagonism with the

State. They were condemned, not for particular acts, but for their position, or for acts which denoted, not so much a hostile design, as an incompatible habit. By the *loi des suspects*, which was provoked by this conflict between the form of government and the real state of the country, whole classes, rather than ill-disposed individuals, were declared objects of alarm. Hence the proscription was wholesale. Criminals were judged and executed in categories; and the merits of individual cases were, therefore, of little account. For this reason, leading men of ability, bitterly hostile to the new system, were saved by Danton; for it was often indifferent who were the victims, provided the group to which they belonged was struck down. The question was not, what crimes has the prisoner committed? but, does he belong to one of those classes whose existence the Republic cannot tolerate? From this point of view, there were not so many unjust judgments pronounced, at least in Paris, as is generally believed. It was necessary to be prodigal of blood, or to abandon the theory of liberty and equality, which had commanded, for a whole generation, the enthusiastic devotion of educated men, and for the truth of which thousands of its believers were ready to die. The truth of that doctrine was tested by a terrible alternative; but the fault lay with those who believed it, not exclusively with those who practised it. There were few who could administer such a system without any other motive but devotion to the idea, or who could retain the coolness and indifference of which St. Just is an extraordinary example. Most of the Terrorists were swayed by fear for themselves, or by the frenzy which is produced by familiarity with slaughter. But this is of small account. The significance of that sanguinary drama lies in the fact, that a political abstraction was powerful enough to make men think themselves right in destroying masses of their countrymen in the attempt to impose it on their country. The horror of that system and its failure have given vitality to the communistic theory. It was unreasonable to attack the effect instead of the cause, and cruel to destroy the proprietor, while the danger lay in the property. For private property necessarily produces that inequality which the Jacobin theory condemned; and the Constitution of 1793 could not be maintained by Terrorism without Communism, by proscribing the rich while riches were tolerated. The Jacobins were guilty of inconsistency in omitting to attack inequality in its source. Yet no man who admits their theory has a right to complain of their acts. The one proceeded from the other with the inflexible logic of history. The Reign of Terror was nothing else than the reign of those who conceive that liberty and equality can co-exist.

One more quotation will sufficiently justify what we have said of the sincerity and ignorance which Mr. Goldwin Smith shows in his remarks on Catholic subjects. After calling the Bull of Adrian IV. "the stumbling-block and the despair of Catholic historians," he proceeded to say:—

> Are Catholics filled with perplexity at the sight of infallibility sanctioning rapine? They can scarcely be less perplexed by the title which infallibility puts forward to the dominion of Ireland. . . . But this perplexity arises entirely from the assumption, which may be an article of faith, but is not an article of history, that the infallible morality of the Pope has never changed (pp. 46, 47).

It is hard to understand how a man of honour and ability can entertain such notions of the character of the Papacy as these words imply, or where he can have found authorities for so monstrous a caricature. We will only say that infallibility is no attribute of the political system of the Popes, and that the Bulls of Adrian and Alexander are not instances of infallible morality.

Great as the errors which we have pointed out undoubtedly are, the book itself is of real value, and encourages us to form sanguine hopes of the future services of its author to historical science, and ultimately to religion. We are hardly just in complaining of Protestant writers who fail to do justice to the Church.

There are not very many amongst ourselves who take the trouble to ascertain her real character as a visible institution, or to know how her nature has been shown in her history. We know the doctrine which she teaches; we are familiar with the outlines of her discipline. We know that sanctity is one of her marks, and that beneficence has characterised her influence. In a general way we are confident that historical accusations are as false as dogmatic attacks, and most of us have some notion of the way in which the current imputations are to be met. But as to her principles of action in many important things, how they have varied in course of time, what changes have been effected by circumstances, and what rules have never been broken,—few are at the pains to inquire. As adversaries imagine that in exposing a Catholic they strike Catholicism, and that the defects of the men are imperfections in the institution and a proof that it is not divine, so we grow accustomed to confound in our defence that which is defective and that which is indefectible, and to discover in the Church merits as self-contradictory as are the accusations of her different foes. At one moment we are told that Catholicism teaches contempt, and therefore neglect of wealth; at another, that it is false to say that the Church does not promote temporal prosperity. If a great point is made against persecution, it will be denied that she is intolerant, whilst at another time it will be argued that heresy and unbelief deserve to be punished.

We cannot be surprised that Protestants do not know the Church better than we do ourselves, or that, while we allow no evil to be spoken of her human elements, those who deem her altogether human should discover in her the defects of human institutions. It is intensely difficuit to enter into the spirit of a system not our own. Particular principles and doctrines are easily mastered; but a system answering all the spiritual cravings, all the intellectual capabilities of man, demands more than a mere mental effort,—a submission of the intellect, an act of faith, a temporary suspension of the critical faculty.

This applies not merely to the Christian religion, with its unfathomable mysteries and its inexhaustible fund of truth, but to the fruits of human speculation. Nobody has ever succeeded in writing a history of philosophy without incurring either the reproach that he is a mere historian, incapable of entering into the genius of any system, or a mere metaphysician, who can discern in all other philosophies only the relation they bear to his own. In religion the difficulty is greater still, and greatest of all with Catholicism. For the Church is to be seen, not in books, but in life. No divine can put together the whole body of her doctrine; no canonist the whole fabric of her law; no historian the infinite vicissitudes of her career. The Protestant who wishes to be informed on all these things can be advised to rely on no one manual, on no encyclopædia of her deeds and of her ideas; if he seeks to know what these have been, he must be told to look around. And to one who surveys her teaching and her fortunes through all ages and all lands, ignorant or careless of that which is essential, changeless, and immortal in her, it will not be easy to discern through so much outward change a regular development, amid such variety of forms the unchanging substance, in so many modifications fidelity to constant laws; or to recognise, in a career so chequered with failure, disaster, and suffering, with the apostasy of heroes, the weakness of rulers, and the errors of doctors, the unfailing hand of a heavenly Guide.

IX

NATIONALITY[1]

WHENEVER great intellectual cultivation has been combined with that suffering which is inseparable from extensive changes in the condition of the people, men of speculative or imaginative genius have sought in the contemplation of an ideal society a remedy, or at least a consolation, for evils which they were practically unable to remove. Poetry has always preserved the idea, that at some distant time or place, in the Western islands or the Arcadian region, an innocent and contented people, free from the corruption and restraint of civilised life, have realised the legends of the golden age. The office of the poets is always nearly the same, and there is little variation in the features of their ideal world; but when philosophers attempt to admonish or reform mankind by devising an imaginary state, their motive is more definite and immediate, and their commonwealth is a satire as well as a model. Plato and Plotinus, More and Campanella, constructed their fanciful societies with those materials which were omitted from the fabric of the actual communities, by the defects of which they were inspired. The Republic, the Utopia, and the City of the Sun were protests against a state of things which the experience of their authors taught them to condemn, and from the faults of which they took refuge in the opposite extremes. They remained without influence, and have never passed from literary into political history, because something more than discontent and speculative ingenuity is needed in order to invest a political idea with power over the masses

[1] *Home and Foreign Review*, July 1862.

of mankind. The scheme of a philosopher can command the practical allegiance of fanatics only, not of nations; and though oppression may give rise to violent and repeated outbreaks, like the convulsions of a man in pain, it cannot mature a settled purpose and plan of regeneration, unless a new notion of happiness is joined to the sense of present evil.

The history of religion furnishes a complete illustration. Between the later mediæval sects and Protestantism there is an essential difference, that outweighs the points of analogy found in those systems which are regarded as heralds of the Reformation, and is enough to explain the vitality of the last in comparison with the others. Whilst Wycliffe and Hus contradicted certain particulars of the Catholic teaching, Luther rejected the authority of the Church, and gave to the individual conscience an independence which was sure to lead to an incessant resistance. There is a similar difference between the Revolt of the Netherlands, the Great Rebellion, the War of Independence, or the rising of Brabant, on the one hand, and the French Revolution on the other. Before 1789, insurrections were provoked by particular wrongs, and were justified by definite complaints and by an appeal to principles which all men acknowledged. New theories were sometimes advanced in the cause of controversy, but they were accidental, and the great argument against tyranny was fidelity to the ancient laws. Since the change produced by the French Revolution, those aspirations which are awakened by the evils and defects of the social state have come to act as permanent and energetic forces throughout the civilised world. They are spontaneous and aggressive, needing no prophet to proclaim, no champion to defend them, but popular, unreasoning, and almost irresistible. The Revolution effected this change, partly by its doctrines, partly by the indirect influence of events. It taught the people to regard their wishes and wants as the supreme criterion of right. The rapid vicissitudes of power, in which each party successively appealed to the favour of the masses as the arbiter of success, accustomed the masses to be arbitrary as well as insubordinate. The fall of many governments, and the frequent redistribution of territory, deprived all settlements of the dignity of permanence. Tradition and prescription ceased to be guardians of authority ; and the arrangements which proceeded from revolutions, from the triumphs of war, and from treaties of peace, were equally regardless of established rights. Duty cannot be dissociated from right, and nations refuse to be controlled by laws which are no protection.

In this condition of the world, theory and action follow close upon each other, and practical evils easily give birth to opposite systems. In the realms of free-will, the regularity of natural progress is preserved by the conflict of extremes. The impulse of the reaction carries men from one extremity towards another. The pursuit of a remote and ideal object, which captivates the imagination by its splendour and the reason by its simplicity, evokes an energy which would not be inspired by a rational, possible end, limited by many antagonistic claims, and confined to what is reasonable, practicable, and just. One excess or exaggeration is the corrective of the other, and error promotes truth, where the masses are concerned, by counterbalancing a contrary error. The few have not strength to achieve great changes unaided ; the many have not wisdom to be moved by truth unmixed. Where the disease is various, no particular definite remedy can meet the wants of all. Only the attraction of an abstract idea, or of an ideal state, can unite in a common action multitudes who seek a universal cure for many special evils, and a common restorative applicable to many different conditions. And hence false principles, which correspond with the bad as well as with the just aspirations of mankind, are a normal and necessary element in the social life of nations.

Theories of this kind are just, inasmuch as they are provoked by definite ascertained evils, and undertake their removal. They are useful in opposition, as a warning or a threat, to modify existing things, and keep awake the consciousness of wrong. They cannot serve as a basis for the reconstruction of civil society, as medicine cannot serve for food; but they may influence it with advantage, because they point out the direction, though not the measure, in which reform is needed. They oppose an order of things which is the result of a selfish and violent abuse of power by the ruling classes, and of artificial restriction on the natural progress of the world, destitute of an ideal element or a moral purpose. Practical extremes differ from the theoretical extremes they provoke, because the first are both arbitrary and violent, whilst the last, though also revolutionary, are at the same time remedial. In one case the wrong is voluntary, in the other it is inevitable. This is the general character of the contest between the existing order and the subversive theories that deny its legitimacy. There are three principal theories of this kind, impugning the present distribution of power, of property, and of territory, and attacking respectively the aristocracy, the middle class, and the sovereignty. They are the theories of equality, communism, and nationality. Though sprung from a common origin, opposing cognate evils, and connected by many links, they did not appear simultaneously. Rousseau proclaimed the first, Babœuf the second, Mazzini the third; and the third is the most recent in its appearance, the most attractive at the present time, and the richest in promise of future power.

In the old European system, the rights of nationalities were neither recognised by governments nor asserted by the people. The interest of the reigning families, not those of the nations, regulated the frontiers; and the administration was conducted generally without any reference to popular desires. Where all liberties were suppressed, the claims of national independence were necessarily ignored, and a princess, in the words of Fénelon, carried a monarchy in her wedding portion. The eighteenth century acquiesced in this oblivion of corporate rights on the Continent, for the absolutists cared only for the State, and the liberals only for the individual. The Church, the nobles, and the nation had no place in the popular theories of the age;

and they devised none in their own defence, for they were not openly attacked. The aristocracy retained its privileges, and the Church her property; and the dynastic interest, which overruled the natural inclination of the nations and destroyed their independence, nevertheless maintained their integrity. The national sentiment was not wounded in its most sensitive part. To dispossess a sovereign of his hereditary crown, and to annex his dominions, would have been held to inflict an injury upon all monarchies, and to furnish their subjects with a dangerous example, by depriving royalty of its inviolable character. In time of war, as there was no national cause at stake, there was no attempt to rouse national feeling. The courtesy of the rulers towards each other was proportionate to the contempt for the lower orders. Compliments passed between the commanders of hostile armies; there was no bitterness, and no excitement; battles were fought with the pomp and pride of a parade. The art of war became a slow and learned game. The monarchies were united not only by a natural community of interests, but by family alliances. A marriage contract sometimes became the signal for an interminable war, whilst family connections often set a barrier to ambition. After the wars of religion came to an end in 1648, the only wars were those which were waged for an inheritance or a dependency, or against countries whose system of government exempted them from the common law of dynastic States, and made them not only unprotected but obnoxious. These countries were England and Holland, until Holland ceased to be a republic, and until, in England, the defeat of the Jacobites in the forty-five terminated the struggle for the Crown. There was one country, however, which still continued to be an exception; one monarch whose place was not admitted in the comity of kings.

Poland did not possess those securities for stability which were supplied by dynastic connections and the theory of legitimacy, wherever a crown could be obtained by marriage or inheritance. A monarch without royal blood, a crown bestowed by the nation, were an anomaly and an outrage in that age of dynastic absolutism. The country was excluded from the European system by the nature of its institutions. It excited a cupidity which could not be satisfied. It gave the reigning families of Europe no hope of permanently strengthening themselves by intermarriage with its rulers, or of obtaining it by bequest or by inheritance. The Habsburgs had contested the possession of Spain and the Indies with the French Bourbons, of Italy with the Spanish Bourbons, of the empire with the house of Wittelsbach, of Silesia with the house of Hohenzollern. There had been wars between rival houses for half the territories of Italy and Germany. But none could hope to redeem their losses or increase their power in a country to which marriage and descent gave no claim. Where they could not permanently inherit they endeavoured, by intrigues, to prevail at each election, and after contending in support of candidates who were their partisans, the neighbours at last appointed an instrument for the final demolition of the Polish State. Till then no nation had been deprived of its political existence by the Christian Powers, and whatever disregard had been shown for national interests and sympathies, some care had been taken to conceal the wrong by a hypocritical perversion of law. But the partition of Poland was an act of wanton violence, committed in open defiance not only of popular feeling but of public law. For the first time in modern history a great State was suppressed, and a whole nation divided among its enemies.

This famous measure, the most revolutionary act of the old absolutism, awakened the theory of nationality in Europe, converting a dormant right into an aspiration, and a sentiment into a political claim. "No wise or honest man," wrote Edmund Burke, "can approve of that partition, or can contemplate it without prognosticating great mischief from it to all countries at some future time." [1] Thenceforward there was a nation demanding

[1] "Observations on the Conduct of the Minority," *Works*, v. 112.

to be united in a State,—a soul, as it were, wandering in search of a body in which to begin life over again; and, for the first time, a cry was heard that the arrangement of States was unjust—that their limits were unnatural, and that a whole people was deprived of its right to constitute an independent community. Before that claim could be efficiently asserted against the overwhelming power of its opponents,—before it gained energy, after the last partition, to overcome the influence of long habits of submission, and of the contempt which previous disorders had brought upon Poland,—the ancient European system was in ruins, and a new world was rising in its place.

The old despotic policy which made the Poles its prey had two adversaries,—the spirit of English liberty, and the doctrines of that revolution which destroyed the French monarchy with its own weapons; and these two contradicted in contrary ways the theory that nations have no collective rights. At the present day, the theory of nationality is not only the most powerful auxiliary of revolution, but its actual substance in the movements of the last three years. This, however, is a recent alliance, unknown to the first French Revolution. The modern theory of nationality arose partly as a legitimate consequence, partly as a reaction against it. As the system which overlooked national division was opposed by liberalism in two forms, the French and the English, so the system which insists upon them proceeds from two distinct sources, and exhibits the character either of 1688 or of 1789. When the French people abolished the authorities under which it lived, and became its own master, France was in danger of dissolution: for the common will is difficult to ascertain, and does not readily agree. "The laws," said Vergniaud, in the debate on the sentence of the king, "are obligatory only as the presumptive will of the people, which retains the right of approving or condemning them. The instant it manifests its wish the work of the national representation, the law, must disappear." This doctrine resolved society into its natural elements, and threatened to break up the country into as many republics as there were communes. For true republicanism is the principle of self-government in the whole and in all the parts. In an extensive country, it can prevail only by the union of several independent communities in a single confederacy, as in Greece, in Switzerland, in the Netherlands, and in America; so that a large republic not founded on the federal principle must result in the government of a single city, like Rome and Paris, and, in a less degree, Athens, Berne, and Amsterdam; or, in other words, a great democracy must either sacrifice self-government to unity, or preserve it by federalism.

The France of history fell together with the French State, which was the growth of centuries. The old sovereignty was destroyed. The local authorities were looked upon with aversion and alarm. The new central authority needed to be established on a new principle of unity. The state of nature, which was the ideal of society, was made the basis of the nation; descent was put in the place of tradition, and the French people was regarded as a physical product: an ethnological, not historic, unit. It was assumed that a unity existed separate from the representation and the government, wholly independent of the past, and capable at any moment of expressing or of changing its mind. In the words of Sieyès, it was no longer France, but some unknown country to which the nation was transported. The central power possessed authority, inasmuch as it obeyed the whole, and no divergence was permitted from the universal sentiment. This power, endowed with volition, was personified in the Republic One and Indivisible. The title signified that a part could not speak or act for the whole,—that there was a power supreme over the State, distinct from, and independent of, its members; and it expressed, for the first time in history, the notion of an abstract nationality. In this manner the idea of the sovereignty of the people, uncontrolled by the past, gave birth to the idea of nationality independent of the political influence of history. It sprang from the rejection of the two authorities,—of the State and of the past. The kingdom of France was, geographically as well as politically, the product of a long series of events, and the same influences which built up the State formed the territory. The Revolution repudiated alike the agencies to which France owed her boundaries and those to which she owed her government. Every effaceable trace and relic of national history was carefully wiped away,—the system of administration, the physical divisions of the country, the classes of society, the corporations, the weights and measures, the calendar. France was no longer bounded by the limits she had received from the condemned influence of her history; she could recognise only those which were set by nature. The definition of the nation was borrowed from the material world, and, in order to avoid a loss of territory, it became not only an abstraction but a fiction.

There was a principle of nationality in the ethnological character of the movement, which is the source of the common observation that revolution is more frequent in Catholic than in Protestant countries. It is, in fact, more frequent in the Latin than in the Teutonic world, because it depends partly on a national impulse, which is only awakened where there is an alien element, the vestige of a foreign dominion, to expel. Western Europe has undergone two conquests—one by the Romans and one by the Germans, and twice received laws from the invaders. Each time it rose again against the victorious race; and the two great reactions, while they differ according to the different characters of the two conquests, have the phenomenon of imperialism in common. The Roman republic laboured to crush the subjugated nations into a homogeneous and obedient mass; but the increase which the proconsular authority obtained in the process subverted the republican government, and the reaction of the provinces against Rome assisted in establishing the empire. The Cæsarean system gave an unprecedented freedom to the dependencies, and raised them to a civil equality which put an end to the dominion of race over race and of class over class. The monarchy was hailed as a refuge from the pride and cupidity of the Roman people; and the love of equality, the hatred of nobility, and the tolerance of despotism implanted by Rome became, at least in Gaul, the chief feature of the national character. But among the nations whose vitality had been broken down by the stern republic, not one retained the materials necessary to enjoy independence, or to develop a new history. The political faculty which organises states and finds society in a moral order was exhausted, and the Christian doctors looked in vain over the waste of ruins for a people by whose aid the Church might survive the decay of Rome. A new element of national life was brought to that declining world by the enemies who destroyed it. The flood of barbarians settled over it for a season, and then subsided; and when the landmarks of civilisation appeared once more, it was found that the soil had been impregnated with a fertilising and regenerating influence, and that the inundation had laid the germs of future states and of a new society. The political sense and energy came with the new blood, and was exhibited in the power exercised by the younger race upon the old, and in the establishment of a graduated freedom. Instead of universal equal rights, the actual enjoyment of which is necessarily contingent on, and commensurate with, power, the rights of the people were made dependent on a variety of conditions, the first of which was the distribution of property. Civil society became a classified organism instead of a formless combination of atoms, and the feudal system gradually arose.

Roman Gaul had so thoroughly adopted the ideas of absolute authority and undistinguished equality during the five centuries between Cæsar and Clovis, that the people could never be reconciled to the new system. Feudalism remained a foreign importation, and the feudal aristocracy an alien race, and the common people of France sought protection against both in the Roman jurisprudence and the power of the crown. The development of absolute monarchy by the help of democracy is the one constant character of French history. The royal power, feudal at first, and limited by the immunities and the great vassals, became more popular as it grew more absolute; while the suppression of aristocracy, the removal of the intermediate authorities, was so particularly the object of the nation, that it was more energetically accomplished after the fall of the throne. The monarchy which had been engaged from the thirteenth century in curbing the nobles, was at last thrust aside by the democracy, because it was too dilatory in the work, and was unable to deny its own origin and effectually ruin the class from which it sprang. All those things which constitute the peculiar character of the French Revolution,—the demand for equality, the hatred of nobility and feudalism, and of the Church which was connected with them, the constant reference to pagan examples, the suppression of monarchy, the new code of law, the breach with tradition, and the substitution of an ideal system for everything that had proceeded from the mixture and mutual action of the races,—all these exhibit the common type of a reaction against the effects of the Frankish invasion. The hatred of royalty was less than the hatred of aristocracy; privileges were more detested than tyranny; and the king perished because of the origin of his authority rather than because of its abuse. Monarchy unconnected with aristocracy became popular in France, even when most uncontrolled; whilst the attempt to reconstitute the throne, and to limit and fence it with its peers, broke down, because the old Teutonic elements on which it relied—hereditary nobility, primogeniture, and privilege—were no longer tolerated. The substance of the ideas of 1789 is not the limitation of the sovereign power, but the abrogation of intermediate powers. These powers, and the classes which enjoyed them, come in Latin Europe from a barbarian origin; and the movement which calls itself liberal is essentially national. If liberty were its object, its means would be the establishment of great independent authorities not derived from the State, and its model would be England. But its object is equality; and it seeks, like France in 1789, to cast out the elements of inequality which were introduced by the Teutonic race. This is the object which Italy and Spain have had in common with France, and herein consists the natural league of the Latin nations.

This national element in the movement was not understood by the revolutionary leaders. At first, their doctrine appeared entirely contrary to the idea of nationality. They taught that certain general principles of government were absolutely right in all States; and they asserted in theory the unrestricted freedom of the individual, and the supremacy of the will over every external necessity or obligation. This is in apparent contradiction to the national theory, that certain natural forces ought to determine the character, the form, and the policy of the State, by which a kind of fate is put in the place of freedom. Accordingly the national sentiment was not developed directly out of the revolution in which it was involved, but was exhibited first in resistance to it, when the attempt to emancipate had been absorbed in the desire to subjugate, and the republic had been succeeded by the empire. Napoleon called a new power into existence by attacking nationality in Russia, by delivering it in Italy, by governing in defiance of it in Germany and Spain. The sovereigns of these countries were deposed or degraded; and a system of administration was introduced which was French in its origin, its spirit, and its instruments. The people resisted the change. The movement against it was popular and spontaneous, because the rulers were absent or helpless; and it was national, because it was directed against foreign institutions. In Tyrol, in Spain, and afterwards in Prussia, the people did not receive the impulse from the government, but undertook of their own accord to cast out the armies and the ideas of revolutionised France. Men were made conscious of the national element of the revolution by its conquests, not in its rise. The three things which the Empire most openly oppressed—religion, national independence, and political liberty—united in a short-lived league to animate the great uprising by which Napoleon fell. Under the influence of that memorable alliance a political spirit was called forth on the Continent, which clung to freedom and abhorred revolution, and sought to restore, to develop, and to reform the decayed national institutions. The men who proclaimed these ideas, Stein and Görres, Humboldt, Müller, and De Maistre,[1] were as hostile to Bonapartism as to the absolutism of the old governments, and insisted on the national rights, which had been invaded equally by both, and which they hoped to restore by the destruction of the French supremacy. With the cause that triumphed at Waterloo the friends of the Revolution had no sympathy, for they had learned to identify their doctrine with the cause of France. The Holland House Whigs in England, the Afrancesados in Spain, the Muratists in Italy, and the partisans of the Confederation of the Rhine, merging patriotism in their revolutionary affections, regretted the fall of the French power, and looked with alarm at those new and unknown forces which the War of Deliverance had evoked, and which were as menacing to French liberalism as to French supremacy.

But the new aspirations for national and popular rights were crushed at the restoration. The liberals of those days cared for freedom, not in the shape of national independence, but of French institutions; and they combined against the nations with the ambition of the governments. They were as ready to sacrifice nationality to their ideal as the Holy Alliance was to the interests of absolutism. Talleyrand indeed declared at Vienna that the Polish

[1] There are some remarkable thoughts on nationality in the State Papers of the Count de Maistre: "En premier lieu les nations sont quelque chose dans le monde, il n'est pas permis de les compter pour rien, de les affliger dans leurs convenances, dans leurs affections, dans leurs intérêts les plus chers. . . . Or le traité du 30 mai anéantit complétement la Savoie; il divise l'indivisible; il partage en trois portions une malheureuse nation de 400,000 hommes, une par la langue, une par la religion, une par le caractère, une par l'habitude invétérée, une enfin par les limites naturelles. . . . L'union des nations ne souffre pas de difficultés sur la carte géographique; mais dans la réalité, c'est autre chose; il y a des nations *immiscibles*. . . . Je lui parlai par occasion de l'esprit italien qui s'agite dans ce moment; il (Count Nesselrode) me répondit: 'Oui, Monsieur; mais cet esprit est un grand mal, car il peut gêner les arrangements de l'Italie'" (*Correspondance Diplomatique de J. de Maistre*, ii. 7, 8, 21, 25). In the same year, 1815, Görres wrote: "In Italien wie allerwarts ist das Volk gewecht; es will etwas grossartiges, es will Ideen haben, die, wenn es sie auch nicht ganz begreift, doch einen freien unendlichen Gesichtskreis seiner Einbildung eröffnen. . . . Es ist reiner Naturtrieb, dass ein Volk, also scharf und deutlich in seine natürlichen Gränzen eingeschlossen, aus der Zerstreuung in die Einheit sich zu sammeln sucht" (*Werke*, ii. 20).

question ought to have precedence over all other questions, because the partition of Poland had been one of the first and greatest causes of the evils which Europe had suffered; but dynastic interests prevailed. All the sovereigns represented at Vienna recovered their dominions, except the King of Saxony, who was punished for his fidelity to Napoleon; but the States that were unrepresented in the reigning families—Poland, Venice, and Genoa—were not revived, and even the Pope had great difficulty in recovering the Legations from the grasp of Austria. Nationality, which the old *régime* had ignored, which had been outraged by the revolution and the empire, received, after its first open demonstration, the hardest blow at the Congress of Vienna. The principle which the first partition had generated, to which the revolution had given a basis of theory, which had been lashed by the empire into a momentary convulsive effort was matured by the long error of the restoration into a consistent doctrine, nourished and justified by the situation of Europe.

The governments of the Holy Alliance devoted themselves to suppress with equal care the revolutionary spirit by which they had been threatened, and the national spirit by which they had been restored. Austria, which owed nothing to the national movement, and had prevented its revival after 1809, naturally took the lead in repressing it. Every disturbance of the final settlements of 1815, every aspiration for changes or reforms, was condemned as sedition. This system repressed the good with the evil tendencies of the age; and the resistance which it provoked, during the generation that passed away from the restoration to the fall of Metternich, and again under the reaction which commenced with Schwarzenberg and ended with the administrations of Bach and Manteuffel, proceeded from various combinations of the opposite forms of liberalism. In the successive phases of that struggle, the idea that national claims are above all other rights gradually rose to the supremacy which it now possesses among the revolutionary agencies.

The first liberal movement, that of the Carbonari in the south of Europe, had no specific national character, but was supported by the Bonapartists both in Spain and Italy. In the following years the opposite ideas of 1813 came to the front, and a revolutionary movement, in many respects hostile to the principles of revolution, began in defence of liberty, religion, and nationality. All these causes were united in the Irish agitation, and in the Greek, Belgian, and Polish revolutions. Those sentiments which had been insulted by Napoleon, and had risen against him, rose against the governments of the restoration. They had been oppressed by the sword, and then by the treaties. The national principle added force, but not justice, to this movement, which, in every case but Poland, was successful. A period followed in which it degenerated into a purely national idea, as the agitation for repeal succeeded emancipation, and Panslavism and Panhellenism arose under the auspices of the Eastern Church. This was the third phase of the resistance to the settlement of Vienna, which was weak, because it failed to satisfy national or constitutional aspirations, either of which would have been a safeguard against the other, by a moral if not by a popular justification. At first, in 1813, the people rose against their conquerors, in defence of their legitimate rulers. They refused to be governed by usurpers. In the period between 1825 and 1831, they resolved that they would not be misgoverned by strangers. The French administration was often better than that which it displaced, but there were prior claimants for the authority exercised by the French, and at first the national contest was a contest for legitimacy. In the second period this element was wanting. No dispossessed princes led the Greeks, the Belgians, or the Poles. The Turks, the Dutch, and the Russians were attacked, not as usurpers, but as oppressors,—because they misgoverned, not because they were of a different race. Then began a time when the text simply was, that nations would not be governed by foreigners. Power legitimately obtained, and exercised with moderation, was declared invalid. National rights, like religion, had borne part in the previous combinations, and had been auxiliaries in the struggles for freedom, but now nationality became a paramount claim, which was to assert itself alone, which might put forward as pretexts the rights of rulers, the liberties of the people, the safety of religion, but which, if no such union could be formed, was to prevail at the expense of every other cause for which nations make sacrifices.

Metternich is, next to Napoleon, the chief promoter of this theory; for the anti-national character of the restoration was most distinct in Austria, and it is in opposition to the Austrian Government that nationality grew into a system. Napoleon, who, trusting to his armies, despised moral forces in politics, was overthrown by their rising. Austria committed the same fault in the government of her Italian provinces. The kingdom of Italy had united all the northern part of the Peninsula in a single State; and the national feelings, which the French repressed elsewhere, were encouraged as a safeguard of their power in Italy and in Poland. When the tide of victory turned, Austria invoked against the French the aid of the new sentiment they had fostered. Nugent announced, in his proclamation to the Italians, that they should become an independent nation. The same spirit served different masters, and contributed first to the destruction of the old States, then to the expulsion of the French, and again, under Charles Albert, to a new revolution. It was appealed to in the name of the most contradictory principles of government, and served all parties in succession, because it was one in which all could unite. Beginning by a protest against the dominion of race over race, its mildest and least-developed form, it grew into a condemnation of every State that included different races, and finally became the complete and consistent theory, that the State and the nation must be co-extensive. "It is," says Mr. Mill, "in general a necessary condition of free institutions, that the boundaries of governments should coincide in the main with those of nationalities."[1]

[1] *Considerations on Representative Government*, p. 298.

The outward historical progress of this idea from an indefinite aspiration to be the keystone of a political system, may be traced in the life of the man who gave to it the element in which its strength resides,—Giuseppe Mazzini. He found Carbonarism impotent against the measures of the governments, and resolved to give new life to the liberal movement by transferring it to the ground of nationality. Exile is the nursery of nationality, as oppression is the school of liberalism; and Mazzini conceived the idea of Young Italy when he was a refugee at Marseilles. In the same way, the Polish exiles are the champions of every national movement; for to them all political rights are absorbed in the idea of independence, which, however they may differ with each other, is the one aspiration common to them all. Towards the year 1830 literature also contributed to the national idea. "It was the time," says Mazzini, "of the great conflict between the romantic and the classical school, which might with equal truth be called a conflict between the partisans of freedom and of authority." The romantic school was infidel in Italy, and Catholic in Germany; but in both it had the common effect of encouraging national history and literature, and Dante was as great an authority with the Italian democrats as with the leaders of the mediæval revival at Vienna, Munich, and Berlin. But neither the influence of the exiles, nor that of the poets and critics of the new party, extended over the masses. It was a sect without popular sympathy or encouragement, a conspiracy founded not on a grievance, but on a doctrine; and when the attempt to rise was made in Savoy, in 1834, under a banner with the motto "Unity, Independence, God and Humanity," the people were puzzled at its object, and indifferent to its failure. But Mazzini continued his propaganda, developed his *Giovine Italia* into a *Giovine Europa*, and established in 1847 the international league of nations. "The people," he said, in his opening address, "is penetrated with only one idea, that of unity and nationality. . . . There is no international question as to forms of government, but only a national question."

The revolution of 1848, unsuccessful in its national purpose, prepared the subsequent victories of nationality in two ways. The first of these was the restoration of the Austrian power in Italy, with a new and more energetic centralisation, which gave no promise of freedom. Whilst that system prevailed, the right was on the side of the national aspirations, and they were revived in a more complete and cultivated form by Manin. The policy of the Austrian Government, which failed during the ten years of the reaction to convert the tenure by force into a tenure by right, and to establish with free institutions the condition of allegiance, gave a negative encouragement to the theory. It deprived Francis Joseph of all active support and sympathy in 1859, for he was more clearly wrong in his conduct than his enemies in their doctrines. The real cause of the energy which the national theory has acquired is, however, the triumph of the democratic principle in France, and its recognition by the European Powers. The theory of nationality is involved in the democratic theory of the sovereignty of the general will. "One hardly knows what any division of the human race should be free to do, if not to determine with which of the various collective bodies of human beings they choose to associate themselves."[1] It is by this act that a nation constitutes itself. To have a collective will, unity is necessary, and independence is requisite in order to assert it. Unity and nationality are still more essential to the notion of the sovereignty of the people than the cashiering of monarchs, or the revocation of laws. Arbitrary acts of this kind may be prevented by the happiness of the people or the popularity of the king, but a nation inspired by the democratic idea cannot with consistency allow a part of itself to belong to a foreign State, or the whole to be divided into several native States. The theory of nationality therefore proceeds from both the principles which divide the political world,—from legitimacy, which ignores its claims, and from the revolution, which assumes them; and for the

[1] Mill's *Considerations*, p. 296.

same reason it is the chief weapon of the last against the first.

In pursuing the outward and visible growth of the national theory we are prepared for an examination of its political character and value. The absolutism which has created it denies equally that absolute right of national unity which is a product of democracy, and that claim of national liberty which belongs to the theory of freedom. These two views of nationality, corresponding to the French and to the English systems, are connected in name only, and are in reality the opposite extremes of political thought. In one case, nationality is founded on the perpetual supremacy of the collective will, of which the unity of the nation is the necessary condition, to which every other influence must defer, and against which no obligation enjoys authority, and all resistance is tyrannical. The nation is here an ideal unit founded on the race, in defiance of the modifying action of external causes, of tradition, and of existing rights. It overrules the rights and wishes of the inhabitants, absorbing their divergent interests in a fictitious unity; sacrifices their several inclinations and duties to the higher claim of nationality, and crushes all natural rights and all established liberties for the purpose of vindicating itself.[1] Whenever a single definite object is made the supreme end of the State, be it the advantage of a class, the safety or the power of the country, the greatest happiness of the greatest number, or the support of any speculative idea, the State becomes for the time inevitably absolute. Liberty alone demands for its realisation the limitation of the public authority, for liberty is the only object which benefits all alike, and provokes no sincere opposition. In supporting the claims of national unity, governments must be subverted in whose title there is no flaw, and whose policy is beneficent and

1 "Le sentiment d'indépendance nationale est encore plus général et plus profondément gravé dans le cœur des peuples que l'amour d'une liberté constitutionnelle. Les nations les plus soumises au despotisme éprouvent ce sentiment avec autant de vivacité que les nations libres; les peuples les plus barbares le sentent même encore plus vivement que les nations policées" (*L'Italie au Dix-neuvième Siècle*, p. 148, Paris, 1821).

equitable, and subjects must be compelled to transfer their allegiance to an authority for which they have no attachment, and which may be practically a foreign domination. Connected with this theory in nothing except in the common enmity of the absolute state, is the theory which represents nationality as an essential, but not a supreme element in determining the forms of the State. It is distinguished from the other, because it tends to diversity and not to uniformity, to harmony and not to unity; because it aims not at an arbitrary change, but at careful respect for the existing conditions of political life, and because it obeys the laws and results of history, not the aspirations of an ideal future. While the theory of unity makes the nation a source of despotism and revolution, the theory of liberty regards it as the bulwark of self-government, and the foremost limit to the excessive power of the State. Private rights, which are sacrificed to the unity, are preserved by the union of nations. No power can so efficiently resist the tendencies of centralisation, of corruption, and of absolutism, as that community which is the vastest that can be included in a State, which imposes on its members a consistent similarity of character, interest, and opinion, and which arrests the action of the sovereign by the influence of a divided patriotism. The presence of different nations under the same sovereignty is similar in its effect to the independence of the Church in the State. It provides against the servility which flourishes under the shadow of a single authority, by balancing interests, multiplying associations, and giving to the subject the restraint and support of a combined opinion. In the same way it promotes independence by forming definite groups of public opinion, and by affording a great source and centre of political sentiments, and of notions of duty not derived from the sovereign will. Liberty provokes diversity, and diversity preserves liberty by supplying the means of organisation. All those portions of law which govern the relations of men with each other, and regulate social life, are the varying result of national custom and the creation of private society.

In these things, therefore, the several nations will differ from each other; for they themselves have produced them, and they do not owe them to the State which rules them all. This diversity in the same State is a firm barrier against the intrusion of the government beyond the political sphere which is common to all into the social department which escapes legislation and is ruled by spontaneous laws. This sort of interference is characteristic of an absolute government, and is sure to provoke a reaction, and finally a remedy. That intolerance of social freedom which is natural to absolutism is sure to find a corrective in the national diversities, which no other force could so efficiently provide. The co-existence of several nations under the same State is a test, as well as the best security of its freedom. It is also one of the chief instruments of civilisation; and, as such, it is in the natural and providential order, and indicates a state of greater advancement than the national unity which is the ideal of modern liberalism.

The combination of different nations in one State is as necessary a condition of civilised life as the combination of men in society. Inferior races are raised by living in political union with races intellectually superior. Exhausted and decaying nations are revived by the contact of a younger vitality. Nations in which the elements of organisation and the capacity for government have been lost, either through the demoralising influence of despotism, or the disintegrating action of democracy, are restored and educated anew under the discipline of a stronger and less corrupted race. This fertilising and regenerating process can only be obtained by living under one government. It is in the cauldron of the State that the fusion takes place by which the vigour, the knowledge, and the capacity of one portion of mankind may be communicated to another. Where political and national boundaries coincide, society ceases to advance, and nations relapse into a condition corresponding to that of men who renounce intercourse with their fellow-men. The difference between the two unites mankind not only by the benefits it confers on those who live together, but because it connects society either by a political or a national bond, gives to every people an interest in its neighbours, either because they are under the same government or because they are of the same race, and thus promotes the interests of humanity, of civilisation, and of religion.

Christianity rejoices at the mixture of races, as paganism identifies itself with their differences, because truth is universal, and errors various and particular. In the ancient world idolatry and nationality went together, and the same term is applied in Scripture to both. It was the mission of the Church to overcome national differences. The period of her undisputed supremacy was that in which all Western Europe obeyed the same laws, all literature was contained in one language, and the political unity of Christendom was personified in a single potentate, while its intellectual unity was represented in one university. As the ancient Romans concluded their conquests by carrying away the gods of the conquered people, Charlemagne overcame the national resistance of the Saxons only by the forcible destruction of their pagan rites. Out of the mediæval period, and the combined action of the German race and the Church, came forth a new system of nations and a new conception of nationality. Nature was overcome in the nation as well as in the individual. In pagan and uncultivated times, nations were distinguished from each other by the widest diversity, not only in religion, but in customs, language, and character. Under the new law they had many things in common; the old barriers which separated them were removed, and the new principle of self-government, which Christianity imposed, enabled them to live together under the same authority, without necessarily losing their cherished habits, their customs, or their laws. The new idea of freedom made room for different races in one State. A nation was no longer what it had been to the ancient world,—the progeny of a common ancestor, or the aboriginal product of a particular region,—a result of merely physical and material causes,—but a moral and political being;

not the creation of geographical or physiological unity, but developed in the course of history by the action of the State. It is derived from the State, not supreme over it. A State may in course of time produce a nationality; but that a nationality should constitute a State is contrary to the nature of modern civilisation. The nation derives its rights and its power from the memory of a former independence.

The Church has agreed in this respect with the tendency of political progress, and discouraged wherever she could the isolation of nations; admonishing them of their duties to each other, and regarding conquest and feudal investiture as the natural means of raising barbarous or sunken nations to a higher level. But though she has never attributed to national independence an immunity from the accidental consequences of feudal law, of hereditary claims, or of testamentary arrangements, she defends national liberty against uniformity and centralisation with an energy inspired by perfect community of interests. For the same enemy threatens both; and the State which is reluctant to tolerate differences, and to do justice to the peculiar character of various races, must from the same cause interfere in the internal government of religion. The connection of religious liberty with the emancipation of Poland or Ireland is not merely the accidental result of local causes; and the failure of the Concordat to unite the subjects of Austria is the natural consequence of a policy which did not desire to protect the provinces in their diversity and autonomy, and sought to bribe the Church by favours instead of strengthening her by independence. From this influence of religion in modern history has proceeded a new definition of patriotism.

The difference between nationality and the State is exhibited in the nature of patriotic attachment. Our connection with the race is merely natural or physical, whilst our duties to the political nation are ethical. One is a community of affections and instincts infinitely important and powerful in savage life, but pertaining more to the animal than to the civilised man; the other is an authority governing by laws, imposing obligations, and giving a moral sanction and character to the natural relations of society. Patriotism is in political life what faith is in religion, and it stands to the domestic feelings and to home-sickness as faith to fanaticism and to superstition. It has one aspect derived from private life and nature, for it is an extension of the family affections, as the tribe is an extension of the family. But in its real political character, patriotism consists in the development of the instinct of self-preservation into a moral duty which may involve self-sacrifice. Self-preservation is both an instinct and a duty, natural and involuntary in one respect, and at the same time a moral obligation. By the first it produces the family; by the last the State. If the nation could exist without the State, subject only to the instinct of self-preservation, it would be incapable of denying, controlling, or sacrificing itself; it would be an end and a rule to itself. But in the political order moral purposes are realised and public ends are pursued to which private interests and even existence must be sacrificed. The great sign of true patriotism, the development of selfishness into sacrifice, is the product of political life. That sense of duty which is supplied by race is not entirely separated from its selfish and instinctive basis; and the love of country, like married love, stands at the same time on a material and a moral foundation. The patriot must distinguish between the two causes or objects of his devotion. The attachment which is given only to the country is like obedience given only to the State—a submission to physical influences. The man who prefers his country before every other duty shows the same spirit as the man who surrenders every right to the State. They both deny that right is superior to authority.

There is a moral and political country, in the language of Burke, distinct from the geographical, which may be possibly in collision with it. The Frenchmen who bore arms against the Convention were as patriotic as the Englishmen who bore arms against King Charles, for they recognised a higher duty than that of obedience to the actual sovereign. "In an address to France," said Burke, "in an attempt to treat with it, or in considering any scheme at all relative to it, it is impossible we should mean the geographical, we must always mean the moral and political, country. . . . The truth is, that France is out of itself—the moral France is separated from the geographical. The master of the house is expelled, and the robbers are in possession. If we look for the corporate people of France, existing as corporate in the eye and intention of public law (that corporate people, I mean, who are free to deliberate and to decide, and who have a capacity to treat and conclude), they are in Flanders and Germany, in Switzerland, Spain, Italy, and England. There are all the princes of the blood, there are all the orders of the State, there are all the parliaments of the kingdom. . . . I am sure that if half that number of the same description were taken out of this country, it would leave hardly anything that I should call the people of England."[1] Rousseau draws nearly the same distinction between the country to which we happen to belong and that which fulfils towards us the political functions of the State. In the *Emile* he has a sentence of which it is not easy in a translation to convey the point: "Qui n'a pas une patrie a du moins un pays." And in his tract on Political Economy he writes: "How shall men love their country if it is nothing more for them than for strangers, and bestows on them only that which it can refuse to none?" It is in the same sense he says, further on, "La patrie ne peut subsister sans la liberté."[2]

The nationality formed by the State, then, is the only one to which we owe political duties, and it is, therefore, the only one which has political rights. The Swiss are

[1] Burke's "Remarks on the Policy of the Allies" (*Works*, v. 26, 29, 30).

[2] *Œuvres*, i. 593, 595, ii. 717. Bossuet, in a passage of great beauty on the love of country, does not attain to the political definition of the word: "La société humaine demande qu'on aime la terre où l'on habite ensemble, ou la regarde comme une mère et une nourrice commune. . . . Les hommes en effet se sentent liés par quelque chose de fort, lorsqu'ils songent, que la même terre qui les a portés et nourris étant vivants, les recevra dans son sein quand ils seront morts" ("Politique tirée de l'Ecriture Sainte," *Œuvres*, x. 317).

ethnologically either French, Italian, or German; but no nationality has the slightest claim upon them, except the purely political nationality of Switzerland. The Tuscan or the Neapolitan State has formed a nationality, but the citizens of Florence and of Naples have no political community with each other. There are other States which have neither succeeded in absorbing distinct races in a political nationality, nor in separating a particular district from a larger nation. Austria and Mexico are instances on the one hand, Parma and Baden on the other. The progress of civilisation deals hardly with the last description of States. In order to maintain their integrity they must attach themselves by confederations, or family alliances, to greater Powers, and thus lose something of their independence. Their tendency is to isolate and shut off their inhabitants, to narrow the horizon of their views, and to dwarf in some degree the proportions of their ideas. Public opinion cannot maintain its liberty and purity in such small dimensions, and the currents that come from larger communities sweep over a contracted territory. In a small and homogeneous population there is hardly room for a natural classification of society, or for inner groups of interests that set bounds to sovereign power. The government and the subjects contend with borrowed weapons. The resources of the one and the aspirations of the other are derived from some external source, and the consequence is that the country becomes the instrument and the scene of contests in which it is not interested. These States, like the minuter communities of the Middle Ages, serve a purpose, by constituting partitions and securities of self-government in the larger States; but they are impediments to the progress of society, which depends on the mixture of races under the same governments.

The vanity and peril of national claims founded on no political tradition, but on race alone, appear in Mexico. There the races are divided by blood, without being grouped together in different regions. It is, therefore, neither possible to unite them nor to convert them into the elements of an organised State. They are fluid, shapeless, and unconnected, and cannot be precipitated, or formed into the basis of political institutions. As they cannot be used by the State, they cannot be recognised by it; and their peculiar qualities, capabilities, passions, and attachments are of no service, and therefore obtain no regard. They are necessarily ignored, and are therefore perpetually outraged. From this difficulty of races with political pretensions, but without political position, the Eastern world escaped by the institution of castes. Where there are only two races there is the resource of slavery; but when different races inhabit the different territories of one Empire composed of several smaller States, it is of all possible combinations the most favourable to the establishment of a highly developed system of freedom. In Austria there are two circumstances which add to the difficulty of the problem, but also increase its importance. The several nationalities are at very unequal degrees of advancement, and there is no single nation which is so predominant as to overwhelm or absorb the others. These are the conditions necessary for the very highest degree of organisation which government is capable of receiving. They supply the greatest variety of intellectual resource; the perpetual incentive to progress, which is afforded not merely by competition, but by the spectacle of a more advanced people; the most abundant elements of self-government, combined with the impossibility for the State to rule all by its own will; and the fullest security for the preservation of local customs and ancient rights. In such a country as this, liberty would achieve its most glorious results, while centralisation and absolutism would be destruction.

The problem presented to the government of Austria is higher than that which is solved in England, because of the necessity of admitting the national claims. The parliamentary system fails to provide for them, as it presupposes the unity of the people. Hence in those countries in which different races dwell together, it has not satisfied their desires, and is regarded as an imperfect form of freedom. It brings out more clearly than before the differences it does not recognise, and thus continues the work of the old absolutism, and appears as a new phase of centralisation. In those countries, therefore, the power of the imperial parliament must be limited as jealously as the power of the crown, and many of its functions must be discharged by provincial diets, and a descending series of local authorities.

The great importance of nationality in the State consists in the fact that it is the basis of political capacity. The character of a nation determines in great measure the form and vitality of the State. Certain political habits and ideas belong to particular nations, and they vary with the course of the national history. A people just emerging from barbarism, a people effete from the excesses of a luxurious civilisation, cannot possess the means of governing itself; a people devoted to equality, or to absolute monarchy, is incapable of producing an aristocracy; a people averse to the institution of private property is without the first element of freedom. Each of these can be converted into efficient members of a free community only by the contact of a superior race, in whose power will lie the future prospects of the State. A system which ignores these things, and does not rely for its support on the character and aptitude of the people, does not intend that they should administer their own affairs, but that they should simply be obedient to the supreme command. The denial of nationality, therefore, implies the denial of political liberty.

The greatest adversary of the rights of nationality is the modern theory of nationality. By making the State and the nation commensurate with each other in theory, it reduces practically to a subject condition all other nationalities that may be within the boundary. It cannot admit them to an equality with the ruling nation which constitutes the State, because the State would then cease to be national, which would be a contradiction of the principle of its existence. According, therefore, to the degree of humanity and civilisation in that dominant body which claims all the rights of the community, the inferior races are exterminated, or reduced to servitude, or outlawed, or put in a condition of dependence.

If we take the establishment of liberty for the realisation of moral duties to be the end of civil society, we must conclude that those states are substantially the most perfect which, like the British and Austrian Empires, include various distinct nationalities without oppressing them. Those in which no mixture of races has occurred are imperfect; and those in which its effects have disappeared are decrepit. A State which is incompetent to satisfy different races condemns itself; a State which labours to neutralise, to absorb, or to expel them, destroys its own vitality; a State which does not include them is destitute of the chief basis of self-government. The theory of nationality, therefore, is a retrograde step in history. It is the most advanced form of the revolution, and must retain its power to the end of the revolutionary period, of which it announces the approach. Its great historical importance depends on two chief causes.

First, it is a chimera. The settlement at which it aims is impossible. As it can never be satisfied and exhausted, and always continues to assert itself, it prevents the government from ever relapsing into the condition which provoked its rise. The danger is too threatening, and the power over men's minds too great, to allow any system to endure which justifies the resistance of nationality. It must contribute, therefore, to obtain that which in theory it condemns,—the liberty of different nationalities as members of one sovereign community. This is a service which no other force could accomplish; for it is a corrective alike of absolute monarchy, of democracy, and of constitutionalism, as well as of the centralisation which is common to all three. Neither the monarchical, nor the revolutionary, nor the parliamentary system can do this; and all the ideas which have excited enthusiasm in past times are impotent for the purpose except nationality alone.

And secondly, the national theory marks the end of the revolutionary doctrine and its logical exhaustion. In proclaiming the supremacy of the rights of nationality, the system of democratic equality goes beyond its own extreme boundary, and falls into contradiction with itself. Between the democratic and the national phase of the revolution, socialism had intervened, and had already carried the consequences of the principle to an absurdity. But that phase was passed. The revolution survived its offspring, and produced another further result. Nationality is more advanced than socialism, because it is a more arbitrary system. The social theory endeavours to provide for the existence of the individual beneath the terrible burdens which modern society heaps upon labour. It is not merely a development of the notion of equality, but a refuge from real misery and starvation. However false the solution, it was a reasonable demand that the poor should be saved from destruction ; and if the freedom of the State was sacrificed to the safety of the individual, the more immediate object was, at least in theory, attained. But nationality does not aim either at liberty or prosperity, both of which it sacrifices to the imperative necessity of making the nation the mould and measure of the State. Its course will be marked with material as well as moral ruin, in order that a new invention may prevail over the works of God and the interests of mankind. There is no principle of change, no phase of political speculation conceivable, more comprehensive, more subversive, or more arbitrary than this. It is a confutation of democracy, because it sets limits to the exercise of the popular will, and substitutes for it a higher principle. It prevents not only the division, but the extension of the State, and forbids to terminate war by conquest, and to obtain a security for peace. Thus, after surrendering the individual to the collective will, the revolutionary system makes the collective will subject to conditions which are independent of it, and rejects all law, only to be controlled by an accident.

Although, therefore, the theory of nationality is more

absurd and more criminal than the theory of socialism, it has an important mission in the world, and marks the final conflict, and therefore the end, of two forces which are the worst enemies of civil freedom,—the absolute monarchy and the revolution.

X

DÖLLINGER ON THE TEMPORAL POWER[1]

AFTER half a year's delay, Dr. Döllinger has redeemed his promise to publish the text of those lectures which made so profound a sensation in the Catholic world.[2] We are sorry to find that the report which fell into our hands at the time, and from which we gave the account that appeared in our May Number, was both defective and incorrect; and we should further regret that we did not follow the example of those journals which abstained from comment so long as no authentic copy was accessible, if it did not appear that, although the argument of the lecturer was lost, his meaning was not, on the whole, seriously misrepresented. Excepting for the sake of the author, who became the object, and of those who unfortunately made themselves the organs, of so much calumny, it is impossible to lament the existence of the erroneous statements which have caused the present publication. Intending at first to prefix an introduction to the text of his lectures, the Professor has been led on by the gravity of the occasion, the extent of his subject, and the abundance of materials, to compose a book of 700 pages. Written with all the author's perspicuity of style, though without his usual compression; with the exhaustless information which never fails him, but with an economy of quotation suited to the general public for whom it is designed, it betrays the circumstances of its origin. Subjects are sometimes introduced out of their

[1] *The Rambler*, November 1861.

[2] *Kirche und Kirchen*, Munich, 1861 ("Papstum und Kirchenstaat").

proper place and order; and there are occasional repetitions, which show that he had not at starting fixed the proportions of the different parts of his work. This does not, however, affect the logical sequence of the ideas, or the accuracy of the induction. No other book contains—no other writer probably could supply—so comprehensive and so suggestive a description of the state of the Protestant religion, or so impartial an account of the causes which have brought on the crisis of the temporal power.

The *Symbolik* of Möhler was suggested by the beginning of that movement of revival and resuscitation amongst the Protestants, of which Döllinger now surveys the fortunes and the result. The interval of thirty years has greatly altered the position of the Catholic divines towards their antagonists. Möhler had to deal with the ideas of the Reformation, the works of the Reformers, and the teaching of the confessions; he had to answer in the nineteenth century the theology of the sixteenth. The Protestantism for which he wrote was a complete system, antagonistic to the whole of Catholic theology, and he confuted the one by comparing it with the other, dogma for dogma. But that of which Döllinger treats has lost, for the most part, those distinctive doctrines, not by the growth of unbelief, but in consequence of the very efforts which its most zealous and religious professors have made to defend and to redeem it. The contradictions and errors of the Protestant belief were formerly the subject of controversy with its Catholic opponents, but now the controversy is anticipated and prevented by the undisguised admissions of its desponding friends. It stands no longer as a system consistent, complete, satisfying the judgment and commanding the unconditional allegiance of its followers, and fortified at all points against Catholicism; but disorganised as a church, its doctrines in a state of dissolution, despaired of by its divines, strong and compact only in its hostility to Rome, but with no positive principle of unity, no ground of resistance, nothing to have faith in but the determination to reject authority. This, therefore, is the point which

Döllinger takes up. Reducing the chief phenomena of religious and social decline to the one head of failing authority, he founds on the state of Protestantism the apology of the Papacy. He abandons to the Protestant theology the destruction of the Protestant Church, and leaves its divines to confute and abjure its principles in detail, and to arrive by the exhaustion of the modes of error, through a painful but honourable process, at the gates of truth; he meets their arguments simply by a chapter of ecclesiastical history, of which experience teaches them the force; and he opposes to their theories, not the discussions of controversial theology, but the character of a single institution. The opportunity he has taken to do this, the assumed coincidence between the process of dissolution among the Protestants and the process of regeneration in the Court of Rome, is the characteristic peculiarity of the book. Before we proceed to give an analysis of its contents, we will give some extracts from the Preface, which explains the purpose of the whole, and which is alone one of the most important contributions to the religious discussions of the day.

This book arose from two out of four lectures which were delivered in April this year. How I came to discuss the most difficult and complicated question of our time before a very mixed audience, and in a manner widely different from that usually adopted, I deem myself bound to explain. It was my intention, when I was first requested to lecture, only to speak of the present state of religion in general, with a comprehensive view extending over all mankind. It happened, however, that from those circles which had given the impulse to the lectures, the question was frequently put to me, how the position of the Holy See, the partly consummated, partly threatening, loss of its secular power is to be explained. What answer, I was repeatedly asked, is to be given to those out of the Church who point with triumphant scorn to the numerous Episcopal manifestoes, in which the States of the Church are declared essential and necessary to her existence although the events of the last thirty years appear with increasing distinctness to announce their downfall? I had found the hope often expressed in newspapers, books, and periodicals, that after the destruction of the temporal power of the Popes, the Church herself would not escape dissolution. At the same time, I was struck by finding in the memoirs of Chateaubriand that Cardinal Bernetti, Secretary of State to Leo

XII., had said, that if he lived long, there was a chance of his beholding the fall of the temporal power of the Papacy. I had also read, in the letter of a well-informed and trustworthy correspondent from Paris, that the Archbishop of Rheims had related on his return from Rome that Pius IX. had said to him, "I am under no illusions, the temporal power must fall. Goyon will abandon me; I shall then disband my remaining troops. I shall excommunicate the king when he enters the city; and shall calmly await my death."

I thought already, in April, that I could perceive, what has become still more clear in October, that the enemies of the secular power of the Papacy are determined, united, predominant, and that there is nowhere a protecting power which possesses the will, and at the same time the means, of averting the catastrophe. I considered it therefore probable that an interruption of the temporal dominion would soon ensue—an interruption which, like others before it, would also come to an end, and would be followed by a restoration. I resolved, therefore, to take the opportunity, which the lectures gave me, to prepare the public for the coming events, which already cast their shadows upon us, and thus to prevent the scandals, the doubt, and the offence which must inevitably arise if the States of the Church should pass into other hands, although the pastorals of the Bishops had so energetically asserted that they belonged to the integrity of the Church. I meant, therefore, to say, the Church by her nature can very well exist, and did exist for seven centuries, without the territorial possessions of the Popes; afterwards this possession became necessary, and, in spite of great changes and vicissitudes, has discharged in most cases its function of serving as a foundation for the independence and freedom of the Popes. As long as the present state and arrangement of Europe endures, we can discover no other means to secure to the Holy See its freedom, and with it the confidence of all. But the knowledge and the power of God reach farther than ours, and we must not presume to set bounds to the Divine wisdom and omnipotence, or to say to it, In this way and no other! Should, nevertheless, the threatening consummation ensue, and should the Pope be robbed of his land, one of three eventualities will assuredly come to pass. Either the loss of the State is only temporary, and the territory will revert, after some intervening casualties, either whole or in part, to its legitimate sovereign; or Providence will bring about, by ways unknown to us, and combinations which we cannot divine, a state of things in which the object, namely, the independence and free action of the Holy See, will be attained without the means which have hitherto served; or else we are approaching great catastrophes in Europe, the doom of the whole edifice of the present social order,—events of which the ruin of the Roman State is only the precursor and the herald.

The reasons for which, of these three possibilities, I think the first the most probable, I have developed in this book. Concerning the second alternative, there is nothing to be said; it is an unknown, and therefore, indescribable, quantity. Only we must retain it against certain over-confident assertions which profess to know the secret things to come, and, trespassing on the divine domain, wish to subject the Future absolutely to the laws of the immediate Past. That the third possibility must also be admitted, few of those who studiously observe the signs of the time will dispute. One of the ablest historians and statesmen—Niebuhr—wrote on the 5th October 1830: "If God does not miraculously aid, a destruction is in store for us such as the Roman world underwent in the middle of the third century—destruction of prosperity, of freedom, of civilisation, and of literature." And we have proceeded much farther on the inclined plane since then. The European Powers have overturned, or have allowed to be overturned, the two pillars of their existence,—the principle of legitimacy, and the public law of nations. Those monarchs who have made themselves the slaves of the Revolution, to do its work, are the active agents in the historical drama; the others stand aside as quiet spectators, in expectation of inheriting something, like Prussia and Russia, or bestowing encouragement and assistance, like England; or as passive invalids, like Austria and the sinking empire of Turkey. But the Revolution is a permanent chronic disease, breaking out now in one place, now in another, sometimes seizing several members together. The Pentarchy is dissolved; the Holy Alliance, which, however defective or open to abuse, was one form of political order, is buried; the right of might prevails in Europe. Is it a process of renovation or a process of dissolution in which European society is plunged? I still think the former; but I must, as I have said, admit the possibility of the other alternative. If it occurs, then, when the powers of destruction have done their work, it will be the business of the Church at once to co-operate actively in the reconstruction of social order out of the ruins, both as a connecting civilising power, and as the preserver and dispenser of moral and religious tradition. And thus the Papacy, with or without territory, has its own function and its appointed mission.

These, then, were the ideas from which I started; and it may be supposed that my language concerning the immediate fate of the temporal power of the Pope necessarily sounded ambiguous, that I could not well come with the confidence which is given to other—perhaps more far-sighted—men before my audience, and say, Rely upon it, the States of the Church—the land from Radicofani to Ceperano, from Ravenna to Cività Vecchia, shall and must and will invariably remain to the Popes. Heaven and earth shall pass away before the Roman State shall pass away. I could not do this, because I did not at that time believe it, nor do I now; but am only confident that the Holy See will not be permanently deprived of the conditions necessary for the fulfilment of its mission. Thus the substance of my words was this: Let no one lose faith in the Church if the secular principality of the Pope should disappear for a season, or for ever. It is not essence, but accident; not end, but means; it began late; it was formerly something quite different from what it is now. It justly appears to us indispensable, and as long as the existing order lasts in Europe, it must be maintained at any price; or if it is violently interrupted, it must be restored. But a political settlement of Europe is conceivable in which it would be superfluous, and then it would be an oppressive burden. At the same time I wished to defend Pope Pius IX. and his government against many accusations, and to point out that the inward infirmities and deficiencies which undeniably exist in the country, by which the State has been reduced to so deplorable a condition of weakness and helplessness, were not attributable to him; that, on the contrary, he has shown, both before and since 1848, the best will to reform; and that by him, and under him, much has been really improved.

The newspaper reports, written down at home from memory, gave but an inaccurate representation of a discourse which did not attempt in the usual way to cut the knot, but which, with buts and ifs, and referring to certain elements in the decision which are generally left out of the calculation, spoke of an uncertain future, and of various possibilities. This was not to be avoided. Any reproduction which was not quite literal must, in spite of the good intentions of the reporter, have given rise to false interpretations. When, therefore, one of the most widely read papers reported the first lecture, without any intentional falsification, but with omissions which altered the sense and the tendency of my words, I immediately proposed to the conductors to print my manuscript; but this offer was declined. In other accounts in the daily press, I was often unable to recognise my ideas; and words were put into my mouth which I had never uttered. And here I will admit that, when I gave the lectures, I did not think that they would be discussed by the press, but expected that, like others of the same kind, they would at most be mentioned in a couple of words, *in futuram oblivionem*. Of the controversy which sprang up at once, in separate works and in newspaper articles, in Germany, France, England, Italy, and even in America, I shall not speak. Much of it I have not read. The writers often did not even ask themselves whether the report which accident put into their hands, and which they carelessly adopted, was at all accurate. But I must refer to an account in one of the most popular English periodicals, because I am there brought into a society to which I do not belong. The author of an article in the July Number of the *Edinburgh Review* . . . appeals to me, misunderstanding the drift of my words, and erroneously believing that I had already published an apology of my orthodoxy. . . . A sharp attack upon me in the *Dublin Review* I know only from extracts in English papers; but I can see from the vehemence with which the writer pronounces himself against liberal institutions, that, even after the appearance of this book, I cannot reckon on coming to an understanding with him. . . .

The excitement which was caused by my lectures, or rather by the accounts of them in the papers, had this advantage, that it brought to light, in a way which to many was unexpected, how widely, how deeply, and how firmly the attachment of the people to the See of St. Peter is rooted. For the sake of this I was glad to accept all the attacks and animosity which fell on me in consequence. But why, it will be asked—and I have been asked innumerable times—why not cut short misunderstandings by the immediate publication of the lectures, which must, as a whole, have been written beforehand? why wait for five months? For this I had two reasons: first, it was not merely a question of misunderstanding. Much of what I had actually said had made an unpleasant impression in many quarters, especially among our optimists. I should, therefore, with my bare statements, have become involved in an agitating discussion in pamphlets and newspapers, and that was not an attractive prospect. The second reason was this: I expected that the further progress of events in Italy, the irresistible logic of facts, would dispose minds to receive certain truths. I hoped that people would learn by degrees, in the school of events, that it is not enough always to be reckoning with the figures "revolution," "secret societies," "Mazzinism," "Atheism," or to estimate things only by the standard supplied by the "Jew of Verona," but that other factors must be admitted into the calculation; for instance, the condition of the Italian clergy, and its position towards the laity. I wished, therefore, to let a few months go by before I came before the public. Whether I judged rightly, the reception of this book will show.

I thoroughly understand those who think it censurable that I should have spoken in detail of situations and facts which are gladly ignored, or touched with a light and hasty hand, and that especially at the present crisis. I myself was restrained for ten years by these considerations, in spite of the feeling which urged me to speak on the question of the Roman government, and it required the circumstances I have described, I may almost say, to compel me to speak publicly on the subject. I beg of these persons to weigh the following points. First, when an author openly exposes a state of things already abundantly discussed in the press, if he draws away the necessarily very transparent covering from the gaping wounds which are not on the Church herself, but on an institution nearly connected with her, and whose infirmities she is made to feel, it may fairly be supposed that he does it, in agreement with the example of earlier friends and great men of the Church, only to show the possibility and the necessity of the cure, in order, so far as in him lies, to weaken the reproach that the defenders of the Church see only the mote in the eyes of others, not the beam in their own, and with narrow-hearted prejudice endeavour to soften, or to dissimulate, or to deny every fact which is or which appears unfavourable to their cause. He does it in order that it may be understood that where the powerlessness of men to effect a cure becomes manifest, God interposes in order to sift on

His threshing-floor the chaff from the wheat, and to consume it with the fire of the catastrophes which are only His judgments and remedies. Secondly, I could not, as a historian, present the effects without going back to their causes; and it was therefore my duty, as it is that of every religious inquirer and observer, to try to contribute something to the *Theodicée.* He that undertakes to write on such lofty interests, which nearly affect the weal and woe of the Church, cannot avoid examining and displaying the wisdom and justice of God in the conduct of terrestrial events regarding them. The fate which has overtaken the Roman States must above all be considered in the light of a Divine ordinance for the advantage of the Church. Seen by that light, it assumes the character of a trial, which will continue until the object is attained, and the welfare of the Church so far secured.

It seemed evident to me, that as a new order of things in Europe lies in the design of Providence, the disease, through which for the last half-century the States of the Church unquestionably have passed, might be the transition to a new form. To describe this malady without overlooking or concealing any of the symptoms was, therefore, an undertaking which I could not avoid. The disease has its source in the inward contradiction and discord of the institutions and conditions of the government; for the modern French institutions stand there, without any reconciling qualifications, besides those of the mediæval hierarchy. Neither of these elements is strong enough to expel the other; and either of them would, if it prevailed alone, be again a form of disease. Yet, in the history of the last few years I recognise symptoms of convalescence, however feeble, obscure, and equivocal its traces may appear. What we behold is not death or hopeless decay, it is a purifying process, painful, consuming, penetrating bone and marrow,—such as God inflicts on His chosen persons and institutions. There is abundance of dross, and time is necessary before the gold can come pure out of the furnace. In the course of this process it may happen that the territorial dominion will be interrupted, that the State may be broken up or pass into other hands; but it will revive, though perhaps in another form, and with a different kind of government. In a word, *sanabilibus laboramus malis*—that is what I wished to show; that, I believe, I have shown. Now, and for the last forty years, the condition of the Roman States is the heel of Achilles of the Catholic Church, the standing reproach for adversaries throughout the world, and a stumbling-block for thousands. Not as though the objections, which are founded on the fact of this transitory disturbance and discord in the social and political sphere, possessed any weight in a theological point of view, but it cannot be denied that they are of incalculable influence on the disposition of the world external to the Church.

Whenever a state of disease has appeared in the Church, there has been but one method of cure,—that of an awakened, renovated, healthy consciousness and of an enlightened public opinion in the

Church. The goodwill of the ecclesiastical rulers and heads has not been able to accomplish the cure, unless sustained by the general sense and conviction of the clergy and of the laity. The healing of the great malady of the sixteenth century, the true internal reformation of the Church, only became possible when people ceased to disguise or to deny the evil, and to pass it by with silence and concealment,—when so powerful and irresistible a public opinion had formed itself in the Church, that its commanding influence could no longer be evaded. At the present day, what we want is the whole truth, not merely the perception that the temporal power of the Pope is required by the Church,—for that is obvious to everybody, at least out of Italy, and everything has been said that can be said about it; but also the knowledge of the conditions under which this power is possible for the future. The history of the Popes is full of instances where their best intentions were not fulfilled, and their strongest resolutions broke down, because the interests of a firmly compacted class resisted like an impenetrable hedge of thorns. Hadrian VI. was fully resolved to set about the reformation in earnest; and yet he achieved virtually nothing, and felt himself, though in possession of supreme power, altogether powerless against the passive resistance of all those who should have been his instruments in the work. Only when public opinion, even in Italy, and in Rome itself, was awakened, purified, and strengthened; when the cry for reform resounded imperatively on every side,—then only was it possible for the Popes to overcome the resistance in the inferior spheres, and gradually, and step by step, to open the way for a more healthy state. May, therefore, a powerful, healthy, unanimous public opinion in Catholic Europe come to the aid of Pius IX.! . . .

Concerning another part of this book I have a few words to say. I have given a survey of all the Churches and ecclesiastical communities now existing. The obligation of attempting this presented itself to me, because I had to explain both the universal importance of the Papacy as a power for all the world, and the things which it actually performs. This could not be done fully without exhibiting the internal condition of the Churches which have rejected it, and withdrawn from its influence. It is true that the plan increased under my hands, and I endeavoured to give as clear a picture as possible of the development which has accomplished itself in the separated Churches since the Reformation, and through it, in consequence of the views and principles which had been once for all adopted. I have, therefore, admitted into my description no feature which is not, in my opinion, an effect, a result, however remote, of those principles and doctrines. There is doubtless room for discussion in detail upon this point, and there will unavoidably be a decided opposition to this book, if it should be noticed beyond the limits of the Church to which I belong. I hope that there also the justice will be done me of believing that I was far from having any intention of offending; that I have only said what must be said, if we would go to the bottom of these questions; that I had to do with institutions which, because of the dogmas and principles from which they spring, must, like a tree that is nailed to a wall, remain in one position, however unnatural it may be. I am quite ready to admit that, on the opposite side, the men are often better than the system to which they are, or deem themselves, attached; and that, on the contrary, in the Church the individuals are, on the average, inferior in theory and in practice to the system under which they live. . . .

The union of the two religions, which would be socially and politically the salvation of Germany and of Europe, is not possible at present; first because the greater, more active, and more influential portion of the German Protestants do not desire it, for political or religious reasons, in any form or under any practicable conditions. It is impossible, secondly, because negotiations concerning the mode and the conditions of union can no longer be carried on. For this, plenipotentiaries on both sides are required; and these only the Catholic Church is able to appoint, by virtue of her ecclesiastical organisation, not the Protestants. . . .

Nevertheless, theologically, Protestants and Catholics have come nearer each other; for those capital doctrines, those articles with which the Church was to stand or fall, for the sake of which the Reformers declared separation from the Catholic Church to be necessary, are now confuted and given up by Protestant theology, or are retained only nominally, whilst other notions are connected with the words. . . . Protestant theology is at the present day less hostile, so to speak, than the theologians. For whilst theology has levelled the strongest bulwarks and doctrinal barriers which the Reformation had set up to confirm the separation, the divines, instead of viewing favourably the consequent facilities for union, often labour, on the contrary, to conceal the fact, or to provide new points of difference. Many of them probably agree with Stahl of Berlin, who said, shortly before his death, "Far from supposing that the breach of the sixteenth century can be healed, we ought, if it had not already occurred, to make it now." This, however, will not continue; and a future generation, perhaps that which is even now growing up, will rather adopt the recent declaration of Heinrich Leo, "In the Roman Catholic Church a process of purification has taken place since Luther's day; and if the Church had been in the days of Luther what the Roman Catholic Church in Germany actually is at present, it would never have occurred to him to assert his opposition so energetically as to bring about a separation." Those who think thus will then be the right men and the chosen instruments for the acceptable work of the reconciliation of the Churches, and the true unity of Germany. Upon the day when, on both sides, the conviction shall arise vivid and strong that Christ really desires the unity of His Church, that the division of Christendom, the multiplicity of

Churches, is displeasing to God, that he who helps to prolong the situation must answer for it to the Lord,—on that day four-fifths of the traditional polemics of the Protestants against the Church will with one blow be set aside, like chaff and rubbish; for four-fifths consist of misunderstandings, logomachies, and wilful falsifications, or relate to personal, and therefore accidental, things, which are utterly insignificant where only principles and dogmas are at stake.

On that day, also, much will be changed on the Catholic side. Thenceforward the character of Luther and the Reformers will no more be dragged forward in the pulpit. The clergy, mindful of the saying, *interficite errores*, *diligite homines*, will always conduct themselves towards members of other Churches in conformity with the rules of charity, and will therefore assume, in all cases where there are no clear proofs to the contrary, the *bona fides* of opponents. They will never forget that no man is convinced and won over by bitter words and violent attacks, but that every one is rather repelled by them. Warned by the words of the Epistle to the Romans (xiv. 13), they will be more careful than heretofore to give to their separate brethren no scandal, no grounds of accusation against the Church. Accordingly, in popular instruction and in religious life, they will always make the great truths of salvation the centre of all their teaching: they will not treat secondary things in life and doctrine as though they were of the first importance; but, on the contrary, they will keep alive in the people the consciousness that such things are but means to an end, and are only of inferior consequence and subsidiary value.

Until that day shall dawn upon Germany, it is our duty as Catholics, in the words of Cardinal Diepenbrock, "to bear the religious separation in a spirit of penance for guilt incurred in common." We must acknowledge that here also God has caused much good as well as much evil to proceed from the errors of men, from the contests and passions of the sixteenth century; that the anxiety of the German nation to see the intolerable abuses and scandals in the Church removed was fully justified, and sprang from the better qualities of our people, and from their moral indignation at the desecration and corruption of holy things, which were degraded to selfish and hypocritical purposes.

We do not refuse to admit that the great separation, and the storms and sufferings connected with it, was an awful judgment upon Catholic Christendom, which clergy and laity had but too well deserved—a judgment which has had an improving and salutary effect. The great conflict of intellects has purified the European atmosphere, has impelled the human mind on to new courses, and has promoted a rich scientific and literary life. Protestant theology, with its restless spirit of inquiry, has gone along by the side of the Catholic, exciting and awakening, warning and vivifying; and every eminent Catholic divine in Germany will gladly admit that he owes much to the writings of Protestant scholars.

We must also acknowledge that in the Church the rust of abuses and of a mechanical superstition is always forming afresh; that the spiritual in religion is sometimes materialised, and therefore degraded, deformed, and applied to their own loss, by the servants of the Church, through their indolence and want of intelligence, and by the people, through their ignorance. The true spirit of reform must, therefore, never depart from the Church, but must periodically break out with renovating strength, and penetrate the mind and the will of the clergy. In this sense we do not refuse to admit the justice of a call to penance, when it proceeds from those who are not of us,—that is, of a warning carefully to examine our religious life and pastoral conduct, and to remedy what is found defective.

At the same time it must not be forgotten that the separation did not ensue in consequence of the abuses of the Church. For the duty and necessity of removing these abuses has always been recognised; and only the difficulty of the thing, the not always unjustifiable fear lest the wheat should be pulled up with the tares, prevented for a time the Reformation, which was accomplished in the Church and through her. Separation on account merely of abuses in ecclesiastical life, when the doctrine is the same, is rejected as criminal by the Protestants as well as by us. It is, therefore, for doctrine's sake that the separation occurred; and the general discontent of the people, the weakening of ecclesiastical authority by the existence of abuses, only facilitated the adoption of the new doctrines. But now on one side some of these defects and evils in the life of the Church have disappeared; the others have greatly diminished since the reforming movement; and on the other side, the principal doctrines for which they separated, and on the truth of which, and their necessity for salvation, the right and duty of secession was based, are given up by Protestant science, deprived of their Scriptural basis by exegesis, or at least made very uncertain by the opposition of the most eminent Protestant divines. Meanwhile we live in hopes, comforting ourselves with the conviction that history, or that process of development in Europe which is being accomplished before our eyes, as well in society and politics as in religion, is the powerful ally of the friends of ecclesiastical union; and we hold out our hands to Christians on the other side for a combined war of resistance against the destructive movements of the age.

There are two circumstances which make us fear that the work will not be received in the spirit in which it is written, and that its object will not immediately be attained. The first of these is the extraordinary effect which was produced by the declaration which the author made on the occasion of the late assembly of the Catholic associations of Germany at Munich. He stated simply, what is understood by every Catholic out of Italy, and intelligible to every reasonable Protestant, that the freedom of the Church imperatively requires that, in order to protect the Pope from the perils which menace him, particularly in our age, he should possess a sovereignty not merely nominal, and that his right to his dominions is as good as that of all other legitimate sovereigns. In point of fact, this expression of opinion, which occurs even in the garbled reports of the lectures, leaves all those questions on which it is possible for serious and dispassionate men to be divided entirely open. It does not determine whether there was any excuse for the disaffection of the Papal subjects; whether the security afforded by a more extensive dominion is greater than the increased difficulty of administration under the conditions inherited from the French occupation; whether an organised system of tribute or domains might be sufficient, in conjunction with a more restricted territory; whether the actual loss of power is or is not likely to improve a misfortune for religion. The storm of applause with which these words, simply expressing that in which all agree, were received, must have suggested to the speaker that his countrymen in general are unprepared to believe that one, who has no other aspiration in his life and his works than the advancement of the Catholic religion, can speak without a reverent awe of the temporal government, or can witness without dismay its impending fall. They must have persuaded themselves that not only the details, but the substance of his lectures had been entirely misreported, and that his views were as free from novelty as destitute of offence. It is hard to believe that such persons will be able to reconcile themselves to the fearless and straightforward spirit in which the first of Church historians discusses the history of his own age.

Another consideration, almost equally significant with the attitude of the great mass of Catholics, is the silence of the minority who agree with Döllinger. Those earnest Catholics who, in their Italian patriotism, insist on the possibility of reconciling the liberty of the Holy See with the establishment of an ideal unity, Passaglia, Tosti, the followers of Gioberti, and the disciples of Rosmini, have not hesitated to utter openly their honest but most inconceivable persuasion. But on the German side of the Alps, where no political agitation affects the religious judgment, or drives men into disputes, those eminent thinkers who agree with Döllinger are withheld by various considerations from publishing their views. Sometimes it is the hopelessness of making an impression, sometimes the grave inconvenience of withstanding the current of opinion that makes them keep silence; and their silence leaves those who habitually follow them not only without means of expressing their views, but often without decided views to express. The same influences which deprive Döllinger of the open support of these natural allies will impede the success of his work, until events have outstripped ideas, and until men awake to the discovery that what they refused to anticipate or to prepare for, is already accomplished.

Piety sometimes gives birth to scruples, and faith to superstition, when they are not directed by wisdom and knowledge. One source of the difficulty of which we are speaking is as much a defect of faith as a defect of knowledge. Just as it is difficult for some Catholics to believe that the supreme spiritual authority on earth could ever be in unworthy hands, so they find it hard to reconcile the reverence due to the Vicar of Christ, and the promises made to him, with the acknowledgment of intolerable abuses in his temporal administration. It is a comfort to make the best of the case, to draw conclusions from the exaggerations, the inventions, and the malice of the accusers against the justice of the accusation, and in favour of the accused. It is a temptation to our weakness and to our consciences to defend the Pope as we would defend ourselves—with the same care and zeal, with the same uneasy secret consciousness that there are weak points in the case which can best be concealed by diverting attention from them. What the defence gains in energy it loses in sincerity; the cause of the Church, which is the cause of truth, is mixed up and confused with human elements, and is injured by a degrading alliance. In this way even piety may lead to immorality, and devotion to the Pope may lead away from God.

The position of perpetual antagonism to a spirit which we abhor; the knowledge that the clamour against the temporal power is, in very many instances, inspired by hatred of the spiritual authority; the indignation at the impure motives mixed up with the movement—all these things easily blind Catholics to the fact that our attachment to the Pope as our spiritual Head, our notion that his civil sovereignty is a safeguard of his freedom, are the real motives of our disposition to deny the truth of the accusations made against his government. It is hard to believe that imputations which take the form of insults, and which strike at the Church through the State, are well founded, and to distinguish the design and the occasion from the facts. It is, perhaps, more than we can expect of men, that, after defending the Pope as a sovereign, because he is a pontiff, and adopting against his enemies the policy of unconditional defence, they will consent to adopt a view which corroborates to a great extent the assertions they have combated, and implicitly condemns their tactics. It is natural to oppose one extreme by another; and those who avoid both easily appear to be capitulating with error. The effects of this spirit of opposition are not confined to those who are engaged in resisting the No-popery party in England, or the revolution in Italy. The fate of the temporal power hangs neither on the Italian ministry nor on English influence, but on the decision of the Emperor of the French; and the loudest maintainers of the rights of the Holy See are among that party who have been the most zealous adversaries of the Imperial system. The French Catholics behold in the Roman policy of the emperor a scheme for obtaining over the Church a power of which they would be the first victims. Their religious freedom is in jeopardy while he has the fate of the Pope in his hands. That which is elsewhere simply a manifestation of opinion and a moral influence is in France an active interference and a political power. They alone among Catholic subjects can bring a pressure to bear on him who has had the initiative in the Italian movement. They fear by silence to incur a responsibility for criminal acts. For them it is a season for action, and the time has not yet come when they can speak with judicial impartiality, or with the freedom of history, or determine how far, in the pursuit of his ambitious ends, Napoleon III. is the instrument of Providence, or how far, without any merit of his own, he is likely to fulfil the expectations of those who see in him a new Constantine. Whilst they maintain this unequal war, they naturally identify the rights of the Church with her interests; and the wrongs of the Pope are before their eyes so as to eclipse the realities of the Roman government. The most vehement and one-sided of those who have dwelt exclusively on the crimes of the Revolution and the justice of the Papal cause, the Bishop of Orleans for instance, or Count de Montalembert, might without inconsistency, and doubtless would without hesitation, subscribe to almost every word in Döllinger's work; but in the position they have taken they would probably deem such adhesion a great rhetorical error, and fatal to the effect of their own writings. There is, therefore, an allowance to be made, which is by no means a reproach, for the peculiar situation of the Catholics in France.

When Christine of Sweden was observed to gaze long and intently at the statue of Truth in Rome, a court-like prelate observed that this admiration for Truth did her honour, as it was seldom shared by persons in her station. "That," said the Queen, "is because truths are not all made of marble." Men are seldom zealous for an idea in which they do not perceive some reflection of themselves, in which they have not embarked some portion of their individuality, or which they cannot connect with some subjective purpose of their own. It is often more easy to sympathise with a person in whose opposite views we discern a weakness corresponding to our own, than with one who unsympathetically avoids to colour the objectivity of truth, and is guided in his judgment by facts, not by wishes. We endeavoured not many months ago to show how remote the theology of Catholic Germany is in its scientific spirit from that of other countries, and how far asunder are science and policy. The same method applied to the events of our own day must be yet more startling, and for a time we can scarcely anticipate that the author of this work will escape an apparent isolation between the reserve of those who share his views, but are not free to speak, and the foregone conclusions of most of those who have already spoken. But a book which treats of contemporary events in accordance with the signs of the time, not with the aspirations of men, possesses in time itself an invincible auxiliary. When the lesson which this great writer draws from the example of the mediæval Popes has borne its fruit; when the purpose for which he has written is attained, and the freedom of the Holy See from revolutionary aggression and arbitrary protection is recovered by the heroic determination to abandon that which in the course of events has ceased to be a basis of independence—he will be the first, but no longer the only, proclaimer of new ideas, and he will not have written in vain.

The Christian religion, as it addresses and adapts itself to all mankind, bears towards the varieties of national character a relation of which there was no example in the religions of antiquity, and which heresy repudiates and inevitably seeks to destroy. For heresy, like paganism, is national, and dependent both on the particular disposition of the people and on the government of the State. It is identified with definite local conditions, and moulded by national and political peculiarities. Catholicity alone is universal in its character and mission, and independent of those circumstances by which States are established, and nations are distinguished from each other. Even Rome had not so far extended her limits, nor so thoroughly subjugated and amalgamated the races that obeyed her, as to secure the Church from the natural reaction of national spirit against a religion which claimed a universality beyond even that of the Imperial power. The first and most terrible assault of ethnicism was in Persia, where Christianity appeared as a Roman, and therefore a foreign and a hostile, system. As the Empire gradually declined, and the nationalities, no longer oppressed beneath a vigorous central force, began to revive, the heresies, by a natural affinity, associated themselves with them. The Donatist schism, in which no other country joined, was an attempt of the African people to establish a separate national Church. Later on, the Egyptians adopted the Monophysite heresy as the national faith, which has survived to this day in the Coptic Church. In Armenia similar causes produced like effects.

In the twelfth century—not, as is commonly supposed, in the time of Photius and Cerularius, for religious communion continued to subsist between the Latins and the Greeks at Constantinople till about the time of Innocent III., but after the Crusades had embittered the antagonism between East and West—another great national separation occurred. In the Eastern Empire the communion with Rome was hateful to the two chief authorities. The patriarch was ambitious to extend his own absolute jurisdiction over the whole Empire, the emperor wished to increase that power as the instrument of his own: out of this threefold combination of interests sprang the Byzantine system. It was founded on the ecclesiastical as well as civil despotism of the emperor, and on the exclusive pride of the people in its nationality; that is, on those things which are most essentially opposed to the Catholic spirit, and to the nature of a universal Church. In consequence of the schism, the sovereign became supreme over the canons of the Church and the laws of the State; and to this imperial papacy the Archbishop of Thessalonica, in the beginning of the fifteenth century, justly attributes the ruin and degradation of the Empire. Like the Eastern schism, the schism of the West in the fourteenth century arose from the predominance of national interests in the Church: it proceeded from the endeavour to convert the Holy See into a possession of the French people and a subject of the French crown. Again, not long after, the Hussite revolution sprang from the union of a new doctrine with the old antipathy of the Bohemians for the Germans, which had begun in times when the boundaries of Christianity ran between the two nations, and which led to a strictly national separation, which has not yet exhausted its political effects. Though the Reformation had not its origin in national feelings, yet they became a powerful instrument in the hands of Luther, and ultimately prevailed over the purely theological elements of the movement.

The Lutheran system was looked on by the Germans with patriotic pride as the native fruit, and especial achievement of the genius of their country, and it was adopted out of Germany only by the kindred races of Scandinavia. In every other land to which it has been transplanted by the migrations of this century, Lutheranism appears as eradicated from its congenial soil, loses gradually its distinctive features, and becomes assimilated to the more consolatory system of Geneva. Calvinism exhibited from the first no traces of the influence of national character, and to this it owes its greater extension ; whilst in the third form of Protestantism, the Anglican Church, nationality is the predominant characteristic. In whatever country and in whatever form Protestantism has prevailed, it has always carried out the principle of separation and local limitation by seeking to subject itself to the civil power, and to confine the Church within the jurisdiction of the State. It is dependent not so much on national character as on political authority, and has grafted itself rather on the State than on the people. But the institution which Christ founded in order to collect all nations together in one fold under one shepherd, while tolerating and respecting the natural historical distinctions of nations and of States, endeavours to reconcile antagonism, and to smooth away barriers between them, instead of estranging them by artificial differences, and erecting new obstacles to their harmony. The Church can neither submit as a whole to the influence of a particular people, nor impose on one the features or the habits of another; for she is exalted in her catholicity above the differences of race, and above the claims of political power. At once the most firm and the most flexible institution in the world, she is all things to all nations—educating each in her own spirit, without violence to its nature, and assimilating it to herself without prejudice to the originality of its native character. Whilst she thus transforms them, not by reducing them to a uniform type, but by raising them towards a common elevation, she receives from them services in return. Each healthy and vigorous nation that is converted is a dynamic as well as a numerical increase in the resources of the Church, by bringing an accession of new and peculiar qualities, as well as of quantity and numbers. So far from seeking sameness, or flourishing only in one atmosphere, she is enriched and strengthened by all the varieties of national character and intellect. In the mission of the Catholic Church, each nation has its function, which its own position and nature indicate and enable it to fulfil. Thus the extinct nations of antiquity survive in the beneficial action they continue to exert within her, and she still feels and acknowledges the influence of the African or of the Cappadocian mind.

The condition of this immunity from the predominant influence of national and political divisions, and of this indifference to the attachment of particular States and races,—the security of unity and universality,—consists in the existence of a single, supreme, independent head. The primacy is the bulwark, or rather the corner-stone, of Catholicism; without it, there would be as many churches as there are nations or States. Not one of those who have denounced the Papacy as a usurpation has ever attempted to show that the condition which its absence necessarily involves is theologically desirable, or that it is the will of God. It remains the most radical and conspicuous distinction between the Catholic Church and the sects. Those who attempt to do without it are compelled to argue that there is no earthly office divinely appointed for the government of the Church, and that nobody has received the mission to conduct ecclesiastical affairs, and to preserve the divine order in religion. The several local churches may have an earthly ruler, but for the whole Church of Christ there is no such protection. Christ, therefore, is the only head they acknowledge, and they must necessarily declare separation, isolation, and discord to be a principle and the normal condition of His Church. The rejection of the primacy of St. Peter has driven men on to a slippery course, where all the steps are downwards. The Greeks first proclaimed that they recognised no Pope, that each patriarch ruled over a portion of the Church. The Anglicans rejected both Pope and patriarch, and admitted no ecclesiastical order higher than the Episcopate. Foreign Protestanism refused to tolerate even bishops, or any authority but the parish clergy under the supremacy of the ruler of the land. Then the sects abolished the local jurisdiction of the parish clergy, and retained only preachers. At length the ministry was rejected as an office altogether, and the Quakers made each individual his own prophet, priest, and doctor.

The Papacy, that unique institution, the Crown of the Catholic system, exhibits in its history the constant working of that law which is at the foundation of the life of the Church, the law of continuous organic development. It shared the vicissitudes of the Church, and had its part in everything which influences the course and mode of her existence. In early times it grew in silence and obscurity, its features were rarely and imperfectly distinguishable; but even then the Popes exerted their authority in all directions, and while the wisdom with which it was exercised was often questioned, the right itself was undisputed. So long as the Roman Empire upheld in its strong framework and kept together the Church, which was confined mostly within its bounds, and checked with the stern discipline of a uniform law the manifestations of national and local divergence, the interference of the Holy See was less frequently required, and the reins of Church government did not need to be tightly drawn. When a new order of States emerged from the chaos of the great migration, the Papacy, which alone stood erect amid the ruins of the empire, became the centre of a new system and the moderator of a new code. The long contest with the Germanic empire exhausted the political power both of the empire and of the Papacy, and the position of the Holy See, in the midst of a multitude of equal States, became more difficult and more unfavourable. The Popes were forced to rely on the protection of France, their supremacy over the States was at an end, and the resistance of the nations commenced. The schism, the opposition of the general Councils, the circumstances which plunged the Holy See into the intrigues of Italian politics, and at last the Reformation, hastened the decline of that extensive social and political power, the echoes and reminiscences of which occasioned disaster and repulse whenever an attempt was made to exercise it. Ever since the Tridentine age, the Popes have confined themselves more and more exclusively to the religious domain; and here the Holy See is as powerful and as free at the present day as at any previous period of its history. The perils and the difficulties which surround it arise from temporal concerns,—from the state of Italy, and from the possessions of the pontifical dominions.

As the Church advances towards fulness and maturity in her forms, bringing forward her exhaustless resources, and calling into existence a wealth of new elements,—societies, corporations, and institutions,—so is the need more deeply felt for a powerful supreme guide to keep them all in health and harmony, to direct them in their various spheres, and in their several ways towards the common ends and purposes of all, and thus to provide against decay, variance, and confusion. Such an office the Primacy alone can discharge, and the importance of the Papacy increases as the organisation of the Church is more complete. One of its most important but most delicate duties is to act as an independent, impartial, and dispassionate mediator between the churches and the governments of the different States, and between the conflicting claims and contradictory idiosyncrasies of the various nations. Yet, though the Papacy is so obviously an essential part of a Church whose mission is to all mankind, it is the chosen object of attack both to enemies of Catholicism and to discontented Catholics. Serious and learned men complain of its tyranny, and say that it claims universal dominion, and watches for an opportunity of obtaining it; and yet, in reality, there is no power on earth whose action is restricted by more sacred and irresistible bonds than that of the Holy See. It is only by the closest fidelity to the laws and tradition of the Church that the Popes are able to secure the obedience and the confidence of Catholics. Pius VII., who, by sweeping away the ancient church of France, and depriving thirty-seven protesting bishops of their sees, committed the most arbitrary act ever done by a Pope, has himself described the rules which guided the exercise of his authority:—

> The nature and constitution of the Catholic Church impose on the Pope, who is the head of the Church, certain limits which he cannot transgress. . . . The Bishops of Rome have never believed that they could tolerate any alteration in those portions of the discipline which are directly ordained by Jesus Christ; or in those which, by their nature, are connected with dogma, or in those which heretics assail in support of their innovations.

The chief points urged against the ambition of Rome are the claim of the deposing Power, according to the theory that all kinds of power are united in the Church, and the protest against the Peace of Westphalia, the basis of the public law and political order of modern Europe. It is enough to cite one of the many authorities which may be cited in refutation of the first objection. Cardinal Antonelli, Prefect of Propaganda, states in his letter to the Irish bishops, 1791, that "the See of Rome has never taught that faith is not to be kept with those of another religion, or that an oath sworn to kings who are separated from the Catholic communion may be broken, or that the Pope is permitted to touch their temporal rights and possessions." The Bull in which Boniface VIII. set up the theory of the supremacy of the spiritual over the secular power was retracted soon after his death.

The protest of Innocent X. against the Peace of Westphalia is one of the glories of the Papacy. That peace was concluded on an unchristian and tyrannical principle, introduced by the Reformation, that the subjects may be compelled to follow the religion of the ruler. This was very different in principle and in effect from the intolerance of the ages of faith, when prince and people were members of one religion, and all were agreed that no other could be permitted in the State. Every heresy that arose in the Middle Ages involved revolutionary consequences, and would inevitably have overthrown State and society, as well as Church, wherever it prevailed. The Albigenses, who provoked the cruel legislation against heretics, and who were exterminated by fire and sword, were the Socialists of those days. They assailed the fundamental institutions of society, marriage, family, and property, and their triumph would have plunged Europe into the barbarism and licence of pagan times. The principles of the Waldenses and the Lollards were likewise incompatible with European civilisation. In those days the law relating to religion was the same for all. The Pope as well as the king would have lost his crown if he had fallen into heresy. During a thousand years, from the fall of Rome to the appearance of Luther, no Catholic prince ever made an attempt to introduce a new religion into his dominions, or to abandon the old. But the Reformation taught that this was the supreme duty of princes; whilst Luther declared that in matters of faith the individual is above every authority, and that a child could understand the Scriptures better than Popes or Councils, he taught at the same time, with an inconsistency which he never attempted to remove, that it is the duty of the civil power to exterminate popery, to set up the Gospel, and to suppress every other religion.

The result was a despotism such as the world had never seen. It was worse than the Byzantine system; for there no attempt was made to change the faith of the people. The Protestant princes exercised an ecclesiastical authority more arbitrary than the Pope had ever possessed; for the papal authority can only be used to maintain an existing doctrine, whilst theirs was aggressive and wholly unlimited. Possessing the power to command, and to alter in religion, they naturally acquired by degrees a corresponding absolutism in the civil order. The consistories, the office by which the sovereign ruled the Church, were the commencement of bureaucratic centralisation. A great lawyer of those days says, that after the treaties of Westphalia had recognised the territorial supremacy over religion, the business of administration in the German States increased tenfold. Whilst that system remained in its integrity, there could be no peaceful neighbourhood between Catholics and Protestants. From this point of view, the protest of the Pope was entirely justified. So far from having been made in the spirit of the mediæval authority, which would have been fatal to the work of the Congress, it was never used by any Catholic prince to invalidate the treaties. They took advantage of the law in their own territories to exercise the *jus reformandi*. It was not possible for them to tolerate a body which still refused to tolerate the Catholic religion by the side of its own, which accordingly eradicated it wherever it had the means, and whose theory made the existence of every religion depend on the power and the will of the sovereign. A system which so resolutely denied that two religions could coexist in the same State, put every attempt at mutual toleration out of the question. The Reformation was a great movement against the freedom of conscience—an effort to subject it to a new authority, the arbitrary initiative of a prince who might differ in religion from all his subjects. The extermination of obstinate Catholics was a matter of course; Melanchthon insisted that the Anabaptists should be put to death, and Beza was of opinion that Anti-Trinitarians ought to be executed, even after recantation. But no Lutheran could complain when the secular arm converted him into a Calvinist. "Your conscience is in error," he would say, "but under the circumstances you are not only justified, but compelled, on my own principles, to act as you do."[1]

The resistance of the Catholic Governments to the progress of a religion which announced that it would destroy them as soon as it had the power, was an instinct of self-preservation. No Protestant divine denied or disguised the truth that his party sought the destruction of Catholicism, and would accomplish it whenever they could. The Calvinists, with their usual fearless consistency, held that as civil and ecclesiastical power must be in the same hands, no prince had any right to govern who did not belong to them. Even in the Low Countries, where other sects were free, and the notion of unity abandoned, the Catholics were oppressed.

This new and aggressive intolerance infected even Catholic countries, where there was neither, as in Spain, religious unity to be preserved; nor, as in Austria, a menacing danger to be resisted. For in Spain the persecution of the Protestants might be defended on the mediæval principle of unity, whilst under Ferdinand II. it was provoked in the hereditary dominions by the imminent peril which threatened to dethrone the monarch, and to ruin every faithful Catholic. But in France the Protestant doctrine that every good subject must follow the religion of his king grew out of the intensity of personal absolutism. At the revocation of the Edict of Nantes, the official argument was the will of the sovereign — an argument which in Germany had reigned so

[1] So late as 1791 Pius VI. wrote: "Discrimen intercedit inter homines, qui extra gremium Ecclesiae semper fuerunt, quales sunt Infideles atque Judaei, atque inter illos qui se Ecclesiae ipsi per susceptum baptismi sacramentum subjecerunt. Primi enim constringi ad catholicam obedientiam non debent, contra vero alteri sunt cogendi." If this theory had, like that of the Protestants, been put in practice by the Government, it would have furnished the Protestants with an argument precisely similar to that by which the Catholics justified the severity they exercised towards them.

triumphantly that a single town, which had ten times changed masters, changed its religion ten times in a century. Bayle justly reproaches the Catholic clergy of France with having permitted, and even approved, a proceeding so directly contrary to the spirit of their religion, and to the wishes of the Pope. A convert, who wrote a book to prove that Huguenots were in conscience bound to obey the royal edict which proscribed their worship, met with applause a hundred years later. This fault of the French clergy was expiated in the blood of their successors.

The excess of evil led to its gradual cure. In England Protestantism lost its vigour after the victory over the Catholic dynasty ; religion faded away, and with it that religious zeal which leads to persecution : when the religious antagonism was no longer kept alive by a political controversy, the sense of right and the spirit of freedom which belongs to the Anglo-Saxon race accomplished the work which indifference had begun. In Germany the vitality of the Lutheran theology expired after it had lasted for about two hundred years. The intellectual contradictions and the social consequences of the system had become intolerable to the German mind. Rationalism had begun to prevail, when Frederick II. declared that his subjects should work out their salvation in their own way. That generation of men, who looked with contempt on religious zeal, looked with horror on religious persecution. The Catholic Church, which had never taught that princes are supreme over the religion of their subjects, could have no difficulty in going along with public opinion when it disapproved of compulsion in matters of conscience. It was natural that in the new order of things, when Christendom had lost its unity, and Protestantism its violence, she should revert to the position she occupied of old, when she admitted other religions to equal rights with herself, and when men like St. Ambrose, St. Martin, and St. Leo deprecated the use of violence against heretics. Nevertheless, as the preservation of morality depends on the preservation of faith, both alike are in the interest and within the competence of the State. The Church of her own strength is not strong enough to resist the advance of heresy and unbelief. Those enemies find an auxiliary in the breast of every man whose weakness and whose passions repel him from a Church which imposes such onerous duties on her members. But it is neither possible to define the conditions without which liberty must be fatal to the State, nor the limits beyond which protection and repression become tyrannical, and provoke a reaction more terrible than the indifference of the civil power. The events of the last hundred years have tended in most places to mingle Protestants and Catholics together, and to break down the social and political lines of demarcation between them ; and time will show the providential design which has brought about this great change.

These are the subjects treated in the first two chapters on "The Church and the Nations," and on the Papacy in connection with the universality of Catholicism, as contrasted with the national and political dependence of heresy. The two following chapters pursue the topic farther in a general historical retrospect, which increases in interest and importance as it proceeds from the social to the religious purpose and influence of the Papacy, and from the past to the present time. The third chapter, "The Churches and Civil Liberty," examines the effects of Protestantism on civil society. The fourth, entitled "The Churches without a Pope," considers the actual theological and religious fruits of separation from the visible Head of the Church.

The independence of the Church, through that of her Supreme Pontiff, is as nearly connected with political as with religious liberty, since the ecclesiastical system which rejects the Pope logically leads to arbitrary power. Throughout the north of Europe—in Sweden and Denmark, in Mecklenburg and Pomerania, in Prussia, Saxony, and Brunswick—the power which the Reformation gave to the State introduced an unmitigated despotism. Every security was removed which protected the people against the abuse of the sovereign power, and the lower against the oppression of the upper class. The crown became, sooner or later, despotic ; the peasantry, by a long series of enactments, extending to the end of the seventeeth century, was reduced to servitude ; the population grew scanty, and much of the land went out of cultivation. All this is related by the Protestant historians and divines, not in the tone of reluctant admission, but with patriotic indignation, commensurate with the horrors of the truth. In all these countries Lutheran unity subsisted. If Calvinism had ever succeeded in obtaining an equal predominance in the Netherlands, the power of the House of Orange would have become as despotic as that of the Danish or the Prussian sovereigns. But its triumph was impeded by sects, and by the presence of a large Catholic minority, destitute indeed of political rights or religious freedom, but for that very reason removed from the conflicts of parties, and therefore an element of conservatism, and a natural ally of those who resisted the ambition of the Stadtholders. The absence of religious unity baffled their attempts to establish arbitrary power on the victory of Calvinism, and upheld, in conjunction with the brilliant policy abroad, a portion of the ancient freedom. In Scotland, the other home of pure Calvinism, where intolerance and religious tyranny reached a pitch equalled only among the Puritans in America, the perpetual troubles hindered the settlement of a fixed political system, and the restoration of order after the union with England stripped the Presbyterian system of its exclusive supremacy, and opened the way for tolerance and freedom.

Although the political spirit of Anglicanism was as despotic as that of every other Protestant system, circumstances prevented its full development. The Catholic Church had bestowed on the English the great elements of their political prosperity,—the charter of their liberties, the fusion of the races, and the abolition of villeinage,—that is, personal and general freedom, and national unity. Hence the people were so thoroughly impregnated with

Catholicism that the Reformation was imposed on them by foreign troops in spite of an armed resistance; and the imported manufacture of Geneva remained so strange and foreign to them, that no English divine of the sixteenth century enriched it with a single original idea. The new Church, unlike those of the Continent, was the result of an endeavour to conciliate the Catholic disposition of the people, by preserving as far as possible the externals to which they were attached; whilst the queen—who was a Protestant rather by policy than by conviction—desired no greater change than was necessary for her purpose. But the divines whom she placed at the head of the new Church were strict Calvinists, and differed from the Puritans only in their submission to the court. The rapidly declining Catholic party accepted Anglicanism as the lesser evil; while zealous Protestants deemed that the outward forms ought to correspond to the inward substance, and that Calvinistic doctrines required a Calvinistic constitution. Until the end of the century there was no Anglican theology; and the attempt to devise a system in harmony with the peculiar scheme and design of the institution, began with Hooker. The monarch was absolute master in the Church, which had been established as an instrument of royal influence; and the divines acknowledged his right by the theory of passive obedience. The consistent section of the Calvinists was won over, for a time, by the share which the gentry obtained in the spoils of the Church, and by the welcome concession of the penal laws against her, until at last they found that they had in their intolerance been forging chains for themselves. One thing alone, which our national jurists had recognised in the fifteenth century as the cause and the sign of our superiority over foreign States—the exclusion of the Roman code, and the unbroken preservation of the common law—kept England from sinking beneath a despotism as oppressive as that of France or Sweden.

As the Anglican Church under James and Charles was the bulwark of arbitrary power, the popular resistance took the form of ecclesiastical opposition. The Church continued to be so thoroughly committed to the principle of unconditional submission to the power from which it derived its existence, that James II. could reckon on this servile spirit as a means of effecting the subversion of the Establishment; and Defoe reproached the bishops with having by their flattery led on the king, whom they abandoned in the moment of his need. The Revolution, which reduced the royal prerogative, removed the oppressiveness of the royal supremacy. The Established Church was not emancipated from the crown, but the Nonconformists were emancipated from the tyranny of the Established Church. Protestantism, which in the period of its power dragged down by its servility the liberties of the nation, did afterwards, in its decay and disorganisation, by the surrender of its dogmatic as well as of its political principle, promote their recovery and development. It lost its oppressiveness in proportion as it lost its strength, and it ceased to be tyrannical when divines had been forced to give up its fundamental doctrine, and when its unity had been dissolved by the sects. The revival of those liberties which, in the Middle Ages, had taken root under the influence of the Church, coincided with the progress of the Protestant sects, and with the decay of the penal laws. The contrast between the political character of those countries in which Protestantism integrally prevailed, and that of those in which it was divided against itself, and could neither establish its system nor work out its consequences, is as strongly marked as the contrast between the politics of Catholic times and those which were introduced by the Reformation. The evil which it wrought in its strength was turned to good by its decline.

Such is the sketch of the effects of the Protestant apostasy in the political order, considered chiefly in relation to the absence of a supreme ecclesiastical authority independent of political control. It would require far more space to exhibit the positive influence of heretical principles on the social foundations of political life; and the picture would not be complete without showing the contrast exhibited by Catholic States, and tracing their passage from the mediæval system under the influence of the reaction against the Reformation. The third chapter covers only a portion of this extensive subject; but it shows the action of the new mode of ecclesiastical government upon the civil order, and proves that the importance of the Papacy is not confined to its religious sphere. It thus prepares the way for the subject discussed in the fourth chapter,—the most comprehensive and elaborate in the book.

Dr. Döllinger begins his survey of the churches that have renounced the Pope with those of the Eastern schism. The Patriarch of Constantinople, whose ecclesiastical authority is enormous, and whose opportunities of extorting money are so great that he is generally deposed at the end of two or three years, in order that many may succeed each other in the enjoyment of such advantages, serves not as a protection, but as an instrument for the oppression of the Christians. The Greek clergy have been the chief means by which the Turks have kept down both the Greek and the Slavonic population, and the Slavs are by degrees throwing off their influence. Submission to the civil power is so natural in communities separated from the Universal Church, that the Greeks look up to the Turkish authorities as arbiters in ecclesiastical matters. When there was a dispute between Greeks and Armenians respecting the mixture of water with the wine in the chalice, the question was referred for decision to the proper quarter, and the Reis Effendi decided that, wine being condemned by the Koran, water alone might be used. Yet to this pusillanimous and degenerate Church belong the future of European Turkey, and the inheritance of the sinking power of the Turks. The vitality of the dominant race is nearly exhausted, and the Christians—on whose pillage they live—exceed them, in increasing proportions, in numbers, prosperity, intelligence, and enterprise.

The Hellenic Church, obeying the general law of schismatical communities, has exchanged the authority of the patriarch for that of the crown, exercised through a synod, which is appointed on the Russian model by the Government. The clergy, disabled for religious purposes by the necessity of providing for their families, have little education and little influence, and have no part in the revival of the Grecian intellect. But the people are attached to their ecclesiastical system, not for religion's sake, for infidelity generally accompanies education, but as the defence of their nationality.

In Russia the Catholic Church is considered heretical because of her teaching on the procession of the Holy Ghost, and schismatical in consequence of the claims of the Pope. In the doctrine of purgatory there is no essential difference; and on this point an understanding could easily be arrived at, if none had an interest in widening the breach. In the seventeenth century, the Russian Church retained so much independence that the Metropolitan of Kiev could hold in check the power of the Czar, and the clergy were the mediators between the people and the nobles or the crown. This influence was swept away by the despotism of Peter the Great; and under Catherine II. the property of the Church was annexed to the crown lands, in order, it was said, to relieve the clergy of the burden of administration. Yet even now the Protestant doctrine that the sovereign is supreme in all matters of religion has not penetrated among the Russians. But though the Czar does not possess this authority over the national Church, of which he is a member, the Protestant system has conceded it to him in the Baltic provinces. Not only are all children of mixed marriages between Protestants and schismatics brought up in the religion of the latter, by which the gradual decline of Protestanism is provided for, but conversions to Protestanism, even of Jews, Mohammedans, and heathens, are forbidden; and, in all questions of doctrine or of liturgy, the last appeal is to the emperor. The religious despotism usually associated with the Russian monarchy subsists only for the Protestants.

The Russian Church is dumb; the congregation does not sing, the priest does not preach. The people have no prayer-books, and are therefore confined to the narrow circle of their own religious ideas. Against the cloud of superstition which naturally gathers in a religion of ceremonies, destitute of the means of keeping alive or cultivating the religious sentiments of the people, there is no resource. In spite of the degeneracy of their clergy, which they are unable to feel, the Russians cling with patriotic affection to their Church, and identify its progress and prosperity with the increase of their empire. As it is an exclusively national institution, every war may become a war of religion, and it is the attachment to the Church which creates the longing and the claim to possess the city from which it came. From the Church the empire derives its tendency to expand, and the Czar the hopes of that universal dominion which was promised to him by the Synod of Moscow in 1619, and for which a prayer was then appointed. The schismatical clergy of Eastern Europe are the channel of Russian influence, the pioneers of Russian aggression. The political dependence of the Church corresponds to its political influence; subserviency is the condition of the power it possesses. The certificate of Easter confession and communion is required for every civil act, and is consequently an object of traffic. In like manner, the confessor is bound to betray to the police all the secrets of confession which affect the interest of the Government. In this deplorable state of corruption, servitude, and decay within, and of threatening hostility to Christian civilisation abroad, the Russian Church pays the penalty of its Byzantine descent.

The Established Church and the sects in England furnish few opportunities of treating points which would be new to our readers. Perhaps the most suggestive portion is the description of the effects of Protestantism on the character and condition of the people. The plunder and oppression of the poor has everywhere followed the plunder of the Church, which was the guardian and refuge of the poor. The charity of the Catholic clergy aimed not merely at relieving, but at preventing poverty. It was their object not only to give alms, but to give to the lower orders the means of obtaining a livelihood. The Reformation at once checked alms-giving; so that, Selden says, in places where twenty pounds a year had been distributed formerly, not a handful of meal was given away in his time, for the wedded clergy could not afford it. The confiscation of the lands where thousands had tilled the soil under the shadow of the monastery or the Church, was followed by a new system of cultivation, which deprived the peasants of their homes. The sheep, men said, were the cause of all the woe; and whole towns were pulled down to make room for them. The prelates of the sixteenth century lament the decline of charity since the Catholic times; and a divine attributed the growing selfishness and harshness to the doctrine of justification by faith. The alteration in the condition of the poor was followed by severe enactments against vagrancy; and the Protestant legislature, after creating a proletariate, treated it as a crime. The conversion of Sunday into a Jewish Sabbath cut off the holiday amusements and soured the cheerfulness of the population. Music, singing, and dancing, the favourite relaxation of a contented people, disappeared, and, especially after the war in the Low Countries, drunkenness began to prevail among a nation which in earlier times had been reckoned the most sober of Northern Europe. The institution which introduced these changes has become a State, not a national Church, whose services are more attended by the rich than by the poor.

After describing the various parties in the Anglican system, the decay of its divinity, and the general aversion to theological research, Döllinger concludes that its dissolution is a question of time. No State Church can long subsist in modern society which professes the religion of the minority. Whilst the want of a definite system of doctrine, allowing every clergyman to be the mouthpiece, not of a church, but of a party, drives an increasing portion of the people to join the sects which have a fixed doctrine and allow less independence to their preachers, the great danger which menaces the Church comes from the State itself. The progress of dissent and of democracy in the legislature will make the Church more and more entirely dependent on the will of the majority, and will drive the best men from the communion of a servile establishment. The rise and fortunes of Methodism are related with peculiar predilection by the author, who speaks of John Wesley as the greatest intellect English Protestantism has produced, next to Baxter.

The first characteristic of Scottish Presbyterianism is the absence of a theology. The only considerable divines that have appeared in Scotland since the Reformation, Leighton and Forbes, were prelates of the Episcopal Church. Calvinism was unable to produce a theological literature, in spite of the influence of English writers, of the example of Holland, and of the great natural intelligence of the Scots. "Their theology," says a distinguished Lutheran divine, "possesses no system of Christian ethics." This Döllinger attributes to the strictness with which they have held to the doctrine of imputation, which is incompatible with any system of moral theology. In other countries it was the same; where that doctrine prevailed, there was no ethical system, and where ethics were cultivated, the doctrine was abandoned. For a century after Luther, no moral theology was written in Germany. The first who attempted it, Calixtus, gave up the Lutheran doctrine. The Dutch historians of Calvinism in the Netherlands record, in like manner, that there the dread of a collision with the dogma silenced the teaching of ethics both in literature and at the universities. Accordingly, all the great Protestant moralists were opposed to the Protestant doctrine of justification. In Scotland the intellectual lethargy of churchmen is not confined to the department of ethics; and Presbyterianism only prolongs its existence by suppressing theological writing, and by concealing the contradictions which would otherwise bring down on the clergy the contempt of their flocks.

Whilst Scotland has clung to the original dogma of Calvin, at the price of complete theological stagnation, the Dutch Church has lost its primitive orthodoxy in the progress of theological learning. Not one of the several schools into which the clergy of the Netherlands are divided has remained faithful to the five articles of the synod of Dortrecht, which still command so extensive an allegiance in Great Britain and America. The conservative party, headed by the statesman and historian, Groen van Prinsterer, who holds fast to the theology which is so closely interwoven with the history of his country and with the fortunes of the reigning house, and who invokes the aid of the secular arm in support of pure Calvinism, is not represented at the universities. For all the Dutch divines know that the system cannot be revived without sacrificing the theological activity by which it has been extinguished. The old confessional writings have lost their authority; and the general synod of 1854 decided that, "as it is impossible to reconcile all opinions and wishes, even in the shortest confession, the Church tolerates divergence from the symbolical books." The only unity, says Groen, consists in this, that all the preachers are paid out of the same fund. The bulk of the clergy are Arminians or Socinians. From the spectacle of the Dutch Church, Dr. Döllinger comes to the following result: first, that without a code of doctrine laid down in authoritative confessions of faith, the Church cannot endure; secondly, that the old confessional writings cannot be maintained, and are universally given up; and thirdly, that it is impossible to draw up new ones.

French Protestantism suffered less from the Revolution than the Catholic Church, and was treated with tenderness, and sometimes with favour. The dissolution of Continental Protestantism began in France. Before their expulsion in 1685, the French divines had cast off the yoke of the Dortrecht articles, and in their exile they afterwards promoted the decline of Calvinism in the Netherlands. The old Calvinistic tradition has never been restored, the works of the early writers are forgotten, no new theological literature has arisen, and the influence of Germany has borne no considerable fruit. The evangelical party, or Methodists, as they are called, are accused by the rest of being the cause of their present melancholy state. The rationalism of the *indifférens* generally prevails among the clergy, either in the shape of the naturalism of the eighteenth century (Coquerel), or in the more advanced form of modern criticism, as it is carried out by the faculty of Strasburg, with the aid of German infidelity. Payment by the State and hatred of Catholicism are the only common marks of French Protestant divines. They have no doctrine, no discipline, no symbol, no theology. Nobody can define the principle or the limits of their community.

The Calvinism of Switzerland has been ruined in its doctrine by the progress of theology, and in its constitution by the progress of democracy. In Geneva the Church of Calvin fell in the revolutions of 1841 and 1846. The symbolical books are abolished; the doctrine is based on the Bible; but the right of free inquiry is granted to all; the ruling body consists of laymen. "The faith of our fathers," says Merle d'Aubigné, "counts but a small group of adherents amongst us." In the canton of Vaud, where the whole ecclesiastical power was in the hands of the Government, the yoke of the democracy became insupportable, and the excellent writer, Vinet, seceded with 180 ministers out of 250. The people of Berne are among the most bitter enemies of Catholicism in Europe. Their fanaticism crushed the Sonderbund; but the recoil drove them towards infidelity, and hastened the decrease of devotion and of the influence of the clergy. None of the German Swiss, and few of the French, retain in its purity the system of Calvin. The unbelief of the clergy lays the Church open to the attacks of a Cæsaro-papistic democracy. A Swiss Protestant divine said recently: "Only a Church with a Catholic organisation could have maintained itself without a most extraordinary descent of the Holy Spirit against the assaults of Rationalism." "What we want," says another, "in order to have a free Church, is pastors and flocks; dogs and wolves there are in plenty."

In America it is rare to find people who are openly irreligious. Except some of the Germans, all Protestants generally admit the truth of Christianity and the authority of Scripture. But above half of the American population belongs to no particular sect, and performs no religious functions. This is the result of the voluntary principle, of the dominion of the sects, and of the absence of an established Church, to receive each individual from his birth, to adopt him by baptism, and to bring him up in the atmosphere of a religious life. The majority of men will naturally take refuge in indifference and neutrality from the conflict of opinions, and will persuade themselves that where there are so many competitors, none can be the lawful spouse. Yet there is a blessing on everything that is Christian, which can never be entirely effaced or converted into a curse. Whatever the imperfections of the form in which it exists, the errors mixed up with it, or the degrading influence of human passion, Christianity never ceases to work immeasurable social good. But the great theological characteristic of American Protestantism is the absence of the notion of the Church. The prevailing belief is, that in times past there was always a war of opinions and of parties, that there never was one unbroken vessel, and that it is necessary, therefore, to put up with fragments, one of which is nearly as good as another. Sectarianism, it is vaguely supposed, is the normal condition of religion. Now a sect is, by its very nature, instinctively adverse to a scientific theology; it feels that it is short-lived, without a history, and unconnected with the main stream of ecclesiastical progress, and it is inspired with hatred and with contempt for the past, for its teaching and its writings. Practically, sectaries hold that a tradition is the more surely to be rejected the older it is, and the more valuable in proportion to the lateness of its origin. As a consequence of the want of roots in the past, and of the thirst for novelty, the history of those sects which are not sunk in lethargy consists in sudden transitions to opposite extremes. In the religious world ill weeds grow apace; and those communities which strike root, spring up, and extend most rapidly are the least durable and the least respectable. The sects of Europe were transplanted into America: but there the impatience of authority, which is the basis of social and political life, has produced in religion a variety and a multiplicity, of which Europe has no experience.

Whilst these are the fruits of religious liberty and ecclesiastical independence among a people generally educated, the Danish monarchy exhibits unity of faith strictly maintained by keeping the people under the absolute control of the upper class, on whose behalf the Reformation was introduced, and in a state of ignorance corresponding to their oppression. Care was taken that they should not obtain religious instruction, and in the beginning of the eighteenth century the celebrated Bishop Pontoppidan says, "an almost heathen blindness pervades the land." About the same time the Norwegian prelates declared, in a petition to the King of Denmark: "If we except a few children of God, there is only this difference between us and our heathen ancestors, that we bear the name of Christians." The Danish Church has given no signs of life, and has shown no desire for independence since the Reformation; and in return for this submissiveness, the Government suppressed every tendency towards dissent. Things were not altered when the tyranny of the nobles gave way to the tyranny of the crown; but when the revolution of 1848 had given the State a democratic basis, its confessional character was abrogated, and whilst Lutheranism was declared the national religion, conformity was no longer exacted. The king is still the head of the Church, and is the only man in Denmark who must be a Lutheran. No form of ecclesiastical government suitable to the new order of things has yet been devised, and the majority prefer to remain in the present provisional state, subject to the will of a Parliament, not one member of which need belong to the Church which it governs. Among the clergy, those who are not Rationalists follow the lead of Grundtvig. During many years this able man has conducted an incessant resistance against the progress of unbelief and of the German influence, and against the Lutheran system, the royal supremacy, and the parochial constitution. Not unlike the Tractarians, he desires the liberty of establishing a system which shall exclude Lutheranism, Rationalism, and Erastianism ; and he has united in his school nearly all who profess positive Christianity in Denmark. In Copenhagen, out of 150,000 inhabitants, only 6000 go regularly to church. In Altona, there is but one church for 45,000 people. In Schleswig the churches are few and empty. "The great evil," says a Schleswig divine, "is not the oppression which falls on the German tongue, but the irreligion and consequent demoralisation which Denmark has imported into Schleswig. A moral and religious tone is the exception, not the rule, among the Danish clergy."

The theological literature of Sweden consists almost entirely of translations from the German. The clergy, by renouncing study, have escaped Rationalism, and remain faithful to the Lutheran system. The king is supreme in spirituals, and the Diet discusses and determines religious questions. The clergy, as one of the estates, has great political influence, but no ecclesiastical independence. No other Protestant clergy possesses equal privileges or less freedom. It is usual for the minister after the sermon to read out a number of trivial local announcements, sometimes half an hour long; and in a late Assembly the majority of the bishops pronounced in favour of retaining this custom, as none but old women and children would come to church for the service alone.

In no other country in Europe is the strict Lutheran system preached but in Sweden. The doctrine is preserved, but religion is dead, and the Church is as silent and as peaceful as the churchyard. The Church is richly endowed ; there are great universities, and Swedes are among the foremost in almost every branch of science, but no Swedish writer has ever done anything for religious thought. The example of Denmark and its Rationalist clergy brought home to them the consequences of theological study. In one place the old system has been preserved, like a frail and delicate curiosity, by excluding the air of scientific inquiry, whilst in the other Lutheranism is decomposing under its influence. In Norway, where the clergy have no political representation, religious liberty was established in 1844.

Throughout the north of Europe the helpless decline of Protestantism is betrayed by the numerical disproportion of preachers to the people. Norway, with a population of 1,500,000, thinly scattered over a very large territory, has 485 parishes, with an average of 3600 souls apiece. But the clergy are pluralists, and as many as five parishes are often united under a single incumbent. Holstein has only 192 preachers for an almost exclusively Lutheran population of 544,000. In Schleswig many parishes have been deserted because they were too poor to maintain a clergyman's family. Sometimes there are only two ministers for 13,000 persons. In the Baltic provinces the proportion is one to 4394. In this way the people have to bear the burden of a clergy with families to support.

The most brilliant and important part of this chapter is devoted to the state of Protestantism in the author's native country. He speaks with the greatest authority and effect when he comes near home, describes the opinions of men who have been his rivals in literature, or his adversaries in controversy, and touches on discussions which his own writings have influenced. There is a difference also in the tone. When he speaks of the state of other countries, with which he has made himself acquainted as a traveller, or through the writings of others, he preserves the calmness and objectivity of a historian, and adds few reflections to the simple description of facts. But in approaching the scenes and the thoughts of his own country, the interests and the most immediate occupations of his own life, the familiarity of long experience gives greater confidence, warmth, and vigour to his touch ; the historian gives way to the divine, and the narrative sometimes slides into theology. Besides the position of the author, the difference of the subject justifies a change in the treatment. The examination of Protestantism in the rest of the world pointed with monotonous uniformity to a single conclusion. Everywhere there was the same spectacle and the same alternative: either religion sacrificed to the advancement of learning, or learning relinquished for the preservation of religion. Everywhere the same antagonism between intellectual progress and fidelity to the fundamental doctrines of Protestantism: either religion has become stark and stagnant in States which protect unity by the proscription of knowledge, or the progress of thought and inquiry has undermined belief in the Protestant system, and driven its professors from one untenable position to another, or the ascendency of the sectarian spirit has been equally fatal to its dogmatic integrity and to its intellectual development. But in the home of the Reformation a league has been concluded in our time between theology and religion, and many schools of Protestant divines are labouring, with a vast expenditure of ability and learning, to devise, or to restore, with the aid of theological science, a system of positive Christianity. Into this great scene of intellectual exertion and doctrinal confusion the leading adversary of Protestantism in Germany conducts his readers, not without sympathy for the high aims which inspire the movement, but with the almost triumphant security which belongs to a Church possessing an acknowledged authority, a definite organisation, and a system brought down by tradition from the apostolic age. Passing by the schools of infidelity, which have no bearing on the topic of his work, he addresses himself to the believing Protestantism of Germany, and considers its efforts to obtain a position which may enable it to resist unbelief without involving submission to the Church.

The character of Luther separates the German Protestants from those of other countries. His was the master-spirit, in whom his contemporaries beheld the incarnation of the genius of their nation. In the strong lineaments of his character they recognised, in heroic proportions, the reflection of their own; and thus his name has survived, not merely as that of a great man, the mightiest of his age, but as the type of a whole period in the history of the German people, the centre of a new world of ideas, the personification of those religious and ethical opinions which the country followed, and whose influence even their adversaries could not escape. His writings have long ceased to be popular, and are read only as monuments of history; but the memory of his person has not yet grown dim. His name is still a power in his own country, and from its magic the Protestant doctrine derives a portion of its life. In other countries men dislike to be described by the name of the founder of their religious system, but in Germany and Sweden there are thousands who are proud of the name of Lutheran.

The results of his system prevail in the more influential and intelligent classes, and penetrate the mass of the modern literature of Germany. The Reformation had introduced the notion that Christianity was a failure, and had brought far more suffering than blessings on mankind; and the consequences of that movement were not calculated to impress educated men with the belief that things were changed for the better, or that the reformers had achieved the work in which the Apostles were unsuccessful. Thus an atmosphere of unbelief and of contempt for everything Christian gradually arose, and Paganism appeared more cheerful, more human, and more poetical than the repulsive Galilean doctrine of holiness and privation. This spirit still governs the educated class. Christianity is abominated both in life and in literature, even under the form of believing Protestantism.

In Germany theological study and the Lutheran system subsisted for two centuries together. The controversies that arose from time to time developed the theory, but brought out by degrees its inward contradictions. The danger of biblical studies was well understood, and the Scriptures were almost universally excluded from the universities in the seventeenth century; but in the middle of the eighteenth Bengel revived the study of the Bible, and the dissolution of the Lutheran doctrine began. The rise of historical learning hastened the process. Frederic the Great says of himself, that the notion that the history of the Church is a drama, conducted by rogues and hypocrites, at the expense of the deceived masses, was the real cause of his contempt for the Christian religion. The Lutheran theology taught, that after the Apostolic age God withdrew from the Church, and abandoned to the devil the office which, according to the Gospel, was reserved for the Holy Spirit. This diabolical millennium lasted till the appearance of Luther. As soon, therefore, as the reverence for the symbolical books began to wane, the belief in the divine foundation departed with the belief in the divine guidance of the Church, and the root was judged by the stem, the beginning by the continuation. As research went on, unfettered now by the authorities of the sixteenth century, the clergy became Rationalists, and stone after stone of the temple was carried away by its own priests. The infidelity which at the same time flourished in France, did not, on the whole, infect the priesthood. But in Germany it was the divines who destroyed religion, the pastors who impelled their flocks to renounce the Christian faith.

In 1817 the Prussian Union added a new Church to the two original forms of Protestantism. But strict Calvinism is nearly extinct in Germany, and the old Lutheran Church itself has almost disappeared. It subsists, not in any definite reality, but only in the aspirations of certain divines and jurists. The purpose of the union was to bring together, in religious communion, the reigning family of Prussia, which had adopted Calvinism in 1613, and the vast Lutheran majority among the people. It was to be, in the words of the king, a merely ritual union, not an amalgamation of dogmas. In some places there was resistance, which was put down by military execution. Some thousands emigrated to America; but the public press applauded the measures, and there was no general indignation at their severity. The Lutherans justly perceived that the union would promote religious indifference; but at the accession of the late king there came a change; religious faith was once more sought after, believing professors were appointed in almost all the German universities, after the example of Prussia; Jena and Giessen alone continued to be seats of Rationalism. As soon as theology had begun to recover a more religious and Christian character, two very divergent tendencies manifested themselves. Among the disciples of Schleiermacher and of Neander a school of unionists arose who attempted a conciliatory intermediate theology. At the same time a strictly Lutheran theology flourished at the universities of Erlangen, Leipzig, Rostock, and Dorpat, which sought to revive the doctrine of the sixteenth century, clothed in the language of the nineteenth. But for men versed in Scripture theology this was an impossible enterprise, and it was abandoned by the divines to a number of parochial clergymen, who are represented in literature by Rudelbach, and who claim to be the only surviving Protestants whom Luther would acknowledge as his sons and the heirs of his spirit.

The Lutheran divines and scholars formed the new Lutheran party,[1] whose most illustrious lay champion was the celebrated Stahl. They profess the Lutheran doctrine of justification, but reject the notion of the invisible Church and the universal priesthood. Holding to the divine institution of the offices of the Church, in opposition to the view which refers them to the congregation, they are led to assume a sacrament of orders, and to express opinions on ordination, sacraments, and sacrifice, which involve them in the imputation of Puseyism, or even of Catholicism. As they remain for the most part in the State Church, there is an open war between their confessional spirit and the syncretism of the union. In 1857 the Evangelical Alliance met at Berlin in order to strengthen the unionist principles, and to testify against these Pharisees. Baptists, Methodists, and Presbyterians —sects connected by nothing but a common hatred of

[1] The works contained in Clark's library of translations are chiefly of this school.

Catholicism—were greeted by the union divines as bone of their bone, and welcome allies in the contest with an exclusive Lutheranism and with Rome. The confusion in the minds of the people was increased by this spectacle. The union already implied that the dogma of the Lord's Supper, on which Lutherans and Calvinists disagree, was uncertain, and therefore not essential. The alliance of so many denominations added baptism to the list of things about which nothing is positively known. The author of this measure was Bunsen, who was full of the idea of uniting all Protestant sects in a union against the Catholic Church and catholicising tendencies.

For the last fifteen years there has been an active agitation for the improvement of the Church among the Protestant divines. The first question that occupies and divides them is that of Church government and the royal Episcopate, which many deem the chief cause of the ecclesiastical decay. The late King of Prussia, a zealous and enlightened friend of the Protestant Church, declared that "the territorial system and the Episcopal authority of the sovereign are of such a nature that either of them would alone be enough to kill the Church if the Church was mortal," and that he longed to be able to abdicate his rights into the hands of the bishops. In other countries, as in Baden, a new system has been devised, which transfers political constitutionalism to the Church, and makes it a community, not of those who believe in Christ, but, in the words of the Government organ, of those who believe in a moral order. Hopes were entertained that the introduction of Synods would be an improvement, and in 1856 and 1857 a beginning was made at Berlin; but it was found that the existence of great evils and disorders in the Church, which had been a secret of the initiated, would be published to the world, and that government by majorities, the ecclesiastical democracy which was Bunsen's ideal, would soon destroy every vestige of Christianity.

In their doctrinal and theological literature resides at the present day the strength and the renown of the

Protestants; for a scientific Protestant theology exists only in Germany. The German Protestant Church is emphatically a Church of theologians; they are its only authority, and, through the princes, its supreme rulers. Its founder never really divested himself of the character of a professor, and the Church has never emancipated itself from the lecture-room: it teaches, and then disappears. Its hymns are not real hymns, but versified theological dissertations, or sermons in rhyme. Born of the union of princes with professors, it retains the distinct likeness of both its parents, not altogether harmoniously blended; and when it is accused of worldliness, of paleness of thought, of being a police institution rather than a Church, that is no more than to say that the child cannot deny its parentage.

Theology has become believing in Germany, but it is very far from being orthodox. No writer is true to the literal teaching of the symbolical books, and for a hundred years the pure doctrine of the sixteenth century has never been heard. No German divine could submit to the authority of the early articles and formulas without hypocrisy and violence to his conscience, and yet they have nothing else to appeal to. That the doctrine of justification by faith only is the principal substance of the symbolical writings, the centre of the antagonism against the Catholic Church, all are agreed. The neo-Lutherans proclaim it "the essence and treasure of the Reformation," "the doctrine of which every man must have a clear and vivid comprehension who would know anything of Christianity," "the banner which must be unfurled at least once in every sermon," "the permanent death that gnaws the bones of Catholics," "the standard by which the whole of the Gospel must be interpreted, and every obscure passage explained," and yet this article of a standing or falling Church, on the strength of which Protestants call themselves evangelical, is accepted by scarcely one of their more eminent divines, even among the Lutherans. The progress of biblical studies is too great to admit of a return to the doctrine which has been exploded by the advancement of religious learning. Dr. Döllinger gives a list (p. 430) of the names of the leading theologians, by all of whom it has been abandoned. Yet it was for the sake of this fundamental and essential doctrine that the epistle of St. James was pronounced an epistle of straw, that the Augsburg Confession declared it to have been the belief of St. Augustine, and that when the author of the Confession had for very shame omitted this falsehood in the published edition, the passage was restored after his death. For its sake Luther deliberately altered the sense of several passages in the Bible, especially in the writings of St. Paul. To save this doctrine, which was unknown to all Christian antiquity, the breach was made with all ecclesiastical tradition, and the authority of the dogmatic testimony of the Church in every age was rejected. While the contradiction between the Lutheran doctrine and that of the first centuries was disguised before the laity, it was no secret among the Reformers. Melanchthon confessed to Brenz that in the Augsburg Confession he had lied. Luther admitted that his theory was new, and sought in consequence to destroy the authority of the early Fathers and Councils. Calvin declared that the system was unknown to tradition. All these men and their disciples, and the whole of the Lutheran and Calvinistic theology of the sixteenth and seventeenth centuries, professed to find their doctrine of imputation laid down distinctly in the Bible. The whole modern scientific theology of the Protestants rejects both the doctrine and the Lutheran exegesis of the passages in question. But it is the supreme evangelical principle, that the Scripture is perfectly clear and sufficient on all fundamental points. Yet the point on which this great divergence subsists is a doctrine which is decisive for the existence of the Church, and most important in its practical influence on life. The whole edifice of the Protestant Church and theology reposes therefore on two principles, one material, the other formal—the doctrine of imputation, and the sufficiency of the Bible. But the material principle is given up by exegesis and by dogmatic theology; and as to the formal principle, for the sufficiency of the Bible, or even for the inspiration of the writings of the disciples of the Apostles, not the shadow of a scriptural argument can be adduced. The significance of this great fact is beginning to make its way. "Whilst Rationalism prevailed," says a famous Lutheran divine, "we could impute to its action that our churches were deserted and empty. But now that Christ crucified is everywhere preached, and no serious effect is to be observed, it is necessary to abandon this mistake, and not to conceal from ourselves that preaching is unable to revive religious life."

The religious indifference of the educated classes is the chief security for the existence of the Protestant Church. If they were to take an interest in matters of worship and doctrine, and to inform themselves as to the present relation of theological science to the teaching of the pulpit, the day of discovery and exposure would come, and confidence in the Church would be at an end. The dishonesty of Luther in those very things on which the Reformation depended could not be concealed from them. In Prussia there was a conscientious clergyman who taught his parishioners Greek, and then showed them all the passages, especially in the Epistles of St. Paul, which were intentionally altered in the translation. But one of the Protestant leaders impresses on the clergy the danger of allowing the people to know that which ought to be kept a secret among the learned. At most, he says, it may be necessary to admit that the translation is not perspicuous. The danger of this discovery does not, however, appear to be immediate, for no book is less familiar to the laity than the Bible. "There is scarcely one Christian family in a hundred," says Tholuck, "in which the Holy Scriptures are read." In the midst of this general downfall of Christianity, in spite of the great efforts of Protestants, some take refuge in the phrase of an invisible Church, some in a Church of the future. Whilst there exists a real, living, universal Church, with a settled system and means of salvation, the invisible

Church is offered in her stead, wrapped up in the swaddling clothes of rhetoric, like the stone which Rhea gave her husband instead of the child. In a novel of Jean Paul, a Swedish clergyman is advised in the middle of winter to walk about with a bit of orange-sugar in his mouth, in order to realise with all his senses the sunny climes of the South. It requires as much imagination to realise the Church by taking a "spiritual league" into one's mouth.

Another acknowledgment, that the Church has become estranged from the people, and subsists only as a ruin of a past age, is the widely spread hope of a new Pentecost. Eminent theologians speak of it as the only conceivable salvation, though there is no such promise in Scripture, no example in history of a similar desire. They rest their only hope in a miracle, such as has not happened since the Apostles, and thereby confess that, in the normal process of religious life by which Christ has guided His Church till now, their cause is lost. A symptom of the same despair is the rise of chiliastic aspirations, and the belief in the approaching end of the world. To this party belongs the present minister of public worship and education in Berlin. Shortly before his appointment he wrote: "Both Church and State must perish in their earthly forms, that the kingdom of Christ may be set up over all nations, that the bride of the Lamb, the perfect community, the new Jerusalem, may descend from heaven." Not long before this was published another Prussian statesman, Bunsen, had warned his Protestant readers to turn away from false prophets, who announce the end of the world because they have come to the end of their own wisdom.

In the midst of this desperate weakness, although Catholics and Protestants are so mixed up with each other that toleration must soon be universal throughout Germany, the thoughts of the Protestants are yet not turned towards the Catholic Church; they still show a bitter animosity against her, and the reproach of Catholic tendencies has for twenty years been the strongest argument against every attempt to revive religion and worship. The attitude of Protestantism towards Rome, says Stahl, is that of the Borghese gladiator. To soften this spirit of animosity the only possible resource is to make it clear to all Protestants who still hold to Christianity, what their own internal condition is, and what they have come to by their rejection of the unity and the authority which the Catholic Church possesses in the Holy See. Having shown the value of the Papacy by the results which have ensued on its rejection, Döllinger proceeds, with the same truth and impartiality, to trace the events which have injured the influence and diminished the glory and attractiveness of the Holy See, and have converted that which should be the safeguard of its spiritual freedom into a calamity and a dishonour in the eyes of mankind. It seems as though he wished to point out, as the moral to be learnt from the present condition of the religious world, that there is a coincidence in time and in providential purpose between the exhaustion and the despair at which enlightened Protestantism has arrived, from the failure of every attempt to organise a form of church government, to save the people from infidelity, and to reconcile theological knowledge with their religious faith,—between this and that great drama which, by destroying the bonds which linked the Church to an untenable system, is preparing the restoration of the Holy See to its former independence, and to its just influence over the minds of men.

The Popes, after obtaining a virtual independence under the Byzantine sceptre, transferred their allegiance to the revived empire of the West. The line between their authority and that of the emperor in Rome was never clearly drawn. It was a security for the freedom and regularity of the election, which was made by the lay as well as ecclesiastical dignitaries of the city, that it should be subject to the imperial ratification; but the remoteness of the emperors, and the inconvenience of delay, caused this rule to be often broken. This prosperous period did not long continue. When the dynasty of

Charlemagne came to an end, the Roman clergy had no defence against the nobles, and the Romans did all that men could do to ruin the Papacy. There was little remaining of the state which the Popes had formed in conjunction with the emperors. In the middle of the tenth century the Exarchate and the Pentapolis were in the power of Berengarius, and Rome in the hands of the Senator Alberic. Alberic, understanding that a secular principality could not last long, obtained the election of his son Octavian, who became Pope John XII. Otho the Great, who had restored the empire, and claimed to exercise its old prerogative, deposed the new Pope ; and when the Romans elected another, sent him also into exile beyond the Alps. For a whole century after this time there was no trace of freedom of election. Without the emperor, the Popes were in the hands of the Roman factions, and dependence on the emperor was better for the Church than dependence on the nobles. The Popes appointed under the influence of the prelates, who were the ecclesiastical advisers of the Imperial Government, were preferable to the nominees of the Roman chiefs, who had no object or consideration but their own ambition, and were inclined to speculate on the worthlessness of their candidates. During the first half of the eleventh century they recovered their predominance, and the deliverance of the Church came once more from Germany. A succession of German Popes, named by the emperor, opened the way for the permanent reform which is associated with the name of Gregory VII. Up to this period the security of the freedom of the Holy See was the protection of the emperor, and Gregory was the last Pope who asked for the imperial confirmation.

Between the middle of the ninth century and the middle of the eleventh the greater part of the Roman territory had passed into the hands of laymen. Some portions were possessed by the emperor, some by the great Italian families, and the revenues of the Pope were derived from the tribute of his vassals. Sylvester II. complains that this was very small, as the possessions of the Church had been given away for very little. Besides the tribute, the vassals owed feudal service to the Pope; but the government was not in his hands, and the imperial suzerainty remained. The great families had obtained from the Popes of their making such extensive grants that there was little remaining, and Otho III. tried to make up for it by a new donation. The loss of the patrimonies in Southern Italy established a claim on the Norman conquerors, and they became papal vassals for the kingdom of Sicily. But throughout the twelfth century the Popes had no firm basis of their power in Italy. They were not always masters of Rome, and there was not a single provincial town they could reckon on. Seven Popes in a hundred years sought a refuge in France; two remained at Verona. The donation of Matilda was disputed by the emperors, and brought no material accession of territory, until Innocent III., with his usual energy, secured to the Roman Church the south of Tuscany. He was the first Pope who governed a considerable territory, and became the real founder of the States of the Church. Before him, the Popes had possessions for which they claimed tribute and service, but no State that they administered. Innocent obtained the submission of Benevento and Romagna. He left the towns to govern themselves by their own laws, demanding only military aid in case of need, and a small tribute, which was not always exacted; Viterbo, for instance, paid nothing until the fifteenth century.

The contest with Frederic II. stripped the Holy See of most of these acquisitions. In many cases its civil authority was no longer acknowledged; in many it became a mere title of honour, while the real power had passed into the hands of the towns or of the nobles, sometimes into those of the bishops. Rudolph of Habsburg restored all that had been lost, and surrendered the imperial claims. But while the German influence was suspended, the influence of France prevailed over the Papacy; and during the exile at Avignon the Popes were as helpless as if they had possessed not an acre of their own in Italy. It was during their absence that the Italian Republics fell under the tyrannies, and their dominions were divided among a swarm of petty princes. The famous expedition of Cardinal Albornoz put an end to these disorders. He recovered the territories of the Church, and became, by the Ægidian Constitutions, which survived for ages, the legislator of Romagna. In 1376 eighty towns rose up in the space of three days, declared themselves free, or recalled the princes whom Albornoz had expelled. Before they could be reduced, the schism broke out, and the Church learnt the consequences of the decline of the empire, and the disappearance of its advocacy and protectorate over the Holy See. Boniface IX. sold to the republics and the princes, for a sum of money and an annual tribute, the ratification of the rights which they had seized.

The first great epoch in the history of the temporal power after the schism is the election of Eugenius IV. He swore to observe a statute which had been drawn up in conclave, by which all vassals and officers of State were to swear allegiance to the College of Cardinals in conjunction with the Pope. As he also undertook to abandon to the cardinals half the revenue, he shared in fact his authority with them. This was a new form of government, and a great restriction of the papal power; but it did not long endure.

The centrifugal tendency, which broke up Italy into small principalities, had long prevailed, when at last the Popes gave way to it. The first was Sixtus IV., who made one of his nephews lord of Imola, and another of Sinigaglia. Alexander VI. subdued all the princes in the States of the Church except the Duke of Montefeltro, and intended to make the whole an hereditary monarchy for his son. But Julius II. recovered all these conquests for the Church, added new ones to them, and thus became, after Innocent III. and Albornoz, the third founder of the Roman State. The age which beheld this restoration was marked in almost every country by the establishment of political unity on the ruins of the mediæval independence, and of monarchical absolutism at the expense of mediæval freedom. Both of these tendencies asserted themselves in the States of the Church. The liberties of the towns were gradually destroyed. This was accomplished by Clement VII. in Ancona, in 1532; by Paul III. in Perugia, in 1540. Ravenna, Faenza, Jesi had, under various pretexts, undergone the same fate. By the middle of the sixteenth century all resistance was subdued. In opposition, however, to this centralising policy, the nepotism introducted by Sixtus IV. led to dismemberment. Paul III. gave Parma and Piacenza to his son Pier Luigi Farnese, and the duchy was lost to the Holy See for good. Paul IV. made a similar attempt in favour of his nephew Caraffa, but he was put to death under Pius IV.; and this species of nepotism, which subsisted at the expense of the papal territory, came to an end. Pius V. forbade, under pain of excommunication, to invest any one with a possession of the Holy See, and this law was extended even to temporary concessions.

In the eighteenth century a time came when the temporal power was a source of weakness, and a weapon by which the courts compelled the Pope to consent to measures he would otherwise never have approved. It was thus that the suppression of the Jesuits was obtained from Clement XIV. Under his successors the world had an opportunity of comparing the times when Popes like Alexander III. or Innocent IV. governed the Church from their exile, and now, when men of the greatest piety and conscientiousness virtually postponed their duty as head of the Church to their rights as temporal sovereigns, and, like the senators of old, awaited the Gauls upon their throne. There is a lesson not to be forgotten in the contrast between the policy and the fate of the great mediæval pontiffs, who preserved their liberty by abandoning their dominions, and that of Pius VI. and Pius VII., who preferred captivity to flight.

The nepotism of Urban VIII. brought on the war of Castro, and in its train increase of debt, of taxes, impoverishment of the State, and the odious union of spiritual with temporal arms, which became a permanent calamity for the Holy See. This attachment to the interest of their families threw great discredit on the Popes, who were dishonoured by the faults, the crimes, and the punishment of their relatives. But since the death of Alexander VIII., in 1691, even that later form of nepotism which aimed at wealth only, not at political power, came to an end, and has never reappeared except in the case of the Braschi. The nepotism of the cardinals and prelates has survived that of the Popes. If the statute of Eugenius IV. had remained in force, the College of Cardinals would have formed a wholesome restraint in the temporal government, and the favouritism of the papal relations would have been prevented. But the Popes acted with the absolute power which was in the spirit of the monarchies of that age. When Paul IV. announced to the Sacred College that he had stripped the house of Colonna of its possessions to enrich his nephew, and that he was at war with Spain, they listened in silence, and have been passive ever since. No European sovereignty enjoyed so arbitrary an authority. Under Julius II. the towns retained considerable privileges, and looked on their annexation to the Papal State as a deliverance from their former oppressors. Machiavelli and Guicciardini say that the Popes required neither to defend nor to administer their dominions, and that the people were content in the enjoyment of their autonomy. In the course of the sixteenth century the administration was gradually centralised in Rome, and placed in the hands of ecclesiastics. Before 1550 the governors were ordinarily laymen, but the towns themselves preferred to be governed by prelates. By the close of the century the independence of the corporations had disappeared; but the centralisation, though complete, was not vigorous, and practically the towns and the barons, though not free, were not oppressed.

The modern system of government in the Roman States originated with Sixtus V. He introduced stability and regularity in the administration, and checked the growth of nepotism, favouritism, and arbitrary power, by the creation of permanent congregations. In connection with this measure the prelates became the upper class of official persons in the State, and were always expected to be men of fortune. A great burden for the country was the increase of offices, which were created only to be sold. No important duties and no fixed salary were attached to them, and the incumbent had to rely on fees and extortion. In the year 1470 there were 650 places of this kind. In eighty years they had increased to 3500. The theory was, that the money raised by the sale of places saved the people from the imposition of new taxes. Innocent XII., in 1693, put an end to this traffic; but it had continued so long that the ill-effects survived.

There was a great contrast between the ecclesiastical administration, which exhibited a dignified stability, resting on fixed rules and ancient traditions, and the civil government, which was exposed to continual fluctuation by the change of persons, of measures, and of systems; for few Popes continued the plans of their predecessors. The new Pontiff commenced his reign generally with a profound sense of the abuses and of the discontent which prevailed before his elevation, and naturally sought to obtain favour and improvement by opposite measures. In the cultivation of the Roman Campagna, for instance, it was observed that each Pope followed a different system, so that little was accomplished. The persons were almost always changed by the new Pope, so that great offices rarely remained long in the same hands. The Popes themselves were seldom versed in affairs of State, and therefore required the assistance of statesmen of long experience. In the eleventh, twelfth, and thirteenth centuries, when the election was free from outward influence, men were generally chosen who had held under one or two Popes the highest office of state,—Gregory VII., Urban II., Gelasius II., Lucius II., Alexander III., Gregory VIII., Gregory IX., Alexander IV. But in modern times it has been the rule that the Secretary of State should not be elected, and that the new Pope should dismiss the heads of the administration. Clement IX. was the first who gave up this practice, and retained almost all those who had been employed under his predecessor.

The burdens of the State increased far beyond its resources from the aid which the Popes gave to the Catholic Powers, especially in the Turkish wars. At the beginning of the seventeenth century the debt amounted to 12,242,620 *scudi*, and the interest absorbed three-fourths of the whole income. In 1655 it had risen to 48,000,000 *scudi*. The financial administration was secret, free from the control of public accounts, and the *Tesoriere*, being necessarily a cardinal, was irresponsible. There was no industry in the towns; they remained for the most part small and poor; almost all articles of common use were imported, and the country had little to give in exchange. All the interest of the public debt went to foreign creditors. As early as 1595 the discontent was very great, and so many emigrated, in order to escape the heavy burdens, that Cardinal Sacchetti said, in 1664, that the population was reduced by one-half. In the year 1740 the president De Brosses found the Roman Government the most defective but the mildest in Europe. Becattini, in his panegyrical biography of Pius VI., declares that it was the worst after that of Turkey. There were none of those limitations which in other countries restrained the power of the monarch, no fundamental laws, no coronation oath, no binding decrees of predecessors, no provincial estates, no powerful corporations. But, in reality, this unlimited absolutism was softened by custom, and by great indulgence towards individuals.

When Consalvi adopted the French institutions, he did not understand that an absolute government is intolerable, and must sink under the weight of its responsibility, unless it recognises the restraint of custom and tradition, and of subordinate, but not dependent forces. The unity and uniformity he introduced were destructive. He restored none of the liberties of the towns, and confided the administration to ecclesiastics superficially acquainted with law, and without knowledge of politics or of public economy. In the ecclesiastical States of Germany, the civil and religious departments were separate; and it is as wrong to say that the double position of the head must repeat itself throughout the administration, as to say that a king, because he is the head of the army as well as of the civil government, ought to mix the two spheres throughout the State. It would, in reality, be perfectly possible to separate the political and ecclesiastical authorities.

Leo XII. attempted to satisfy the *Zelanti*, the adversaries of Consalvi, by restoring the old system. He abolished the provincial Councils, revived the Inquisition, and subjected official honesty and public morality to a strict espionage. Leo saw the error of Consalvi, but mistook the remedy; and his government was the most unpopular that had been seen for a century. Where the laity are excluded from the higher offices, and the clergy enjoy the monopoly of them, that moral power which modern bureaucracy derives from the corporate spirit, and the feelings of honour which it inspires, cannot subsist. One class becomes demoralised by its privileged position, the other by its limited prospects and insufficient pay. Leo tried to control them by the *congregazione di vigilanze*, which received and examined all charges against official persons; but it was suppressed by his successor.

The famous Memorandum of the Powers, 31st May 1831, recommended the admission of the laity to all secular offices, the restoration of the provincial Councils, and the introduction of elective communal Councils with the power of local government; and finally, a security against the changes incident to an elective sovereignty. The historian Coppi, who was charged to draw up a plan of reform in reply to these demands, relates that the Pope and the majority of the cardinals rejected every serious change, and were resolved to uphold the old principles, and to concede nothing to the lay party, "because, if anything was voluntarily conceded, there would be no right of recalling it afterwards." Two things in particular it was determined not to grant—elective Councils in the towns and provinces, and a lay Council of State beside the Sacred College. In a general way, vague reforms were promised; but the promise was not redeemed. Austria would not tolerate any liberal concessions in Italy which were in contradiction with her own system and her own interests; thus all Italian aspirations for reforms were concentrated in the wish to get rid of the foreign yoke, and Austria never succeeded in forming a party amongst the Italians favourable to her power. Yet Gregory XVI. knew that great changes were needed. In 1843 he said:—

> The civil administration requires a great reform. I was too old when I was elected; I did not expect to live so long, and had not the courage to begin the undertaking. For whoever begins, must accomplish it. I have now only a few more years to live; perhaps only a few days. After me they will choose a young Pope, whose mission it will be to perform the act, without which it is impossible to go on.

The Austrian occupation caused the Roman Government to be identified with the foreign supremacy, and transferred to it the hatred of the patriots. The disaffection of the subjects of the Pope had deeper motives. Except the clergy, that overshadows all, there are no distinct orders in the society of the Roman State; no country nobility, no wealthy class of peasant proprietors; nothing but the population of the towns, and a degenerate class of patricians. These were generally hostile to the ecclesiastical system. The offices are so distributed, that the clergy govern, and the laity are their instruments. In the principal departments, no amount of services or ability could raise a layman above a certain level, beyond which younger and less competent ecclesiastics were promoted over his head. This subordination, which led to a regular dependence of the lay officials on the prelates, drove the best men away from the service of the State, and disposed the rest to long for a government which should throw open to them the higher prizes of their career. Even the country people, who were never tainted with the ideas of the secret societies, were not always well affected.

It is more difficult for a priest than for a layman to put aside his private views and feelings in the administration of justice. He is the servant and herald of grace, of forgiveness, of indulgence, and easily forgets that in human concerns the law is inexorable, that favour to one is often injury to many or to all, and that he has no right to place his own will above the law. He is still more disqualified for the direction of the police, which, in an absolute State and in troubled times, uses its unlimited power without reference to Christian ideas, leaves unpunished acts which are grievous sins, and punishes others which in a religious point of view are innocent. It is hard for the people to distinguish clearly the priestly character from the action of its bearer in the administration of police. The same indifference to the strict letter of the law, the same confusion between breaches of divine and of human ordinances, led to a practice of arbitrary imprisonment, which contrasts painfully with the natural gentleness of a priestly government. Hundreds of persons were cast into prison without a trial or even an examination; only on suspicion, and kept there more than a year for greater security.

The immunities of the clergy were as unpopular as their power. The laws and decrees of the Pope as a temporal sovereign were not held to be binding on them unless it was expressly said, or was clear from the context, that they were given also in his character of Head of the Church. Ecclesiastics were tried before their own tribunals, and had the right to be more lightly punished than laymen for the same delinquency. Those events in the life of Achilli, which came out at his trial, had not only brought down on him no severe punishment, but did not stand in the way of his promotion.

With all these privileges, the bulk of the Roman clergy had little to do; little was expected of them, and their instruction was extremely deficient.

At the end of the pontificate of Gregory XVI. the demand for reforms was loud and universal, and men began to perceive that the defects of the civil government were undermining the religious attachment of the people. The conclave which raised Pius IX. to the Papal throne was the shortest that had occurred for near three hundred years. The necessity of choosing a Pontiff disposed to understand and to satisfy the pressing requirements of the time, made it important to hasten matters in order to escape the interference of Austria. It was expected that Cardinal Gizzi or Cardinal Mastai would be elected. The latter had been pointed out by Gregory XVI. as his fittest successor, and he made Gizzi Secretary of State. The first measure of the new reign, the amnesty, which, as Metternich said, threw open the doors of the house to the professional robbers, was taken not so much as an act of policy, as because the Pope was resolved to undo an accumulation of injustice. The reforms which followed soon made Pius the most popular of Italian princes, and all Catholics rejoiced that the reconciliation of the Papacy with modern freedom was at length accomplished, and that the shadow which had fallen on the priesthood throughout the world was removed with the abuses in the Roman Government. The Constitution was, perhaps, an inevitable though a fatal necessity. "The Holy Father must fall," said his minister, "but at least he will fall with honour." The preliminary conditions of constitutional life were wanting—habits of self-government in the towns and provinces, security from the vexations of the police, separation of spiritual and temporal jurisdiction. It could not be but that the existence of an elective chamber must give to the lay element a preponderance in the State, whilst in the administration the contrary position was maintained. There could be no peaceful solution of this contradiction, and it is strange that the cardinals, who were unanimously in favour of the statute, should not have seen that it would lead to the destruction of the privileges of the clergy. But in the allocution of 20th April 1849, the Pope declared that he had never intended to alter the character of his government; so that he must have thought the old system of administration by ecclesiastics compatible with the working of the new Constitution. At his return from exile all his advisers were in favour of abrogating all the concessions of the first years of his reign. Balbo and Rosmini visited him at Gaeta, to plead for the Constitution, but they obtained nothing. Pius IX. was persuaded that every concession would be a weapon in the hands of the Radicals. A lay *consulta* gave to the laity a share of the supreme government; but the chief offices and the last decision remained, as before, in the hands of the prelates. Municipal reforms were promised. In general the old defects continued, and the old discontent was not conciliated.

It is manifest that Constitutionalism, as it is ordinarily understood, is not a system which can be applied to the States of the Church. It could not be tolerated that a warlike faction, by refusing supplies, should compel the Pope to go to war with a Christian nation, as they sought to compel him to declare war against Austria in 1848. His sovereignty must be real, not merely nominal. It makes no difference whether he is in the power of a foreign State or of a parliamentary majority. But real sovereignty is compatible with a participation of the people in legislation, the autonomy of corporations, a moderate freedom of the press, and the separation of religion and police.

Recent events would induce one to suppose that the enormous power of the press and of public opinion, which it forms and reflects, is not understood in Rome. In 1856 the Inquisitor at Ancona issued an edict, threatening with the heaviest censures all who should omit to denounce the religious or ecclesiastical faults of their neighbours, relatives, or superiors; and in defiance of the general indignation, and of the despondency of those who, for the sake of religion, desired reforms in the States of the Church, the *Civilta Cattolica* declared that the Inquisitor had done his duty. Such cases as this, and those of Achilli and Mortara, weighed more heavily in the scale in which the Roman State is weighed than a lost battle. Without discussing the cases themselves, it is clear what their influence has been on public opinion, with which it is more important at the present day to treat than with the governments which depend on it. This branch of diplomacy has been unfortunately neglected, and hence the Roman Government cannot rely on lay support.

After describing the evils and disorders of the State, which the Pope so deeply felt that he put his own existence in peril, and inflamed half of Europe with the spirit of radical change in the attempt to remove them, Dr. Döllinger contrasts, with the gloomy picture of decay and failure, the character of the Pontiff who attempted the great work of reform.

Nevertheless, the administration of Pius IX. is wise, benevolent, indulgent, thrifty, attentive to useful institutions and improvements. All that proceeds from Pius IX. personally is worthy of a head of the Church—elevated, liberal in the best sense of the term. No sovereign spends less on his court and his own private wants. If all thought and acted as he does, his would be a model State. Both the French and the English envoys affirm that the financial administration had improved, that the value of the land was increasing, agriculture flourishing, and that many symptoms of progress might be observed. Whatever can be expected of a monarch full of affection for his people, and seeking his sole recreation in works of beneficence, Pius richly performs. *Pertransiit benefaciendo*,—words used of one far greater,—are simply the truth applied to him. In him we can clearly perceive how the Papacy, even as a temporal state, might, so far as the character of the prince is concerned, through judicious elections, be the most admirable of human institutions. A man in the prime of life, after an irreproachable youth and a conscientious discharge of Episcopal duties, is elevated to the highest dignity and to sovereign power. He knows nothing of expensive amusements; he has no other passion but that of doing good, no other ambition but to be beloved by his subjects. His day is divided between prayer and the labours of government; his relaxation is a walk in the garden, a visit to a church, a prison, or a charitable institution. Free from personal desires and from terrestrial bonds, he has no relatives, no favourites to provide for. For him the rights and powers of his office exist only for the sake of its duties. . . . Grievously outraged, injured, rewarded with ingratitude, he has never harboured a thought of revenge, never committed an act of severity, but ever forgiven and ever pardoned. The cup of sweetness and of bitterness, the cup of human favour and of human aversion, he has not only tasted, but emptied to the dregs ; he heard them cry "Hosannah !" and soon after "Crucifige !" The man of his confidence, the first intellectual power of his nation, fell beneath the murderer's knife ; the bullet of an insurgent struck down the friend by his side. And yet no feeling of hatred, no breath of anger could ever obscure, even for a moment, the spotless mirror of his soul. Untouched by human folly, unmoved by human malice, he proceeds with a firm and regular step on his way, like the stars of heaven.

Such I have seen the action of this Pope in Rome, such it has been described to me by all, whether near him or afar ; and if he now seems to be appointed to pass through all the painful and discouraging experience which can befall a monarch, and to continue to the end the course of a prolonged martyrdom, he resembles in this, as in so many other things, the sixteenth Louis ; or rather ; to go up higher, he knows that the disciple is not above the Master, and that the pastor of a church, whose Lord and Founder died upon the cross, cannot wonder and cannot refuse that the cross should be laid also upon him (pp. 624-627).

It is a common opinion, that the Pope, as a sovereign, is bound by the common law to the forms and ideas of the Middle Ages ; and that in consequence of the progress of society, of the difference between the thirteenth century and the nineteenth, there is an irreconcilable discord between the Papacy and the necessities of civil government. All Catholics are bound to oppose this opinion. Only that which is of Divine institution is unchangeable through all time. But the sovereignty of the Popes is extremely elastic, and has already gone through many forms. No contrast can be stronger than that between the use which the Popes made of their power in the thirteenth or the fifteenth century, and the system of Consalvi. There is no reason, therefore, to doubt, that it will now, after a violent interruption, assume the form best adapted to the character of the age and the requirements of the Italian people. There is nothing chimerical in the vision of a new order of things, in which the election shall fall on men in the prime of their years and their strength; in which the people shall be reconciled to their government by free institutions and a share in the conduct of their own concerns, and the upper classes satisfied by the opening of a suitable career in public affairs. Justice publicly and speedily administered would obtain the confidence of the people; the public service would be sustained by an honourable *esprit de corps;* the chasm between laity and priesthood would be closed by equality in rights and duties; the police would not rely on the help of religion, and religion would no longer drag itself along on the crutches of the police. The integrity of the Papal States would be under the joint guardianship of the Powers, who have guaranteed even the dominions of the Sultan; and the Pope would have no enemies to fear, and his subjects would be delivered from the burden of military service and of a military budget.

Religious liberty is not, as the enemies of the Holy See declare, and some even of its friends believe, an insurmountable difficulty. Events often cut the knots which appear insoluble to theory. Attempts at proselytising have not hitherto succeeded among the subjects of the Pope; but if it had been otherwise, would it have been possible for the Inquisition to proceed against a Protestant? The agitation that must have ensued would be a welcome opportunity to put an end to what remains of the temporal power. It is true that the advance of Protestantism in Italy would raise up a barrier between the Pope and his subjects; but no such danger is to be apprehended. At the time when the doctrines of the Reformation exercised an almost magical power over mankind, they never took root in Italy beyond a few men of letters; and now that their power of attraction and expansion has long been exhausted, neither Sardinian policy nor English gold will succeed in seducing the Italians to them.

The present position of helpless and humiliating dependence will not long endure. The determination of the Piedmontese Government to annex Rome is not more certain than the determination of the Emperor Napoleon to abrogate the temporal power. Pius IX. would enjoy greater security in Turkey than in the hands of a State which combines the tyranny of the Convention, the impudent sophistry of a government of advocates, and the ruthless brutality of military despotism. Rather than trust to Piedmont, may Pius IX. remember the example of his greatest predecessors, who, relying on the spiritual might of the Papacy, sought beyond the Alps the freedom which Italy denied to them. The Papacy has beheld the rise and the destruction of many thrones, and will assuredly outlive the kingdom of Italy, and other monarchies besides. It can afford to wait; *patiens quia æternus.* The Romans need the Pope more than the Pope needs Rome. Above the Catacombs, among the Basilicas, beside the Vatican, there is no place for a tribune or for a king. We shall see what was seen in the fourteenth century: envoys will come from Rome to entreat the Pope to return to his faithful city.

Whilst things continue as they are, the emperor can, by threatening to withdraw his troops, compel the Pope to consent to anything not actually sinful. Such a situation is alarming in the highest degree for other countries. But for the absolute confidence that all men have in the fidelity and conscientiousness of the present Pope, and for the providential circumstance that there is no ecclesiastical complication which the French Government could use for its own ends, it would not be tolerated by the rest of the Catholic world. Sooner or later these conditions of security will disappear, and the interest of the Church demands that before that happens, the peril should be averted, even by a catastrophe.

The hostility of the Italians themselves to the Holy See is the tragic symptom of the present malady. In other ages, when it was assailed, the Italians were on its side, or at least were neutral. Now they require the destruction of the temporal power, either as a necessary sacrifice for the unity and greatness of their country, or as a just consequence of incurable defects. The time will come, however, when they will be reconciled with the Papacy, and with its presence as a Power among them. It was the dependence of the Pope on the Austrian arms, and his identification in popular opinion with the cause of the detested foreigner, that obscured his lofty position as the moral bulwark and protector of the nation. For 1500 years the Holy See was the pivot of Italian history, and the source of the Italian influence in Europe. The nation and the See shared the same fortunes, and grew powerful or feeble together. It was not until the vices of Alexander VI. and his predecessors had destroyed the reverence which was the protection of Italy, that she became the prey of the invaders. None of the great Italian historians has failed to see that they would ruin themselves in raising their hands against Rome. The old prophecy of the *Papa Angelico*, of an Angel Pope, who was to rise up to put an end to discord and disorder, and to restore piety and peace and happiness in Italy, was but the significant token of the popular belief that the Papacy and the nation were bound up together, and that one was the guardian of the other. That belief slumbers, now that the idea of unity prevails, whilst the Italians are attempting to put the roof on a building without walls and without foundations, but it will revive again, when centralisation is compelled to yield to federalism, and the road to the practicable has been found in the search after impossibilities.

The tyrannical character of the Piedmontese Government, its contempt for the sanctity of public law, the principles on which it treats the clergy at home, and the manner in which it has trampled on the rights of the Pope and the interests of religion, the perfidy and despotism it exhibits, render it impossible that any securities it may offer to the Pope can possess a real value. Moreover, in the unsettled state of the kingdom, the uncertain succession of parties, and the fluctuation of power, whatever guarantee is proposed by the ministry, there is nobody to guarantee the guarantor. It is a system without liberty and without stability; and the Pope can never be reconciled to it, or become a dweller in the new Italian kingdom.

If he must choose between the position of a subject and of an exile, he is at home in the whole Catholic world, and wherever he goes he will be surrounded by children who will greet him as their father. It may become an inevitable, but it must always be a heroic resolution. The court and the various congregations for the administration of the affairs of the Church are too numerous to be easily moved. In former times the machinery was more simple, and the whole body of the pontifical government could be lodged in a single French monastery. The absence of the Pope from Rome will involve great difficulties and annoyance; but it is a lesser evil than a surrender of principle, which cannot be recalled.

To remove the Holy See to France would, under present circumstances, be an open challenge to a schism, and would afford to all who wish to curtail the papal rights, or to interrupt the communication between the Pope and the several churches, the most welcome pretexts, and it would put arms in the hands of governments that wish to impede the action of his authority within their States.

The conclusion of the book is as follows:—

If the Court of Rome should reside for a time in Germany, the Roman prelates will doubtless be agreeably surprised to discover that our people is able to remain Catholic and religious without the leading-strings of a police, and that its religious sentiments are a better protection to the Church than the episcopal *carceri*, which, thank God, do not exist. They will learn that the Church in Germany is able to maintain herself without the Holy Office; that our bishops, although, or because, they use no physical compulsion, are reverenced like princes by the people, that they are received with triumphal arches, that their arrival in a place is a festival for the inhabitants. They will see how the Church with us rests on the broad, strong, and healthy basis of a well-organised system of pastoral administration and of popular religious instruction. They will perceive that we Catholics have maintained for years the struggle for the deliverance of the Church from the bonds of bureaucracy straightforwardly and without reservation; that we cannot entertain the idea of denying to the Italians what we have claimed for ourselves; and that therefore we are far from thinking that it is anywhere an advantage to fortify the Church with the authority of the police and with the power of the secular arm. Throughout Germany we have been taught by experience the truth of Fénelon's saying, that the spiritual power must be carefully kept separate from the civil, because their union is pernicious. They will find, further, that the whole of the German clergy is prepared to bless the day when it shall learn that the free sovereignty of the Pope is assured, without sentence of death being still pronounced by ecclesiastics, without priests continuing to discharge the functions of treasury-clerks or police directors, or to conduct the business of the lottery. And, finally, they will convince themselves that all the Catholics of Germany will stand up as one man for the independence of the Holy See, and the legitimate rights of the Pope; but that they are no admirers of a form of government of very recent date, which is, in fact, nothing else than the product of the mechanical polity of Napoleon combined with a clerical administration. And this information will bear good fruit when the hour shall strike for the return, and restitution shall be made. . . .

Meanwhile Pius IX. and the men of his Council will "think upon the days of old, and have in their minds the eternal years." They will read the future in the earlier history of the Papacy, which has already seen many an exile and many a restoration. The example of the resolute, courageous Popes of the Middle Ages will light the way. It is no question now of suffering martyrdom, of clinging to the tombs of the Apostles, or of descending into the catacombs; but of quitting the land of bondage, in order to exclaim on a free soil, "Our bonds are broken, and we are free!" For the rest God will provide, and the unceasing gifts and sympathies of the Catholic world. And the parties in Italy, when they have torn and exhausted the land which has become a battle-field; when the sobered and saddened people, tired of the rule of lawyers and of soldiers, has understood the worth of a moral and spiritual authority, then will be the time to think of returning to the Eternal City. In the interval, the things will have disappeared for whose preservation such pains are taken; and then there will be better reason than Consalvi had, in the preface to the *Motu Proprio* of 6th July 1816, to say: "Divine Providence, which so conducts human affairs that out of the greatest calamity innumerable benefits proceed, seems to have intended that the interruption of the papal government should prepare the way for a more perfect form of it."

We have written at a length for which we must apologise to our readers; and yet this is but a meagre sketch of the contents of a book which deals with a very large proportion of the subjects that occupy the thoughts and move the feelings of religious men. We will attempt to sum up in a few words the leading ideas of the author. Addressing a mixed audience, he undertakes to controvert two different interpretations of the events which are being fulfilled in Rome. To the Protestants, who triumph in the expected downfall of the Papacy, he shows the consequences of being without it. To the Catholics, who see in the Roman question a great peril to the Church, he explains how the possession of the temporal sovereignty had become a greater misfortune than its loss for a time would be. From the opposite aspects of the religious camps of our age he endeavours to awaken the misgivings of one party, and to strengthen the confidence of the other. There is an inconsistency between the Protestant system and the progress of modern learning; there is none between the authority of the Holy See and the progress of modern society. The events which are tending to deprive the Pope of his territory are not to be, therefore, deplored, if we consider the preceding causes, because they made this catastrophe inevitable; still less if, looking to the future, we consider the state of Protestantism, because they remove an obstacle to union which is humanly almost insurmountable. In a former work Döllinger exhibited the moral and intellectual exhaustion of Paganism as the prelude to Christianity. In like manner he now confronts the dissolution and spiritual decay of Protestantism with the Papacy. But in order to complete the contrast, and give force to the vindication, it was requisite that the true function and character of the Holy See should not be concealed from the unpractised vision of strangers by the mask of that system of government which has grown up around it in modern times. The importance of this violent disruption of the two authorities consists in the state of religion throughout the world. Its cause lies in the deficiences of the temporal power; its end in the mission of the spiritual.

The interruption of the temporal sovereignty is the only way we can discern in which these deficiences can be remedied and these ends obtained. But this interruption cannot be prolonged. In an age in which the State throughout the Continent is absolute, and tolerates no immunities; when corporations have therefore less freedom than individuals, and the disposition to restrict their action increases in proportion to their power, the Pope cannot be independent as a subject. He must, therefore, be a sovereign, the free ruler of an actual territory, protected by international law and a European guarantee. The restoration consequently is necessary, though not as an immediate consequence of the revolution. In this revolutionary age the protection of the Catholic Powers is required against outward attack. They must also be our security that no disaffection is provoked within; that there shall be no recurrence of the dilemma between the right of insurrection against an arbitrary government and the duty of obedience to the Pope; and that civil society shall not again be convulsed, nor the pillars of law and order throughout Europe shaken, by a revolution against the Church, of which, in the present instance, the conservative powers share the blame, and have already felt the consequences.

In the earnest and impressive language of the conclusion, in which Döllinger conveys the warnings which all Transalpine Catholicism owes to its Head as an Italian sovereign, it seems to us that something more definite is intended than the expression of the wish, which almost every Catholic feels, to receive the Pope in his own country. The anxiety for his freedom which would be felt if he took refuge in France, would be almost equally justified by his presence in Austria. A residence in an exclusively Catholic country, such as Spain, would be contrary to the whole spirit of this book, and to the moral which it inculcates, that the great significance of the crisis is in the state of German Protestantism. If the position of the Catholics in Germany would supply useful lessons and examples to the Roman court, it is also from the vicinity of the Protestant world that the full benefit can best be drawn from its trials, and that the crimes of the Italians, which have begun as calamities, may be turned to the advantage of the Church. But against such counsels there is a powerful influence at work. Napoleon has declared his determination to sweep away the temporal power. The continuance of the occupation of Rome, and his express prohibition to the Piedmontese government to proceed with the annexation during the life of the present Pope, signify that he calculates on greater advantages in a conclave than from the patient resolution of Pius IX. This policy is supported by the events in Italy in a formidable manner. The more the Piedmontese appear as enemies and persecutors, the more the emperor will appear as the only saviour ; and the dread of a prolonged exile in any Catholic country, and of dependence for subsistence on the contributions of the faithful, must exhibit in a fascinating light the enjoyment of the splendid hospitality and powerful protection of France. On these hopes and fears, and on the difficulties which are pressing on the cardinals from the loss of their revenues, the emperor speculates, and persuades himself that he will be master of the next election. On the immovable constancy of her Supreme Pontiff the Catholic Church unconditionally relies ; and we are justified in believing that, in an almost unparalleled emergency, he will not tremble before a resolution of which no Pope has given an example since the consolidation of the temporal power.

XI

DÖLLINGER'S HISTORICAL WORK[1]

WHEN first seen, at Würzburg, in the diaries of Platen the poet, Dr. Döllinger was an eager student of general literature, and especially of Schlegel and the romantic philosophy. It was an epoch in which the layman and the *dilettante* prevailed. In other days a divine had half a dozen distinct schools of religious thought before him, each able to develop and to satisfy a receptive mind; but the best traditions of western scholarship had died away when the young Franconian obtained a chair in the reorganised university of Munich. His own country, Bavaria, his time, the third decade of the century, furnished no guide, no master, and no model to the new professor. Exempt, by date and position, from the discipline of a theological party, he so continued, and never turned elsewhere for the dependence he escaped at home. No German theologian, of his own or other churches, bent his course; and he derived nothing from the powerful writer then dominant in the North. To a friend describing Herder as the one unprofitable classic, he replied, "Did you ever learn anything from Schleiermacher?" And if it is doubtful which way this stroke was aimed, it is certain that he saw less than others in the Berlin teacher.

Very young he knew modern languages well, though with a defective ear, and having no local or contemporary attachments he devoted himself systematically to the study of foreign divines. The characteristic universality of his later years was not the mere result of untiring

[1] *English Historical Review*, 1890.

energy and an unlimited command of books. His international habit sprang from the inadequacy of the national supply, and the search for truth in every century naturally became a lecturer whose function it was to unfold from first to last the entire life of the Church, whose range extended over all Christian ages, and who felt the inferiority of his own. Döllinger's conception of the science which he was appointed to carry forward, in conformity with new requirements and new resources, differed from the average chiefly by being more thorough and comprehensive. At two points he was touched by currents of the day. Savigny, the legal expert of a school recruited from both denominations and gravitating towards Catholicism, had expounded law and society in that historic spirit which soon pervaded other sciences, and restored the significance of national custom and character. By his writings Protestant literature overlapped. The example of the conspicuous jurist served as a suggestion for divines to realise the patient process of history; and Döllinger continued to recognise him as a master and originator of true scientific methods when his influence on jurisprudence was on the wane. On the same track, Drey, in 1819, defended the theory of development as the vital prerogative of Rome over the fixity of other churches. Möhler was the pupil of Drey, and they made Tübingen the seat of a positive theology, broader and more progressive than that of Munich.

The first eminent thinker whom he saw and heard was Baader, the poorest of writers, but the most instructive and impressive talker in Germany, and the one man who appears to have influenced the direction of his mind. Bishop Martensen has described his amazing powers; and Döllinger, who remembered him with more scant esteem, bore equal testimony to the wealth and worth of his religious philosophy. He probably owed to him his persistent disparagement of Hegel, and more certainly that familiarity with the abstruse literature of mysticism which made him as clear and sure of vision in the twilight of Petrucci and St.

Martin as in the congenial company of Duperron. Baader is remembered by those who abstain from sixteen volumes of discordant thought, as the inventor of that system of political insurance which became the Holy Alliance. That authority is as sacred and sovereignty as absolute in the Church as in the State, was an easy and obvious inference, and it had been lately drawn with an energy and literary point to which Baader was a stranger, by the Count de Maistre, who was moreover a student of St. Martin. When the ancient mystic welcomed his new friend, he was full of the praises of De Maistre. He impressed upon his earnest listener the importance of the books on the pope and on the Gallican church, and assured him that the spirit which animates them is the genuine Catholicism. These conversations were the origin of Döllinger's specific ultramontanism. It governed one half of his life, and his interest in De Maistre outlasted the assent which he once gave to some of his opinions. Questions arising from the Savoyard's indictment against Bacon, which he proposed to Liebig, formed the connection between the two laboured attacks on the founder of English philosophy.

Much of that which at any time was unhistoric or presumptive in his mind may be ascribed to this influence; and it divided him from Möhler, who was far before him in the fulness of the enjoyment of his powers and his fame, whom he survived half a century, and never ceased to venerate as the finest theological intellect he had known. The publication of the *Symbolik* made it difficult for the author to remain in Wirtemberg; Tübingen, he said, was a place where he could neither live nor die happy; and having made Döllinger's acquaintance, he conceived an ardent wish to become his colleague at Munich.

Im Verkehre mit Ihnen, und dem Kreise in dem Sie leben, habe ich mich aufs anmuthigste erheitert, sittlich gestärkt, und religiös getröstet und ermuthigt gefunden; ein Verein von Einwirkungen auf mich wurde mir gewährt, deren aller ich in fast gleichein Grade bedürftig war.

Döllinger negotiated his appointment, overcame the resisting ministerial medium through the intervention of the king, and surrendered his own department of theology which they both regarded as the most powerful agency in religious instruction. Möhler had visited Göttingen and Berlin, and recognised their superiority. A public address to Planck, praising the Protestant treatment of history, was omitted by Döllinger from the edition of his miscellaneous writings. They differed so widely that one of them hesitated to read Bossuet's *Defensio,* and generally kept the stronger Gallicans out of sight, whilst the other warmly recommended Richer, and Launoy, and Dupin, and cautioned his pupils against Baronius, as a forger and a cheat, who dishonestly attributed to the primitive Church ideas quite foreign to its constitution. He found fault with his friend for undue favour to the Jesuits, and undue severity towards Jansenism. The other advised him to read Fénelon, and succeeded in modifying this opinion.

Sie werden vielleicht um so geneigter sein, mir zu verzeihen, wenn ich Ihnen melde, dass ich inzwischen recht fleissig die Jansenistischen Streitigkeiten, durch Ihre freundliche Zuschrift angeregt, studirt habe, und Ihrer Darstellung ohne Zweifel jetzt weit näher stehe als früher. Selbst die Bulle Unigenitus erscheint mir in einem weit günstigeren Lichte als früher, obschon ich die Censur mancher Quesnel'scher Sätze immer noch nicht begreifen kann. Sie schrieben mir, dass die Fénelon'sche Correspondenz einen grossen Einfluss auf Ihre Betrachtungsweise ausgeübt habe. Auch bei mir ist dieses der Fall.

But in describing the failure of scholastic theology, the exaggeration of De Maistre, the incompetence of the Roman censorship, the irreligion of Leo X., and the strength of Luther's case against the Papacy, the sensitive Suabian made a contrast, then, and long after, with Döllinger's disciplined coolness and reserve.

Dann war wirklich die bestehende Form der Kirche im höchsten Grade tadelhaft, und bedurfte der Reinigung. Die Päpste waren Despoten, willkührliche Herrscher geworden. Gebräuche hatten sich angehäuft, die im höchsten Grade dem Glauben und der christlichen Frömmigkeit entgegen waren. In vielen Punkten hatte Luther immer Recht, wenn er von Missbräuchen der Römischen Gewalt spricht, dass dort alles feil sei.—Tetzel verfuhr ohnediess auf die empörendste Weise, und übertrieb, mit einer religiösen Rohheit und einem Stumpfsinn ohne Gleichen, das Bedenkliche der Sache auf die äusserste Spitze.

The disagreement which made itself felt from time to time between the famous colleagues was not removed when one of them wished the other to change his confessor before his last illness.

Möhler claimed the supreme chair of ecclesiastical history as a matter of course, and by right of seniority. He apologised for venturing to supersede one who had gained distinction in that lecture-room, but he hinted that he himself was the least fit of the two for dogmatics.

Ich habe mich für die historischen Fächer entschieden. Ihr Opfer, wenn Sie Dogmatik lesen, anerkenne ich, aber ich bitte das meinige nicht zu übersehen. Welcher Entschluss, ich möchte sagen, welche Unverschämtheit ist es, nach Ihnen und bei Ihren Lebzeiten, Kirchengeschichte in München zu doziren?

Döllinger took that branch for the time, but he never afterwards taught theology proper. As Möhler, who was essentially a theologian, deserted divinity to compose inferior treatises on the gnostics and the false decretals, Döllinger, by choice and vocation a divine, having religion as the purpose of his life, judged that the loftier function, the more spiritual service, was historical teaching. The problem is to know how it came to pass that a man who was eminently intelligent and perspicuous in the exposition of doctrines, but who, in narrative, description, and knowledge of character, was neither first nor second, resolved that his mission was history.

In early life he had picked up chance copies of Baronius and Petavius, the pillars of historic theology; but the motives of his choice lay deeper. Church history had long been the weakest point and the cause of weakness among the Catholics, and it was the rising strength of the German Protestants. Therefore it was the post of danger; and it gave to a theologian the command of a public of laymen. The restoration of history coincided with the euthanasia of metaphysic; when the foremost philosophic genius of the time led over to the historic treatment both of philosophy and religion, and Hamilton, Cousin, Comte, severally converted the science into its history. Many men better equipped for speculation than for erudition went the same way; the systematic theology was kept up in the universities by the influence of Rome, where scholasticism went on untouched by the romantic transformation. Writing of England, Wiseman said: "There is still a scholastic hardness in our controversial theology, an unbendingness of outward forms in our explanations of Catholic principles, which renders our theologians dry and unattractive to the most catholicly inclined portion of our Protestants." The choice which these youths made, towards 1830, was, though they did not know it, the beginning of a rift that widened.

Döllinger was more in earnest than others in regarding Christianity as history, and in pressing the affinity between catholic and historical thought. Systems were to him nearly as codes to Savigny, when he exhorted his contemporaries not to consolidate their law, lest, with their wisdom and knowledge, they should incorporate their delusions and their ignorance, and usurp for the state what belonged to the nation. He would send an inquiring student to the *Historia Congregationis de Auxiliis* and the *Historia Pelagiana* rather than to Molina or Lemos, and often gave the advice which, coming from Oriel, disconcerted Morris of Exeter: "I am afraid you will have to read the Jesuit Petavius." He dreaded the predominance of great names which stop the way, and everything that interposes the notions of an epoch, a region, or a school between the Church and the observer.

To an Innsbruck professor, lamenting that there was no philosophy which he could heartily adopt, he replied that philosophies do not subsist in order to be adopted. A Thomist or a Cartesian seemed to him as a captive, or a one-armed combatant. Prizing metaphysicians for the unstrung pearls which they drop beyond the seclusion of system, he loved the *disjecta membra* of Coleridge, and preferred the *Pensieri*, and *Parerga und Paralipomena* to the constructed work of Gioberti and Schopenhauer. He knew Leibniz chiefly in his letters, and was perceptibly affected by his law of continuous progression, his general optimism, and his eclectic art of extracting from men and books only the good that is in them; but of monadology or pre-established harmony there was not a trace. His colleague, Schelling, no friend to the friends of Baader, stood aloof. The elder Windischmann, whom he particularly esteemed, and who acted in Germany as the interpreter of De Maistre, had hailed Hegel as a pioneer of sound philosophy, with whom he agreed both in thought and word. Döllinger had no such condescension. Hegel remained, in his eyes, the strongest of all the enemies of religion, the guide of Tübingen in its aberrations, the reasoner whose abstract dialectics made a generation of clever men incapable of facing facts. He went on preferring former historians of dogma, who were untainted by the trail of pantheism, Baumgarten-Crusius, and even Muenscher, and by no means admitted that Baur was deeper than the early Jesuits and Oratorians, or gained more than he lost by constriction in the Hegelian coil. He took pleasure in pointing out that the best recent book on the penitential system, Kliefoth's fourth volume, owed its substance to Morinus. The dogmas of pantheistic history offended him too much to give them deep study, and he was ill prepared with counsel for a wanderer lost in the pervading haze. Hegelians said of him that he lacked the constructive unity of idea, and knew the way from effect to cause, but not from cause to law.

His own lectures on the philosophy of religion, which have left no deep furrow, have been praised by Ketteler, who was not an undiscriminating admirer. He sent on one of his pupils to Rosmini, and set another to begin metaphysics with Suarez; and when Lady Ashburton consulted him on the subject, he advised her to read

Norris and Malebranche. He encouraged the study of remoter luminaries, such as Cusa and Raymundus, whose *Natural Theology* he preferred to the *Analogy;* and would not have men overlook some who are off the line, like Postel. But although he deemed it the mark of inferiority to neglect a grain of the gold of obsolete and eccentric writers, he always assigned to original speculation a subordinate place, as a good servant but a bad master, without the certainty and authority of history. What one of his English friends writes of a divine they both admired, might fitly be applied to him:

> He was a disciple in the school of Bishop Butler, and had learned as a first principle to recognise the limitations of human knowledge, and the unphilosophical folly of trying to round off into finished and pretentious schemes our fragmentary yet certain notices of our own condition and of God's dealing with it.

He alarmed Archer Gurney by saying that all hope of an understanding is at an end, if logic be applied for the rectification of dogma, and to Dr. Plummer, who acknowledged him as the most capable of modern theologians and historians, he spoke of the hopelessness of trying to discover the meaning of terms used in definitions. To his archbishop he wrote that men may discuss the mysteries of faith to the last day without avail; "we stand here on the solid ground of history, evidence, and fact." Expressing his innermost thought, that religion exists to make men better, and that the ethical quality of dogma constitutes its value, he once said: "Tantum valet quantum ad corrigendum, purgandum, sanctificandum hominem confert." In theology as an intellectual exercise, beyond its action on the soul, he felt less interest, and those disputes most satisfied him which can be decided by appeal to the historian.

From his early reputation and his position at the outpost, confronting Protestant science, he was expected to make up his mind over a large area of unsettled thought and disputed fact, and to be provided with an opinion—a freehold opinion of his own—and a reasoned answer to every difficulty. People had a right to know what he knew about the end of the sixteenth chapter of St. Mark, and the beginning of the eighth chapter of St. John, the lives of St. Patrick and the sources of Erigena, the author of the *Imitation* and of the *Twelve Articles*, the *Nag's Head* and the *Casket Letters*. The suspense and poise of the mind, which is the pride and privilege of the unprofessional scholar, was forbidden him. Students could not wait for the master to complete his studies; they flocked for dry light of knowledge, for something defined and final, to their keen, grave, unemotional professor, who said sometimes more than he could be sure of, but who was not likely to abridge thought by oracular responses, or to give aphorism for argument. He accepted the necessity of the situation. A time came when everybody was invited, once a week, to put any imaginable question from the whole of Church history, and he at once replied. If this was a stimulus to exertion during the years spent in mastering and pondering the immense materials, it served less to promote originality and care than premature certitude and the craving for quick returns. Apart from the constant duty of teaching, his knowledge might not have been so extensive, but his views would have been less decided and therefore less liable to change.

As an historian, Döllinger regarded Christianity as a force more than as a doctrine, and displayed it as it expanded and became the soul of later history. It was the mission and occupation of his life to discover and to disclose how this was accomplished, and to understand the history of civilised Europe, religious and profane, mental and political, by the aid of sources which, being original and authentic, yielded certainty. In his vigorous prime, he thought that it would be within his powers to complete the narrative of the conquest of the world by Christ in a single massive work. The separated churches, the centrifugal forces, were to have been treated apart, until he adopted the ampler title of a history of Christianity. We who look back upon all that the combined and divided labour of a thousand earnest, gifted, and often instructed men has done and left undone in sixty years, can estimate the scientific level of an age where such a dream could be dreamed by such a man, misled neither by imagination nor ambition, but knowing his own limitations and the immeasurable world of books. Experience slowly taught him that he who takes all history for his province is not the man to write a compendium.

The four volumes of *Church History* which gave him a name in literature appeared between 1833 and 1838, and stopped short of the Reformation. In writing mainly for the horizon of seminaries, it was desirable to eschew voyages of discovery and the pathless border-land. The materials were all in print, and were the daily bread of scholars. A celebrated Anglican described Döllinger at that time as more intentional than Fleury; while Catholics objected that he was a candid friend; and Lutherans, probing deeper, observed that he resolutely held his ground wherever he could, and as resolutely abandoned every position that he found untenable. He has since said of himself that he always spoke sincerely, but that he spoke as an advocate—a sincere advocate who pleaded only for a cause which he had convinced himself was just. The cause he pleaded was the divine government of the Church, the fulfilment of the promise that it would be preserved from error, though not from sin, the uninterrupted employment of the powers committed by Christ for the salvation of man. By the absence of false arts he acquired that repute for superior integrity which caused a Tyrolese divine to speak of him as the most chivalrous of the Catholic celebrities; and the nuncio who was at Munich during the first ten years called him the "professeur le plus éclairé, le plus religieux, en un mot le plus distingué de l'université."

Taking his survey from the elevation of general history, he gives less space to all the early heresies together than to the rise of Mohammedanism. His way lies between Neander, who cares for no institutions, and Baur, who cares for no individuals. He was entirely exempt from that impersonal idealism which Sybel laid down at the foundation of his review, which causes Delbrück to complain that Macaulay, who could see facts so well, could not see that they are revelations, which Baur defines without disguise in his *Dreieinigkeitslehre*: "Alle geschichtlichen Personen sind für uns blosse Namen." The two posthumous works of Hegel which turned events into theories had not then appeared. Döllinger, setting life and action above theory, omitted the progress of doctrine. He proposed that Möhler should take that share of their common topic, and the plan, entertained at first, was interrupted, with much besides, by death. He felt too deeply the overwhelming unity of force to yield to that atomic theory which was provoked by the Hegelian excess: "L'histoire n'est pas un simple jeu d'abstractions, et les hommes y sont plus que les doctrines. Ce n'est pas une certaine théorie sur la justification et la rédemption qui a fait la Réforme: c'est Luther, c'est Calvin." But he allows a vast scope to the variable will and character of man. The object of religion upon earth is saintliness, and its success is shown in holy individuals. He leaves law and doctrine, moving in their appointed orbits, to hold up great men and examples of Christian virtue.

Döllinger, who had in youth acted as secretary to Hohenlohe, was always reserved in his use of the supernatural. In the vision of Constantine and the rebuilding of the temple, he gives his reader both the natural explanation and the miraculous. He thought that the witness of the fathers to the continuance of miraculous powers could not be resisted without making history *a priori*, but later on, the more he sifted and compared authorities, the more severe he became. He deplored the uncritical credulity of the author of the *Monks of the West*; and, in examining the Stigmata, he cited the experience of a Spanish convent where they were so common that it became a sign of reprobation to be without them. Historians, he said, have to look for natural causes: enough will remain for the action of Providence, where we cannot penetrate. In his unfinished book on *Ecclesiastical Prophecy* he enumerates the illusions of mediæval saints when they spoke of the future, and describes them, as he once described Carlyle and Ruskin, as prophets having nothing to foretell. At Frankfort, where he spoilt his watch by depositing it in unexpected holy water, and it was whispered that he had put it there to mend it, everybody knew that there was hardly a Catholic in the Parliament of whom such a fable could be told with more felicitous unfitness.

For twenty years of his life at Munich, Görres was the impressive central figure of a group reputed far and wide, the most intellectual force in the Catholic world. Seeing things by the light of other days, Nippold and Maurenbrecher describe Döllinger himself as its most eminent member. There was present gain and future peril in living amongst a clever but restricted set, sheltered, supported, and restrained by friends who were united in aims and studies, who cherished their sympathies and their enmities in common, and who therefore believed that they were divided by no deep cleft or ultimate principle. Döllinger never outlived the glamour of the eloquence and ascendancy of Görres, and spoke of him long after his death as a man of real knowledge, and of greater religious than political insight. Between the imaginative rhetorician and the measured, scrutinising scholar, the contrast was wide. One of the many pupils and rare disciples of the former complained that his friend supplied interminable matter for the sterile and unavailing *Mystik*, in order to amuse him with ropes of sand: and the severest censure of Döllinger's art as an historian was pronounced by Görres when he said, "I always see analogies, and you always see differences."

At all times, but in his early studies especially, he owed much to the Italians, whose ecclesiastical literature was the first that he mastered, and predominates in his Church history. Several of his countrymen, such as Savigny and Raumer, had composed history on the shoulders of Bolognese and Lombard scholars, and some of their most conspicuous successors to the present day have lived under heavy obligations to Modena and San

Marino. During the tranquil century before the Revolution, Italians studied the history of their country with diligence and success. Even such places as Parma, Verona, Brescia, became centres of obscure but faithful work. Osimo possessed annals as bulky as Rome. The story of the province of Treviso was told in twenty volumes. The antiquities of Picenum filled thirty-two folios. The best of all this national and municipal patriotism was given to the service of religion. Popes and cardinals, dioceses and parish churches became the theme of untiring enthusiasts. There too were the stupendous records of the religious orders, their bulls and charters, their biography and their bibliography. In this immense world of patient, accurate, devoted research, Döllinger laid the deep foundations of his historical knowledge. Beginning like everybody with Baronius and Muratori, he gave a large portion of his life to Noris, and to the solid and enlightened scholarship that surrounded Benedict XIV., down to the compilers, Borgia, Fantuzzi, Marini, with whom, in the evil days of regeneration by the French, the grand tradition died away. He has put on record his judgment that Orsi and Saccarelli were the best writers on the general history of the Church. Afterwards, when other layers had been superposed, and the course he took was his own, he relied much on the canonists, Ballerini and Berardi; and he commended Bianchi, De Bennettis, and the author of the anonymous *Confutazione*, as the strongest Roman antidote to Blondel, Buckeridge, and Barrow. Italy possessed the largest extant body of Catholic learning; the whole sphere of Church government was within its range, and it enjoyed something of the official prerogative.

Next to the Italians he gave systematic attention to the French. The conspicuous Gallicans, the Jansenists, from whom at last he derived much support, Richer, Van Espen, Launoy, whom he regarded as the original of Bossuet, Arnauld, whom he thought his superior, are absent from his pages. He never overcame his distrust of Pascal, for his methodical scepticism and his endeavour to dissociate religion from learning; and he rated high Daniel's reply to the *Provinciales.* He esteemed still more the French Protestants of the seventeenth century, who transformed the system of Geneva and Dort. English theology did not come much in his way until he had made himself at home with the Italians and the primary French. Then it abounded. He gathered it in quantities on two journeys in 1851 and 1858, and he possessed the English divines in perfection, at least down to Whitby, and the nonjurors. Early acquaintance with Sir Edward Vavasour and Lord Clifford had planted a lasting prejudice in favour of the English Catholic families, which sometimes tinged his judgments. The neglected literature of the Catholics in England held a place in his scheme of thought, which it never obtained in the eyes of any other scholar, native or foreign. This was the only considerable school of divines who wrote under persecution, and were reduced to an attitude of defence. In conflict with the most learned, intelligent, and conciliatory of controversialists, they developed a remarkable spirit of moderation, discriminating inferior elements from the original and genuine growth of Catholic roots; and their several declarations and manifestoes, from the Restoration onwards, were an inexhaustible supply for irenics. Therefore they powerfully attracted one who took the words of St. Vincent of Lérins not merely for a flash of illumination, but for a scientific formula and guiding principle. Few writers interested him more deeply than Stapleton, Davenport, who anticipated Number XC., Irishmen, such as Caron and Walshe, and the Scots, Barclay, the adversary and friend of Bellarmine, Ramsay, the convert and recorder of Fénelon. It may be that, to an intellect trained in the historic process, stability, continuity, and growth were terms of more vivid and exact significance than to the doctors of Pont-à-Mousson and Lambspring. But when he came forward arrayed in the spoils of Italian libraries and German universities, with the erudition of centuries and the criticism of to-day, he sometimes was content to follow where forgotten Benedictines or Franciscans had preceded, under the later Stuarts.

He seldom quotes contemporary Germans, unless to dispute with them, prefers old books to new, and speaks of the necessary revision and renovation of history. He suspected imported views and foregone conclusions even in Neander; and although he could not say, with Macaulay, that Gieseler was a rascal, of whom he had never heard, he missed no opportunity of showing his dislike for that accomplished artificer in mosaic. Looking at the literature before him, at England, with Gibbon for its one ecclesiastical historian; at Germany, with the most profound of its divines expecting the Church to merge in the State, he inferred that its historic and organic unity would only be recognised by Catholic science, while the soundest Protestant would understand it least. In later years, Kliefoth, Ritschl, Gass, perhaps also Dorner and Uhlhorn, obliged him to modify an opinion which the entire school of Schleiermacher, including the illustrious Rothe, served only to confirm. Germany, as he found it when he began to see the world, little resembled that of his old age, when the work he had pursued for seventy years was carried forward, with knowledge and power like his own, by the best of his countrymen. The proportion of things was changed. There was a religious literature to be proud of, to rely on: other nations, other epochs, had lost their superiority. As his own people advanced, and dominated in the branches of learning to which his life was given, in everything except literary history and epigraphics, and there was no more need to look abroad, Döllinger's cosmopolitan characteristic diminished, he was more absorbed in the national thought and work, and did not object to be called the most German of the Germans.

The idea that religious science is not so much science as religion, that it should be treated differently from other matters, so that he who treats it may rightly display his soul, flourished in his vicinity, inspiring the lives of Saint Elizabeth and Joan of Arc, Möhler's fine lectures on the early fathers, and the book which Gratry chose to entitle a *Commentary on St. Matthew*. Döllinger came early to the belief that history ought to be impersonal, that the historian does well to keep out of the way, to be humble and self-denying, making it a religious duty to prevent the intrusion of all that betrays his own position and quality, his hopes and wishes. Without aspiring to the calm indifference of Ranke, he was conscious that, in early life, he had been too positive, and too eager to persuade. The Belgian scholar who, conversing with him in 1842, was reminded of Fénelon, missed the acuter angles of his character. He, who in private intercourse sometimes allowed himself to persist, to contradict, and even to baffle a bore by frankly falling asleep, would have declined the evocation of Versailles. But in reasonableness, moderation, and charity, in general culture of mind and the sense of the demands of the progress of civilisation, in the ideal church for which he lived, he was more in harmony with Fénelon than with many others who resembled him in the character of their work.

He deemed it catholic to take ideas from history, and heresy to take them into it. When men gave evidence for the opposite party, and against their own, he willingly took for impartiality what he could not always distinguish from indifference or subdivision. He felt that sincere history was the royal road to religious union, and he specially cultivated those who saw both sides. He would cite with complacency what clever Jesuits, Raynaud and Faure, said for the Reformation, Mariana and Cordara against their society. When a Rhenish Catholic and a Genevese Calvinist drew two portraits of Calvin which were virtually the same, or when, in Ficker's revision of Böhmer, the Catholic defended the Emperor Frederic II. against the Protestant, he rejoiced as over a sign of the advent of science. As the Middle Ages, rescued from polemics by the genial and uncritical sympathy of Müller, became an object of popular study, and Royer Collard said of Villemain, *Il a fait, il fait, et il fera toujours son Grégoire VII.*, there were Catholics who desired, by a prolonged *sorites*, to derive advantage from the new spirit. Wiseman consulted Döllinger for the purpose. "Will you be kind enough to write me a list of what you consider the best books for the history of the Reformation; Menzel and Buchholz I know; especially any exposing the characters of the leading reformers?" In the same frame of mind he asked him what pope there was whose good name had not been vindicated; and Döllinger's reply, that Boniface VIII. wanted a friend, prompted both Wiseman's article and Tosti's book.

In politics, as in religion, he made the past a law for the present, and resisted doctrines which are ready-made, and are not derived from experience. Consequently, he undervalued work which would never have been done from disinterested motives; and there were three of his most eminent contemporaries whom he decidedly underestimated. Having known Thiers, and heard him speak, he felt profoundly the talent of the extraordinary man, before Lanfrey or Taine, Häusser and Bernhardi had so ruined his credit among Germans that Döllinger, disgusted by his advocacy, whether of the Revolution, of Napoleon, or of France, neglected his work. Stahl claims to be accounted an historian by his incomparably able book on the Church government of the Reformation. As a professor at Munich, and afterwards as a parliamentary leader at Berlin, he was always an avowed partisan. Döllinger depreciated him accordingly, and he had the mortification that certain remarks on the sovereign dialectician of European conservatism were on the point of appearing when he died. He so far made it good in his preface that the thing was forgotten when Gerlach came to see the assailant of his friend. But once, when I spoke of Stahl as the greatest man born of a Jewish mother since Titus, he thought me unjust to Disraeli.

Most of all, he misjudged Macaulay, whose German admirers are not always in the higher ranks of literature, and of whom Ranke even said that he could hardly be called an historian at all, tried by the stricter test. He had no doubt seen how his unsuggestive fixity and assurance could cramp and close a mind; and he felt more beholden to the rivals who produced d'Adda, Barillon, and Bonnet, than to the author of so many pictures and so much bootless decoration. He tendered a course of Bacon's Essays, or of Butler's and Newman's Sermons, as a preservative against intemperate dogmatism. He denounced Macaulay's indifference to the merits of the inferior cause, and desired more generous treatment of the Jacobites and the French king. He deemed it hard that a science happily delivered from the toils of religious passion should be involved in political, and made to pass from the sacristy to the lobby, by the most brilliant example in literature. To the objection that one who celebrates the victory of parliaments over monarchs, of democracy over aristocracy, of liberty over authority, declares, not the tenets of a party, but manifest destiny and the irrevocable decree, he would reply that a narrow induction is the bane of philosophy, that the ways of Providence are not inscribed on the surface of things, that religion, socialism, militarism, and revolution possibly reserve a store of cogent surprises for the economist, utilitarian, and whig.

In 1865 he was invited to prepare a new edition of his Church history. Whilst he was mustering the close ranks of folios which had satisfied a century of historians, the world had moved, and there was an increase of raw material to be measured by thousands of volumes. The archives which had been sealed with seven seals had become as necessary to the serious student as his library. Every part of his studies had suffered transformation, except the fathers, who had largely escaped the crucible, and the canon law, which had only just been caught by the historical current. He had begun when Niebuhr was lecturing at Bonn and Hegel at Berlin; before Tischendorf unfolded his first manuscript; before Baur discovered the Tübingen hypothesis in the congregation of Corinth; before Rothe had planned his treatise on the primitive church, or Ranke had begun to pluck the plums for his modern popes. Guizot had not founded the *École des Chartes*, and the school of method was not yet opened at Berlin. The application of instruments of precision was just beginning, and what Prynne calls the heroic study of records had scarcely molested the ancient reign of lives and chronicles. None had worked harder at his science and at himself than Döllinger; and the change around him was not greater than the change within. In his early career as a teacher of religion he had often shrunk from books which bore no stamp of orthodoxy. It was long before he read Sarpi or the *Lettres Provinciales*, or even Ranke's *Popes*, which appeared when he was thirty-five, and which astonished him by the serene ease with which a man who knew so much touched on such delicate ground. The book which he had written in that state of mind, and with that conception of science and religion, had only a prehistoric interest for its author. He refused to reprint it, and declared that there was hardly a sentence fit to stand unchanged. He lamented that he had lost ten years of life in getting his bearings, and in learning, unaided, the most difficult craft in the world. Those years of apprenticeship without a master were the time spent on his *Kirchengeschichte*. The want of training remained. He could impart knowledge better than the art of learning. Thousands of his pupils have acquired connected views of religion passing through the ages, and gathered, if they were intelligent, some notion of the meaning of history; but nobody ever learnt from him the mechanism by which it is written.

Brougham advised the law-student to begin with Dante; and a distinguished physician informs us that Gibbon, Grote, and Mill made him what he is. The men to whom Döllinger owed his historic insight and who mainly helped to develop and strengthen and direct his special faculty, were not all of his own cast, or remarkable in the common description of literary talent. The assistants were countless, but the masters were few, and he looked up with extraordinary gratitude to men like Sigonius, Antonius Augustinus, Blondel, Petavius, Leibniz, Burke, and Niebuhr, who had opened the passes for him as he struggled and groped in the illimitable forest.

He interrupted his work because he found the materials too scanty for the later Middle Ages, and too copious for the Reformation. The defective account of the Albigensian theology, which he had sent to one of his translators, never appeared in German. At Paris he searched the library for the missing information, and he asked Rességuier to make inquiry for the records of the Inquisition in Languedoc, thus laying the foundations of that *Sektengeschichte* which he published fifty years later. Munich offered such inexhaustible supplies for the Reformation that his collections overran all bounds. He completed only that part of his plan which included Lutheranism and the sixteenth century. The third volume, published in 1848, containing the theology of the Reformation, is the most solid of his writings. He had miscalculated, not his resources, of which only a part had come into action, but the possibilities of concentration and compression. The book was left a fragment when he had to abandon his study for the Frankfort barricades.

The peculiarity of his treatment is that he contracts the Reformation into a history of the doctrine of justification. He found that this and this alone was the essential point in Luther's mind, that he made it the basis of his argument, the motive of his separation, the root and principle of his religion. He believed that Luther was right in the cardinal importance he attributed to this doctrine in his system, and he in his turn recognised that it was the cause of all that followed, the source of the reformer's popularity and success, the sole insurmountable obstacle to every scheme of restoration. It was also, for him, the centre and the basis of his antagonism. That was the point that he attacked when he combated Protestantism, and he held all other elements of conflict cheap in comparison, deeming that they are not invariable, or not incurable, or not supremely serious. Apart from this, there was much in Protestantism that he admired, much in its effects for which he was grateful. With the Lutheran view of imputation, Protestant and Catholic were separated by an abyss. Without it, there was no lasting reason why they should be separate at all. Against the communities that hold it he stood in order of battle, and believed that he could scarcely hit too hard. But he distinguished very broadly the religion of the reformers from the religion of Protestants. Theological science had moved away from the symbolical books, the root dogma had been repudiated and contested by the most eminent Protestants, and it was an English bishop who wrote: "Fuit haec doctrina jam a multis annis ipsissimum Reformatae Ecclesiae opprobrium ac dedecus.—Est error non levis, error putidissimus." Since so many of the best writers resist or modify that which was the main cause, the sole ultimate cause, of disunion, it cannot be logically impossible to discover a reasonable basis for discussion. Therefore conciliation was always in his thoughts; even his *Reformation* was a treatise on the conditions of reunion. He long purposed to continue it, in narrower limits, as a history of that central doctrine by which Luther meant his church to stand or fall, of the reaction against it, and of its decline. In 1881, when Ritschl, the author of the chief work upon the subject, spent some days with Döllinger, he found him still full of these ideas, and possessing Luther at his fingers' ends.

This is the reason why Protestants have found him so earnest an opponent and so warm a friend. It was this that attracted him towards Anglicans, and made very many of them admire a Roman dignitary who knew the Anglo-Catholic library better than De Lugo or Ripalda. In the same spirit he said to Pusey: "Tales cum sitis jam nostri estis," always spoke of Newman's *Justification* as the greatest masterpiece of theology that England has produced in a hundred years, and described Baxter and Wesley as the most eminent of English Protestants—meaning Wesley as he was after 1st December 1767, and Baxter as the life-long opponent of that theory which was the source and the soul of the Reformation. Several Englishmen who went to consult him—Hope Scott and Archdeacon Wilberforce—became Catholics. I know not whether he urged them. Others there were, whom he did not urge, though his influence over them might have been decisive. In a later letter to Pusey he wrote: "I am convinced by reading your *Eirenicon* that we are united inwardly in our religious convictions, although externally we belong to two separated churches." He followed attentively the parallel movements that went on in his own country, and welcomed with serious respect the overtures which came to him, after 1856, from eminent historians. When they were old men, he and Ranke, whom, in hot youth, there was much to part, lived on terms of mutual goodwill. Döllinger had pronounced the theology of the *Deutsche Reformation* slack and trivial, and Ranke at one moment was offended by what he took for an attack on the popes, his patrimony. In 1865, after a visit to Munich, he allowed that in religion there was no dispute between them, that he had no fault to find with the Church as Döllinger understood it. He added that one of his colleagues, a divine whose learning filled him with unwonted awe, held the same opinion. Döllinger's growing belief that an approximation of part of Germany to sentiments of conciliation was only a question of time, had much to do with his attitude in Church questions after the year 1860. If history cannot confer faith or virtue, it can clear away the misconceptions and misunderstandings that turn men against one another. With the progress of incessant study and meditation his judgment on many points underwent revision; but with regard to the Reformation the change was less than he supposed. He learnt to think more favourably of the religious influence of Protestantism, and of its efficacy in the defence of Christianity; but he thought as before of the spiritual consequences of Lutheranism proper. When people said of Luther that he does not come well out of his matrimonial advice to certain potentates, to Henry and to Philip, of his exhortations to exterminate the revolted peasantry, of his passage from a confessor of toleration to a teacher of intolerance, he would not have the most powerful conductor of religion that Christianity has produced in eighteen centuries condemned for two pages in a hundred volumes. But when he had refused the test of the weakest link, judging the man by his totals, he was not less severe on his theological ethics.

Meinerseits habe ich noch eine andre schwere Anklage gegen ihn zu erheben, nämlich die, dass er durch seine falsche Imputationslehre das sittlich-religiöse Bewusstseyn der Menschen auf zwei Jahrhunderte hinaus verwirrt und corrumpirt hat (3rd July 1888).

The revolution of 1848, during which he did not hold his professorship, brought him forward uncongenially in active public life, and gave him the means of telling the world his view of the constitution and policy of the Church, and the sense and limits of liability in which he gave his advocacy. When lecturing on canon law he was accustomed to dwell on the strict limit of all ecclesiastical authority, admitting none but spiritual powers, and invoking the maxims of pontiffs who professed themselves guardians, not masters, of the established legislation—"Canones ecclesiae solvere non possumus, qui custodes canonum sumus." Acting on these principles, in the Paulskirche, and at Ratisbon, he vindicated Rome against the reproach of oppression, argued that society can only gain by the emancipation of the Church, as it claims no superiority over the State, and that both Gallicans and Jesuits are out of date. Addressing the bishops of Germany in secret session at Würzburg, he exhorted them to avail themselves fully of an order of things which was better than the old, and to make no professions of unconditional allegiance. He told them that freedom is the breath of the Catholic life, that it belongs to the Church of God by right divine, and that whatever they claimed must be claimed for others.

From these discourses, in which the scholar abandoned the details by which science advances for the general principles of the popular orator, the deductions of liberalism proceed as surely as the revolution from the title-page of Sieyès. It should seem that the key to his career lies there. It was natural to associate him with the men whom the early promise of a reforming pope inspired to identify the cause of free societies with the papacy which had Rosmini for an adviser, Ventura for a preacher,

Gioberti for a prophet, and to conclude that he thus became a trusted representative, until the revolving years found him the champion of a vanished cause, and the Syllabus exposed the illusion and bore away his ideal. Harless once said of him that no good could be expected from a man surrounded by a ring of liberals. When Döllinger made persecution answer both for the decline of Spain and the fall of Poland, he appeared to deliver the common creed of Whigs; and he did not protest against the American who called him the acknowledged head of the liberal Catholics. His hopefulness in the midst of the movement of 1848, his ready acquiescence in the fall of ancient powers and institutions, his trust in Rome, and in the abstract rights of Germans, suggested a reminiscence of the *Avenir* in 1830.

Lamennais, returning with Montalembert after his appeal to Rome, met Lacordaire at Munich, and during a banquet given in their honour he learnt, privately, that he was condemned. The three friends spent that afternoon in Döllinger's company; and it was after he had left them that Lamennais produced the encyclical and said: *Dieu a parlé*. Montalembert soon returned, attracted as much by Munich art as by religion or literature. The fame of the Bavarian school of Catholic thought spread in France among those who belonged to the wider circles of the *Avenir*; and priests and laymen followed, as to a scientific shrine. In the *Mémoires d'un Royaliste* Falloux has preserved, with local colour, the spirit of that pilgrimage:

> Munich lui fut indiqué comme le foyer d'une grande rénovation religieuse et artistique. Quels nobles et ardents entretiens, quelle passion pour l'Eglise et pour sa cause! Rien n'a plus ressemblé aux discours d'un portique chrétien que les apologies enflammées du vieux Görres, les savantes déductions de Döllinger, la verve originale de Brentano.

Rio, who was the earliest of the travellers, describes Döllinger as he found him in 1830:

> Par un privilège dont il serait difficile de citer un autre exemple,

il avait la passion des études théologiques comme s'il n'avait été que prêtre, et la passion des études littéraires appliquées aux auteurs anciens et modernes comme s'il n'avait été que littérateur ; à quoi il faut ajouter un autre don qu'il y aurait ingratitude à oublier, celui d'une exposition lucide, patiente et presque affectueuse, comme s'il n'avait accumulé tant de connaissances que pour avoir le plaisir de les communiquer.

For forty years he remained in correspondence with many of these early friends, who, in the educational struggle which ended with the ministry of Falloux in 1850, revived the leading maxims of the rejected master. As Lacordaire said, on his deathbed: "La parole de l'Avenir avait germé de son tombeau comme une cendre féconde." Döllinger used to visit his former visitors in various parts of France, and at Paris he attended the salon of Madame Swetchine. One day, at the seminary, he inquired who were the most promising students ; Dupanloup pointed out a youth, who was the hope of the Church, and whose name was Ernest Renan.

Although the men who were drawn to him in this way formed the largest and best-defined cluster with which he came in contact, there was more private friendship than mutual action or consultation between them. The unimpassioned German, who had no taste for ideas released from controlling fact, took little pleasure in the impetuous declamation of the Breton, and afterwards pronounced him inferior to Loyson. Neither of the men who were in the confidence of both has intimated that he made any lasting impression on Lamennais, who took leave of him without discussing the action of Rome. Döllinger never sought to renew acquaintance with Lacordaire, when he had become the most important man in the church of France. He would have a prejudice to overcome against him whom Circourt called the most ignorant man in the Academy, who believed that Erasmus ended his days at Rotterdam, unable to choose between Rome and Wittemberg, and that the Irish obtained through O'Connell the right to worship in their own way. He saw more of Dupanloup, without feeling, as deeply as Renan, the rare charm of the combative prelate. To an exacting and reflective scholar, to whom even the large volume of heavy erudition in which Rosmini defended the *Cinque Piaghe* seemed superficial, there was incongruity in the attention paid to one of whom he heard that he promoted the council, that he took St. Boniface for St. Wilfrid, and that he gave the memorable advice: *Surtout méfiez-vous des sources.* After a visit from the Bishop of Orleans he sat down in dismay to compose the most elementary of his books. Seeing the inferiority of Falloux as a historian, he never appreciated the strong will and cool brain of the statesman who overawed Tocqueville. Eckstein, the obscure but thoughtful originator of much liberal feeling among his own set, encouraged him in the habit of depreciating the attainments of the French clergy, which was confirmed by the writings of the most eminent among them, Darboy, and lasted until the appearance of Duchesne. The politics of Montalembert were so heavily charged with conservatism, that in defiance of such advisers as Lacordaire, Ravignan, and Dupanloup, he pronounced in favour of the author of the *coup d'état*, saying: "Je suis pour l'autorité contre la révolte"; and boasted that, in entering the Academy he had attacked the Revolution, not of '93 but '89, and that Guizot, who received him, had nothing to say in reply. There were many things, human and divine, on which they could not feel alike; but as the most urgent, eloquent, and persevering of his Catholic friends, gifted with knowledge and experience of affairs, and dwelling in the focus, it may be that on one critical occasion, when religion and politics intermingled, he influenced the working of Döllinger's mind. But the plausible reading of his life which explains it by his connection with such public men as Montalembert, De Decker, and Mr. Gladstone is profoundly untrue; and those who deem him a liberal in any scientific use of the term, miss the keynote of his work.

The political party question has to be considered here, because, in fact, it is decisive. A liberal who thinks his thought out to the end without flinching is forced to certain conclusions which colour to the root every phase and scene of universal history. He believes in upward progress, because it is only recent times that have striven deliberately, and with a zeal according to knowledge, for the increase and security of freedom. He is not only tolerant of error in religion, but is specially indulgent to the less dogmatic forms of Christianity, to the sects which have restrained the churches. He is austere in judging the past, imputing not error and ignorance only, but guilt and crime, to those who, in the dark succession of ages, have resisted and retarded the growth of liberty, which he identifies with the cause of morality, and the condition of the reign of conscience. Döllinger never subjected his mighty vision of the stream of time to correction according to the principles of this unsympathising philosophy, never reconstituted the providential economy in agreement with the Whig Théodicée. He could understand the Zoroastrian simplicity of history in black and white, for he wrote: "obgleich man allerdings sagen kann, das tiefste Thema der Weltgeschichte sei der Kampf der Knechtschaft oder Gebundenheit, mit der Freiheit, auf dem intellectuellen, religiösen, politischen und socialen Gebiet." But the scene which lay open before his mind was one of greater complexity, deeper design, and infinite intellect. He imagined a way to truth through error, and outside the Church, not through unbelief and the diminished reign of Christ. Lacordaire in the cathedral pulpit offering his thanks to Voltaire for the good gift of religious toleration, was a figure alien to his spirit. He never substituted politics for religion as the test of progress, and never admitted that they have anything like the dogmatic certainty and sovereignty of religious, or of physical, science. He had all the liberality that consists of common sense, justice, humanity, enlightenment, the wisdom of Canning or Guizot. But revolution, as the breach of continuity, as the renunciation of history, was odious to him, and he not only refused to see method in the madness of Marat, or dignity in the end of Robespierre, but believed that the best measures of Leopold, the most intelligent reformer in the era of repentant monarchy, were vitiated and frustrated by want of adaptation to custom. Common party divisions represented nothing scientific to his mind, and he was willing, like De Quincey, to accept them as corresponding halves of a necessary whole. He wished that he knew half as much as his neighbour, Mrs. Somerville; but he possessed no natural philosophy, and never acquired the emancipating habit which comes from a life spent in securing progress by shutting one's eyes to the past. "Alle Wissenschaft steht und ruht auf ihrer historischen Entwicklung, sie lebt von ihrer traditionellen Vergangenheit, wie der Baum von seiner Wurzel."

He was moved, not by the gleam of reform after the conclave of Pius IX., but by Pius VII. The impression made upon him by the character of that pope, and his resistance to Napoleon, had much to do with his resolution to become a priest. He took orders in the Church in the days of revival, as it issued from oppression and the eclipse of hierarchy; and he entered its service in the spirit of Sailer, Cheverus, and Doyle. The mark of that time never left him. When Newman asked him what he would say of the Pope's journey to Paris, for the coronation of the emperor, he hardly recognised the point of the question. He opposed, in 1853, the renewal of that precedent; but to the end he never felt what people mean when they remark on the proximity of Notre-Dame to Vincennes.

Döllinger was too much absorbed in distant events to be always a close observer of what went on near him; and he was, therefore, not so much influenced by contact with contemporary history as men who were less entirely at home in other centuries. He knew about all that could be known of the ninth: in the nineteenth his superiority deserted him. Though he informed himself assiduously his thoughts were not there. He collected from Hormayr, Radowitz, Capponi, much secret matter of the last generation; and where Brewer had told him about Oxford, and Plantier about Louis Philippe, there were landmarks, as when Knoblecher, the missionary, set down

Krophi and Mophi on his map of Africa. He deferred, at once, to the competent authority. He consulted his able colleague Hermann on all points of political economy, and used his advice when he wrote about England. Having satisfied himself, he would not reopen these questions, when, after Hermann's death, he spent some time in the society of Roscher, a not less eminent economist, and of all men the one who most resembled himself in the historian's faculty of rethinking the thoughts and realising the knowledge, the ignorance, the experience, the illusions of a given time.

He had lived in many cities, and had known many important men; he had sat in three parliamentary assemblies, had drawn constitutional amendments, had been consulted upon the policy and the making of ministries, and had declined political office; but as an authority on recent history he was scarcely equal to himself. Once it became his duty to sketch the character of a prince whom he had known. There was a report that this sovereign had only been dissuaded from changing his religion and abolishing the constitution by the advice of an archbishop and of a famous parliamentary jurist; and the point of the story was that the Protestant doctrinaire had prevented the change of religion, and the archbishop had preserved the constitution. It was too early to elucidate these court mysteries; instead of which there is a remarkable conversation about religion, wherein it is not always clear whether the prince is speaking, or the professor, or Schelling.

Although he had been translated into several languages and was widely known in his own country, he had not yet built himself a European name. At Oxford, in 1851, when James Mozley asked whom he would like to see, he said, the men who had written in the *Christian Remembrancer* on Dante and Luther. Mozley was himself one of the two, and he introduced him to the other at Oriel. After thirty-two years, when the writer on Dante occupied a high position in the Church and had narrowly escaped the highest, that visit was returned. But he had no idea that he had once received Döllinger in his college rooms and hardly believed it when told. In Germany, the serried learning of the *Reformation*, the author's energy and decisiveness in public assemblies, caused him to stand forth as an accepted spokesman, and, for a season, threw back the reticent explorer, steering between the shallows of anger and affection.

In that stage the *Philosophumena* found him, and induced him to write a book of controversy in the shape of history. Here was an anonymous person who, as Newman described it, "calls one pope a weak and venal dunce, and another a sacrilegious swindler, an infamous convict, and an heresiarch *ex cathedrâ*." In the Munich Faculty there was a divine who affirmed that the Church would never get over it. Döllinger undertook to vindicate the insulted See of Rome; and he was glad of the opportunity to strike a blow at three conspicuous men of whom he thought ill in point both of science and religion. He spoke of Gieseler as the flattest and most leathern of historians; he accused Baur of frivolity and want of theological conviction; and he wished that he knew as many circumlocutions for untruth as there are Arabian synonyms for a camel, that he might do justice to Bunsen without violation of courtesy. The weight of the new testimony depended on the discovery of the author. Adversaries had assigned it to Hippolytus, the foremost European writer of the time, venerated as a saint and a father of the Church. Döllinger thought them right, and he justified his sincerity by giving further reasons for a conclusion which made his task formidable even for such dexterity as his own. Having thus made a concession which was not absolutely inevitable, he resisted the inference with such richness of illustration that the fears of the doubting colleague were appeased. In France, by Pitra's influence, the book was reviewed without making known that it supported the authorship of Hippolytus, which is still disputed by some impartial critics, and was always rejected by Newman. *Hippolytus und Kallistus*, the high-water mark of Döllinger's official assent and concurrence, came out in 1853. His next book showed the ebb.

He came originally from the romantic school, where history was honeycombed with imagination and conjecture; and the first important book he gave to a pupil in 1850 was Creuzer's *Mythology*. In 1845 he denounced the rationalism of Lobeck in investigating the *Mysteries*; but in 1857 he preferred him as a guide to those who proceed by analogy. With increase of knowledge had come increase of restraining caution and sagacity. The critical acumen was not greater in the *Vorhalle* that when he wrote on the *Philosophumena*, but instead of being employed in a chosen cause, upon fixed lines, for welcome ends, it is applied impartially. Ernst von Lasaulx, a man of rich and noble intellect, was lecturing next door on the philosophy and religion of Greece, and everybody heard about his indistinct mixture of dates and authorities, and the spell which his unchastened idealism cast over students. Lasaulx, who brilliantly carried on the tradition of Creuzer, who had tasted of the mythology of Schelling, who was son-in-law to Baader and nephew to Görres, wrote a volume on the fall of Hellenism which he brought in manuscript and read to Döllinger at a sitting. The effect on the dissenting mind of the hearer was a warning; and there is reason to date from those two hours in 1853 a more severe use of materials, and a stricter notion of the influence which the end of an inquiry may lawfully exert on the pursuit of it.

Heidenthum und Judenthum, which came out in 1857, gave Lasaulx his revenge. It is the most positive and self-denying of histories, and owes nothing to the fancy. The author refused the aid of Scandinavia to illustrate German mythology, and he was rewarded long after, when Caspari of Christiania and Conrad Maurer met at his table and confirmed the discoveries of Bugge. But the account of Paganism ends with a significant parallel. In December 69 a torch flung by a soldier burnt the temple on the Capitol to the ground. In August 70 another Roman soldier set fire to the temple on Mount

Sion. The two sanctuaries perished within a year making way for the faith of men still hidden in the back streets of Rome. When the Hellenist read this passage it struck him deeply. Then he declared that it was hollow. All was over at Jerusalem; but at Rome the ruin was restored, and the smoke of sacrifice went up for centuries to come from the altar of Capitoline Jove.

In this work, designed as an introduction to Christian history, the apologist betrays himself when he says that no Greek ever objected to slavery, and when, out of 730 pages on paganism, half a page is allotted to the moral system of Aristotle. That his Aristotelian chapter was weak, the author knew; but he said that it was not his text to make more of it. He did not mean that a Christian divine may be better employed than in doing honour to a heathen; but, having to narrate events and the action of causes, he regarded Christianity more as an organism employing sacramental powers than as a body of speculative ideas. To cast up the total of moral and religious knowledge attained by Seneca, Epictetus, and Plutarch, to measure the line and rate of progress since Socrates, to compare the point reached by Hermas and Justin, is an inquiry of the highest interest for writers yet to come. But the quantitative difference of acquired precept between the later pagan and the early Christian is not the key to the future. The true problem is to expose the ills and errors which Christ, the Healer, came to remove. The measure must be taken from the depth of evil from which Christianity had to rescue mankind, and its history is more than a continued history of philosophical theories. Newman, who sometimes agreed with Döllinger in the letter, but seldom in the spirit, and who distrusted him as a man in whom the divine lived at the mercy of the scholar, and whose burden of superfluous learning blunted the point and the edge of his mind, so much liked what he heard of this book that, being unable to read it, he had it translated at the Oratory.

The work thus heralded never went beyond the first volume, completed in the autumn of 1860, which was received by the *Kirchenzeitung* of Berlin as the most acceptable narrative of the founding of Christianity, and as the largest concession ever made by a Catholic divine. The author, following the ancient ways, and taking, with Reuss, the New Testament as it stands, made no attempt to establish the position against modern criticism. Up to this, prescription and tradition held the first place in his writings, and formed his vantage-ground in all controversy. His energy in upholding the past as the rule and measure of the future distinguished him even among writers of his own communion. In *Christenthum und Kirche* he explained his theory of development, under which flag the notion of progress penetrates into theology, and which he held as firmly as the balancing element of perpetuity: "In dem Maass als dogmenhistorische Studien mehr getrieben werden, wird die absolute innere Nothwendigkeit und Wahrheit der Sache immer allgemeiner einleuchten." He conceived no bounds to the unforeseen resources of Christian thought and faith. A philosopher in whose works he would not have expected to find the scientific expression of his own idea, has a passage bearing close analogy to what he was putting forward in 1861:

It is then in the change to a higher state of form or composition that development differs from growth. We must carefully distinguish development from mere increase; it is the acquiring, not of greater bulk, but of new forms and structures, which are adapted to higher conditions of existence.

It is the distinction which Uhhorn draws between the terms *Entfaltung* and *Entwickelung*. Just then, after sixteen years spent in the Church of Rome, Newman was inclined to guard and narrow his theory. On the one hand he taught that the enactments and decisions of ecclesiastical law are made on principles and by virtue of prerogatives which *jam antea latitavere* in the Church of the apostles and fathers. But he thought that a divine of the second century on seeing the Roman catechism, would have recognised his own belief in it, without surprise, as soon as he understood its meaning. He once wrote: "If

I have said more than this, I think I have not worked out my meaning, and was confused—whether the minute facts of history will bear me out in this view, I leave to others to determine." Döllinger would have feared to adopt a view for its own sake, without knowing how it would be borne out by the minute facts of history. His own theory of development had not the same ingenious simplicity, and he thought Newman's brilliant book unsound in detail. But he took high ground in asserting the undeviating fidelity of Catholicism to its principle. In this, his last book on the Primitive Church, as in his early lectures, he claims the unswerving unity of faith as a divine prerogative. In a memorable passage of the *Symbolik* Möhler had stated that there is no better security than the law which pervades human society, which preserves harmony and consistency in national character, which makes Lutheranism perpetually true to Luther, and Islamism to the Koran.

Speaking in the name of his own university, the rector described him as a receptive genius. Part of his career displays a quality of assimilation, acquiescence, and even adaptation, not always consistent with superior originality or intense force of character. His *Reformation*, the strongest book, with the *Symbolik*, which Catholics had produced in the century, was laid down on known lines, and scarcely effected so much novelty and change as the writings of Kampschulte and Kolde. His book on the first age of the Church takes the critical points as settled, without special discussion. He appeared to receive impulse and direction, limit and colour, from his outer life. His importance was achieved by the force within. Circumstances only conspired to mould a giant of commonplace excellence and average ideas, and their influence on his view of history might long be traced. No man of like spirituality, of equal belief in the supreme dignity of conscience, systematically allowed as much as he did for the empire of chance surroundings and the action of home, and school, and place of worship upon conduct. He must have known that his own mind and character as an historian was not formed by effort and design. From early impressions, and a life spent, to his fiftieth year, in a rather unvaried professional circle, he contracted homely habits in estimating objects of the greater world ; and his imagination was not prone to vast proportions and wide horizons. He inclined to apply the rules and observation of domestic life to public affairs, to reduce the level of the heroic and sublime ; and history, in his hands, lost something both in terror and in grandeur. He acquired his art in the long study of earlier times, where materials are scanty. All that can be known of Cæsar or Charlemagne, or Gregory VII., would hold in a dozen volumes ; a library would not be sufficient for Charles V. or Lewis XVI. Extremely few of the ancients are really known to us in detail, as we know Socrates, or Cicero, or St. Augustine. But in modern times, since Petrarca, there are at least two thousand actors on the public stage whom we see by the revelations of private correspondence. Besides letters that were meant to be burnt, there are a man's secret diaries, his autobiography and table-talk, the recollections of his friends, self-betraying notes on the margins of books, the report of his trial if he is a culprit, and the evidence for beatification if he is a saint. Here we are on a different footing, and we practise a different art when dealing with Phocion or Dunstan, or with Richelieu or Swift. In one case we remain perforce on the surface of character, which we have not the means of analysing : we have to be content with conjecture, with probable explanations and obvious motives. We must constantly allow the benefit of the doubt, and reserve sentence. The science of character comes in with modern history. Döllinger had lived too long in the ages during which men are seen mostly in outline, and never applied an historical psychology distinct from that of private experience. Great men are something different from an enlarged repetition of average and familiar types, and the working and motive of their minds is in many instances the exact contrary of ordinary men, living to avoid contingencies of danger, and pain, and sacrifice, and the weariness of constant thinking and far-seeing precaution.

We are apt to judge extraordinary men by our own standard, that is to say, we often suppose them to possess, in an extraordinary degree, those qualities which we are conscious of in ourselves or others. This is the easiest way of conceiving their characters, but not the truest. They differ in kind rather than in degree.

We cannot understand Cromwell or Shaftesbury, Sunderland or Penn, by studies made in the parish. The study of intricate and subtle character was not habitual with Döllinger, and the result was an extreme dread of unnecessary condemnation. He resented being told that Ferdinand I. and II., that Henry III. and Lewis XIII., were, in the coarse terms of common life, assassins; that Elizabeth tried to have Mary made away with, and that Mary, in matters of that kind, had no greater scruples; that William III. ordered the extirpation of a clan, and rewarded the murderers as he had rewarded those of De Witt; that Lewis XIV. sent a man to kill him, and James II. was privy to the Assassination Plot. When he met men less mercifully given than himself, he said that they were hanging judges with a Malthusian propensity to repress the growth of population. This indefinite generosity did not disappear when he had long outgrown its early cause. It was revived, and his view of history was deeply modified, in the course of the great change in his attitude in the Church which took place between the years 1861 and 1867.

Döllinger used to commemorate his visit to Rome in 1857 as an epoch of emancipation. He had occasionally been denounced; and a keen eye had detected latent pantheism in his *Vorhalle*, but he had not been formally censured. If he had once asserted the value of nationality in the Church, he was vehement against it in religion; and if he had joined in deprecating the dogmatic decree in 1854, he was silent afterwards. By Protestants he was still avoided as the head and front of offending ultra montanism; and when the historical commission was instituted at Munich, by disciples of the Berlin school, he was passed over at first, and afterwards opposed. When public matters took him to Berlin in 1857, he sought no intercourse with the divines of the faculty. The common idea of his *Reformation* was expressed by Kaulbach in a drawing which represented the four chief reformers riding on one horse, pursued by a scavenger with the unmistakable features of their historian. He was received with civility at Rome, if not with cordiality. The pope sent to Cesena for a manuscript which it was reported that he wished to consult; and his days were spent profitably between the Minerva and the Vatican, where he was initiated in the mysteries of Galileo's tower. It was his fortune to have for pilot and instructor a prelate classified in the pigeon-holes of the Wilhelmsstrasse as the chief agitator against the State, "dessen umfangreiches Wissen noch durch dessen Feinheit und geistige Gewandtheit übertroffen wird." He was welcomed by Passaglia and Schrader at the Collegio Romano, and enjoyed the privilege of examining San Callisto with De Rossi for his guide. His personal experience was agreeable, though he strove unsuccessfully to prevent the condemnation of two of his colleagues by the Index.

There have been men connected with him who knew Rome in his time, and whose knowledge moved them to indignation and despair. One bishop assured him that the Christian religion was extinct there, and only survived in its forms; and an important ecclesiastic on the spot wrote: *Delenda est Carthago.* The archives of the Culturkampf contain a despatch from a Protestant statesman sometime his friend, urging his government to deal with the Papacy as they would deal with Dahomey. Döllinger's impression on his journey was very different. He did not come away charged with visions of scandal in the spiritual order, of suffering in the temporal, or of tyranny in either. He was never in contact with the sinister side of things. Theiner's *Life of Clement the Fourteenth* failed to convince him, and he listened incredulously to his indictment of the Jesuits. Eight years later Theiner wrote to him that he hoped they would now agree better on that subject than when they discussed it in Rome. "Ich freue mich, dass Sie jetzt erkennen, dass mein Urtheil über die Jesuiten und ihr Wirken gerecht war.—Im kommenden Jahr, so Gott will, werden wir uns hoffentlich besser verstehen als im Jahr 1857." He thought the governing body unequal to the task of ruling both Church and State; but it was the State that seemed to him to suffer from the combination. He was anxious about the political future, not about the future of religion. The persuasion that government by priests could not maintain itself in the world as it is, grew in force and definiteness as he meditated at home on the things he had seen and heard. He was despondent and apprehensive; but he had no suspicion of what was then so near. In the summer of 1859, as the sequel of Solferino began to unfold itself, he thought of making his observations known. In November a friend wrote: "Je ne me dissimule aucune des misères de tout ordre qui vous ont frappé à Rome." For more than a year he remained silent and uncertain, watching the use France would make of the irresistible authority acquired by the defeat of Austria and the collapse of government in Central Italy.

The war of 1859, portending danger to the temporal power, disclosed divided counsels. The episcopate supported the papal sovereignty, and a voluntary tribute, which in a few years took shape in tens of millions, poured into the treasury of St. Peter. A time followed during which the Papacy endeavoured, by a series of connected measures, to preserve its political authority through the aid of its spiritual. Some of the most enlightened Catholics, Dupanloup and Montalembert, proclaimed a sort of holy war. Some of the most enlightened Protestants, Guizot and Leo, defended the Roman government, as the most legitimate, venerable, and necessary of governments. In Italy there were ecclesiastics like Liverani, Tosti, Capecelatro, who believed with Manzoni that there could be no deliverance without unity, or calculated that political loss might be religious gain. Passaglia, the most celebrated Jesuit living, and a confidential adviser of the pope, both in dogma and in the preparation of the Syllabus, until Perrone refused to meet him, quitted the Society, and then fled from Rome, leaving the Inquisition in possession of his papers, in order to combat the use of theology in defence of the temporal power. Forty thousand priests, he said, publicly or privately agreed with him; and the diplomatists reported the names of nine cardinals who were ready to make terms with Italian unity, of which the pope himself said: "Ce serait un beau rêve." In this country, Newman did not share the animosity of conservatives against Napoleon III. and his action in Italy. When the flood, rising, reached the papal throne, he preserved an embarrassed silence, refusing, in spite of much solicitation, to commit himself even in private. An impatient M.P. took the train down to Edgbaston, and began, trying to draw him: "What times we live in, Father Newman! Look at all that is going on in Italy."—"Yes, indeed! And look at China too, and New Zealand!" Lacordaire favoured the cause of the Italians more openly, in spite of his Paris associates. He hoped, by federation, to save the interests of the Holy See, but he was reconciled to the loss of provinces, and he required religious liberty at Rome. Lamoricière was defeated in September 1860, and in February the fortress of Gaëta, which had become the last Roman outwork, fell. Then Lacordaire, disturbed in his reasoning by the logic of events, and by an earnest appeal to his priestly conscience, as his biographer says: "ébranlé un moment par une lettre éloquente," broke away from his friends:—

Que Montalembert, notre ami commun, ne voie pas dans ce qui se passe en Italie, sauf le mal, un progrès sensible dans ce que nous avons toujours cru le bien de l'église, cela tient à sa nature passionnée. Ce qui le domine aujourd'hui c'est la haine du gouvernement français.—Dieu se sert de tout, même du despotisme, même de l'égoïsme; et il y a même des choses qu'il ne peut accomplir par des mains tout à fait pures.—Qu'y puis-je? Me déclarer contre l'Italie parce que ses chaînes tombent mal à propos? Non assurément: je laisse à d'autres une passion aussi profonde, et j'aime mieux accepter ce que j'estime un bien de quelque part qu'il vienne.—Il est vrai que la situation temporelle du Pape souffre présentement de la libération de l'Italie, et peut-être en souffrira-t-elle encore assez longtemps: mais c'est un malheur qui a aussi ses fins dans la politique mystérieuse de la Providence. Souffrir n'est pas mourir, c'est quelquefois expier et s'éclairer.

This was written on 22nd February 1861. In April Döllinger spoke on the Roman question in the Odeon at Munich, and explained himself more fully in the autumn, in the most popular of all his books.

The argument of *Kirche und Kirchen* was, that the churches which are without the pope drift into many troubles, and maintain themselves at a manifest disadvantage, whereas the church which energetically preserves the principle of unity has a vast superiority which would prevail, but for its disabling and discrediting failure in civil government. That government seemed to him as legitimate as any in the world, and so needful to those for whose sake it was instituted, that if it should be overthrown, it would, by irresistible necessity, be restored. Those for whose sake it was instituted were, not the Roman people, but the catholic world. That interest, while it lasted, was so sacred, that no sacrifice was too great to preserve it, not even the exclusion of the clerical order from secular office.

The book was an appeal to Catholics to save the papal government by the only possible remedy, and to rescue the Roman people from falling under what the author deemed a tyranny like that of the Convention. He had acquired his politics in the atmosphere of 1847, from the potential liberality of men like Radowitz, who declared that he would postpone every political or national interest to that of the Church, Capponi, the last Italian federalist, and Tocqueville, the minister who occupied Rome. His object was not materially different from that of Antonelli and Mérode, but he sought it by exposing the faults of the papal government during several centuries, and the hopelessness of all efforts to save it from the Revolution unless reformed. He wrote to an English minister that it could not be our policy that the head of the Catholic Church should be subject to a foreign potentate :—

Das harte Wort, mit welchem Sie im Parlamente den Stab über Rom gebrochen haben—*hopelessly incurable*, oder *incorrigible*,—kann ich mir nicht aneignen ; ich hoffe vielmehr, wie ich es in dem Buche dargelegt habe, das Gegentheil. An die Dauerhaftigkeit eines ganz Italien umfassenden Piemontesisch-Italiänischen Reiches glaube ich nicht.—Inzwischen tröste ich mich mit dem Gedanken, dass in Rom zuletzt doch *vexatio dabit intellectum*, und dann wird noch alles gut werden.

To these grateful vaticinations his correspondent replied :—

You have exhibited the gradual departure of the government in the states of the church from all those conditions which made it tolerable to the sense and reason of mankind, and have, I think, completely justified, in principle if not in all the facts, the conduct of those who have determined to do away with it.

The policy of exalting the spiritual authority though at the expense of sacrifices in the temporal, the moderation even in the catalogue of faults, the side blow at the Protestants, filling more than half the volume, disarmed for a moment the resentment of outraged Rome. The Pope, on a report from Theiner, spoke of the book as one that might do good. Others said that it was pointless, that its point was not where the author meant it to be, that the handle was sharper than the blade. It was made much more clear that the Pope had governed badly than that Russia or Great Britain would gain by his supremacy. The cold analysis, the diagnosis by the bedside of the sufferer, was not the work of an observer dazzled by admiration or blinded by affection. It was a step, a first unconscious, unpremeditated step, in the process of detachment. The historian here began to prevail over the divine, and to judge Church matters by a law which was not given from the altar. It was the outcome of a spirit which had been in him from the beginning. His English translator had uttered a mild protest against his severe treatment of popes. His censure of the Reformation had been not as that of Bossuet, but as that of Baxter and Bull. In 1845 Mr. Gladstone remarked that he would answer every objection, but never proselytised. In 1848 he rested the claims of the Church on the common law, and bade the hierarchy remember that national character is above free will: "Die Nationalität ist etwas der Freiheit des menschlichen Willens entrücktes, geheimnissvolles und in ihrem letzen Grunde selbst etwas von Gott gewolltes." In his *Hippolytus* he began by surrendering the main point, that a man who so vilified the papacy might yet be an undisputed saint. In the *Vorhalle* he flung away a favourite argument, by avowing that paganism developed by its own lines and laws, untouched by Christianity, until the second century; and as with the Gentiles, so with the sects; he taught, in the suppressed chapter of his history, that their doctrines followed a normal course. And he believed so far in the providential mission of Protestantism, that it was idle to talk of reconciliation until it had borne all its fruit. He exasperated a Munich colleague by refusing to pronounce whether Gregory and Innocent had the right to depose emperors, or Otho and Henry to depose popes; for he thought that historians should not fit theories to facts, but should be content with showing how things worked. Much secret and suppressed antagonism found vent in 1858, when one who had been his assistant in writing the *Reformation* and was still his friend, declared that he would be a heretic whenever he found a backing.

Those with whom he actively coalesced felt at times that he was incalculable, that he pursued a separate line, and was always learning, whilst others busied themselves less with the unknown. This note of distinctness and solitude set him apart from those about him, during his intimacy with the most catholic of Anglican prelates, Forbes, and with the lamented Liddon. And it appeared still more when the denominational barrier of his sympathy was no longer marked, and he, who had stood in the rank almost with De Maistre and Perrone, found himself acting for the same ends with their enemies, when he delivered a studied eulogy on Mignet, exalted the authority of Laurent in religious history and of Ferrari in civil, and urged the Bavarian academy to elect Taine, as a writer who had but one rival in France, leaving it to uncertain conjecture whether the man he meant was Renan. In theory it was his maxim that a man should guard against his friends. When he first addressed the university as Rector, saying that as the opportunity might never come again, he would employ it to utter the thoughts closest to his heart, he exhorted the students to be always true to their convictions and not to yield to surroundings; and he invoked, rightly or wrongly, the example of Burke, his favourite among public men, who, turning from his associates to obey the light within, carried the nation with him. A gap was apparent now between the spirit in which he devoted himself to the service of his Church and that of the men whom he most esteemed. At that time he was nearly the only German who knew Newman well and appreciated the grace and force of his mind. But Newman, even when he was angry, assiduously distinguished the pontiff from his court:

> There will necessarily always be round the Pope second-rate people, who are not subjects of that supernatural wisdom which is his prerogative. For myself, certainly I have found myself in a different atmosphere, when I have left the Curia for the Pope himself.

Montalembert protested that there were things in *Kirche und Kirchen* which he would not have liked to say in public:

> Il est certain que la seconde partie de votre livre déplaira beaucoup, non seulement à Rome, mais encore à la très grande majorité des Catholiques. Je ne sais donc pas si, dans le cas où vous m'eussiez consulté préalablement, j'aurais eu le courage d'infliger cette blessure à mon père et à mes frères.

Döllinger judged that the prerogative even of natural wisdom was often wanting in the government of the Church; and the sense of personal attachment, if he ever entertained it, had worn away in the friction and familiarity of centuries.

After the disturbing interlude of the Roman question he did not resume the history of Christianity. The second century with its fragments of information, its scope for piercing and conjecture, he left to Lightfoot. With increasing years he lost the disposition to travel on common ground, impregnably occupied by specialists, where he had nothing of his own to tell; and he preferred to work where he could be a pathfinder. Problems of Church government had come to the front, and he proposed to retraverse his subject, narrowing it into a history of the papacy. He began by securing his foundations and eliminating legend. He found so much that was legendary that his critical preliminaries took the shape of a history of fables relating to the papacy. Many of these were harmless: others were devised for a purpose, and he fixed his attention more and more on those which were the work of design. The question, how far the persistent production of spurious matter had permanently affected the genuine constitution and theology of the Church arose before his mind as he composed the *Papstfabeln des Mittelalters*. He indicated the problem without discussing it. The matter of the volume was generally neutral, but its threatening import was perceived, and twenty-one hostile critics sent reviews of it to one theological journal

Since he first wrote on these matters, thirty years earlier, the advance of competitive learning had made it a necessity to revise statements by all accessible lights, and to subject authorities to a closer scrutiny. The increase in the rigour of the obligation might be measured by Tischendorf, who, after renewing the text of the New Testament in seven editions, had more than three thousand changes to make in the eighth. The old pacific superficial method yielded no longer what would be accepted as certain knowledge. Having made himself master of the reconstructive process that was carried on a little apart from the main chain of durable literature, in academic transactions, in dissertations and periodicals, he submitted the materials he was about to use to the exigencies of the day. Without it, he would have remained a man of the last generation, distanced by every disciple of the new learning. He went to work with nothing but his trained and organised common sense, starting from no theory, and aiming at no conclusion. If he was beyond his contemporaries in the mass of expedient knowledge, he was not before them in the strictness of his tests, or in sharpness or boldness in applying them. He was abreast as a critic, he was not ahead. He did not innovate. The parallel studies of the time kept pace with his; and his judgments are those which are accepted generally. His critical mind was pliant, to assent where he must, to reject where he must, and to doubt where he must. His submission to external testimony appeared in his panegyric of our Indian empire, where he overstated the increase of population. Informed of his error by one of his translators, he replied that the figures had seemed incredible also to him, but having verified, he found the statement so positively made that he did not venture to depart from it. If inclination ever swayed his judgment, it was in his despair of extracting a real available Buddha from the fables of Southern India, which was conquered at last by the ablest of Mommsen's pupils.

He was less apprehensive than most of his English friends in questions relating to the Old Testament; and in the New, he was disposed, at times, to allow some force to Muratori's fragment as to the person of the evangelist who is least favourable to St. Peter; and was puzzled at the zeal of the Speaker's commentator as to the second epistle of the apostle. He held to the epistles of St. Ignatius with the tenacity of a Caroline prelate, and was grateful to De Rossi for a chronological point in their favour. He rejected the attacks of Lucius on the most valued passages in Philo, and stood with Gass against Weingarten's argument on the life of St. Anthony and the origin of Monasticism. He resisted Overbeck on the epistle to Diognetus, and thought Ebrard all astray as to the Culdees. There was no conservative antiquarian whom he prized higher than Le Blant: yet he considered Ruinart credulous in dealing with acts of early martyrs. A pupil on whose friendship he relied, made an effort to rescue the legends of the conversion of Germany; but the master preferred the unsparing demolitions of Rettberg. Capponi and Carl Hegel were his particular friends; but he abandoned them without hesitation for Scheffer Boichorst, the iconoclast of early Italian chronicles, and never consented to read the learned reply of Da Lungo.

The *Pope Fables* carried the critical inquiry a very little way; but he went on with the subject. After the Donation of Constantine came the Forged Decretals, which were just then printed for the first time in an accurate edition. Döllinger began to be absorbed in the long train of hierarchical fictions, which had deceived men like Gregory VII., St. Thomas Aquinas, and Cardinal Bellarmine, which he traced up to the false Areopagite, and down to the Laminæ Granatenses. These studies became the chief occupation of his life; they led to his excommunication in 1871, and carried him away from his early system. For this, neither syllabus nor ecumenical council was needed; neither crimes nor scandals were its distant cause. The history of Church government was the influence which so profoundly altered his position. Some trace of his researches, at an early period of their progress, appears in what he wrote on the occasion of the Vatican Council, especially in the fragment of an ecclesiastical pathology which was published under the name of Janus. But the history itself, which was the main and characteristic work of his life, and was pursued until the end, was never published or completed. He died without making it known to what extent, within what limit, the ideas with which he had been so long identified were changed by his later studies, and how wide a trench had opened between his earlier and his later life. Twenty years of his historical work are lost for history.

The revolution in method since he began to write was partly the better use of old authorities, partly the accession of new. Döllinger had devoted himself to the one in 1863; he passed to the other in 1864. For definite objects he had often consulted manuscripts, but the harvest was stacked away, and had scarcely influenced his works. In the use and knowledge of unpublished matter he still belonged to the old school, and was on a level with Neander. Although, in later years, he printed six or seven volumes of Inedita, like Mai and Theiner he did not excel as an editor: and this part of his labours is notable chiefly for its effect on himself. He never went over altogether to men like Schottmüller, who said of him that he made no research—*er hat nicht geforscht*—meaning that he had made his mind up about the Templars by the easy study of Wilkins, Michelet, Schottmüller himself, and perhaps a hundred others, but had not gone underground to the mines they delved in. Fustel de Coulanges, at the time of his death, was promoting the election of the Bishop of Oxford to the Institute, on the ground that he surpassed all other Englishmen in his acquaintance with manuscripts. Döllinger agreed with their French rival in his estimate of our English historian, but he ascribed less value to that part of his acquirements. He assured the Bavarian Academy that Mr. Freeman, who reads print, but nevertheless mixes his colours with brains, is the author of the most profound work on the Middle Ages ever written in this country, and is not only a brilliant writer and a sagacious critic, but the most learned of all our countrymen. Ranke once drew a line at 1514, after which, he said, we still want help from unprinted sources. The world had moved a good deal since that cautious innovation, and after 1860, enormous and excessive masses of archive were brought into play. The Italian Revolution opened tempting horizons. In 1864 Döllinger spent his vacation in the libraries of Vienna and Venice. At

Vienna, by an auspicious omen, Sickel, who was not yet known to Greater Germany as the first of its mediæval palæographers, showed him the sheets of a work containing 247 Carolingian acts unknown to Böhmer, who had just died with the repute of being the best authority on Imperial charters. During several years Döllinger followed up the discoveries he now began. Theiner sent him documents from the *Archivio Segreto*; one of his friends shut himself up at Trent, and another at Bergamo. Strangers ministered to his requirements, and huge quantities of transcripts came to him from many countries. Conventional history faded away; the studies of a lifetime suddenly underwent transformation; and his view of the last six centuries was made up from secret information gathered in thirty European libraries and archives. As many things remote from current knowledge grew to be certainties, he became more confident, more independent, and more isolated. The ecclesiastical history of his youth went to pieces against the new criticism of 1863, and the revelation of the unknown which began on a very large scale in 1864.

During four years of transition occupied by this new stage of study, he abstained from writing books. Whenever some local occasion called upon him to speak, he spoke of the independence and authority of history. In cases of collision with the Church, he said that a man should seek the error in himself; but he spoke of the doctrine of the universal Church, and it did not appear that he thought of any living voice or present instructor. He claimed no immunity for philosophy; but history, he affirmed, left to itself and pursued disinterestedly, will heal the ills it causes; and it was said of him that he set the university in the place of the hierarchy. Some of his countrymen were deeply moved by the measures which were being taken to restore and to confirm the authority of Rome; and he had impatient colleagues at the university who pressed him with sharp issues of uncompromising logic. He himself was reluctant to bring down serene research into troublesome disputation, and wished to keep history and controversy apart. His hand was forced at last by his friends abroad. Whilst he pursued his isolating investigations he remained aloof from a question which in other countries and other days was a summary and effective test of impassioned controversy. Persecution was a problem that had never troubled him. It was not a topic with theoretical Germans; the necessary books were hardly available, and a man might read all the popular histories and theologies without getting much further than the Spanish Inquisition. Ranke, averse from what is unpleasant, gave no details. The gravity of the question had never been brought home to Döllinger in forty years of public teaching. When he approached it, as late as 1861, he touched lightly, representing the intolerance of Protestants to their disadvantage, while that of Catholics was a bequest of Imperial Rome, taken up in an emergency by secular powers, in no way involving the true spirit and practice of the Church. With this light footfall the topic which has so powerful a leverage slipped into the current of his thought. The view found favour with Ambrose de Lisle, who, having read the *Letters to a Prebendary*, was indignant with those who commit the Church to a principle often resisted or ignored. Newman would admit to no such compromise:

> Is not the miraculous infliction of judgments upon blasphemy, lying, profaneness, etc., in the apostles' day a sanction of infliction upon the same by a human hand in the times of the Inquisition? Ecclesiastical rulers may punish with the sword, if they can, and if it is expedient or necessary to do so. The church has a right to make laws and to enforce them with temporal punishments.

The question came forward in France in the wake of the temporal power. Liberal defenders of a government which made a principle of persecution had to decide whether they approved or condemned it. Where was their liberality in one case, or their catholicity in the other? It was the simple art of their adversaries to press this point, and to make the most of it; and a French priest took upon him to declare that intolerance, far from being a hidden shame, was a pride and a glory: "L'Eglise regarde l'Inquisition comme l'apogée de la civilisation chrétienne, comme le fruit naturel des époques de foi et de catholicisme national." Gratry took the other side so strongly that there would have been a tumult at the Sorbonne, if he had said from his chair what he wrote in his book; and certain passages were struck out of the printed text by the cautious archbishop's reviser. He was one of those French divines who had taken in fuel at Munich, and he welcomed *Kirche und Kirchen*: "Quant au livre du docteur Döllinger sur la Papauté, c'est, selon moi, le livre décisif. C'est un chef-d'œuvre admirable à plusieurs égards, et qui est destiné à produire un bien incalculable et à fixer l'opinion sur ce sujet; c'est ainsi que le juge aussi M. de Montalembert. Le docteur Döllinger nous a rendu à tous un grand service." This was not the first impression of Montalembert. He deplored the Odeon lectures as usurping functions divinely assigned not to professors, but to the episcopate, as a grief for friends and a joy for enemies. When the volume came he still objected to the policy, to the chapter on England, and to the cold treatment of Sixtus V. At last he admired without reserve. Nothing better had been written since Bossuet; the judgment on the Roman government, though severe, was just, and contained no more than the truth. There was not a word which he would not be able to sign. A change was going on in his position and his affections, as he came to regard toleration as the supreme affair. At Malines he solemnly declared that the Inquisitor was as horrible as the Terrorist, and made no distinction in favour of death inflicted for religion against death for political motives: "Les bûchers allumés par une main catholique me font autant d'horreur que les échafauds où les Protestants ont immolé tant de martyrs." Wiseman, having heard him once, was not present on the second day; but the Belgian cardinal assured him that he had spoken like a sound divine. He described Dupanloup's defence of the Syllabus as a masterpiece of eloquent subterfuge, and repudiated his *interpréta-*

tions équivoques. A journey to Spain in 1865 made him more vehement than ever; although, from that time, the political opposition inflamed him less. He did not find imperialism intolerable. His wrath was fixed on the things of which Spain had reminded him: "C'est là qu'il faut aller pour voir ce que le catholicisme exclusif a su faire d'une des plus grandes et des plus héroïques nations de la terre.—Je rapporte un surcroît d'horreur pour les doctrines fanatiques et absolutistes qui ont cours aujourd'hui chez les catholiques du monde entier." In 1866 it became difficult, by the aid of others, to overcome Falloux's resistance to the admission of an article in the *Correspondant*, and by the end of the year his friends were unanimous to exclude him. An essay on Spain, his last work—"dernier soupir de mon âme indignée et attristée"—was, by Dupanloup's advice, not allowed to appear. Repelled by those whom he now designated as spurious, servile, and prevaricating liberals, he turned to the powerful German with whom he thought himself in sympathy. He had applauded him for dealing with one thing at a time, in his book on Rome: "Vous avez bien fait de ne rien dire de l'absolutisme spirituel, quant à présent. *Sat prata biberunt.* Le reste viendra en son temps." He avowed that spiritual autocracy is worse than political; that evil passions which had triumphed in the State were triumphant in the Church; that to send human beings to the stake, with a crucifix before them, was the act of a monster or a maniac. He was dying; but whilst he turned his face to the wall, lamenting that he had lived too long, he wished for one more conference with the old friend with whom, thirty-five years before, in a less anxious time, he had discussed the theme of religion and liberty. This was in February 1867; and for several years he had endeavoured to teach Döllinger his clear-cut antagonism, and to kindle in him something of his gloomy and passionate fervour, on the one point on which all depended.

Döllinger arrived slowly at the contemplation of deeper issues than that of churchmen or laymen in political offices, of Roman or German pupils in theological chairs. After seeing Baron Arnim, in 1865, he lost the hope of saving the papal government, and ceased to care about the things he had contended for in 1861; and a time came when he thought it difficult to give up the temporal power, and yet revere the Holy See. He wrote to Montalembert that his illusions were failing: "Ich bin sehr ernüchtert.—Es ist so vieles in der Kirche anders gekommen, als ich es mir vor 20-30 Jahren gedacht, und rosenfarbig ausgemalt hatte." He learnt to speak of spiritual despotism almost in the words of his friend. The point of junction between the two orders of ideas is the use of fire for the enforcement of religion on which the French were laying all their stress: "In Frankreich bewegt sich der Gegensatz blos auf dem socialpolitischen Gebiete, nicht auf dem theologisch-wissenschaftlichen, weil es dort genau genommen eine theologische Wissenschaft nicht gibt" (16th October 1865). The Syllabus had not permanently fixed his attention upon it. Two years later, the matter was put more definitely, and he found himself, with little real preparation, turning from antiquarian curiosities, and brought face to face with the radical question of life and death. If ever his literary career was influenced by his French alliances, by association with men in the throng, for whom politics decided, and all the learning of the schools did not avail, the moment was when he resolved to write on the Inquisition.

The popular account which he drew up appeared in the newspapers in the summer of 1867; and although he did not mean to burn his ships, his position as an official defender of the Holy See was practically at an end. He wrote rapidly, at short notice, and not in the steady course of progressive acquisition. Ficker and Winkelmann have since given a different narrative of the step by which the Inquisition came into existence; and the praise of Gregory X., as a man sincerely religious who kept aloof, was a mark of haste. In the work which he was using, there was no act by that pontiff; but if he had had time to look deeper he would not have found him, in this respect, different from his contemporaries. There is no uncertainty as to the author's feeling towards the infliction of torture and death for religion, and the purpose of his treatise is to prevent the nailing of the Catholic colours to the stake. The spirit is that of the early lectures, in which he said : " Diese Schutzgewalt der Kirche ist rein geistlich. Sie kann also auch einen solchen öffentlichen hartnäckigen und sonst unheilbaren Gegner der Kirche nur seiner rein geistlichen kirchlichen Rechte berauben." Compared with the sweeping vehemence of the Frenchmen who preceded, the restrained moderation of language, the abstinence from the use of general terms, leaves us in doubt how far the condemnation extended, and whether he did more, in fact, than deplore a deviation from the doctrine of the first centuries. " Kurz darauf trat ein Umschwung ein, den man wohl einen Abfall von der alten Lehre nennen darf, und der sich ausnimmt, als ob die Kaiser die Lehrmeister der Bischöfe geworden seien." He never entirely separated himself in principle from the promoters, the agents, the apologists. He did not believe, with Hefele, that the spirit survives, that there are men, not content with eternal flames, who are ready to light up new Smithfields. Many of the defenders were his intimate friends. The most conspicuous was the only colleague who addressed him with the familiar German *Du*. Speaking of two or three men, of whom one, Martens, had specially attacked the false liberalism which sees no good in the Inquisition, he wrote : " Sie werden sich noch erinnern . . . wie hoch ich solche Männer stelle." He differed from them widely, but he differed academically ; and this was not the polish or precaution of a man who knows that to assail character is to degrade and to betray one's cause. The change in his own opinions was always before him. Although convinced that he had been wrong in many of the ideas and facts with which he started, he was also satisfied that he had been as sincere and true to his lights in 1835 as in 1865. There was no secret about the Inquisition, and its observances were published and republished in fifty books; but in his early days he had not read them, and there was not a German, from Basel to Königsberg, who could have faced a *viva voce* in the *Directorium* or the *Arsenale*, or who had ever read Percin or Paramo. If Lacordaire disconnected St. Dominic from the practice of persecution, Döllinger had done the same thing before him.

Weit entfernt, wie man ihm wohl vorgeworfen hat, sich dabei Gewalt und Verfolgung zu erlauben, oder gar der Stifter der Inquisition zu werden, wirkte er, nicht den Irrenden, sondern den Irrthum befehdend, nur durch ruhige Belehrung und Erörterung.

If Newman, a much more cautious disputant, thought it substantial truth to say that Rome never burnt heretics, there were things as false in his own early writings. If Möhler, in the religious wars, diverted attention from Catholic to Protestant atrocities, he took the example from his friend's book, which he was reviewing. There may be startling matter in Locatus and Pegna, but they were officials writing under the strictest censorship, and nobody can tell when they express their own private thoughts. There is a copy of Suarez on which a priest has written the marginal ejaculation : " Mon Dieu, ayez pitié de nous ! " But Suarez had to send the manuscript of his most aggressive book to Rome for revision, and Döllinger used to insist, on the testimony of his secretary, in Walton's *Lives*, that he disavowed and detested the interpolations that came back.

The French group, unlike him in spirit and motive, but dealing with the same opponents, judged them freely, and gave imperative utterance to their judgments. While Döllinger said of Veuillot that he meant well, but did much good and much evil, Montalembert called him a hypocrite : " L'Univers, en déclarant tous les jours qu'il ne veut pas d'autre liberté que la sienne, justifie tout ce que nos pires ennemis ont jamais dit sur la mauvaise foi et l'hypocrisie des polémistes chrétiens." Lacordaire wrote to a hostile bishop : " L'Univers est à mes yeux la négation de tout esprit chrétien et de tout bon sens humain. Ma consolation au milieu de si grandes misères morales est de vivre solitaire, occupé d'une œuvre que

Dieu bénit, et de protester par mon silence, et de temps en temps par mes paroles, contre la plus grande insolence qui se soit encore autorisée au nom de Jésus-Christ." Gratry was a man of more gentle nature, but his tone is the same: "Esprits faux ou nuls, consciences intellectuelles faussées par l'habitude de l'apologie sans franchise: *partemque ejus cum hypocritis ponet.*—Cette école est bien en vérité une école de mensonge.—C'est cette école qui est depuis des siècles, et surtout en ce siècle, l'opprobre de notre cause et le fléau de la religion. Voilà notre ennemi commun; voilà l'ennemi de l'Eglise."

Döllinger never understood party divisions in this tragic way. He was provided with religious explanations for the living and the dead; and his maxims in regard to contemporaries governed and attenuated his view of every historical problem. For the writers of his acquaintance who were unfaltering advocates of the Holy Office, for Philips and Gams, and for Theiner, who expiated devious passages of early youth, amongst other penitential works, with large volumes in honour of Gregory XIII., he had always the same mode of defence: "Mir begegnet es noch jede Woche, dass ich irgend einem Irrthum, mitunter einem lange gepflegten, entsage, ihn mir gleichsam aus der Brust herausreissen muss. Da sollte man freilich höchst duldsam und nachsichtig gegen fremde Irrthümer werden" (5th October 1866). He writes in the same terms to another correspondent sixteen years later: "Mein ganzes Leben ist ein successives Abstreifen von Irrthümern gewesen, von Irrthümern, die ich mit Zähigkeit festhielt, gewaltsam gegen die mir aufdämmernde bessere Erkenntniss mich stemmend; und doch meine ich sagen zu dürfen, dass ich dabei nicht *dishonest* war. Darf ich andre verurtheilen *in eodem luto mecum haerentes?*" He regretted as he grew old the hardness and severity of early days, and applied the same inconclusive deduction from his own experience to the past. After comparing Baronius and Bellarmine with Bossuet and Arnauld he goes on: "Wenn ich solche Männer auf einem Irrthum treffe, so sage ich mir: 'Wenn Du damals gelebt, und an seiner Stelle gestanden wärest, hättest Du nicht den allgemeinen Wahn getheilt; und er, wenn er die Dir zu Theil gewordenen Erkenntnissmittel besessen, würde er nicht besseren Gebrauch davon gemacht haben, die Wahrheit nicht früher erkannt und bekannt haben, als Du?'"

He sometimes distrusted his favourite argument of ignorance and early prepossessions, and felt that there was presumption and unreality in tendering such explanations to men like the Bollandist De Buck, De Rossi, whom the Institute elected in preference to Mommsen, or Windischmann, whom he himself had been accused of bringing forward as a rival to Möhler. He would say that knowledge may be a burden and not a light, that the faculty of doing justice to the past is among the rarest of moral and intellectual gifts: "Man kann viel wissen, viele Notizen im Kopf haben, ohne das rechte wissenschaftliche Verständniss, ohne den historischen Sinn. Dieser ist, wie Sie wohl wissen, gar nicht so häufig; und wo er fehlt, da fehlt auch, scheint mir, die volle Verantwortlichkeit für das gewusste."

In 1879 he prepared materials for a paper on the Massacre of St. Bartholomew. Here he was breaking new ground, and verging on that which it was the policy and the aspiration of his life to avoid. Many a man who gives no tears to Cranmer, Servetus, or Bruno, who thinks it just that the laws should be obeyed, who deems that actions done by order are excused, and that legality implies morality, will draw the line at midnight murder and wholesale extermination. The deed wrought at Paris and in forty towns of France in 1572, the arguments which produced it, the arguments which justified it, left no room for the mists of mitigation and compromise. The passage from the age of Gregory IX. to that of Gregory XIII., from the Crusades to the wars of Religion, brought his whole system into jeopardy. The historian who was at the heels of the divine in 1861, and level with him in 1867, would have come to the front. The discourse was never delivered, never composed. But the subject of toleration was absent no more from his thoughts, filling space once occupied by Julian of Eclanum and Duns Scotus, the Variata and the Five Propositions. To the last days of 1889 he was engaged in following the doctrines of intolerance back to their root, from Innocent III. to the Council of Rheims, from Nicholas I. to St. Augustine, narrowing the sphere of individual responsibility, defending agents, and multiplying degrees so as to make them imperceptible. Before the writings of Priscillian were published by the Vienna Academy the nature of their strange contents was disclosed. It then appeared that a copy of the *Codex unicus* had been sent to Döllinger from Würzburg years before; and that he had never adverted to the fact that the burning of heretics came, fully armed, from the brain of one man, and was the invention of a heretic who became its first victim.

At Rome he discussed the council of Trent with Theiner, and tried to obtain permission for him to publish the original acts. Pius IX. objected that none of his predecessors had allowed it, and Theiner answered that none of them had defined the Immaculate Conception. In a paper which Döllinger drew up, he observed that Pallavicini cannot convince; that far from proving the case against the artful Servite, the pettiness of his charges indicates that he has no graver fault to find; so that nothing but the production of the official texts can enforce or disprove the imputation that Trent was a scene of tyranny and intrigue. His private belief then was that the papers would disprove the imputation and vindicate the council. When Theiner found it possible to publish his *Acta Authentica*, Döllinger also printed several private diaries, chiefly from Mendham's collection at the Bodleian. But the correspondence between Rome and the legates is still, in its integrity, kept back. The two friends had examined it; both were persuaded that it was decisive; but they judged that it decided in opposite ways. Theiner, the official guardian of the records, had been forbidden to communicate them during the Vatican Council; and he deemed the concealment prudent. What passed in Rome under Pius IX. would, he averred, suffer by comparison. According to Döllinger, the suppressed papers told against Trent.

Wenn wir nicht allen unseren henotischen Hoffnungen entsagen und uns nicht in schweren Konflikt mit der alten (vormittelalterigen) Kirche bringen wollen, werden wir doch auch da das Korrektiv des Vincentianischen Prinzips (*semper*, *ubique*, *ab omnibus*) zur Anwendung bringen müssen.

After his last visit to the Marciana he thought more favourably of Father Paul, sharing the admiration which Venetians feel for the greatest writer of the Republic, and falling little short of the judgments which Macaulay inscribed, after each perusal, in the copy at Inveraray. Apart from his chief work he thought him a great historian, and he rejected the suspicion that he professed a religion which he did not believe. He even fancied that the manuscript, which in fact was forwarded with much secrecy to Archbishop Abbot, was published against his will. The intermediate seekers, who seem to skirt the border, such as Grotius, Ussher, Praetorius, and the other celebrated Venetian, De Dominis, interested him deeply, in connection with the subject of Irenics, and the religious problem was part motive of his incessant study of Shakespeare, both in early life, and when he meditated joining in the debate between Simpson, Rio, Bernays, and the *Edinburgh Review*.

His estimate of his own work was low. He wished to be remembered as a man who had written certain books, but who had not written many more. His collections constantly prompted new and attractive schemes, but his way was strewn with promise unperformed, and abandoned from want of concentration. He would not write with imperfect materials, and to him the materials were always imperfect. Perpetually engaged in going over his own life and reconsidering his conclusions, he was not depressed by unfinished work. When a sanguine friend hoped that all the contents of his hundred note-books would come into use, he answered that perhaps they might, if he lived for a hundred and fifty years. He seldom wrote a book without compulsion, or the aid of energetic assistants.

The account of mediæval sects, dated 1890, was on the stocks for half a century. The discourse on the Templars, delivered at his last appearance in public, had been always before him since a conversation with Michelet about the year 1841. Fifty-six years lay between his text to the *Paradiso* of Cornelius and his last return to Dante.

When he began to fix his mind on the constitutional history of the Church, he proposed to write, first, on the times of Innocent XI. It was the age he knew best, in which there was most interest, most material, most ability, when divines were national classics, and presented many distinct types of religious thought, when biblical and historical science was founded, and Catholicism was presented in its most winning guise. The character of Odescalchi impressed him, by his earnestness in sustaining a strict morality. Fragments of this projected work reappeared in his lectures on Louis XIV., and in his last publication on the Casuists. The lectures betray the decline of the tranquil idealism which had been the admiration and despair of friends. Opposition to Rome had made him, like his ultramontane allies in France, more indulgent to the ancient Gallican enemy. He now had to expose the vice of that system, which never roused the king's conscience, and served for sixty years, from the remonstrance of Caussin to the anonymous warning of Fénelon, as the convenient sanction of absolutism. In the work on seventeeth-century ethics, which is his farthest, the moral point of view prevails over every other, and conscience usurps the place of theology, canon law, and scholarship. This was his tribute to a new phase of literature, the last he was to see, which was beginning to put ethical knowledge above metaphysics and politics, as the central range of human progress. Morality, veracity, the proper atmosphere of ideal history, became the paramount interest.

When he was proposed for a degree, the most eloquent lips at Oxford, silenced for ever whilst I write this page, pointed to his excellence in those things which are the merit of Germans. "Quaecunque in Germanorum indole admiranda atque imitanda fere censemus, ea in Doellingerc maxime splendent." The patriotic quality was recognised in the address of the Berlin professors, who say that by upholding the independence of the national thought, whilst he enriched it with the best treasure of other lands, he realised the ideal of the historian. He became more German in extreme old age, and less impressive in his idiomatic French and English than in his own language. The lamentations of men he thought good judges, Mazade and Taine, and the first of literary critics, Montégut, diluted somewhat his admiration for the country of St. Bernard and Bossuet. In spite of politics, his feeling for English character, for the moral quality of English literature, never changed; and he told his own people that their faults are not only very near indeed to their virtues, but are sometimes more apparent to the observer. The belief in the fixity and influence of national type, confirmed by his authorities, Ganganelli and Möhler, continued to determine his judgments. In his last letter to Mr. Gladstone, he illustrated the Irish question by means of a chronicle describing Ireland a thousand years ago.

Everybody has felt that his power was out of proportion to his work, and that he knew too much to write. It was so much better to hear him than to read all his books, that the memory of what he was will pass away with the children whom he loved. Hefele called him the first theologian in Germany, and Höfler said that he surpassed all men in the knowledge of historical literature; but Hefele was the bishop of his predilection, and Höfler had been fifty years his friend, and is the last survivor of the group which once made Munich the capital of citramontane Catholicity. Martensen, the most brilliant of Episcopalian divines, describes him as he talked with equal knowledge and certainty of every age, and understood all characters and all situations as if he had lived in the midst of them. The best ecclesiastical historian now living is the fittest judge of the great ecclesiastical historian who is dead. Harnack has assigned causes which limited his greatness as a writer, perhaps even as a thinker; but he has declared that no man had the same knowledge and intelligence of history in general, and of religious history which is its most essential element, and he affirms, what some have doubted, that he possessed the rare faculty of entering into alien thought. None of those who knew Professor Döllinger best, who knew him in the third quarter of the century, to which he belonged by the full fruition of his powers and the completeness of his knowledge, will ever qualify these judgments. It is right to add that, in spite of boundless reading, there was no lumber in his mind, and in spite of his classical learning, little ornament. Among the men to be commemorated here, he stands alone. Throughout the measureless distance which he traversed, his movement was against his wishes, in pursuit of no purpose, in obedience to no theory, under no attraction but historical research alone. It was given to him to form his philosophy of history on the largest induction ever available to man; and whilst he owed more to divinity than any other historian, he owed more to history than any other divine.

XII

CARDINAL WISEMAN AND THE HOME AND FOREIGN REVIEW[1]

IT is one of the conditions inseparable from a public career to be often misunderstood, and sometimes judged unfairly even when understood the best. No one who has watched the formation of public opinion will be disposed to attribute all the unjust judgments which assail him to the malice of individuals, or to imagine that he can prevent misconceptions or vindicate his good name by words alone. He knows that even where he has committed no errors he must pay tribute to the fallibility of mankind, and that where he is in fault he must also pay tribute to his own. This is a natural law; and the purer a man's conscience is, and the more single his aim, the less eager will he be to evade it, or to defend himself from its penalties.

The man whose career is bound up with that of some school or party will estimate the value of his opponents' censures by the worth which he attributes to the undiscriminating praise of his friends; but he who has devoted himself to the development of principles which will not always bend to the dictates of expediency will have no such short way of dealing with objections. His independence will frequently and inexorably demand the sacrifice of interests to truth—of what is politic to what is right;

[1] "Rome and the Catholic Episcopate. Reply of His Eminence Cardinal Wiseman to an Address presented by the Clergy, Secular and Regular, of the Archdiocese of Westminster, on Tuesday, the 5th of August 1862." London: Burns and Lambert. (*Home and Foreign Review*, 1862.)

and, whenever he makes that sacrifice, he will appear a traitor to those whom he is most anxious to serve, while his act will be hailed by those who are farthest from sharing his opinions as a proof of secret sympathy, and harbinger of future alliance. Thus, the censure which he incurs will most often come from those whose views are essentially his own; and the very matter which calls it forth will be that which elicits the applause of adversaries who cannot bring themselves to believe either in the truth of his opinions, in the integrity of his motives, or in the sincerity of his aims.

There are few men living whose career has been more persistently misinterpreted, more bitterly assailed, or more ignorantly judged, than the illustrious person who is the head in England of the Church to which we belong. Cardinal Wiseman has been for many years the chief object of the attacks of those who have desired to injure or degrade our community. He is not only the canonical chief of English Catholics, but his ability, and the devotion of his life to their cause, have made him their best representative and their most powerful champion. No prelate in Christendom is more fully trusted by the Holy See, or exercises a more extensive personal influence, or enjoys so wide a literary renown. Upon him, therefore, intolerance and fanaticism have concentrated their malice. He has had to bear the brunt of that hatred which the holiness of Catholicism inspires in its enemies; and the man who has never been found wanting when the cause of the Church was at stake may boast, with a not unworthy pride, of the indifference with which he has encountered the personal slander of a hostile press.

The Catholics of this country are attached to Cardinal Wiseman by warmer feelings and more personal ties than those of merely ecclesiastical subordination. It has been his privilege to gather the spiritual fruits of the Catholic Emancipation Act; and the history of English Catholicism has been, for a whole generation, bound up with his name. That immense change in the internal condition of the Church in England which distinguishes our days from the time of Milner has grown up under his influence, and has been in great part his work. We owe it to him that we have been brought into closer intercourse with Rome, and into contact with the rest of Europe. By his preaching and his spiritual direction he has transformed the devotions of our people; while his lectures and writings have made Protestants familiar with Catholic ideas, and have given Catholics a deeper insight into their own religion. As a controversialist he influenced the Oxford movement more deeply than any other Catholic. As director of the chief literary organ of Catholics during a quarter of a century he rendered services to our literature, and overcame difficulties, which none are in a better position to appreciate than those who are engaged in a similar work. And as President of Oscott, he acquired the enduring gratitude of hundreds who owed to his guidance the best portion of their training.

These personal relations with English Catholics, which have made him a stranger to none and a benefactor to all, have at the same time given him an authority of peculiar weight amongst them. With less unity of view and tradition than their brethren in other lands, they were accustomed, in common with the rest of Englishmen, to judge more independently and to speak more freely than is often possible in countries more exclusively Catholic. Their minds are not all cast in the same mould, nor their ideas derived from the same stock; but all alike, from bishop to layman, identify their cause with that of the Cardinal, and feel that, in the midst of a hostile people, no diversity of opinion ought to interfere with unity of action, no variety of interest with identity of feeling, no controversy with the universal reverence which is due to the position and character of the Archbishop of Westminster.

In this spirit the Catholic body have received Cardinal Wiseman's latest publication—his "Reply to the Address of his Clergy on his return from Rome." He speaks in it of the great assemblage of the Episcopate, and of their address to the Holy Father. Among the bishops there present he was the most conspicuous, and he was President of the Commission to which the preparation of their address was intrusted. No account of it, therefore, can be more authentic than that which he is able to give. The reserve imposed by his office, and by the distinguished part he had to bear, has been to some extent neutralised by the necessity of refuting false and exaggerated rumours which were circulated soon after the meeting, and particularly two articles which appeared in *The Patrie* on the 4th and 5th of July, and in which it was stated that the address written by Cardinal Wiseman contained "most violent attacks on all the fundamental principles of modern society."

After replying in detail to the untruths of this newspaper, the Cardinal proceeds as follows:—

With far greater pain I feel compelled to advert to a covert insinuation of the same charges, in a publication avowedly Catholic, and edited in my own diocese, consequently canonically subject to my correction. Should such a misstatement, made under my own eyes, be passed over by me, it might be surmised that it could not be contradicted; and whether chronologically it preceded or followed the French account it evidently becomes my duty to notice it, as French bishops have considered it theirs to correct the inaccuracies of their native writers.

Otherwise, in a few years, we might find reference made, as to a recognised Catholic authority, for the current and unreproved statement of what occurred at Rome, to *The Home and Foreign Review*. And that in a matter on which reprehension would have been doubly expected, if merited. In its first number the Address, which has, I believe, wonderfully escaped the censure of Protestant and infidel journals, is thus spoken of: "This Address is said to be a compromise between one which took the violent course of recommending that major excommunication should be at once pronounced against the chief enemies of the temporal power by name, and one still more moderate than the present" (*The Home and Foreign Review*, p. 264). Now this very charge about recommending excommunication is the one made by the French paper against my Address. But, leaving to the writer the chance of an error, in this application of his words, I am bound to correct it, to whomever it refers. He speaks of only two addresses: the distinction between them implies severe censure on one. I assure you that neither contained the recommendation or the sentiment alluded to.

My Brethren, I repeat that it pains me to have to contradict the repetition, in my own diocese, of foreign accusations, without the smallest pains taken to verify or disprove them with means at hand. But this can hardly excite surprise in us who know the antecedents of that journal under another name, the absence for years of all reserve or reverence in its treatment of persons or of things deemed sacred, its grazing over the very edges of the most perilous abysses of error, and its habitual preferences of uncatholic to catholic instincts, tendencies, and motives. In uttering these sad thoughts, and entreating you to warn your people, and especially the young, against such dangerous leadership, believe me I am only obeying a higher direction than my own impulses, and acting under much more solemn sanctions. Nor shall I stand alone in this unhappily necessary correction.

But let us pass to more cheerful and consoling thoughts. If my connection with the preparation of the Address, from my having held, though unworthy, office in its Committee, enables and authorises me to rebut false charges against it, it has further bestowed upon me the privilege of personal contact with a body of men who justly represented the entire Episcopate, and would have represented it with equal advantage in any other period of the Church. I know not who selected them, nor do I venture to say that many other equal committees of eighteen could not have been extracted from the remainder. I think they might; but I must say that a singular wisdom seemed to me to have presided over the actual, whatever might have been any other possible, choice.

Deliberations more minute, more mutually respectful, more courteous, or at the same time more straightforward and unflinching, could hardly have been carried on. More learning in theology and canon law, more deep religious feeling, a graver sense of the responsibility laid upon the Commission, or a more scrupulous regard to the claims of justice, and no less of mercy, could scarcely have been exhibited. Its spirit was one of mildness, of gentleness, and of reverence to all who rightly claimed it. "Violent courses," invitations to "draw the sword and rush on enemies," or to deal about "the major excommunication by name," I deliberately assure you, were never mentioned, never insinuated, and I think I may say, never thought of by any one in that Council. In the sketches proposed by several, there was not a harsh or disrespectful word about any sovereign or government; in anything I ever humbly proposed, there was not a single allusion to "King or Kaiser."

Our duty to the Cardinal and our duty to our readers alike forbid us to pass by these remarks without notice. Silence would imply either that we admitted the charge, or that we disregarded the censure; and each of these suppositions would probably be welcome to the enemies of our common cause, while both of them are, in fact, untrue. The impossibility of silence, however, involves the necessity of our stating the facts on which charges so definite and so formidable have been founded. In doing so, we shall endeavour both to exhibit the true sequence of events, and to explain the origin of the Cardinal's misapprehension; and in this way we shall reply to the charges made against us.

But we must first explicitly declare, as we have already implied, that in the Cardinal's support and approbation of our work we should recognise an aid more valuable to the cause we are engaged in than the utmost support which could be afforded to us by any other person; and that we cannot consider the terms he has used respecting us otherwise than as a misfortune to be profoundly regretted, and a blow which might seriously impair our power to do service to religion.

A Catholic Review which is deprived of the countenance of the ecclesiastical authorities is placed in an abnormal position. A germ of distrust is planted in the ground where the good seed should grow; the support which the suspected organ endeavours to lend to the Church is repudiated by the ecclesiastical rulers; and its influence in Protestant society, as an expositor of Catholic ideas, is in danger of being destroyed, because its exposition of them may be declared unsound and unfair, even when it represents them most faithfully and defends them most successfully. The most devoted efforts of its conductors are liable to be misconstrued, and perversely turned either against the Church or against the *Review* itself; its best works are infected with the suspicion with which it is regarded, and its merits become almost more perilous than its faults.

These considerations could not have been overlooked by the Cardinal when he resolved to take a step which threatened to paralyse one of the few organs of Catholic opinion in England. Yet he took that step. If an enemy had done this, it would have been enough to vindicate ourselves, and to leave the burden of an unjust accusation to be borne by its author. But since it has been done by an ecclesiastical superior, with entire foresight of the grave consequences of the act, it has become necessary for us, in addition, to explain the circumstances by which he was led into a course we have so much reason to deplore, and to show how an erroneous and unjust opinion could arise in the mind of one whom obvious motives would have disposed to make the best use of a publication, the conductors of which are labouring to serve the community he governs, and desired and endeavoured to obtain his sanction for their work. If we were unable to reconcile these two necessities,—if we were compelled to choose between a forbearance dishonourable to ourselves, and a refutation injurious to the Cardinal, we should be placed in a painful and almost inextricable difficulty. For a Catholic who defends himself at the expense of an ecclesiastical superior sacrifices that which is generally of more public value than his own fair fame; and an English Catholic who casts back on Cardinal Wiseman the blame unjustly thrown on himself, hurts a reputation which belongs to the whole body, and disgraces the entire community of Catholics. By such a course, a Review which exists only for public objects would stultify its own position and injure its own cause, and *The Home and Foreign Review* has no object to attain, and no views to advance, except objects and views in which the Catholic Church is interested. The ends for which it labours, according to its light and ability, are ends by which the Church cannot but gain; the doctrine it receives, and the authority it obeys, are none other than those which command the acceptance and submission of the Cardinal himself. It desires to enjoy his support; it has no end to gain by opposing him. But we are not in this painful dilemma. We can show that the accusations of the Cardinal are unjust; and, at the same time, we can explain how naturally the suppositions on which they are founded have arisen, by giving a distinct and ample statement of our own principles and position.

The complaint which the Cardinal makes against us contains, substantially, five charges: (1) that we made a misstatement, affirming something historically false to be historically true; (2) that the falsehood consists in the statement that only two addresses were proposed in the Commission—one violent, the other very moderate,—and that the address finally adopted was a compromise between these two; (3) that we insinuated that the Cardinal himself was the author of the violent address; (4) that we cast, by implication, a severe censure on that address and its author; and (5) that our narrative was derived from the same sources, and inspired by the same motives, as that given in *The Patrie*,—for the Cardinal distinctly connects the two accounts, and quotes passages indifferently from both, in such a way that words which we never used might by a superficial reader be supposed to be ours.

To these charges our reply is as follows: (1) We gave the statement of which the Cardinal complains as a mere rumour current on any good authority at the time of our publication, and we employed every means in our power to test its accuracy, though the only other narratives which had then reached England were, as the Cardinal says (p. 9), too "partial and perverted" to enable us to sift it to the bottom. We stated that a rumour was current, not that its purport was true. (2) We did not speak of "only two addresses" actually submitted to the Commission. We supposed the report to mean, that of the three possible forms of address, two extreme and one mean, each of which actually had partisans in the Commission, the middle or moderate form was the one finally adopted. (3) We had no suspicion that the Cardinal had proposed any violent address at all; we did not know that such a proposal had been, or was about to be, attributed to him; and there was no connection whatever between him and it either in our mind or in our language. (4) We implied no censure either on the course proposed or on its proposer, still less on the Cardinal personally. (5) The articles in *The Patrie* first appeared—and that in France—some days after our Review was in the hands of the public; we know nothing of the authority on which their statements were founded, and we have not the least sympathy either with the politics or the motives of that newspaper.

This reply would be enough for our own defence; but it is right that we should show, on the other side, how it came to pass that the Cardinal was led to subject our words to that construction which we have so much reason to regret. Reading them by the light of his own knowledge, and through the medium of the false reports which afterwards arose with regard to himself, his interpretation of them may easily have appeared both plausible and likely. For there were more draft addresses than one: one was his; the actual address was a compromise between them, and he had been falsely accused of, and severely censured for, proposing violent courses in his address. Knowing this, he was tempted to suspect a covert allusion to himself under our words, and the chronological relation between our own article and those of *The Patrie* was easily forgotten, or made nugatory by the supposition of their both being derived from the same sources of information.

But this will be made clearer by the following narrative of facts: A Commission was appointed to draw up the address of the bishops; Cardinal Wiseman, its president, proposed a draft address, which was not obnoxious to any of the criticisms made on any other draft, and is, in substance, the basis of the address as it was ultimately settled. It was favourably received by the Commission; but, after some deliberation, its final adoption was postponed.

Subsequently, a prelate who had been absent from the previous discussion presented another draft, not in competition with that proposed by the president, nor as an amendment to it, but simply as a basis for discussion. This second draft was also favourably received; and the Commission, rather out of consideration for the great services and reputation of its author than from any dissatisfaction with the address proposed by the president, resolved to amalgamate the two drafts. All other projects were set aside; and, in particular, two proposals were deliberately rejected. One of these proposals was, to pay a tribute of acknowledgment for the services of the French nation to the Holy See; the other was, to denounce the perfidious and oppressive policy of the Court of Turin in terms which we certainly should not think either exaggerated or undeserved. We have neither right nor inclination to complain of the ardent patriotism which has been exhibited by the illustrious Bishop of Orleans in the two publications he has put forth since his return to his See, or of the indignation which the system prevailing at Turin must excite in every man who in his heart loves the Church, or whose intelligence can appreciate the first principles of government. Whatever may have been the censure proposed, it certainly did not surpass the measure of the offence. Nevertheless, the impolicy of a violent course, which could not fail to cause irritation, and to aggravate the difficulties of the Church, appears to have been fully recognised by the Commission; and we believe that no one was more prompt in exposing the inutility of such a measure than the Cardinal himself. The idea that anything imprudent or aggressive was to be found in his draft is contradicted by all the facts of the case, and has not a shadow of foundation in anything that is contained in the address as adopted.

We need say no more to explain what has been very erroneously called our covert insinuation. From this narrative of facts our statement comes out, no longer as a mere report, but as a substantially accurate summary of events, questioned only on one point,—the extent of the censure which was proposed. So that in the account which the Cardinal quoted from our pages there was no substantial statement to correct, as in fact no correction of any definite point but one has been attempted.

How this innocent statement has come to be suspected of a hostile intent, and to be classed with the calumnies of *The Patrie*, is another question. The disposition with which the Cardinal sat in judgment upon our words was founded, not on anything they contained, but, as he declares, on the antecedents of the conductors of *The Home and Foreign Review*, and on the character of a journal which no longer exists. That character he declares to consist in "the absence for years of all reserve or reverence in its treatment of persons or of things deemed sacred, its grazing over the very edges of the most perilous abysses of error, and its habitual preferences of uncatholic to catholic instincts, tendencies, and motives." In publishing this charge, which amounts to a declaration that we hold opinions and display a spirit not compatible with an entire attachment and submission of intellect and will to the doctrine and authority of the Catholic Church, the Cardinal adds, "I am only obeying a higher direction than my own impulses, and acting under much more solemn sanctions. Nor shall I stand alone in this unhappily necessary correction."

There can be little doubt of the nature of the circumstances to which this announcement points. It is said that certain papers or propositions, which the report does not specify, have been extracted from the journal which the Cardinal identifies with this Review, and forwarded to Rome for examination; that the Prefect of Propaganda has characterised these extracts, or some of them, in terms which correspond to the Cardinal's language; and that the English bishops have deliberated whether they should issue similar declarations. We have no reason to doubt that the majority of them share the Cardinal's view, which is also that of a large portion both of the rest of the clergy and also of the laity; and, whatever may be the precise action which has been taken in the matter, it is unquestionable that a very formidable mass of ecclesiastical authority and popular feeling is united against certain principles or opinions which, whether rightly or wrongly, are attributed to us. No one will suppose that an impression so general can be entirely founded on a mistake. Those who admit the bare orthodoxy of our doctrine will, under the circumstances, naturally conclude that in our way of holding or expounding it there must be something new and strange, unfamiliar and bewildering, to those who are accustomed to the prevalent spirit of Catholic literature; something which our fellow-Catholics are not prepared to admit; something which can sufficiently explain misgivings so commonly and so sincerely entertained. Others may perhaps imagine that we are unconsciously drifting away from the Church, or that we only professedly and hypocritically remain with her. But the Catholic critic will not forget that charity is a fruit of our religion, and that his anxiety to do justice to those from whom he must differ ought always to be in equal proportion with his zeal. Relying, then, upon this spirit of fairness, convinced of the sincerity of the opposition we encounter, and in order that there may remain a distinct and intelligible record of the aim to which we dedicate our labours, we proceed to make that declaration which may be justly asked of nameless writers, as a testimony of the purpose which has inspired our undertaking, and an abiding pledge of our consistency.

This Review has been begun on a foundation which its conductors can never abandon without treason to their own convictions, and infidelity to the objects they have publicly avowed. That foundation is a humble faith in the infallible teaching of the Catholic Church, a devotion to her cause which controls every other interest, and an attachment to her authority which no other influence can supplant. If in anything published by us a passage can be found which is contrary to that doctrine, incompatible with that devotion, or disrespectful to that authority, we sincerely retract and lament it. No such passage was ever consciously admitted into the pages either of the late *Rambler* or of this Review. But undoubtedly we may have committed errors in judgment, and admitted errors of fact; such mistakes are unavoidable in secular matters, and no one is exempt from them in spiritual things except by the constant assistance of Divine grace. Our wish and purpose are not to deny faults, but to repair them; to instruct, not to disturb our readers; to take down the barriers which shut out our Protestant countrymen from the Church, not to raise up divisions within her pale; and to confirm and deepen, not to weaken, alter, or circumscribe the faith of Catholics.

The most exalted methods of serving religion do not lie in the path of a periodical which addresses a general audience. The appliances of the spiritual life belong to a more retired sphere—that of the priesthood, of the sacraments, of religious offices ; that of prayer, meditation, and self-examination. They are profaned by exposure, and choked by the distractions of public affairs. The world cannot be taken into the confidence of our inner life, nor can the discussion of ascetic morality be complicated with the secular questions of the day. To make the attempt would be to usurp and degrade a holier office. The function of the journalist is on another level. He may toil in the same service, but not in the same rank, as the master-workman. His tools are coarser, his method less refined, and if his range is more extended, his influence is less intense. Literature, like government, assists religion, but it does so indirectly, and from without. The ends for which it works are distinct from those of the Church, and yet subsidiary to them ; and the more independently each force achieves its own end, the more complete will the ultimate agreement be found, and the more will religion profit. The course of a periodical publication in its relation to the Church is defined by this distinction of ends ; its sphere is limited by the difference and inferiority of the means which it employs, while the need for its existence and its independence is vindicated by the necessity there is for the service it performs.

It is the peculiar mission of the Church to be the channel of grace to each soul by her spiritual and pastoral action—she alone has this mission ; but it is not her only work. She has also to govern and educate, so far as government and education are needful subsidiaries to her great work of the salvation of souls. By her discipline, her morality, her law, she strives to realise the divine order upon earth ; while by her intellectual labour she seeks an even fuller knowledge of the works, the ideas, and the nature of God. But the ethical and intellectual offices of the Church, as distinct from her spiritual office, are not hers exclusively or peculiarly. They were discharged, however imperfectly, before she was founded ; and they are discharged still, independently of her, by two other authorities,—science and society ; the Church cannot perform all these functions by herself, nor, consequently, can she absorb their direction. The political and intellectual orders remain permanently distinct from the spiritual. They follow their own ends, they obey their own laws, and in doing so they support the cause of religion by the discovery of truth and the upholding of right. They render this service by fulfilling their own ends independently and unrestrictedly, not by surrendering them for the sake of spiritual interests. Whatever diverts government and science from their own spheres, or leads religion to usurp their domains, confounds distinct authorities, and imperils not only political right and scientific truths, but also the cause of faith and morals. A government that, for the interests of religion, disregards political right, and a science that, for the sake of protecting faith, wavers and dissembles in the pursuit of knowledge, are instruments at least as well adapted to serve the cause of falsehood as to combat it, and never can be used in furtherance of the truth without that treachery to principle which is a sacrifice too costly to be made for the service of any interest whatever.

Again, the principles of religion, government, and science are in harmony, always and absolutely ; but their interests are not. And though all other interests must yield to those of religion, no principle can succumb to any interest. A political law or a scientific truth may be perilous to the morals or the faith of individuals, but it cannot on this ground be resisted by the Church. It may at times be a duty of the State to protect freedom of conscience, yet this freedom may be a temptation to apostasy. A discovery may be made in science which will shake the faith of thousands, yet religion cannot refute it or object to it. The difference in this respect between a true and a false religion is, that one judges all things by the standard of their truth, the other by the touchstone of its own interests. A false religion fears the progress of all truth; a true religion seeks and recognises truth wherever it can be found, and claims the power of regulating and controlling, not the progress, but the dispensation of knowledge. The Church both accepts the truth and prepares the individual to receive it.

The religious world has been long divided upon this great question: Do we find principles in politics and in science? Are their methods so rigorous that we may not bend them, their conclusions so certain that we may not dissemble them, in presence of the more rigorous necessity of the salvation of souls and the more certain truth of the dogmas of faith? This question divides Protestants into rationalists and pietists. The Church solves it in practice, by admitting the truths and the principles in the gross, and by dispensing them in detail as men can bear them. She admits the certainty of the mathematical method, and she uses the historical and critical method in establishing the documents of her own revelation and tradition. Deny this method, and her recognised arguments are destroyed. But the Church cannot and will not deny the validity of the methods upon which she is obliged to depend, not indeed for her existence, but for her demonstration. There is no opening for Catholics to deny, in the gross, that political science may have absolute principles of right, or intellectual science of truth.

During the last hundred years Catholic literature has passed through three phases in relation to this question. At one time, when absolutism and infidelity were in the ascendant, and the Church was oppressed by governments and reviled by the people, Catholic writers imitated, and even caricatured the early Christian apologists in endeavouring to represent their system in the light most acceptable to one side or the other, to disguise antagonism, to modify old claims, and to display only that side of their religion which was likely to attract toleration and good will. Nothing which could give offence was allowed to appear. Something of the fulness, if not of the truth, of religion was sacrificed for the sake of conciliation. The great Catholic revival of the present century gave birth to an opposite school. The attitude of timidity and concession was succeeded by one of confidence and triumph. Conciliation passed into defiance. The unscrupulous falsehoods of the eighteenth century had thrown suspicion on all that had ever been advanced by the adversaries of religion; and the belief that nothing could be said for the Church gradually died away into the conviction that nothing which was said against her could be true. A school of writers arose strongly imbued with a horror of the calumnies of infidel philosophers and hostile controversialists, and animated by a sovereign desire to revive and fortify the spirit of Catholics. They became literary advocates. Their only object was to accomplish the great work before them; and they were often careless in statement, rhetorical and illogical in argument, too positive to be critical, and too confident to be precise. In this school the present generation of Catholics was educated; to it they owe the ardour of their zeal, the steadfastness of their faith, and their Catholic views of history, politics, and literature. The services of these writers have been very great. They restored the balance, which was leaning terribly against religion, both in politics and letters. They created a Catholic opinion and a great Catholic literature, and they conquered for the Church a very powerful influence in European thought. The word "ultramontane" was revived to designate this school, and that restricted term was made to embrace men as different as De Maistre and Bonald, Lamennais and Montalembert, Balmez and Donoso Cortes, Stolberg and Schlegel, Phillips and Tapparelli.

There are two peculiarities by which we may test this whole group of eminent writers: their identification of Catholicism with some secular cause, such as the interests of a particular political or philosophical system, and the use they make of Protestant authorities. The views which they endeavoured to identify with the cause of the Church, however various, agreed in giving them the air of partisans. Like advocates, they were wont to defend their cause with the ingenuity of those who know that all points are not equally strong, and that nothing can be conceded except what they can defend. They did much for the cause of learning, though they took little interest in what did not immediately serve their turn. In their use of Protestant writers they displayed the same partiality. They estimated a religious adversary, not by his knowledge, but by his concessions; and they took advantage of the progress of historical criticism, not to revise their opinions, but to obtain testimony to their truth. It was characteristic of the school to be eager in citing the favourable passages from Protestant authors, and to be careless of those which were less serviceable for discussion. In the principal writers this tendency was counteracted by character and learning; but in the hands of men less competent or less suspicious of themselves, sore pressed by the necessities of controversy, and too obscure to challenge critical correction, the method became a snare for both the writer and his readers. Thus the very qualities which we condemn in our opponents, as the natural defences of error and the significant emblems of a bad cause, came to taint both our literature and our policy.

Learning has passed on beyond the range of these men's vision. Their greatest strength was in the weakness of their adversaries, and their own faults were eclipsed by the monstrous errors against which they fought. But scientific methods have now been so perfected, and have come to be applied in so cautious and so fair a spirit, that the apologists of the last generation have collapsed before them. Investigations have become so impersonal, so colourless, so free from the prepossessions which distort truth, from predetermined aims and foregone conclusions, that their results can only be met by investigations in which the same methods are yet more completely and conscientiously applied. The sounder scholar is invincible by the brilliant rhetorician, and the eloquence and ingenuity of De Maistre and Schlegel would be of no avail against researches pursued with perfect mastery of science and singleness of purpose. The apologist's armour would be vulnerable at the point where his religion and his science were forced into artificial union. Again, as science widens and deepens, it escapes from the grasp of dilettantism. Such knowledge as existed formerly could be borrowed, or superficially acquired, by men whose lives were not devoted to its pursuit, and subjects as far apart as the controversies of Scripture, history, and physical science might be respectably discussed by a single writer. No such shallow versatility is possible now. The new accuracy and certainty of criticism have made science unattainable except by those who devote themselves systematically to its study. The training of a skilled labourer has become indispensable for the scholar, and science yields its results to none but those who have mastered its methods. Herein consists the distinction between the apologists we have described and that school of writers and thinkers which is now growing up in foreign countries, and on the triumph of which the position of the Church in modern society depends. While she was surrounded with men whose learning was sold to the service of untruth, her defenders naturally adopted the artifices of the advocate, and wrote as if they were pleading for a human cause. It was their concern only to promote those precise kinds and portions of knowledge which would confound an adversary, or support a claim. But learning ceased to be hostile to Christianity when it ceased to be pursued merely as an instrument of controversy—when facts came to be acknowledged, no longer because they were useful, but simply because they were true. Religion had no occasion to rectify the results of learning when irreligion had ceased to pervert them, and the old weapons of controversy became repulsive as soon as they had ceased to be useful.

By this means the authority of political right and of scientific truth has been re-established, and they have become, not tools to be used by religion for her own interests, but conditions which she must observe in her actions and arguments. Within their respective spheres, politics can determine what rights are just, science what truths are certain. There are few political or scientific problems which affect the doctrines of religion, and none of them are hostile to it in their solution. But this is not the difficulty which is usually felt. A political principle or a scientific discovery is more commonly judged, not by its relation to religious truth, but by its bearings on some manifest or probable religious interests. A fact may be true, or a law may be just, and yet it may, under certain conditions, involve some spiritual loss.

And here is the touchstone and the watershed of principles. Some men argue that the object of government is to contribute to the salvation of souls; that certain measures may imperil this end, and that therefore they must be condemned. These men only look to interests; they cannot conceive the duty of sacrificing them to independent political principle or idea. Or, again, they will say, "Here is a scientific discovery calculated to overthrow many traditionary ideas, to undo a prevailing system of theology, to disprove a current interpretation, to cast discredit on eminent authorities, to compel men to revise their most settled opinions, to disturb the foundation on which the faith of others stands." These are sufficient reasons for care in the dispensation of truth; but the men we are describing will go on to say, "This is enough to throw suspicion on the discovery itself; even if it is true, its danger is greater than its value. Let it, therefore, be carefully buried, and let all traces of it be swept away."

A policy like this appears to us both wrong in itself and derogatory to the cause it is employed to serve. It argues either a timid faith which fears the light, or a false morality which would do evil that good might come. How often have Catholics involved themselves in hopeless contradiction, sacrificed principle to opportunity, adapted their theories to their interests, and staggered the world's reliance on their sincerity by subterfuges which entangle the Church in the shifting sands of party warfare, instead of establishing her cause on the solid rock of principles! How often have they clung to some plausible chimera which seemed to serve their cause, and nursed an artificial ignorance where they feared the discoveries of an impertinent curiosity! As ingenious in detraction as in silence and dissimulation, have they not too often answered imputations which they could not disprove with accusations which they could not prove, till the slanders they had invented rivalled in number and intensity the slanders which had been invented against them? For such men principles have had only temporary value and local currency. Whatever force was the strongest in any place and at any time, with that they have sought to ally the cause of religion. They have, with equal zeal, identified her with freedom in one country and with absolutism in another; with conservatism where she had privileges to keep, and with reform where she had oppression to withstand. And for all this, what have they gained? They have betrayed duties more sacred than the privileges for which they fought; they have lied before God and man; they have been divided into fractions by the supposed interests of the Church, when they ought to have been united by her principles and her doctrines; and against themselves they have justified those grave accusations of falsehood, insincerity, indifference to civil rights and contempt for civil authorities which are uttered with such profound injustice against the Church.

The present difficulties of the Church—her internal dissensions and apparent weakness, the alienation of so much intellect, the strong prejudice which keeps many away from her altogether, and makes many who had approached her shrink back,—all draw nourishment from this rank soil. The antagonism of hostile doctrines and the enmity of governments count for little in comparison. It is in vain to point to her apostolic tradition, the unbroken unity of her doctrine, her missionary energy, or her triumphs in the region of spiritual life, if we fail to remove the accumulated prejudice which generations of her advocates have thrown up around her. The world can never know and recognise her divine perfection while the pleas of her defenders are scarcely nearer to the truth than the crimes which her enemies impute to her. How can the stranger understand where the children of the kingdom are deceived?

Against this policy a firm and unyielding stand is of supreme necessity. The evil is curable and the loss recoverable by a conscientious adherence to higher principles, and a patient pursuit of truth and right. Political science can place the liberty of the Church on principles so certain and unfailing, that intelligent and disinterested Protestants will accept them; and in every branch of learning with which religion is in any way connected, the progressive discovery of truth will strengthen faith by promoting knowledge and correcting opinion, while it destroys prejudices and superstitions by dissipating the errors on which they are founded. This is a course which conscience must approve in the whole, though against each particular step of it conscience may itself be tempted to revolt. It does not always conduce to immediate advantage; it may lead across dangerous and scandalous ground. A rightful sovereign may exclude the Church from his dominions, or persecute her members. Is she therefore to say that his right is no right, or that all intolerance is necessarily wrong? A newly discovered truth may be a stumbling-block to perplex or to alienate the minds of men. Is she therefore to deny or smother it? By no means. She must in every case do right. She must prefer the law of her own general spirit to the exigencies of immediate external occasion, and leave the issue in the hands of God.

Such is the substance of those principles which shut out *The Home and Foreign Review* from the sympathies of a large portion of the body to which we belong. In common with no small or insignificant section of our fellow-Catholics, we hold that the time has gone by when defects in political or scientific education could be alleged as an excuse for depending upon expediency or mistrusting knowledge; and that the moment has come when the best service that can be done to religion is to be faithful to principle, to uphold the right in politics though it should require an apparent sacrifice, and to seek truth in science though it should involve a possible risk. Modern society has developed no security for freedom, no instrument of progress, no means of arriving at truth, which we look upon with indifference or suspicion. We see no necessary gulf to separate our political or scientific convictions from those of the wisest and most intelligent men who may differ from us in religion. In pursuing those studies in which they can sympathise, starting from principles which they can accept, and using methods which are theirs as well as ours, we shall best attain the objects which alone can be aimed at in a Review,—our own instruction, and the conciliation of opponents.

There are two main considerations by which it is necessary that we should be guided in our pursuit of these objects. First, we have to remember that the scientific method is most clearly exhibited and recognised in connection with subjects about which there are no prepossessions to wound, no fears to excite, no interests to threaten. Hence, not only do we exclude from our range all that concerns the ascetic life and the more intimate relations of religion, but we most willingly devote ourselves to the treatment of subjects quite remote from all religious bearing. Secondly, we have to remember that the internal government of the Church belongs to a sphere exclusively ecclesiastical, from the discussion of which we are shut out, not only by motives of propriety and reverence, but also by the necessary absence of any means for forming a judgment. So much ground is fenced off by these two considerations, that a secular sphere alone remains. The character of a scientific Review is determined for it. It cannot enter on the domains of ecclesiastical government or of faith, and neither of them can possibly be affected by its conclusions or its mode of discussion.

In asserting thus absolutely that all truth must render service to religion, we are saying what few perhaps will deny in the abstract, but what many are not prepared to admit in detail. It will be vaguely felt. that views which take so little account of present inconvenience and manifest danger are perilous and novel, though they may seem to spring from a more unquestioning faith, a more absolute confidence in truth, and a more perfect submission to the general laws of morality. There is no articulate theory, and no distinct view, but there is long habit, and there are strong inducements of another kind which support this sentiment.

To understand the certainty of scientific truth, a man must have deeply studied scientific method; to understand the obligation of political principle requires a similar mental discipline. A man who is suddenly introduced from without into a society where this certainty and obligation are currently acknowledged is naturally bewildered. He cannot distinguish between the dubious impressions of his second-hand knowledge and the certainty of that primary direct information which those who possess it have no power to deny. To accept a criterion which may condemn some cherished opinion has hitherto seemed to him a mean surrender and a sacrifice of position. He feels it simple loss to give up an idea; and even if he is prepared to surrender it when compelled by controversy, still he thinks it quite unnecessary and gratuitous to engage voluntarily in researches which may lead to such an issue. To enter thus upon the discussion of questions which have been mixed up with religion, and made to contribute their support to piety, seems to the idle spectator, or to the person who is absorbed in defending religion, a mere useless and troublesome meddling, dictated by the pride of intellectual triumph, or by the moral cowardice which seeks unworthily to propitiate enemies.

Great consideration is due to those whose minds are not prepared for the full light of truth and the grave responsibilities of knowledge; who have not learned to distinguish what is divine from what is human—defined dogma from the atmosphere of opinion which surrounds it,—and who honour both with the same awful reverence. Great allowances are also due to those who are constantly labouring to nourish the spark of belief in minds perplexed by difficulties, or darkened by ignorance and prejudice. These men have not always the results of research at command ; they have no time to keep abreast with the constant progress of historical and critical science ; and the solutions which they are obliged to give are consequently often imperfect, and adapted only to uninstructed and uncultivated minds. Their reasoning cannot be the same as that of the scholar who has to meet error in its most vigorous, refined, and ingenious form. As knowledge advances, it must inevitably happen that they will find some of their hitherto accepted facts contradicted, and some arguments overturned which have done good service. They will find that some statements, which they have adopted under stress of controversy, to remove prejudice and doubt, turn out to be hasty and partial replies to the questions they were meant to answer, and that the true solutions would require more copious explanation than they can give. And thus will be brought home to their minds that, in the topics upon which popular controversy chiefly turns, the conditions of discussion and the resources of arguments are subject to gradual and constant change.

A Review, therefore, which undertakes to investigate political and scientific problems, without any direct subservience to the interests of a party or a cause, but with the belief that such investigation, by its very independence and straightforwardness, must give the most valuable indirect assistance to religion, cannot expect to enjoy at once the favour of those who have grown up in another school of ideas. Men who are occupied in the special functions of ecclesiastical life, where the Church is all-sufficient and requires no extraneous aid, will naturally see at first in the problems of public life, the demands of modern society, and the progress of human learning, nothing but new and unwelcome difficulties,—trial and distraction to themselves, temptation and danger to their flocks. In time they will learn that there is a higher and a nobler course for Catholics than one which begins in fear and does not lead to security. They will come to see how vast a service they may render to the Church by vindicating for themselves a place in every movement that promotes the study of God's works and the advancement of mankind. They will remember that, while the office of ecclesiastical authority is to tolerate, to warn, and to guide, that of religious intelligence and zeal is not to leave the great work of intellectual and social civilisation to be the monopoly and privilege of others, but to save it from debasement by giving to it for leaders the children, not the enemies, of the Church. And at length, in the progress of political right and scientific knowledge, in the development of freedom in the State and of truth in literature, they will recognise one of the first among their human duties and the highest of their earthly rewards.

XIII

CONFLICTS WITH ROME[1]

AMONG the causes which have brought dishonour on the Church in recent years, none have had a more fatal operation than those conflicts with science and literature which have led men to dispute the competence, or the justice, or the wisdom, of her authorities. Rare as such conflicts have been, they have awakened a special hostility which the defenders of Catholicism have not succeeded in allaying. They have induced a suspicion that the Church, in her zeal for the prevention of error, represses that intellectual freedom which is essential to the progress of truth; that she allows an administrative interference with convictions to which she cannot attach the stigma of falsehood; and that she claims a right to restrain the growth of knowledge, to justify an acquiescence in ignorance, to promote error, and even to alter at her arbitrary will the dogmas that are proposed to faith. There are few faults or errors imputed to Catholicism which individual Catholics have not committed or held, and the instances on which these particular accusations are founded have sometimes been supplied by the acts of authority itself. Dishonest controversy loves to confound the personal with the spiritual element in the Church—to ignore the distinction between the sinful agents and the divine institution. And this confusion makes it easy to deny, what otherwise would be too evident to question, that knowledge has a freedom in the Catholic Church which it can find in no other religion;

[1] *Home and Foreign Review*, April 1864.

though there, as elsewhere, freedom degenerates unless it has to struggle in its own defence.

Nothing can better illustrate this truth than the actual course of events in the cases of Lamennais and Frohschammer. They are two of the most conspicuous instances in point; and they exemplify the opposite mistakes through which a haze of obscurity has gathered over the true notions of authority and freedom in the Church. The correspondence of Lamennais and the later writings of Frohschammer furnish a revelation which ought to warn all those who, through ignorance, or timidity, or weakness of faith, are tempted to despair of the reconciliation between science and religion, and to acquiesce either in the subordination of one to the other, or in their complete separation and estrangement. Of these alternatives Lamennais chose the first, Frohschammer the second; and the exaggeration of the claims of authority by the one and the extreme assertion of independence by the other have led them, by contrary paths, to nearly the same end.

When Lamennais surveyed the fluctuations of science, the multitude of opinions, the confusion and conflict of theories, he was led to doubt the efficacy of all human tests of truth. Science seemed to him essentially tainted with hopeless uncertainty. In his ignorance of its methods he fancied them incapable of attaining to anything more than a greater or less degree of probability, and powerless to afford a strict demonstration, or to distinguish the deposit of real knowledge amidst the turbid current of opinion. He refused to admit that there is a sphere within which metaphysical philosophy speaks with absolute certainty, or that the landmarks set up by history and natural science may be such as neither authority nor prescription, neither the doctrine of the schools nor the interest of the Church, has the power to disturb or the right to evade. These sciences presented to his eyes a chaos incapable of falling into order and harmony by any internal self-development, and requiring the action of an external director to clear up its darkness and remove its uncertainty. He thought that no research, however rigorous, could make sure of any fragment of knowledge worthy the name. He admitted no certainty but that which relied on the general tradition of mankind, recorded and sanctioned by the infallible judgment of the Holy See. He would have all power committed, and every question referred, to that supreme and universal authority. By its means he would supply all the gaps in the horizon of the human intellect, settle every controversy, solve the problems of science, and regulate the policy of states.

The extreme Ultramontanism which seeks the safeguard of faith in the absolutism of Rome he believed to be the keystone of the Catholic system. In his eyes all who rejected it, the Jesuits among them, were Gallicans; and Gallicanism was the corruption of the Christian idea.[1] "If my principles are rejected," he wrote on the 1st of November 1820, "I see no means of defending religion effectually, no decisive answer to the objections of the unbelievers of our time. How could these principles be favourable to them? they are simply the development of the great Catholic maxim, *quod semper, quod ubique, quod ab omnibus*." Joubert said of him, with perfect justice, that when he destroyed all the bases of human certainty, in order to retain no foundation but authority, he destroyed authority itself. The confidence which led him to confound the human element with the divine in the Holy See was destined to be tried by the severest of all tests; and his exaggeration of the infallibility of the Pope proved fatal to his religious faith.

In 1831 the Roman Breviary was not to be bought in Paris. We may hence measure the amount of opposition with which Lamennais's endeavours to exalt Rome would be met by the majority of the French bishops and clergy, and by the school of St. Sulpice. For him, on the other hand, no terms were too strong to express his animosity against those who rejected his

[1] Lamennais, *Correspondence*, Nouvelle édition (Paris: Didier).

teaching and thwarted his designs. The bishops he railed at as idiotic devotees, incredibly blind, supernaturally foolish. "The Jesuits," he said, "were *grenadiers de la folie*, and united imbecility with the vilest passions."[1] He fancied that in many dioceses there was a conspiracy to destroy religion, that a schism was at hand, and that the resistance of the clergy to his principles threatened to destroy Catholicism in France. Rome, he was sure, would help him in his struggle against her faithless assailants, on behalf of her authority, and in his endeavour to make the clergy refer their disputes to her, so as to receive from the Pope's mouth the infallible oracles of eternal truth.[2] Whatever the Pope might decide, would, he said, be right, for the Pope alone was infallible. Bishops might be sometimes resisted, but the Pope never.[3] It was both absurd and blasphemous even to advise him. "I have read in the *Diario di Roma*," he said, "the advice of M. de Chateaubriand to the Holy Ghost. At any rate, the Holy Ghost is fully warned; and if he makes a mistake this time, it will not be the ambassador's fault."

Three Popes passed away, and still nothing was done against the traitors he was for ever denouncing. This reserve astounded him. Was Rome herself tainted with Gallicanism, and in league with those who had conspired for her destruction? What but a schism could ensue from this inexplicable apathy? The silence was a grievous trial to his faith. "Let us shut our eyes," he said, "let us invoke the Holy Spirit, let us collect all the powers of our soul, that our faith may not be shaken."[4] In his perplexity he began to make distinctions between the Pope and the Roman Court. The advisers of the Pope were traitors, dwellers in the outer darkness, blind and deaf; the Pope himself and he alone was infallible, and would never act so as to injure the faith, though meanwhile he was not aware of the real state of things, and was evidently deceived by false

[1] April 12 and June 25, 1830.
[2] Feb. 27, 1831.
[3] March 30, 1831.
[4] May 8 and June 15, 1829.

reports.[1] A few months later came the necessity for a further distinction between the Pontiff and the Sovereign. If the doctrines of the *Avenir* had caused displeasure at Rome, it was only on political grounds. If the Pope was offended, he was offended not as Vicar of Christ, but as a temporal monarch implicated in the political system of Europe. In his capacity of spiritual head of the Church he could not condemn writers for sacrificing all human and political considerations to the supreme interests of the Church, but must in reality agree with them.[2] As the Polish Revolution brought the political questions into greater prominence, Lamennais became more and more convinced of the wickedness of those who surrounded Gregory XVI., and of the political incompetence of the Pope himself. He described him as weeping and praying, motionless, amidst the darkness which the ambitious, corrupt, and frantic idiots around him were ever striving to thicken.[3] Still he felt secure. When the foundations of the Church were threatened, when an essential doctrine was at stake, though, for the first time in eighteen centuries, the supreme authority might refuse to speak,[4] at least it could not speak out against the truth. In this belief he made his last journey to Rome. Then came his condemnation. The staff on which he leaned with all his weight broke in his hands; the authority he had so grossly exaggerated turned against him, and his faith was left without support. His system supplied no resource for such an emergency. He submitted, not because he was in error, but because Catholics had no right to defend the Church against the supreme will even of an erring Pontiff.[5] He was persuaded that his silence would injure religion, yet he deemed it his duty to be silent and to abandon theology. He had ceased to believe that the Pope could not err, but he still believed that he could not lawfully be disobeyed. In the two years during which he still remained in the Church

[1] Feb. 8, 1830. [2] Aug. 15, 1831. [3] Feb. 10, 1832.
[4] July 6, 1829. [5] Sept. 15, 1832.

his faith in her system fell rapidly to pieces. Within two months after the publication of the Encyclical he wrote that the Pope, like the other princes, seemed careful not to omit any blunder that could secure his annihilation.[1] Three weeks afterwards he denounced in the fiercest terms the corruption of Rome. He predicted that the ecclesiastical hierarchy was about to depart with the old monarchies; and, though the Church could not die, he would not undertake to say that she would revive in her old forms.[2] The Pope, he said, had so zealously embraced the cause of antichristian despotism as to sacrifice to it the religion of which he was the chief. He no longer felt it possible to distinguish what was immutable in the external organisation of the Church. He admitted the personal fallibility of the Pope, and declared that, though it was impossible, without Rome, to defend Catholicism successfully, yet nothing could be hoped for from her, and that she seemed to have condemned Catholicism to die.[3] The Pope, he soon afterwards said, was in league with the kings in opposition to the eternal truths of religion, the hierarchy was out of court, and a transformation like that from which the Church and Papacy had sprung was about to bring them both to an end, after eighteen centuries, in Gregory XVI.[4] Before the following year was over he had ceased to be in communion with the Catholic Church.

The fall of Lamennais, however impressive as a warning, is of no great historical importance; for he carried no one with him, and his favourite disciples became the ablest defenders of Catholicism in France. But it exemplifies one of the natural consequences of dissociating secular from religious truth, and denying that they hold in solution all the elements necessary for their reconciliation and union. In more recent times, the same error has led, by a contrary path, to still more lamentable results, and scepticism on the possibility of harmonising reason and faith has once more driven a philosopher into

[1] Oct. 9, 1832.
[2] Jan. 25, 1833.
[3] Feb. 5, 1833.
[4] March 25, 1833.

heresy. Between the fall of Lamennais and the conflict with Frohschammer many metaphysical writers among the Catholic clergy had incurred the censures of Rome. It is enough to cite Bautain in France, Rosmini in Italy, and Günther in Austria. But in these cases no scandal ensued, and the decrees were received with prompt and hearty submission. In the cases of Lamennais and Frohschammer no speculative question was originally at issue, but only the question of authority. A comparison between their theories will explain the similarity in the courses of the two men, and at the same time will account for the contrast between the isolation of Lamennais and the influence of Frohschammer, though the one was the most eloquent writer in France, and the head of a great school, and the other, before the late controversy, was not a writer of much name. This contrast is the more remarkable since religion had not revived in France when the French philosopher wrote, while for the last quarter of a century Bavaria has been distinguished among Catholic nations for the faith of her people. Yet Lamennais was powerless to injure a generation of comparatively ill-instructed Catholics, while Frohschammer, with inferior gifts of persuasion, has won educated followers even in the home of Ultramontanism.

The first obvious explanation of this difficulty is the narrowness of Lamennais's philosophy. At the time of his dispute with the Holy See he had somewhat lost sight of his traditionalist theory; and his attention, concentrated upon politics, was directed to the problem of reconciling religion with liberty,—a question with which the best minds in France are still occupied. But how can a view of policy constitute a philosophy? He began by thinking that it was expedient for the Church to obtain the safeguards of freedom, and that she should renounce the losing cause of the old *régime*. But this was no more philosophy than the similar argument which had previously won her to the side of despotism when it was the stronger cause. As Bonald, however, had erected absolute monarchy into a dogma, so Lamennais proceeded to do with freedom. The Church, he said, was on the side of freedom, because it was the just side, not because it was the stronger. As De Maistre had seen the victory of Catholic principles in the Restoration, so Lamennais saw it in the revolution of 1830.

This was obviously too narrow and temporary a basis for a philosophy. The Church is interested, not in the triumph of a principle or a cause which may be dated as that of 1789, or of 1815, or of 1830, but in the triumph of justice and the just cause, whether it be that of the people or of the Crown, of a Catholic party or of its opponents. She admits the tests of public law and political science. When these proclaim the existence of the conditions which justify an insurrection or a war, she cannot condemn that insurrection or that war. She is guided in her judgment on these causes by criteria which are not her own, but are borrowed from departments over which she has no supreme control. This is as true of science as it is of law and politics. Other truths are as certain as those which natural or positive law embraces, and other obligations as imperative as those which regulate the relations of subjects and authorities. The principle which places right above expedience in the political action of the Church has an equal application in history or in astronomy. The Church can no more identify her cause with scientific error than with political wrong. Her interests may be impaired by some measure of political justice, or by the admission of some fact or document. But in neither case can she guard her interests at the cost of denying the truth.

This is the principle which has so much difficulty in obtaining recognition in an age when science is more or less irreligious, and when Catholics more or less neglect its study. Political and intellectual liberty have the same claims and the same conditions in the eyes of the Church. The Catholic judges the measures of governments and the discoveries of science in exactly the same manner. Public law may make it imperative to overthrow a Catholic monarch, like James II., or to uphold a

Protestant monarch, like the King of Prussia. The demonstrations of science may oblige us to believe that the earth revolves round the sun, or that the *donation of Constantine* is spurious. The apparent interests of religion have much to say against all this; but religion itself prevents those considerations from prevailing. This has not been seen by those writers who have done most in defence of the principle. They have usually considered it from the standing ground of their own practical aims, and have therefore failed to attain that general view which might have been suggested to them by the pursuit of truth as a whole. French writers have done much for political liberty, and Germans for intellectual liberty; but the defenders of the one cause have generally had so little sympathy with the other, that they have neglected to defend their own on the grounds common to both. There is hardly a Catholic writer who has penetrated to the common source from which they spring. And this is the greatest defect in Catholic literature, even to the present day.

In the majority of those who have afforded the chief examples of this error, and particularly in Lamennais, the weakness of faith which it implies has been united with that looseness of thought which resolves all knowledge into opinion, and fails to appreciate methodical investigation or scientific evidence. But it is less easy to explain how a priest, fortified with the armour of German science, should have failed as completely in the same inquiry. In order to solve the difficulty, we must go back to the time when the theory of Frohschammer arose, and review some of the circumstances out of which it sprang.

For adjusting the relations between science and authority, the method of Rome had long been that of economy and accommodation. In dealing with literature, her paramount consideration was the fear of scandal. Books were forbidden, not merely because their statements were denied, but because they seemed injurious to morals, derogatory to authority, or dangerous to faith. To be so, it was not necessary that they should be untrue.

For isolated truths separated from other known truths by an interval of conjecture, in which error might find room to construct its works, may offer perilous occasions to unprepared and unstable minds. The policy was therefore to allow such truths to be put forward only hypothetically, or altogether to suppress them. The latter alternative was especially appropriated to historical investigations, because they contained most elements of danger. In them the progress of knowledge has been for centuries constant, rapid, and sure; every generation has brought to light masses of information previously unknown, the successive publication of which furnished ever new incentives, and more and more ample means of inquiry into ecclesiastical history. This inquiry has gradually laid bare the whole policy and process of ecclesiastical authority, and has removed from the past that veil of mystery wherewith, like all other authorities, it tries to surround the present. The human element in ecclesiastical administration endeavours to keep itself out of sight, and to deny its own existence, in order that it may secure the unquestioning submission which authority naturally desires, and may preserve that halo of infallibility which the twilight of opinion enables it to assume. Now the most severe exposure of the part played by this human element is found in histories which show the undeniable existence of sin, error, or fraud in the high places of the Church. Not, indeed, that any history furnishes, or can furnish, materials for undermining the authority which the dogmas of the Church proclaim to be necessary for her existence. But the true limits of legitimate authority are one thing, and the area which authority may find it expedient to attempt to occupy is another. The interests of the Church are not necessarily identical with those of the ecclesiastical government. A government does not desire its powers to be strictly defined, but the subjects require the line to be drawn with increasing precision. Authority may be protected by its subjects being kept in ignorance of its faults, and by their holding it in superstitious admiration. But religion has no communion with any manner of error: and the conscience can only be injured by such arts, which, in reality, give a far more formidable measure of the influence of the human element in ecclesiastical government than any collection of detached cases of scandal can do. For these arts are simply those of all human governments which possess legislative power, fear attack, deny responsibility, and therefore shrink from scrutiny.

One of the great instruments for preventing historical scrutiny had long been the Index of prohibited books, which was accordingly directed, not against falsehood only, but particularly against certain departments of truth. Through it an effort had been made to keep the knowledge of ecclesiastical history from the faithful, and to give currency to a fabulous and fictitious picture of the progress and action of the Church. The means would have been found quite inadequate to the end, if it had not been for the fact that while society was absorbed by controversy, knowledge was only valued so far as it served a controversial purpose. Every party in those days virtually had its own prohibitive Index, to brand all inconvenient truths with the note of falsehood. No party cared for knowledge that could not be made available for argument. Neutral and ambiguous science had no attractions for men engaged in perpetual combat. Its spirit first won the naturalists, the mathematicians, and the philologists; then it vivified the otherwise aimless erudition of the Benedictines; and at last it was carried into history, to give new life to those sciences which deal with the tradition, the law, and the action of the Church.

The home of this transformation was in the universities of Germany, for there the Catholic teacher was placed in circumstances altogether novel. He had to address men who had every opportunity of becoming familiar with the arguments of the enemies of the Church, and with the discoveries and conclusions of those whose studies were without the bias of any religious object. Whilst he lectured in one room, the next might be occupied by a pantheist, a rationalist, or a Lutheran, descanting on the same topics. When he left the desk his place might be taken by some great original thinker or scholar, who would display all the results of his meditations without regard for their tendency, and without considering what effects they might have on the weak. He was obliged often to draw attention to books lacking the Catholic spirit, but indispensable to the deeper student. Here, therefore, the system of secrecy, economy, and accommodation was rendered impossible by the competition of knowledge, in which the most thorough exposition of the truth was sure of the victory, and the system itself became inapplicable as the scientific spirit penetrated ecclesiastical literature in Germany.

In Rome, however, where the influences of competition were not felt, the reasons of the change could not be understood, nor its benefits experienced; and it was thought absurd that the Germans of the nineteenth century should discard weapons which had been found efficacious with the Germans of the sixteenth. While in Rome it was still held that the truths of science need not be told, and ought not to be told, if, in the judgment of Roman theologians, they were of a nature to offend faith, in Germany Catholics vied with Protestants in publishing matter without being diverted by the consideration whether it might serve or injure their cause in controversy, or whether it was adverse or favourable to the views which it was the object of the Index to protect. But though this great antagonism existed, there was no collision. A moderation was exhibited which contrasted remarkably with the aggressive spirit prevailing in France and Italy. Publications were suffered to pass unnoted in Germany which would have been immediately censured if they had come forth beyond the Alps or the Rhine. In this way a certain laxity grew up side by side with an unmeasured distrust, and German theologians and historians escaped censure.

This toleration gains significance from its contrast to the severity with which Rome smote the German philosophers like Hermes and Günther when they erred.

Here, indeed, the case was very different. If Rome had insisted upon suppressing documents, perverting facts, and resisting criticism, she would have been only opposing truth, and opposing it consciously, for fear of its inconveniences. But if she had refrained from denouncing a philosophy which denied creation or the personality of God, she would have failed to assert her own doctrines against her own children who contradicted them. The philosopher cannot claim the same exemption as the historian. God's handwriting exists in history independently of the Church, and no ecclesiastical exigence can alter a fact. The divine lesson has been read, and it is the historian's duty to copy it faithfully without bias and without ulterior views. The Catholic may be sure that as the Church has lived in spite of the fact, she will also survive its publication. But philosophy has to deal with some facts which, although as absolute and objective in themselves, are not and cannot be known to us except through revelation, of which the Church is the organ. A philosophy which requires the alteration of these facts is in patent contradiction against the Church. Both cannot coexist. One must destroy the other.

Two circumstances very naturally arose to disturb this equilibrium. There were divines who wished to extend to Germany the old authority of the Index, and to censure or prohibit books which, though not heretical, contained matter injurious to the reputation of ecclesiastical authority, or contrary to the common opinions of Catholic theologians. On the other hand, there were philosophers of the schools of Hermes and Günther who would not retract the doctrines which the Church condemned. One movement tended to repress even the knowledge of demonstrable truth, and the other aimed at destroying the dogmatic authority of the Holy See. In this way a collision was prepared, which was eventually brought about by the writings of Dr. Frohschammer.

Ten years ago, when he was a very young lecturer on philosophy in the university of Munich, he published a work on the origin of the soul, in which he argued against the theory of pre-existence, and against the common opinion that each soul is created directly by Almighty God, defending the theory of Generationism by the authority of several Fathers, and quoting, among other modern divines, Klee, the author of the most esteemed treatise of dogmatic theology in the German language It was decided at Rome that his book should be condemned, and he was informed of the intention, in order that he might announce his submission before the publication of the decree.

His position was a difficult one, and it appears to be admitted that his conduct at this stage was not prompted by those opinions on the authority of the Church in which he afterwards took refuge, but must be explained by the known facts of the case. His doctrine had been lately taught in a book generally read and approved. He was convinced that he had at least refuted the opposite theories, and yet it was apparently in behalf of one of these that he was condemned. Whatever errors his book contained, he might fear that an act of submission would seem to imply his acceptance of an opinion he heartily believed to be wrong, and would therefore be an act of treason to truth. The decree conveyed no conviction to his mind. It is only the utterances of an infallible authority that men can believe without argument and explanation, and here was an authority not infallible, giving no reasons, and yet claiming a submission of the reason. Dr. Frohschammer found himself in a dilemma. To submit absolutely would either be a virtual acknowledgment of the infallibility of the authority, or a confession that an ecclesiastical decision necessarily bound the mind irrespectively of its truth or justice. In either case he would have contradicted the law of religion and of the Church. To submit, while retaining his own opinion, to a disciplinary decree, in order to preserve peace and avoid scandal, and to make a general acknowledgment that his work contained various ill-considered and equivocal statements which might bear a bad construction,—such a conditional submission either would not have been that which the Roman Court desired and intended, or, if made without explicit statement of its meaning, would have been in some measure deceitful and hypocritical. In the first case it would not have been received, in the second case it could not have been made without loss of self-respect. Moreover, as the writer was a public professor, bound to instruct his hearers according to his best knowledge, he could not change his teaching while his opinion remained unchanged. These considerations, and not any desire to defy authority, or introduce new opinions by a process more or less revolutionary, appear to have guided his conduct. At this period it might have been possible to arrive at an understanding, or to obtain satisfactory explanations, if the Roman Court would have told him what points were at issue, what passages in his book were impugned, and what were the grounds for suspecting them. If there was on both sides a peaceful and conciliatory spirit, and a desire to settle the problem, there was certainly a chance of effecting it by a candid interchange of explanations. It was a course which had proved efficacious on other occasions, and in the then recent discussion of Günther's system it had been pursued with great patience and decided success.

Before giving a definite reply, therefore, Dr. Frohschammer asked for information about the incriminated articles. This would have given him an opportunity of seeing his error, and making a submission *in foro interno.* But the request was refused. It was a favour, he was told, sometimes extended to men whose great services to the Church deserved such consideration, but not to one who was hardly known except by the very book which had incurred the censure. This answer instantly aroused a suspicion that the Roman Court was more anxious to assert its authority than to correct an alleged error, or to prevent a scandal. It was well known that the mistrust of German philosophy was very deep at Rome; and it seemed far from impossible that an intention existed to put it under all possible restraint.

This mistrust on the part of the Roman divines was fully equalled, and so far justified, by a corresponding literary contempt on the part of many German Catholic scholars. It is easy to understand the grounds of this feeling. The German writers were engaged in an arduous struggle, in which their antagonists were sustained by intellectual power, solid learning, and deep thought, such as the defenders of the Church in Catholic countries have never had to encounter. In this conflict the Italian divines could render no assistance. They had shown themselves altogether incompetent to cope with modern science. The Germans, therefore, unable to recognise them as auxiliaries, soon ceased to regard them as equals, or as scientific divines at all. Without impeaching their orthodoxy, they learned to look on them as men incapable of understanding and mastering the ideas of a literature so very remote from their own, and to attach no more value to the unreasoned decrees of their organ than to the undefended *ipse dixit* of a theologian of secondary rank. This opinion sprang, not from national prejudice or from the self-appreciation of individuals comparing their own works with those of the Roman divines, but from a general view of the relation of those divines, among whom there are several distinguished Germans, to the literature of Germany. It was thus a corporate feeling, which might be shared even by one who was conscious of his own inferiority, or who had written nothing at all. Such a man, weighing the opinion of the theologians of the Gesù and the Minerva, not in the scale of his own performance, but in that of the great achievements of his age, might well be reluctant to accept their verdict upon them without some aid of argument and explanation.

On the other hand, it appeared that a blow which struck the Catholic scholars of Germany would assure to the victorious congregation of Roman divines an easy supremacy over the writers of all other countries. The case of Dr. Frohschammer might be made to test what degree of control it would be possible to exercise over his countrymen, the only body of writers at whom alarm was felt, and who insisted, more than others, on their freedom. But the suspicion of such a possibility was likely only to confirm him in the idea that he was chosen to be the experimental body on which an important principle was to be decided, and that it was his duty, till his dogmatic error was proved, to resist a questionable encroachment of authority upon the rights of freedom. He therefore refused to make the preliminary submission which was required of him, and allowed the decree to go forth against him in the usual way. Hereupon it was intimated to him—though not by Rome—that he had incurred excommunication. This was the measure which raised the momentous question of the liberties of Catholic science, and gave the impulse to that new theory on the limits of authority with which his name has become associated.

In the civil affairs of mankind it is necessary to assume that the knowledge of the moral code and the traditions of law cannot perish in a Christian nation. Particular authorities may fall into error; decisions may be appealed against; laws may be repealed, but the political conscience of the whole people cannot be irrecoverably lost. The Church possesses the same privilege, but in a much higher degree, for she exists expressly for the purpose of preserving a definite body of truths, the knowledge of which she can never lose. Whatever authority, therefore, expresses that knowledge of which she is the keeper must be obeyed. But there is no institution from which this knowledge can be obtained with immediate certainty. A council is not *à priori* œcumenical; the Holy See is not separately infallible. The one has to await a sanction, the other has repeatedly erred. Every decree, therefore, requires a preliminary examination.

A writer who is censured may, in the first place, yield an external submission, either for the sake of discipline, or because his conviction is too weak to support him against the weight of authority. But if the question at issue is more important than the preservation of peace, and if his conviction is strong, he inquires whether the authority which condemns him utters the voice of the Church. If he finds that it does, he yields to it, or ceases to profess the faith of Catholics. If he finds that it does not, but is only the voice of authority, he owes it to his conscience, and to the supreme claims of truth, to remain constant to that which he believes, in spite of opposition. No authority has power to impose error, and, if it resists the truth, the truth must be upheld until it is admitted. Now the adversaries of Dr. Frohschammer had fallen into the monstrous error of attributing to the congregation of the Index a share in the infallibility of the Church. He was placed in the position of a persecuted man, and the general sympathy was with him. In his defence he proceeded to state his theory of the rights of science, in order to vindicate the Church from the imputation of restricting its freedom. Hitherto his works had been written in defence of a Christian philosophy against materialism and infidelity. Their object had been thoroughly religious, and although he was not deeply read in ecclesiastical literature, and was often loose and incautious in the use of theological terms, his writings had not been wanting in catholicity of spirit; but after his condemnation by Rome he undertook to pull down the power which had dealt the blow, and to make himself safe for the future. In this spirit of personal antagonism he commenced a long series of writings in defence of freedom and in defiance of authority.

The following abstract marks, not so much the outline of his system, as the logical steps which carried him to the point where he passed beyond the limit of Catholicism. Religion, he taught, supplies materials but no criterion for philosophy; philosophy has nothing to rely on, in the last resort, but the unfailing veracity of our nature, which is not corrupt or weak, but normally healthy, and unable to deceive us.[1] There is not greater division or uncertainty in matters of speculation than on questions of faith.[2] If at

[1] *Naturphilosophie*, p. 115; *Einleitung in die Philosophie*, pp. 40, 54; *Freiheit der Wissenschaft*, pp. 4, 89; *Athenäum*, i. 17.
[2] *Athenäum*, i. 92.

any time error or doubt should arise, the science possesses in itself the means of correcting or removing it, and no other remedy is efficacious but that which it applies to itself.[1] There can be no free philosophy if we must always remember dogma.[2] Philosophy includes in its sphere all the dogmas of revelation, as well as those of natural religion. It examines by its own independent light the substance of every Christian doctrine, and determines in each case whether it be divine truth.[3] The conclusions and judgments at which it thus arrives must be maintained even when they contradict articles of faith.[4] As we accept the evidence of astronomy in opposition to the once settled opinion of divines, so we should not shrink from the evidence of chemistry if it should be adverse to transubstantiation.[5] The Church, on the other hand, examines these conclusions by her standard of faith, and decides whether they can be taught in theology.[6] But she has no means of ascertaining the philosophical truth of an opinion, and cannot convict the philosopher of error. The two domains are as distinct as reason and faith; and we must not identify what we know with what we believe, but must separate the philosopher from his philosophy. The system may be utterly at variance with the whole teaching of Christianity, and yet the philosopher, while he holds it to be philosophically true and certain, may continue to believe all Catholic doctrine, and to perform all the spiritual duties of a laymen or a priest. For discord cannot exist between the certain results of scientific investigation and the real doctrines of the Church. Both are true, and there is no conflict of truths. But while the teaching of science is distinct and definite, that of the Church is subject to alteration. Theology is at no time absolutely complete, but always liable to be modified, and cannot, therefore, be made a fixed test of truth.[7] Consequently there is no reason against the union of the Churches. For the liberty of private judgment, which is

[1] *Freiheit der Wissenschaft*, p. 32.
[2] *Athenäum*, i. 167.
[3] *Einleitung*, pp. 305, 317, 397.
[4] *Athenäum*, i. 208.
[5] *Ibid.* ii. 655.
[6] *Ibid.* ii. 676.
[7] *Ibid.* ii. 661.

the formal principle of Protestantism, belongs to Catholics; and there is no actual Catholic dogma which may not lose all that is objectionable to Protestants by the transforming process of development.[1]

The errors of Dr. Frohschammer in these passages are not exclusively his own. He has only drawn certain conclusions from premisses which are very commonly received. Nothing is more usual than to confound religious truth with the voice of ecclesiastical authority. Dr. Frohschammer, having fallen into this vulgar mistake, argues that because the authority is fallible the truth must be uncertain. Many Catholics attribute to theological opinions which have prevailed for centuries without reproach a sacredness nearly approaching that which belongs to articles of faith: Dr. Frohschammer extends to defined dogmas the liability to change which belongs to opinions that yet await a final and conclusive investigation. Thousands of zealous men are persuaded that a conflict may arise between defined doctrines of the Church and conclusions which are certain according to all the tests of science: Dr. Frohschammer adopts this view, and argues that none of the decisions of the Church are final, and that consequently in such a case they must give way. Lastly, uninstructed men commonly impute to historical and natural science the uncertainty which is inseparable from pure speculation: Dr. Frohschammer accepts the equality, but claims for metaphysics the same certainty and independence which those sciences possess.

Having begun his course in company with many who have exactly opposite ends in view, Dr. Frohschammer, in a recent tract on the union of the Churches, entirely separates himself from the Catholic Church in his theory of development. He had received the impulse to his new system from the opposition of those whom he considered the advocates of an excessive uniformity and the enemies of progess, and their contradiction has driven him to a point where he entirely sacrifices unity to change. He now affirms that our Lord desired no unity or perfect

[1] *Wiedervereinigung der Katholiken und Protestanten*, pp. 26, 35.

conformity among His followers, except in morals and charity;[1] that He gave no definite system of doctrine; and that the form which Christian faith may have assumed in a particular age has no validity for all future time, but is subject to continual modification.[2] The definitions, he says, which the Church has made from time to time are not to be obstinately adhered to; and the advancement of religious knowledge is obtained by genius, not by learning, and is not regulated by traditions and fixed rules.[3] He maintains that not only the form but the substance varies; that the belief of one age may be not only extended but abandoned in another; and that it is impossible to draw the line which separates immutable dogma from undecided opinions.[4]

The causes which drove Dr. Frohschammer into heresy would scarcely have deserved great attention from the mere merit of the man, for he cannot be acquitted of having, in the first instance, exhibited very superficial notions of theology. Their instructiveness consists in the conspicuous example they afford of the effect of certain errors which at the present day are commonly held and rarely contradicted. When he found himself censured unjustly, as he thought, by the Holy See, it should have been enough for him to believe in his conscience that he was in agreement with the true faith of the Church. He would not then have proceeded to consider the whole Church infected with the liability to err from which her rulers are not exempt, or to degrade the fundamental truths of Christianity to the level of mere school opinions. Authority appeared in his eyes to stand for the whole Church; and therefore, in endeavouring to shield himself from its influence, he abandoned the first principles of the ecclesiastical system. Far from having aided the cause of freedom, his errors have provoked a reaction against it, which must be looked upon with deep anxiety, and of which the first significant symptom remains to be described.

On the 21st of December 1863, the Pope addressed

[1] *Wiedervereinigung*, pp. 8, 10.
[2] *Ibid.* p. 15.
[3] *Ibid.* p. 21.
[4] *Ibid.* pp. 25, 26.

a Brief to the Archbishop of Munich, which was published on the 5th of March. This document explains that the Holy Father had originally been led to suspect the recent Congress at Munich of a tendency similar to that of Frohschammer, and had consequently viewed it with great distrust; but that these feelings were removed by the address which was adopted at the meeting, and by the report of the Archbishop. And he expresses the consolation he has derived from the principles which prevailed in the assembly, and applauds the design of those by whom it was convened. He asked for the opinion of the German prelates, in order to be able to determine whether, in the present circumstances of their Church, it is right that the Congress should be renewed.

Besides the censure of the doctrines of Frohschammer, and the approbation given to the acts of the Munich Congress, the Brief contains passages of deeper and more general import, not directly touching the action of the German divines, but having an important bearing on the position of this *Review*. The substance of these passages is as follows: In the present condition of society the supreme authority in the Church is more than ever necessary, and must not surrender in the smallest degree the exclusive direction of ecclesiastical knowledge. An entire obedience to the decrees of the Holy See and the Roman congregations cannot be inconsistent with the freedom and progress of science. The disposition to find fault with the scholastic theology, and to dispute the conclusions and the method of its teachers, threatens the authority of the Church, because the Church has not only allowed theology to remain for centuries faithful to their system, but has urgently recommended it as the safest bulwark of the faith, and an efficient weapon against her enemies. Catholic writers are not bound only by those decisions of the infallible Church which regard articles of faith. They must also submit to the theological decisions of the Roman congregations, and to the opinions which are commonly received in the schools. And it is wrong, though not heretical, to reject those decisions or opinions.

In a word, therefore, the Brief affirms that the common opinions and explanations of Catholic divines ought not to yield to the progress of secular science, and that the course of theological knowledge ought to be controlled by the decrees of the Index.

There is no doubt that the letter of this document might be interpreted in a sense consistent with the habitual language of the *Home and Foreign Review*. On the one hand, the censure is evidently aimed at that exaggerated claim of independence which would deny to the Pope and the Episcopate any right of interfering in literature, and would transfer the whole weight heretofore belonging to the traditions of the schools of theology to the incomplete, and therefore uncertain, conclusions of modern science. On the other hand, the *Review* has always maintained, in common with all Catholics, that if the one Church has an organ it is through that organ that she must speak; that her authority is not limited to the precise sphere of her infallibility; and that opinions which she has long tolerated or approved, and has for centuries found compatible with the secular as well as religious knowledge of the age, cannot be lightly supplanted by new hypotheses of scientific men, which have not yet had time to prove their consistency with dogmatic truth. But such a plausible accommodation, even if it were honest or dignified, would only disguise and obscure those ideas which it has been the chief object of the *Review* to proclaim. It is, therefore, not only more respectful to the Holy See, but more serviceable to the principles of the *Review* itself, and more in accordance with the spirit in which it has been conducted, to interpret the words of the Pope as they were really meant, than to elude their consequences by subtle distinctions, and to profess a formal adoption of maxims which no man who holds the principles of the *Review* can accept in their intended signification.

One of these maxims is that theological and other opinions long held and allowed in the Church gather truth from time, and an authority in some sort binding from the implied sanction of the Holy See, so that they cannot be rejected without rashness; and that the decrees of the congregation of the Index possess an authority quite independent of the acquirements of the men composing it. This is no new opinion; it is only expressed on the present occasion with unusual solemnity and distinctness. But one of the essential principles of this *Review* consists in a clear recognition, first, of the infinite gulf which in theology separates what is of faith from what is not of faith,—revealed dogmas from opinions unconnected with them by logical necessity, and therefore incapable of anything higher than a natural certainty—and next, of the practical difference which exists in ecclesiastical discipline between the acts of infallible authority and those which possess no higher sanction than that of canonical legality. That which is not decided with dogmatic infallibility is for the time susceptible only of a scientific determination, which advances with the progress of science, and becomes absolute only where science has attained its final results. On the one hand, this scientific progress is beneficial, and even necessary, to the Church; on the other, it must inevitably be opposed by the guardians of traditional opinion, to whom, as such, no share in it belongs, and who, by their own acts and those of their predecessors, are committed to views which it menaces or destroys. The same principle which, in certain conjunctures, imposes the duty of surrendering received opinions imposes in equal extent, and under like conditions, the duty of disregarding the fallible authorities that uphold them.

It is the design of the Holy See not, of course, to deny the distinction between dogma and opinion, upon which this duty is founded, but to reduce the practical recognition of it among Catholics to the smallest possible limits. A grave question therefore arises as to the position of a *Review* founded in great part for the purpose of exemplifying this distinction.[1] In considering the solution of this

[1] The prospectus of the *Review* contained these words: "It will abstain from direct theological discussion, as far as external circumstances will allow; and in dealing with those mixed questions into which theology indirectly enters, its aim will be to combine devotion to the Church with discrimination and candour in the

question two circumstances must be borne in mind: first, that the antagonism now so forcibly expressed has always been known and acknowledged; and secondly, that no part of the Brief applies directly to the *Review*. The *Review* was as distinctly opposed to the Roman sentiment before the Brief as since, and it is still as free from censure as before. It was at no time in virtual sympathy with authority on the points in question, and it is not now in formal conflict with authority.

But the definiteness with which the Holy See has pronounced its will, and the fact that it has taken the initiative, seem positively to invite adhesion, and to convey a special warning to all who have expressed opinions contrary to the maxims of the Brief. A periodical which not only has done so, but exists in a measure for the purpose of doing so, cannot with propriety refuse to survey the new position in which it is placed by this important act. For the conduct of a *Review* involves more delicate relations with the government of the Church than the authorship of an isolated book. When opinions which an author defends are rejected at Rome, he either makes his submission, or, if his mind remains unaltered, silently leaves his book to take its chance, and to influence men according to its merits. But such passivity, however right and seemly in the author of a book, is inapplicable to the case of a *Review*. The periodical iteration of rejected propositions would amount to insult and defiance, and would probably provoke more definite measures; and thus the result would be to commit authority yet more irrevocably to an opinion which otherwise might take no deep root, and might yield ultimately to the influence of time. For it is hard to surrender a cause on behalf of which a struggle has been sustained, and spiritual evils have been inflicted. In an isolated book, the author need discuss no more topics than he likes, and any want of

treatment of her opponents; to reconcile freedom of inquiry with implicit faith, and to discountenance what is untenable and unreal, without forgetting the tenderness due to the weak, or the reverence rightly claimed for what is sacred. Submitting without reserve to infallible authority, it will encourage a habit of manly investigation on subjects of scientific interest."

agreement with ecclesiastical authority may receive so little prominence as to excite no attention. But a continuous *Review*, which adopted this kind of reserve, would give a negative prominence to the topics it persistently avoided, and by thus keeping before the world the position it occupied would hold out a perpetual invitation to its readers to judge between the Church and itself. Whatever it gained of approbation and assent would be so much lost to the authority and dignity of the Holy See. It could only hope to succeed by trading on the scandal it caused.

But in reality its success could no longer advance the cause of truth. For what is the Holy See in its relation to the masses of Catholics, and where does its strength lie? It is the organ, the mouth, the head of the Church. Its strength consists in its agreement with the general conviction of the faithful. When it expresses the common knowledge and sense of the age, or of a large majority of Catholics, its position is impregnable. The force it derives from this general support makes direct opposition hopeless, and therefore disedifying, tending only to division and promoting reaction rather than reform. The influence by which it is to be moved must be directed first on that which gives its strength, and must pervade the members in order that it may reach the head. While the general sentiment of Catholics is unaltered, the course of the Holy See remains unaltered too. As soon as that sentiment is modified, Rome sympathises with the change. The ecclesiastical government, based upon the public opinion of the Church, and acting through it, cannot separate itself from the mass of the faithful, and keep pace with the progress of the instructed minority. It follows slowly and warily, and sometimes begins by resisting and denouncing what in the end it thoroughly adopts. Hence a direct controversy with Rome holds out the prospect of great evils, and at best a barren and unprofitable victory. The victory that is fruitful springs from that gradual change in the knowledge, the ideas, and the convictions of the Catholic body, which, in due time, overcomes the natural reluctance to forsake a beaten path, and by insensible degrees constrains the mouthpiece of tradition to conform itself to the new atmosphere with which it is surrounded. The slow, silent, indirect action of public opinion bears the Holy See along, without any demoralising conflict or dishonourable capitulation. This action belongs essentially to the graver scientific literature to direct: and the inquiry what form that literature should assume at any given moment involves no question which affects its substance, though it may often involve questions of moral fitness sufficiently decisive for a particular occasion.

It was never pretended that the *Home and Foreign Review* represented the opinions of the majority of Catholics. The Holy See has had their support in maintaining a view of the obligations of Catholic literature very different from the one which has been upheld in these pages; nor could it explicitly abandon that view without taking up a new position in the Church. All that could be hoped for on the other side was silence and forbearance, and for a time they have been conceded. But this is the case no longer. The toleration has now been pointedly withdrawn; and the adversaries of the Roman theory have been challenged with the summons to submit.

If the opinions for which submission is claimed were new, or if the opposition now signalised were one of which there had hitherto been any doubt, a question might have arisen as to the limits of the authority of the Holy See over the conscience, and the necessity or possibility of accepting the view which it propounds. But no problem of this kind has in fact presented itself for consideration. The differences which are now proclaimed have all along been acknowledged to exist; and the conductors of this *Review* are unable to yield their assent to the opinions put forward in the Brief.

In these circumstances there are two courses which it is impossible to take. It would be wrong to abandon principles which have been well considered and are sincerely held, and it would also be wrong to assail the authority which contradicts them. The principles have not ceased to be true, nor the authority to be legitimate, because the two are in contradiction. To submit the intellect and conscience without examining the reasonableness and justice of this decree, or to reject the authority on the ground of its having been abused, would equally be a sin, on one side against morals, on the other against faith. The conscience cannot be relieved by casting on the administrators of ecclesiastical discipline the whole responsibility of preserving religious truth; nor can it be emancipated by a virtual apostasy. For the Church is neither a despotism in which the convictions of the faithful possess no power of expressing themselves and no means of exercising legitimate control, nor is it an organised anarchy where the judicial and administrative powers are destitute of that authority which is conceded to them in civil society—the authority which commands submission even where it cannot impose a conviction of the righteousness of its acts.

No Catholic can contemplate without alarm the evil that would be caused by a Catholic journal persistently labouring to thwart the published will of the Holy See, and continuously defying its authority. The conductors of this *Review* refuse to take upon themselves the responsibility of such a position. And if it were accepted, the *Review* would represent no section of Catholics. But the representative character is as essential to it as the opinions it professes, or the literary resources it commands. There is no lack of periodical publications representing science apart from religion, or religion apart from science. The distinctive feature of the *Home and Foreign Review* has been that it has attempted to exhibit the two in union; and the interest which has been attached to its views proceeded from the fact that they were put forward as essentially Catholic in proportion to their scientific truth, and as expressing more faithfully than even the voice of authority the genuine spirit of the Church in relation to intellect. Its object has been to elucidate the harmony which exists between religion and the established conclusions of secular knowledge, and to exhibit the real amity and sympathy between the methods of science and the methods employed by the Church. That amity and sympathy the enemies of the Church refuse to admit, and her friends have not learned to understand. Long disowned by a large part of our Episcopate, they are now rejected by the Holy See; and the issue is vital to a *Review* which, in ceasing to uphold them, would surrender the whole reason of its existence.

Warned, therefore, by the language of the Brief, I will not provoke ecclesiastical authority to a more explicit repudiation of doctrines which are necessary to secure its influence upon the advance of modern science. I will not challenge a conflict which would only deceive the world into a belief that religion cannot be harmonised with all that is right and true in the progress of the present age. But I will sacrifice the existence of the *Review* to the defence of its principles, in order that I may combine the obedience which is due to legitimate ecclesiastical authority, with an equally conscientious maintenance of the rightful and necessary liberty of thought. A conjuncture like the present does not perplex the conscience of a Catholic; for his obligation to refrain from wounding the peace of the Church is neither more nor less real than that of professing nothing beside or against his convictions. If these duties have not been always understood, at least the *Home and Foreign Review* will not betray them; and the cause it has imperfectly expounded can be more efficiently served in future by means which will neither weaken the position of authority nor depend for their influence on its approval.

If, as I have heard, but now am scarcely anxious to believe, there are those, both in the communion of the Church and out of it, who have found comfort in the existence of this *Review*, and have watched its straight short course with hopeful interest, trusting it as a sign that the knowledge deposited in their minds by study, and transformed by conscience into inviolable convictions, was not only tolerated among Catholics, but might be reasonably held to be of the very essence of their system; who were willing to accept its principles as a possible solution of the difficulties they saw in Catholicism, and were even prepared to make its fate the touchstone of the real spirit of our hierarchy; or who deemed that while it lasted it promised them some immunity from the overwhelming pressure of uniformity, some safeguard against resistance to the growth of knowledge and of freedom, and some protection for themselves, since, however weak its influence as an auxiliary, it would, by its position, encounter the first shock, and so divert from others the censures which they apprehended; who have found a welcome encouragement in its confidence, a satisfaction in its sincerity when they shrank from revealing their own thoughts, or a salutary restraint when its moderation failed to satisfy their ardour; whom, not being Catholics, it has induced to think less hardly of the Church, or, being Catholics, has bound more strongly to her;—to all these I would say that the principles it has upheld will not die with it, but will find their destined advocates, and triumph in their appointed time. From the beginning of the Church it has been a law of her nature, that the truths which eventually proved themselves the legitimate products of her doctrine, have had to make their slow way upwards through a phalanx of hostile habits and traditions, and to be rescued, not only from open enemies, but also from friendly hands that were not worthy to defend them. It is right that in every arduous enterprise some one who stakes no influence on the issue should make the first essay, whilst the true champions, like the Triarii of the Roman legions, are behind, and wait, without wavering, until the crisis calls them forward.

And already it seems to have arrived. All that is being done for ecclesiastical learning by the priesthood of the Continent bears testimony to the truths which are now called in question; and every work of real science written by a Catholic adds to their force. The example of great writers aids their cause more powerfully than many theoretical discussions. Indeed, when the principles of the antagonism which divides Catholics have been brought clearly out, the part of theory is accomplished, and most of the work of a *Review* is done. It remains that the principles which have been made intelligible should be translated into practice, and should pass from the arena of discussion into the ethical code of literature. In that shape their efficacy will be acknowledged, and they will cease to be the object of alarm. Those who have been indignant at hearing that their methods are obsolete and their labours vain, will be taught by experience to recognise in the works of another school services to religion more momentous than those which they themselves have aspired to perform ; practice will compel the assent which is denied to theory ; and men will learn to value in the fruit what the germ did not reveal to them. Therefore it is to the prospect of that development of Catholic learning which is too powerful to be arrested or repressed that I would direct the thoughts of those who are tempted to yield either to a malignant joy or an unjust despondency at the language of the Holy See. If the spirit of the *Home and Foreign Review* really animates those whose sympathy it enjoyed, neither their principles, nor their confidence, nor their hopes will be shaken by its extinction. It was but a partial and temporary embodiment of an imperishable idea—the faint reflection of a light which still lives and burns in the hearts of the silent thinkers of the Church.

XIV

THE VATICAN COUNCIL[1]

THE intention of Pius IX. to convene a General Council became known in the autumn of 1864, shortly before the appearance of the Syllabus. They were the two principal measures which were designed to restore the spiritual and temporal power of the Holy See. When the idea of the Council was first put forward it met with no favour. The French bishops discouraged it; and the French bishops holding the talisman of the occupying army, spoke with authority. Later on, when the position had been altered by the impulse which the Syllabus gave to the ultramontane opinions, they revived the scheme they had first opposed. Those who felt their influence injured by the change persuaded themselves that the Court of Rome was more prudent than some of its partisans, and that the Episcopate was less given to extremes than the priesthood and laity. They conceived the hope that an assembly of bishops would curb the intemperance of a zeal which was largely directed against their own order, and would authentically sanction such an exposition of Catholic ideas as would reconcile the animosity that feeds on things spoken in the heat of controversy, and on the errors of incompetent apologists. They had accepted the Syllabus; but they wished to obtain canonicity for their own interpretation of it. If those who had succeeded in assigning an acceptable meaning to its censures could appear in a body to plead their cause before the Pope, the pretensions which compromised the Church might be permanently repressed.

[1] *The North British Review*, October 1870.

Once, during the struggle for the temporal power, the question was pertinently asked, how it was that men so perspicacious and so enlightened as those who were its most conspicuous champions, could bring themselves to justify a system of government which their own principles condemned. The explanation then given was, that they were making a sacrifice which would be compensated hereafter, that those who succoured the Pope in his utmost need were establishing a claim which would make them irresistible in better times, when they should demand great acts of conciliation and reform. It appeared to these men that the time had come to reap the harvest they had arduously sown.

The Council did not originate in the desire to exalt beyond measure the cause of Rome. It was proposed in the interest of moderation; and the Bishop of Orleans was one of those who took the lead in promoting it. The Cardinals were consulted, and pronounced against it. The Pope overruled their resistance. Whatever embarrassments might be in store, and however difficult the enterprise, it was clear that it would evoke a force capable of accomplishing infinite good for religion. It was an instrument of unknown power that inspired little confidence, but awakened vague hopes of relief for the ills of society and the divisions of Christendom. The guardians of immovable traditions, and the leaders of progress in religious knowledge, were not to share in the work. The schism of the East was widened by the angry quarrel between Russia and the Pope; and the letter to the Protestants, whose orders are not recognised at Rome, could not be more than a ceremonious challenge. There was no promise of sympathy in these invitations or in the answers they provoked; but the belief spread to many schools of thought, and was held by Dr. Pusey and by Dean Stanley, by Professor Hase and by M. Guizot, that the auspicious issue of the Council was an object of vital care to all denominations of Christian men.

The Council of Trent impressed on the Church the stamp of an intolerant age, and perpetuated by its decrees the spirit of an austere immorality. The ideas embodied in the Roman Inquisition became characteristic of a system which obeyed expediency by submitting to indefinite modification, but underwent no change of principle. Three centuries have so changed the world that the maxims with which the Church resisted the Reformation have become her weakness and her reproach, and that which arrested her decline now arrests her progress. To break effectually with that tradition and eradicate its influence, nothing less is required than an authority equal to that by which it was imposed. The Vatican Council was the first sufficient occasion which Catholicism had enjoyed to reform, remodel, and adapt the work of Trent. This idea was present among the motives which caused it to be summoned. It was apparent that two systems which cannot be reconciled were about to contend at the Council; but the extent and force of the reforming spirit were unknown.

Seventeen questions submitted by the Holy See to the bishops in 1867 concerned matters of discipline, the regulation of marriage and education, the policy of encouraging new monastic orders, and the means of making the parochial clergy more dependent on the bishops. They gave no indication of the deeper motives of the time. In the midst of many trivial proposals, the leading objects of reform grew more defined as the time approached, and men became conscious of distinct purposes based on a consistent notion of the Church. They received systematic expression from a Bohemian priest, whose work, *The Reform of the Church in its Head and Members*, is founded on practical experience, not only on literary theory, and is the most important manifesto of these ideas. The author exhorts the Council to restrict centralisation, to reduce the office of the Holy See to the ancient limits of its primacy, to restore to the Episcopate the prerogatives which have been confiscated by Rome, to abolish the temporal government, which is the prop of hierarchical despotism, to revise the matrimonial discipline, to suppress many religious orders and the solemn vows for all, to modify the absolute rule of celibacy for the clergy, to admit the use of the vernacular in the Liturgy, to allow a larger share to the laity in the management of ecclesiastical affairs, to encourage the education of the clergy at universities, and to renounce the claims of mediæval theocracy, which are fruitful of suspicion between Church and State.

Many Catholics in many countries concurred in great part of this programme; but it was not the symbol of a connected party. Few agreed with the author in all parts of his ideal church, or did not think that he had omitted essential points. Among the inveterate abuses which the Council of Trent failed to extirpate was the very one which gave the first impulse to Lutheranism. The belief is still retained in the superficial Catholicism of Southern Europe that the Pope can release the dead from Purgatory; and money is obtained at Rome on the assurance that every mass said at a particular altar opens heaven to the soul for which it is offered up. On the other hand, the Index of prohibited books is an institution of Tridentine origin, which has become so unwieldy and opprobrious that even men of strong Roman sympathies, like the bishops of Würzburg and St. Pölten, recommended its reform. In France it was thought that the Government would surrender the organic articles, if the rights of the bishops and the clergy were made secure under the canon law, if national and diocesan synods were introduced, and if a proportionate share was given to Catholic countries in the Sacred College and the Roman congregations. The aspiration in which all the advocates of reform seemed to unite was that those customs should be changed which are connected with arbitrary power in the Church. And all the interests threatened by this movement combined in the endeavour to maintain intact the papal prerogative. To proclaim the Pope infallible was their compendious security against hostile States and Churches, against human liberty and authority, against disintegrating tolerance and rationalising science, against error and sin. It became the common refuge of those who shunned what was called the liberal influence in Catholicism.

Pius IX. constantly asserted that the desire of obtaining the recognition of papal infallibility was not originally his motive in convoking the Council. He did not require that a privilege which was practically undisputed should be further defined. The bishops, especially those of the minority, were never tired of saying that the Catholic world honoured and obeyed the Pope as it had never done before. Virtually he had exerted all the authority which the dogma could confer on him. In his first important utterance, the Encyclical of November 1846, he announced that he was infallible; and the claim raised no commotion. Later on he applied a more decisive test, and gained a more complete success, when the bishops summoned to Rome, not as a Council but as an audience, received from him an additional article of their faith. But apart from the dogma of infallibility he had a strong desire to establish certain cherished opinions of his own on a basis firm enough to outlast his time. They were collected in the Syllabus, which contained the essence of what he had written during many years, and was an abridgment of the lessons which his life had taught him. He was anxious that they should not be lost. They were part of a coherent system. The Syllabus was not rejected; but its edge was blunted and its point broken by the zeal which was spent in explaining it away; and the Pope feared that it would be contested if he repudiated the soothing interpretations. In private he said that he wished to have no interpreter but himself. While the Jesuit preachers proclaimed that the Syllabus bore the full sanction of infallibility, higher functionaries of the Court pointed out that it was an informal document, without definite official value. Probably the Pope would have been content that these his favourite ideas should be rescued from evasion by being incorporated in the canons of the Council. Papal infallibility was implied rather than included among them. Whilst the authority of his acts was not resisted, he was not eager to disparage his right by exposing the need of a more exact definition. The opinions which Pius IX. was anxiously promoting were not the mere fruit of his private meditations; they belonged to the doctrines of a great party, which was busily pursuing its own objects, and had not been always the party of the Pope. In the days of his trouble he had employed an advocate; and the advocate had absorbed the client. During his exile a Jesuit had asked his approbation for a Review, to be conducted by the best talents of the Order, and to be devoted to the papal cause; and he had warmly embraced the idea, less, it should seem, as a prince than as a divine. There were his sovereign rights to maintain; but there was also a doctrinaire interest, there were reminiscences of study as well as practical objects that recommended the project. In these personal views the Pope was not quite consistent. He had made himself the idol of Italian patriots, and of the liberal French Catholics; he had set Theiner to vindicate the suppresser of the Jesuits; and Rosmini, the most enlightened priest in Italy, had been his trusted friend. After his restoration he submitted to other influences; and the writers of the *Civiltà Cattolica*, which followed him to Rome and became his acknowledged organ, acquired power over his mind. These men were not identified with their Order. Their General, Roothan, had disliked the plan of the Review, foreseeing that the Society would be held responsible for writings which it did not approve, and would forfeit the flexibility in adapting itself to the moods of different countries, which is one of the secrets of its prosperity. The Pope arranged the matter by taking the writers under his own protection, and giving to them a sort of exemption and partial immunity under the rule of their Order. They are set apart from other Jesuits; they are assisted and supplied from the literary resources of the Order, and are animated more than any of its other writers by its genuine and characteristic spirit; but they act on their own judgment under the guidance of the Pope, and are a bodyguard, told off from the army, for the personal protection of the Sovereign. It is their easy function to fuse into one system the interests and ideas of the Pope and those of their Society. The result has been, not to weaken by compromise and accommodation, but to intensify both. The prudence and sagacity which are sustained in the government of the Jesuits by their complicated checks on power, and their consideration for the interests of the Order under many various conditions, do not always restrain men who are partially emancipated from its rigorous discipline and subject to a more capricious rule. They were chosen in their capacity as Jesuits, for the sake of the peculiar spirit which their system develops. The Pope appointed them on account of that devotion to himself which is a quality of the Order, and relieved them from some of the restraints which it imposes. He wished for something more papal than other Jesuits; and he himself became more subject to the Jesuits than other pontiffs. He made them a channel of his influence, and became an instrument of their own.

The Jesuits had continued to gain ground in Rome ever since the Pope's return. They had suffered more than others in the revolution that dethroned him; and they had their reward in the restoration. They had long been held in check by the Dominicans; but the theology of the Dominicans had been discountenanced and their spirit broken in 1854, when a doctrine which they had contested for centuries was proclaimed a dogma of faith. In the strife for the Pope's temporal dominion the Jesuits were most zealous; and they were busy in the preparation and in the defence of the Syllabus. They were connected with every measure for which the Pope most cared; and their divines became the oracles of the Roman congregations. The papal infallibility had been always their favourite doctrine. Its adoption by the Council promised to give to their theology official warrant, and to their Order the supremacy in the Church. They were now in power; and they snatched their opportunity when the Council was convoked.

Efforts to establish this doctrine had been going on for years. The dogmatic decree of 1854 involved it so distinctly that its formal recognition seemed to be only a question of time and zeal. People even said that it was the real object of that decree to create a precedent which should make it impossible afterwards to deny papal infallibility. The Catechisms were altered, or new ones were substituted, in which it was taught. After 1852 the doctrine began to show itself in the Acts of provincial synods, and it was afterwards supposed that the bishops of those provinces were committed to it. One of these synods was held at Cologne; and three surviving members were in the Council at Rome, of whom two were in the minority, and the third had continued in his writings to oppose the doctrine of infallibility, after it had found its way into the Cologne decree. The suspicion that the Acts had been tampered with is suggested by what passed at the synod of Baltimore in 1866. The Archbishop of St. Louis signed the Acts of that synod under protest, and after obtaining a pledge that his protest would be inserted by the apostolic delegate. The pledge was not kept. "I complain," writes the archbishop, "that the promise which had been given was broken. The Acts ought to have been published in their integrity, or not at all."[1] This process was carried on so boldly that men understood what was to come. Protestants foretold that the Catholics would not rest until the Pope was formally declared infallible; and a prelate returning from the meeting of bishops at Rome in 1862 was startled at being asked by a clear-sighted friend whether infallibility had not been brought forward.

It was produced not then, but at the next great meeting, in 1867. The Council had been announced; and the bishops wished to present an address to the Pope. Haynald, Archbishop of Colocza, held the pen, assisted by Franchi, one of the clever Roman prelates and by

[1] Fidem mihi datam non servatam fuisse queror. Acta supprimere, aut integra dare oportebat. He says also: Omnia ad nutum delegati Apostolici fiebant.

some bishops, among whom were the Archbishop of Westminster and the Bishop of Orleans. An attempt was made to get the papal infallibility acknowledged in the address. Several bishops declared that they could not show themselves in their dioceses if they came back without having done anything for that doctrine. They were resisted in a way which made them complain that its very name irritated the French. Haynald refused their demand, but agreed to insert the well-known words of the Council of Florence; and the bishops did not go away empty-handed.

A few days before this attempt was made, the *Civiltà Cattolica* had begun to agitate, by proposing that Catholics should bind themselves to die, if need be, for the truth of the doctrine; and the article was printed on a separate sheet, bearing the papal *imprimatur*, and distributed widely. The check administered by Haynald and his colleagues brought about a lull in the movement; but the French bishops had taken alarm, and Maret, the most learned of them, set about the preparation of his book.

During the winter of 1868-69 several commissions were created in Rome to make ready the materials for the Council. The dogmatic commission included the Jesuits Perrone, Schrader, and Franzelin. The question of infallibility was proposed to it by Cardoni, Archbishop of Edessa, in a dissertation which, having been revised, was afterwards published, and accepted by the leading Roman divines as an adequate exposition of their case. The dogma was approved unanimously, with the exception of one vote, Alzog of Freiberg being the only dissentient. When the other German divines who were in Rome learned the scheme that was on foot in the Dogmatic Commission, they resolved to protest, but were prevented by some of their colleagues. They gave the alarm in Germany. The intention to proclaim infallibility at the Council was no longer a secret. The first bishop who made the wish public was Fessler of St. Pölten. His language was guarded, and he only prepared his readers for a probable contingency; but he was soon followed by the Bishop of Nîmes, who thought the discussion of the dogma superfluous, and foreshadowed a vote by acclamation. The *Civiltà* on the 6th of February gave utterance to the hope that the Council would not hesitate to proclaim the dogma and confirm the Syllabus in less than a month. Five days later the Pope wrote to some Venetians who had taken a vow to uphold his infallibility, encouraging their noble resolution to defend his supreme authority and all his rights. Until the month of May Cardinal Antonelli's confidential language to diplomatists was that the dogma was to be proclaimed, and that it would encounter no difficulty.

Cardinal Reisach was to have been the President of the Council. As Archbishop of Munich he had allowed himself and his diocese to be governed by the ablest of all the ultramontane divines. During his long residence in Rome he rose to high estimation, because he was reputed to possess the secret, and to have discovered the vanity, of German science. He had amused himself with Christian antiquities; and his friendship for the great explorer De' Rossi brought him for a time under suspicion of liberality. But later he became unrelenting in his ardour for the objects of the *Civiltà*, and regained the confidence of the Pope. The German bishops complained that he betrayed their interests, and that their church had suffered mischief from his paramount influence. But in Rome his easy temper and affable manners made him friends; and the Court knew that there was no cardinal on whom it was so safe to rely.

Fessler, the first bishop who gave the signal of the intended definition, was appointed Secretary. He was esteemed a learned man in Austria, and he was wisely chosen to dispel the suspicion that the conduct of the Council was to be jealously retained in Roman hands, and to prove that there are qualities by which the confidence of the Court could be won by men of a less favoured nation. Besides the President and Secretary, the most conspicuous of the Pope's theological advisers was a

German. At the time when Passaglia's reputation was great in Rome, his companion Clement Schrader shared the fame of his solid erudition. When Passaglia fell into disgrace, his friend smote him with reproaches and intimated the belief that he would follow the footsteps of Luther and debauch a nun. Schrader is the most candid and consistent asserter of the papal claims. He does not shrink from the consequences of the persecuting theory; and he has given the most authentic and unvarnished exposition of the Syllabus. He was the first who spoke out openly what others were variously attempting to compromise or to conceal. While the Paris Jesuits got into trouble for extenuating the Roman doctrine, and had to be kept up to the mark by an abbé who reminded them that the Pope, as a physical person, and without co-operation of the Episcopate, is infallible, Schrader proclaimed that his will is supreme even against the joint and several opinions of the bishops.[1]

When the proceedings of the dogmatic commission, the acts of the Pope, and the language of French and Austrian bishops, and of the press serving the interests of Rome, announced that the proclamation of infallibility had ceased to be merely the aspiration of a party and was the object of a design deliberately set on foot by those to whom the preparation and management of the Council pertained, men became aware that an extraordinary crisis was impending, and that they needed to make themselves familar with an unforeseen problem. The sense of its gravity made slow progress. The persuasion was strong among divines that the episcopate would not surrender to a party which was odious to many of them; and politicians were reluctant to believe that schemes were ripening such as Fessler described, schemes intended to alter the relations between Church and State. When the entire plan was made public by the *Allgemeine Zeitung* in March 1869, many refused to be convinced.

[1] Citra et contra singulorum suffragia, imo praeter et supra omnium vota pontificis solius declarationi atque sententiae validam vim atque irreformabilem adesse potestatem.

It happened that a statesman was in office who had occasion to know that the information was accurate. The Prime Minister of Bavaria, Prince Hohenlohe, was the brother of a cardinal; the University of Munich was represented on the Roman commissions by an illustrious scholar; and the news of the thing that was preparing came through trustworthy channels. On the 9th of April Prince Hohenlohe sent out a diplomatic circular on the subject of the Council. He pointed out that it was not called into existence by any purely theological emergency, and that the one dogma which was to be brought before it involved all those claims which cause collisions between Church and State, and threaten the liberty and the security of governments. Of the five Roman Commissions, one was appointed for the express purpose of dealing with the mixed topics common to religion and to politics. Besides infallibility and politics, the Council was to be occupied with the Syllabus, which is in part directed against maxims of State. The avowed purpose of the Council being so largely political, the governments could not remain indifferent to its action; lest they should be driven afterwards to adopt measures which would be hostile, it would be better at once to seek an understanding by friendly means and to obtain assurance that all irritating deliberations should be avoided, and no business touching the State transacted except in presence of its representatives. He proposed that the governments should hold a conference to arrange a plan for the protection of their common interest.

Important measures proposed by small States are subject to suspicion of being prompted by a greater Power. Prince Hohenlohe, as a friend of the Prussian alliance, was supposed to be acting in this matter in concert with Berlin. This good understanding was suspected at Vienna; for the Austrian Chancellor was more conspicuous as an enemy of Prussia than Hohenlohe as a friend. Count Beust traced the influence of Count Bismarck in the Bavarian circular. He replied, on behalf of the Catholic empire of Austria, that there were no grounds to impute political objects to the Council, and that repression and not prevention was the only policy compatible with free institutions. After the refusal of Austria, the idea of a conference was dismissed by the other Powers; and the first of the storm clouds that darkened the horizon of infallibilty passed without breaking.

Although united action was abandoned, the idea of sending ambassadors to the Council still offered the most inoffensive and amicable means of preventing the danger of subsequent conflict. Its policy or impolicy was a question to be decided by France. Several bishops, and Cardinal Bonnechose among the rest, urged the Government to resume its ancient privilege, and send a representative. But two powerful parties, united in nothing else, agreed in demanding absolute neutrality. The democracy wished that no impediment should be put in the way of an enterprise which promised to sever the connection of the State with the Church. M. Ollivier set forth this opinion in July 1868, in a speech which was to serve him in his candidature for office; and in the autumn of 1869 it was certain that he would soon be in power. The ministers could not insist on being admitted to the Council, where they were not invited, without making a violent demonstration in a direction they knew would not be followed. The ultramontanes were even more eager than their enemies to exclude an influence that might embarrass their policy. The Archbishop of Paris, by giving the same advice, settled the question. He probably reckoned on his own power of mediating between France and Rome. The French Court long imagined that the dogma would be set aside, and that the mass of the French bishops opposed it. At last they perceived that they were mistaken, and the Emperor said to Cardinal Bonnechose, "You are going to give your signature to decrees already made." He ascertained the names of the bishops who would resist; and it was known that he was anxious for their success. But he was resolved that it should be gained by them, and not by the pressure of his diplomacy at the cost of displeasing the Pope. The Minister of Foreign Affairs and his chief secretary were counted by the Court of Rome among its friends; and the ordinary ambassador started for his post with instructions to conciliate, and to run no risk of a quarrel. He arrived at Rome believing that there would be a speculative conflict between the extremes of Roman and German theology, which would admit of being reconciled by the safer and more sober wisdom of the French bishops, backed by an impartial embassy. His credulity was an encumbrance to the cause which it was his mission and his wish to serve.

In Germany the plan of penetrating the Council with lay influence took a strange form. It was proposed that the German Catholics should be represented by King John of Saxony. As a Catholic and a scholar, who had shown, in his Commentary on Dante, that he had read St. Thomas, and as a prince personally esteemed by the Pope, it was conceived that his presence would be a salutary restraint. It was an impracticable idea; but letters which reached Rome during the winter raised an impression that the King regretted that he could not be there. The opinion of Germany would still have some weight if the North and South, which included more than thirteen millions of Catholics, worked together. It was the policy of Hohenlohe to use this united force, and the ultramontanes learned to regard him as a very formidable antagonist. When their first great triumph, in the election of the Commission on Doctrine, was accomplished, the commentary of a Roman prelate was, "Che colpo per il Principe Hohenlohe!" The Bavarian envoy in Rome did not share the views of his chief, and he was recalled in November. His successor had capacity to carry out the known policy of the prince; but early in the winter the ultramontanes drove Hohenlohe from office, and their victory, though it was exercised with moderation, and was not followed by a total change of policy, neutralised the influence of Bavaria in the Council.

The fall of Hohenlohe and the abstention of France

hampered the Federal Government of Northern Germany. For its Catholic subjects, and ultimately in view of the rivalry with France, to retain the friendship of the papacy is a fixed maxim at Berlin. Count Bismarck laid down the rule that Prussia should display no definite purpose in a cause which was not her own, but should studiously keep abreast of the North German bishops. Those bishops neither invoked, nor by their conduct invited, the co-operation of the State; and its influence would have been banished from the Council but for the minister who represented it in Rome. The vicissitudes of a General Council are so far removed from the normal experience of statesmen that they could not well be studied or acted upon from a distance. A government that strictly controlled and dictated the conduct of its envoy was sure to go wrong, and to frustrate action by theory. A government that trusted the advice of its minister present on the spot enjoyed a great advantage. Baron Arnim was favourably situated. A Catholic belonging to any but the ultramontane school would have been less willingly listened to in Rome than a Protestant who was a conservative in politics, and whose regard for the interests of religion was so undamaged by the sectarian taint that he was known to be sincere in the wish that Catholics should have cause to rejoice in the prosperity of their Church. The apathy of Austria and the vacillation of France contributed to his influence, for he enjoyed the confidence of bishops from both countries; and he was able to guide his own government in its course towards the Council.

The English Government was content to learn more and to speak less than the other Powers at Rome. The usual distrust of the Roman Court towards a Liberal ministry in England was increased at the moment by the measure which the Catholics had desired and applauded. It seemed improbable to men more solicitous for acquired rights than for general political principle, that Protestant statesmen who disestablished their own Church could feel a very sincere interest in the welfare of another.

Ministers so utopian as to give up solid goods for an imaginary righteousness seemed, as practical advisers, open to grave suspicion. Mr. Gladstone was feared as the apostle of those doctrines to which Rome owes many losses. Public opinion in England was not prepared to look on papal infallibility as a matter of national concern, more than other dogmas which make enemies to Catholicism. Even if the Government could have admitted the Prussian maxim of keeping in line with the bishops, it would have accomplished nothing. The English bishops were divided; but the Irish bishops, who are the natural foes of the Fenian plot, were by an immense majority on the ultramontane side. There was almost an ostentation of care on the part of the Government to avoid the appearance of wishing to influence the bishops or the Court of Rome. When at length England publicly concurred in the remonstrances of France, events had happened which showed that the Council was raising up dangers for both Catholic and liberal interests. It was a result so easy to foresee, that the Government had made it clear from the beginning that its extreme reserve was not due to indifference.

The lesser Catholic Powers were almost unrepresented in Rome. The government of the Regent of Spain possessed no moral authority over bishops appointed by the Queen; and the revolution had proved so hostile to the clergy that they were forced to depend on the Pope. Diplomatic relations being interrupted, there was nothing to restrain them from seeking favour by unqualified obedience.

Portugal had appointed the Count de Lavradio ambassador to the Council; but when he found that he was alone he retained only the character of envoy to the Holy See. He had weight with the small group of Portuguese bishops; but he died before he could be of use, and they drifted into submission.

Belgium was governed by M. Frère Orban, one of the most anxious and laborious enemies of the hierarchy, who had no inducement to interfere with an event which justified his enmity, and was, moreover, the unanimous wish of the Belgian Episcopate. When Protestant and Catholic Powers joined in exhorting Rome to moderation, Belgium was left out. Russia was the only Power that treated the Church with actual hostility during the Council, and calculated the advantage to be derived from decrees which would intensify the schism.

Italy was more deeply interested in the events at Rome than any other nation. The hostility of the clergy was felt both in the political and financial difficulties of the kingdom; and the prospect of conciliation would suffer equally from decrees confirming the Roman claims, or from an invidious interposition of the State. Public opinion watched the preparations for the Council with frivolous disdain; but the course to be taken was carefully considered by the Menabrea Cabinet. The laws still subsisted which enabled the State to interfere in religious affairs; and the government was legally entitled to prohibit the attendance of the bishops at the Council, or to recall them from it. The confiscated church property was retained by the State, and the claims of the episcopate were not yet settled. More than one hundred votes on which Rome counted belonged to Italian subjects. The means of applying administrative pressure were therefore great, though diplomatic action was impossible. The Piedmontese wished that the resources of their ecclesiastical jurisprudence should be set in motion. But Minghetti, who had lately joined the Ministry, warmly advocated the opinion that the supreme principle of the liberty of the Church ought to override the remains of the older legislation, in a State consistently free; and, with the disposition of the Italians to confound Catholicism with the hierarchy, the policy of abstention was a triumph of liberality. The idea of Prince Hohenlohe, that religion ought to be maintained in its integrity and not only in its independence, that society is interested in protecting the Church even against herself, and that the enemies of her liberty are ecclesiastical as well as political, could find no favour in Italy. During the session of 1869, Menabrea gave no pledge to Parliament as to the

Council; and the bishops who inquired whether they would be allowed to attend it were left unanswered until October. Menabrea then explained in a circular that the right of the bishops to go to the Council proceeded from the liberty of conscience, and was not conceded under the old privileges of the crown, or as a favour that could imply responsibility for what was to be done. If the Church was molested in her freedom, excuse would be given for resisting the incorporation of Rome. If the Council came to decisions injurious to the safety of States, it would be attributed to the unnatural conditions created by the French occupation, and might be left to the enlightened judgment of Catholics.

It was proposed that the fund realised by the sale of the real property of the religious corporations should be administered for religious purposes by local boards of trustees representing the Catholic population, and that the State should abdicate in their favour its ecclesiastical patronage, and proceed to discharge the unsettled claims of the clergy. So great a change in the plans by which Sella and Rattazzi had impoverished the Church in 1866 and 1867 would, if frankly carried into execution, have encouraged an independent spirit among the Italian bishops; and the reports of the prefects represented about thirty of them as being favourable to conciliation. But the Ministry fell in November, and was succeeded by an administration whose leading members, Lanza and Sella, were enemies of religion. The Court of Rome was relieved from a serious peril.

The only European country whose influence was felt in the attitude of its bishops was one whose government sent out no diplomatists. While the Austrian Chancellor regarded the issue of the Council with a profane and supercilious eye, and so much indifference prevailed at Vienna that it was said that the ambassador at Rome did not read the decrees, and that Count Beust did not read his despatches, the Catholic statesmen in Hungary were intent on effecting a revolution in the Church. The system which was about to culminate in the proclamation of infallibility, and which tended to absorb all power from the circumference into the centre, and to substitute authority for autonomy, had begun at the lower extremities of the hierarchical scale. The laity, which once had its share in the administration of Church property and in the deliberations of the clergy, had been gradually compelled to give up its rights to the priesthood, the priests to the bishops, and the bishops to the Pope. Hungary undertook to redress the process, and to correct centralised absolutism by self-government. In a memorandum drawn up in April 1848, the bishops imputed the decay of religion to the exclusion of the people from the management of all Church affairs, and proposed that whatever is not purely spiritual should be conducted by mixed boards, including lay representatives elected by the congregations. The war of the revolution and the reaction checked this design; and the Concordat threw things more than ever into clerical hands. The triumph of the liberal party after the peace of Prague revived the movements; and Eötvös called on the bishops to devise means of giving to the laity a share and an interest in religious concerns. The bishops agreed unanimously to the proposal of Deàk, that the laity should have the majority in the boards of administration; and the new constitution of the Hungarian Church was adopted by the Catholic Congress on the 17th of October 1869, and approved by the King on the 25th. The ruling idea of this great measure was to make the laity supreme in all that is not liturgy and dogma, in patronage, property, and education; to break down clerical exclusiveness and government control; to deliver the people from the usurpations of the hierarchy, and the Church from the usurpations of the State. It was an attempt to reform the Church by constitutional principles, and to crush ultramontanism by crushing Gallicanism. The Government, which had originated the scheme, was ready to surrender its privileges to the newly-constituted authorities; and the bishops acted in harmony with the ministers and with public opinion. Whilst this good understanding lasted, and while the bishops were engaged in applying the impartial principles of self-government at home, there was a strong security that they would not accept decrees that would undo their work. Infallibility would not only condemn their system, but destroy their position. As the winter advanced the influence of these things became apparent. The ascendency which the Hungarian bishops acquired from the beginning was due to other causes.

The political auspices under which the Council opened were very favourable to the papal cause. The promoters of infallibility were able to coin resources of the enmity which was shown to the Church. The danger which came to them from within was averted. The policy of Hohenlohe, which was afterwards revived by Daru, had been, for a time, completely abandoned by Europe. The battle between the papal and the episcopal principle could come off undisturbed, in closed lists. Political opposition there was none; but the Council had to be governed under the glare of inevitable publicity, with a free press in Europe, and hostile views prevalent in Catholic theology. The causes which made religious science utterly powerless in the strife, and kept it from grappling with the forces arrayed against it, are of deeper import than the issue of the contest itself.

While the voice of the bishops grew louder in praise of the Roman designs, the Bavarian Government consulted the universities, and elicited from the majority of the Munich faculty an opinion that the dogma of infallibility would be attended with serious danger to society. The author of the Bohemian pamphlet affirmed that it had not the conditions which would enable it ever to become the object of a valid definition. Janus compared the primacy, as it was known to the Fathers of the Church, with the ultramontane ideal, and traced the process of transformation through a long series of forgeries. Maret published his book some weeks after Janus and the Reform. It had been revised by several French bishops and divines, and was to serve as a vindication of the Sorbonne and the Gallicans, and as the manifesto of men who were to be present at the Council. It had not the merit of novelty or the fault of innovation, but renewed with as little offence as possible the language of the old French school.[1] While Janus treated infallibility as the critical symptom of an ancient disease, Maret restricted his argument to what was directly involved in the defence of the Gallican position. Janus held that the doctrine was so firmly rooted and so widely supported in the existing constitution of the Church, that much must be modified before a genuine Œcumenical Council could be celebrated. Maret clung to the belief that the real voice of the Church would make itself heard at the Vatican. In direct contradiction with Janus, he kept before him the one practical object, to gain assent by making his views acceptable even to the unlearned.

At the last moment a tract appeared which has been universally attributed to Döllinger, which examined the evidences relied on by the infallibilists, and stated briefly the case against them. It pointed to the inference that their theory is not merely founded on an illogical and uncritical habit, but on unremitting dishonesty in the use of texts. This was coming near the secret of the whole controversy, and the point that made the interference of the Powers appear the only availing resource. For the sentiment on which infallibility is founded could not be reached by argument, the weapon of human reason, but resided in conclusions transcending evidence, and was the inaccessible postulate rather than a demonstrable consequence of a system of religious faith. The two doctrines opposed, but never met each other. It was as much an instinct of the ultramontane theory to elude the tests of science as to resist the control of States. Its opponents,

[1] Nous restons dans les doctrines de Bossuet parce que nous les croyons généralement vraies ; nous les défendons parce qu'elles sont attaquées, et qu'un parti puissant veut les faire condamner. Ces doctrines de l'épiscopat français, de l'école de Paris, de notre vieille Sorbonne, se ramènent pour nous à trois propositions, à trois vérités fondamentales : 1° l'Église est une monarchie efficacement tempérée d'aristocratie ; 2° la souveraineté spirituelle est essentiellement composée de ces deux éléments quoique le second soit subordonné au premier ; 3° le concours de ces éléments est nécessaire pour établir la règle absolue de la foi, c'est-à-dire, pour constituer l'acte par excellence de la souveraineté spirituelle.

baffled and perplexed by the serene vitality of a view which was impervious to proof, saw want of principle where there was really a consistent principle, and blamed the ultramontane divines for that which was of the essence of ultramontane divinity. How it came that no appeal to revelation or tradition, to reason or conscience, appeared to have any bearing whatever on the issue, is a mystery which Janus and Maret and Döllinger's reflections left unexplained.

The resources of mediæval learning were too slender to preserve an authentic record of the growth and settlement of Catholic doctrine. Many writings of the Fathers were interpolated; others were unknown, and spurious matter was accepted in their place. Books bearing venerable names—Clement, Dionysius, Isidore—were forged for the purpose of supplying authorities for opinions that lacked the sanction of antiquity. When detection came, and it was found that fraud had been employed in sustaining doctrines bound up with the peculiar interests of Rome and of the religious Orders, there was an inducement to depreciate the evidences of antiquity, and to silence a voice that bore obnoxious testimony. The notion of tradition underwent a change; it was required to produce what it had not preserved. The Fathers had spoken of the unwritten teaching of the apostles, which was to be sought in the churches they had founded, of esoteric doctrines, and views which must be of apostolic origin because they are universal, of the inspiration of general Councils, and a revelation continued beyond the New Testament. But the Council of Trent resisted the conclusions which this language seemed to countenance, and they were left to be pursued by private speculation. One divine deprecated the vain pretence of arguing from Scripture, by which Luther could not be confuted, and the Catholics were losing ground;[1] and at

[1] Si hujus doctrinae memores fuissemus, haereticos scil cet non esse infirmandos vel convincendos ex Scripturis, meliore sane loco essent res nostrae; sed dum ostentandi ingenii et eruditionis gratia cum Luthero in certamen descenditur Scripturarum, excitatum est hoc, quod, proh dolor! nunc videmus, incendium (Pighius).

Trent a speaker averred that Christian doctrine had been so completely determined by the Schoolmen that there was no further need to recur to Scripture. This idea is not extinct, and Perrone uses it to explain the inferiority of Catholics as Biblical critics.[1] If the Bible is inspired, says Peresius, still more must its interpretation be inspired. It must be interpreted variously, says the Cardinal of Cusa, according to necessity; a change in the opinion of the Church implies a change in the will of God.[2] One of the greatest Tridentine divines declares that a doctrine must be true if the Church believes it, without any warrant from Scripture. According to Petavius, the general belief of Catholics at a given time is the work of God, and of higher authority than all antiquity and all the Fathers. Scripture may be silent, and tradition contradictory, but the Church is independent of both. Any doctrine which Catholic divines commonly assert, without proof, to be revealed, must be taken as revealed. The testimony of Rome, as the only remaining apostolic Church, is equivalent to an unbroken chain of tradition.[3] In this way, after Scripture had been subjugated, tradition itself was deposed; and the constant belief of the past yielded to the general conviction of the present. And, as antiquity had given way to universality, universality made way for authority. The Word of God and the authority of the Church came to be declared the two sources of religious knowledge. Divines of this school, after preferring the Church to the Bible, preferred the modern Church to the ancient, and ended by sacrificing both to the Pope. "We have not the authority of Scripture," wrote Prierias in his defence of Indulgences, "but we have

[1] Catholici non admondum solliciti sunt de critica et hermeneutica biblica . . . Ipsi, ut verbo dicam, jam habent aedificium absolutum sane ac perfectum, in cujus possessione firme ac secure consistant.

[2] Praxis Ecclesiae uno tempore interpretatur Scripturam uno modo et alio tempore alio modo, nam intellectus currit cum praxi.—Mutato judicio Ecclesiae mutatum est Dei judicium.

[3] Si viri ecclesiastici, sive in concilio oecumenico congregati, sive seorsim scribentes, aliquod dogma vel unamquamque consuetudinem uno ore ac diserte testantur ex traditione divina haberi, sine dubio certum argumentum est, uti ita esse credamus.—Ex testimonio hujus solius Ecclesiae sumi potest certum argumentum ad probandas apostolicas traditiones (Bellarmine).

the higher authority of the Roman pontiffs."[1] A bishop who had been present at Trent confesses that in matters of faith he would believe a single Pope rather than a thousand Fathers, saints, and doctors.[2] The divine training develops an orthodox instinct in the Church, which shows itself in the lives of devout but ignorant men more than in the researches of the learned, and teaches authority not to need the help of science, and not to heed its opposition. All the arguments by which theology supports a doctrine may prove to be false, without diminishing the certainty of its truth. The Church has not obtained, and is not bound to sustain it, by proof. She is supreme over fact as over doctrine, as Fénelon argues, because she is the supreme expounder of tradition, which is a chain of facts.[3] Accordingly, the organ of one ultramontane bishop lately declared that infallibility could be defined without arguments; and the Bishop of Nîmes thought that the decision need not be preceded by long and careful discussion. The Dogmatic Commission of the Council proclaims that the existence of tradition has nothing to do with evidence, and that objections taken from history are not valid when contradicted by ecclesiastical decrees.[4] Authority must conquer history.

This inclination to get rid of evidence was specially associated with the doctrine of papal infallibility, because

[1] Veniae sive indulgentiae autoritate Scripturae nobis non innotuere, sed autoritate ecclesiae Romanae Romanorumque Pontificum, quae major est.

[2] Ego, ut ingenue fatear, plus uni summo pontifici crederem, in his, quae fidei mysteria tangunt, quam mille Augustinis, Hieronymis, Gregoriis (Cornelius Mussus).

[3] The two views contradict each other; but they are equally characteristic of the endeavour to emancipate the Church from the obligation of proof. Fénelon says: "Oseroit-on soutenir que l'Église après avoir mal raisonné sur tous les textes, et les avoir pris à contre-sens, est tout à coup saisie par un enthousiasme aveugle, pour juger bien, en raisonnant mal?" And Möhler: "Die ältesten ökumenischen Synoden führten daher für ihre dogmatischen Beschlüsse nicht einmal bestimmte biblische Stellen an; und die katholischen Theologen lehren mit allgemeiner Uebereinstimmung und ganz aus dem Geiste der Kirche heraus, dass selbst die biblische Beweisführung eines für untrüglich gehaltenen Beschlusses nicht untrüglich sei, sondern eben nur das ausgesprochene Dogma selbst."

[4] Cujuscumque ergo scientiae, etiam historiae ecclesiasticae conclusiones, Romanorum Pontificum infallibilitati adversantes, quo manifestius haec ex revelationis fontibus infertur, eo certius veluti totidem errores habendas esse consequitur.

it is necessary that the Popes themselves should not testify against their own claim. They may be declared superior to all other authorities, but not to that of their own see. Their history is not irrelevant to the question of their rights. It could not be disregarded; and the provocation to alter or to deny its testimony was so urgent that men of piety and learning became a prey to the temptation of deceit. When it was discovered in the manuscript of the *Liber Diurnus* that the Popes had for centuries condemned Honorius in their profession of faith, Cardinal Bona, the most eminent man in Rome, advised that the book should be suppressed if the difficulty could not be got over; and it was suppressed accordingly.[1] Men guilty of this kind of fraud would justify it by saying that their religion transcends the wisdom of philosophers, and cannot submit to the criticism of historians. If any fact manifestly contradicts a dogma, that is a warning to science to revise the evidence. There must be some defect in the materials or in the method. Pending its discovery, the true believer is constrained humbly but confidently to deny the fact.

The protest of conscience against this fraudulent piety grew loud and strong as the art of criticism became more certain. The use made of it by Catholics in the literature of the present age, and their acceptance of the conditions of scientific controversy, seemed to ecclesiastical authorities a sacrifice of principle. A jealousy arose that ripened into antipathy. Almost every writer who really served Catholicism fell sooner or later under the disgrace or the suspicion of Rome. But its censures had lost efficacy; and it was found that the progress of literature could only be brought under control by an increase of authority. This could be obtained if a general council declared the decisions of the Roman congregations absolute, and the Pope infallible.

The division between the Roman and the Catholic

[1] Cum in professione fidei electi pontificis damnetur Honorius Papa, ideo quia pravis haereticorum assertionibus fomentum impendit, si verba delineata sint vere in autographo, nec ex notis apparere possit, quomodo huic vulneri medelam offerat, praestat non divulgari opus.

elements in the Church made it hopeless to mediate between them ; and it is strange that men who must have regarded each other as insincere Christians or as insincere Catholics, should not have perceived that their meeting in Council was an imposture. It may be that a portion, though only a small portion, of those who failed to attend, stayed away from that motive. But the view proscribed at Rome was not largely represented in the episcopate ; and it was doubtful whether it would be manifested at all. The opposition did not spring from it, but maintained itself by reducing to the utmost the distance that separated it from the strictly Roman opinions, and striving to prevent the open conflict of principles. It was composed of ultramontanes in the mask of liberals, and of liberals in the mask of ultramontanes. Therefore the victory or defeat of the minority was not the supreme issue of the Council. Besides and above the definition of infallibility arose the question how far the experience of the actual encounter would open the eyes and search the hearts of the reluctant bishops, and how far their language and their attitude would contribute to the impulse of future reform. There was a point of view from which the failure of all attempts to avert the result by false issues and foreign intrusion, and the success of the measures which repelled conciliation and brought on an open struggle and an overwhelming triumph, were means to another and a more importunate end.

Two events occurred in the autumn which portended trouble for the winter. On the 6th of September nineteen German bishops, assembled at Fulda, published a pastoral letter in which they affirmed that the whole episcopate was perfectly unanimous, that the Council would neither introduce new dogmas nor invade the civil province, and that the Pope intended its deliberations to be free. The patent and direct meaning of this declaration was that the bishops repudiated the design announced by the *Civiltà* and the *Allgemeine Zeitung*, and it was received at Rome with indignation. But it soon appeared that it was worded with studied ambiguity, to be signed by men of opposite opinions, and to conceal the truth. The Bishop of Mentz read a paper, written by a professor of Würzburg, against the wisdom of raising the question, but expressed his own belief in the dogma of papal infallibility; and when another bishop stated his disbelief in it, the Bishop of Paderborn assured him that Rome would soon strip him of his heretical skin. The majority wished to prevent the definition, if possible, without disputing the doctrine; and they wrote a private letter to the Pope warning him of the danger, and entreating him to desist. Several bishops who had signed the pastoral refused their signatures to the private letter. It caused so much dismay at Rome that its nature was carefully concealed; and a diplomatist was able to report, on the authority of Cardinal Antonelli, that it did not exist.

In the middle of November, the Bishop of Orleans took leave of his diocese in a letter which touched lightly on the learned questions connected with papal infallibility, but described the objections to the definition as of such a kind that they could not be removed. Coming from a prelate who was so conspicuous as a champion of the papacy, who had saved the temporal power and justified the Syllabus, this declaration unexpectedly altered the situation at Rome. It was clear that the definition would be opposed, and that the opposition would have the support of illustrious names.

The bishops who began to arrive early in November were received with the assurance that the alarm which had been raised was founded on phantoms. It appeared that nobody had dreamed of defining infallibility, or that, if the idea had been entertained at all, it had been abandoned. Cardinals Antonelli, Berardi, and De Luca, and the Secretary Fessler disavowed the *Civiltà*. The ardent indiscretion that was displayed beyond the Alps contrasted strangely with the moderation, the friendly candour, the majestic and impartial wisdom, which were found to reign in the higher sphere of the hierarchy. A bishop, afterwards noted among the opponents of the dogma, wrote home that the idea that infallibility was to be defined was entirely unfounded. It was represented as a mere fancy, got up in Bavarian newspapers, with evil intent; and the Bishop of Sura had been its dupe. The insidious report would have deserved contempt if it had caused a revival of obsolete opinions. It was a challenge to the Council to herald it with such demonstrations, and it unfortunately became difficult to leave it unnoticed. The decision must be left to the bishops. The Holy See could not restrain their legitimate ardour, if they chose to express it; but it would take no initiative. Whatever was done would require to be done with so much moderation as to satisfy everybody, and to avoid the offence of a party triumph. Some suggested that there should be no anathema for those who questioned the doctrine; and one prelate imagined that a formula could be contrived which even Janus could not dispute, and which yet would be found in reality to signify that the Pope is infallible. There was a general assumption that no materials existed for contention among the bishops, and that they stood united against the world.

Cardinal Antonelli openly refrained from connecting himself with the preparation of the Council, and surrounded himself with divines who were not of the ruling party. He had never learned to doubt the dogma itself; but he was keenly alive to the troubles it would bring upon him, and thought that the Pope was preparing a repetition of the difficulties which followed the beginning of his pontificate. He was not trusted as a divine, or consulted on questions of theology; but he was expected to ward off political complications, and he kept the ground with unflinching skill.

The Pope exhorted the diplomatic corps to aid him in allaying the alarm of the infatuated Germans. He assured one diplomatist that the *Civiltà* did not speak in his name. He told another that he would sanction no proposition that could sow dissension among the bishops. He said to a third, "You come to be present at a scene of pacification." He described his object in summoning the Council to be to obtain a remedy for old abuses and for recent errors. More than once, addressing a group of bishops, he said that he would do nothing to raise disputes among them, and would be content with a declaration in favour of intolerance. He wished of course that Catholicism should have the benefit of toleration in England and Russia, but the principle must be repudiated by a Church holding the doctrine of exclusive salvation. The meaning of this intimation, that persecution would do as a substitute for infallibility, was that the most glaring obstacle to the definition would be removed if the Inquisition was recognised as consistent with Catholicism. Indeed it seemed that infallibility was a means to an end which could be obtained in other ways, and that he would have been satisfied with a decree confirming the twenty-third article of the Syllabus, and declaring that no Pope has ever exceeded the just bounds of his authority in faith, in politics, or in morals.[1]

Most of the bishops had allowed themselves to be reassured, when the Bull *Multiplices inter*, regulating the procedure at the Council, was put into circulation in the first days of December. The Pope assumed to himself the sole initiative in proposing topics, and the exclusive nomination of the officers of the Council. He invited the bishops to bring forward their own proposals, but required that they should submit them first of all to a Commission which was appointed by himself, and consisted half of Italians. If any proposal was allowed to pass by this Commission, it had still to obtain the sanction of the Pope, who could therefore exclude at will any topic, even if the whole Council wished to discuss it. Four elective Commissions were to mediate between the Council and the Pope. When a decree had been discussed and opposed, it was to be referred, together with the amendments, to one of these Commissions, where it was to be reconsidered, with the aid of divines. When it came back from the

1 That article condemns the following proposition : "Romani Pontifices et Concilia oecumenica a limitibus suae potestati recesserunt, jura Principum usurparunt, atque etiam in rebus fidei et morum definiendis errarunt."

Commission with corrections and remarks, it was to be put to the vote without further debate. What the Council discussed was to be the work of unknown divines: what it voted was to be the work of a majority in a Commission of twenty-four. It was in the election of these Commissions that the episcopate obtained the chance of influencing the formation of its decrees. But the papal theologians retained their predominance, for they might be summoned to defend or alter their work in the Commission, from which the bishops who had spoken or proposed amendments were excluded. Practically, the right of initiative was the deciding point. Even if the first regulation had remained in force, the bishops could never have recovered the surprises, and the difficulty of preparing for unforeseen debates. The regulation ultimately broke down under the mistake of allowing the decree to be debated only once, and that in its crude state, as it came from the hands of the divines. The authors of the measure had not contemplated any real discussion. It was so unlike the way in which business was conducted at Trent, where the right of the episcopate was formally asserted, where the envoys were consulted, and the bishops discussed the questions in several groups before the general congregations, that the printed text of the Tridentine Regulation was rigidly suppressed. It was further provided that the reports of the speeches should not be communicated to the bishops; and the strictest secrecy was enjoined on all concerning the business of the Council. The bishops, being under no obligation to observe this rule, were afterwards informed that it bound them under grievous sin.

This important precept did not succeed in excluding the action of public opinion. It could be applied only to the debates; and many bishops spoke with greater energy and freedom before an assembly of their own order than they would have done if their words had been taken down by Protestants, to be quoted against them at home. But printed documents, distributed in seven hundred copies, could not be kept secret. The rule was subject to exceptions which destroyed its efficacy; and the Roman cause was discredited by systematic concealment, and advocacy that abounded in explanation and colour, but abstained from the substance of fact. Documents couched in the usual official language, being dragged into the forbidden light of day, were supposed to reveal dark mysteries. The secrecy of the debates had a bad effect in exaggerating reports and giving wide scope to fancy. Rome was not vividly interested in the discussions; but its cosmopolitan society was thronged with the several adherents of leading bishops, whose partiality compromised their dignity and envenomed their disputes. Everything that was said was repeated, inflated, and distorted. Whoever had a sharp word for an adversary, which could not be spoken in Council, knew of an audience that would enjoy and carry the matter. The battles of the Aula were fought over again, with anecdote, epigram, and fiction. A distinguished courtesy and nobleness of tone prevailed at the beginning. When the Archbishop of Halifax went down to his place on the 28th of December, after delivering the speech which taught the reality of the opposition, the Presidents bowed to him as he passed them. The denunciations of the Roman system by Strossmayer and Darboy were listened to in January without a murmur. Adversaries paid exorbitant compliments to each other, like men whose disagreements were insignificant, and who were one at heart. As the plot thickened, fatigue, excitement, friends who fetched and carried, made the tone more bitter. In February the Bishop of Laval described Dupanloup publicly as the centre of a conspiracy too shameful to be expressed in words, and professed that he would rather die than be associated with such iniquity. One of the minority described his opponents as having disported themselves on a certain occasion like a herd of cattle. By that time the whole temper of the Council had been changed; the Pope himself had gone into the arena; and violence of language and gesture had become an artifice adopted to hasten the end.

When the Council opened, many bishops were bewildered and dispirited by the Bull *Multiplices*. They feared that a struggle could not be averted, as, even if no dogmatic question was raised, their rights were cancelled in a way that would make the Pope absolute in dogma. One of the Cardinals caused him to be informed that the Regulation would be resisted. But Pius IX. knew that in all that procession of 750 bishops one idea prevailed. Men whose word is powerful in the centres of civilisation, men who three months before were confronting martyrdom among barbarians, preachers at Notre Dame, professors from Germany, Republicans from Western America, men with every sort of training and every sort of experience, had come together as confident and as eager as the prelates of Rome itself, to hail the Pope infallible. Resistance was improbable, for it was hopeless. It was improbable that bishops who had refused no token of submission for twenty years would now combine to inflict dishonour on the Pope. In their address of 1867 they had confessed that he is the father and teacher of all Christians; that all the things he has spoken were spoken by St. Peter through him; that they would believe and teach all that he believed and taught. In 1854 they had allowed him to proclaim a dogma, which some of them dreaded and some opposed, but to which all submitted when he had decreed without the intervention of a Council. The recent display of opposition did not justify serious alarm. The Fulda bishops feared the consequences in Germany; but they affirmed that all were united, and that there would be no new dogma. They were perfectly informed of all that was being got ready in Rome. The words of their pastoral meant nothing if they did not mean that infallibility was no new dogma, and that all the bishops believed in it. Even the Bishop of Orleans avoided a direct attack on the doctrine, proclaimed his own devotion to the Pope, and promised that the Council would be a scene of concord.[1] It was

[1] J'en suis convaincu: à peine aurai-je touché la terre sacrée, à peine aurai-je baisé le tombeau des Apôtres, que je me sentirai dans la paix, hors de la bataille,

certain that any real attempt that might be made to prevent the definition could be overwhelmed by the preponderance of those bishops whom the modern constitution of the Church places in dependence on Rome.

The only bishops whose position made them capable of resisting were the Germans and the French; and all that Rome would have to contend with was the modern liberalism and decrepit Gallicanism of France, and the science of Germany. The Gallican school was nearly extinct; it had no footing in other countries, and it was essentially odious to the liberals. The most serious minds of the liberal party were conscious that Rome was as dangerous to ecclesiastical liberty as Paris. But, since the Syllabus made it impossible to pursue the liberal doctrines consistently without collision with Rome, they had ceased to be professed with a robust and earnest confidence, and the party was disorganised. They set up the pretence that the real adversary of their opinions was not the Pope, but a French newspaper; and they fought the King's troops in the King's name. When the Bishop of Orleans made his declaration, they fell back, and left him to mount the breach alone. Montalembert, the most vigorous spirit among them, became isolated from his former friends, and accused them, with increasing vehemence, of being traitors to their principles. During the last disheartening year of his life he turned away from the clergy of his country, which was sunk in Romanism, and felt that the real abode of his opinions was on the Rhine.[1] It was only lately that the ideas of the Coblentz

au sein d'une assemblée présidée par un Père et composée de Frères. Là, tous les bruits expireront, toutes les ingérences téméraires cesseront, toutes les imprudences disparaîtront, les flots et les vents seront apaisés.

[1] Vous admirez sans doute beaucoup l'évêque d'Orléans, mais vous l'admireriez bien plus encore, si vous pouviez vous figurer l'abîme d'idolatrie où est tombé le clergé français. Cela dépasse tout ce que l'on aurait jamais pu l'imaginer aux jours de ma jeunesse, au temps de Frayssinous et de La Mennais. Le pauvre Mgr. Maret, pour avoir exposé des idées tres modérées dans un langage plein d'urbanité et de charité, est traité publiquement dans les journaux soi-disant religieux d'hérésiarque et d'apostat, par les derniers de nos curés. De tous les mystères que présente en si grand nombre l'histoire de l'Église je n'en connais pas qui égale ou dépasse cette transformation si prompte et si complète de la France Catholique en une basse-cour de *l'anticamera du Vatican.* J'en serais encore plus désesperé

address, which had so deeply touched the sympathies of Montalembert, had spread widely in Germany. They had their seat in the universities; and their transit from the interior of lecture-rooms to the outer world was laborious and slow. The invasion of Roman doctrines had given vigour and popularity to those which opposed them, but the growing influence of the universities brought them into direct antagonism with the episcopate. The Austrian bishops were generally beyond its reach, and the German bishops were generally at war with it. In December, one of the most illustrious of them said: "We bishops are absorbed in our work, and are not scholars. We sadly need the help of those that are. It is to be hoped that the Council will raise only such questions as can be dealt with competently by practical experience and common sense." The force that Germany wields in theology was only partially represented in its episcopate.

At the opening of the Council the known opposition consisted of four men. Cardinal Schwarzenberg had not published his opinion, but he made it known as soon as he came to Rome. He brought with him a printed paper, entitled *Desideria patribus Concilii oecumenici proponenda*, in which he adopted the ideas of the divines and canonists who are the teachers of his Bohemian clergy. He entreated the Council not to multiply unnecessary articles of faith, and in particular to abstain from defining papal infallibility, which was beset with difficulties, and would make the foundations of faith to tremble even in the devoutest souls. He pointed out that the Index could not continue on its present footing, and urged that the Church should seek her strength in the cultivation of liberty and learning, not in privilege and coercion; that she should rely on popular institutions, and obtain popular support. He warmly advocated the system of autonomy

qu'humilié, si là, comme partout dans les régions illuminées par la foi, la miséricorde et l'esperance ne se laissaient entrevoir à travers les ténèbres. "C'est du Rhin aujourd'hui que nous vient la lumière." L'Allemagne a été choisie pour opposer une digue à ce torrent de fanatisme servile que menaçait de tout englouter (Nov. 7, 1869).

that was springing up in Hungary.[1] Unlike Schwarzenberg, Dupanloup, and Maret, the Archbishop of Paris had taken no hostile step in reference to the Council, but he was feared the most of all the men expected at Rome. The Pope had refused to make him a cardinal, and had written to him a letter of reproof such as has seldom been received by a bishop. It was felt that he was hostile, not episodically, to a single measure, but to the peculiar spirit of this pontificate. He had none of the conventional prejudices and assumed antipathies which are congenial to the hierarchical mind. He was without passion or pathos or affectation; and he had good sense, a perfect temper, and an intolerable wit. It was characteristic of him that he made the Syllabus an occasion to impress moderation on the Pope: "Your blame has power, O Vicar of Jesus Christ; but your blessing is more potent still. God has raised you to the apostolic See between the two halves of this century, that you may absolve the one and inaugurate the other. Be it yours to reconcile reason with faith, liberty with authority, politics with the Church. From the height of that triple majesty with which religion, age, and misfortune adorn you, all that you do and all that you say reaches far, to disconcert or to encourage the nations. Give them from your large priestly heart one word to amnesty the past, to reassure the present, and to open the horizons of the future."

The security into which many unsuspecting bishops

[1] Non solum ea quae ad scholas theologicas pertinent scholis relinquantur, sed etiam doctrinae quae a fidelibus pie tenentur et coluntur, sine gravi causa in codicem dogmatum ne inferantur. In specie ne Concilium declaret vel definiat infallibilitatem Summi Pontificis, a doctissimis et prudentissimis fidelibus Sanctae sedi intime addictis, vehementer optatur. Gravia enim mala exinde oritura timent tum fidelibus tum infidelibus. Fideles enim, qui Primatum magisterii et jurisdictionis in Summo Pontifice ultro agnoscunt, quorum pietas et obedientia erga Sanctam Sedem nullo certe tempore major fuit, corde turbarentur magis quam erigerentur, ac si nunc demum fundamentum Ecclesiae et verae doctrinae stabiliendum sit; infideles vero novam calumniarum et derisionum materiam lucrarentur. Neque desunt, qui ejusmodi definitionem logice impossibilem vocant. . . . Nostris diebus defensio veritatis ac religionis tum praesertim efficax et fructuosa est, si sacerdotes a lege caeterorum civium minus recedunt, sed communibus omnium juribus utuntur, ita ut vis defensionis sit in veritate interna non per tutelam externae exemtionis. . . . Praesertim Ecclesia se scientiarum, quae hominem ornant perficiuntque, amicam et patronam exhibeat, probe noscens, omne verum a Deo esse, et profunda ac seria literarum studia opitulari fidei.

had been lulled quickly disappeared ; and they understood that they were in presence of a conspiracy which would succeed at once if they did not provide against acclamation, and must succeed at last if they allowed themselves to be caught in the toils of the Bull *Multiplices*. It was necessary to make sure that no decree should be passed without reasonable discussion, and to make a stand against the regulation. The first congregation, held on the 10th of December, was a scene of confusion ; but it appeared that a bishop from the Turkish frontier had risen against the order of proceeding, and that the President had stopped him, saying that this was a matter decided by the Pope, and not submitted to the Council. The bishops perceived that they were in a snare. Some began to think of going home. Others argued that questions of Divine right were affected by the regulation, and that they were bound to stake the existence of the Council upon them. Many were more eager on this point of law than on the point of dogma, and were brought under the influence of the more clear-sighted men, with whom they would not have come in contact through any sympathy on the question of infallibility. The desire of protesting against the violation of privileges was an imperfect bond. The bishops had not yet learned to know each other ; and they had so strongly impressed upon their flocks at home the idea that Rome ought to be trusted, that they were going to manifest the unity of the Church and to confound the insinuations of her enemies, that they were not quick to admit all the significance of the facts they found. Nothing vigorous was possible in a body of so loose a texture. The softer materials had to be eliminated, the stronger welded together by severe and constant pressure, before an opposition could be made capable of effective action. They signed protests that were of no effect. They petitioned ; they did not resist.

It was seen how much Rome had gained by excluding the ambassadors ; for this question of forms and regulations would have admitted the action of diplomacy. The idea of being represented at the Council was revived in

France; and a weary negotiation began, which lasted several months, and accomplished nothing but delay. It was not till the policy of intervention had ignominiously failed, and till its failure had left the Roman court to cope with the bishops alone, that the real question was brought on for discussion. And as long as the chance remained that political considerations might keep infallibility out of the Council, the opposition abstained from declaring its real sentiments. Its union was precarious and delusive, but it lasted in this state long enough to enable secondary influences to do much towards supplying the place of principles.

While the protesting bishops were not committed against infallibility, it would have been possible to prevent resistance to the bull from becoming resistance to the dogma. The Bishop of Grenoble, who was reputed a good divine among his countrymen, was sounded in order to discover how far he would go; and it was ascertained that he admitted the doctrine substantially. At the same time, the friends of the Bishop of Orleans were insisting that he had questioned not the dogma but the definition; and Maret, in the defence of his book, declared that he attributed no infallibility to the episcopate apart from the Pope. If the bishops had been consulted separately, without the terror of a decree, it is probable that the number of those who absolutely rejected the doctrine would have been extremely small. There were many who had never thought seriously about it, or imagined that it was true in a pious sense, though not capable of proof in controversy. The possibility of an understanding seemed so near that the archbishop of Westminster, who held the Pope infallible apart from the episcopate, required that the words should be translated into French in the sense of independence, and not of exclusion. An ambiguous formula embodying the view common to both parties, or founded on mutual concession, would have done more for the liberty than the unity of opinion, and would not have strengthened the authority of the Pope. It was resolved to proceed with caution, putting in motion the strong machinery of Rome, and exhausting the advantages of organisation and foreknowledge.

The first act of the Council was to elect the Commission on Dogma. A proposal was made on very high authority that the list should be drawn up so as to represent the different opinions fairly, and to include some of the chief opponents. They would have been subjected to other influences than those which sustain party leaders; they would have been separated from their friends and brought into frequent contact with adversaries; they would have felt the strain of official responsibility; and the opposition would have been decapitated. If these sagacious counsels had been followed, the harvest of July might have been gathered in January, and the reaction that was excited in the long struggle that ensued might have been prevented. Cardinal de Angelis, who ostensibly managed the elections, and was advised by Archbishop Manning, preferred the opposite and more prudent course. He caused a lithographed list to be sent to all the bishops open to influence, from which every name was excluded that was not on the side of infallibility.

Meantime the bishops of several nations selected those among their countrymen whom they recommended as candidates. The Germans and Hungarians, above forty in number, assembled for this purpose under the presidency of Cardinal Schwarzenberg; and their meetings were continued, and became more and more important, as those who did not sympathise with the opposition dropped away. The French were divided into two groups, and met partly at Cardinal Mathieu's, partly at Cardinal Bonnechose's. A fusion was proposed, but was resisted, in the Roman interest, by Bonnechose. He consulted Cardinal Antonelli, and reported that the Pope disliked large meetings of bishops. Moreover, if all the French had met in one place, the opposition would have had the majority, and would have determined the choice of the candidates. They voted separately; and the Bonnechose list was represented to foreign bishops as the united choice of the French episcopate. The Mathieu group believed that this had been done fraudulently, and resolved to make their complaint to the Pope; but Cardinal Mathieu, seeing that a storm was rising, and that he would be called on to be the spokesman of his friends, hurried away to spend Christmas at Besançon. All the votes of his group were thrown away. Even the bishop of Grenoble, who had obtained twenty-nine votes at one meeting, and thirteen at the other, was excluded from the Commission. It was constituted as the managers of the election desired, and the first trial of strength appeared to have annihilated the opposition. The force under entire control of the court could be estimated from the number of votes cast blindly for candidates not put forward by their own countrymen, and unknown to others, who had therefore no recommendation but that of the official list. According to this test Rome could dispose of 550 votes.

The moment of this triumph was chosen for the production of an act already two months old, by which many ancient censures were revoked, and many were renewed. The legislation of the Middle Ages and of the sixteenth century appointed nearly two hundred cases by which excommunication was incurred *ipso facto*, without inquiry or sentence. They had generally fallen into oblivion, or were remembered as instances of former extravagance; but they had not been abrogated, and, as they were in part defensible, they were a trouble to timorous consciences. There was reason to expect that this question, which had often occupied the attention of the bishops, would be brought before the Council; and the demand for a reform could not have been withstood. The difficulty was anticipated by sweeping away as many censures as it was thought safe to abandon, and deciding, independently of the bishops, what must be retained. The Pope reserved to himself alone the faculty of absolving from the sin of harbouring or defending the members of any sect, of causing priests to be tried by secular courts, of violating asylum or alienating the real property of the Church. The prohibition of anonymous writing was restricted to works on theology, and the excommunication hitherto incurred by reading books which are on the Index was confined to readers of heretical books. This Constitution had no other immediate effect than to indicate the prevailing spirit, and to increase the difficulties of the partisans of Rome. The organ of the Archbishop of Cologne justified the last provision by saying, that it does not forbid the works of Jews, for Jews are not heretics; nor the heretical tracts and newspapers, for they are not books; nor listening to heretical books read aloud, for hearing is not reading.

At the same time, the serious work of the Council was begun. A long dogmatic decree was distributed, in which the special theological, biblical, and philosophical opinions of the school now dominant in Rome were proposed for ratification. It was so weak a composition that it was as severely criticised by the Romans as by the foreigners; and there were Germans whose attention was first called to its defects by an Italian cardinal. The disgust with which the text of the first decree was received had not been foreseen. No real discussion had been expected. The Council hall, admirable for occasions of ceremony, was extremely ill adapted for speaking, and nothing would induce the Pope to give it up. A public session was fixed for the 6th of January, and the election of Commissions was to last till Christmas. It was evident that nothing would be ready for the session, unless the decree was accepted without debate, or infallibility adopted by acclamation.

Before the Council had been assembled a fortnight, a store of discontent had accumulated which it would have been easy to avoid. Every act of the Pope, the Bull *Multiplices*, the declaration of censures, the text of the proposed decree, even the announcement that the Council should be dissolved in case of his death, had seemed an injury or an insult to the episcopate. These measures undid the favourable effect of the caution with which the bishops had been received. They did what the dislike of infallibility alone would not have done. They broke the spell of veneration for Pius IX. which fascinated the Catholic Episcopate. The jealousy with which he guarded his prerogative in the appointment of officers, and of the great Commission, the pressure during the elections, the prohibition of national meetings, the refusal to hold the debates in a hall where they could be heard, irritated and alarmed many bishops. They suspected that they had been summoned for the very purpose they had indignantly denied, to make the papacy more absolute by abdicating in favour of the official prelature of Rome. Confidence gave way to a great despondency, and a state of feeling was aroused which prepared the way for actual opposition when the time should come.

Before Christmas the Germans and the French were grouped nearly as they remained to the end. After the flight of Cardinal Mathieu, and the refusal of Cardinal Bonnechose to coalesce, the friends of the latter gravitated towards the Roman centre, and the friends of the former held their meetings at the house of the Archbishop of Paris. They became, with the Austro-German meeting under Cardinal Schwarzenberg, the strength and substance of the party that opposed the new dogma; but there was little intercourse between the two, and their exclusive nationality made them useless as a nucleus for the few scattered American, English, and Italian bishops whose sympathies were with them. To meet this object, and to centralise the deliberations, about a dozen of the leading men constituted an international meeting, which included the best talents, but also the most discordant views. They were too little united to act with vigour, and too few to exercise control. Some months later they increased their numbers. They were the brain but not the will of the opposition. Cardinal Rauscher presided. Rome honoured him as the author of the Austrian Concordat; but he feared that infallibility would bring destruction on his work, and he was the most constant, the most copious, and the most emphatic of its opponents.

When the debate opened, on the 28th of December, the idea of proclaiming the dogma by acclamation had not been abandoned. The Archbishop of Paris exacted a promise that it should not be attempted. But he was warned that the promise held good for the first day only, and that there was no engagement for the future. Then he made it known that one hundred bishops were ready, if a surprise was attempted, to depart from Rome, and to carry away the Council, as he said, in the soles of their shoes. The plan of carrying the measure by a sudden resolution was given up, and it was determined to introduce it with a demonstration of overwhelming effect. The debate on the dogmatic decree was begun by Cardinal Rauscher. The Archbishop of St. Louis spoke on the same day so briefly as not to reveal the force and the fire within him. The Archbishop of Halifax concluded a long speech by saying that the proposal laid before the Council was only fit to be put decorously under ground. Much praise was lavished on the bishops who had courage, knowledge, and Latin enough to address the assembled Fathers; and the Council rose instantly in dignity and in esteem when it was seen that there was to be real discussion. On the 30th, Rome was excited by the success of two speakers. One was the Bishop of Grenoble, the other was Strossmayer, the bishop from the Turkish frontier, who had again assailed the regulation, and had again been stopped by the presiding Cardinal. The fame of his spirit and eloquence began to spread over the city and over the world. The ideas that animated these men in their attack on the proposed measure were most clearly shown a few days later in the speech of a Swiss prelate. "What boots it," he exclaimed, "to condemn errors that have been long condemned, and tempt no Catholic? The false beliefs of mankind are beyond the reach of your decrees. The best defence of Catholicism is religious science. Give to the pursuit of sound learning every encouragement and the widest field; and prove by deeds as well as words that the progress of nations in liberty and light is the mission of the Church."[1]

[1] Quid enim expedit damnare quae damnata jam sunt, quidve juvat errores proscribere quos novimus jam esse proscriptos? . . . Falsa sophistarum dogmata, veluti cineres a turbine venti evanuerunt, corrupuerunt, fateor, permultos,

The tempest of criticism was weakly met; and the opponents established at once a superiority in debate. At the end of the first month nothing had been done; and the Session imprudently fixed for the 6th of January had to be filled up with tedious ceremonies. Everybody saw that there had been a great miscalculation. The Council was slipping out of the grasp of the Court, and the regulation was a manifest hindrance to the despatch of business. New resources were required.

A new president was appointed. Cardinal Reisach had died at the end of December without having been able to take his seat, and Cardinal De Luca had presided in his stead. De Angelis was now put into the place made vacant by the death of Reisach. He had suffered imprisonment at Turin, and the glory of his confessorship was enhanced by his services in the election of the Commissions. He was not suited otherwise to be the moderator of a great assembly; and the effect of his elevation was to dethrone the accomplished and astute De Luca, who had been found deficient in thoroughness, and to throw the management of the Council into the hands of the junior Presidents, Capalti and Bilio. Bilio was a Barnabite monk, innocent of court intrigues, a friend of the most enlightened scholars in Rome, and a favourite of the Pope. Cardinal Capalti had been distinguished as a canonist. Like Cardinal Bilio, he was not reckoned among men of the extreme party; and they were not always in harmony with their colleagues, De Angelis and Bizarri. But they did not waver when the policy they had to execute was not their own.

infecerunt genium saeculi hujus, sed numquid credendum est, corruptionis contaginem non contigisse, si ejusmodi errores decretorum anathemate prostrati fuissent? . . . Pro tuenda et tute servanda religione Catholica praeter gemitus et preces ad Deum aliud medium praesidiumque nobis datum non est nisi Catholica scientia, cum recta fide per omnia concors. Excolitur summopere apud heterodoxos fidei inimica scientia, excolatur ergo oportet et omni opere augeatur apud Catholicos vera scientia, Ecclesiae amica. . . . Obmutescere faciamus ora obtrectantium qui falso nobis imputare non desistunt, Catholicam Ecclesiam opprimere scientiam, et quemcumque liberum cogitandi modum ita cohibere, ut neque scientia, nec ulla alia animi libertas in ea subsistere vel florescere possit. . . . Propterea monstrandum hoc est, et scriptis et factis manifestandum, in Catholica Ecclesia veram pro populis esse libertatem, verum profectum, verum lumen, veramque prosperitatem.

The first decree was withdrawn, and referred to the Commission on Doctrine. Another, on the duties of the episcopate, was substituted; and that again was followed by others, of which the most important was on the Catechism. While they were being discussed, a petition was prepared, demanding that the infallibility of the Pope should be made the object of a decree. The majority undertook to put a strain on the prudence or the reluctance of the Vatican. Their zeal in the cause was warmer than that of the official advisers. Among those who had the responsibility of conducting the spiritual and temporal government of the Pope, the belief was strong that his infallibility did not need defining, and that the definition could not be obtained without needless obstruction to other papal interests. Several Cardinals were inopportunists at first, and afterwards promoted intermediate and conciliatory proposals. But the business of the Council was not left to the ordinary advisers of the Pope, and they were visibly compelled and driven by those who represented the majority. At times this pressure was no doubt convenient. But there were also times when there was no collusion, and the majority really led the authorities. The initiative was not taken by the great mass whose zeal was stimulated by personal allegiance to the Pope. They added to the momentum, but the impulse came from men who were as independent as the chiefs of the opposition. The great Petition, supported by others pointing to the same end, was kept back for several weeks, and was presented at the end of January.

At that time the opposition had attained its full strength, and presented a counter-petition, praying that the question might not be introduced. It was written by Cardinal Rauscher, and was signed, with variations, by 137 bishops. To obtain that number the address avoided the doctrine itself, and spoke only of the difficulty and danger in defining it; so that this, their most imposing act, was a confession of inherent weakness, and a signal to the majority that they might force on the dogmatic discussion. The bishops stood on the negative. They showed no sense of their mission to renovate Catholicism; and it seemed that they would compound for the concession they wanted, by yielding in all other matters, even those which would be a practical substitute for infallibility. That this was not to be, that the forces needed for a great revival were really present, was made manifest by the speech of Strossmayer on the 24th of January, when he demanded the reformation of the Court of Rome, decentralisation in the government of the Church, and decennial Councils. That earnest spirit did not animate the bulk of the party. They were content to leave things as they were, to gain nothing if they lost nothing, to renounce all premature striving for reform if they could succeed in avoiding a doctrine which they were as unwilling to discuss as to define. The words of Ginoulhiac to Strossmayer, "You terrify me with your pitiless logic," expressed the inmost feelings of many who gloried in the grace and the splendour of his eloquence. No words were too strong for them if they prevented the necessity of action, and spared the bishops the distressing prospect of being brought to bay, and having to resist openly the wishes and the claims of Rome.

Infallibility never ceased to overshadow every step of the Council,[1] but it had already given birth to a deeper question. The Church had less to fear from the violence of the majority than from the inertness of their opponents. No proclamation of false doctrines could be so great a disaster as the weakness of faith which would prove that the power of recovery, the vital force of Catholicism, was extinct in the episcopate. It was better to be overcome after openly attesting their belief than to strangle both discussion and definition, and to disperse without having uttered a single word that could reinstate the authorities of the Church in the respect of men. The future depended less on the outward struggle between two

[1] Il n'y a au fond qu'une question devenue urgente et inévitable, dont la décision faciliterait le cours et la décision de toutes les autres, dont le retard paralyse tout. Sans cela rien n'est commencé ni même abordable (*Univers*, February 9).

parties than on the process by which the stronger spirit within the minority leavened the mass. The opposition was as averse to the actual dogmatic discussion among themselves as in the Council. They feared an inquiry which would divide them. At first the bishops who understood and resolutely contemplated their real mission in the Council were exceedingly few. Their influence was strengthened by the force of events, by the incessant pressure of the majority, and by the action of literary opinion.

Early in December the Archbishop of Mechlin brought out a reply to the letter of the Bishop of Orleans, who immediately prepared a rejoinder, but could not obtain permission to print it in Rome. It appeared two months later at Naples. Whilst the minority were under the shock of this prohibition, Gratry published at Paris the first of four letters to the Archbishop of Mechlin, in which the case of Honorius was discussed with so much perspicuity and effect that the profane public was interested, and the pamphlets were read with avidity in Rome. They contained no new research, but they went deep into the causes which divided Catholics. Gratry showed that the Roman theory is still propped by fables which were innocent once, but have become deliberate untruths since the excuse of mediæval ignorance was dispelled; and he declared that this school of lies was the cause of the weakness of the Church, and called on Catholics to look the scandal in the face, and cast out the religious forgers. His letters did much to clear the ground and to correct the confusion of ideas among the French. The bishop of St. Brieuc wrote that the exposure was an excellent service to religion, for the evil had gone so far that silence would be complicity.[1] Gratry was no sooner

[1] Gratry had written: "Cette apologétique sans franchise est l'une des causes de notre décadence religieuse depuis des siècles. . . . Sommes-nous les prédicateurs du mensonge ou les apôtres de la vérité? Le temps n'est-il pas venu de rejeter avec dégoût les fraudes, les interpolations, et les mutilations que les menteurs et les faussaires, nos plus cruels ennemis, ont pu introduire parmi nous?" The bishop wrote: "Jamais parole plus puissante, inspirée par la conscience et le savoir, n'est arrivée plus à propos que la vôtre. . . . Le mal est tel et le danger si effrayant que le silence deviendrait de la complicité."

approved by one bishop than he was condemned by a great number of others. He had brought home to his countrymen the question whether they could be accomplices of a dishonest system, or would fairly attempt to root it out.

While Gratry's letters were disturbing the French, Döllinger published some observations on the petition for infallibility, directing his attack clearly against the doctrine itself. During the excitement that ensued, he answered demonstrations of sympathy by saying that he had only defended the faith which was professed, substantially, by the majority of the episcopate in Germany. These words dropped like an acid on the German bishops. They were writhing to escape the dire necessity of a conflict with the Pope; and it was very painful to them to be called as compurgators by a man who was esteemed the foremost opponent of the Roman system, whose hand was suspected in everything that had been done against it, and who had written many things on the sovereign obligations of truth and faith which seemed an unmerciful satire on the tactics to which they clung. The notion that the bishops were opposing the dogma itself was founded on their address against the regulation; but the petition against the definition of infallibility was so worded as to avoid that inference, and had accordingly obtained nearly twice as many German and Hungarian signatures as the other. The Bishop of Mentz vehemently repudiated the supposition for himself, and invited his colleagues to do the same. Some followed his example, others refused; and it became apparent that the German opposition was divided, and included men who accepted the doctrines of Rome. The precarious alliance between incompatible elements was prevented from breaking up by the next act of the Papal Government.

The defects in the mode of carrying on the business of the Council were admitted on both sides. Two months had been lost; and the demand for a radical change was publicly made in behalf of the minority by a letter communicated to the *Moniteur*. On the 22nd of

February a new regulation was introduced, with the avowed purpose of quickening progress. It gave the Presidents power to cut short any speech, and provided that debate might be cut short at any moment when the majority pleased. It also declared that the decrees should be carried by majority—*id decernetur quod majori Patrum numero placuerit.* The policy of leaving the decisive power in the hands of the Council itself had this advantage, that its exercise would not raise the question of liberty and coercion in the same way as the interference of authority. By the Bull *Multiplices*, no bishop could introduce any matter not approved by the Pope. By the new regulation he could not speak on any question before the Council, if the majority chose to close the discussion, or if the Presidents chose to abridge his speech. He could print nothing in Rome, and what was printed elsewhere was liable to be treated as contraband. His written observations on any measure were submitted to the Commission, without any security that they would be made known to the other bishops in their integrity. There was no longer an obstacle to the immediate definition of papal infallibility. The majority was omnipotent.

The minority could not accept this regulation without admitting that the Pope is infallible. Their thesis was, that his decrees are not free from the risk of error unless they express the universal belief of the episcopate. The idea that particular virtue attaches to a certain number of bishops, or that infallibility depends on a few votes more or less, was defended by nobody. If the act of a majority of bishops in the Council, possibly not representing a majority in the Church, is infallible, it derives its infallibility from the Pope. Nobody held that the Pope was bound to proclaim a dogma carried by a majority. The minority contested the principle of the new Regulation, and declared that a dogmatic decree required virtual unanimity. The chief protest was drawn up by a French bishop. Some of the Hungarians added a paragraph asserting that the authority and œcumenicity of the

Council depended on the settlement of this question; and they proposed to add that they could not continue to act as though it were legitimate unless this point was given up. The author of the address declined this passage, urging that the time for actual menace was not yet come. From that day the minority agreed in rejecting as invalid any doctrine which should not be passed by unanimous consent. On this point the difference between the thorough and the simulated opposition was effaced, for Ginoulhiac and Ketteler were as positive as Kenrick or Hefele. But it was a point which Rome could not surrender without giving up its whole position. To wait for unanimity was to wait for ever, and to admit that a minority could prevent or nullify the dogmatic action of the papacy was to renounce infallibility. No alternative remained to the opposing bishops but to break up the Council. The most eminent among them accepted this conclusion, and stated it in a paper declaring that the absolute and indisputable law of the Church had been violated by the Regulation allowing articles of faith to be decreed on which the episcopate was not morally unanimous; and that the Council, no longer possessing in the eyes of the bishops and of the world the indispensable condition of liberty and legality, would be inevitably rejected. To avert a public scandal, and to save the honour of the Holy See, it was proposed that some unopposed decrees should be proclaimed in solemn session, and the Council immediately prorogued.

At the end of March a breach seemed unavoidable. The first part of the dogmatic decree had come back from the Commission so profoundly altered that it was generally accepted by the bishops, but with a crudely expressed sentence in the preamble, which was intended to rebuke the notion of the reunion of Protestant Churches. Several bishops looked upon this passage as an uncalled-for insult to Protestants, and wished it changed; but there was danger that if they then joined in voting the decree they would commit themselves to the lawfulness of the Regulation against which they had protested. On the 22nd of March Strossmayer raised both questions. He said that it was neither just nor charitable to impute the progress of religious error to the Protestants. The germ of modern unbelief existed among the Catholics before the Reformation, and afterwards bore its worst fruits in Catholic countries. Many of the ablest defenders of Christian truth were Protestants, and the day of reconciliation would have come already but for the violence and uncharitableness of the Catholics. These words were greeted with execrations, and the remainder of the speech was delivered in the midst of a furious tumult. At length, when Strossmayer declared that the Council had forfeited its authority by the rule which abolished the necessity of unanimity, the Presidents and the multitude refused to let him go on.[1] On the following day he drew up

[1] Pace eruditissimorum virorum dictum esto: mihi haecce nec veritati congrua esse videntur, nec caritati. Non veritati; verum quidem est Protestantes gravissimam commisisse culpam, dum spreta et insuperhabita divina Ecclesiae auctoritate, aeternas et immutabiles fidei veritates subjectivae rationis judicio et arbitrio subjecissent. Hoc superbiae humanae fomentum gravissimis certe malis, rationalismo, criticismo, etc. occasionem dedit. Ast hoc quoque respectu dici debet, protestantismi ejus qui cum eodem in nexu existit rationalismi germen saeculo xvi. praeextitisse in sic dicto humanismo et classicismo, quem in sanctuario ipso quidam summae auctoritatis viri incauto consilio fovebant et nutriebant; et nisi hoc germen praeextitisset concipi non posset quomodo tam parva scintilla tantum in medio Europae excitare potuisset incendium, ut illud ad hodiernum usque diem restingui non potuerit. Accedit et illud: fidei et religionis, Ecclesiae et omnis auctoritatis contemptum absque ulla cum Protestantismo cognatione et parentela in medio Catholicae gentis saeculo xviii. temporibus Voltarii et encyclopaedistarum enatum fuisse. . . . Quidquid interim sit de rationalismo, puto venerabilem deputationem omnino falli dum texendo genealogiam naturalismi, materialismi, pantheismi, atheismi, etc., omnes omnino hos errores foetus Protestantismi esse asserit. . . . Errores superius enumerati non tantum nobis verum et ipsis Protestantibus horrori sunt et abominationi, ut adeo Ecclesiae et nobis Catholicis in iis oppugnandis et refellendis auxilio sint et adjumento. Ita Leibnitius erat certe vir eruditus et omni sub respectu praestans; vir in dijudicandis Ecclesiae Catholicae institutis aequus; vir in debellandis sui temporis erroribus strenuus; vir in revehenda inter Christianas communitates concordia optime animatus et meritus. [Loud cries of "Oh! Oh!" The President de Angelis rang the bell and said, "Non est hicce locus laudandi Protestantes."] . . . Hos viros quorum magna copia existit in Germania, in Anglia, item et in America septentrionali, magna hominum turba inter Protestantes sequitur, quibus omnibus applicari potest illud magni Augustini: "Errant, sed bona fide errant; haeretici sunt, sed illi nos haereticos tenent. Ipsi errorem non invenerunt, sed a perversis et in errorem inductis parentibus haereditaverunt, parati errorem deponere quamprimum convicti fuerint." [Here there was a long interruption and ringing of the bell, with cries of "Shame! shame!" "Down with the heretic!"] Hi omnes etiamsi non spectent ad Ecclesiae corpus, spectant tamen ad ejus animam, et de muneribus Redemptionis aliquatenus participant. Hi omnes in amore quo erga Iesum Christum Dominum nostrum feruntur, atque in illis positivis veritatibus quas ex fidei naufragio salvarunt, totidem gratiae divinae

a protest, declaring that he could not acknowledge the validity of the Council if dogmas were to be decided by a majority,[1] and sent it to the Presidents after it had been approved at the meeting of the Germans, and by bishops of other nations. The preamble was withdrawn, and another was inserted in its place, which had been written in great haste by the German Jesuit Kleutgen, and was received with general applause. Several of the Jesuits obtained credit for the ability and moderation with which the decree was drawn up. It was no less than a victory over extreme counsels. A unanimous vote was insured for the public session of 24th April; and harmony was restored. But the text proposed originally in the Pope's name had undergone so many changes as to make it appear that his intentions had been thwarted. There was a supplement to the decree, which the bishops had understood would be withdrawn, in order that the festive concord and good feeling might not be disturbed. They were informed at the last moment that it would be put to the vote, as its withdrawal would be a confession of

momenta possident, quibus misericordia Dei utetur, ut eos ad priscam fidem et Ecclesiam reducat, nisi nos exaggerationibus nostris et improvidis charitatis ipsis debitae laesionibus tempus misericordiae divinae elongaverimus. Quantum autem ad charitatem, ei certe contrarium est vulnera aliena alio fine tangere quam ut ipsa sanentur; puto autem hac enumeratione errorum, quibus Protestantismus occasionem dedisset, id non fieri. . . . Decreto, quod in supplementum ordinis interioris nobis nuper communicatum est, statuitur res in Concilio hocce suffragiorum majoritate decidendas fore. Contra hoc principium, quod omnem praecedentium Conciliorum praxim funditus evertit, multi episcopi reclamarunt, quin tamen aliquod responsum obtinuerint. Responsum autem in re tanti momenti dari debuisset clarum, perspicuum et omnis ambiguitatis expers. Hoc ad summas Concilii hujus calamitates spectat, nam hoc certe et praesenti generationi et posteris praebebit ansam dicendi: huic concilio libertatem et veritatem defuisse. Ego ipse convictus sum, aeternam ac immutabilem fidei et traditionis regulam semper fuisse semperque mansuram communem, adminus moraliter unanimem consensum. Concilium, quod hac regula insuperhabita, fidei et morum dogmata majoritate numerica definire intenderet, juxta meam intimam convictionem eo ipso excideret jure conscientiam orbis Catholici sub sanctione vitae ac mortis aeternae obligandi.

[1] Dum autem ipse die hesterno ex suggestu hanc quaestionem posuissem et verba de consensu moraliter unanimi in rebus fidei definiendis necessario protulissem, interruptus fui, mihique inter maximum tumultum et graves comminationes possibilitas sermonis continuandi adempta est. Atque haec gravissima sane circumstantia magis adhuc comprobat necessitatem habendi responsi, quod clarum sit omnisque ambiguitatis expers. Peto itaque humillime, ut hujusmodi responsum in proxima congregatione generali detur. Nisi enim haec fierent anceps haererem an manere possem in Concilio, ubi libertas Episcoporum ita opprimitur, quemadmodum heri in me oppressa fuit, et ubi dogmata fidei definirentur novo et in Ecclesia Dei adusque inaudito modo.

defeat for Rome. The supplement was an admonition that the constitutions and decrees of the Holy See must be observed even when they proscribe opinions not actually heretical.[1] Extraordinary efforts were made in public and in private to prevent any open expression of dissent from this paragraph. The Bishop of Brixen assured his brethren, in the name of the Commission, that it did not refer to questions of doctrine, and they could not dispute the general principle that obedience is due to lawful authority. The converse proposition, that the papal acts have no claim to be obeyed, was obviously untenable. The decree was adopted unanimously. There were some who gave their vote with a heavy heart, conscious of the snare.[2] Strossmayer alone stayed away.

The opposition was at an end. Archbishop Manning afterwards reminded them that by this vote they had implicitly accepted infallibility. They had done even

[1] Quoniam vero satis non est, haereticam pravitatem devitare, nisi ii quoque errores diligenter fugiantur, qui ad illam plus minusve accedunt, omnes officii monemus, servandi etiam Constitutiones et Decreta quibus pravae eiusmodi opiniones, quae isthic diserte non enumerantur, ab hac Sancta Sede proscriptae et prohibitae sunt.

[2] In the speech on infallibility which he prepared, but never delivered, Archbishop Kenrick thus expressed himself: "Inter alia quae mihi stuporem injecerunt dixit Westmonasteriensis, nos additamento facto sub finem Decreti de Fide, tertia Sessione lati, ipsam Pontificiam Infallibilitatem, saltem implicite, jam agnovisse, nec ab ea recedere nunc nobis licere. Si bene intellexerim R^m^ Relatorem, qui in Congregatione generali hoc additamentum, prius oblatum, deinde abstractum, nobis mirantibus quid rei esset, illud iterum inopinato commendavit—dixit, verbis clarioribus, per illud nullam omnino doctrinam edoceri; sed eam quatuor capitibus ex quibus istud decretum compositum est imponi tanquam eis coronidem convenientem; eamque disciplinarem magis quam doctrinalem characterem habere. Aut deceptus est ipse, si vera dixit Westmonasteriensis; aut nos sciens in errorem induxit, quod de viro tam ingenuo minime supponere licet. Utcumque fuerit, ejus declarationi fidentes, plures suffragia sua isti decreto haud deneganda censuerunt ob istam clausulam; aliis, inter quos egomet, dolos parari metuentibus, et aliorum voluntati hac in re aegre cedentibus. In his omnibus non est mens mea aliquem ex Reverendissimis Patribus malae fidei incusare; quos omnes, ut par est, veneratione debita prosequor. Sed extra concilium adesse dicuntur viri religiosi—forsan et pii—qui maxime in illud influunt; qui calliditati potius quam bonis artibus confisi, rem Ecclesiae in maximum ex quo orta sit discrimen adduxerunt; qui ab inito concilio effecerunt ut in Deputationes conciliares ii soli eligerentur qui eorum placitis fovere aut noscerentur aut crederentur; qui nonnullorum ex eorum praedecessoribus vestigia prementes in schematibus nobis propositis, et ex eorum officina prodeuntibus, nihil magis cordi habuisse videntur quam Episcopalem auctoritatem deprimere, Pontificiam autem extollere; et verborum ambagibus incautos decipere velle videntur, dum alia ab aliis in eorum explicationem dicantur. Isti grave hoc incendium in Ecclesia excitarunt, et in illud insufflare non desinunt, scriptis eorum, pietatis speciem prae se ferentibus sed veritate ejus vacuis, in populos spargentibus.

more. They might conceivably contrive to bind and limit dogmatic infallibility with conditions so stringent as to evade many of the objections taken from the examples of history; but, in requiring submission to papal decrees on matters not articles of faith, they were approving that of which they knew the character, they were confirming without let or question a power they saw in daily exercise, they were investing with new authority the existing Bulls, and giving unqualified sanction to the Inquisition and the Index, to the murder of heretics and the deposing of kings. They approved what they were called on to reform, and solemnly blessed with their lips what their hearts knew to be accursed. The Court of Rome became thenceforth reckless in its scorn of the opposition, and proceeded in the belief that there was no protest they would not forget, no principle they would not betray, rather than defy the Pope in his wrath. It was at once determined to bring on the discussion of the dogma of infallibility. At first, when the minority knew that their prayers and their sacrifices had been vain, and that they must rely on their own resources, they took courage in extremity. Rauscher, Schwarzenberg, Hefele, Ketteler, Kenrick, wrote pamphlets, or caused them to be written, against the dogma, and circulated them in the Council. Several English bishops protested that the denial of infallibility by the Catholic episcopate had been an essential condition of emancipation, and that they could not revoke that assurance after it had served their purpose, without being dishonoured in the eyes of their countrymen.[1] The Archbishop of St. Louis, admitting the force of the argument, derived from the fact

[1] The author of the protest afterwards gave the substance of his argument as follows: "Episcopi et theologi publice a Parlamento interrogati fuerunt, utrum Catholici Angliae tenerent Papam posse definitiones relativas ad fidem et mores populis imponere absque omni consensu expresso vel tacito Ecclesiae. Omnes Episcopi et theologi responderunt Catholicos hoc non tenere. Hisce responsionibus confisum Parlamentum Angliae Catholicos admisit ad participationem iurium civilium. Quis Protestantibus persuadebit Catholicos contra honorem et bonam fidem non agere, qui quando agebatur de iuribus sibi acquirendis publice professi sunt ad fidem Catholicam non pertinere doctrinam infallibilitatis Romani Pontificis, statim autem ac obtinuerint quod volebant, a professione publice facta recedunt et contrarium affirmant?"

that a dogma was promulgated in 1854 which had long been disputed and denied, confessed that he could not prove the Immaculate Conception to be really an article of faith.[1]

An incident occurred in June which showed that the experience of the Council was working a change in the fundamental convictions of the bishops. Döllinger had written in March that an article of faith required not only to be approved and accepted unanimously by the Council, but that the bishops united with the Pope are not infallible, and that the œcumenicity of their acts must be acknowledged and ratified by the whole Church. Father Hötzl, a Franciscan friar, having published a pamphlet in defence of this proposition, was summoned to Rome, and required to sign a paper declaring that the confirmation of a Council by the Pope alone makes it œcumenical. He put his case into the hands of German bishops who were eminent in the opposition, asking first their opinion on the proposed declaration, and, secondly, their advice on his own conduct. The bishops whom he consulted replied that they believed the declaration to be erroneous; but they added that they had only lately arrived at the conviction, and had been shocked at first by Döllinger's doctrine. They could not require him to suffer the consequences of being condemned at Rome as a rebellious friar and obstinate heretic for a view which they themselves had doubted only three months before. He followed the advice, but he perceived that his advisers had considerately betrayed him.

When the observations on infallibility which the bishops had sent in to the Commission appeared in print it seemed that the minority had burnt their ships. They affirmed that the dogma would put an end to the conversion of Protestants, that it would drive devout men out of the Church and make Catholicism indefensible in controversy,

[1] Archbishop Kenrick's remarkable statement is not reproduced accurately in his pamphlet *De Pontificia infallibilitate.* It is given in full in the last pages of the *Observationes*, and is abridged in his *Concio habenda sed non habita*, where he concludes: "Eam fidei doctrinam esse neganti, non video quomodo responderi possit, cum objiceret Ecclesiam errorem contra fidem divinitus revelatam diu tolerare non potuisse, quin, aut quod ad fidei depositum pertineret non scivisse, aut errorem manifestum tolerasse videretur."

that it would give governments apparent reason to doubt the fidelity of Catholics, and would give new authority to the theory of persecution and of the deposing power. They testified that it was unknown in many parts of the Church, and was denied by the Fathers, so that neither perpetuity nor universality could be pleaded in its favour; and they declared it an absurd contradiction, founded on ignoble deceit, and incapable of being made an article of faith by Pope or Council.[1] One bishop protested that he would die rather than proclaim it. Another thought it would be an act of suicide for the Church.

What was said, during the two months' debate, by men perpetually liable to be interrupted by a majority acting less from conviction than by command,[2] could be of no

[1] Certissimum ipsi esse fore ut infallibilitate ista dogmatice definita, in dioecesi sua, in qua ne vestigium quidem traditionis de infallibilitate S. P. hucusque inveniatur, et in aliis regionibus multi, et quidem non solum minoris, sed etiam optimae notae, a fide deficiant.—Si edatur, omnis progressus conversionum in Provinciis Foederatis Americae funditus extinguetur. Episcopi et sacerdotes in disputationibus cum Protestantibus quid respondere possent non haberent.—Per eiusmodi definitionem acatholicis, inter quos haud pauci iique optimi hisce praesertim temporibus firmum fidei fundamentum desiderant, ad Ecclesiam reditus redditur difficilis, imo impossibilis.—Qui Concilii decretis obsequi vellent, invenient se maximis in difficultatibus versari. Gubernia civilia eos tanquam subditos minus fidos, haud sine verisimilitudinis specie, habebunt. Hostes Ecclesiae eos lacessere non verebuntur, nunc eis objicientes errores quos Pontifices aut docuisse, aut sua agendi ratione probasse, dicuntur et risu excipient responsa quae sola afferri possint.—Eo ipso definitur in globo quidquid per diplomata apostolica huc usque definitum est. . . . Poterit, admissa tali definitione, statuere de dominio temporali, de eius mensura, de potestate deponendi reges, de usu coercendi haereticos.—Doctrina de Infallibilitate Romani Pontificis nec in Scriptura Sacra, nec in traditione ecclesiastica fundata mihi videtur. Immo contrariam, ni fallor, Christiana antiquitas tenuit doctrinam.—Modus dicendi Schematis supponit existere in Ecclesia duplicem infallibilitatem, ipsius Ecclesiae et Romani Pontificis, quod est absurdum et inauditum.—Subterfugiis quibus theologi non pauci in Honorii causa usi sunt, derisui me exponerem. Sophismata adhibere et munere episcopali et natura rei, quae in timore Domini pertractanda est, indignum mihi videtur.—Plerique textus quibus eam comprobant etiam melioris notae theologi, quos Ultramontanos vocant, mutilati sunt, falsificati, interpolati, circumtruncati, spurii, in sensum alienum detorti.—Asserere audeo eam sententiam, ut in schemate jacet, non esse fidei doctrinam, nec talem devenire posse per quamcumque definitionem etiam conciliarem.

[2] This, at least, was the discouraging impression of Archbishop Kenrick: Semper contigit ut Patres surgendo assensum sententiae deputationis praebuerint. Primo quidem die suffragiorum, cum quaestio esset de tertia parte primae emendationis, nondum adhibita indicatione a subsecretario, deinde semper facta, plures surrexerunt adeo ut necesse foret numerum surgentium capere, ut constaret de suffragiis. Magna deinde confusio exorta est, et ista emendatio, quamvis majore forsan numero sic acceptata, in crastinum diem dilata est. Postero die R^ms Relator ex ambone Patres monuit, deputationem emendationem istam admittere nolle. Omnes fere eam rejiciendam surgendo statim dixerunt.

practical account, and served for protest, not for persuasion. Apart from the immediate purpose of the discussion, two speeches were memorable—that of Archbishop Conolly of Halifax, for the uncompromising clearness with which he appealed to Scripture and repudiated all dogmas extracted from the speculations of divines, and not distinctly founded on the recorded Word of God,[1] and that of Archbishop Darboy, who foretold that a decree which increased authority without increasing power, and claimed for one man, whose infallibility was only now defined, the obedience which the world refused to the whole Episcopate, whose right had been unquestioned in the Church for 1800 years, would raise up new hatred and new suspicion, weaken the influence of religion over society, and wreak swift ruin on the temporal power.[2]

[1] Quodcumque Dominus Noster non dixerit etiam si metaphysice aut physice certissimum nunquam basis esse poterit dogmatis divinae fidei. Fides enim per auditum, auditus autem non per scientiam sed per verba Christi. . . . Non ipsa verba S. Scripturae igitur, sed genuinus sensus, sive litteralis, sive metaphoricus, prout in mente Dei revelantis fuit, atque ab Ecclesiae patribus semper atque ubique concorditer expositus, et quem nos omnes juramento sequi abstringimur, hic tantummodo sensus Vera Dei revelatio dicendus est. . . . Tota antiquitas silet vel contraria est. . . . Verbum Dei volo et hoc solum, quaeso et quidem indubitatum, ut dogma fiat.

[2] Hanc de infallibilitate his conditionibus ortam et isto modo introductam aggredi et definire non possumus, ut arbitror, quin eo ipso tristem viam sternamus tum cavillationibus impiorum, tum etiam objectionibus moralem hujus Concilii auctoritatem minuentibus. Et hoc quidem eo magis cavendum est, quod jam prostent et pervulgentur scripta et acta quae vim ejus et rationem labefactare attentant; ita ut nedum animos sedare queat et quae pacis sunt afferre, e contra nova dissensionis et discordiarum semina inter Christianos spargere videatur. . . . Porro, quod in tantis Ecclesiae angustiis laboranti mundo remedium affertur? Iis omnibus qui ab humero indocili excutiunt onera antiquitus imposita, et consuetudine Patrum veneranda, novum ideoque grave et odiosum onus imponi postulant schematis auctores. Eos omnes qui infirmae fidei sunt novo et non satis opportuno dogmate quasi obruunt, doctrina scilicet hucusque nondum definita, praesentis discussionis vulnere nonnihil sauciata, et a Concilio cujus libertatem minus aequo apparere plurimi autumant et dicunt pronuntianda. . . . Mundus aut aeger est aut perit, non quod ignorat veritatem vel veritatis doctores, sed quod ab ea refugit eamque sibi non vult imperari. Igitur, si eam respuit, quum a toto docentis Ecclesiae corpore, id est ab 800 episcopis per totum orbem sparsis et simul cum S. Pontifice infallibilibus praedicatur, quanto magis quum ab unico Doctore infallibili, et quidem ut tali recenter declarato praedicabitur? Ex altera parte, ut valeat et efficaciter agat auctoritas necesse est non tantum eam affirmari, sed insuper admitti. . . . Syllabus totam Europam pervasit at cui malo mederi potuit etiam ubi tanquam oraculum infallibile susceptus est? Duo tantum restabant regna in quibus religio florebat, non de facto tantum, sed et de jure dominans: Austria scilicet et Hispania. Atqui in his duobus regnis ruit iste Catholicus ordo, quamvis ab infallibili auctoritate commendatus, imo forsan saltem in Austria eo praecise quod ab hac commendatus. Audeamus igitur res uti sunt considerare. Nedum

The general debate had lasted three weeks, and forty-nine bishops were still to speak, when it was brought to a close by an abrupt division on the 3rd of June. For twenty-four hours the indignation of the minority was strong. It was the last decisive opportunity for them to reject the legitimacy of the Council. There were some who had despaired of it from the beginning, and held that the Bull *Multiplices* deprived it of legal validity. But it had not been possible to make a stand at a time when no man knew whether he could trust his neighbour, and when there was fair ground to hope that the worst rules would be relaxed. When the second regulation, interpreted according to the interruptors of Strossmayer, claimed the right of proclaiming dogmas which part of the Episcopate did not believe, it became doubtful whether the bishops could continue to sit without implicit submission. They restricted themselves to a protest, thinking that it was sufficient to meet words with words, and that it would be time to act when the new principle was actually applied. By the vote of the 3rd of June the obnoxious regulation was enforced in a way evidently injurious to the minority and their cause. The chiefs of the opposition were now convinced of the invalidity of the Council, and advised that they should all abstain from speaking, and attend at St. Peter's only to negative by their vote the decree which they disapproved. In this way they thought that the claim to œcumenicity would be abolished without breach or violence. The greater number were averse to so vigorous a demonstration; and Hefele threw the great weight of his authority into their scale. He contended that they would be worse than their word if they proceeded to extremities on this occasion. They had announced that they would do it only to prevent the promulgation of a dogma which was opposed. If that were done the Council would be revolutionary and tyrannical; and they ought to keep their strongest

Sanctissimi Pontificis independens infallibilitas praejudicia et objectiones destruat quae permultos a fide avertunt, ea potius auget et aggravat. . . . Nemo non videt si politicae gnarus, quae semina dissensionum schema nostrum contineat et quibus periculis exponatur ipsa temporalis Sanctae sedis potestas.

measure in reserve for that last contingency. The principle of unanimity was fundamental. It admitted no ambiguity, and was so clear, simple, and decisive, that there was no risk in fixing on it. The Archbishops of Paris, Milan, Halifax, the Bishops of Djakovar, Orleans, Marseilles, and most of the Hungarians, yielded to these arguments, and accepted the policy of less strenuous colleagues, while retaining the opinion that the Council was of no authority. But there were some who deemed it unworthy and inconsistent to attend an assembly which they had ceased to respect.

The debate on the several paragraphs lasted till the beginning of July, and the decree passed at length with eighty-eight dissentient votes. It was made known that the infallibility of the Pope would be promulgated in solemn session on the 18th, and that all who were present would be required to sign an act of submission. Some bishops of the minority thereupon proposed that they should all attend, repeat their vote, and refuse their signature. They exhorted their brethren to set a conspicuous example of courage and fidelity, as the Catholic world would not remain true to the faith if the bishops were believed to have faltered. But it was certain that there were men amongst them who would renounce their belief rather than incur the penalty of excommunication, who preferred authority to proof, and accepted the Pope's declaration, "La tradizione son' io." It was resolved by a small majority that the opposition should renew its negative vote in writing, and should leave Rome in a body before the session. Some of the most conscientious and resolute adversaries of the dogma advised this course. Looking to the immediate future, they were persuaded that an irresistible reaction was at hand, and that the decrees of the Vatican Council would fade away and be dissolved by a power mightier than the Episcopate and a process less perilous than schism. Their disbelief in the validity of its work was so profound that they were convinced that it would perish without violence, and they resolved to spare the Pope and themselves the indignity of a rupture. Their last manifesto, *La dernière Heure*, is an appeal for patience, an exhortation to rely on the guiding, healing hand of God.[1] They deemed that they had assigned the course which was to save the Church, by teaching the Catholics to reject a Council which was neither legitimate in constitution, free in action, nor unanimous in doctrine, but to observe moderation in contesting an authority over which great catastrophes impend. They conceived that it would thus be possible to save the peace and unity of the Church without sacrifice of faith and reason.

[1] Espérons que l'excès du mal provoquera le retour du bien. Ce Concile n'aura eu qu'un heureux résultat, celui d'en appeler un autre, réuni dans la liberté. . . . Le Concile du Vatican demeurera stérile, comme tout ce qui n'est pas éclos sous le souffle de l'Esprit Saint. Cependant il aura révélé non seulement jusqu'à quel point l'absolutisme peut abuser des meilleures institutions et des meilleurs instincts, mais aussi ce que vaut encore le droit, alors même qu'il n'a plus que le petit nombre pour le deféndre. . . . Si la multitude passe quand même nous lui prédisons qu'elle n'ira pas loin. Les Spartiates, qui étaient tombés aux Thermopyles pour défendre les terres de la liberté, avaient preparé au flot impitoyable au despotisme la défaite de Salamis.

XV

A HISTORY OF THE INQUISITION OF THE MIDDLE AGES. By HENRY CHARLES LEA[1]

A GOOD many years ago, when Bishop Wilberforce was at Winchester, and the Earl of Beaconsfield was a character in fiction, the bishop was interested in the proposal to bring over the Utrecht Psalter. Mr. Disraeli thought the scheme absurd. "Of course," he said, "you won't get it." He was told that, nevertheless, such things are, that public manuscripts had even been sent across the Atlantic in order that Mr. Lea might write a history of the Inquisition. "Yes," he replied, "but they never came back again." The work which has been awaited so long has come over at last, and will assuredly be accepted as the most important contribution of the new world to the religious history of the old. Other books have shown the author as a thoughtful inquirer in the remunerative but perilous region where religion and politics conflict, where ideas and institutions are as much considered as persons and events, and history is charged with all the elements of fixity, development, and change. It is little to say, now, that he equals Buckle in the extent, and surpasses him in the intelligent choice and regulation, of his reading. He is armed at all points. His information is comprehensive, minute, exact, and everywhere sufficient, if not everywhere complete. In this astonishing press of digested facts there is barely space to discuss the ideas which they exhibit and the law which they obey. M. Molinier lately wrote that a work with this scope and title "serait, à notre sens, une

[1] *English Historical Review*, 1888.

entreprise à peu près chimérique." It will be interesting to learn whether the opinion of so good a judge has been altered or confirmed.

The book begins with a survey of all that led to the growth of heresy, and to the creation, in the thirteenth century, of exceptional tribunals for its suppression. There can be no doubt that this is the least satisfactory portion of the whole. It is followed by a singularly careful account of the steps, legislative and administrative, by which Church and State combined to organise the intermediate institution, and of the manner in which its methods were formed by practice. Nothing in European literature can compete with this, the centre and substance of Mr. Lea's great history. In the remaining volumes he summons his witnesses, calls on the nations to declare their experience, and tells how the new force acted upon society to the end of the Middle Ages. History of this undefined and international cast, which shows the same wave breaking upon many shores, is always difficult, from the want of visible unity and progression, and has seldom succeeded so well as in this rich but unequal and disjointed narrative. On the most significant of all the trials, those of the Templars and of Hus, the author spends his best research; and the strife between Avignon and the Franciscans, thanks to the propitious aid of Father Ehrle, is better still. Joan of Arc prospers less than the disciples of Perfect Poverty; and after Joan of Arc many pages are allotted, rather profusely, to her companion in arms, who survives in the disguise of Bluebeard. The series of dissolving scenes ends, in order of time, at Savonarola; and with that limit the work is complete. The later Inquisition, starting with the Spanish and developing into the Roman, is not so much a prolongation or a revival as a new creation. The mediæval Inquisition strove to control states, and was an engine of government. The modern strove to coerce the Protestants, and was an engine of war. One was subordinate, local, having a kind of headquarters in the house of Saint Dominic at Toulouse. The other was sovereign, universal, centred in the Pope, and exercising its domination, not against obscure men without a literature, but against bishop and archbishop, nuncio and legate, primate and professor; against the general of the Capuchins and the imperial preacher; against the first candidate in the conclave, and the president of the œcumenical council. Under altered conditions, the rules varied and even principles were modified. Mr. Lea is slow to take counsel of the voluminous moderns, fearing the confusion of dates. When he says that the laws he is describing are technically still in force, he makes too little of a fundamental distinction. In the eye of the polemic, the modern Inquisition eclipses its predecessor, and stops the way.

The origin of the Inquisition is the topic of a lasting controversy. According to common report, Innocent III. founded it, and made Saint Dominic the first inquisitor; and this belief has been maintained by the Dominicans against the Cistercians, and by the Jesuits against the Dominicans themselves. They affirm that the saint, having done his work in Languedoc, pursued it in Lombardy: "Per civitates et castella Lombardiae circuibat, praedicans et evangelizans regnum Dei, atque contra haereticos inquirens, quos ex odore et aspectu dignoscens, condignis suppliciis puniebat" (Fontana, *Monumenta Dominicana*, 16). He transferred his powers to Fra Moneta, the brother in whose bed he died, and who is notable as having studied more seriously than any other divine the system which he assailed: "Vicarium suum in munere inquisitionis delegerat dilectissimum sibi B. Monetam, qui spiritu illius loricatus, tanquam leo rugiens contra haereticos surrexit. . . . Iniquos cum haereticos ex corde insectaretur, illisque nullo modo parceret, sed igne ac ferro consumeret." Moneta is succeeded by Guala, who brings us down to historic times, when the Inquisition flourished undisputed: "Facta promotione Guallae constitutus est in eius locum generalis inquisitor P. F. Guidottus de Sexto, a Gregorio Papa IX., qui innumeros propemodum haereticos igne consumpsit" (Fontana, *Sacrum Theatrum Dominicanum*, 595). Sicilian inquisitors produce an imperial privilege of December 1224, which shows the tribunal in full action under Honorius III.: "Sub nostrae indignationis fulmine praesenti edicto districtius praecipiendo mandamus, quatenus inquisitoribus haereticae pravitatis, ut suum libere officium prosequi et exercere valeant, prout decet, omne quod potestis impendatis auxilium" (Franchina, *Inquisizione di Sicilia*, 1774, 8). This document may be a forgery of the fifteenth century; but the whole of the Dominican version is dismissed by Mr. Lea with contempt. He has heard that their founder once rescued a heretic from the flames; "but Dominic's project only looked to their peaceful conversion, and to performing the duties of instruction and exhortation." Nothing is better authenticated in the life of the saint than the fact that he condemned heretics and exercised the right of deciding which of them should suffer and which should be spared. "Contigit quosdam haereticos captos et per eum convictos, cum redire nollent ad fidem catholicam, tradi judicio saeculari. Cumque essent incendio deputati, aspiciens inter alios quemdam Raymundum de Grossi nomine, ac si aliquem eo divinae praedestinationis radium fuisset intuitus, istum, inquit officialibus curiae, reservate, nec aliquo modo cum caeteris comburatur" (Constantinus, *Vita S. Dominici*; Echard, *Scriptores O. P.*, I. 33). The transaction is memorable in Dominican annals as the one link distinctly connecting Saint Dominic with the system of executions, and the only security possessed by the order that the most conspicuous of its actions is sanctioned by the spirit and example of the founder. The original authorities record it, and it is commemorated by Bzovius and Malvenda, by Fontana and Percin, by Echard and Mamachi, as well as in the *Acta Sanctorum*. Those are exactly the authors to whom in the first instance a man betakes himself who desires to understand the inception and early growth of the Inquisition. I cannot remember that any one of them appears in Mr. Lea's notes. He says indeed that Saint Dominic's inquisitorial activity "is affirmed by all the historians of the order," and he is a workman who knows his tools so well that we may hesitate to impute this grave omission to inacquaintance with necessary literature. It is one of his characteristics to be suspicious of the *Histoire Intime* as the seat of fable and proper domain of those problems in psychology against which the certitude of history is always going to pieces. Where motives are obscure, he prefers to contemplate causes in their effects, and to look abroad over his vast horizon of unquestioned reality. The difference between outward and interior history will be felt by any one who compares the story of Dolcino here given with the account in Neander. Mr. Lea knows more about him and has better materials than the ponderous professor of pectoral theology. But he has not all Neander's patience and power to read significance and sense in the musings of a reckless erratic mind.

He believes that Pope Gregory IX. is the intellectual originator, as well as the legislative imponent, of the terrific system which ripened gradually and experimentally in his pontificate. It does not appear whether he has read, or knows through Havet the investigations which conducted Ficker to a different hypothesis. The transition of 1231 from the saving of life to the taking of life by fire was nearly the sharpest that men can conceive, and in pursuance of it the subsequent legal forms are mere detail. The spirit and practice of centuries were renounced for the opposite extreme; and between the mercy of 1230 and the severity of 1231 there was no intervening stage of graduated rigour. Therefore it is probable that the new idea of duty, foreign to Italian and specifically to Roman ways, was conveyed by a new man, that a new influence just then got possession of the Pope. Professor Ficker signals Guala as the real contriver of the *régime* of terror, and the man who acquired the influence imported the idea and directed the policy. Guala was a Dominican prior whom the Pope trusted in emergencies. In the year 1230 he negotiated the treaty of San Germano between Frederic II. and the Church, and was made Bishop of Brescia. In that year Brescia, first among Italian cities, inserted in its statutes the emperor's Lombard law of 1224, which sent the heretic to the stake. The inference is that the Dominican prelate caused its insertion, and that nobody is so likely to have expounded its available purport to the pontiff as the man who had so lately caused it to be adopted in his own see, and who stood high just then in merit and in favour. That Guala was bishop-elect on 28th August, half a year before the first burnings at Rome, we know; that he caused the adoption of Frederic's law at Brescia or at Rome is not in evidence. Of that abrupt and unexplained enactment little is told us, but this we are told, that it was inspired by Honorius: "Leges quoque imperiales per quondam Fredericum olim Romanorum imperatorem, tunc in devotione Romane sedis persistentem, procurante eadem sede, fuerunt edite et Padue promulgate" (Bern. Guidonis, *Practica Inquisitionis*, 173). At any rate, Gregory, who had seen most things since the elevation of Innocent, knew how Montfort dealt with Albigensian prisoners at Minerve and Lavaur, what penalties were in store at Toulouse, and on what principles Master Conrad administered in Germany the powers received from Rome. The Papacy which inspired the coronation laws of 1220, in which there is no mention of capital punishment, could not have been unobservant of the way in which its own provisions were transformed; and Gregory, whom Honorius had already called "magnum et speciale ecclesie Romane membrum," who had required the university of Bologna to adopt and to expound the new legislation, and who knew the Archbishop of Magdeburg, had little to learn from Guala about the formidable weapon supplied to that prelate for the government of Lombardy. There is room for further conjecture.

In those days it was discovered that Arragon was infested with heresy; and the king's confessor proposed that the Holy See be applied to for means of active suppression. With that object, in 1230 he was sent to Rome. The envoy's name was Raymond, and his home was on the coast of Catalonia in the town of Pennaforte. He was a Bolognese jurist, a Dominican, and the author of the most celebrated treatise on morals made public in the generation preceding the scholastic theology. The five years of his abode in Rome changed the face of the Church. He won the confidence of Gregory, became penitentiary, and was employed to codify the acts of the popes militant since the publication of Gratian. Very soon after Saint Raymond appeared at the papal court, the use of the stake became law, the inquisitorial machinery had been devised, and the management given to the priors of the order. When he departed he left behind him instructions for the treatment of heresy, which the pope adopted and sent out where they were wanted. He refused a mitre, rose to be general, it is said in opposition to Albertus Magnus, and retired early, to become, in his own country, the oracle of councils on the watch for heterodoxy. Until he came, in spite of much violence and many laws, the popes had imagined no permanent security against religious error, and were not formally committed to death by burning. Gregory himself, excelling all the priesthood in vigour and experience, had for four years laboured, vaguely and in vain, with the transmitted implements. Of a sudden, in three successive measures, he finds his way, and builds up the institution which is to last for centuries. That this mighty change in the conditions of religious thought and life and in the functions of the order was suggested by Dominicans is probable. And it is reasonable to suppose that it was the work of the foremost Dominican then living, who at that very moment had risen to power and predominance at Rome.

No sane observer will allow himself to overdraw the influence of national character on events. Yet there was that in the energetic race that dwell with the Pyrenees above them and the Ebro below that suited a leading part in the business of organised persecution. They are among the nations that have been inventors in politics, and both the constitution of Arragon and that of the society of Jesus prove their constructive science. While people in other lands were feeling their way, doubtful and debonair, Arragon went straight to the end. Before the first persecuting pope was elected, before the Child of Apulia, who was to be the first persecuting emperor, was born, Alfonso proscribed the heretics. King and clergy were in such accord that three years later the council of Girona decreed that they might be beaten while they remained, and should be burnt if they came back. It was under this government, amid these surroundings, that Saint Dominic grew up, whom Sixtus V., speaking on authority which we do not possess, entitled the First Inquisitor. Saint Raymond, who had more to do with it than Saint Dominic, was his countryman. Eymerici, whose *Directorium* was the best authority until the *Practica* of Guidonis appeared, presided during forty years over the Arragonese tribunal; and his commentator Pegna, the Coke upon Littleton of inquisitorial jurisprudence, came from the same stern region.

The *Histoire Générale de Languedoc* in its new shape has supplied Mr. Lea with so good a basis that his obligations to the present editors bring him into something like dependence on French scholarship. He designates monarchs by the names they bear in France—Louis le Germanique, Charles le Sage, Philippe le Bon, and even Philippe; and this habit, with Foulques and Berenger of Tours, with Aretino for Arezzo, Oldenburg for Altenburg, Torgau for Zürich, imparts an exotic flavour which would be harmless but for a surviving preference for French books. Compared with Bouquet and Vaissète, he is unfamiliar with Böhmer and Pertz. For Matthew Paris he gets little or no help from Coxe, or Madden, or Luard, or Liebermann, or Huillard. In France few things of importance have escaped him. His account of Marguerite Porrette differs from that given by Hauréau in the *Histoire Littéraire*, and the difference is left unexplained. No man can write about Joan of Arc without suspicion who discards the publications of Quicherat, and even of Wallon, Beaucourt, and Luce. Etienne de Bourbon was an inquisitor of long experience, who knew the original comrade and assistant of Waldus. Fragments of him scattered up and down in the works of learned men have caught the author's eye; but it is uncertain how much he knows of the fifty pages from Stephanus printed in

Echard's book on Saint Thomas, or of the volume in which Lecoy de la Marche has collected all, and more than all, that deserves to live of his writings. The "Historia Pontificalis," attributed to John of Salisbury, in the twentieth volume of the *Monumenta*, should affect the account of Arnold of Brescia. The analogy with the Waldenses, amongst whom his party seems to have merged, might be more strongly marked. "Hominum sectam fecit que adhuc dicitur heresis Lumbardorum. . . . Episcopis non parcebat ob avariciam et turpem questum, et plerumque propter maculam vite, et quia ecclesiam Dei in sanguinibus edificare nituntur." He was excommunicated and declared a heretic. He was reconciled and forgiven. Therefore, when he resumed his agitation his portion was with the obstinate and relapsed. "Ei populus Romanus vicissim auxilium et consilium contra omnes homines et nominatim contra domnum papam repromisit, eum namque excommunicaverat ecclesia Romana. . . . Post mortem domni Innocentii reversus est in Italiam, et promissa satisfactione et obediencia Romane ecclesie, a domno Eugenio receptus est apud Viterbum." And it is more likely that the fear of relics caused them to reduce his body to ashes than merely to throw the ashes into the Tiber.

The energy with which Mr. Lea beats up information is extraordinary even when imperfectly economised. He justly makes ample use of the *Vitae Paparum Avenionensium*, which he takes apparently from the papal volume of Muratori. These biographies were edited by Baluze, with notes and documents of such value that Avignon without him is like Athenæus without Casaubon, or the Theodosian Code without Godefroy. But if he neglects him in print, he constantly quotes a certain Paris manuscript in which I think I recognise the very one which Baluze employed. Together with Guidonis and Eymerici, the leading authority of the fourteenth century is Zanchini, who became an inquisitor at Rimini in 1300, and died in 1340. His book was published with a commentary by Campeggio, one of the Tridentine fathers; and Campeggio was further annotated by Simancas, who exposes the disparity between

Italian and Spanish usage. It was reprinted, with other treatises of the same kind, in the eleventh volume of the *Tractatus.* Some of these treatises, and the notes of Campeggio and Simancas, are passed over by Mr. Lea without notice. But he appreciates Zanchini so well that he has had him copied from a manuscript in France. Very much against his habit, he prints one entire sentence, from which it appears that his copy does not agree to the letter with the published text. It is not clear in every case whether he is using print or manuscript. One of the most interesting directions for inquisitors, and one of the earliest, was written by Cardinal Fulcodius, better known as Clement IV. Mr. Lea cites him a dozen times, always accurately, always telling us scrupulously which of the fifteen chapters to consult. The treatise of Fulcodius occupies a few pages in Carena, *De Officio S.S. Inquisitionis*, in which, besides other valuable matter, there are notes by Carena himself, and a tract by Pegna, the perpetual commentator of the Inquisition. This is one of the first eight or ten books which occur to any one whose duty it is to lay in an inquisitor's library. Not only we are never told where to find Fulcodius, but when Carena is mentioned it is so done as to defy verification. Inartistic references are not, in this instance, a token of inadequate study. But a book designed only for readers who know at a glance where to lay their finger on *S. Francis. Collat. Monasticae*, *Collat.* 20, or *Post constt. IV. XIX. Cod. I. v.* will be slow in recovering outlay.

Not his acquaintance with rare books only, which might be the curiosity of an epicurean, but with the right and appropriate book, amazes the reader. Like most things attributed to Abbot Joachim, the *Vaticinia Pontificum* is a volume not in common use, and decent people may be found who never saw a copy. Mr. Lea says: "I have met with editions of Venice issued in 1589, 1600, 1605, and 1646, of Ferrara in 1591, of Frankfort in 1608, of Padua in 1625, and of Naples in 1660, and there are doubtless numerous others." This is the general level throughout; the rare failures disappear in the imposing supererogation of knowledge. It could not be exceeded by the pupils of the Göttingen seminary or the École des Chartes. They have sometimes a vicious practice of overtopping sufficient proof with irrelevant testimony: but they transcribe all deciding words in full, and for the rest, quicken and abridge our toil by sending us, not to chapter and verse, but to volume and page, of the physical and concrete book. We would gladly give Bluebeard and his wife—he had but one after all—in exchange for the best quotations from sources hard of access which Mr. Lea must have hoarded in the course of labours such as no man ever achieved before him, or will ever attempt hereafter. It would increase the usefulness of his volumes, and double their authority. There are indeed fifty pages of documentary matter not entirely new or very closely connected with the text. Portions of this, besides, are derived from manuscripts explored in France and Italy, but not it seems in Rome, and in this way much curious and valuable material underlies the pages; but it is buried without opportunity of display or scrutiny. Line upon line of references to the Neapolitan archives only bewilder and exasperate. Mr. Lea, who dealt more generously with the readers of *Sacerdotal Celibacy*, has refused himself in these overcrowded volumes that protection against overstatement. The want of verifiable indication of authorities is annoying, especially at first; and it may be possible to find one or two references to Saint Bonaventure or to Wattenbach which are incorrect. But he is exceedingly careful in rendering the sense of his informants, and neither strains the tether nor outsteps his guide. The original words in very many cases would add definiteness and a touch of surprise to his narrative.

If there is anywhere the least infidelity in the statement of an author's meaning, it is in the denial that Marsilius, the imperial theorist, and the creator with Ockam of the Ghibelline philosophy that has ruled the world, was a friend of religious liberty. Marsilius assuredly was not a Whig. Quite as much as any Guelph, he desired to concentrate power, not to limit or divide it. Of the sacred immunities of conscience he had no clearer vision than Dante. But he opposed persecution in the shape in which he knew it, and the patriarchs of European emancipation have not done more. He never says that there is no case in which a religion may be proscribed; but he speaks of none in which a religion may be imposed. He discusses, not intolerance, but the divine authority to persecute, and pleads for a secular law. It does not appear how he would deal with a Thug. "Nemo quantumcumque peccans contra disciplinas speculativas aut operativas quascumque punitur vel arcetur in hoc saeculo praecise in quantum huiusmodi, sed in quantum peccat contra praeceptum humanae legis. . . . Si humana lege prohibitum fuerit haereticum aut aliter infidelem in regione manere, qui talis in ipsa repertus fuerit, tanquam legis humanae transgressor, poena vel supplicio huic transgressioni eadem lege statutis, in hoc saeculo debet arceri." The difference is slight between the two readings. One asserts that Marsilius was tolerant in effect; the other denies that he was tolerant in principle.

Mr. Lea does not love to recognise the existence of much traditional toleration. Few lights are allowed to deepen his shadows. If a stream of tolerant thought descended from the early ages to the time when the companion of Vespucci brought his improbable tale from Utopia, then the views of Bacon, of Dante, of Gerson cannot be accounted for by the ascendency of a unanimous persuasion. It is because all men were born to the same inheritance of enforced conformity that we glide so easily towards the studied increase of pain. If some men were able to perceive what lay in the other scale, if they made a free choice, after deliberation, between well-defined and well-argued opinions, then what happened is not assignable to invincible causes, and history must turn from general and easy explanation to track the sinuosities of a tangled thread. In Mr. Lea's acceptation of ecclesiastical history intolerance was handed down as a rule of life from the days of St. Cyprian, and the few who shrank half-hearted from the gallows and the flames were exceptions, were men navigating craft of their own away from the track of St. Peter. Even in his own age he is not careful to show that the Waldenses opposed persecution, not in self-defence, but in the necessary sequence of thought. And when he describes Eutychius as an obscure man, who made a point at the fifth general council, for which he was rewarded with the patriarchate of Constantinople—Eutychius, who was already patriarch when the council assembled; and when he twice tears Formosus from his grave to parade him in his vestments about Rome,—we may suspect that the perfect grasp of documentary history from the twelfth century does not reach backwards in a like degree.

If Mr. Lea stands aloft, in his own domain, as an accumulator, his credit as a judge of testimony is nearly as high. The deciding test of his critical sagacity is the masterly treatment of the case against the Templars. They were condemned without mercy, by Church and State, by priest and jurist, and down to the present day cautious examiners of evidence, like Prutz and Lavocat, give a faltering verdict. In the face of many credulous forerunners and of much concurrent testimony Mr. Lea pronounces positively that the monster trial was a conspiracy to murder, and every adverse proof a lie. His immediate predecessor, Schottmüller, the first writer who ever knew the facts, has made this conclusion easy. But the American does not move in the retinue of the Prussian scholar. He searches and judges for himself; and in his estimate of the chief actor in the tragedy, Clement V., he judges differently. He rejects, as forgeries, a whole batch of unpublished confessions, and he points out that a bull disliked by inquisitors is not reproduced entire in the *Bullarium Dominicanum.* But he fails to give the collation, and is generally jealous about admitting readers to his confidence, taking them into consultation and producing the scales. In the case of Delicieux, which nearly closes the drama of Languedoc, he consults his own sources, independently of Hauréau, and in the end adopts the marginal statement in Limborch, that the pope aggravated the punishment. In other places, he puts his trust in the

Historia Tribulationum, and he shows no reason for dismissing the different account there given of the death of Delicieux: "Ipsum fratrem Bernardum sibi dari a summo pontifice petierunt. Et videns summus pontifex quod secundum accusationes quas de eo fecerant fratres minores justitiam postularent, tradidit eis eum. Qui, quum suscepissent eum in sua potestate, sicut canes, cum vehementer furiunt, lacerant quam capiunt bestiam, ita ipsi diversis afflictionibus et cruciatibus laniaverunt eum. Et videntes quod neque inquisitionibus nec tormentis poterant pompam de eo facere in populo, quam quaerebant, in arctissimo carcere eum reduxerunt, ibidem eum taliter tractantes, quod infra paucos menses, quasi per ignem et aquam transiens, de carcere corporis et minorum et praedicatorum liberatus gloriose triumphans de mundi principe, migravit ad coelos."

We obtain only a general assurance that the fate of Cecco d' Ascoli is related on the strength of unpublished documents at Florence. It is not stated what they are. There is no mention of the epitaph pronounced by the pope who had made him his physician: "Cucullati Minores recentiorum Peripateticorum principem perdiderunt." We do not learn that Cecco reproached Dante with the same fatalistic leaning for which he himself was to die: "Non è fortuna cui ragion non vinca." Or how they disputed: "An ars natura fortior ac potentior existeret," and argument was supplanted by experiment: "Aligherius, qui opinionem oppositam mordicus tuebatur, felem domesticam Stabili objiciebat, quam ea arte instituerat, ut ungulis candelabrum teneret, dum is noctu legeret, vel coenaret. Cicchius igitur, ut in sententiam suam Aligherium pertraheret, scutula assumpta, ubi duo musculi asservabantur inclusi, illos in conspectum felis dimisit; quae naturae ingenio inemendabili obsequens, muribus vix inspectis, illico in terram candelabrum abjecit, et ultro citroque cursare ac vestigiis praedam persequi instituit." Either Appiani's defence of Cecco d' Ascoli has escaped Mr. Lea, who nowhere mentions Bernino's *Historia di tutte l' Heresie* where it is printed; or he may distrust Bernino for calling Dante a schismatic; or it may be that he rejects all this as legend, beneath the certainty of history. But he does not disdain the legendary narrative of the execution: "Tradition relates that he had learned by his art that he should die between Africa and Campo Fiore, and so sure was he of this that on the way to the stake he mocked and ridiculed his guards; but when the pile was about to be lighted he asked whether there was any place named Africa in the vicinage, and was told that that was the name of a neighbouring brook flowing from Fiesole to the Arno. Then he recognised that Florence was the Field of Flowers, and that he had been miserably deceived." The Florentine document before me, whether the same or another I know not, says nothing about untimely mockery or miserable deception: "Aveva inteso dal demonio dover lui morire di morte accidentale infra l' Affrica e campo di fiore; per lo che cercando di conservare la reputazione sua, ordinò di non andar mai nelle parti d' Affrica; e credendo tal fallacia è di potere sbeffare la gente, pubblicamente in Italia esecutava l'arte della negromanzia, et essendo per questo preso in Firenze e per la sua confessione essendo già giudicato al fuoco e legato al palo, nè vedendo alcun segno della sua liberazione, avendo prima fatto i soliti scongiuri, domandò alle persone che erano all' intorno, se quivi vicino era alcun luogo che si chiamasse Affrica, et essendogli risposto di si, cioè un fiumicello che correva ivi presso, il quale discende da Fiesole ed è chiamato Affrica, considerando che il demonio per lo campo de' fiori aveva inteso Fiorenza, e per l' Affrica quel fiumicello, ostinato nella sua perfidia, disse al manigoldo che quanto prima attaccasse il fuoco."

Mr. Lea thinks that the untenable conditions offered to the count of Toulouse by the council of Arles in 1211 are spurious. M. Paul Meyer has assigned reasons on the other side in his notes to the translation of the *Chanson de la Croisade*, pp. 75-77; and the editors of Vaissète (vi. 347) are of the same opinion as M. Paul Meyer. It happens that Mr. Lea reads the *Chanson* in the *editio princeps* of Fauriel; and in this particular place he cites the *Histoire du Languedoc* in the old and superseded edition. From a letter lately brought to light in the *Archiv für Geschichte des Mittelalters*, he infers that the decree of Clement V. affecting the privilege of inquisitors was tampered with before publication. A Franciscan writes from Avignon when the new canons were ready: "Inquisitores etiam heretice pravitatis restinguuntur et supponuntur episcopis"—which he thinks would argue something much more decisive than the regulations as they finally appeared. Ehrle, who publishes the letter, remarks that the writer exaggerated the import of the intended change; but he says it not of this sentence, but of the next preceding. Mr. Lea has acknowledged elsewhere the gravity of this Clementine reform. As it stands, it was considered injurious by inquisitors, and elicited repeated protests from Bernardus Guidonis: "Ex predicta autem ordinatione seu restrictione nonnulla inconvenientia consecuntur, que liberum et expeditum cursum officii inquisitoris tam in manibus dyocesanorum quam etiam inquisitorum diminuunt seu retardant. . . . Que apostolice sedis circumspecta provisione ac provida circumspectione indigent, ut remedientur, aut moderentur in melius, seu pocius totaliter suspendantur propter nonnulla inconvenientia que consecuntur ex ipsis circa liberum et expeditum cursum officii inquisitoris."

The feudal custom which supplied Beaumarchais with the argument of his play recruits a stout believer in the historian of the Inquisition, who assures us that the authorities may be found on a certain page of his *Sacerdotal Celibacy*. There, however, they may be sought in vain. Some dubious instances are mentioned, and the dissatisfied inquirer is passed on to the Fors de Béarn, and to Lagrèze, and is informed that M. Louis Veuillot raised an unprofitable dust upon the subject. I remember that M. Veuillot, in his boastful scorn for book learning, made no secret that he took up the cause because the Church was attacked, but got his facts from somebody else. Graver men than Veuillot have shared his conclusion. Sir Henry Maine, having looked into the matter in his quick, decisive way, declared that an instance of the *droit du seigneur* was as rare as the Wandering Jew. In resting his case on the Pyrenees, Mr. Lea shows his usual judgment. But his very confident note is a too easy and contemptuous way of settling a controversy which is still wearily extant from Spain to Silesia, in which some new fact comes to light every year, and drops into obscurity, riddled with the shafts of critics.

An instance of too facile use of authorities occurs at the siege of Béziers. "A fervent Cistercian contemporary informs us that when Arnaud was asked whether the Catholics should be spared, he feared the heretics would escape by feigning orthodoxy, and fiercely replied, 'Kill them all, for God knows his own.'" Caesarius, to whom we owe the *locus classicus*, was a Cistercian and a contemporary, but he was not so fervent as that, for he tells it as a report, not as a fact, with a caution which ought not to have evaporated. "Fertur dixisse: Caedite eos. Novit enim Dominus qui sunt eius!" The Catholic defenders had been summoned to separate from the Cathari, and had replied that they were determined to share their fate. It was then resolved to make an example, which we are assured bore fruit afterwards. The hasty zeal of Citeaux adopted the speech of the abbot and gave it currency. But its rejection by the French scholars, Tamizey de Larroque and Auguste Molinier, was a warning against presenting it with a smooth surface, as a thing tested and ascertained. Mr. Lea, in other passages, has shown his disbelief in Caesarius of Heisterbach, and knows that history written in reliance upon him would be history fit for the moon. Words as ferocious are recorded of another legate at a different siege (Langlois, *Règne de Philippe le Hardi*, p. 156). Their tragic significance for history is not in the mouth of an angry crusader at the storming of a fortress, but in the pen of an inoffensive monk, watching and praying under the peaceful summit of the Seven Mountains.

Mr. Lea undertakes to dispute no doctrine and to propose no moral. He starts with an avowed desire not to say what may be construed injuriously to the character or feelings of men. He writes pure history, and is methodically oblivious of applied history. The broad and sufficient realm of fact is divided by a scientific frontier from the outer world of interested argument. Beyond the frontier he has no cognisance, and neither aspires to inflame passions nor to compose the great eirenikon. Those who approach with love or hatred are to go empty away; if indeed he does not try by turns to fill them both. He seeks his object not by standing aloof, as if the name that perplexed Polyphemus was the proper name for historians, but by running successively on opposing lines. He conceives that civilised Europe owes its preservation to the radiant centre of religious power at Rome, and is grateful to Innocent III. for the vigour with which he recognised that force was the only cure for the pestiferous opinions of misguided zealots. One of his authorities is the inquisitor Bernardus Guidonis, and there is no writer whom, in various shapes, he quotes so often. But when Guidonis says that Dolcino and Margarita suffered *per juditium ecclesie*, Mr. Lea is careful to vindicate the clergy from the blame of their sufferings.

From a distinction which he draws between despotism and its abuse, and from a phrase, disparaging to elections, about rivers that cannot rise above the level of their source, it would appear that Mr. Lea is not under compulsion to that rigid liberalism which, by repressing the time-test and applying the main rules of morality all round, converts history into a frightful monument of sin. Yet, in the wake of passages which push the praises of authority to the verge of irony, dire denunciations follow. When the author looks back upon his labours, he discerns "a scene of almost unrelieved blackness." He avers that "the deliberate burning alive of a human being simply for difference of belief, is an atrocity," and speaks of a "fiendish legislation," "an infernal curiosity," a "seemingly causeless ferocity which appears to persecute for the mere pleasure of persecuting." The Inquisition is "energetic only in evil"; it is "a standing mockery of justice, perhaps the most iniquitous that the arbitrary cruelty of man has ever devised."

This is not the protest of wounded humanity. The righteous resolve to beware of doctrine has not been strictly kept. In the private judgment of the writer, the thinking of the Middle Ages was sophistry and their belief superstition. For the erring and suffering mass of mankind he has an enlightened sympathy; for the intricacies of speculation he has none. He cherishes a disbelief, theological or inductive it matters not, in sinners rescued by repentance and in blessings obtained by prayer. Between remitted guilt and remitted punishment he draws a vanishing line that makes it doubtful whether Luther started from the limits of purgatory or the limits of hell. He finds that it was a universal precept to break faith with heretics, that it was no arbitrary or artificial innovation to destroy them, but the faithful outcome of the traditional spirit of the Church. He hints that the horror of sensuality may be easily carried too far, and that Saint Francis of Assisi was in truth not very much removed from a worshipper of the devil. Prescott, I think, conceived a resemblance between the god of Montezuma and the god of Torquemada; but he saw and suspected less than his more learned countryman. If any life was left in the Strappado and the Samarra, no book would deserve better than this description of their vicissitudes to go the way of its author, and to fare with the flagrant volume, snatched from the burning at Champel, which is still exhibited to Unitarian pilgrims in the Rue de Richelieu.

In other characteristic places we are taught to observe the agency of human passion, ambition, avarice, and pride; and wade through oceans of unvaried evil with that sense of dejection which comes from Digby's *Mores Catholici* or the *Origines de la France Contemporaine*, books which affect the mind by the pressure of repeated instances. The Inquisition is not merely "the monstrous offspring of mistaken zeal," but it is "utilised by selfish greed and lust of power." No piling of secondary motives will confront us with the true cause. Some of those who fleshed their swords with preliminary bloodshed on their way to the holy war may have owed their victims money; some who in 1348 shared the worst crime that Christian nations have committed perhaps believed that Jews spread the plague. But the problem is not there. Neither credulity nor cupidity is equal to the burden. It needs no weighty scholar, pressed down and running over with the produce of immense research, to demonstrate how common men in a barbarous age were tempted and demoralised by the tremendous power over pain, and death, and hell. We have to learn by what reasoning process, by what ethical motive, men trained to charity and mercy came to forsake the ancient ways and made themselves cheerfully familiar with the mysteries of the torture-chamber, the perpetual prison, and the stake. And this cleared away, when it has been explained why the gentlest of women chose that the keeper of her conscience should be Conrad of Marburg, and, inversely, how that relentless slaughterer directed so pure a penitent as Saint Elizabeth, a larger problem follows. After the first generation, we find that the strongest, the most original, the most independent minds in Europe—men born for opposition, who were neither awed nor dazzled by canon law and scholastic theology, by the master of sentences, the philosopher and the gloss—fully agreed with Guala and Raymond. And we ask how it came about that, as the rigour of official zeal relaxed, and there was no compulsion, the fallen cause was taken up by the Council of Constance, the University of Paris, the States-General, the House of Commons, and the first reformers; that Ximenes outdid the early Dominicans, while Vives was teaching toleration; that Fisher, with his friend's handy book of revolutionary liberalism in his pocket, declared that violence is the best argument with Protestants; that Luther, excommunicated for condemning persecution, became a persecutor? Force of habit will not help us, nor love and fear of authority, nor the unperceived absorption of circumambient fumes.

Somewhere Mr. Lea, perhaps remembering Maryland, Rhode Island, and Pennsylvania, speaks of "what was universal public opinion from the thirteenth to the seventeenth century." The obstacle to this theory, as of a ship labouring on the Bank, or an orb in the tail of a comet, is that the opinion is associated with no area of time, and remains unshaken. The Dominican democrat who took his seat with the Mountain in 1848 never swerved from the principles of his order. More often, and, I think, more deliberately, Mr. Lea urges that intolerance is implied in the definition of the mediæval Church, that it sprang from the root and grew with "the very law of its being." It is no desperate expedient of authority at bay, for "the people were as eager as their pastors to send the heretic to the stake." Therefore he does not blame the perpetrator, but his inherited creed. "No firm believer in the doctrine of exclusive salvation could doubt that the truest mercy lay in sweeping away the emissaries of Satan with fire and sword." What we have here is the logic of history, constraining every system to utter its last word, to empty its wallets, and work its consequences out to the end. But this radical doctrine misguides its author to the anachronism that as early as the first Leo "the final step had been taken, and the Church was definitely pledged to the suppression of heresy at whatever cost."

We do not demand that historians shall compose our opinions or relieve us from the purifying pains of thought. It is well if they discard dogmatising, if they defer judgment, or judge, with the philosopher, by precepts capable of being a guide for all. We may be content that they should deny themselves, and repress their sentiments and wishes. When these are contradictory, or such as evidently to tinge the medium, an unholy curiosity is engendered to learn distinctly not only what the writer knows, but what he thinks. Mr. Lea has a malicious pleasure in baffling inquiry into the principle of his judgments. Having found, in the Catechism of Saint Sulpice, that devout Catholics are much on a par with the fanatics whose sympathy with Satan made the holy office a requisite of civilisation, and having, by his exuberant censure, prepared us to hear that this requisite of civilisation "might well seem the invention of demons," he arrives at the inharmonious conclusion that it was wrought and worked, with benefit to their souls, by sincere and godly men. The condemnation of Hus is the proper test, because it was the extreme case of all. The council was master of the situation, and was crowded with men accustomed to disparage the authority of the Holy See and to denounce its acts. Practically, there was no pope either of Rome or Avignon. The Inquisition languished. There was the plausible plea of deference to the emperor and his passport; there was the imperative consideration for the religious future of Bohemia. The reforming divines were free to pursue their own scheme of justice, of mercy, and of policy. The scheme they pursued has found an assiduous apologist in their new historian. "To accuse the good fathers of Constance of conscious bad faith" is impossible. To observe the safe-conduct would have seemed absurd "to the most conscientious jurists of the council." In a nutshell, "if the result was inevitable, it was the fault of the system and not of the judges, and their conscience might well feel satisfied."

There may be more in this than the oratorical precaution of a scholar wanting nothing, who chooses to be discreet rather than explicit, or the wavering utterance of a mind not always strung to the same pitch. It is not the craving to rescue a favourite or to clear a record, but a fusion of unsettled doctrines of retrospective contempt. There is a demonstration of progress in looking back without looking up, in finding that the old world was wrong in the grain, that the kosmos which is inexorable to folly is indifferent to sin. Man is not an abstraction, but a manufactured product of the society with which he stands or falls, which is answerable for crimes that are the shadow and the echo of its own nobler vices, and has no right to hang the rogue it rears. Before you lash the detected class, mulct the undetected. Crime without a culprit, the unavenged victim who perishes by no man's fault, law without responsibility, the virtuous agent of a vicious cause—all these are the signs and pennons of a philosophy not recent, but rather inarticulate still and inchoate, which awaits analysis by Professor Flint.

No propositions are simpler or more comprehensive

than the two, that an incorrigible misbeliever ought to burn, or that the man who burns him ought to hang. The world as expanded on the liberal and on the hegemonic projection is patent to all men, and the alternatives, that Lacordaire was bad and Conrad good, are clear in all their bearings. They are too gross and palpable for Mr. Lea. He steers a subtler course. He does not sentence the heretic, but he will not protect him from his doom. He does not care for the inquisitor, but he will not resist him in the discharge of his duty. To establish a tenable footing on that narrow but needful platform is the epilogue these painful volumes want, that we may not be found with the traveller who discovered a precipice to the right of him, another to the left, and nothing between. Their profound and admirable erudition leads up, like Hellwald's *Culturgeschichte*, to a great note of interrogation. When we find the Carolina and the savage justice of Tudor judges brought to bear on the exquisitely complex psychological revolution that proceeded, after the year 1200, about the Gulf of Lyons and the Tyrrhene Sea, we miss the historic question. When we learn that Priscillian was murdered (i. 214), but that Lechler has no business to call the sentence on John Hus "ein wahrer Justizmord" (ii. 494), and then again that the burning of a heretic is a judicial murder after all (i. 552), we feel bereft of the philosophic answer.

Although Mr. Lea gives little heed to Pani and Hefele, Gams and Du Boys, and the others who write for the Inquisition without pleading ignorance, he emphasises a Belgian who lately wrote that the Church never employed direct constraint against heretics. People who never heard of the Belgian will wonder that so much is made of this conventional figleaf. Nearly the same assertion may be found, with varieties of caution and of confidence, in a catena of divines, from Bergier to Newman. To appear unfamiliar with the defence exposes the writer to the thrust that you cannot know the strength or the weakness of a case until you have heard its advocates. The liberality of Leo XIII., which has yielded a splendid and impartial harvest to Ehrle, and Schottmüller, and the École Française, raises the question whether the Abbé Duchesne or Father Denifle supplied with all the resources of the archives which are no longer secret would produce a very different or more complete account. As a philosophy of religious persecution the book is inadequate. The derivation of sects, though resting always upon good supports, stands out from an indistinct background of dogmatic history. The intruding maxims, darkened by shadows of earth, fail to ensure at all times the objective and delicate handling of mediæval theory. But the vital parts are protected by a panoply of mail. From the Albigensian crusade to the fall of the Templars and to that Franciscan movement wherein the key to Dante lies, the design and organisation, the activity and decline of the Inquisition constitute a sound and solid structure that will survive the censure of all critics. Apart from surprises still in store at Rome, and the manifest abundance of Philadelphia, the knowledge which is common property, within reach of men who seriously invoke history as the final remedy for untruth and the sovereign arbiter of opinion, can add little to the searching labours of the American.

XVI

THE AMERICAN COMMONWEALTH. By James Bryce[1]

The American Commonwealth cancels that sentence of Scaliger which Bacon amplifies in his warning against bookish politicians: "Nec ego nec alius doctus possumus scribere in politicis." The distinctive import of the book is its power of impressing American readers. Mr. Bryce is in a better position than the philosopher who said of another, "Ich hoffe, wir werden uns recht gut verständigen können; und wenn auch keiner den andern ganz versteht, wird doch jeder dem andern dazu helfen, dass er sich selbst besser verstehe." He writes with so much familiarity and feeling—the national, political, social sympathy is so spontaneous and sincere—as to carry a very large measure indeed of quiet reproach. The perfect tone is enough to sweeten and lubricate a medicine such as no traveller since Hippocrates has administered to contrite natives. Facts, not comments, convey the lesson; and I know no better illustration of a recent saying: "Si un livre porte un enseignement, ce doit être malgré son auteur, par la force même des faits qu'il raconte."

If our countryman has not the chill sententiousness of his great French predecessor, his portable wisdom and detached thoughts, he has made a far deeper study of real life, apart from comparative politics and the European investment of transatlantic experience. One of the very few propositions which he has taken straight from Tocqueville is also one of the few which a de-

[1] *English Historical Review*, 1889.

termined fault-finder would be able to contest. For they both say that the need for two chambers has become an axiom of political science. I will admit that the doctrine of Paine and Franklin and Samuel Adams, which the Pennsylvanian example and the authority of Turgot made so popular in France, is confuted by the argument of Laboulaye: "La division du corps législatif est une condition essentielle de la liberté. C'est la seule garantie qui assure la nation contre l'usurpation de ses mandataires." But it may be urged that a truth which is disputed is not an axiom; and serious men still imagine a state of things in which an undivided legislature is necessary to resist a too powerful executive, whilst two chambers can be made to curb and neutralise each other. Both Tocqueville and Turgot are said to have wavered on this point.

It has been said that Tocqueville never understood the federal constitution. He believed, to his last edition, that the opening words of the first section, "all legislative powers herein granted," meant "tous les pouvoirs législatifs déterminés par les représentants." Story thought that he "has borrowed the greater part of his reflections from American works [meaning his own and Lieber's] and little from his own observation." The French minister at Washington described his book as "intéressant mais fort peu exact"; and even the *Nation* calls it "brilliant, superficial, and attractive." Mr. Bryce can never be accused of imperfect knowledge or penetration, of undue dependence upon others, or of writing up to a purpose. His fault is elsewhere. This scholar, distinguished not only as a successful writer of history, which is said to be frequent, but as a trained and professed historian, which is rare, altogether declines the jurisdiction of the HISTORICAL REVIEW. His contumacy is in gross black and white: "I have had to resist another temptation, that of straying off into history." Three stout volumes tell how things are, without telling how they came about. I should have no title to bring them before this tribunal, if it were not for an occasional glimpse at the past; if it were not for a strongly marked and personal philosophy of American history which looms behind the Boss and the Boom, the Hoodlum and the Mugwump.

There is a valid excuse for preferring to address the unhistoric mind. The process of development by which the America of Tocqueville became the America of Lincoln has been lately described with a fulness of knowledge which no European can rival. Readers who thirst for the running stream can plunge and struggle through several thousand pages of Holst's *Verfassungsgeschichte*, and it is better to accept the division of labour than to take up ground so recently covered by a work which, if not very well designed or well composed, is, by the prodigious digestion of material, the most instructive ever written on the natural history of federal democracy. The author, who has spent twenty years on American debates and newspapers, began during the pause between Sadowa and Wörth, when Germany was in the throes of political concentration that made the empire. He explains with complacency how another irrepressible conflict between centre and circumference came and went, and how the welfare of mankind is better served by the gathering than by the balance or dispersion of forces. Like Gneist and Tocqueville, he thinks of one country while he speaks of another; he knows nothing of reticence or economy in the revelation of private opinion; and he has none of Mr. Bryce's cheery indulgence for folly and error. But when the British author refuses to devote six months to the files of Californian journalism, he leaves the German master of his allotted field.

The actual predominates so much with Mr. Bryce that he has hardly a word on that extraordinary aspect of democracy, the union in time of war; and gives no more than a passing glance at the confederate scheme of government, of which a northern writer said: "The invaluable reforms enumerated should be adopted by the United States, with or without a reunion of the seceded States, and as soon as possible." There are points on which some additional light could be drawn from the roaring loom of time. In the chapter on Spoils it is not stated that the idea belongs to the ministers of George III. Hamilton's argument against removals is mentioned, but not the New York edition of *The Federalist* with the marginal note that "Mr. H. had changed his view of the constitution on that point." The French wars of speculation and plunder are spoken of; but, to give honour where honour is due, it should be added that they were an American suggestion. In May 1790, Morris wrote to two of his friends at Paris: "I see no means of extricating you from your troubles, but that which most men would consider as the means of plunging you into greater—I mean a war. And you should make it to yourselves a war of men, to your neighbours a war of money. . . . I hear you cry out that the finances are in a deplorable situation. This should be no obstacle. I think that they may be restored during war better than in peace. You want also something to turn men's attention from their present discontents." There is a long and impartial inquiry into parliamentary corruption as practised now; but one wishes to hear so good a judge on the report that money prevailed at some of the turning-points of American history; on the imputations cast by the younger Adams upon his ablest contemporaries; on the story told by another president, of 223 representatives who received accommodation from the bank, at the rate of a thousand pounds apiece, during its struggle with Jackson.

America as known to the man in the cars, and America observed in the roll of the ages, do not always give the same totals. We learn that the best capacity of the country is withheld from politics, that there is what Emerson calls a gradual withdrawal of tender consciences from the social organisation, so that the representatives approach the level of the constituents. Yet it is in political science only that America occupies the first rank. There are six Americans on a level with the foremost Europeans, with Smith and Turgot, Mill and Humboldt. Five of these were secretaries of state, and one was secretary of the treasury. We are told also that the American of to-day regards the national institutions with a confidence sometimes grotesque. But this is a sentiment which comes down, not from Washington and Jefferson, but from Grant and Sherman. The illustrious founders were not proud of their accomplished work; and men like Clay and Adams persisted in desponding to the second and third generation. We have to distinguish what the nation owes to Madison and Marshall, and what to the army of the Potomac; for men's minds misgave them as to the constitution until it was cemented by the ordeal and the sacrifice of civil war. Even the claim put forward for Americans as the providers of humour for mankind seems to me subject to the same limitation. People used to know how often, or how seldom, Washington laughed during the war; but who has numbered the jokes of Lincoln?

Although Mr. Bryce has too much tact to speak as freely as the Americans themselves in the criticism of their government, he insists that there is one defect which they insufficiently acknowledge. By law or custom no man can represent any district but the one he resides in. If ten statesmen live in the same street, nine will be thrown out of work. It is worth while to point out (though this may not be the right place for a purely political problem) that even in that piece of censure in which he believes himself unsupported by his friends in the States, Mr. Bryce says no more than intelligent Americans have said before him. It chances that several of them have discussed this matter with me. One was governor of his State, and another is among the compurgators cited in the preface. Both were strongly persuaded that the usage in question is an urgent evil; others, I am bound to add, judged differently, deeming it valuable as a security against Boulangism—an object which can be attained by restricting the number of constituencies to be addressed by the same candidate. The two American presidents who agreed in saying that Whig and Tory belong to natural history, proposed a dilemma which Mr. Bryce wishes to elude. He prefers to stand halfway between the two, and to resolve general principles into questions of expediency, probability, and degree: "The wisest statesman is he who best holds the balance between liberty and order." The sentiment is nearly that of Croker and De Quincey, and it is plain that the author would discard the vulgar definition that liberty is the end of government, and that in politics things are to be valued as they minister to its security. He writes in the spirit of John Adams when he said that the French and the American Revolution had nothing in common, and of that eulogy of 1688 as the true Restoration, on which Burke and Macaulay spent their finest prose. A sentence which he takes from Judge Cooley contains the brief abstract of his book: "America is not so much an example in her liberty as in the covenanted and enduring securities which are intended to prevent liberty degenerating into licence, and to establish a feeling of trust and repose under a beneficent government, whose excellence, so obvious in its freedom, is still more conspicuous in its careful provision for permanence and stability." Mr. Bryce declares his own point of view in the following significant terms: "The spirit of 1787 was an English spirit, and therefore a conservative spirit. . . . The American constitution is no exception to the rule that everything which has power to win the obedience and respect of men must have its roots deep in the past, and that the more slowly every institution has grown, so much the more enduring is it likely to prove. . . . There is a hearty puritanism in the view of human nature which pervades the instrument of 1787. . . . No men were less revolutionary in spirit than the heroes of the American Revolution. They made a revolution in the name of Magna Charta and the Bill of Rights." I descry a bewildered Whig emerging from the third volume with a reverent appreciation of ancestral wisdom, Burke's *Reflections*, and the eighteen Canons of Dort, and a growing belief in the function of ghosts to make laws for the quick.

When the last Valois consulted his dying mother, she

advised him that anybody can cut off, but that the sewing on is an acquired art. Mr. Bryce feels strongly for the men who practised what Catharine thought so difficult, and he stops for a moment in the midst of his very impersonal treatise to deliver a panegyric on Alexander Hamilton. *Tanto nomini nullum par elogium.* His merits can hardly be overstated. Talleyrand assured Ticknor that he had never known his equal; Seward calls him "the ablest and most effective statesman engaged in organising and establishing the union"; Macmaster, the iconoclast, and Holst, poorly endowed with the gift of praise, unite in saying that he was the foremost genius among public men in the new world; Guizot told Rush that *The Federalist* was the greatest work known to him, in the application of elementary principles of government to practical administration; his paradox in support of political corruption, so hard to reconcile with the character of an honest man, was repeated to the letter by Niebuhr. In estimating Hamilton we have to remember that he was in no sense the author of the constitution. In the convention he was isolated, and his plan was rejected. In *The Federalist*, written before he was thirty, he pleaded for a form of government which he distrusted and disliked. He was out of sympathy with the spirit that prevailed, and was not the true representative of the cause, like Madison, who said of him, "If his theory of government deviated from the republican standard, he had the candour to avow it, and the greater merit of co-operating faithfully in maturing and supporting a system which was not his choice." The development of the constitution, so far as it continued on his lines, was the work of Marshall, barely known to us by the extracts in late editions of the *Commentaries*. "*The Federalist*," says Story, "could do little more than state the objects and general bearing of these powers and functions. The masterly reasoning of the chief-justice has followed them out to their ultimate results and boundaries with a precision and clearness approaching, as near as may be, to mathematical demonstration." Morris, who was as strong as Hamilton on the side of federalism, testifies heavily against him as a leader: "More a theoretic than a practical man, he was not sufficiently convinced that a system may be good in itself, and bad in relation to particular circumstances. He well knew that his favourite form was inadmissible, unless as the result of civil war; and I suspect that his belief in that which he called an approaching crisis arose from a conviction that the kind of government most suitable, in his opinion, to this extensive country, could be established in no other way. . . . He trusted, moreover, that in the changes and chances of time we should be involved in some war, which might strengthen our union and nerve the executive. He was of all men the most indiscreet. He knew that a limited monarchy, even if established, could not preserve itself in this country. . . . He never failed, on every occasion, to advocate the excellence of, and avow his attachment to, monarchical government. . . . Thus, meaning very well, he acted very ill, and approached the evils he apprehended by his very solicitude to keep them at a distance." The language of Adams is more severe; but Adams was an enemy. It has been justly said that "he wished good men, as he termed them, to rule; meaning the wealthy, the well-born, the socially eminent." The federalists have suffered somewhat from this imputation; for a prejudice against any group claiming to serve under that flag is among the bequests of the French Revolution. "Les honnêtes gens ont toujours peur: c'est leur nature," is a maxim of Chateaubriand. A man most divergent and unlike him, Menou, had drawn the same conclusion: "En révolution il ne faut jamais se mettre du côté des honnêtes gens: ils sont toujours balayés." And Royer Collard, with the candour one shows in describing friends, said: "C'est le parti des honnêtes gens qui est le moins honnête de tous les partis. Tout le monde, même dans ses erreurs, était honnête à l'assemblée constituante, excepté le côté droit." Hamilton stands higher as a political philosopher than as an American partisan. Europeans are generally liberal for the sake of something that is not liberty, and conservative for an object to be conserved; and in a jungle of other motives besides the reason of state we cannot often eliminate unadulterated or disinterested conservatism. We think of land and capital, tradition and custom, the aristocracy and the services, the crown and the altar. It is the singular superiority of Hamilton that he is really anxious about nothing but the exceeding difficulty of quelling the centrifugal forces, and that no kindred and coequal powers divide his attachment or intercept his view. Therefore he is the most scientific of conservative thinkers, and there is not one in whom the doctrine that prefers the ship to the crew can be so profitably studied.

In his scruple to do justice to conservative doctrine Mr. Bryce extracts a passage from a letter of Canning to Croker which, by itself, does not adequately represent that minister's views. "Am I to understand, then, that you consider the king as completely in the hands of the Tory aristocracy as his father, or rather as George II. was in the hands of the Whigs? If so, George III. reigned, and Mr. Pitt (both father and son) administered the government, in vain. I have a better opinion of the real vigour of the crown when it chooses to put forth its own strength, and I am not without some reliance on the body of the people." The finest mind reared by many generations of English conservatism was not always so faithful to monarchical traditions, and in addressing the incessant polemist of Toryism Canning made himself out a trifle better than he really was. His intercourse with Marcellus in 1823 exhibits a diluted orthodoxy: "Le système britannique n'est que le butin des longues victoires remportées par les sujets contre le monarque. Oubliez-vous que les rois ne doivent pas donner des institutions, mais que les institutions seules doivent donner des rois? . . . Connaissez-vous un roi qui mérite d'être libre, dans le sens implicite du mot? . . . Et George IV., croyez-vous que je serais son ministre, s'il avait été libre de choisir? . . Quand un roi dénie au peuple les institutions dont le peuple a besoin, quel est le procédé de l'Angleterre? Elle expulse ce roi, et met à sa place un roi d'une famille alliée sans doute, mais qui se trouve ainsi, non plus un fils de la royauté, confiant dans le droit de ses ancêtres, mais le fils des institutions nationales, tirant tous ses droits de cette seule origine. . . . Le gouvernement représentatif est encore bon à une chose que sa majesté a oubliée. Il fait que des ministres essuient sans répliquer les épigrammes d'un roi qui cherche à se venger ainsi de son impuissance."

Mr. Bryce's work has received a hearty welcome in its proper hemisphere, and I know not that any critic has doubted whether the pious founder, with the dogma of unbroken continuity, strikes the just note or covers all the ground. At another angle, the origin of the greatest power and the grandest polity in the annals of mankind emits a different ray. It was a favourite doctrine with Webster and Tocqueville that the beliefs of the pilgrims inspired the Revolution, which others deem a triumph of pelagianism; while J. Q. Adams affirms that "not one of the motives which stimulated the puritans of 1643 had the slightest influence in actuating the confederacy of 1774." The Dutch statesman Hogendorp, returning from the United States in 1784, had the following dialogue with the stadtholder: "La religion, monseigneur, a moins d'influence que jamais sur les esprits. . . . Il y a toute une province de quakers? . . . Depuis la révolution il semble que ces sortes de différences s'évanouissent. . . . Les Bostoniens ne sont-ils pas fort dévots? . . . Ils l'étaient, monseigneur, mais à lire les descriptions faites il y a vingt ou même dix ans, on ne les reconnaît pas de ce côté-là." It is an old story that the federal constitution, unlike that of Hérault de Séchelles, makes no allusion to the Deity; that there is none in the president's oath; and that in 1796 it was stated officially that the government of the United States is not in any sense founded on the Christian religion. No three men had more to do with the new order than Franklin, Adams, and Jefferson. Franklin's irreligious tone was such that his manuscripts, like Bentham's, were suppressed, to the present year. Adams called the Christian faith a horrid blasphemy. Of Jefferson we are assured that, if not an absolute atheist, he had no belief in a future existence; and he hoped that the French arms "would bring at length kings, nobles, and priests to the scaffolds which they have been so long deluging with human blood." If Calvin prompted the Revolution, it was after he had suffered from contact with Tom Paine; and we must make room for other influences which, in that generation, swayed the world from the rising to the setting sun. It was an age of faith in the secular sense described by Guizot: "C'était un siècle ardent et sincère, un siècle plein de foi et d'enthousiasme. Il a eu foi dans la vérité, car il lui a reconnu le droit de régner."

In point both of principle and policy, Mr. Bryce does well to load the scale that is not his own, and to let the jurist within him sometimes mask the philosophic politician. I have to speak of him not as a political reasoner or as an observer of life in motion, but only in the character which he assiduously lays aside. If he had guarded less against his own historic faculty, and had allowed space to take up neglected threads, he would have had to expose the boundless innovation, the unfathomed gulf produced by American independence, and there would be no opening to back the Jeffersonian shears against the darning-needle of the great chief-justice. My misgiving lies in the line of thought of Riehl and the elder Cherbuliez. The first of those eminent conservatives writes: "Die Extreme, nicht deren Vermittelungen und Abschwächungen, deuten die Zukunft vor." The Genevese has just the same remark: "Les idées n'ont jamais plus de puissance que sous leur forme la plus abstraite. Les idées abstraites ont plus remué le monde, elles ont causé plus de révolutions et laissé plus de traces durables que les idées pratiques." Lassalle says, "Kein Einzelner denkt mit der Consequenz eines Volksgeistes." Schelling may help us over the parting ways: "Der erzeugte Gedanke ist eine unabhängige Macht, für sich fortwirkend, ja, in der menschlichen Seele, so anwachsend, dass er seine eigene Mutter bezwingt und unterwirft." After the philosopher, let us conclude with a divine: "C'est de révolte en révolte, si l'on veut employer ce mot, que les sociétés se perfectionnent, que la civilisation s'établit, que la justice règne, que la vérité fleurit."

The anti-revolutionary temper of the Revolution belongs to 1787, not to 1776. Another element was at work, and it is the other element that is new, effective, characteristic, and added permanently to the experience of the world. The story of the revolted colonies impresses us first and most distinctly as the supreme manifestation of the law of resistance, as the abstract revolution in its purest and most perfect shape. No people was so free as the insurgents; no government less oppressive than the government which they overthrew. Those who deem Washington and Hamilton honest can apply the term to few European statesmen. Their example presents a thorn, not a cushion, and threatens all existing political forms, with the doubtful exception of the federal constitution of 1874. It teaches that men ought to be in arms even against a remote and constructive danger to their freedom; that even if the cloud is no bigger than a man's hand, it is their right and duty to stake the national existence, to sacrifice lives and fortunes, to cover the country with a lake of blood, to shatter crowns and sceptres and fling parliaments into the sea. On this principle of subversion they erected their commonwealth, and by its virtue lifted the world out of its orbit and assigned a new course to history. Here or nowhere we have the broken chain, the rejected past, precedent and statute superseded by unwritten law, sons wiser than their fathers, ideas rooted in the future, reason cutting as clean as Atropos. The wisest philosopher of the old world instructs us to take things as they are, and to adore God in the event: "Il faut toujours être content de l'ordre du passé, parce qu'il est conforme à la volonté de Dieu absolue, qu'on connoît par l'évènement." The contrary is the text of Emerson: "Institutions are not aboriginal, though they existed before we were born. They are not superior to the citizen. Every law and usage was a man's expedient to meet a particular case. We may make as good; we may make better." More to the present point is the language of Seward: "The rights asserted by our forefathers were not peculiar to themselves, they were the common rights of mankind. The basis of the constitution was laid broader by far than the superstructure which the conflicting interests and prejudices of the day suffered to be erected. The constitution and laws of the federal government did not practically extend those principles throughout the new system of government; but they were plainly promulgated in the declaration of independence. Their complete development and reduction to practical operation constitute the progress which all liberal statesmen desire to promote, and the end of that progress will be complete political equality among ourselves, and the extension and perfection of institutions similar to our own throughout the world." A passage which Hamilton's editor selects as the keynote of his system expresses well enough the spirit of the Revolution: "The sacred rights of mankind are not to be rummaged for among old parchments or musty records. They are written, as with a sunbeam, in the whole volume of human nature, by the hand of the Divinity itself, and can never be erased or obscured by mortal power. I consider civil liberty, in a genuine, unadulterated sense, as the greatest of terrestrial blessings. I am convinced that the whole human race is entitled to it, and that it can be wrested from no part of them without the blackest and most aggravated guilt." Those were the days when a philosopher divided governments into two kinds, the bad and the good, that is, those which exist and those which do not exist; and when Burke, in the fervour of early liberalism, proclaimed that a revolution was the only thing that could do the world any good: "Nothing less than a convulsion that will shake the globe to its centre can ever restore the European nations to that liberty by which they were once so much distinguished."

XVII

HISTORICAL PHILOSOPHY IN FRANCE AND FRENCH BELGIUM AND SWITZERLAND.

By ROBERT FLINT[1]

WHEN Dr. Flint's former work appeared, a critic, who, it is true, was also a rival, objected that it was diffusely written. What then occupied three hundred and thirty pages has now expanded to seven hundred, and suggests a doubt as to the use of criticism. It must at once be said that the increase is nearly all material gain. The author does not cling to his main topic, and, as he insists that the science he is adumbrating flourishes on the study of facts only, and not on speculative ideas, he bestows some needless attention on historians who professed no philosophy, or who, like Daniel and Velly, were not the best of their kind. Here and there, as in the account of Condorcet, there may be an unprofitable or superfluous sentence. But on the whole the enlarged treatment of the philosophy of history in France is accomplished not by expansion, but by solid and essential addition. Many writers are included whom the earlier volume passed over, and Cousin occupies fewer pages now than in 1874, by the aid of smaller type and the omission of a passage injurious to Schelling. Many necessary corrections and improvements have been made, such as the transfer of Ballanche from theocracy to the liberal Catholicism of which he is supposed to be the founder.

Dr. Flint's unchallenged superiority consists alike in his familiarity with obscure, but not irrelevant authors,

[1] *English Historical Review*, 1895.

whom he has brought into line, and in his scrupulous fairness towards all whose attempted systems he has analysed. He is hearty in appreciating talent of every kind, but he is discriminating in his judgment of ideas, and rarely sympathetic. Where the best thoughts of the ablest men are to be displayed, it would be tempting to present an array of luminous points or a chaplet of polished gems. In the hands of such artists as Stahl or Cousin they would start into high relief with a convincing lucidity that would rouse the exhibited writers to confess that they had never known they were so clever. Without transfiguration the effect might be attained by sometimes stringing the most significant words of the original. Excepting one unduly favoured competitor, who fills two pages with untranslated French, there is little direct quotation. Cournot is one of those who, having been overlooked at first, are here raised to prominence. He is urgently, and justly, recommended to the attention of students. "They will find that every page bears the impress of patient, independent, and sagacious thought. I believe I have not met with a more genuine thinker in the course of my investigations. He was a man of the finest intellectual qualities, of a powerful and absolutely truthful mind." But then we are warned that Cournot never wrote a line for the general reader, and accordingly he is not permitted to speak for himself. Yet it was this thoughtful Frenchman who said: "Aucune idée parmi celles qui se réfèrent à l'ordre des faits naturels ne tient de plus près à la famille des idées religieuses que l'idée du progrès, et n'est plus propre à devenir le principe d'une sorte de foi religieuse pour ceux qui n'en ont pas d'autres. Elle a, comme la foi religieuse, la vertu de relever les âmes et les caractères."

The successive theories gain neither in clearness nor in contrast by the order in which they stand. As other countries are reserved for other volumes, Cousin precedes Hegel, who was his master, whilst Quetelet is barely mentioned in his own place, and has to wait for Buckle, if not for Oettingen and Rümelin, before he comes on for discussion. The finer threads, the underground currents, are not carefully traced. The connection between the *juste milieu* in politics and eclecticism in philosophy was already stated by the chief eclectic; but the subtler link between the Catholic legitimists and democracy seems to have escaped the author's notice. He says that the republic proclaimed universal suffrage in 1848, and he considers it a triumph for the party of Lafayette. In fact, it was the triumph of an opposite school—of those legitimists who appealed from the narrow franchise which sustained the Orleans dynasty to the nation behind it. The chairman of the constitutional committee was a legitimist, and he, inspired by the abbé de Genoude, of the *Gazette de France*, and opposed by Odilon Barrot, insisted on the pure logic of absolute democracy.

It is an old story now that the true history of philosophy is the true evolution of philosophy, and that when we have eliminated whatever has been damaged by contemporary criticism or by subsequent advance, and have assimilated all that has survived through the ages, we shall find in our possession not only a record of growth, but the full-grown fruit itself. This is not the way in which Dr. Flint understands the building up of his department of knowledge. Instead of showing how far France has made a way towards the untrodden crest, he describes the many flowery paths, discovered by the French, which lead elsewhere, and I expect that in coming volumes it will appear that Hegel and Buckle, Vico and Ferrari, are scarcely better guides than Laurent or Littré. Fatalism and retribution, race and nationality, the test of success and of duration, heredity and the reign of the invincible dead, the widening circle, the emancipation of the individual, the gradual triumph of the soul over the body, of mind over matter, reason over will, knowledge over ignorance, truth over error, right over might, liberty over authority, the law of progress and perfectibility, the constant intervention of providence, the sovereignty of the developed conscience—neither these nor other alluring theories are accepted as more than illusions or half-truths. Dr. Flint scarcely avails himself of them even for his foundations or his skeleton framework. His critical faculty, stronger than his gift of adaptation, levels obstructions and marks the earth with ruin. He is more anxious to expose the strange unreason of former writers, the inadequacy of their knowledge, their want of aptitude in induction, than their services in storing material for the use of successors. The result is not to be the sifted and verified wisdom of two centuries, but a future system, to be produced when the rest have failed by an exhaustive series of vain experiments. We may regret to abandon many brilliant laws and attractive generalisations that have given light and clearness and simplicity and symmetry to our thought; but it is certain that Dr. Flint is a close and powerful reasoner, equipped with satisfying information, and he establishes his contention that France has not produced a classic philosophy of history, and is still waiting for its Adam Smith or Jacob Grimm.

The kindred topic of development recurs repeatedly, as an important factor in modern science. It is still a confused and unsettled chapter, and in one place Dr. Flint seems to attribute the idea to Bossuet; in another he says that it was scarcely entertained in those days by Protestants, and not at all by Catholics; in a third he implies that its celebrity in the nineteenth century is owing in the first place to Lamennais. The passage, taken from Vinet, in which Bossuet speaks of the development of religion is inaccurately rendered. His words are the same which, on another page, are rightly translated "the course of religion"—*la suite de la religion.* Indeed, Bossuet was the most powerful adversary the theory ever encountered. It was not so alien to Catholic theology as is here stated, and before the time of Jurieu is more often found among Catholic than Protestant writers. When it was put forward, in guarded, dubious, and evasive terms, by Petavius, the indignation in England was as great as in 1846. The work which contained it, the most learned that Christian theology had then produced, could not be reprinted over here, lest it should supply the Socinians with inconvenient texts. Nelson hints that the great Jesuit may have been a secret Arian, and Bull stamped upon his theory amid the grateful applause of Bossuet and his friends. Petavius was not an innovator, for the idea had long found a home among the Franciscan masters: "Proficit fides secundum statum communem, quia secundum profectum temporum efficiebantur homines magis idonei ad percipienda et intelligenda sacramenta fidei.—Sunt multae conclusiones necessario inclusae in articulis creditis, sed antequam sunt per Ecclesiam declaratae et explicatae non oportet quemcumque eas credere. Oportet tamen circa eas sobrie opinari, ut scilicet homo sit paratus eas tenere pro tempore, pro quo veritas fuerit declarata." Cardinal Duperron said nearly the same thing as Petavius a generation before him: "L'Arien trouvera dans sainct Irénée, Tertullien et autres qui nous sont restez en petit nombre de ces siècles-là, que le Fils est l'instrument du Père, que le Père a commandé au Fils lors qu'il a esté question de la création des choses, que le Père et le Fils sont *aliud et aliud;* choses que qui tiendroit aujourd'huy, que le langage de l'Eglise est plus examiné, seroit estimé pour Arien luy-mesme." All this does not serve to supply the pedigree which Newman found it so difficult to trace. Development, in those days, was an expedient, an hypothesis, and not even the thing so dear to the Oxford probabilitarians, a working hypothesis. It was not more substantial than the gleam in Robinson's farewell to the pilgrims: "I am very confident that the Lord has more truth yet to break forth out of His holy word." The reason why it possessed no scientific basis is explained by Duchesne: "Ce n'est guère avant la seconde moitié du xviie siècle qu'il devint impossible de soutenir l'authenticité des fausses décrétales, des constitutions apostoliques, des 'Récognitions Clémentines,' du faux Ignace, du pseudo-Dionys et de l'immense fatras d'œuvres anonymes ou pseudonymes qui grossissait souvent du tiers ou de la moitié l'héritage littéraire des auteurs les plus considérables. Qui aurait pu même songer à un développement dogmatique?" That it was little understood, and lightly and loosely employed, is proved by Bossuet himself, who alludes to it in one passage as if he did not know that it was the subversion of his theology: "Quamvis ecclesia omnem veritatem funditus norit, ex haeresibus tamen discit, ut aiebat magni nominis Vincentius Lirinensis, aptius, distinctius, clariusque eandem exponere."

The account of Lamennais suffers from the defect of mixing him up too much with his early friends. No doubt he owed to them the theory that carried him through his career, for it may be found in Bonald, and also in De Maistre, though not, perhaps, in the volumes he had already published. It was less original than he at first imagined, for the English divines commonly held it from the seventeenth century, and its dirge was sung only the other day by the Bishop of Gloucester and Bristol.[1] A Scottish professor would even be justified in claiming it for Reid. But of course it was Lamennais who gave it most importance, in his programme and in his life. And his theory of the common sense, the theory that we can be certain of truth only by the agreement of mankind, though vigorously applied to sustain authority in State and Church, gravitated towards multitudinism, and marked him off from his associates. When he said *quod semper*, *quod ubique*, *quod ab omnibus*, he was not thinking of the Christian Church, but of Christianity as old as the creation; and the development he meant led up to the Bible, and ended at the New Testament instead of beginning there. That is the theory which he made so famous, which founded his fame and governed his fate, and to which Dr. Flint's words apply when he speaks of celebrity. In that sense it is a mistake to connect Lamennais with Möhler and Newman; and I do not believe that he anticipated their teaching, in spite of one or two passages which do not, on the face of them, bear date B.C., and may, no doubt, be quoted for the opposite opinion.

In the same group Dr. Flint represents De Maistre as

[1] [Dr. Ellicott.]

the teacher of Savigny, and asserts that there could never be a doubt as to the liberalism of Chateaubriand. There was none after his expulsion from office; but there was much reason for doubting in 1815, when he entreated the king to set bounds to his mercy; in 1819, when he was contributing to the *Conservateur*; and in 1823, when he executed the mandate of the absolute monarchs against the Spanish constitution. His zeal for legitimacy was at all times qualified with liberal elements, but they never became consistent or acquired the mastery until 1824. De Maistre and Savigny covered the same ground at one point; they both subjected the future to the past. This could serve as an argument for absolutism and theocracy, and on that account was lovely in the eyes of De Maistre. If it had been an argument the other way he would have cast it off. Savigny had no such ulterior purpose. His doctrine, that the living are not their own masters, could serve either cause. He rejected a mechanical fixity, and held that whatever has been made by process of growth shall continue to grow and suffer modification. His theory of continuity has this significance in political science, that it supplied a basis for conservatism apart from absolutism and compatible with freedom. And, as he believed that law depends on national tradition and character, he became indirectly and through friends a founder of the theory of nationality.

The one writer whom Dr. Flint refuses to criticise, because he too nearly agrees with him, is Renouvier. Taking this avowal in conjunction with two or three indiscretions on other pages, we can make a guess, not at the system itself, which is to console us for so much deviation, but at its tendency and spirit. The fundamental article is belief in divine government. As Kant beheld God in the firmament of heaven, so too we can see him in history on earth. Unless a man is determined to be an atheist, he must acknowledge that the experience of mankind is a decisive proof in favour of religion. As providence is not absolute, but reigns over men destined to freedom, its method is manifested in the law of progress. Here, however, Dr. Flint, in his agreement with Renouvier, is not eager to fight for his cause, and speaks with a less jubilant certitude. He is able to conceive that providence may attain its end without the condition of progress, that the divine scheme would not be frustrated if the world, governed by omnipotent wisdom, became steadily worse. Assuming progress as a fact, if not a law, there comes the question wherein it consists, how it is measured, where is its goal. Not religion, for the Middle Ages are an epoch of decline. Catholicism has since lost so much ground as to nullify the theories of Bossuet; whilst Protestantism never succeeded in France, either after the Reformation, when it ought to have prevailed, nor after the Revolution, when it ought not. The failure to establish the Protestant Church on the ruins of the old *régime*, to which Quinet attributes the breakdown of the Revolution, and which Napoleon regretted almost in the era of his concordat, is explained by Mr. Flint on the ground that Protestants were in a minority. But so they were in and after the wars of religion; and it is not apparent why a philosopher who does not prefer orthodoxy to liberty should complain that they achieved nothing better than toleration. He disproves Bossuet's view by that process of deliverance from the Church which is the note of recent centuries, and from which there is no going back. On the future I will not enlarge, because I am writing at present in the HISTORICAL, not the PROPHETICAL, REVIEW. But some things were not so clear in France in 1679 as they are now at Edinburgh. The predominance of Protestant power was not foreseen, except by those who disputed whether Rome would perish in 1710 or about 1720. The destined power of science to act upon religion had not been proved by Newton or Simon. No man was able to forecast the future experience of America, or to be sure that observations made under the reign of authority would be confirmed by the reign of freedom.

If the end be not religion, is it morality, humanity, civilisation, knowledge? In the German chapters of

1874 Dr. Flint was severe upon Hegel, and refused his notion that the development of liberty is the soul of history, as crude, one-sided, and misunderstood. He is more lenient now, and affirms that liberty occupies the final summit, that it profits by all the good that is in the world, and suffers by all the evil, that it pervades strife and inspires endeavour, that it is almost, if not altogether, the sign, and the prize, and the motive in the onward and upward advance of the race for which Christ was crucified. As that refined essence which draws sustenance from all good things it is clearly understood as the product of civilisation, with its complex problems and scientific appliances, not as the elementary possession of the noble savage, which has been traced so often to the primeval forest. On the other hand, if sin not only tends to impair, but does inevitably impair and hinder it, providence is excluded from its own mysterious sphere, which, as it is not the suppression of all evil and present punishment of wrong, should be the conversion of evil into an instrument to serve the higher purpose. But although Dr. Flint has come very near to Hegel and Michelet, and seemed about to elevate their teaching to a higher level and a wider view, he ends by treating it coldly, as a partial truth requiring supplement, and bids us wait until many more explorers have recorded their soundings. That, with the trained capacity for misunderstanding and the smouldering dissent proper to critics, I might not mislead any reader, or do less than justice to a profound though indecisive work, I should have wished to piece together the passages in which the author indicates, somewhat faintly, the promised but withheld philosophy which will crown his third or fourth volume. Any one who compares pages 125, 135, 225, 226, 671, will understand better than I can explain it the view which is the master-key to the book.

APPENDIX

By the kindness of the Abbot Gasquet we are enabled to supplement the Bibliography of Acton's writings published by the Royal Historical Society with the following additional items :—

In *The Rambler*, 1858

April—Burke.
July—[With Simpson] Mr. Buckle's Thesis and Method.
Short Reviews.
August—Mr. Buckle's Philosophy of History.
October—Theiner's *Documents inédits relatifs aux affaires religieuses de France 1790-1800*, pp. 265-267.
December—The Count de Montalembert, pp. 421-428 and note, 432.
Carlyle's *History of Frederick the Great*, vols. i. and ii. p. 429.

1859

January—Political Thoughts on the Church.
February—The Catholic Press.
September—Contemporary Events.

1860

September—National Defence.
Irish Education in Current Events.

1862

Correspondence.
The Danger of the Physical Sciences.

INDEX

Printed in Great Britain by R. & R. CLARK, LIMITED, *Edinburgh.*